THE LETTERS OF

# Henry Wadsworth Longfellow

VOLUME II

1837-1843

# THE LETTERS OF
# Henry Wadsworth Longfellow

EDITED BY

Andrew Hilen

VOLUME II

1837-1843

The Belknap Press of Harvard University Press

Cambridge, Massachusetts

1966

*Distributed in Great Britain by Oxford University Press, London*

*Library of Congress Catalog Card Number 66–18248*

*Typography by Burton Jones*

*Printed in the U.S.A. by Harvard University Printing Office*

# Contents

## Volume II

# ILLUSTRATIONS

## Volume II

*following page 118*



*following page 246*

# ILLUSTRATIONS

*following page 374*

# CHRONOLOGY

1837 Longfellow begins Harvard lectures, May 23. Forms "Five of Clubs" with Charles Sumner, Cornelius Felton, George Hillard, and Henry Cleveland. Publication in the *North American Review* of "The Great Metropolis," April, and "Hawthorne's *Twice Told Tales*" and "Tegnér's *Frithiofs Saga*," July. Tours the White Mountains, July 22 — August 3. Begins residence in Craigie House, August.

1838 Courts Frances Appleton unsuccessfully. Composes "A Psalm of Life," July 26. Publication of "Anglo-Saxon Literature" in the *North American Review*, July. Begins writing *Hyperion*, August–September.

1839 Publication of *Hyperion, A Romance* (New York: Samuel Colman), August, and *Voices of the Night* (Cambridge: John Owen), December. Marriage of Mary Longfellow to James Greenleaf, October 22.

1840 Lectures before the Mercantile Library Association of New York, January. Publication of "The French Language in England" in the *North American Review*, October. Completes first draft of *The Spanish Student*, December.

1841 Death of Mrs. Andrew Craigie, May 6. Publication of *Ballads and Other Poems* (Cambridge: John Owen), December.

1842 Meets Charles Dickens in Boston, January. Departs for Europe, April. Resides at Wasser-Heil-Anstalt Marienberg, Boppard, June 4 — September 17. Forms friendship with Ferdinand Freiligrath. Visits Charles Dickens in London, October. Returns to America, November. Publication of *Poems on Slavery* (Cambridge: John Owen), December.

1843 Publication of *The Spanish Student* (Cambridge: John Owen), May. Marries Frances Appleton, July 13. Nathan Appleton purchases Craigie House, October 14, and transfers title to Frances Appleton Longfellow, November 8.

# PART FIVE

# NEW BEGINNING, HARVARD

# 1837–1838

# NEW BEGINNING, HARVARD

## 1837–1838

UPON HIS ARRIVAL in Cambridge in December 1836, Longfellow took up residence in a rooming house across from the college yard, but in August 1837 he moved to more comfortable quarters in the Craigie House on Brattle Street. He was to live there for the rest of his life. During his first two years as Smith Professor of Modern Languages he wrote 140 letters or more, 92 of which have been recovered for this edition. These letters enable us to follow him as he worked at his college duties, advanced his scholarly and literary reputation with a modest amount of publication, increased his circle of friends and acquaintances, and began his difficult courtship of Fanny Appleton.

Longfellow's duties at Harvard involved the preparation of lectures on linguistic and literary subjects as well as the management of a team of native instructors in French, German, Italian, and Spanish. Of these duties, the preparation of the lectures proved to be the less onerous. In Letter No. 378 he gives a "slight sketch" of his course of lectures, revealing that some were written and others were delivered from notes. In Letter No. 382 he comments on his satisfaction at having begun the lectures (in May 1837) and on his conviction that their presentation was successful: "I lecture from Notes, and have succeeded very much to my own satisfaction; feeling no more embarrassment, than if I were eating dinner. I am rather astonished at this; and very much pleased; for now instead of being a source of anxiety, these Lectures are a source of pleasure to me. I had a presentiment, that all would turn out well; and perhaps this presentiment has had some influence in producing the result. As far as I can percieve and hear, the audience is quite as much pleased as I am; and they sit quite motionless and attentive for nearly an hour."

Whereas at the beginning he enjoyed being the center of attraction at the lectern, he found his administrative duties troublesome. He had inherited from George Ticknor a group of disparate native language teachers whom he described as a "*four-in-hand* of outlandish animals, all pulling the wrong way, except one." "This," he went on, "gives me more trouble than anything else." He eventually worked out this problem by hiring new instructors, but not without difficulties attended by exasperation.

He worked at fulfilling his scholarly commitments by publishing articles in the *North American Review*, by promoting Joseph Bosworth's compendium on the Anglo-Saxon language, and by collecting the materials that he later consolidated into the introductory essays for his anthology *The Poets and Poetry of Europe*. Although he may not at this time have intended that literary rather than scholarly writing should become the staple of his reputation, his interest in contemporary literature was by no means dormant, as his letters to George Washington Greene and Lewis Gaylord Clark reveal. Indeed, his plans and early drafts for *Hyperion* suggest that his literary ambitions were gathering momentum. His occasional poetry for Clark's *Knickerbocker* also enjoyed a remarkable success. Thus, paradoxically, the Harvard professorship that he had earned as a result of his scholarly endeavors in the study of languages became, in fact, a position from which he proceeded almost exclusively to the composition of imaginative and popular poetry and prose.

Longfellow, who had long dreamed of release from Brunswick to the social and cultural attractions of Boston, lost little time in taking advantage of his new opportunities. From Cambridge he took frequent walks to Boston to visit new friends (often the Appleton family on Beacon Street after their return from Europe in September 1837), to attend a lecture or a concert, or merely to display on promenade his imported kid gloves and fashionable waistcoats. In Cambridge he found a congenial family atmosphere in the Shady Hill home of the Reverend Andrews Norton, and as his courtship of Frances Appleton progressed, or rather failed to progress, he turned to Mrs. Norton as a confidante and to young Jane Norton as a platonic substitute for his "dark ladie."

He had his happiest moments in the company of a group of friends with whom he formed an informal society known as the "Five of Clubs." He had known Cornelius Felton for some years, having met him on one of his excursions to Cambridge from Brunswick, and it was presumably Felton who took Longfellow into his group of intimates: Charles Sumner, his law partner George Hillard (1808–1879), and Henry Russell Cleveland (1809–1843), a young man with literary ambitions who had recently been married to an heiress and who could entertain the "club" in a manner to which they were all pleased to become accustomed. Of this group, Sumner became his closest friend, although he was absent abroad from December 1837 to May 1840. Conviviality seems to have been the principal characteristic of the club's meetings, and Longfellow's letters do not indicate that the members occupied themselves with a serious discussion of political and social problems. However, knowing the literary bent of each member, one doubts that all their moments together were devoted merely to "oystering and roistering."

Only occasionally do the letters of 1837–1838 reveal the emotional crosscurrents that moved Longfellow when he was not occupied by his academic duties, his adjustments to a new environment, or the social pleasures provided by his Harvard colleagues and other friends. Yet during this period his love for Frances Appleton slowly grew until it possessed his heart, and when that attractive woman failed to encourage him, he sometimes surrendered to a melancholy fed by visions of his dead wife. If in general he was happy at this time in his new professorship, he was also moving deeper into the frustrations of an unrequited love that would culminate, in 1842, in his emotional and physical collapse.

### 363. *To Parker Cleaveland*

Portland Jan. 1. 1837.

My dear Sir,

Your favor of Dec. 8. did not arrive till I had left town [Portland]. Indeed I did not have the pleasure of receiving it till I arrived here a few days ago, on a second short visit to my parents. It was detained here, as they were expecting me back daily.

I am very sorry, that it is not in my power to make you a visit now. I want to see you very much, and yet I cannot, for I have not time; as I am obliged to return to Cambridge on Wednesday next. To tell the truth I have hardly courage to visit Brunswick yet. There are too many associations with the happy Past — connected with it! It would remind me too vividly of what has been — but is no more. A visit there at this moment,[1] would be too painful.

I hope to hear from you when I return to Cambridge. Thus far they seem disposed to make everything pleasant to me there. All that is *required* of me now is to oversee the various branches of my department and to lecture; which I shall do next Summer.

Remember me particularly to all your family, and to the *Government* [of Bowdoin College] in general and several. Wishing you all a Happy New Year,

I am very truly yours
Henry W. Longfellow

P.S. I leave,[2] to be sent or delivered to you as a New Year's present, a small agate box, which I bought at Chamouni, under the very shadow of Mont Blanc.

MANUSCRIPT: Longfellow Trust Collection. ADDRESS: To/Professor Cleaveland/Brunswick. POSTMARK: PORTLAND ME. JAN 2

1. At this point Longfellow deleted the phrase "and at this season of the year."
2. Longfellow deleted the words "for you" here.

364. *To Frances Appleton*

Boston. Jan. 8. 1837.

My dear Miss Fanny,

As I sat down a few evenings since to translate the piece I here send you, I remembered the time when "by the margin of fair Zurich's waters" we translated together the little ballad of Uhland.[1] I remembered also, the delight you always felt in reading whatever was beautiful in his poems, and I thought it would give you pleasure to see this Elegy of Matthisson, a writer celebrated for the elegance of his style, and the pleasing melancholy of his thoughts. I therefore send it to you as a kind of Valentine; with my warmest wishes of a Happy New Year to all of you. It will serve you likewise as a German lesson, during the master's absence. He hopes to resume hereafter his instructions in the *musical tongue.*

With my best regards to your father and brother,

very truly yours,
Henry W. Longfellow

MANUSCRIPT: Longfellow Trust Collection. ADDRESS: To/Miss Fanny E. Appleton PUBLISHED: *Young Longfellow,* pp. 242–243.

1. Longfellow and Fanny Appleton had translated Johann Ludwig Uhland's "Das Schloss am Meere" ("The Castle by the Sea") while at Zurich together on August 9, 1836. See *Young Longfellow,* p. 397. With this letter Longfellow enclosed his translation of Friedrich von Matthisson's "Elegie in den Ruinen eines alten Bergschlosses geschrieben" ("Elegy. Written in the Ruins of an Old Castle"), first published in the *Knickerbocker,* XIV (September 1839), 211–212, and later in *Poets and Poetry of Europe,* p. 318.

365. *To Mrs. Anna Marie Clarke Greene*[1]

Cambridge Jan. 9. 1837

My dear Mrs Greene,

I did not have the pleasure of receiving your favor until this evening. I have just reached Cambridge on my return from a visit to Portland. This will account for my not sending a more immediate reply.

I regret very much that it will not be in my power to accept your polite invitation for the present. I enter upon my duties here this week; and have so much to attend to that an absence of even a few days would be attended with no little inconvenience. I will come and see you, however, as soon as I can find time.

So George has become a Roman Consul! I should perhaps say *the* Roman Consul. I had not heard of it: and shall straightway write him a letter of congratulation. I am most sincerely glad that his wishes in this particular have been crowned with success. His Article on the

Reformation in Italy was published, on Jan. 1. I have not yet read it, having been away since that time. I wish to forward to him an extra copy of the Article in sheets. Do you know of any opportunity?[2]

For my own part I have done nothing and written nothing for a long, long time; and for a long time to come I shall be occupied in preparing Lectures on German literature. While steam-boats and locomotives traverse field and flood with the speed of light, — there are alas! none on the great streams of thought and the vast fields of learning. Almost single-handed must we breast the stream, and over stocks and stones travel we — on foot. So that the labor of weeks is sometimes necessary for the production of a lecture, which can be delivered in the short space of an hour.

By the way, did you not receive a letter from me, while I was in Heidelberg? — in answer to one you wrote concerning George? I ask, lest in case the letter was lost you might think I never answered yours. I presume my reply reached you safely.[3]

With many thanks for the affectionate interest you take in me, and kind regards to all yr family,

I am very truly yours
Henry W. Longfellow

P.S. — Inclosed I send you $25. which Mr. Felton has just received, from the Editor of the N.A. Review — being the sum due for the Article before mentioned.

Mr. Felton sends his best regards. He recd. a letter from George a few weeks ago. All was well.

MANUSCRIPT: Longfellow Trust Collection. ADDRESS: To/Mrs. Ann Greene/ East Greenwich/Rhode Island POSTMARK: CAMBRIDGE MS. JAN 11 ENDORSEMENT: answered 22 jan. 1837

1. Mrs. Greene (1783–1886) was the mother of George Washington Greene.
2. Greene's review of Thomas Macrie's *History of the Reformation in Italy* (Edinburgh, 1827) appeared in the *North American Review*, XLIV (January 1837), 153–178. He had just begun a career as U. S. Consul in Rome that lasted until 1845.
3. This letter is unrecovered.

## 366. *To Willis Gaylord Clark*

[Cambridge, January 11, 1837]

THIS *is* sinful. I ought to have written you sooner. Day treads upon the heels of day; and one after another they pass away with such gigantic strides, that I cannot keep pace with them; nor unto me do they 'utter forth knowledge'[1] to any remarkable degree. I told your brother why I did not write you from over-sea. After a few short months our tour of pleasure was turned into a funeral procession, as you know. Under such circumstances a man has no heart to write; no, not even to his best friends. GOD grant that you may never know what this meaneth!

LEWIS told me of your engagement.[2] When a good man weds (as when he dies) angels lead his spirit into a quiet land, full of holiness and peace, full of all pleasant sights, and 'beautiful exceedingly.'[3] Your dreams will not be realized: *dreams* never are; but the reality will differ from and be a thousand fold sweeter than any dreams. The blessing of a friend go with you. May you oft enjoy 'a look into a pure, loving eye; a word without falseness to a bride without falseness; and close beside you in the still watches of the night, a soft-breathing breast, in which there is nothing but Paradise, a sermon and a midnight prayer!' These words are from a German writer.[4] Beautiful, are they not? *Apropos* of German writers. In one of your KNICKERBOCKER pieces you introduced some lines from GLUCK, beginning:

> 'METHINKS it were no pain to die
>   On such an eve, when such a sky
> O'er canopies the west,' etc.

Can you send me a copy of the entire piece, and tell me where I can find the original German?[5]

MANUSCRIPT: unrecovered; text from *The Knickerbocker, or New-York Monthly Magazine*, LVII (February 1861), 226–227.

1. Cf. Ps. 19:2.
2. Clark had married Anne Poyntell Caldcleugh on June 1, 1836. She died of consumption in December 1838 (*Clark Letters*, p. 9).
3. Coleridge, *Christabel*, I, 68.
4. Jean Paul Richter, *The Life of Quintus Fixlein*, Eighth Letter-Box.
5. The original is unidentified. In his reply to Longfellow of February 25, 1837, Clark wrote of the translation, "I know not where I first met with it, or whence it came. When I read, it was impressed directly on my memory" (*Clark Letters*, p. 38). He had printed twelve lines from the poem in his "Ollapodiana" essay in the *Knickerbocker*, V (May 1835), 435.

## 367. *To Thomas Gold Appleton*[1]

Cambridge. Jan. 23. 1837.

My dear Sir,

I am going to ask a favor of you, which you must not grant, unless you can do it without the slightest inconvenience. You will find it at the close of this letter. I do not wish to be abrupt; but will lead you gradually to it, through three pages. Let me first say a word in answer to your favor from Schaffhausen, which reached me in Paris.

According to your request I called on Mrs. Wm. Appleton as soon as I reached Boston; and have been frequently since. They cherish William's memory with the most ardent affection; and love to speak of him, and show the things that were once his.[2] The bitterness of their grief is over; unless perhaps in the mother's heart. She still looks very sad; and yet she seems to feel that "graves are the footsteps of angels." [3]

I was very sorry to hear of your misfortunes on the Rhine. I thought you would all enjoy it so highly; and behold that glorious land in all the splendor of Autumn. But it seems, that like Peter Rug in the story-book, wherever you went you were followed by a storm; and at last detained by more serious calamities in that dull town Mayence.[4] I have myself passed through such scenes too recently, not to sympathise with you from my heart of hearts. And yet when these things reached us here, you were safe and warm on the sunny side of the Rue de Rivoli: — where I trust you now "possess yourselves in much quietness" [5] — and enjoy the sunshine and pure air, which may be supposed to come to you over the frozen fountains and leafless trees of the Tuileries. I hope grim-visaged Winter has treated you as gently as he has us. Till within two days he has been very mild, and gives no offence. He has behaved, as Nat Willis would say, "very *gingerly*." But alas! two days ago there came a north-wester; and the snow fell as if the milky way and all the starry heavens were coming down upon us at once. And now we stand breast-high amid the drifts of snow; and all my peace of mind has taken flight, to return only with the Spring; so utterly do I hate the snow.

And what shall I tell you of Boston? The inhabitants of the fair city complain, that it is very dull; — that is that there are no parties. Instead thereof, only Lectures. Waldo Emerson on Tran[s]cendentalism — sufficiently obscure; — Mr. Choate on the "Poetry of the Sea"; — in great demand, and much admired, tho' to me tedious and wishy-washy, like the great sea itself: and Lewis Stackpole on "the March of Mind"; — him I have not heard.[6] And then there is an Oratorio, where the part of David is sung by a very fat man, and the part of Goliah by a very small one; and when the pebble hits Goliah on the head it is represented by a great blow on a bass-drum, and for fear there should be any mistake, *explained in the bill*! [7] The last engagement is Mr. Amory (he of the *aquiline* nose) to Miss. Mary Green, (daughter of the late Gardiner Green), "*both of Boston.*" [8] There is some gossip a-foot, and the wags amuse themselves with the "*Yes, I thank you*" which she is said to have uttered on the occasion, and which was doubtless more pleasant to his ears than "No, I thank you." I see by the papers of to-day, that Dr. Wainwright has arrived in N.Y.[9]

One of the persons, whom I like best in Boston is your most amiable aunt Mrs. S. A. [Samuel Appleton] I was there a short time since and she invited me to join in writing a Valentine for your sisters. I contributed some Translations from the German for Miss Fanny, and a copy of the "Hymn to the Flowers" for Miss. M[ary].[10] This letter will probably reach you sooner, than the package.

And now the favor I have to ask; which is, that you would buy me at *Privat's*, Rue de la Paix, near the Boulevard, one dozen light-colored kid gloves, (a little larger than your own) and one dozen small ladies' gloves *black*. I bought for every one else, save myself, and forgot that my sister [Anne] was in mourning. I advise you to supply yourself before your return very bountifully. With kind regards to your father and sisters

Very truly yours.
H. W. Longfellow

MANUSCRIPT: Longfellow Trust Collection. ADDRESS: To/Mr. Thomas G. Appleton/care of Nathan Appleton Esq/Welles & cie. Place St. George/Paris/New York & Hâvre. ANNOTATION (*by Longfellow*): Paid./Charge. H.W.L./No. 180. POSTMARKS: CAMBRIDGE MS JAN 23/20[?] FEVR 1837/PAYS D'OUTREMER PAR LE HAVRE

1. Son of the prosperous merchant Nathan Appleton and brother of Longfellow's future wife, Tom Appleton (1812–1884) devoted his life to travel, philanthropy, and the cultivation of literature. He first met Longfellow in Switzerland. See *Young Longfellow*, p. 236.

2. In a letter from Schaffhausen of August 25, 1836, Appleton had described the death on August 24 of his second cousin, William Sullivan Appleton (b. 1815), son of the Hon. William and Mrs. Mary Anne Cutler Appleton of Boston. He had subsequently met Longfellow in Strasbourg on August 30 and supplemented his letter with more detail. See Longfellow's MS Journal for that date.

3. This quotation, used by Longfellow in *Hyperion* (*Works*, VIII, 249), came originally from Jean Paul Richter. See Longfellow's translated "Passages from Jean Paul" in the *Boston Notion*, II, No. 24 (March 13, 1841), 1, and in *Roberts' Semi-Monthly Magazine for Town and Country*, I, No. 6 (April 1, 1841), 232.

4. In commenting on the Appletons' ill luck with the weather, Longfellow alludes to William Austin's fable "Peter Rugg, the Missing Man" (1824), already a part of New England folklore. The party had to remain a month or so in Mayence after both Mary and Frances Appleton were attacked by gastric fever, an ailment described by Tom Appleton as "a sort of infliction of these regions for the vile compounds of their kitchen, bred of grease, lard, and all the abominations of the German sausage" (*Life and Letters of Thomas Gold Appleton*, prepared by Susan Hale [New York, 1885], p. 237).

5. Unidentified, but perhaps an echo of Luke 21:19.

6. During the winter of 1835–1836 Emerson delivered a series of twelve lectures on the "Philosophy of History" in the Masonic Temple in Boston (Ralph L. Rusk, *The Life of Ralph Waldo Emerson* [New York, 1949], pp. 245–248). Rufus Choate (1799–1859), lawyer, orator, and congressman, delivered his popular lecture "The Romance of the Sea" on many occasions. His biographer has remarked that he "afterwards lost it, or it was stolen from him, in New York" (Samuel Gilman

Brown, *The Works of Rufus Choate with a Memoir of his Life* [Boston, 1862], I, 42). Joseph Lewis Stackpole (1808–1847), a Boston lawyer, was a close friend of John Lothrop Motley, who became his brother-in-law.

7. *David*, an oratorio by Sigismund, Chevalier von Neukomm (1778–1858), was given the first of many performances by the Boston Handel and Haydn Society on February 28, 1836 (Dr. Frédéric Louis Ritter, *Music in America* [New York, 1883], p. 364).

8. Mary Copley Greene (1817–1892), daughter of the merchant Gardiner Greene (1753–1832) and granddaughter of John Singleton Copley, married James Sullivan Amory (1809–1884) on November 28, 1837.

9. Jonathan Mayhew Wainwright (1792–1854), rector of Trinity Church, Boston (later bishop of the Episcopal Church), had been sent by his parishioners to England to arrange the construction of a new church organ (John N. Norton, *Life of Bishop Wainwright* [New York, 1858], p. 85). While on the Continent, he had met the Appletons at Schaffhausen and had officiated at William Appleton's funeral (T. G. Appleton to Longfellow, August 25, 1835).

10. In addition to the elegy mentioned in Letter No. 364, Longfellow included in his Valentine a translation of Tiedge's poem "Die Welle" ("The Wave"), which he later printed in *Voices of the Night* (*Young Longfellow*, p. 398), and "Hymn to the Flowers" by the English poet Horace Smith (1779–1849).

## 368. *To Lewis Gaylord Clark*

Cambridge Feb. 1. 1837

My dear Clark,

Your favor of Decr. 19. reached me only two days ago. I happened to be at the Tremont House, to see a gentleman residing there, when *something within me* said, "ask at the Bar" — (you need not laugh; it was not for liquor) — "for a bundle or package." I did so; and they answered No. And then they looked again and answered Yes, and gave me your package, which I was very glad to get. It had been lying there time out of mind, and would be lying there still, but for the lucky accident mentioned above. Now, my worthy friend, never send a letter in a package again will you: but by mail as a kind of harbinger announcing to me the speedy coming of the package. Otherwise, ten to one, neither will reach me.

I am much obliged to you for the books. I should like to have the Blackwood regularly: — *Post-Nubila-Phoebus Whitaker*[1] need not come any more. Can't you send the Blackwood and Knickerbocker together to the Agent of K. in Boston — Broaders[2] I mean? If so it will please. If not convenient don't do it.

April 4.

*Toujours pêche qui en prend un*; — he likewise fishes, who catches *one*: and he likewise corresponds, who writes one. The fact is, my friend, it will happen so sometimes. With the best intentions in the world, we put things off from day to day — and then we begin — and then we stop, and then after months have elapsed we find them in old drawers, as Scott did Waverly — and as I did this Epistle.

&c . &c . &c.
&c . &c.
&c.

This will be taken to New York by my most particular and beloved friend Prof. Felton, a ripe scholar, and a most excellent man. He professes the Greek tongue in this University. I hope you will find time to call upon him at the *Domus Astor*. He will bring you likewise, a Translation from the Italian: executed by a young man of Boston, who has passed some time in Italy &c. &c. The Original Story is most quaint and piteous for to read. The Translator informs me, that he has endeavored to preserve this quaintness in his Translation; so that it will not read like a modern polished tale. So much the better, as giving some variety in these stereotype days. Perhaps it may need here and there a touch of your pen. I have not had time to read it: but hope you will find it fit and suitable for your Knickerbocker [which by the way you do not send me.][3] If you do not like it, please send it back by Mr. Felton, who tarries but two or three days in your city.[4] [*remainder of manuscript missing*]

MANUSCRIPT: Longfellow Trust Collection. ADDRESS: Lewis G. Clark Esq/New York.

1. Daniel Kimball Whitaker (1801–1881), a Harvard graduate of 1820, edited the *Southern Literary Journal and Magazine of Arts* in Charlestown from 1835 to 1837. Why Longfellow attached the epithet to his name is not clear. It may refer to Whitaker's decision to spend his life in the South.

2. Clark's agent in Boston was Otis, Broaders & Company, 120 Washington Street.

3. Longfellow's brackets.

4. The "young man of Boston" is unidentified, but his translation of the Romeo and Juliet legend appeared in the *Knickerbocker*, IX (May 1837), 478–487, under the title "The History Lately Discovered, of Two Noble Lovers, with their Piteous Death, which happened in the City of Verona, in the Time of the Sig. Bartolommeo de Scala." See Clark to Longfellow, April 7, 1837 (*Clark Letters*, pp. 96–97).

## 369. *To George Washington Greene*

Cambridge Feb. 1. 1837

My dear Greene,

Two nights ago, as I returned from an evening visit, your letter looked down upon me from the mantle-piece with a most friendly, albeit outlandish aspect, its face being tattooed with post-marks black and red. I sat down and read it through with mournful pleasure, solemn and glad by turns, as the string was touched. It seemed to me like a voice of Eld — like the voice of the Northern God Mimer, who sits by the wave of the Destiny of the Past, and utters traditions. But of the Past, enough. Let me tell you of the present. I have taken up my abode in Cambridge. My chambers are very pleasant; with great trees in front, whose branches almost touch my windows: so that I have a nest not unlike the birds; being high up — in the third story. Right under me, in the second, lives and laughs Cornelius whose surname is Felton. He is engaged! Let me introduce to your acquaintance his beloved — Miss Mary Whitney:[1] rather tall, and plump withal, — dark hair and eyes, and round, red cheeks. You perceive she is not beautiful: but they say her mind is the great charm. I know her very little, and it seems to me she is difficult to get acquainted with; inasmuch as I do not feel any better acquainted with her, than I did the first time I saw her. Perhaps it is my own fault. I am sorry it should be so.

My life here is very quiet and agreeable. Like the clown in Shakespeare I have "no enemy but Winter and rough weather."[2] I never want a worse one. To Boston I go frequently — and generally on foot. It is a pleasant walk, you know: and one has an object in view. I have no classes to hear in College, and in all probability shall never be required to hear any. I am now occupied in preparing a course of Lectures on German Literature, to be delivered next Summer. I do not write them out; but make notes and translations. I think this the best way — most decidedly. In this course something of the Danish and Swedish (the new feathers in my cap) is to be mingled. From all this you will gather, that my occupations are of the most delightful kind. All would be well with me, were it not for the excited state of my nervous system, which grows no quieter, although I have entirely discontinued smoking. When the East-winds of Spring come, what shall I do? It is all delirium *now,* — a pleasant excitement. *Then,* it will be deep dejection, I fear. Think of me, when the next Sirocco blows! and imagine, that I feel as you do, tho' ruder blasts assail me, than will ever dare to breathe on the cheek of the *Roman Consul,* to whom all hail! — all hail! forevermore. Most sincerely do I congratulate you on your success. This letter will reach you in Rome, whither you will have gone to assume the Consular dignity. Remember me to the Pope; and to the good-natured Bottle-Imp (Monsignor Botiglia) who has been made a Cardinal, I hear.[3] The Persianis you will take kindly by the hand, and say it is for me: and that I remember them all with much regard. Kiss the old lady; (on your own hook, though); and show them what I have to say of them and Rome in Outre Mer.[4] Ah! this is a mad world, a mad world!

I am very sorry to hear that your eyes are put out. You sit up too late o'-nights, don't you? Hereafter be more exemplary and go to bed with your wife. And now rises up before [me] a picture of heaven upon earth, which I met with a few days ago in Jean Paul Richter, the most magnificent of the German Prose Writers. Listen to his words. "Look into a pure loving eye; — a word without falseness to a bride without falseness, and then under the coverlid a soft-breathing breast, in which there is nothing but Paradise, a sermon, and an evening prayer. By heaven! with this I will satisfy a Mythic God, who has left his own Heaven, and is seeking a new one among us here below!"[5] There, is not that beautiful? My friend, learn to enjoy the present — that little space of time between the great Past, and the still greater Future. Rome must be delightful to you. Your wife's native city, and the city of your choise. We were there together, likewise, in the days of our youth. Walk with me again in the spirit through the Forum: and visit La Riccia in the Summer time, and all the old, familiar scenes in and around the Eternal City.

I have no news to tell you. Your Article on the Reformation in Italy is published,[6] and is much liked. I have the sheets for you, but did not reach Cambridge in time to correct the proofs. We are looking daily for something more from you.

The cash for the above-mentioned Article I sent to your mother. I had a few lines from her this morning in answer. They are all well. *Mr. Greene*, postmaster of Boston, has translated from the Italian a History of Italy. You will find it noticed in the October No. of [the] N. American. Nathaniel Greene! I thought at first it might be your brother Nat! — but it was not.[7]

My love to your dear little wife: and write me soon and long, long letters. Felton &c. &c.

Yrs. truly
H. W. L.

If Cortés has not left you, give him my most cordial remembrance. I should write to him [did] I not suppose he had left Florence.

Your letter to Felton was recd. a few weeks ago. He will write you soon. Until then console yourself with what I here send.

P.S. Send us your title as Consul: with all the Ill[ustrissi]mos &c. so that we need not lower you in the eyes of the S.P.Q.R.

MANUSCRIPT: Longfellow Trust Collection. ADDRESS: To/George W. Greene Esq/ Florence [*remainder deleted and illegible*] ANNOTATION (*by Longfellow*): Paid. Charge H.W.L. No. 180 POSTMARKS: CAMBRIDGE MS. FEB 2/16 FEVR 1837/PAYS D'OUTREMER PAR LE HAVRE/PAID

1. Felton married Mary Whitney (1815–1845) on July 19, 1838.

2. *As You Like It,* II, v, 43–44.

3. Luigi Bottiglia (1752–1836) became a cardinal in the promotion of June 23, 1834. He had died the previous September and lay buried in the Church of San Silvestro in Capite.

4. Longfellow had boarded with the Persianis in Rome (125.1) and alluded to them in the chapter "Rome in Midsummer" in *Outre-Mer* (*Works,* VII, 239).

5. See 366.4.

6. See 365.2.

7. Nathaniel Greene (1797–1877), minor poet, editor, and Jacksonian Democrat, was the translator of Luigi Sforzosi's *A Compendious History of Italy* (New York, 1836). It was noticed in the *North American Review,* XLIII (October 1836), 532–533.

## 370. *To Charles Folsom*

[Cambridge] Wednesday morng. Feb. 15. '37.

My dear Sir,

I shall have an Article in the next No. of N.A.R.[1] Dr. Palfrey will send it to you forthwith, I presume; unless he find something therein to gainsay. Will you have the goodness to *preserve the M.S. and send it to me with the proofs!*

Very truly yrs.
H. W. Longfellow

MANUSCRIPT: Boston Public Library. ADDRESS: To/Chs. Folsom Esqr./Cambridge ENDORSEMENT: Rec'd 15 Feb. 1837

1. See the *North American Review,* XLIV (April 1837), 461–484. The article is a review of *The Great Metropolis* (New York, 1837), 2 vols.

## 371. *To Stephen Longfellow*

Cambridge March 22. 1837.

My dear Father,

This is quite too bad. When I left you, I intended to write very frequently; and I believe this is only my third letter.[1] The fact is I am occupied in various ways from morn till night; and so often interrupted by visitors &c. that with the best intentions in the world, I give my absent friends too much reason to think that I am forgetful of them: which however is by no means the case. And now having at length my heels tripped up by the influenza, which has confined me for some days to the house, I find time to tell you so: and furthermore to inform you of what has been going forward since I last wrote you.

My first quarter's salary was paid without any ado. As yet, however, I have taken no active part in College instruction, there being no room for it. Therefore you need not be allarmed about my injuring myself with study. If hurt in any way it will be by too little, not too much. There is such a social spirit here and in Boston, that I seldom see a book by candlelight. Indeed, I pass half of my evenings at least in Society: it being almost impossible to avoid it. All that I have done in the way of study is to prepare Lectures for the Summer. I have also written an Article for the April No. of the North American; a Review of a book called "The Great Metropolis." So you perceive, I take things very easily. People here are too agreeable to let a man kill himself with study. I see Dr. [John Gorham] Palfrey frequently; — Mr. [Jared] Sparks every day; — and play Whist with Mr. [Andrews] Norton as often as once a week. My most intimate friend is [Cornelius] Felton, the best fellow in the world — or one of the best. He is full of talent, and good sound sense, and as simple as a child. Moreover, very learned, and a good critic, save being a little inclined to exaggerated praise. The Review of "Ion" in the next N. A. R. is by him. There is also a Review of Bulwer by Willard Phillips. But I will give you a complete list on the next page. In the July No. I shall have two articles; one the Legend of Frithiof, a Swedish poem; the other on a book entitled Twice-told Tales; a beautiful work by a classmate of mine, N. Hawthorne of Salem.[2]

This afternoon I received two Nos. of the new Portland paper. On one of them was written "With respects of J. Furbish. Please give us something of your best." This is a pretty abrupt way of bidding a true man stand and deliver. Is Mr. Furbish the editor?[3]

I believe everything goes very smoothly with Sam. I see him very often — almost every day: so you must not feel any anxiety about him.[4] The vacation commences in a fortnight: at which time I trust the steamboats will be in motion.

Many thanks to Anne for her note and *flannel breastplates*: and most particular regards to Clara and the rest at the Judge's &c. &c.[5]

Very truly yours
Henry W. Longfellow

P.S. I sent to the Dean for the names of the N.A.R. writers; but he says they must not be made known till the Review is published. I will send them soon; or bring them with me.

Second P.S. Alex. I have not seen for more than a week. He never comes out to Cambridge except of a Sunday; so that I do not see him half so often as I wish.[6]

My friend Slidell is here — or rather in Charlestown. He sails soon as 1st Lieut. in the Independence.[7]

MANUSCRIPT: Longfellow Trust Collection. ADDRESS: Hon. Stephen Longfellow/ Portland/Me. POSTMARK: CAMBRIDGE MS. MAR 23

1. Longfellow had left Portland on January 4, but this is his first recorded letter home since that date.

2. Felton reviewed Thomas Talfourd's *Ion; a Tragedy* in the *North American Review*, XLIV (April 1837), 485–503; and Willard Phillips, the Boston jurist, wrote a critique of Bulwer's fiction in the same number, pp. 426–434. Longfellow's essay on Tegnér's *Frithiofs Saga*, with his original translations from the poem, appeared in XLV (July 1837), 149–185; his commendatory review of *Twice-Told Tales* is in the same number, pp. 59–73.

3. James Furbish edited the *Orion*, a Portland literary weekly that lasted from March to December 1837.

4. Samuel Longfellow was in his second year at Harvard College.

5. Clara Crowninshield was on intimate terms with the Potter family of Portland (*Diary of Clara Crowninshield*, Introduction), and during the next few years she made several visits to the Judge's home.

6. After the completion in 1836 of his cruise with the Pacific Squadron (241.2), Alexander Longfellow began the study of engineering with James Hayward, a former professor of mathematics and natural philosophy at Harvard, who at this time was doing preliminary work on the Andover-Haverhill section of the Boston and Maine Railroad.

7. Alexander Slidell Mackenzie spent a two-year tour of duty on the *Independence*, a cruise that took him to the Baltic, Russia, and Brazil. (Alexander Slidell had added Mackenzie to his name in 1837.)

## 372. *To Samuel Ward*

Cambridge April 2. 1837

My dear Ward,

*Warum haben Sie mir nicht geschrieben*? Why the devil have you not written to me? *Weil Sie keine Zeit gehabt haben*? Because you have had no time? *Oder keine Lust dazu*? or because you did not want to?

After this simple wise do I, for my own private diversion, *construe* your silence. On which so ever of the two horns, that silence hangs, I beg thee shake it off. Is this the way you serve your friends? like the spirits in Milton's Paradise, consoling yourself with a "They also serve, who only stand and wait."[1] You have waited sometime, haven't you?

Having let off this pop-gun of small witticisms, you shall anon hear me speak more solemnly. As for example, what followeth on the next page.[2]

["Saturday. April. 2. Rain — rain — rain! and cold weather. Received a letter from Ward, who is in Luxembourg, confined to his chamber with a lame leg, occasioned by a fall from his carriage. He writes: 'A knee, whose amputation crisis has this day passed, saved my life.' I wonder what he means by that."][3]

This is an extract from my last year's Journal, whereby you are reminded of your deplorable condition a twelve month ago this very day.

And now, my friend, allow me the pleasure of introducing, not to your *acquaintance*, but to your *recollection*, our Greek Professor, and in days of yore your instructor at Round Hill; — Mr. C. C. Felton. He is my intimate and beloved friend; and if your spirit moves you to hear of my welfare, he has authentic documents in his heart and brain, from which to give you a short biographical sketch of the absent.

When I last saw you, you told me you had Greene's manuscript of Guizot's — something. You know what I mean. The translation from the French, that you were to get published in New York. If you have not succeeded to your mind, have the goodness to send me the M.S. A gentleman in Boston proposes to publish a Series of Translations from the German and French. If the work goes forward, it would be of service to George W. to have his name connected with the enterprize. Mr. Felton will tell you more of this.[4]

And now, good Ward, blame me not if this letter is short and unsatisfactory. I am not otherwise. It is a bright day, and the birds are singing; — but the heart of man is heavy in his chamber. You will write to me soon, I trust; and when the shuttle of thought gets once fairly in motion, we will weave such a motley and gorgeous epistolary tapestry, as has never yet been woven on the "sounding loom of Time."[5] What do you think of that?

Leben Sie wohl [Farewell].

H. W. L.

MANUSCRIPT: Rosalind Richards, Gardiner, Maine. ADDRESS: To/Samuel Ward Jr./New York.

1. Longfellow's identification is erroneous; the quotation is from Milton's sonnet "On His Blindness."

2. The direction "Volti subito" ("Turn over quickly") follows at the foot of the sheet.

3. The brackets are Longfellow's. The accident occurred at Trèves on March 22, 1836 (see Letter No. 346).

4. See 207.4.

5. Presumably a translation of Goethe, *Faust,* I, 508.

## 373. *To Jørgen Bølling*

Cambridge. April 23. 1837

My dear Sir,

I have at length reached my Native Land; and entered upon the duties of my profession at this University. The sound of a foreign language I seldom hear, and Europe seems far, *very* far away. But within a few days a ship will sail for the Baltic, freighted with a Minister Plenopotentiary for St. Petersburg.[1] I cannot help availing myself of the opportunity, to stretch my arm over the Atlantic ocean, and shake hands with you once more: and already, at the very thought, Copenhagen, with its wide and stately streets, and great squares, and pleasant green alleys, under the ramparts, seem nearer to me. I have always regretted that it was not in my power to stay longer in that fair city; and sometimes think, with deep sorrow, that perhaps, if I had passed the winter there, I should not now be so desolate as I am, and so alone.

I think it was in August of last year that I wrote you a few lines from Heidelberg,[2] and sent you a copy of my little work "Outre Mer." Did they reach you in safety?

What is there new in Danish Literature? You will do me a great favor if you will note down for me the names of your best writers, in the order they hold in your own estimation. What do you think of Henrik Wergeland and his poem "Skabelsen, Mennesket og Messias?" Is he considered a great Poet? [3]

When I last saw you, I think we were speaking of an American book called "A Year in Spain" which, if I mistake not, has been translated into Danish.[4] The person who takes charge of this letter is the author of that book; — by name Alexander Slidell, Lieutenant in the Navy of the U. States. If he can leave the ship at Copenhagen, he will go to see you at the Library. You will find him very intelligent and very agreeable. I beg you to show him that beautiful little M.S. — that precious book, on parchment, with Illuminations.

How is Riise? Do you smoke together as much as you used to do? O, I wish I could step in some evening, and take a friendly pipe with you both, and talk about books! What is the use of living so far apart? Tell Riise, that Cooper was very much delighted to get the translation of his works.[5] Do not forget to remember me most cordially to the friendly man.

Good bye. If you see Mr. [Peder] Petersen, present my regards to him. Write me soon. In the mean time I remain very truly yours

Henry W. Longfellow

P.S. Please say to Professor Rafn, that I have written him a letter [6] by the same ship, which brings you this.

2nd P.S. After making several inquiries concerning your brother, as you requested, — I cannot hear anything of a person, bearing that name. I do not think there are any Danes in Boston.

MANUSCRIPT: Royal Library, Copenhagen. ADDRESS: à Monsieur/Monsieur Bölling./(Bibliothèque Royale)/à Copenhague PUBLISHED: "Eight Unpublished Letters," pp. 172–173.

1. George Mifflin Dallas (1792–1864), President Van Buren's minister to Russia, 1837–1839, and later Vice-President with Polk, 1845–1849.

2. Letter No. 355, actually written on June 24, 1836.

3. Wergeland's *Creation, Man, and Messiah* has been called "one of the most extraordinary masterpieces of Norwegian literature" (Harald Beyer, *A History of Norwegian Literature* [New York, 1956], p. 131). For Longfellow's interest in the poem, see *Longfellow and Scandinavia*, pp. 74–75.

4. *A Year in Spain* does not seem to have appeared in Danish. Longfellow may have been thinking of the Swedish translation (313.6).

5. See Letter No. 325.

6. Letter No. 375.

## 374. *To Anne Longfellow Pierce*

Cambridge April 23. 1837

My dear Anne,

On Thursday morning last, just as the clocks of Boston were seven, I rang at Mrs Mason's door and left your package and letter: and yesterday noon, as I mounted the stone steps, leading from the Common into Beacon street, I met the lady and her daughter Jane, descending the same.[1] She inquired after you — seemed to be *very* much gratified by your present — said it was beautiful exceedingly — and that she should write you very soon. After which we went our several ways; she homeward, and I to Mrs. [Hannah] Welles's, where I passed an hour in the evangelical society of Saint Eliza. I afterward saw Caro Doane at Chs. Welles's. She appears in good health and spirits: and probably begins to "see the difference."[2]

No more Hock-bottles are wanted. With those Mr. [Charles] Amory has procured here, we have enough. Mine came safely. So did I, saving the loss of my cloak. I think you will find it in the porch. I told the boy to put it in the *round house,* meaning on-board the steamer. I fancy he thought it would do as well to take it *round the house,* through the back yard, into the porch. Am I not right?

Dr. [Ichabod] Nichols and his wife came in the boat with us. I was not aware of the fact, till I heard of it here in Cambridge: having gone to bed the moment I stepped on board the boat.

These few lines, my dear Annie, I write in great haste, having sundry letters to write this day. By Monday's boat I shall send two trunks to Judge Potter. Love to all.

Very truly and affectionately your brother

Henry.

Please communicate the following to Clara [Crowninshield]. Extract from a letter from Ritchie[3] in Heidelberg. March. 12.

"The Hepps and especially Eve were overjoyed at the warm salutations you sent them. I whispered into Eve's ear the 'salute particular and by name' as she came with a candle to show me the way down stairs. She seemed a little surprised, very much pleased — said 'Ich hätte es wirklich nicht erwartet: Er ist ein gar zu lieber Mann,'[4] and charged me not to forget to send you a salute from her equally expressive of her good will. Miss. C's letter came in company with yours, and that evening you may be sure we held a long talk about you. Old Mrs. Hepp praised you, and thumped with her fist on the table, and delivered an oration on Miss. Crowninshield. She swore to God (a literal translation) that she had never seen a woman, with whom she could find no fault, except Miss. C——. Even Edward seemed to be *begeistert* [enthusiastic] and talked *vernünftiger* [more sensibly] than at any other time in the last eighteen months. The evening was devoted to the pleasures of remembrance. Please tell Miss. C. that I sent the three last vols. of her Schiller to Paris, together with yours, care of Welles &co to whom [Daniel Raynes] Goodwin sent your address with orders to forward the books immediately. Be so good as to give the enclosed little view of the Stift Neuburg to Miss. C. with my sincerest regards and best wishes."[5]

Tell Clara, also, that Lavy[6] has sent a pair of Russian slippers for her, (not made:) and likewise a pair for Mary Goddard. I send them in the trunk, with Ritchie's present.

I also send her the Outlines by Retch, and one little German book, which she may like to have: viz Moosblüthen: and a Vol. of Herder for Mary.[7]

MANUSCRIPT: Longfellow Trust Collection. ADDRESS: To/Mrs. A. L. Pierce/care of S. Longfellow Esq/Portland. POSTMARK: CAMBRIDGE MS. APR 24

1. Mrs. Mary Means Mason and Jane Mason were the mother and sister, respectively, of Longfellow's classmate Alfred Mason (43.1). The Mason family had moved to Boston in 1832 and lived on Tremont Street.

2. The people mentioned here were all cousins of Longfellow. Eliza Doane (1783–1840) and Caroline Doane (54.5) were the sisters, and Charles Bartlett Wells (1812–1856) the son, of Mrs. Hannah Wells (43.4). The quotation that Longfellow applies to Caroline is from the *Merchant of Venice*, IV, i, 368: "Thou shalt see the difference of our spirits."

3. David Ritchie (1812–1867), a graduate of Jefferson College, had known Longfellow and Clara Crowninshield in Heidelberg, where he received his J.U.D. in 1837. Upon his return to America he practiced law in Pittsburgh and served three terms in the House of Representatives, 1853–1859.

4. "I had really not expected it: he is a very dear man."

5. This paragraph from Ritchie's letter (in response to an unrecovered letter from Longfellow) concerns Frau Hepp, with whom Clara Crowninshield boarded in Heidelberg, her son Edvard, and her granddaughter Eve. See *Diary of Clara Crowninshield.*

6. Charles Lavy, a businessman from Hamburg, had followed the Longfellow party about Sweden in the summer of 1835 in devoted admiration of Clara Crowninshield. For details of his unsuccessful courtship, see the *Diary of Clara Crowninshield.*

7. Longfellow refers here to Moritz Retzsch (1779–1857), German illustrator and engraver; to *Moosblüthen zum Christgeschenk* (Frankfurt, 1830) by Friedrich Wilhelm Carové (1789–1852); and to Johann Gottfried von Herder (1744–1803), philosopher, poet, and critic.

## 375. *To Carl Christian Rafn*

Cambridge. April 23. 1837.

My dear Sir,

Hearing of an opportunity to send direct to Copenhagen, I cannot suffer it to pass, without writing you a few words, to inform you of my safe return to my Native Land. I was disappointed not to hear from you again before leaving Heidelberg; from which place, in June or July of last year, I sent you a Draft on Hamburg for the amount due from me to the Society of Northern Antiquaries, on becoming a member. I hope that this Draft reached you safely.[1] If it did not, I beg of you to inform me, that I may write to Heidelberg and have the matter rectified.

I had the pleasure of receiving yesterday the Report of the Society, addressed to its British and American Members. In return I send you a paper on the Indian Languages of North America, not yet published. It will appear in the North American Review for July next.[2] By sending it now, you will get it probably some months in advance. Pray let me know in what way I can be useful to you here. What books shall I send you? I beg you to let me serve you in any way I can. It will give me much pleasure.

Are you in correspondence with Her[r] Liljegren in Stockholm? If so, have the goodness, when you next write, to present to him my regards, and tell him I have not forgotten his request in reference to the Calendars, but will send them by the first good opportunity.[3]

I beg you to present my respects to your friend Magnuson. To Bölling I write by the same ship which brings you this.[4]

Very truly yours
Longfellow

MANUSCRIPT: Royal Library, Copenhagen. ANNOTATION (*first sheet*): bew[?] Oct.

18, 1838. PUBLISHED: Benedict Grøndal, *Breve fra og til Carl Christian Rafn, med en Biographi* (Copenhagen, 1869), pp. 179–180.

1. See Letter No. 351.
2. XLV (July 1837), 34–59.
3. What Longfellow meant by "Calendars" is obscure. Liljegren (312.6) did not receive them in any event, for overcome by hypochondria, he committed suicide on June 2, 1837.
4. Letter No. 373.

## 376. *To Alexander Slidell Mackenzie*

[Cambridge] May 3. 1837.

My dear Slidell,

I have been so busy since my return from the East, that it has not been in my power to see you: and fearing that before I have a leisure day you may be "far away on the billow," I here send you a couple of letters for Copenhagen with an introductory billet to one of the Librarians, which may perhaps be of service to you.[1]

You do go to Brazil after all, it seems. Wherever you go, and hear outlandish tongues spoken "O, then remember me." Anything in shape of a *Dialect*, or a *Popular Song* in any language will be very welcome to me.

I mean to see you again before you sail. Tomorrow, if possible. If by any accident I should not, I now shake hands with you most cordially, and wish you all prosperity.

Very sincerely your friend
H. W. Longfellow.

MANUSCRIPT: Massachusetts Historical Society. ADDRESS: Lieut. Slidell.

1. Letters No. 373, 375, and 377.

## 377. *To Jørgen Bølling*

[Cambridge] May 3. 1837.

My dear Sir,

Allow me the pleasure of introducing to you my friend Mr. Slidell of the American Navy. If you will have the goodness to show him the curious books and manuscripts, of which you have the charge, or in any other way be of service to him in your city, you will much oblige me.

Very truly yours,
Henry W. Longfellow

MANUSCRIPT: Royal Library, Copenhagen. ADDRESS: Mr. Bölling/at the Royal Library/Copenhagen./Mr. Slidell. PUBLISHED: "Eight Unpublished Letters," p. 175.

378. *To Stephen Longfellow*

Cambridge May 12. 1837

My dear Father,

Since my return to Cambridge I have been pretty busily employed. I have a class in German; and shall soon commence my Lectures; probably next week; at all events not later than the week after. As you may feel some interest to know my plan of proceeding, I will give you a slight sketch of the Course.

1. Introduction. History of the French Language.
2. The other modern Languages of the South of Europe.
3. History of the Northern, or Gothic Languages.
4. Anglo-Saxon Literature.
5 and 6. Swedish Literature.
7. Sketch of German Literature.
8. 9. 10. Life and Writings of Göthe.
11. and 12. Life and Writings of Jean Paul Richter.

Some of them are written lectures; others will be delivered from Notes. If I feel well during the Summer, and am in good spirits, I may extend the course; but what I have noted down above is all I contemplate at present. People seem to feel some curiosity about the lectures, and consequently I am eager to commence; relying mainly for success on the interesting topics, I shall be able to bring forward. Having in my own mind an idea of what Lectures should be; — and a pretty fixed idea also; — I shall work right on, to put this idea into practice, without troubling myself much about the views and theories of others on this object. And having undertaken nothing but what I feel myself competent to do without effort, I have no great anxiety as to the result. I lecture to the Senior Class, and to those members of the Law and Divinity Schools, who choose to attend. How large an audience I shall have is a matter of entire uncertainty.

Alexander was here on Sunday last. He was very well, and in very good spirits. Active life seems to suit his constitution much better than a sedentary one. He returned to Andover on Monday.[1]

The wine is bottled, and turns out to be of the very best quality. The Hock-drinkers in Boston think they never tasted any equal to it. I shall send you by Monday's boat a basket of it, in small bottles. It is of two kinds. That with a cross on the cork is the most delicate. It is Scharlachberger. The other is Johannisberger. It is strong and generous. I hope it will not make your head ache. I wish you would send a few bottles to the Judge; though I do not think he will like it. I do not know as you will. Most people do not. I do not know how many bottles were put into the basket; but there will be enough at all events to give you a taste, and I will send you more, or bring it, when I come, as you may determine advisable, — in other words — as the wine may prove to your taste.[2]

Tell Anne her books and *pipe*! will be sent with the wine. So will Little Red Ridinghood for Clara. Her books were all in good condition and have been sent to Mr. Nichols.[3]

Cambridge is growing very green and pleasant; and your sons thrive in this climate. Two days ago I saw old Dr. Pierce of Brooklyn. He says he used to be your Tutor.[4] They say he is the dullest preacher that ever preached. In which case he must be *very* dull. Mr. Walker's Dudlean Lecture was very excellent.[5] We think in Cambridge, that he is a more powerful man than Dr. Channing.

With much love to all,

very truly yours
H. W. L.

P.S. I am glad to hear that Aunt Lucia has returned in safety from the East; and look forward with much pleasure to seeing her in August.

MANUSCRIPT: Longfellow Trust Collection. ADDRESS: Hon. Stephen Longfellow./ Portland. POSTMARK: CAMBRIDGE MS. May 13 ENDORSEMENT: H W Longfellow to his father/May 13, 1837

1. See 371.6.
2. Longfellow had purchased this wine in Germany (Letter No. 354 and note).
3. In a letter to her brother dated Thursday evening (May 18, 1837), Anne Pierce made it clear that the pipe, presumably bought by Longfellow in Europe, was to be a present for one of her friends. Little Red Ridinghood (*Rothkäppchen*) refers to a pattern for an *Ofenschirm* (fire screen), bought by Clara Crowninshield in Heidelberg (*Diary of Clara Crowninshield*, p. 218). Benjamin Ropes Nichols (1786–1848), Boston lawyer and brother of Rev. Ichabod Nichols, was Clara Crowninshield's former guardian (*Ibid.*, Introduction).
4. Rev. John Pierce (1773–1849) of Brookline, a member of the Harvard class of 1793, was a tutor, 1796–1797.
5. James Walker (1794–1874), pastor of the Unitarian Church in Charlestown and editor of the *Christian Examiner*, became Professor of Moral and Intellectual Philosophy at Harvard in 1839 and president of the college in 1853. According to Samuel Longfellow, the Dudleian Lecture "was annually given on the ancient foundation of Paul Dudley, but has long been discontinued, from the smallness of the fund and the superannuated condition of the appointed subjects" (*Life*, I, 262n).

379. *To Anne Longfellow Pierce*

[Cambridge] Monday morning. May 15. 1837.

My dear Anne,

The Pipe and the Knickerbocker I herewith send; but not the Bible, because I have not found one to please me. I meant to go to Boston with the express purpose of finding one, but have been prevented by other engagements. I will find time soon.

There is no particular haste in regard to the *father-murderers*, as the Germans call them; — alias *Dickies*, as we call them. I think the German name more expressive.

The pipe should have been more thoroughly cleaned. But unfortunately I do not see my servant, very often: generally only once a day, in the morning, when he comes to bring me my Diogenes-tub of cold water, and wake me from my morning dreams with the cry of "Arise, Mister *Long*fellow!" He uses this elegant form of casting out sleep-devils, because he is a negro and has a patent from Nature for all possible elegances of expression. But never being fully awake till about one hour after this crowing of the cock, I have forgotten to tell the said chanticleer to clean, not *his*, but my pipe, which has been standing for ten days in a corner of the room for that purpose. Therefore— I have had to clean it myself.

In regard to the *Father-murderers*, I was going on to say, that next vacation will be soon enough.

Much love to all —

Very truly &c
H. W. L.

MANUSCRIPT: Longfellow Trust Collection. ADDRESS: Anne Pierce

380. *To Clara Crowninshield*

[Cambridge] Monday morning. May 15. 1837.

My dear Clara,

I should have sent you Rothkäppchen sooner, if I had found an opportunity. I am now forced to squeeze it into a place somewhat too small for it; but shall contrive not to injure it.

The books and so forth are safely lodged in South Street.[1] You have nothing to pay for them. I was indebted to you for sundry postages: and let one account balance the other. That is the shortest way.

If Schiller does not arrive soon, I shall write to Paris. Those two youths[2] must have been crazy to send the package to a Banker's care in Paris.

As to Göthe, it is too late. Ri[t]chie was to leave Heidelberg on the first of June. Of course no letter could reach him. He goes to Paris via Switzerland; and did not send me the name of his Parisian Banker.

I saw Miss. Robbins again after my return. She is as sour as a lemon; and I must say, that in the two interviews I have had with her ladyship, I have seen nothing to justify the high eulogisms bestowed upon her conversational powers. She apologized for her voice being bad — having a cold; and would not have me think that "that was a specimen of her usual voice" &c. There is too much of the blood of Ishmaël in her veins; she has assumed a hostile attitude against the whole world; which in any man or woman is a false and unnatural position; and therefore cannot please. Poor soul! she has had but too much to place her in this position. But it would be *greater* in her to return the world's rebuke with a silent and dignified sorrow, rather than with stormy indignation, which only makes her the more unhappy.[3]

I have seen Mr & Mrs [Benjamin Ropes] Nichols since their return. They are very well, and have brought with them from Georgia the tuft, or top of a pine, with great heavy cones, folded in the wiry leaves: the most beautiful thing you can imagine. I was entirely enraptured.

In haste, with much love to Eliza and Margaret [Potter],

yours &c &c
H.W.L.

MANUSCRIPT: Clifton Waller Barrett Collection, University of Virginia. ADDRESS: Miss/Clara Crowninshield/Portland

1. That is, in the care of Mr. Benjamin Ropes Nichols.
2. David Ritchie and Daniel Goodman.
3. Clara Crowninshield's letters to Longfellow do not reveal the identity of this person, but it may be Eliza Robbins (1786–1853), an acquaintance of Longfellow and the spinster daughter of Edward Hutchinson Robbins, a Harvard graduate of 1775 and former lieutenant-governor of Massachusetts.

## 381. *To George Washington Greene*

Cambridge. Sunday. May. 21. 1837.

How fares it with you, my dear George? afar off in your Italy? Do you think of us often? Do you say now and then "I wish some of those good souls were with me"? Do you "walk in soul" with us at home, as we do with you in Florence? We would fain believe all this, and more. But you write very seldom — at least it seems so to us; — and when you do write, your letters are short — at least it seems so to our still insatiate curiosity, which is busied with you and your doings, far more than you imagine — particularly when the scirocco blows *blue*, and the post brings you no letters, or what it does bring are *no great shakes*.

In Cambridge all is peace. Spring has come; bringing birds and blossoms and Nat Willis, from the South. They are all welcome. Willis is writing a Tragedy. The subject is some passage in the history of the Italian Republics. The hero is Luigi Sforzi — or something to that effect. He writes the piece *"to order,"* for Miss Clifton, who gives him one thousand dollars.[1] I can hardly tell you how *very* sorry I am for this. I do not like to see Poetry sold like a slave. When Göthe wrote his Götz von Berlichingen, a Berlin bookseller was so much pleased with it, or with its success more probably, that he straightway sent the author an order for a dozen more such Dramas on topics connected with the History of the Middle Ages! This coolly ordering a dozen, makes the matter ridiculous. But why not order a dozen as well as one? *Non è vero*? [Isn't that right?] Willis is in good spirits, and fat. Dr. [Samuel Gridley] Howe, whom I saw yesterday, is likewise in good spirits, but lean. I see in a Philadelphia paper the death of Joseph Howard — your friend and Clark's. He died in February last at Madeira, whither he had gone *"in pursuit of health,"* as the Obituaries say. I did not know him. But I remember you always spoke highly of him. Indeed "none named him but to praise."[2]

Felton is well. He passes most of his time at this present writing, in getting his miniature painted, and sitting at the feet of his beloved. For my own part, I lead a somewhat more studious life: and take long, solitary walks, through the green fields and woodlands of this fair neighborhood. Yesterday I was at Mount Auburn, and saw my own grave dug; that is, my own tomb. I assure you, I looked quietly down into it without one feeling of dread. It is a beautiful spot, this Mount Auburn. Were you ever there?

When did you see Ticknor last? Where is he now?[3] When you next meet salute him friendly from me. Tell him the Lectures of his successor commence in two days from this date.

Dean Palfrey and the North American flourish very well. Your Article on Balbi is just through the Press. I send you herewith the proofs — or rather the sheets, — together with those of your last Article. Balbi I did not get till a few minutes ago — by special favor from the printer. (In fact this letter and the whole package is entirely extemporaneous, having heard *suddenly* of an opportunity to send to you.) Therefore I have not read the aforesaid Balbi. The Article which follows on a *Swedish Epic* is by me. I should send you the whole of it, if it were possible; but it is now in Press. I have another Art. in this July No. viz. on Hawthorne's Twice-Told Tales.[4]

Do not send any more Statistics of books, but Poetry — poetry — Italian Poetry, and Modern Literature. The Dean says your Art. on Books &c is very interesting &c &c. I do not doubt it: but I would rather have you write a *cracking* paper on the Living Poets; or if you will on Alfieri, and his singularly interesting auto-biography.[5]

I had a few lines from your mother last week. She is kind enough to urge my visiting her. I shall as soon as I have leisure enough.

Felton has just come in with the sheets of Balbi [and] says "I think this an excellent Article of Green[e]'s." So you have beforehand the good opinion of *le bon Felton* as Nat Willis calls [him].

What a shame it was, that I could not make the acquaintance of your friend [Horatio] Greenough! I regret it very much, I assure you.

Give my warmest, most affectionate regards to Maria and believe me your sincere and very faithful friend

Henry W. Longfellow

MANUSCRIPT: Longfellow Trust Collection. ADDRESS: To/George W. Greene Esq/ American Consul/Rome. ENDORSEMENT: Rome/19—— Jan. 1838

1. Nathaniel Parker Willis' blank-verse tragedy, *Bianca Visconti, or the Heart Overtasked,* was written expressly for Josephine Clifton (1813–1847), a popular actress. Its hero was Francesco Sforzi (1401–1466), duke of Milan.

2. Cf. Fitz-Greene Halleck, "On the Death of J. R. Drake." Joseph Howard (1803–1837) was a native of Providence, Rhode Island. According to State Department records he died in Funchal on February 1, 1837.

3. Ticknor had just left Florence after a fortnight's visit (George S. Hillard, ed., *Life, Letters, and Journals of George Ticknor* [Boston, 1876], II, 87). Greene presumably saw him during this period.

4. For Longfellow's articles, see 371.2. Greene's article, which included a review of Adrien Balbi's *Essai statistique sur les bibliothèques de Vienne* (Vienne, 1835), appeared in the *North American Review,* XLV (July 1837), 116–149. "Your last Article" refers to his review of Macrie's *History of the Reformation in Italy* (365.2).

5. Greene did not act on Longfellow's suggestion. Vittorio Alfieri's revealing autobiography was first published in 1804.

## 382. *To Stephen Longfellow*

Cambridge. May. 25. 1837.

My dear Father,

Since I last wrote you I have commenced my Lectures. The first was on Tuesday last — the second to-day, Thursday. I lecture from Notes, and have succeeded very much to my own satisfaction; feeling no more embarrassment, than if I were eating dinner. I am rather astonished at this; and very much pleased; for now instead of being a source of anxiety, these Lectures are a source of pleasure to me. I had a presentiment, that all would turn out well; and perhaps this presentiment has had some influence[1] in producing the result. As far as I can percieve and hear, the audience is quite as much pleased as I am; and they sit[2] motionless and attentive for nearly an hour.

This is the only news I have to send you; except that I intend to change my lodgings. I have found two large and beautiful rooms in the Craigie-house, and thither I go at the close of this term. I shall be sorry to leave Mrs Stearns on many accounts; but I cannot endure boarding homes. In the Craigie rooms, I shall be entirely my own master, and have my meals by myself and at my own hours. So I form to myself a vision of independence, which I do not now enjoy.[3]

Alexander was here to-day; but I did not see him. He took this rainy day to visit us. He leaves a note stating that they have raised his pay to $50 per month. He seems desirous of leaving Mr. Haywood and joining Mr. Fessenden. I have seen Mr. F. on the subject. He has charge of the Eastern Rail-road between Boston and Salem: but his older pupils have the best situations on the road. He thinks he may soon want another assistant: and offers $30 per month, the year throughout — whether in actual service on the road or in the Office. In other words a salary of $365 per annum. If Alexander can get this place, I think he had better take it. Where he now is, all seems uncertain. For my part, I think I should not remain a single day with Haywood. There is evidently no system about his proceedings. Everything seems to be at loose ends; and it is certainly of great importance for Alex to go through a regular system of training. Dont you think so? In my mind the different appearance of the two offices — Fessenden's and Haywood's — would alone be sufficient to decide the question. In the former — neatness — order — activity: in the latter dust, cobwebs and solitude. The one looks thrifty — the other desperate.[4]

Sam is well, and flourishing.

Old Dr. Ware is nearly blind. For two years past he has been deprived of the sight of one eye; and now a cataract is forming in the other. In a few weeks he thinks he shall see the light of heaven no more — in this world.[5]

Did the wine reach you in safety? How do you like it? Nice little bottles, are they not?

May 26.

Our Eastern storm continues. Indeed for most of the past week we have had cold, rainy, disagreeable weather.

In haste yours — with much love to all —

Henry W. Longfellow

MANUSCRIPT: Longfellow Trust Collection. ADDRESS: To/Hon. Stephen Longfellow/Portland. POSTMARK: CAMBRIDGE MS. MAY 26

1. Longfellow first wrote "effect," then deleted it with a pen stroke.

2. Longfellow wrote "quite" after this word, then deleted it with a pen stroke.

3. Upon taking up residence in Cambridge, Longfellow boarded with his friend Cornelius Felton in the home of Asahel Stearns (1774–1839), a Harvard professor of law who lived in the Foxcroft House on the corner of Kirkland and Oxford streets. The Craigie House — where Longfellow spent the rest of his life — was owned at this time by Mrs. Elizabeth Shaw Craigie (1772–1841), who struggled to maintain herself in its splendor by leasing rooms to Harvard students and instructors. See *Life*, I, 268–275, and H. W. L. Dana, "Chronicles of the Craigie House: The Coming of Longfellow," *Proceedings of the Cambridge Historical Society*, XXV (January 1939), 19–60.

4. See 371.6. Fessenden (139.5) was chief engineer for the Eastern Railroad. Longfellow spent the next three years negotiating with Fessenden and others for a railroad position for his brother, but nothing materialized, and in 1840 Alexander joined the Northeast Boundary Survey.

5. Henry Ware (1764–1845), Hollis Professor of Divinity at Harvard and Unitarian polemicist.

## 383. *To Margaret Potter*

[Cambridge]
Friday evening [June 2, 1837][1]

MY GOOD, DEAR MADGE, —

You do not know how sorry I am, that I cannot see you. But for a week past I have hardly left my chamber. I have been so ill as to give up all College duties, Lectures, &c.; and am very happy to get through — (as I trust I shall) without a fever, which I have been expecting for several days past. To-night I am better and have crawled off the sofa, to write you half a dozen lines.

My dear little child; I am truly delighted to know you are in Boston. It is an unexpected pleasure to me. Of course you mean to stay all summer; and I shall see you very often. Write me immediately; and tell me everything about everybody. I shall come and kiss you to death, as soon as my bodily strength will permit.

Till then very truly my little dear,
Yr. BROTHER HENRY.

MANUSCRIPT: unrecovered; text from Higginson, *Longfellow*, p. 148.

1. The date is speculative but conforms to information in Letter No. 385 concerning Longfellow's illness with influenza and Margaret Potter's presence in Boston.

## 384. *To John Gorham Palfrey*

[Cambridge] Friday morn. [June 2, 1837][1]

My dear Sir,

I should like to see the Revise of the last sheets of Frithiof,[2] if you will be so kind as to send it to me.

I am laid up with the influenza again.

Yrs. truly
H. W. L.

MANUSCRIPT: Harvard College Library. ADDRESS: Rev. Dr. Palfrey/Cambridge.

1. The reference in this letter to *Frithiofs Saga* provides the month and year. Since Longfellow complained of the influenza both here and in Letter No. 383, the exact dates of the two have been made to conform.

2. See 371.2.

## 385. *To Stephen Longfellow*

Cambridge June 10. 1837.

My dear Father,

Since I last wrote you I have been quite unwell: in fact I was not well when I wrote. Three weeks ago I was attacked violently with Influenza, I supposed. Unfortunately it was the day before my Lectures commenced. I had announced the Lectures, and expecting to get over my cold, every day, I began to lecture, and fought against bad weather, and influenza, and blue devils, till finally I got the worst of it, and after three Lectures was obliged to give up. That was ten days ago. Since then I have kept pretty closely to the house. The weather has been wet and cold most of the time; and I have hardly been able even to ride out. I am, however, nearly well and hope next week to begin again with College duties.

I was very glad to see Judge Potter. My last letter had not gone from my hands more than half an hour, when he came in and handed me yours, to which mine was virtually an answer, though I did not imagine so while writing it. Margaret [Potter] I have not yet seen; not having been able to go into Boston. I hear of her occasionally. She is in good health and spirits; and seems to enjoy herself very much.

From Col. Fessenden and the Eastern Railroad, I hear nothing farther; so that Alexander's affairs in this particular are at a stand-still. He has not been here since my last.

I am glad you *try to like* the wine. It is now a long time since I have tasted it. I should certainly take a glass at this moment, if I could conveniently reach it. But I should have to make too long an arm — the wine being all in Boston; so that it may not be *too* near.

Nothing new to add. My love to all at home and at the Judge's.

Most truly yours
H. W. L.

Two words to Mary. I thought, my dear, I had sent your music. But a day or two ago I found it — in my closet. I reflected, however, that having been so long on the way, a few weeks more, would be no great matter; particularly, as you cannot play much under your Dr.'s hands. I am rejoiced to hear you are so much better.[1] Mrs. [Nancy Doane] McLellan brings us this good news. She is still at the "*mansion of Mrs.* [Hannah Doane] *Well's*," I suppose; or was at the last accounts; namely, on Sunday last — a week ago, when Mrs. Wells, hearing I was ill, came out to see me, and was astonished to find me "sitting, clothed and in my right mind." Three miles had magnified my cold into a dangerous malady. The simple truth is, the only symptom of ill health remaining is a *yellow coat* on my tongue — which is not *very* uncomfortable, considering the coldness of the weather. I shall leave it off, when I leave off my flannels.

To Anne. The Biblical History is long: I mean *our* Biblical History; and unlike the Jewish or Hebrew Old Testament, begins with *Job* instead of *Genesis*. It is not my fault: inasmuch as I cannot go out of doors.[2]

Wafers, *Masonic* flourish and screen-apology shall receive early and due attention.[3]

Question. Has my cloak been found?

Answer. — —[4]

MANUSCRIPT: Longfellow Trust Collection. ADDRESS: Hon. Stephen Longfellow/ Portland. POSTMARK: CAMBRIDGE MS. JUN 12 ENDORSEMENT: HW Longfellow *June 10. 1837.*/June 16. 1837.

1. Mary Longfellow's illness is explained by Zilpah in an addendum to her husband's letter to Henry dated June 16, 1837: "Mary was quite sick after going to the wedding of a friend, the excitement of the scene was altogether too much for her strength."

2. A reference to the Bible that Longfellow was to have purchased for his sister (see Letter No. 379).

3. In a letter dated "Thursday evening" (May 18, 1837), Anne had asked Longfellow to send her "some decent *little* blk. [sealing-wax] wafers" and to "expatiate upon" her distress in sending to Mrs. Mason (374.1) a screen "in such a large awkward shape."

4. The answer was Yes (Stephen Longfellow to H.W.L., June 16, 1837).

386. *To Stephen Longfellow*

Hanover July 25. 1837[1]

My dear Father,

We have safely reached this place on our way to the Whites: and here we remain for two days. This afternoon Mr Hillard delivered his Oration;[2] and tomorrow is Commencement, with thirty five Orations. If we survive this, we shall start in the evening for Littleton, by way of Haverhill: thence go to Franconia; and then through the Notch to Portland.

Last evening I was at Dr. [Reuben Dimond] Mussey's; where there was music and lemonade. I dine with him to-day, though on his assurance, that at Commencement time, they live not on bread alone.[3]

Hanover stands on the broad level summit of a hill; — surrounded by a valley, like the fosse of a citadel: — and beyond this are pleasant green hills, forming an amphitheatre to the North, East and West, and opening southward upon the plains. In this direction lies Enfield; with its three Shaker villages on the border of a beautiful lake; the most beautiful scene we have beheld on our journey thus far.[4]

July 26.

Hillard's Oration yesterday afternoon was brilliant and *very* highly finished: a truly remarkable production. It has gained him great applause, and in truth does him infinite credit.

Of the thirty five orations I heard *twenty* five:[5] this forenoon. A greater part of the afternoon I have passed on the balcony of the hotel, looking at the great crowd assembled around the carts of the pedlers, who are selling their Wares at auction. Sam's chum is here, and Sam. Eliot, who is under my wing.[6]

This evening I take tea with President Lord. Last evening, was at Mr. Olcott's. He was a member of the Hartford Convention. Do you remember him? A quiet, pleasant man.[7]

We shall probably leave town tomorrow-morning, unless Dr. Howe, one of our travelling companions, who was seized this morning with the *Cholera* should grow better,[8] as we trust he will.

Farewell. My love to all.

Very truly yours
H. W. Longfellow

MANUSCRIPT: Longfellow Trust Collection. ADDRESS: To/Hon. Stephen Longfellow/Portland POSTMARK: HANOVER N.H. JUL 27 ENDORSEMENT: Henry July 28. 1837. PUBLISHED: *Life*, I, 266–267.

1. Longfellow left Cambridge on July 22 with George Hillard, Samuel Gridley

Howe, and Samuel Eliot (below, n. 6) on a tour that took him to Hanover and thence over the White Mountains to Portland. See MS Journal.

2. Before the Social Friends and the United Fraternity, literary societies of Dartmouth College.

3. Mussey was a vegetarian (*Life*, I, 266, n. 1).

4. The Shaker community on Mascoma Lake was founded in 1793.

5. By members of the Dartmouth graduating class.

6. Samuel Longfellow's chum is unidentified. Samuel Eliot (1821–1898), a Harvard student, became an historian and educator of considerable repute.

7. Nathan Lord (1793–1870), a Bowdoin graduate of 1809 and a clergyman noted for his proslavery sentiments, was president of Dartmouth College, 1828–1863. Mills Olcott (1774–1845), a prominent Hanover lawyer and a trustee of Dartmouth College, had attended the Hartford Convention as a delegate from New Hampshire.

8. Longfellow deleted "get worse" for "grow better" and confused the sense. He and Hillard left Hanover on the 27th, as planned, and reached Portland on August 1. Apparently neither Howe nor Eliot accompanied them.

## 387. *To Margaret Boies Bradford Eliot*[1]

[Hanover] Wednesday evening. [July 26, 1837]

My dear Mrs. Eliot

I cannot let Samuel "depart in peace"[2] without writing you a few words to say, how much he added to the pleasure of our journey by his gay spirits, and merry laugh. I trust he has enjoyed his short tour. Mr. Hillard and Dr. Howe have become very much attached to him; and he wins good opinions and good wishes wherever he goes. As much for your sake as for his do I rejoice in this. May it ever be so: and may the same gallant, generous spirit mark the man, which we all love so much in your beautiful, brave, noble boy.

What are you doing all alone in little, solitary Cambridge? Is Margaret very good? Does she remember me? The six months have not yet gone. And Pep — my good friend — the uproarious Pep — what is he doing all this time? Busy as ever. I dare say; — and as happy as the day is long. My love to them.[3]

Farewell, my dear friend. I shall soon have the supreme felicity of drinking *Peko* (is it spelled so?) with you. Good bye.

Yours most truly

H. W. L.

MANUSCRIPT: Boston Athenaeum. ADDRESS: Mrs. W. H. Eliot/Cambridge

1. Mrs. Eliot (1796–1864), the widow of William Havard Eliot and the mother of Samuel Eliot.

2. Luke 2:29.

3. That is, Mrs. Eliot's two other children: Margaret Bradford Eliot (b. 1830) and William Prescott Eliot (b. 1826), nicknamed "Pep."

388. *To Josiah Quincy*

Portland August 5. 1837

Dear Sir,

On reaching this place two days ago, I had the honor of receiving your letter of July 31, with the accompanying scheme of Duties &c.[1] As the plan has been matured by yourself and the other gentlemen of the Committee, I regret that I cannot give my full assent to it at once. But it requires of me more than I am willing to undertake. I therefore return the paper, with such alterations as seem to me desirable.

Allow me to suggest, also, that in your estimate of the number of hours employed, and comparison of my duties with those of other Professors, you have given hardly weight enough to the consideration, that the *kind* and *amount* of preparation necessary for an ordinary recitation, is different from that required by a Lecture — even the simplest oral lecture. Besides, I seriously object to having my usefulness in the College computed by the number of hours occupied with the classes. From the nature of my studies, this would lead to very erroneous conclusions. As you are well aware, many days of hard study are often necessary for the preparation of a single lecture.

I therefore take the liberty of suggesting several changes in your plan of duties, which I here inclose.[2]

Very respectfully yours
Henry W. Longfellow

MANUSCRIPT: Harvard College Papers, VIII, 199. PUBLISHED: *Professor Longfellow of Harvard*, p. 26.

1. President Quincy's letter is unrecovered, but the "accompanying scheme of Duties," which developed in detail the statement that the "duty of the Professor shall be to superintend to instruct and to lecture," is preserved in Harvard College Papers, VIII, 201. See *Professor Longfellow of Harvard*, pp. 24–25.

2. Printed in *Professor Longfellow of Harvard*, p. 25.

389. *To Stephen Longfellow*

Cambridge Tuesday eve[nin]g. August. 23. 1837

My dear Father,

We had a pretty good night of it, and I took pretty good care of Mrs. Jenkins.[1] Seward Porter[2] was on board, as usual. When that man dies, I think — if he goes to Heaven, — his happiness will be to run a steamer on the Styx — or Lake Avernus: or from some sea-port town in the moon to some other town up river. If he goes to Purgatory — his torment will be, *not* to run said steamer, nor take passage in the same.

I passed Monday in town, and came out to Cambridge in the evening. A little parasol was bought for Anne, and sent to Alex Wadsworth's[3] office. I called upon him, but he was not in. Therefore, I cannot tell you when to expect him. The Chinese Puzzle I was puzzled to find: and did not find one worth buying. Will try again tomorrow — perhaps. I have already commenced moving. Carpets are taken up; — books taken down; and things turned topsy-turvy. The new rooms are above all praise — only they do want painting. I have made arrangements for my breakfasts and dinners with Miriam, the giantess, of whom Mrs. Craigie says "take her by and large, she is a good *crittur.*"[4] At the sound of a bell, she is to bring me my breakfast; — at the sound of the same bell, later in the day — namely at five o'clock — my dinner.

Moreover —, and more important.

— I have seen the President. The Committee accede to all my alteration and improvements in the schedule of duties; save one, which is in relation to the No. of Oral Lectures. Therefore my duties are;

1. One Oral Lecture per week the year through.

2. Superintendance of studies and Instructors, by being present at least once a month at the recitation of every student in each Language.

3. In Summer Term Two Lectures on Belles Lettres or Lit. Hist. per week in addition to the Oral Lectures, as above. This is the only point they insist upon — and they say if I find I have too much to do, I may deliver in Summer only *one* written Lecture instead of *two* per week.

Thus everything is settled to my entire satisfaction; and I shall commence the Term in great spirits, and lecture on the Faust of Göthe, of which I shall probably have an edition printed here — *not* at my own expense — which is something unusual.[5]

Disastrous occur[r]ence. From my trunk, which was so long on its way from Boston to Portland some three weeks ago — disappeared an entire suit of clothes; consisting of one black frock coat; — one satin waistcoat: and one pair of summer trousers. Has Anne found any of these? If not, the trunk was opened on the way, and as *Felton* says I shall be obliged "to seek *re-dress.*"

I suppose that the Commodore and his beautiful wife have already departed.[6] All the Bostonians are at Nahant, coughing, shivering — and lying sick a-bed with rheumatism.

My love to all. When Sam comes he must bring the Spanish music of Alex. — *La Contra*; and the others.

Yrs. truly
H. W. Longfellow

MANUSCRIPT: Longfellow Trust Collection. ADDRESS: Hon. Stephen Longfellow/ Portland/Me. POSTMARK: BOSTON MS AUG 24

1. Possibly the widow of Charles Jenkins (1786–1832), who had been minister of the Third Congregational Church, Portland.

2. "In the year 1823, Capt. Seward Porter commenced running a steamboat, 'The Patent,' from Portland to Boston" (J. S. C. Abbott, *The History of Maine* [Boston, 1875], p. 427).

3. Alexander Wadsworth (b. 1806), a civil engineer of Boston, was Longfellow's first cousin.

4. Miriam was the wife of Mrs. Craigie's farmer. In a reminiscence of the Craigie House, Longfellow wrote of her, "She was a giantess, and very pious in words; and when she brought in my breakfast frequently stopped to exhort me. The exorbitant rate at which she charged my board was rather at variance with her preaching. Her name was Miriam; and Felton called her 'Miriam the profit-ess' " (*Life*, I, 274).

5. Longfellow did not carry out this intention.

6. Commodore Alexander Scammell Wadsworth and his family had recently visited the Longfellows in Portland.

## 390. *To Anne Longfellow Pierce*

Cambridge September 21. 1837

My dear little Annie, dear,

I sent you this morning, by the pious hands of Henry Smith,[1] the Prayer-book, which should have been sent some weeks ago, but was put out of my way and out of my mind, in the confusion of changing my lodgings.

In my new abode I dwell like an Italian Prince in his villa. A flight of stone steps, with flower-pots on each hand, conducts you to the door, and then you pass up a vast staircase and knock at the left hand door. You enter, and the first thing, that meets your admiring gaze is the author of Outre Mer reclining on a sofa, in a striped calamanco morning gown: — slippers, red. It is morning; say, eight o'clock. The sun shining brightly in at one long window. In answer to the bell, which was rung a few minutes before — enter a fat woman, bearing a tray, with tea and toast and a plate of waffles. This is breakfast. After breakfast begins the Massacre of the Innocents — namely, the *flies*. Bloody work. Thousands fall beneath the blows of a red silk handkerchief, used like a sling. Their poor souls depart to Beelzebub — King of flies. Thus did the Emperor Domitian amuse himself in days gone by.[2] Thus do I in September '37.

After this, a walk in the great gardens, appertaining to the domain. Then the day goes about its business, till five o'clock, when the same fat woman appears again, bearing in dinner.

Slowly and solemnly the dinner disappears; I sitting near the window, so as to behold all who pass to and fro from Mount Auburn, which is much frequented at this hour.

In the evening — visits till nine.

At nine — return home. Vast entry lighted. Read till twelve. Lights put out. Author sleeps: dreams perchance, but not often.

No smoking, at any time.

No fire, — yet.

Samuel as well as usual.

I was disappointed in not seeing the Commodore [Wadsworth] and his suite. Monday night was so *very* foggy here, that I did not imagine it possible for him to come in the boat — because I supposed no boat would come. He came, however, and passed right on. A note received the day after, told me all.

By the way — the frilled shirt is the queerest looking shirt, when *on*, you ever beheld. Stay thy hand: and wait till I come. I cannot tell you how to alter it — but can show you, anon.

(*Dickeys* wanted: and likewise white linen handkerchiefs. Nothing else, if I remember right.)

The Appletons have returned.
No other news to tell you.
This looks like poetry.
But it isn't. Wrote to the Comdre. yesterday.[3]
Now put a line in here.
Then another here.
And that makes a Letter.
What nonsence. No matter.
My love to all at home
And at the Judge's.

Very truly, *truly* yours.
H. W. L.

P.S. Excuse my levity. I hate to [write] serious letters. I think it better to write nonsence: that is, sometimes. Have you seen anybody lately in Portland with my black coat upon his unworthy shoulders? With the steam-boat agent in Boston, I had a *scene*. He was very abusive and profane: I very cool and civil. Threatened to prosecute him, in as gentle and insinuating a manner, as if I had been asking him to take wine; which I think he had been taking without my asking him. Vale.

MANUSCRIPT: Longfellow Trust Collection. ADDRESS: To/Mrs. Anne L. Pierce/ Care of S. Longfellow Esq/Portland. POSTMARK: CAMBRIDGE MS. SEP 22

1. Henry Boynton Smith (1815–1877), a graduate of Bowdoin College and a tutor there in 1837, later enjoyed a distinguished career as a theologian.

2. In *The Twelve Caesars* Suetonius reports that at the beginning of his reign Domitian spent hours stabbing flies with a sharp pen.

3. This letter is unrecovered.

## 391. *To John Vaughan*[1]

Cambridge. Sept. 25. 1837.

My dear Sir,

I trust I have not faded entirely away from yr. friendly remembrance; and I take the liberty of reviving myself therein, by presenting my friend Mr. Lane,[2] a graduate of this institution, at our last Commencement.

Mr. Lane proposes to establish himself in yr. city as private tutor in some gentleman's family; and takes with him the strongest credentials. If you should know of any situation of the kind, you would confer a great favor by mentioning it to Mr. Lane.

Very respectfully yr. Obt. Ser[v]t.
H. W. Longfellow.

MANUSCRIPT: American Philosophical Society. ADDRESS: To/John Vaughan Esq./ Philadelphia

1. Vaughan (1756–1842), philanthropist and member of the American Philosophical Society, was a prominent Philadelphia merchant.

2. John Foster Williams Lane (1817–1861), who took his M.D. at Harvard in 1840.

## 392. *To George Ticknor*

Cambridge September 28. 1837

My dear Sir,

How shall I begin this letter? Not with apologies, for they take time: but rather as most people *end* theirs, with my most cordial regards and friendly remembrances to you all, after this long silence. Your last letters inform us, that you are now in Munich; — I say *now,* though this *now* has long since floated down the stream of Time, *per aver pace co' seguaci sui* [to find peace with its followers]. Still I have you before me, walking even *now* amid great frescoes of the Nibelungen, or under the trees of English gardens by the margin of those green rivers, whose rushing hath "a soul-like sound."[1] Meanwhile I sit here at home, and do the things you wot of; — namely go up the stone-steps of University Hall, darkening the door of No 5 on summer mornings, and wearing, on Commencement days, the black mantle you let fall upon me, when you were translated into English, — not by fire, but by water: — for all which I thank you. And now let me bear witness to the gentlemanly deportment of the Corporation in all things relating to me, thus far. They do not require me to hear recitations — but to Lecture — four courses a year; *namely*; oral, explanitory lectures on the most distinguished authors in Modern Literature — all the year through, once a week, at least: and in the Summer term, a course on Literary History — on what I choose. This year, I take as follows. Autumn term; — Göthe's Faust: — Spring term, Dante; — Summer term, the Spanish Drama; and for the more elaborate *written* Lectures, German and Northern Literature. I say *written*, but they are not. Last Summer I spoke from notes: and I believe did pretty well. The four-fold team of instructors [2] jogs on its wonted pace; — but during yr absence the harness got very much out of order. The young men treat Surault, as the frogs did King Log: [3] they leap upon him — run over him; and he, fat soul, says nought but "My friend, my friend! — go on — go on!" meaning, with the lesson. With ancient Sales it is hardly otherwise; except that the language of expostulation is changed to "My soul! By George!" As to Bokum (the Portuguese word is *boquim* — signifying the mouth-piece of a wind instrument) I fear matters go still worse with him. He stalks up and down the room, braying, and switching his books with a small black cane, — the students laughing all the while, and trying to persuade him to sing the Rang des Vaches in *Deutsch.* I think he would have left us this year, if any good man and true had been near enough to fill his place. The only person, upon whom we have our eyes fixed, in case of his departure, is Gräter,[4] who still goeth about, looking like a lion, with a broad-brim[m]ed hat; and swathed about in stormy days with a great-coat, which reminds one of that mentioned by Polilla in the Spanish Comedy, which was "lined with slices of pork." [5] So much for the Department of Foreign Affairs, in our College: and I cannot close this subject more gracefully, than by mentioning that the President frequently honors my Lectures with his presence; and as soon as I begin, he gives his spectacles three whirls (you remember the gesture) and then falls into a deep sleep, highly flattering to the lecturer, and highly conducive to decorum among the students.

In Cambridge I live delightfully; — having my own household gods, in the Craigie house, somewhat aloof, as it were; and around me are faces and voices, which constantly remind me of you (this is to Mrs Ticknor) I mean yr. sisters Mrs. [Andrews] N. [Norton] and Mrs. [Benjamin] G. [Guild] whom I see often. They are all well. *Mr* Norton, however, has been but poorly this Summer; and of late, quite ill; though now again recovered.

In town, there is nothing new, save the late arrival of the much beloved Appletons; who have returned more beautiful than ever. Nothing has produced such a sensation here, since the Boston Massacre; — an ominous figure of speech, faintly shadowing forth, that many are to be "slain with darts, most cruelly." I *could* mention two or three *dandylings*, who are likely to be *"hurt by the archers;"*[6] but I *wont.*

Fare ye well. My kindest regards to Mrs. Ticknor and Miss Anna.

Most sincerely yours
Henry W. Longfellow.

P.S. In looking over what I have written I cannot but hope it will reach you in some merciful and lenient hour, so as not to seem *too* nonsensical. Otherwise I shall be obliged, when I next write, to make the *amends honorable,* which Joe:y Worcester defines (vide Dic[t].) *"an infamous punishment."*[7]

2nd P.S. There is a Mechanics Fair, in what Miss Quincy[8] calls *"Fan-you-ill* Hall." The greatest curiosity there is a stick of candy, weighing *four hundred pounds.* Color, red.

MANUSCRIPT: Dartmouth College Library. ADDRESS: To/George Ticknor Esq./ care of Messieurs Hottinguer & Co/Paris/Havre Packet [*direction following addressee's name in another hand*]

1. Cf. Coleridge, "Hymn Before Sunrise in the Vale of Chamouni," l. 61.

2. Longfellow inherited four language instructors from Ticknor when he took over as Smith Professor: François Marie Joseph Surault, French; Francis Sales (1771–1854), French and Spanish; Hermann Bokum (1807–1878), German; and Pietro Bachi, Italian and Spanish. James Russell Lowell described Sales at some length in his "Cambridge Thirty Years Ago" (*Prose Works*, Riverside Edition, I, 97–99). Longfellow's problems involving these gentlemen are described in *Professor Longfellow of Harvard*, pp. 30–31 and *passim.*

3. In the fable by Aesop.

4. Francis Gräter, an eccentric German pedagogue, was a familiar figure in the Boston area, where he struggled for a living as a drawing and language teacher. In the 1820's he taught at the Round Hill School in Northampton and met Sam Ward, who later became his protector in New York City.

5. Polilla is the gracioso disguised as a doctor in *El desdén con el desdén*, a comedy by Agustín Moreto y Cabaña (1618–1689).

6. In borrowing his phraseology from Cowper (*The Task*, III, 108–116), Longfellow obviously includes himself as one of the *dandylings.*

7. Joseph Emerson Worcester (1784–1865), philologist and lexicographer, had compiled the *Comprehensive Pronouncing and Explanatory English Dictionary* (1830). He kept rooms in the Craigie House.

8. Eliza Susan Quincy (1798–1884), daughter and secretary of President Quincy of Harvard.

393. *To Parker Cleaveland*

Cambridge October 3. 1837.

My dear Sir

I was very sorry to be again in Portland, and not have resolution enough to make you a visit in Brunswick. I start from here with the best resolutions in the world; but when I reach Portland a most unmanly sadness comes upon me; and not even my desire to look once more upon your friendly countenance, shake you cordially by the hand, and sitting quietly of an evening in that same familiar study of yours, burn tobacco by way of incense to the Memory of the Past, — not the desire to do all this, and more — can prevail upon me to move one step farther towards the spot, which after all, has more of my heart, than any other spot on earth. However, I am determined not to give way to these feelings any longer. Throw but a stone — the giant dies.[1]

And now tell me, — how could you pass through Portland — pass by our very door — and not stay to look upon us even! And this twice in one week! The first time, I knew you were expected; and should have sought you out; but I was obliged to go out of town that very day, with a friend, who was visiting me. The second time I knew nothing of it.

And how is Mrs. Cleaveland? — and Martha Anne, and Elizabeth and Mary? Does music flourish as of old? Are those pleasant Autumn evenings as they used to be — with cheerful fire-light — and lamps, and songs! And in the midst of all, does any well known, old, familiar tune ever recall the memory of one, who still cherishes a most lively and grateful remembrance of that kindness which in other days made your house a home to him!

Well — things must change — and friends be torn asunder — and whirled away in the current of events, to see each other seldom — or perchance no more. It is a very short text to say, that we must make the best of it. But when we have said this, we have said all; — and may as well light a cigar;

> "And when the smoke ascends on high,
> Behold therein the vanity
> Of earthly stuff, —
> Gone with a puff!
> Thus think, and — smoke tobacco."[2]

Can I be of any service to you in any way in Boston? Can I do anything to advance the Cause of Science; — for instance, slay a rival, and send him to you for next Spring!

Why dont you give a Course of Lectures in Boston? You can have as large an audience as you wish.

Did the President[3] tell you he met me in Washington Street two or three days ago? I was glad to see him. It brought back to me the Government Meetings where we had so much fun. They are dull enough here as you remember probably. All business — no merry quirks, and discussions *de omnibus rebus* &c. Remember me next Monday night; and be merciful in the administration of justice. We are very savage here, in that particular. Almost too severe.

How do John and Nathan[4] like college — and screws and scrapes, and all such matters?

Has [Daniel Raynes] Goodwin returned?

Remember me to everybody.

Most sincerely yours
H. W. Longfellow

MANUSCRIPT: Longfellow Trust Collection. ADDRESS: To/Professor Cleaveland/ Bowdoin College/Brunswick/Me POSTMARK: CAMBRIDGE MS. OCT 4

1. Cf. Matthew Green, *The Spleen*, l. 92.

2. Stanza 3, modified slightly, of an "old Meditation upon smoking Tobacco" called "Smoking Spiritualized" by Ralph Erskine (1685–1752), a Scotch clergyman. Longfellow first saw the poem in the *Knickerbocker*, V (June 1835), 504, and copied its five stanzas in his journal entry for October 25, 1835.

3. President Allen of Bowdoin College.

4. John Appleton Cleaveland (1819–1873) and Nathan Smith Cleaveland (1821–1896), the youngest sons of Professor Cleaveland, were both members of the Bowdoin class of 1840.

## 394. *To Margaret Potter*

CAMBRIDGE, October 29, 1837.

MY DEAR MARGARET, —

I was very much delighted with your present of the slippers. They are too pretty to be trodden under foot; yet such is their destiny, and shall be accomplished, as soon as may be. The colors look beautifully upon the drab ground; much more so than on the black. Don't you think so? I should have answered your note, and sent you my thanks, by Alexander on Wednesday last; but when I last saw him, I had not received the package. Therefore you must not imagine from my delay, that I do not sufficiently appreciate the gift. . .

There is nothing very new in Boston, which after all is a gossiping kind of *Little Peddlington,* if you know what that is; if you don't, you must read the story.[1] People take too much cognizance of their neighbors; interest themselves too much in what no[2] way concerns them. However, it is no great matter.

There are Indians here:[3] savage fellows; — one Black-Hawk and his friends, with naked shoulders and red blankets wrapped about their bodies: — the rest all grease and spanish brown and vermillion. One carries a great war-club, and wears horns on his head; another has his face painted like a grid-iron, all in bars: — another is all red, like a lobster; and another black and blue, in great daubs of paint, laid on not sparingly. Queer fellows! One great champion of the *Fox* nation had a short pipe in his mouth, smoking with great self-complacency as he marched out of the City Hall; and another was smoking a cigar! Withal, they looked very formidable. Hard customers.

Give my love to Eliza: and tell her I will send the Views of the Isle of Wight[4] by first opportunity.

With kind remembrances to your father, (to whom please say, that I have attended to Wiggin's letter)[5]

very truly yours
H. W. L.

MANUSCRIPT: unrecovered; text from Higginson, *Longfellow*, p. 129, and from incomplete photostat, Longfellow Trust Collection. ADDRESS: To/Miss Margaret L. Potter/Care of Hon. B. Potter/Portland. POSTMARK: CAMBRIDGE MS. OCT 30

1. Longfellow had presumably read John Poole's satire on village life in England in the *New Monthly Magazine and Literary Journal*, where it appeared in several installments during 1835 and 1836 (Vols. XLIV–XLVI) under the title "Extracts from a Journal Kept During a Residence in Little Pedlington." *Little Pedlington and the Pedlingtonians* was published in two volumes in London in 1839.

2. Text from photostatic copy of manuscript begins after "what" and continues to end.

3. These Indians had been delegates to a peace conference in Washington between the Fox and Sioux tribes. Among them was Black Hawk (1767–1838), the famous Sauk chief. After the treaty (signed October 21, 1837) the delegates were conducted on a tour of various metropolitan areas, including Boston.

4. *Barber's Picturesque Illustrations of the Isle of Wight, Comprising Views of Every Object of Interest on the Island* (London, n.d.).

5. In a letter to his son dated October 15, 1837, Stephen Longfellow had enclosed a statement received by Judge Potter from Timothy Wiggin, claiming a small balance of $5.56 on Longfellow's account and requesting that it be paid to his agent in Boston.

## 395. *To Stephen Longfellow*

Cambridge October 29. 1837

My dear Father,

Yours of the 15 was duly recd. and would have been answered before, did not every day, and almost every hour, bring with it some demand upon my attention, which cannot be so easily put off, as the writing of a letter can. Hence my correspondence languishes with everyone. I have much to read, — much to write, and still more to think about; and when I think, as I dress myself in the morning, to-day at least I shall have a day of leisure, lo! on my breakfast table lies a note from the President, calling a meeting of the Faculty. In addition to this, I find it impossible to get along without a great deal of exercise; — and the want of exercise seems to increase with its gratification: and thus I have to run about more than I ever did at any former period of my life. Thus time goes.

My Lectures make something of a parade on paper, and require of course some attention, though they are all unwritten, save the Summer Course, — which I think I shall this year write out. The arrangement with the Committee requires me to lecture but once a week. I throw in the other, to show, that I am not reluctant to work; and likewise for my own good; — namely, to make me read attentively — give me practice — and keep me from growing indolent. It is, however, astonishing how little I accomplish during a week. No matter. And then this *four-in-hand* of outlandish animals, all pulling the wrong way, except one — this gives me more trouble than anything else.[1] I have more anxiety about them doing well, than about my own. I think I should be more satisfied, if I did the work all myself. Nevertheless I take things very easily; not expecting perfection, and making the best of all things.

Mr. Wiggin's letter was attended to without delay; and the balance duly paid.

We have had some trouble in College: no great affair: but enough to make a noise in our little meddling community. It is now all over I trust. Sam[ue]l nowise concerned: tho' the difficulty arose in his class.[2]

There is a grand display of Indians in Boston; Black-Hawk and some dozen other bold fellows, all grease and red-paint: — war-clubs, bears-teeth — and buffalo-scalps in profusion. Hair cut close, like a brush; and powdered with vermillion; — one cheek red — one black; — forehead striped with bright yellow; with a sprinkling of flour between the eyes: — this will fit almost any one of them. They are to have a *pow-wow* on the Common to-morrow. You will see it all in the papers.

I was rejoiced to hear from Judge Story, that you were at Wiscasset, and so well. I have only had a glimpse of him since his return. His wife has been quite dangerously ill of late; but is better.

With much love to all,

Very truly
H. W. L.

P.S. My particular friend, Chs. Sumner, Editor of the Jurist &c. &c. will be in Portland this week. I beg you to show him some attention — dine him or tea him — or something. He sails for Europe soon; and wants Neal's acquaintance and letters from him to London.

Chs. Daveis will tell you more of Sumner than I have room to do here.[3]

MANUSCRIPT: Longfellow Trust Collection. ADDRESS: To/Hon. Stephen Longfellow/Portland./Me. POSTMARK: CAMBRIDGE MS. OCT 30

1. See 392.2. Bachi seems to have been the exception.

2. The Faculty Records of Harvard College, Vol. XI, reveal that there was considerable unrest among the students in 1837. Between October 18–26 there were a number of gunpowder explosions in various college buildings, and in one instance a group of students who were "excited by liquor" disrupted chapel prayers.

3. Sumner, whom Longfellow here mentions for the first time in his correspondence, spent November 8 in Portland, where he met both John Neal and Stephen Longfellow at the home of his friend Charles Daveis (*Sumner Memoir and Letters*, I, 199–200). He sailed for Europe on December 8.

## 396. *To Frances Appleton*

[Cambridge, October, 1837][1]

My dear friend

I send you the volume of German Romance containing Jean Paul; which I intended to bring before; but have been rather unwell and could not get into town. I am *almost* sorry, that yr. acquaintance with Jean Paul, the magnificent painter of Spring and blossoms should begin in these minor works, where the genius of the poet has not elbow room. However, perhaps you will be encouraged by glimpses here and there of his grand style of Art, to persevere in reading him, even unto the *great Titan*.[2] I think you cannot fail to like him, though so grotesque.

Very truly yours
H. W. Longfellow

MANUSCRIPT: Longfellow Trust Collection. ADDRESS: Miss Fanny Appleton.

1. The date is approximate.

2. *Titan* (1800–1803) was Jean Paul's most ambitious novel. According to his MS Journal, Longfellow had read it in Heidelberg in April 1836.

## 397. *To Frances Appleton*

[Cambridge] Thursday morng. [October, 1837][1]

Madonna Francesca,

Fearing I may not find you at home this bright morng. I take the liberty of writing this, to tell you what a delightful day I passed with you on Monday; and to say how much I wish these scraps of antiquated song may please you.

The Ballad of Agincourt[2] is old. The other piece,[3] though somewhat "masked like hoar antiquity,"[4] is modern. Yet how quaint and sweet.

Did you ever read Tennison's Poems? He too is quaint, and at times so wondrously beautiful in his expressions, that even the nicest ear can ask no richer melody: — and the most lively imagination no lovlier picture, nor more true. For instance, what words could better describe the falling of those silver streams in the Lauterbrunnen Valley, than these two lines from page 109.

> A land of streams! some like a downward smoke,
> Slow-dropping veils of thinnest lawn, did go.[5]

Or the description of Rosalind on p. 121

> To whom the slope and stream of life,
> The life before, the life behind,
> In the ear, from far and near,
> Shineth musically clear.[6]

Did not the cold night air after the play, give you a cold?

Most sincerely yrs
H. W. Longfellow

MANUSCRIPT: Longfellow Trust Collection. PUBLISHED: *Young Longfellow,* pp. 413–414.

1. The date is approximate.
2. By Michael Drayton.
3. Longfellow's note at this point: "Have left it accidentally in Cam."
4. Coleridge, "Monody on the Death of Chatterton," l. 144.
5. "The Lotus-Eaters," ll. 10–11.
6. From the original version of "Rosalind," which appeared in *Poems* (London, 1833). Longfellow's page references are to this edition.

## 398. *To Julius Eugen Ruhl*[1]

Cambridge, près de Boston — 14 Novembre. 1837

à Monsieur Ruhl.
Mon cher Monsieur,

Permettez-moi de vous présenter un de mes amis les plus intimes, Mr. Sumner, qui voyage pour son plaisir. Je reclame vos amitiés en sa faveur; veuillez bien le recevoir en ami; et recevez d'avance mes remerciements.

J'ai l'honneur d'être

votre très humble Serviteur
H. W. Longfellow

MANUSCRIPT: Longfellow Trust Collection.

TRANSLATION:

Cambridge, near Boston — 14 November. 1837

To Monsieur Ruhl.
My dear Monsieur,

Allow me to present to you one of my most intimate friends, Mr. Sumner, who is traveling for pleasure. I crave your good will towards him; be so good as to receive him as a friend; and accept my thanks in advance.

I have the honor to be

your most humble servant
H. W. Longfellow

1. Ruhl (1796–1871), landscape painter, etcher, and court architect (Hofbaudirektor) of Hesse-Cassel, had been Longfellow's traveling companion in Switzerland for six days in 1836 (July 11–17). In a journal entry Longfellow describes him as "a very agreeable and intelligent person" (July 11, 1836).

## 399. *To La Comtesse de Sailly*

Boston. Nov. 14. 1837

My dear Madam

I beg leave to recall myself to your remembrance, by presenting my near friend, Mr. Sumner, who will pass some months in your gay metropolis *pour son plaisir* [for his pleasure].

I trust you have not wholly forgotten Autueil and the Bois de Boulogne: I visited them not long ago — in the Summer of 1836 — but alas! how changed!

The Maison de Santé (excuse me for calling up that doleful place to your memory) is still standing, and is still a Maison de Santé. But no Mme. de Sailly is there — no Mr. Lambin — no dumb man from Nantes, with a slate and a patient wife: and in fine no *Nigaud*. The garden still exists, and the ice-house, where they deposited the dead body of the English Colonel, who died mad. Sweet recollections of Autueil! Why, it made me sad for five minutes; after which things went on as usual.[1]

I searched Paris from the Arc de Triomphe to Père la Chaise, to find you; but all in vain: and this made me sad for five days; that is, a quarter of the time I was in Paris. I hope my friend will be more fortunate.

I have the honor to be with affectionate regard,

Yr. Obt. Ser[v]t.
H. W. Longfellow

MANUSCRIPT: Longfellow Trust Collection. PUBLISHED: *Life*, I, 277–278.

1. Longfellow had revisited the Maison de Santé (see Letter No. 101) with Clara Crowninshield on September 25, 1836. During that month in Paris he had also made several unsuccessful attempts to see his friend Lambin, a well-to-do Parisian. The English colonel is mentioned in *Outre-Mer* (*Works*, VII, 50). The allusion to "*Nigaud*" [Simpleton] is inexplicable.

## 400. *To Mary Appleton*[1]

[Cambridge] Sunday eve. Decr. 10. [1837]

*Mein liebes Fräulein,*

I return Heine with thanks manifold, and a request, that at some future day, you will lend me all the volumes; as I want to read them again, and am tempted to write a Review of the whole. Verily he is a beautiful writer, and one of the greatest *painters in words* the world ever beheld. Dont you think so? The origin of German Popular Tales in Vol. 1. — and the description of the Italian itinerant musicians in Vol 3. are exquisite. He is a Lord Byron in Prose; with all the fire, wit, feeling of the English poet, and more pathos.[2]

As to the *Faustian* episode of "Belfagor in Beacon Street," I fear to undertake it now. I am too serious and sad. The devil would enter, as he does in the old Miracle Plays, shouting "Ho! ho! ho!" and that is not the vein for your gentlemanly Belfager; who as I had conceived the part, was to be nowise Satanic, but rather a soft and Pelham-devil, with french boots and *gants de buerre frais* [butter-colored gloves].[3]

Meanwhile I am delighted to hear, that you intend to note down your passing thoughts on the Faust of Old Humbug, as some of the gentle critic craft, are pleased to call the brave old German. I wish you would write them in my book instead of your own. At all events, let me read them, wont you? I have just finished the Second Part: and have no more Lectures till January, when I begin Dante — that is the Purgatorio and Paradiso, to please my imagination with sweeter visions than the Inferno; which with all its hor[r]ors I make over to Dr. Bachi forever. I am tired of *Infernos.* I shall however write out, and very soon, (I intended to do it last week) a Lecture upon the Faust. I think one will be enough: and this you shall certainly see, if you think it wont tire you to death. There is only one impediment in the way. I was imprudent enough to take up Dante the other day; and he excites me more than any other poet. I hate to turn back to Göthe. But the lecture must be written; and I think I had better settle with the *Adversary*, while I am in the way with him. Tell me, how can I stop mid-way in an Introductory Lecture on Christian Dante to take up Heathen Göthe? So much for not being systematic. Truly I have a pretty medley in my brain this week; namely Dante, Göthe, Henry Heine, Paul de Kock, Scott's Life, and the Death Song of Regnar Leather-Breeches, the Iceland Scald.[4] These have been mixed up from day to day during the week, in a style which "Shenstone might have envied."[5] There were some other ingredients which I have forgotten; — equal to "Pickwick and the Pequot Wars."[6]

And what have you been doing in the bright parlor? Shall I sit there no more with you, and read in pleasant books! Are those bright autumnal mornings gone forever?[7]

Ach! du schöne Seele! Es wird mir gar traurig zu Muthe, wenn ich daran denke, und sehe, wie der schöne Traum dahin zieht, — wie die Wolke sich theilt, und in Thränen zerfliesst, und um mich wird alles so leer, und in meiner Seele eine dunkle Nacht — eine dunkle sternlose Nacht! Und dass hab' ich Dir auf Deutsch sagen müssen, weil eine fremde Sprache ist eine Art von Dämmerung und Mondlicht, worin man den Frauenzimmern allerlei sagen kann, — und so hertzlich treu! Eben so herzlich grüss mir die liebe, liebe Fanny, die ich immer liebe, wie meine eigen Seele. Ach! dass bisschen Verstand, das einer haben mag, kommt wenig oder gar nicht in Anschlag, wenn Leidenschaft wüthet. Wie wird mir das Herz so voll! Das letzte Mal, das wir zusammen waren, gingen wir aus einander ohne einander verstanden zu haben: denn "auf dieser Welt keiner leicht den andern versteht." Und dass ist gar zu traurig.[8]

I pray you, thank her for remembering Victor Hugo's "Songs of the Gloaming";[9] which came safely last evening, and which I have been reading to-day. Also do me the favor to send the accompanying note to Mrs. W. A. [William Appleton] whose *fête* I shall not have the pleasure of attending.

Good night, *liebes Fräulein.*

Very sincerely yr. friend
H. W. L.

MANUSCRIPT: Longfellow Trust Collection. PUBLISHED: *New Light on Longfellow*, pp. 50–52.

1. Fanny Appleton's elder sister (1813–1889) and Longfellow's confidante during this period of his unsuccessful courtship.

2. Longfellow refers to Heine's *Reisebilder* (Hamburg, 1826–1834), 4 vols. When several years later he published a brief essay on Heine in *Graham's Magazine,* XX (March 1842), 134–137, he quoted liberally from the *Reisebilder,* including the description of the Italian musicians, but his attitude toward Heine was generally unsympathetic, and he concluded that he was "not sufficiently in earnest to be a great poet" (p. 137).

3. Longfellow apparently wrote this paragraph in response to a passage in Mary Appleton's letter dated "Tuesday noon" (December 5, 1837): "I have little faith in yr. Belphagor. Such an impertinent demon to our sex would say nothing but threadbare satires against us, however *as you must try it* — I shd. like to see what might be made of it." Thompson has surmised that Longfellow planned "to write a play which would combine Faust legends and Belfagor themes, with a New England setting" (*Young Longfellow,* p. 402). Henry Pelham was the hero of Edward Bulwer-Lytton's *Pelham; or, The Adventures of a Gentleman* (London, (1828).

4. The last two parts of this "medley" refer to John Gibson Lockhart's *Memoirs of the Life of Sir Walter Scott* and to F. H. von der Hagen's translation of *Ragnar-Lodbroks-Saga, und Norna-Gests-Saga* (Breslau, 1829).

5. William Shenstone (1714–1763), poet and man of taste, created an outstanding example of natural landscape gardening at his estate, the Leasowes.

6. In a letter dated "Monday morning" (December 4, 1837), Mary Appleton had written, "I have before me a confused jumble of Miss Martineau, slavery-questions, Miss Pardoe, Lamartine, Pickwick, Allston's poetry, Mrs. Jameson, and the *Pequot* wars."

7. An implication that Fanny Appleton had discouraged his visits.

8. "Ah! You beautiful soul! It makes me quite sad in spirit when I think about it and see how the lovely dream there is ended, — how the clouds dissolve, and melt into tears, and everything becomes empty around me, and in my soul a gloomy night — a gloomy, starless night! And this I have had to say to you in German, because a foreign voice is a kind of twilight and moonlight, wherein one may say all sorts of things to women, — and so heartfully sincere! Even now greet affectionately my dear, dear Fanny, whom I shall always love as my own soul. Ah! That little bit of judgment that one may have comes hardly into consideration when passion rages. How full becomes my heart! The last time we were together we left one another without understanding one another: for 'in this world no one understands another easily.' And that is very sad." Quotation from Goethe, *Die Leiden des jungen Werthers,* Erstes Buch, Am 12. August.

9. *Les Chants du crépuscule,* 1835.

## 401. *To Stephen Longfellow*

Cambridge December 10. 1837.

My dear Father,

A day or two before I received your last letter, Mr. Abbot[1] came and passed a long evening with me; and a greater part of the time, he was occupied in trying to light a pipe; but so busy was he in talking, that he did not succeed in attempts to smoke. I did not think him anymore deranged, than when I saw him last winter. His great theme was his travels. He was going first to Lake Memphremagog, where he was to meet an Italian, and buy three islands in the lake. Then he was to proceed to Quebec to see Lord Gosford,[2] and then by the way of Niagara south, where he should remain till Spring: at which time he was to start for Europe. Connected with this main idea, was another; namely, a fixed purpose of writing his Travels. He wound up with a long history of Bowdoin College, which pleased me, because it seemed to please him, till it drew near its close. This was the tragic part of the story: and he told me he was resolved not to leave a cent to the College, but to found a great female Academy at Waterford, and to build a Hall here, to be called Abbot's hall, and establish a professorship to be called the Abbot Professorship. The next day, he was going to Brighton to see Gorham Parsons; who was very rich, and ought to make me his heir.[3] He should tell him to do so. He invited me to go with him; and also to accompany him to all the old grave yards in the neighborhood; each of which invitations I very respectfully declined. He was all alone. I asked him where he was going to lodge. He said at Porter's.[4] I told him Porter was himself a lodger now, and lodged at Mt. Auburn. He nodded his head, and said in his curious, comic way: "Then I think I had rather not pass the night with him." So I went down to the tavern, and saw him comfortably provided for. This was the last I saw of him: and I was a good deal surprised at what you say in yr. letter: for he seemed to be only in a quiet, happy hallucination.

Alexander's book, I will get if I can find it. In the book-store, the other day, I saw a work on Civil Engineering by Prof. Mahan of West Point. Does Alex know of this book? I think it new; and from what I know of Mahan, should say it might be valuable.[5]

Samuel is well. We shall certainly be with you at Christmass; and I hope to discharge *some* part tho' no great part, of my debt to the good Judge.[6]

The Little-Peddlington community of Boston is in a great toss, or has been; first about the College, and then about Dr. Channing and the Abolitionists.[7] But all this you see in the papers. Boston is only a great village. The tyranny of public opinion there surpasses all belief.

I have finished my lectures for this term: and am very busy in preparing for next Spring and Summer. It is delightful. I have a great deal of time at my command; and make pretty good use of it.

Tell Alex I saw Col. Fessenden the other day. He thinks he shall have a vacancy in March: and promises to let me know. I shall keep on the look out.

My love to Mother and the girls, at home and at the Judge's, and to Step. and Maryanne.

Affectionately yours
Henry W. Longfellow

MANUSCRIPT: Longfellow Trust Collection. ADDRESS: Hon. Stephen Longfellow/ Portland/Me. POSTMARK: CAMBRIDGE MS. DEC 11

1. John Abbot (44.1), who had been associated with Bowdoin College for many years as a professor of ancient languages, librarian, trustee, and treasurer, was at length retired because of mental infirmity. At this time he was actually committed to a hospital in Charlestown (Stephen Longfellow to Longfellow, November 26, 1837). An affectionate description of him may be found in Nehemiah Cleaveland and Alpheus Spring Packard, *History of Bowdoin College. With Biographical Sketches of its Graduates from 1806 to 1879, Inclusive* (Boston, 1882), pp. 125–126.

2. Archibald Acheson, earl of Gosford (1776–1849), had only recently resigned as governor-general of Canada.

3. Parsons (1768–1844) was the owner of a large estate in Brighton, which he had embellished with a lavish hand (*New England Historical and Genealogical Register*, L, 63).

4. Israel Porter, who died on May 28, 1837, aged 99, had been the proprietor of the noted Blue Anchor Tavern in Cambridge.

5. The book desired by Alexander was Seth Eastman, *Treatise on Topographical Drawing* (New York, 1837). See Stephen Longfellow to Longfellow, November 26, 1837. The other work was Dennis Hart Mahan, *An Elementary Course of Civil Engineering, for the Use of the Cadets of the United States' Military Academy* (New York, 1837).

6. Longfellow reveals in Letter No. 361 that Judge Potter had assisted him financially.

7. After the abolitionist Elijah P. Lovejoy was killed on November 7, 1837, while defending his printing-press against a mob in Alton, Illinois, Channing and others petitioned city officials to use Faneuil Hall for a protest meeting. Their petition was first denied and then granted. The rally was finally held on December 8, and after much heated oratory by abolitionist sympathizers and their opponents the huge crowd passed Channing's resolutions regarding liberty of speech, free discussion, and freedom of the press. For the college trouble, see 395.2.

## 402. *To Frances Appleton*

[Cambridge]
Thursday afternoon. [December 14, 1837][1]

My dear friend,

I take the liberty to send you the *castañuelas* [castanets], it being impossible for me to bring them to you.

Hoping that you will all enjoy yourselves very much this evening, and "sorrowing most of all that I shall not see your face"[2] at the ball,

Very truly yours
Henry W. Longfellow.

MANUSCRIPT: Longfellow Trust Collection.

1. The date is questionable, but the ball referred to may be synonymous with the "*fête*" mentioned in Letter No. 400.

2. Cf. Acts 20:38.

## 403. *To George Stillman Hillard*

Portland. Decr. 21. 1837.

My dear St. George,

It is so cold here that I cannot mend a pen; and my hand trembles like an old man's. Nevertheless I would fain write you a few words, begging you to send the inclosed without delay. I tell you, I shall succeed in this, O thou of little faith! [1]

It is awful cold to-day. They seem to keep all their "cold snaps," here for College Vacations. My mind is like a frozen ink-stand. I believe there are some thoughts in it, but they wont flow out. There is no feeling in my fingers, — under my nails are purple blood-spots. Circulation stops. Send me some news — a "beaker full of the warm South" [2] (say, Beacon Street) to give the currents of my veins full play. Give me some drink: — juices of Mandragora or Love-in-idleness. Touch my mind's eye therewithal.

I left Boston in good spirits; —

"And by the vision splendid
Was on my way attended." [3]

(Pen, do thy duty better). Coming events cast no shadows before them [4] — only luminous outlines; — like the light of the rising moon, shining through the twilight. So shall it ever be; for with a soul within him and a heaven above him, why should man be sad?

This is a dull town not-withstanding. My native place, too; a perfect hornet's-nest of early recollections, insects with stings. I have hardly been out of doors yet: but hear sundry reports about myself. They were brough[t] from Boston by a dress-maker, a cousin of the Hammonds [5] — who dwelling for a time at Russle's in Beacon street,[6] on her return to this place, says to her fair customers, that she saw me walking by at sundry times with Madonna Francesca, — and *describes our dress minutely*! Thus Boston gossip comes with Boston fashions: — both, by change of place assuming an aspect somewhat *outré.*

My travelling companion hitherward was a Brown student — the youth who dined with us Phi Beta day. He spoke of you and your Oration at Providence in delightful praise; showing how you have left yr. footsteps in the soil of Rhode Island, and under them some seed, which is pleasant to think upon.[7]

How goes it with Feltonius — the *Doctor Solidus* of our new School of Philosophic Theology? [8] I shall write to him anon. Tell Cleaveland not to make more than three hundred and sixty *four* engagements to dine out *next* year. We want him on the sixth of January: which I beg you to bear in mind.[9] "*L'Art de diner en Ville*" was sold at Auction last week. He should have bought it. I wonder if the bread of others has indeed such a savour of salt, and if [it] is *so* hard to go up and down other people's stairs — as the poet says it is![10] You had better not ask him, however, for fear he may think the jest unkind. Heaven knows I do not mean it so.

Good bye, good Geordie.

Yrs. truly
H. W. Longfellow

MANUSCRIPT: Maine Historical Society. ADDRESS: George S. Hillard Esq./ Boston ANNOTATION (*by Longfellow*): double paid POSTMARK: PORTLAND ME. DEC 23

1. The enclosed message for Frances Appleton, to whom he refers throughout this letter, is unrecovered.

2. Keats, "Ode to a Nightingale," l. 15.

3. Cf. Wordsworth, "Ode on the Intimations of Immortality," ll. 73–74.

4. Cf. Thomas Campbell, "Lochiel's Warning," l. 56.

5. Samuel Hammond (1766–1833), a Boston entrepreneur, had left a large estate to his wife, Sarah Davis Hammond (1768–1859), and to his several children, one of whom, Mary Ann Hammond (1800–1897), was the wife of John Gorham Palfrey.

6. Nathaniel P. Russell (1779–1848), a director of the Suffolk Bank, lived at 34 Beacon Street (*Boston Directory* for 1837).

7. According to the records of the Brown Chapter of Phi Beta Kappa, Hillard delivered an oration entitled "A Comparison between Ancient and Modern Literature" on September 6, 1837. The *Providence Daily Journal* for September 8 reported that it was "an elaborate and eloquent production, rich in classic illustration and glowing imagery."

8. Longfellow presumably associates Felton with Richard Middleton (fl. 1280), an English Franciscan who was known in Paris as "doctor solidus et copiosus, fundatissimus et authoratus" (*Dictionary of National Biography*, XIII, 356).

9. Longfellow had known Henry Cleveland for about a year but here mentions him for the first time in his letters. January 6, 1838, was presumably the date set for the next meeting of the "Five of Clubs."

10. Charles Joseph Auguste Maximilien de Colnet (1768–1852) published his *L'Art de dîner en ville, à l'usage des gens de lettres*, a poem in four cantos, in 1810. An edition of 1813 appended a list of authors who had died of hunger.

## 404. *To an Unidentified Correspondent*

[1837][1]

in case all does not turn out as he wishes. Mr Felton's package shall be forwarded this week; to remain at the Rail-road depot, until called for.

I am *very* sorry, that an expected visit from me [*five words muti-*

*lated and illegible*] out so much in yr [*one word mutilated and illegible*].

do you call mine? They remind me of a sea-captain who was so tall, that no voyage, except an India voyage, was long enough for him.

With regards to all yr. family

very sincerely yrs.
H. W. Longfellow.

MANUSCRIPT: Longfellow Trust Collection.

1. Date conjectured by H. W. L. Dana. This fragment consists of five lines at the top of a page and five lines (including complimentary closing) on the verso.

## 405. *To Romeo Elton*

Cambridge. Jan. 5. 1838

My dear Sir,

Owing to absence from town I did not have the pleasure of receiving your favor of Dec 23rd until last evening. The package, you mention, from Mr. Greene, I received soon after you were here in August last; and should have sent it to you immediately, had he not requested me to send with it a copy of his Article on Verazzano, a number of which he wished to have struck off separately and done up in a pamphlet form. This delayed me till October; since when I have been waiting for an opportunity to send to you: and not having any address to which I can forward the package in Providence, I think I shall put it into the hands of a Boston bookseller, as the safest way.[1]

The publications of the French Society of Universal Statistics, I never see. You are wrong in supposing me a member of that Society. I am not.[2]

I am much obliged to you for yr. kind offer of the second vol. of the Transactions of the R. I. Historical Society. The first vol. I took with me to Europe and placed in the Library at Upsala; where I trust it continues to produce great wonderment among the Swedish students.[3]

I beg you to present my best regards to President Wayland and Professor Goddard: [4] and believe me

very truly yours, in haste,
Henry W. Longfellow

MANUSCRIPT: Brown University Library.

1. In his letter of December 23 Elton had inquired about a manuscript copy of a letter by the navigator Giovanni da Verrazzano to Francis I, which Greene had included in a parcel sent to Longfellow and which was to have been forwarded by him to the Rhode Island Historical Society "as a proof of the interest he felt in his

native state" (Elton's remark). This transcript of an original letter in the Magliabecchian Library in Florence is now in the society's archives. The pamphlet mentioned by Longfellow is *The Life and Voyages of Verrazzano* (Cambridge, 1837), a reprint of Greene's article in the *North American Review*, XLV (October 1837), 293–311. See 437.4.

2. Elton, who had been elected a member of the society but had paid no dues and knew nothing of its operations, had requested information about it in his letter.

3. See Letter No. 262.

4. William Giles Goddard (1794–1846), Professor of Rhetoric and Belles-Lettres at Brown University.

## 406. *To Charles Folsom*

[Cambridge] Saturday afternoon. Jan. 6. 1838.

Dear Sir,

Will you have this set up, so as to be printed on a page of letter-paper, and send me proof as soon as possible? [1]

Yrs. truly.
H. W. Longfellow

MANUSCRIPT: Boston Public Library. ADDRESS: Chs. Folsom Esq/Cambridge ENDORSEMENT: Received June 8/1838

1. This refers to a prospectus for Rev. Joseph Bosworth's *Dictionary of the Anglo-Saxon Language*, to which Longfellow had contributed a chapter on the "Dialect of Dalecarlia" (*Longfellow and Scandinavia*, p. 31) and which, at Bosworth's request, he had consented to promote in the U. S. The prospectus describes the work and quotes in full a testimonal letter from the philologist John Pickering to Longfellow, December 9, 1837.

## 407. *To George Washington Greene*

Cambridge Jan. 6. 1838.

My dear, good Geordie,

You will hardly believe me when I tell you, that yr. letter of August 9. with the Tasso M.S.[1] has just reached me. It is not an hour since I opened the package. Where it has been all this time I cannot imagine. I presume you have lost all patience with me for not answering a letter I have but just received. I have lost patience with you several times within the year. To my three or four last letters you have sent only notes in reply, begging me not to mistake them for letters. There was no danger of my doing so, my dear boy, even without the *avis au lecteur* [note to the reader]. And now your last warm letter comes like Summer upon my Winter — a "beaker full of the warm South": [2] and I am sorry and ashamed that I have not written you before. Let that suffice; and remember that you, too, are to blame. I am so sorry about your eyes! Dont use them so much. Why will you work so? Is it necessary? Believe me it is wrong. Let all the glad influences of *Italy* play upon you cheerly; let your soul ripen gladly and joyfully in Italian Sunshine. Be a child in the delicious air. O heaven! if I were once more with you in Rome! I would open no books but those of the Four Italian Poets. How gloriously idle I would be! I would live a life of rapture in the study of Art: and the miserable minor poets might rot in their unknown graves, as they deserve to do. I would go mad about Raphael and Michel Angelo: and walk about in churches, and picture galeries and be very happy. Go thou, and do likewise.[3]

I know not what my "fat friend" Felton may have written you; but you throw out hints in your letters, as if he had given you to understand we were leading a merry life here. God knows I have no merriment in my life. A leaden melancholy hangs over me: — and from this I pass at times into feverish excitement, bordering on madness; which confines me to my chamber for weeks. Witness last Summer — witness the present moment. My friends here think nothing of it. They say — oh, you look very well! Alas! they know not what soul-sickness is. And I have come to the conclusion, that there is very little sympathy in the world for mental suffering. A wounded hand excites more commiseration than a wounded soul. The truth is this. My nature craves sympathy — not of friendship, but of Love. This want of my nature is unsatisfied. And the love of some good being is as necessary to my existence as the air I breathe. To tell you the whole truth — I saw in Switzerland and travelled with a fair lady — whom I now love passionately (strange, will this sound to yr. ears) and have loved ever since I knew her. A glorious and beautiful being — young — and a woman *not* of talent but of *genius*! — indeed a most rare, sweet woman whose name is Fanny Appleton. You saw her at Greenough's studio.[4] You cannot have forgotten her. Tall, with a pale face. Well, that pale face is my Fate. Horrible fate it is, too; for she lends no favorable ear to my passion and for my love gives me only friendship. Good friends we are — but she says she loves me not;[5] and I have vowed to win her affection. Ah! my friend! you know not how this is interwoven into my soul. I think that among all my friends you are the *only* one, who can *understand* me, or *appreciate* me in this point. I shall win this lady, or I shall die. I feel this to be true. I am no longer a boy. All feelings — and this most of all — have become earnest with me. This is not wilfulness. I cannot overcome the passion. I cannot change my nature. Ah! few know the force of *good* passions in *good* souls! The event is uncertain. You will see a good friend of mine soon — Chs. Sumner of Boston.[6] He will tell you much more about this, than I can write.

I shall attend to Wilde's Tasso immediately and will have the books sent you, which you desire, and my miniature, if I can get one. Verrazzano I have already written you about.[7] It is an excellent paper. The N. A. Writers you shall have likewise, regularly. Since my return I have written but three Articles namely "*Great Metropolis*"; "*Hawthorne's Tales*"; "*Frithiof's Saga.*" My next letter shall be literary. I have small room left for others having said so much about myself. I no longer live in the same house with Felton but have an owl-tower[8] of my own. Ask Sumner; to whom I refer you for all particulars relating to myself. Remember me cordially to the Persianis. Dont forget it. I am very glad that Julia is married. Whom did she marry? Poor soul![9] And dear Rome — dear Rome! Let me walk with you at times in the Forum as of old — and at *Acqua Paola*![10] Good Heaven!

My most affectionate remembrance to Maria. When I next write you, my dear George, I hope I shall be able to tell you how a "miserable Knight" won the love of the "proud ladie." Meanwhile, with this aching heart and head I have to toil in writing of Lectures. If I get well enough, I begin next week on the Purgatorio and Paradiso of Dante though this Course is *unwritten* — entirely *oral.*

Truly thine
H.W.L.

N.A. Review for January 1838.

Art. I. Cooper['s Novels]. *Francis Bowen.* II. Cicero. *H. R. Cleaveland.* III. [Talfourd's] Lamb. *C. C. Felton.* IV. Hoffman['s Course of Legal Study]. *G. S. Hillard.* V. [De Quincy's] Rafael. *Franklin Dexter. Esq.*[11] VI. Green[e's] Tales [from the German]. *Wm. H. Prescott.* VII. Grund's America[ns]. *Chs. Sumner.* VII. [*sic*] Northern Antiquities. *Ed. Everett.* VIII. Constitutional Law. *C. S. Daveis.* IX. Prescott's Ferd. and Isabel. *Wm. H. Gardiner.*[12] I have put these down from memory, not having a No. near me. The *Order* may be wrong — but the names and Arts. are all right.

MANUSCRIPT: Longfellow Trust Collection. ADDRESS: George Washington Greene Esq/American Consul at Rome./Care of Welles & co. Place St. George/Paris. ANNOTATION (*by Longfellow*): Paid to N. York/Charge. 192 POSTMARKS: CAMBRIDGE MS. JAN 8/NEW YORK JAN 12/PAYS D'OUTREMER PAR LE HAVRE/ [*place name illegible*] 1838/PAID ENDORSEMENT: Rec. Rome 24. Feb. 1838

1. This manuscript, the work of Richard Henry Wilde (1789–1847), a former member of Congress from Georgia residing in Italy, was sent by Greene to Longfellow in the hope that he would find a publisher for it. Although Longfellow was unsuccessful (see Letter No. 437), Wilde eventually published the work under

the title *Conjectures and Researches Concerning the Love, Madness, and Imprisonment of Torquato Tasso* (New York, 1842).

2. Keats, "Ode to a Nightingale," l. 15.

3. Cf. Luke 10:37.

4. In Rome in 1836.

5. Longfellow first wrote "does not love me."

6. Sumner arrived in Rome on May 21, 1839, and saw much of Greene during the next three months (*Sumner Memoir and Letters*, II, 92–93).

7. This letter is unrecovered (see 437.3).

8. Cf. the chapter "Owl-Towers" in *Hyperion* (*Works*, VIII, 78–84).

9. Julia Persiani had married a Frenchman sometime after Longfellow's infatuation with her in 1828. In a letter of January 31, 1839, Greene wrote, "Julia's husband is named De Launoy and lives [at] Rue D'Anjou S. Honoré No. 42 [Paris]."

10. Longfellow describes this largest and most abundant of the Roman fountains and his visit there with a "friend from my native land" in *Outre-Mer* (*Works*, VII, 241–242 and 243–244).

11. A Boston lawyer and public official (1793–1857).

12. William Howard Gardiner (1796–1882), Prescott's classmate, friend, and legal counselor.

## 408. *To John Gorham Palfrey*

[Cambridge] Saturday morning Jan. 6. 1838.

My dear Sir,

I have just received the accompanying Article from Mr. Greene.[1] It seems to be introductory to another on the same subject: as he writes me, that he is engaged in preparing a notice of Manzoni and others. I suppose he has thus divided his Article; for fear of being too long.

I should come to see you but am confined to my chamber, with all kinds of fever-pains and nervous disorders.

My best and warmest regards to Mrs. Palfrey.

Very truly y[r]s.
H. W. Longfellow

P.S. Wish the children a Happy New Year from me.

MANUSCRIPT: Harvard College Library.

1. Presumably the article "Historical Romance in Italy" (see 437.6).

## 409. *To Samuel Ward*

Harvard University. Sunday morning. Jan. 21. 1838

My dear Ward,

"Vous avez un grand talent pour le silence [You have a great talent for silence]": so great that on the very eve of your marriage you say not a word to me about it, but send a special messenger (Mr. Cogswell) to announce the great event, which throws no shadow before it, only a luminous outline. Receive my warmest congratulations — my most cordial good wishes. May you live very long and very happily with your young bride;

> "And when with envy Time transported
> Shall think to rob you of your joys,
> She in her girls again be courted
> And you go wooing in your boys." [1]

Several months — nearly a year ago — a box of books came to me from Germany — in which was one of yours; namely "Gmelin's Chemie" in 4 vols. 8 vo.[2] I suppose, that by this time *you are in a hurry for it.* The truth is I have had no opportunity to send it; and have put off writing to you on the subject from day to day, down to this late "period of recorded Time." [3] I shall be in N. York in April next; and will bring the books with me. Or do you want them sooner?

I send you a Prospectus of an Anglo-Saxon Dictionary.[4] *Can* you do anything for the author, if you *will*! — and *will* you if you *can*?

Yours most sincerely
Henry W. Longfellow

P. S. What has become of the M. S. Romances etc? [5]

MANUSCRIPT: unrecovered; text from photostat, Longfellow Trust Collection.

1. Cf. last stanza of "Winifreda" in Thomas Percy, *Reliques of Ancient English Poetry.* Ward married Emily Astor (1819–1841), granddaughter of John Jacob Astor, on January 25, 1838.

2. Leopold Gmelin, *Handbuch der theoretischen Chemie* (3rd ed., Frankfurt am Main, 1827–1829), 4 vols.

3. Cf. *Macbeth,* V, v, 21.

4. See 406.1.

5. In his reply of January 27, 1838, Ward says of his projected romances, "They have not left me — yet no longer haunt me in shadowy outlines of heavenly forms for the visions of youth and hope and loveliness have become one glorious and thrilling reality — out of the perfumed incense I have so long burnt to my unknown divinity the goddess herself hath appeared even as from the wizards chafing dish in the faërys legend arose the forms he sought to confine." The goddess, of course, was Emily Astor.

## 410. *To the Harvard Corporation*

Cambridge Feb. 1. 1838 [1]

Gentlemen,

When I had the honor of meeting a committee of your body last Summer, to discuss and determine the duties of my office, it was proposed as an experiment, that I should attend the recitations of every class in the Modern Languages at least once a month, in order to see how the various instructers performed their duties &c.

This I tried during the last Term. I do not see, however, that any good results from this, but, rather, evil. It seems to assume in the eyes of some of the Instructers an appearance of *espionnage.*

I therefore respectfully request to be excused from any regular attendance on the classes; as before this provision was made, attending only such classes and at such times, as in my judgement may be useful or necessary.

I would also request, that during the next Term, I may have the use either of the Chapel or of the Philosophical Room, once a week, for a Course of Public Lectures on Literary History.[2]

Very respectfully, Yr. Obt. Ser[v]t.
Henry W. Longfellow

MANUSCRIPT: Harvard College Papers, VIII, 106. PUBLISHED: *Professor Longfellow of Harvard,* pp. 28–29.

1. Longfellow mistakenly wrote "1837."
2. At its meeting of March 15, 1838, the Corporation voted that it was "inexpedient" to grant Longfellow's requests (*Professor Longfellow of Harvard,* p. 29).

## 411. *To Stephen Longfellow*

Cambridge. Feb. 8. 1838

My dear Father,

Nothing new nor wonderful has taken place here, since I last wrote you; except the explosion of a bomb-shell in the College Chapel, some nights ago. We cannot yet trace it to anyone: and indeed are unwilling to suspect a student of such an offence. The students evidently feel that matters are going too far: that such things disgrace the college and them individually; and have published a *Disapproval* of such outrages in the Boston papers, as you have seen probably. This is the only event which has broken even for a moment the tranquillity of college: and this is almost forgotten already. Things are lost sight of here very quickly.[1]

All my time, save recreation, is taken up with Lectures. I am now upon Dante as you know: unwritten lectures: but have petitioned the Corporation for the use of the chapel next Summer for a course of written, *public* lectures; — by public, I mean free to any and every one, who chooses to attend, whether in College or out of college. What the gentlemen of the corporation will think of such a plan, I know not yet, but shall know soon. In the mean time I am preparing: and devote the whole day to it. After which — about sunset, I generally walk to town, which gives me the necessary exercise. Time passes almost too quickly. The middle of April is not far off — when I suppose I shall go to Washington.

Tell Alexander that I have the Water-Report for him.[2] Shall I send it by mail? — or wait for a private opportunity. I have a short talk now and then with Col. Fessenden, and I think the affair is in *good train*: tho' as yet nothing determinate.

As to *Ale,* so long as you can get such as suits you in Portland, I see no object in purchasing in Boston, with the risk of its not suiting you so well. I dare say all *domestic* ales can be bought as well in Portland as in Boston. The imported perhaps better here.

Samuel flourishes as usual, and thrives. Every body else has been out of health this beautiful winter. Colds and rheumatisms never so prevalent. Among others Mrs. Sumner is *much* out of health: something worse than a cold; — Mr. Sumner has been once more unfortunate and lost all his property by the breaking of one of the Pet Banks.[3] This quite overcomes Mrs. S. — who has been confined to her bed for some weeks.

My love unto all. I shall probably write to Annie before long. Farewell.

Very truly yours
Henry W. Longfellow

P.S. There is a *troupe* of French Opera-dancers in Boston. People hardly know what to make of them. Some look and are pleased: others behold such things with pretty much such feelings as Michal Saul's daughter, beheld David dancing and leaping before the ark; — namely "despise them in their heart." [4]

MANUSCRIPT: Longfellow Trust Collection. ADDRESS: Hon. Stephen Longfellow/ Portland. POSTMARK: CAMBRIDGE MS. FEB 9

1. The Boston *Daily Evening Transcript,* IX (Saturday, February 3, 1838), No. 2302, records this explosion as having taken place on Thursday, February 1, "at deep midnight." The Faculty Meeting of February 5 voted the seniors permission to call a meeting of the undergraduates "in order to express their disapprobation" of the outrage (Faculty Records, Harvard College, XI, 335–336), and the students' statement of disapproval appeared in the *Transcript,* IX (Wednesday, February 7, 1838), No. 2305.

2. Presumably the *Report of the Commissioners Appointed under an Order of the City Council of March 16th, 1837, to Devise a Plan for Supplying the City of Boston with Pure Water* (Boston, 1837).

3. Jesse Sumner and his wife Harriot (77.8) were old friends of the Longfellows. The "pet banks" were state banks chosen by the Jackson Administration for government deposits, several of which failed in Boston early in 1838.

4. Cf. II Sam. 7:16.

412. *To Esaias Tegnér*

Harvard University. Cambridge. U.S. America.
Feb. 21. 1838.

Reverend Sir,

The greatest regret I felt on leaving your country, which I visited in the year 1835, was, that I had found no opportunity of making your acquaintance. Your writings were among the first I read in Swedish; and I hardly need say, are those which most delight me.

I herewith send you a No. of our principal Literary Review. You will find in it an attempt to convey to my countrymen some idea of your great poem, Frithiofs Saga: — at best a feeble idea, and yet, perhaps, better than could have been obtained by them otherwise: for the Swedish Language is almost wholly unknown here, and the only English Translation of Frithiof, which has reached this country is the Anonymous one, which is worthy of no praise, and which, as you will see, I have not hesitated to condemn.[1]

I am sorry, that my own task has not been executed more worthily. But such as it is, I take the liberty of sending it to you; that you may know your fame has reached our distant land; and that in New England, a country much resembling yours, your high song has found an echo.

Wishing you many years of happiness, and God's peace, I have the honor to be

Very sincerely your friend,
Henry W. Longfellow

MANUSCRIPT: Lund University Library. PUBLISHED: "Some Unpublished Longfellow Letters," pp. 181–182.

1. Longfellow's translations from *Frithiofs Saga* appear in an essay on the poem in the *North American Review*, XLV (July 1837), 149–185. For details of its composition and of Longfellow's relationship with Tegnér, see *Longfellow and Scandinavia*, Chap. IV. Tegnér's answer to this letter dated July 10, 1841, is printed in his *Samlade Skrifter*, ed. Wrangel och Böök (Stockholm, 1918–1925), IX, 422.

413. *To Anne Longfellow Pierce*

Cambridge. Feb. 27. 1838.

My dear Anna Matilda

Yesterday as I was going down to Lecture, I had the pleasure of taking your letter out of the post-office, and putting it in my pocket, till lecture was over. Then I read it; and then walked to town to see a collection of beautiful Italian paintings, for sale; — price of *one* of them, a Madonna, fifteen thousand dollars![1] I think of purchasing it: so you need not get the shirts!

After this I went to dine with a friend; — and on my way stopped to shake hands with Amory, when an individual came up the street and said "Mr. Amory your brother's house is on fire!" We looked down Beacon Street; and lo; smoke was rolling from the windows of the stone palace: together with tables, chairs and sofas. In the course of an hour or so, the smoke was put out. The fire caught from one of the furnace-flues! [2] So be careful!

Well, coming from town, and going in, I meditated sufficiently on the content of your letter. Six shirts I must have. I am all in rags. Get me six. I will send you the wherewithal. No matter about exchanging the other. Use it for anything you may happen to want. I will make Mother a present of it: or as much as she may want of it. If there is any left, I should like a pair of sheets and pillow-cases, likewise.

As to dickeys, six are enough. I dont want any more. Have you a cotton shirt of mine, with pearl buttons on the bosom? If so, have *three* made like that, and *three* with button-holes, like the linen one I left.

Mr. Higbee seems to be in great distress.[3] I think I had better call for him on my way to Washington. Perhaps he will lend me some shirts. If you cannot find nice linen in Portland, I can get the *duds* done up here, and save you all the trouble which upon the whole seems to be superfluous, and unnecessary. Shall I?

It is my birth-day to-day. I am twenty seven years old. Only think of it! How old are you? [4]

Samuel is well. We both send many friendly greeting to you all, — to Ann Sophia, and to the girls at the Judges.[5]

Affectionately yours
Henry W. Longw.

P.S. for Alex. Yesterday in town I tried to find Mr. Fessenden, but could not. Alex. Wadsworth says that the Eastern Rail-road will not be carried on, unless there be a loan from the State. This is not yet decided. He more-over says, that Mr. Fessenden is a "Bag of wind," which I think not unlikely.

However, I shall be in town again tomorrow, and will make another attempt. Perhaps I shall get a definite answer. I will write you, as soon as I can upon the subject.

In no great haste

yours truly
H. W. L.

MANUSCRIPT: Longfellow Trust Collection. ADDRESS: To/Mrs. Anne L. Pierce/ Care of Hon. S. Longfellow/Portland. POSTMARK: CAMBRIDGE MS. FEB 28

1. The exhibition, at the Boston Athenaeum, featured a collection of paintings brought from Florence by a Count Celestini as well as another group offered by a dealer named William Hayward (Mabel Munson Swan, *The Athenaeum Gallery 1827–1873* [Boston, 1940], p. 99).

2. This event is listed under "Fires in Boston, during the Year 1838" in S. N. Dickinson's *The Boston Almanac, for the Year 1839*, I, No. 4, 47. William Amory (1804–1888), who lived at 42 Beacon Street, was the brother of Charles Amory.

3. Rev. Edward Young Higbee (1801–1871) of Trinity Church, New York, had met Longfellow through Commodore Wadsworth, whose niece by marriage — Frances Henley of Washington, D.C. — Higbee had married in December 1837. The nature of his distress is not known.

4. Longfellow's jest makes him younger than Anne. He was, of course, thirty-one years old on this date.

5. That is, to Anne Sophia Longfellow (b. 1818), his first cousin, and to Madge and Eliza Potter, his sisters-in-law.

## 414. *To Alexander Wadsworth Longfellow*

Cambridge. March 1. 1838

My dear boy,

I saw Col. Fessenden yesterday. He seems to be very friendly to you; and offers you a place on the Eastern Rail-road, to oversee the laying of rails. He hopes to begin in April; as the rails are expected soon. You will have a chief engineer over you; who will give you definite instructions; your duty will be to see them put into execution. This will last some three or four months only. Whether they continue the road is doubtful: and he says he cannot give more than $1.25 per day, that is $8.75 per week. He seems to think that a situation with Long would be more advantageous to you, and offers you letters of introduction. He gave me the *Notice* I send you.[1] The Water report[2] I shall send in a few days, by private hand.

The Col. says he will wait for you to write to Long, and get definite proposals from him. Then you can take your choice. Of course this must be done without delay: as it is quite a favor from the Colonel, to reserve you a place, and give you this opportunity of doing better if you can. He thinks you had better send duplicates of yr. letter to Long: one to Cassville, the other Marietta; as he passes to and from between these places.

In great haste yrs.
Henry W. Longfellow

MANUSCRIPT: Longfellow Trust Collection.

1. Stephen Harriman Long (1784–1864), the Western explorer, was at this time chief engineer for the Western and Atlantic Railroad in Georgia. The *Notice* was presumably an announcement of the new road and a call for engineers. A position with Long did not materialize for Alexander.

2. See 411.2.

415. *To Anne Longfellow Pierce*

Cambridge March 18. 1838.

My dear Anne,

I am quite astonished in looking at the date of your last to find it was written as long ago as the 6th. It must be a mistake. However, we will not stop to investigate the matter now.

Do you know, I *have* half given up the idea of going to Washington — or rather *had* half given it up. To-day I have resumed the original plan again; and should not be surprised to find myself on the way any time next week. Much good may the new shirts do me, say you. Make *three* with neat pearl buttons *sewed on*. How are they to be sent? Mercy on us, I want some handkerchiefs likewise. But those I will get here. That will be the shortest way. No *round cornered* dickeys, if you please; only make half of them a thought higher than the old ones.

How do you all flourish in Portland? I shall pass next summer vacation with you. I have made up my mind on that point. I am going to Lecture there. Dont you think I can get an Audience for a course of Literary matters? But why do I ask you? You dont know anything about it. My own opinion is, that I can.

To-day, snow-storm tremendous: with North-wind. No getting out of doors; though the church-bells seemed to be crying for help. It is now quite late at night; — I should say near eleven; but cannot stop to take out my watch. Storm continues. Winter has come back after his umbrella. Begone, old man, and do not wag thy gray beard at me.

What does Aunt Lucia write? When do they expect me? Is she coming back under my wing? Suppose I dont go, what then?[1] I shall give two lectures this week, and wind up. Then see how I feel.

There are some beautiful Italian paintings in Boston. I wish you could see them. But now I remember, this is an old story.

What a flat letter Mrs. Jones *did write*. Who was imprudent enough to publish it? Was it she herself: — or her father? Desperate bad.[2] My own — I mean this — is not very good. Rather incoherent, and showing marks of haste, and the like. I shall write again before I go: and tell you all the particulars.

Love to all.

Truly &c
H. W. L.

MANUSCRIPT: Longfellow Trust Collection. ADDRESS: To/Mrs. Anne L. Pierce/ Care of Hon. S. Longfellow/Portland/Me. POSTMARK: CAMBRIDGE MS. MAR 19

1. Lucia Wadsworth was in Washington visiting her brother, Commodore Wadsworth.

2. On February 24, 1838, Jonathan Cilley (1802–1838), Longfellow's classmate at Bowdoin and a member of Congress, had been killed in a duel with William Jordan Graves (1805–1848), congressman from Kentucky. A letter written to Cilley's wife by Mrs. Paulina Cony Jones (1809–1845), filled with effusive sentimentality and datelined Washington, February 25, 1838, appeared in the *Daily Evening Transcript*, IX (March 10, 1838), No. 2332. Mrs. Jones was the daughter of Senator Ruel Williams (1783–1862) of Maine.

## 416. *To William Whitewell Greenough*[1]

Cambridge March 23. 1838

My dear Sir

I had the pleasure of receiving your letter last evening. Dr. Palfrey had already told me that Prof. Stuart's Article had turned out so much longer than he expected, that it would be impossible to publish yours. From Prof. Stuart he expected some twenty pages, and received about forty! It is even too late to reduce your article to a Critical Notice; and upon the whole, I think, if there were time, it would be a pity to do it. You had better publish it in the Repository, or some other Review, entire.[2]

Have you Turner's Hist. Anglo-Saxons from the Library? If so when shall you get through with it? Also Vol. 4 of Henry's History of Great Britain?[3] If you have them, and would return them as soon as you can conveniently, you would oblige me.

In great haste, yours truly
Henry W. Longfellow

MANUSCRIPT: University of California Library, Berkeley. ADDRESS: Mr. W. W. Greenough/Theol. Seminary/Andover. POSTMARK: CAMBRIDGE MS. MAR 24 ENDORSEMENT: Prof. Longfellow./March 23rd/Rec 26th/ans 27th

1. Greenough (1818–1899), a Harvard graduate of 1837 and a man of scholarly tastes, later became a successful Boston businessman.

2. Moses Stuart (1780–1852), Congregational clergyman and professor at the Andover Theological Seminary, wrote a review of William L. Roy's *A Complete Hebrew and English Critical and Pronouncing Dictionary* (New York, 1837) for the *North American Review*, XLVI (April 1838), 487–532. Greenough subsequently printed his review of Joseph Bosworth's *Dictionary of the Anglo-Saxon Language*, not in the Boston *Repository, a Magazine for the Christian Home*, but in the *New York Review*, III (October 1838), 362–377.

3. Sharon Turner, *The History of the Anglo-Saxons from their first appearance above the Elbe, to the death of Egbert* (London, 1799–1805), 4 vols.; and Robert Henry, *The History of Great Britain, from the first invasion of it by the Romans under Julius Caesar* (London, 1771–1793), 6 vols. Both works appeared in later editions.

## 417. *To Stephen Longfellow*

Cambridge March. 28. 1838

My dear father,

I have had the pleasure of receiving yours of the 18th. and write to tell you, that I have given up the journey to Washington.[1] As soon therefore as the steamers begin to run, I shall come and spend a week with you in Portland. I have had a letter from Uncle Alex. and answered it this morning. I am sorry, on some accounts, to relinquish the plan: but upon the whole think it best.

On Saturday I drove down to Salem, by way of recreation. Clara is there, at old Capt. Nichols's. The old gentleman is ninety; and seems to be tumbling to pieces.[2] On Sunday, I dined with your old friend Mr. Leveret Saltinstall. I like him very much. He is cordial and simple in his manners; is Lord Mayor of Salem; leader of the choir in church: — chief of the Sunday-school, and has the gout.[3]

Judge Story has returned. We were on the point of losing him from the Supreme Court and from the University. He was a candidate for Dr. Bowditch's vacant place of President of the Life Insurance company, with a salary of four thousand. They, finally, elected another person; and the judge remains as before; though, I hear, much tired of his associates on the bench.[4]

This morning I received the following letter from Mr. Abbot. It makes me reproach myself not a little. The only excuse I have is that I was misinformed in regard to the regulations of the Institution. I thought they did not want visitors.

"East Cambridge. March 13. 1838. Professor Longfw. My dear Sir, could I ever have expected that my young friend H. L. a son of the most precious friend I have in Maine, the Hon. S. L. and wife, should live since the 20" November last, now about four months, within two miles of me, without once calling to see me? A very respectable man living [in] Roxbury, who was my *Senior* in college, and whom I had not seen for more than fifty years, not aware that I was in Massachusetts, this day accidentally found me here, and gave me a cordial shake by the hand. I am therefore prepared, if Prof. L. call soon, and tell me that he was ignorant, that I was so near him, to shake him most cordially by the hand and receive to my wanted confidence and friendship. I am, my dear Sir, very truly your friend and obedient servant. John Abbot."[5]

I shall go over to see him this afternoon. It is too bad. I am provoked with myself.

I have nothing new for Alex. save the Report of the Engineers of the Western Rail-Road, which I shall send or bring soon.

With much love to all,

truly yours
H. W. L.

MANUSCRIPT: Longfellow Trust Collection. ADDRESS: Hon. Stephen Longfellow/ Portland/Me POSTMARK: CAMBRIDGE MS. MAR 28

1. Longfellow explains his decision in his journal entry for March 24: "I have given up my journey to Washington. My funds are too low. Thus for a few pieces of silver my cherished plan of recreation and delight with which I have fed my imagination through the Winter, as on cut hay, ends in disappointment!" Instead, he spent the period April 6–16 in Portland.

2. Capt. Ichabod Nichols (1749–1839), father of Rev. Ichabod Nichols of Portland and of Benjamin Ropes Nichols, lived at 14 Washington Street, Salem. Clara Crowninshield was tending him in his old age (*Diary of Clara Crowninshield*, p. xxviii).

3. Leverett Saltonstall (1783–1845) had practiced law in Salem since 1805, and Stephen Longfellow undoubtedly knew him professionally. He served as the first mayor of Salem, 1836–1838, and as a member of Congress, 1838–1843.

4. Nathaniel Bowditch (1773–1838), the navigator and mathematician, had been actuary of the Massachusetts Hospital Life Insurance Company from 1823 until his death on March 16, 1838. Justice Story may have considered leaving the bench and his chair as Dane Professor of Law at Harvard because of disagreements with Chief Justice Taney. Bowditch's position went to Joseph Tilden of Boston.

5. The original of this letter, differing only slightly from Longfellow's copy, is in the Longfellow Trust Collection. See 401.1.

## 418. *To Charles Stewart Daveis*

[Portland] April. 16. 1838.

My dear sir

In answer to your inquiries concerning Alexander's studies at Brunswick, I would inform you, that during his residence with me, at that place, his time was chiefly devoted to scientific pursuits. He attended Professor Cleaveland's Lectures on Mineralogy and Geology for two successive years; and likewise his Lectures on Chemistry and Natural Philosophy. He always seemed much devoted to these studies, particularly Mineralogy, and I had every reason to suppose he improved the great advantages he there enjoyed.

Since his return from the Pacific, he has, as you know devoted himself to Civil Engineering: and last Summer had charge of a division of the Boston and Haverhill rail-road and gave I believe entire satisfaction to the Chief Engineer.

He thinks the situation of Assistant in the Geological survey would be of great utility to him in many points of view. I agree with him, and hope he may obtain it: and that it will be in your power to advance his wishes in this respect.[1]

Very truly yours
Henry W Longfellow

MANUSCRIPT: Longfellow Trust Collection. ADDRESS: To/Charles S. Daveis Esq/ Portland.

1. Longfellow's journal entry for April 15 suggests that he and Charles Daveis had already discussed Alexander's future: "In the evening at Chs. Daveis's. He as usual, sparkling and talkative. I very stupid. Retreated soon." This letter, therefore, was an attempt to accomplish what he had failed to do in conversation, that is, to promote Alexander's application for an assistantship on the Maine Geological Survey. Despite the support of Daveis and others, Alexander did not get the job.

## 419. *To an Unidentified Correspondent*

Cambridge April 18. 1838

Gentlemen

Yrs. of the 10th inclosing Bill for Books reached me yesterday. I am sorry I have not the money to send you. It will be very inconvenient for me to pay it before our next Quarter day, June 2nd. If you can wait so long, you will much oblige me.

Respectfully yours
Henry W. Longfellow

MANUSCRIPT: unrecovered; text from typewritten transcript, Longfellow Trust Collection (Longfellow House).

## 420. *To Ann Sophia Stephens*

Cambridge April 20. 1838

Dear Madam,

On returning to town a few days since, I had the honor of receiving your favor of the 12th. In reply I send you a song from Salis; which I hope will please you. I believe it has never before been translated.[1]

I have the honor to be, Madam, with good wishes for your success,
your obt. ser[v]t.
||Henry W. Longfellow||

MANUSCRIPT: Clifton Waller Barrett Collection, University of Virginia. ADDRESS: To/Mrs. Ann S. Stephens/Office of Ladies' Companion/New York. POSTMARK: CAMBRIDGE MS. APR 24

1. Ann Sophia Stephens (1813–1886), to whose *Portland Sketch Book* (Portland, 1836) Longfellow had contributed an abridgment of the chapter "The Village of Autueil" from *Outre-Mer*, was now editor of the *Ladies' Companion* in New York. In her letter of April 12 she had solicited a "short article" from Longfellow. He responded with his translation of Johann Gaudenz von Salis' "Lied: Ins Stille

Land" ("Song of the Silent Land"), which he had translated in his journal on February 6, 1836. See *Ladies' Companion*, IX (June 1838), 57.

## 421. *To Charles Sumner*

[Cambridge] April 20, 1838.

Your warm-hearted letter, written on my birthday, did not reach me till yesterday. You knew, all the time, that you were touching me on my weak side when you chose that date. I confess I was pleased you should remember it. (We did not remember it here; it was not celebrated!) I now indulge the pleasing fancy that at times, as you walk metropolitan streets, — London or Paris, — you do ever and anon remember that the wondrous objects you behold have at a former day had their reflected image in my eye as now in yours, exciting in me thoughts akin to those that rise in you. This shall be a bond of union between us, as you go from city to city, begging your bread and butter in unknown tongues.

Having let off this sentimental sky-rocket or blue-light, I proceed to inform you that your friend —— is engaged. Henry Cleveland has got back from his bridal tour, but I have not seen him. They say he is very happy. Felton is to be married next July, at the beginning of the summer vacation.[1] I am lonely. When you come back, with your great soul brimful of wondrous impressions of that world to which "the streets of the sea"[2] lead, my soul will rejoice at your coming and go out to meet you. They who have read in the same book understand each other better. You will reassure me of the reality of many things which are growing unreal in my imagination. Is it not glorious to see what a great and convenient world we live in! And to go sailing aloft over it all, looking down into the strange nests man has made for himself and called cities! Therefore, while you may, soar! revel in the sunshine and be glad. And, finally, if you have, like Edgar in Lear, a fancy "to curl your hair and wear gloves,"[3] — do it now, and not when you come back!

Hillard I have not seen for a week. I go seldom to town. I am making myself very busy now, so as to have a vacation when you return. We will then dig up the Five of Clubs, which, since you went your ways, has been buried, — covered over with a *spade*! We have no recreations, now, not one. All hard work and dull boys! This very pen I write you with, thus late in the night, has been hard at work all day for the Dean, — an article on Anglo-Saxon literature,[4] which I am condemned to write, and which you will be condemned to read, friendship forcing you thereunto. . . . Of your friends here I have to say only that they are well, — all well, I believe. I strut about among them with your letter in my pocket, and am welcome. I say to them, "I have just received a letter from Sumner." And they say, "Ah, have you? how is he? what is he doing? Paris? London? date?" and so forth. . . . To the Ticknors my kindest regards. Tell them everybody stands tiptoe here to see who shall have the first glimpse of them as they rise over the verge of the Atlantic, home-bound. . . . There! I wish this sheet were larger, — how I would bore you. But I forbear. I scorn to take advantage of your position. I will not write a double letter!

MANUSCRIPT: unrecovered; text from *Life*, I, 293–295.

1. See 369.1. Cleveland had married Sarah Paine Perkins (1818–1893), daughter of James Perkins, on February 1, 1838.
2. Longfellow's translation of the Homeric metaphor *hugra keleutha.*
3. Cf. *King Lear,* III, iv, 83.
4. John Gorham Palfrey was dean of the theological faculty at Harvard, as well as editor of the *North American Review,* where Longfellow's article "Anglo-Saxon Literature" appeared (XLVII [July 1838], 90–134).

## 422. *To John Vaughan*

Cambridge April 29. 1838

My dear Sir,

It is a very long time since I have had the pleasure of seeing you, or communicating directly with you: and I am glad of an opportunity of renewing my friendly intercourse with you, by thanking you for Mr. DuPonceau's most valuable work which came to me through your hands. Have the goodness to present to him my respects, and to renew the thanks, which I have already expressed to him by letter.[1]

Allow me at the same time to ask your influence in behalf of my friend Dr. Bosworth who has lately published this Anglo-Saxon Dictionary, by showing the Prospectus of his works to any of your friends, who you may think feel an interest in such studies.[2]

I have also one more favor to ask, in behalf of an Italian gentleman, Signor Mariotti, who has applied for the situation of Italian instructer in the Girard College.[3] He has lived some years here, and in this neighborhood; — an excellent young man, and a scholar of very distinguished ability, and I should think every way calculated to take charge of classes in your Institution.

I hope you will not think me too free in recommending persons to your friendly notice. I seek not therein my own good but another's;

and know how willing and desirous you always are to lend a friendly hand to those who need and deserve it.

I beg you to present my regards to Dr. Thos. McEuen[4] and my other friends in Phila. With the warmest feelings of friendship,

Truly yrs.
Wadsworth Longfellow

MANUSCRIPT: American Philosophical Society, Philadelphia. ADDRESS: To/John Vaughan Esq/Philadelphia ANNOTATION (*by Longfellow*): Paid. 192 POSTMARKS: CAMBRIDGE MS. APR 30/PAID ENDORSEMENT: 1838./Longfellow. W./Cambridge — April 29th./recd. May 2d./recom[mendin]g Berwith's [*sic*] Anglo-Saxon/dictionary —/do — Sr. Mariotti/for Italian Instructor in the/ Girard College —

1. Peter Stephen Du Ponceau (1760–1844), an eminent lawyer and ethnologist in Philadelphia, had come to America from France as Baron von Steuben's secretary and interpreter. The work to which Longfellow alludes was his *Grammatical System of Some of the Languages of the Indian Nations of North America*, which had just been published. Longfellow's letter to him is unrecovered.

2. This letter is written on the back of a "Prospectus for Bosworth's *A Dictionary of the Anglo-Saxon Language*," which bears the printed signature "Wadsworth Longfellow." See 406.1.

3. Luigi Mariotti was the pseudonym of Antonio Carlo Napoleone Gallenga (1810–1895), an Italian patriot who had come to America in 1836 as a political refugee. Girard College had not yet opened its doors, and no position was available for him. He subsequently returned to Europe, where he had a distinguished career as politician and author.

4. Thomas McEuen (1799–1873) matriculated at the University of Pennsylvania in 1816 and received his M.D. in 1821. A member of the American Philosophical Society and the Franklin Institute, he was one of the original trustees of Girard College.

## 423. *To Stephen Longfellow*

[Cambridge] April 30. 1838

My dear Father,

You must not blame me that I have not written you sooner. Since my return I have been very busy, as I foretold you I should be, working with a cheerful alacrity, in good health and good spirits. The Article on Anglo-Saxon Literature was finished last week. It is long and elaborate; and I think will interest and amuse you. I do not give a dry review of the Dictionary;[1] but after mentioning it with due praise, go on to show what there is in the Literature of the language to induce people to study it, and consequently buy the Dictionary. A heavy, learned Article would have sunk the whole affair. I have therefore tried to write a pleasant and agreeable paper. You shall judge how well I have succeeded. Well for me, was it, that I was prepared for the task by previous study of some years ago; or I could not have accomplished it. I now feel confident that I have done it well; knowing the whole ground; and therefore have no apprehensions nor care for the opinions of people in general. I take the liberty to think well of my essay, because it cost me no little labor; and I do not mean to disparage my own handiwork by false modesty.

Tomorrow is Exhibition-day. Wednesday, the day after, I begin my Lectures on Literature and Literary Life. I have been writing busily all this evening at the Second, and in the course of the week shall have three in advance, and the whole will go merrily.

I see by the Advertiser, (or rather hear *from* the Advertiser) that Alexander has been unhorsed in his Geological aspirations. I hope he looks upon the disappointment with sufficient coolness, and philosophic indifference. It is good to learn betimes in life, that disappointments may be turned to good account: sometimes to better account than success even. I trust it will be so with yours, Don Alejandro! The books at the Foreign Book Store I inquired about to-day. The best of them are no longer to be had: Only a few Geometries and Algebras left; and they did not look as if they were going in a hurry. I think they will wait till you come.

Samuel is well and studious. The Historian Prescott was thrown from his horse two days ago, and came down upon the paved sidewalk of Winter Street, all bent up, like a Hindoo god. Miraculously preserved, with only a strained muscle or so.[2] Have you seen Dean Palfrey's and "Gentleman George" Bancroft's controversy? Foolish enough. Boys quarrelling about marbles! The Dean maintains a dignified silence now, which is certainly the best course. Mr. B. did a shameful thing in "appealing to the sympathies of the Public." Tempest in a tea-pot![3] Good night. With much love

Truly yours
Henry.

MANUSCRIPT: Longfellow Trust Collection. ADDRESS: To/Hon. Stephen Longfellow/Portland/Me ANNOTATION (*by Longfellow*): single POSTMARK: CAMBRIDGE MS. MAY 1 ENDORSEMENT: H W. Longfellow/Apr. 30. 1838/ May 27 —

1. Bosworth's *Dictionary of the Anglo-Saxon Language.*

2. Prescott seems to have developed a reputation for falling off horses. George Ticknor wrote that "as he loved a spirited horse and was often thinking more of his intellectual pursuits than of anything else while he was riding, he sometimes caught a fall" (*Life of William Hickling Prescott* [Boston, 1864], p. 120). In this instance he was thrown not on April 28, as implied here, but on the 24th (MS Journal).

3. George Bancroft had been angered by what he thought was Palfrey's tampering with his article on historians in the *North American Review*, XLVI (April 1838), 475–487. After an acrimonious correspondence Palfrey returned one of

Bancroft's letters unopened, whereupon Bancroft reviewed the entire controversy in an address "To the Literary Public" in the *Boston Post* for April 16, 1838. The quarrel is summarized by M. A. DeWolfe Howe in the *Life and Letters of George Bancroft* (New York, 1908), I, 227–229.

## 424. *To Charles Folsom*

[Cambridge, May 9, 1838]

Dear Sir

I here send you the books. Morton's History [1] I cannot obtain. What shall be done?

Yrs. truly
Longw.

MANUSCRIPT: Boston Public Library. ENDORSEMENT: Rec'd 10 May, 1838.

1. Nathaniel Morton (1613–1686), a nephew of William Bradford, compiled *New-England's Memoriall* (Cambridge, Mass., 1669) in large part from the manuscript of his uncle's *Of Plimoth Plantation.*

## 425. *To Alexander Wadsworth Longfellow*

Cambridge May 10. 1838

My dear Alex,

I write you a few words only, being in haste. A day or two since I saw Col. Fessenden. He says the place on the Eastern Rail-road is still vacant. The rails have not yet arrived: and you can have it, if you wish. He moreover says, that if you wish to pursue your studies in Boston, you can have a desk at his office — a foot-hold, where you can be upon the look-out, and take the best thing that turns up. I think you had better come on, as soon as you can conveniently.

There is to be a new rail-road survey somewhere in this neighborhood this summer, from Taunton to Providence I believe. Mr. Felton — (my friend's brother,) — will probably have charge of it.[1] I have mentioned your name to him, — in case he succeeds; and Prof. Felton will back you, in case of need.

This is all I have to send you in your line. Do you feel much disappointed in the Geological failure? Never mind it. Doubtless it is all for the best. You will not run off your track now: but come to Boston, and be in the way of doing something.

Yesterday a smiling youth spoke to me in the street, and asked about you. One of your fellow students under Haywood, I suppose: though I could not recall his name. He says he hopes to go South. Has light hair, and wears a cap, and snuff-colored frock-coat. Do you recognize him?

Much love to all. I passed some pleasant hours with Pitt [Fessenden] last week; and should have passed more, tell him, if he had not departed so unexpectedly. I went up the Tremont steps, just as he was starting in the stage for Portland.

Yours truly
H. W. Longw.

P.S. When shall I see Ch. Daveis, Judge Potter and Eliza? Bring or send Sam's case of small round seals.

MANUSCRIPT: Longfellow Trust Collection. ADDRESS: To/Mr. A. W. Longfellow/ Portland/Me. POSTMARK: CAMBRIDGE MS. MAY 11 ENDORSEMENT: H. W. Longfellow/Cambridge/May *10. 1838./May 23d*/Resp[ectin]g Appointment on the/Eastern R.R. offered by Col./Fessenden. —

1. Samuel Morse Felton (1809–1889) had recently begun his career as a civil engineer and did not begin railroad engineering until 1841, when he built the Fresh Pond Railroad, designed to bring ice to Boston.

## 426. *To the Harvard Corporation*

[Cambridge] May. 12. 1838

Gentlemen,

I respectfully request that the following works may be purchased for the College Library. They are for sale at Chs. Little's.[1]

1. Turner on the Ancient British Poetry. 8vo. 1 vol. $3.12

2. The German Pulpit: Selections from Celebrated German Divines. 8 vo. 1 vol. $2.25.[2]

Respectfully Yr. Obt. S[er]vt.
Henry W. Longfellow

MANUSCRIPT: Harvard College Papers, VIII, 323. PUBLISHED: *Professor Longfellow of Harvard*, p. 20.

1. Charles Coffin Little (1799–1869) had formed in 1837 the firm that grew eventually into Little, Brown & Co.

2. Sharon Turner, *A Vindication of the Genuineness of the Ancient British Poems of Aneurin, Taliesin, Llywarch Hen, and Merdhin, with Specimens of the Poems* (London, 1803); and *The German Pulpit; being a selection of sermons by the most eminent modern divines of Germany*, trans. by R. Baker (London, 1829). Longfellow's request seems to have been denied, for the library acquired neither volume at this time.

## 427. *To Clara Crowninshield*

Cambridge May 31. 1838.

My dear Clara

I received your note late on Saturday night, on my return from Brooklyne, where I had been to dine with Henry Cleaveland. I felt quite offended, that you should not have let me know of your being in Boston, till you were just stepping into the stage to depart. I hope you wont do so again.

Eliza [Potter] has at length arrived. They came Tuesday morning. I dined with *them* at Dr. Howard's in Brook[li]ne on Wednesday; and saw her again yesterday. She seems about as usual, in regard to her health; but is in good spirits; and will rally famously in Boston, I doubt not.

Mrs. Bliss's engagement rather astonished me. She always seemed to me too much of an icicle to want a husband. I should have thought her ideas on matrimony more like those of *Cathos* in Molières *Precieuses Ridicules, Scene V.* — which I think I will not quote, though they are very funny.[1] What do *you* think of the match? Were you not surprised? What a turmoil it will produce in Hingham! I should like to hear the matter properly discussed. The worst of it is the bringing together of children. A step-father and step-mother in the house; — old reminiscences living in children's faces — rivalries, heart-burnings and sorrow sufficient, no doubt. However, if they think it best, I have no particular objection.[2]

*Pale and low-spirited.*[3] If they had said *lank and silver-haired,* it would have been nearer the truth; though not exactly true. One's spirits rise and fall, more or less, you know; but I am most of the time cheerful; and should be *ashamed* to be unhappy; as every man ought to be.

In Charles' Street yesterday I met *Gräter* walking with his eldest son. He says he has another, fourteen days old. He was in good spirits and not at all drunk: and said; "Ich wünsche dass Sie ein mal *in meines armes Haus* kommen würden. Ich wohne in dem so genanten *Cholera-Hospital!*" Und danach lachte er, etwas leut und sturmisch, nach seiner Art. Wahrhaftig, es that mir Weh, wenn er so lächelnd-traurig, *mein armes Haus,* sagte.[4]

I should have written you before, my dear child, ||but|| since my return I have been so busy, that everything that could be postponed, has been *aufgeschoben* [pushed aside] from day to day. I have had a lecture to write every week; and a long article for the Dean on Anglo-Saxon Literature; in order to recommend Dr. *Bosworth's* dictionary; which with my college duties and the usual interruptions, have hurried me a little.

*"Einsam bin ich"* I have never translated.[5]

The Klopstockian Ode I have not; either original nor translated. My Tr. was only verbal; thus "How they so softly rest — All they the holy ones! — Unto their dwelling-place. Now doth my soul draw near: —" *und so weiter.* If you wish it, I will get a copy for you; though you can translate it better with yr. eyes shut.[6]

I can get very little information about Mr *Röcher,*[7] or whatever his name is. Dr. Follen[8] wrote me a short letter in answer to my enquiries, and said he should soon be in Camb. and would tell me more. I have not yet seen him. Adieu.

Very truly yours
H. W. L.

MANUSCRIPT: Berg Collection, New York Public Library. ADDRESS: To Miss Clara Crowninshield/Care of Ichabod Nichols Esq/Salem POSTMARK: CAMBRIDGE MS. ||JUN|| 1

1. Longfellow delicately refrains from quoting the last lines by Cathos in scene v: "Pour moi, mon oncle, tout ce que je puis vous dire, c'est que je trouve le mariage une chose tout à fait choquante. Comment est-ce qu'on peut souffrir la pensée de coucher contre un homme vraiment nu?" ("As for me, uncle, all that I can tell you is that I find marriage a very shocking business. How can one bear the thought of lying down beside a really naked man?")

2. George Bancroft's second marriage, to Mrs. Elizabeth Davis Bliss (1803–1886) of Boston, took place on August 16, 1838. Despite Longfellow's misgivings, it endured for forty-eight years.

3. In an obvious allusion to Longfellow's unsuccessful courtship of Fanny Appleton, Clara Crowninshield had written: "I hear you have grown *pale* and *low spirited* — Is it so?" (Letter undated; MS, Longfellow Trust Collection [Longfellow House]).

4. " 'I wish that you would come *into my poor house* sometime. I live in the so-called *Cholera Hospital!*' And afterwards he laughed, somewhat loud and impetuously, according to his habit. Really, it made me sad, when he said so comically-tragically *my poor house.*"

5. "Einsam bin ich nicht alleine" is a song from the play *Preciosa* by Pius Alexander Wolff (1782–1828), which had been set to music by von Weber in 1820.

6. Clara's desire for the "Klopstockian ode" seems to have stimulated Longfellow to take up his translation again, for shortly afterwards he included "The Dead. From the German of Klopstock" (the first four lines of which are quoted here) in *Voices of the Night.* In later editions of his poetry he retrieved his error in ascription and described the ode as "From the German of Stockmann"; but in *Works,* VI, 262, his editors finally and mistakenly attributed it to Ernst Stockmann (1634–1712). Actually, "The Dead" is a translation of "Wie sie so sanft ruhn, alle die Seligen," a well-known lyric by August Cornelius Stockmann (1751–1821).

7. Bernard Rölker (1816–1888), a native of Westphalia, was acting as tutor at this time in the family of Samuel Jones, Chief Justice of the Superior Court of New York City. Longfellow interviewed him in July in New York for the post of instructor in German at Harvard. See Letter No. 432. James T. Hatfield discusses Rölker's long friendship with Longfellow in *New Light on Longfellow,* pp. 63–65.

8. Charles Theodore Christian Follen (1796–1840), German-born doctor of jurisprudence, had for several years been Professor of German literature at Harvard, but in 1834 the corporation failed to reappoint him because of his abolitionist sympathies. An ordained Unitarian minister, he was now preaching on occasion in Washington, New York, and Boston.

428. *To Stephen Longfellow*

Cambridge June 2. 1838.

My dear Father,

You have found me a very poor correspondent of late. Letters being of all things the most easily postponed from day to day, always have the preference given them in that particular. For the last month I have had a great deal of writing to do, as you are aware; and the only letters I have written have been business letters.

Two days ago I had a proposition from the Society [for Diffusion] of Useful Knowledge to deliver several lectures before them next winter. They offer me thirty dollars each. I am not sure that I shall not accept. What do you think?? The only objection I have is; that I propose to deliver *a course* there, which might interfere somewhat.[1] I have almost given up the Portland plan.[2] It does not promise much; and I fear would look like *spunging,* in these hard times.

I was very glad to hear from you the other day. I did not see much of the Judge [Barrett Potter], being engaged the morning he was in Cambridge. Eliza is in very good spirits. I have no doubt her visit will do her much good.

Nothing can well surpass the beauty of Cambridge at this season. Every tree is heavy with blossoms and the whole air laden with perfume. My residence here in the old Craigie house is a paradise: and occasionally I drive over to Brookline, where I have many friends from Boston, ruralizing. This, with the College engagements, makes a very pleasant life to lead. Only the Winter is rather solitary; and we are to remedy that now, by a long Vacation. Some changes are to take place soon in our College affairs. We are henceforth to have only two terms and two vacations a year. The first vacation from middle of July to first of August, as now; the second, from middle of January to beginning of March. In addition to this the voluntary system is to be introduced into the classical department, after the Freshman year; — and one step farther taken toward the *beau ideal* of a University. As to my own Department, I know of no changes proposed.

I suppose Sam wrote you, that he had the honor of being elected into the Phi Beta Kappa Society; — which is really an honor. He does very well; tho' I forgot to ask him this morning whether he had got up into the first section again. He is *very* capable: and stands *easily* among the first scholars in his class. I dont think it will hurt him to have a rap over the knuckles now and then, such as he got by being marched down into No. 2 last term. I think he will retrieve ||No. 1|| again soon.

I have not seen Dr. Nichols; nor heard even whether he has been in Cambridge. The various meetings of Societies in Boston this last week I have not attended. The town is quite a-float wtih strangers.

My love to all.

Truly yrs.
H. W. L.

P. S. *for Anne.*

I can find but two pairs of linen drawers. I think the others are in Portland. Those I have are in a sad condition; and I cannot spare *either* for a pattern. What is to be done? I think I will get a pair or two here and wait for the others till vacation. This will be the best way. I shall come home looking like a *tatterdemalion*. What are you doing in Portland? Why did not Mary[3] come with Eliza? I will give her the room opposite mine here; and she can be housekeeper.

MANUSCRIPT: Longfellow Trust Collection. ADDRESS: To/Hon. Stephen Longfellow/Portland/Me POSTMARK: CAMBRIDGE MS. ||JUN|| 4

1. Longfellow ultimately decided against these lectures (*Young Longfellow*, p. 312).
2. The plan to deliver summer lectures there (see Letter No. 415).
3. His sister Mary.

## 429. *To Romeo Elton*

Cambridge June 11. 1838

My dear Sir,

I must beg you to excuse me for suffering so many weeks to elapse, before answering yr. favor of April 23. and thanking you for the volume of Historical Transactions.[1] I have been more than usually busy this summer in preparing and delivering; and my correspondence with my friends has consequently languished a good deal. You know, as every literary man does, how these things come to pass. A letter is of all things the most easily put off till tomorrow, and "this little space of time"[2] creeps in so quickly and so often, that at last we find ourselves justly exposed to a charge of negligence, and begin with an apology; as I now do.

I have read with great interest your memoir of Callender; with the Notes and Biographical Sketches.[3] They make a very valuable book, upon a subject, which seemed, at first glance, to offer but a small foot-hold for the historian. You have certainly wrought your materials up with the greatest success. The short sketch of Bishop Berkeley is delightful. I hope to have it in my power to visit Newport in the course of the Summer; and shall certainly look with new interest upon the spot, where the "gentleman of middle stature, of an agreeable pleasant and erect aspect" arrived, "in a pretty large ship."[4]

In answer to your question, how one may best send a package to our friend Greene, I can only say, that I am in precisely the same doubt with you. I know not. I have several things I wish to send him, but have no way. Is there no Tuscan Consul or Neopolitan, in New York? If there be, I think our best way would be to send every thing to his care, to go by first vessels to Leghorn or Naples. I think Mrs. Greene could inform you. Perhaps we might send to the Wards of New York, who are friends and relatives.

Professor Felton desires his cordial regards to you. I beg you to present mine to Dr. Wayland and Professor Goddard.

Very truly yours
H. W. Longfellow

Professor Elton.

MANUSCRIPT: Brown University Library. ADDRESS: Professor Romeo Elton/Brown University/Providence POSTMARKS: CAMBRIDGE MS. JUN [*date obscure*]/PAID POSTAL ANNOTATION (*by Longfellow*): PAID. charge 192.

1. *Collections of the Rhode-Island Historical Society* (Providence, 1838), Vol. IV.

2. Possibly a garbled reference to the "Tomorrow, and tomorrow, and tomorrow" speech in *Macbeth*, V, v, 19–20.

3. The volume sent to Longfellow consisted of a reprint of John Callender's *An Historical Discourse, on the Civil and Religious Affairs of the Colony of Rhode-Island* (1739) with Elton's voluminous annotation.

4. From Elton's sketch of Dean George Berkeley (1684–1753), later bishop of Cloyne, in the notes to his memoir of Callender, p. 31.

## 430. *To George Washington Greene*

Cambridge. June 11 1838

My dear Greene,

I have much pleasure in making you acquainted with the bearers of this — Mr. McLellan of Boston; and Mr. Brown of Andover; who are on their first travels through Italy, as we were ten years ago.

McLellan you know already as a poet. You will know him better now; particularly when I tell you he is an old college friend of mine, and one of the best fellows in the world. Mr. Brown is principal of the Young Ladies High School in Andover; and son of the former President of Dartmouth.[1]

I think you will enjoy the society of these gentlemen very highly; and I hardly need ask your friendly civilities in their behalf; as I am sure you will do all unasked, which can render their stay in Rome agreeable.

With kindest regards to the Signora,

most truly yours
Longfellow

MANUSCRIPT: Berg Collection, New York Public Library.

1. Isaac McLellan (44.2) and Samuel Gilman Brown (1813–1885) spent two years abroad. Upon his return Brown, son of Francis Brown, the plaintiff in the Dartmouth College Case, became Professor of Oratory and Belles-Lettres at Dartmouth. He later served as president of Hamilton College, 1867–1881.

## 431. *To Nathaniel Hawthorne*

[Cambridge] June 30 [1831][1]

My Dear Hawthorne, —

Mr. Duyckinck and his friend Mr. Beekman, of New York,[2] having read your "Twice-Told Tales" with great wonderment and delight, "desire you of more acquaintance." I therefore am happy to make you known to each other.

Yours truly
Longfellow.

MANUSCRIPT: unrecovered; text from Rose Hawthorne Lathrop, *Memories of Hawthorne* (Boston and New York, 1898), p. 148.

1. The more likely date of this letter was June 27, 1838, when Duyckinck and Beekman called on Longfellow in Cambridge (MS Journal). Longfellow was in New York on June 30. Rose Hawthorne Lathrop mistakenly supplied 1851 as the year.

2. Both Evert Augustus Duyckinck (1816–1878) and James William Beekman (1815–1877) had graduated from Columbia, studied law, and were interested in literary matters. Duyckinck's later career as author, editor, and anthologist frequently crossed Longfellow's. Beekman, a man of inherited wealth and owner of the historic Beekman Mansion, became well known for his public service in New York.

## 432. *To Josiah Quincy*

Harvard College July 13. 1838

President Quincy.
Dear Sir,

In pursuance of frequent conversations held with you, I have requested Mr. Bokum and Mr. Surault to resign the places they now hold in this Institution. In Mr. Bokum's place, I propose Mr. Bernard Rölker.[1] For Mr. Surault I have not yet found a substitute: but shall probably be able to do so before the close of the vacation.

I take this opportunity of asking an increase of Dr. Bachi's Salary, if it be possible. Otherwise, I have some reason to fear, that we shall lose his very important services; as I understand, that overtures have been made to him from another quarter. He has been here now twelve years. The Salary of $500: — is not so great now as it was twelve years ago. His experience as a teacher is far greater; and his services far more valuable. You know how very efficient he is. I therefore respectfully urge this matter upon yr. consideration; and request you to bring it before the Corporation at their next meeting.[2]

I have the honor to be

yr. Obt. Ser[v]t.
Henry W. Longfellow

P.S. Inclosed is a list of students who were absent from my Examinations on Friday last. Would you have the goodness to send for them, that I may know the reason of their absence.[3]

MANUSCRIPT: Harvard College Papers, IX, 21. PUBLISHED: *Professor Longfellow of Harvard*, p. 30.

1. Rölker became instructor in German in place of Bokum by action of the Harvard Corporation on July 19, 1838 (*Professor Longfellow of Harvard*, p. 31). He continued in that post for eighteen years.
2. The Corporation referred the matter of Bachi's salary to a committee composed of President Quincy, Justice Story, and Mr. John Amory Lowell, who left it unchanged (*Professor Longfellow of Harvard*, p. 31).
3. This list has not survived.

## 433. *To Stephen Longfellow*

Cambridge July. 14. 1838

My dear Father

I have returned in safety from the fiery city of New York, going round to cool myself at the Springs.[1] The main object of my journey was to find a German Instructer to take the place of Mr. Bokum, who leaves us this Summer. I am also on the look out for a new French instructer — the present one not being much to my taste. This changing is unpleasant. It is not flattering a man to ask him to resign his place. But in these two instances I have had to do it.

I shall not be in Portland for a week or ten days: on account of my friend Felton's wedding, and the great Webster dinner, which I wish to attend.[2] I shall, however, come at the earliest moment I can.

In New York I saw Mrs. Henley[3] and the Higbees, though only once. They did not seem to like it, that I did not seek them out earlier. But I could not. I had too many people to see, and the weather was too hot. Mrs. Higbee is beautiful. Mr. H. is not. They thought it too bad for me not to go to Washington — *when I was so near.* They call New York *near*! The heat was too great to think of such a movement.

We have just closed our Examinations. Exhibition is on Monday. Sam's part is very good: and written in a very flowing simple and beautiful style. I think he will do himself great credit.

I have nothing new to tell you; and write these few lines in great haste, having many letters to write, and papers to make out at the close of the Term.

Eliza P. [Potter] returned from Walpole yesterday. I went down for her. She seems feeble: and languid. The oppressive heat overcomes her strength.

Affectionately yours
Henry W. Longfellow.

MANUSCRIPT: Longfellow Trust Collection. ADDRESS: Hon. S. Longfellow/Portland/Me POSTMARK: CAMBRIDGE MS. JUL 16

1. Longfellow had left Cambridge for New York on June 29 and had returned on July 9, having gone up the Hudson to Albany and from there overland through Stockbridge and Springfield (MS Journal, July 10, 1838; Letter No. 436).

2. Longfellow attended Felton's wedding on July 19 (see 369.1), but he seems not to have been among the 1500 present at the Webster dinner in Fanueil Hall on July 29. His journal entry for that date makes no mention of the affair. He left Cambridge for Portland on July 31.

3. Elizabeth Denison Henley (b. 1788), sister of Louisa Denison Wadsworth (92.4), was the widow of Capt. John Dandridge Henley, U.S.N. (1781–1835). Her daughter Frances was the wife of Rev. Higbee (413.3).

## 434. *To Clara Crowninshield*

Cambridge July 28. 1838.

My dear Clara,

I know not where thou art — whether in the City of Peace or among the roses of Sharon, which, I understand, are few.[1] But wheresoever it may be, I trust thou will love to look upon the spiritual face of one Thos. Carlyle, as imprinted in the two volumes, which I here send thee. Carlyle is now lecturing in London. Ticknor heard him; and speaks of him as rather so-so-ish. Sumner has also heard him, and calls him the *Zena Colburn* of thought! (Is *Zena* right; or is it something else?)[2] A good figure of speech, for one who deals with the *square-roots* of thought, and can give you any *power* at a moment's warning.

Strange, how unwilling many are to acknowledge any merit in Carlyle, because he is fantastic. Mr. [Andrews] Norton, for instance, absolutely *hates* him; and seems to take it as a *personal insult,* that anybody should write in such a style! As a general rule the young all like — the old all *dislike the Schoolmaster of Craigenputtock.*

Emerson continues to make a stir. Not long ago he preached a most extraordinary sermon here; concerning which the Reverend Dean Palfrey said that "what in it was not folly was impiety!" Oh! After all, it was only a stout *humanitarian* discourse; in which Christ and Göthe were mentioned together as great Philosophers.[3]

I believe nothing else has happened to set people by the ears, since I last saw you; which is a very long while, my dear child. I was very sorry I could not wait for you the other day at Dr. Storer's.[4] I had a *particular* engagement.

I have been in New York lately. Saw the [William Cullen] Bryants, who have not changed in the slightest degree.[5] Had I shut my eyes, I should have thought myself in the *Hauptstrasse* of Heidelberg. Fanny says just such things as she used to say, and in just the same tones; — with German phrases and little scraps of song intermingled. *Jülchen* is thin and blue, with that patient look of child-martyrdom, — that beseeching, *vergiss-mein-nicht* [do not forget me] expression of one, who is going to die and never see you again, which that fragile little creature always had. Monsieur and Madame as usual. They expressed much desire to see you; as did yr. friend Elizth. Peirce, who prays and entreats you to visit her in New York.[6]

Finally, Mr. Bokum has resigned his situation, wishing to pursue *Theology* exclusively. Mr. Rölker takes his place here. He is a tall and pleasant youth; and looks like *Schminke*, which grieves me a little.[7] Monsieur *Surault* likewise takes his departure. I know not yet whom to put in his place. *Surault* dies hard. I am detained here now on this business, when I ought to be in Portland. I hope to go on Monday next; and remain till the close of the vacation. I wish you were going with me. Why cant you; — you and Eliza [Potter]? I shall be in town on Monday, and shall look for you: though I have not at this moment the least idea *where* to look. Moreover I would fain hear from you; but you will not answer my letters. Why?

Affectionately your friend
H. W. Longw.

MANUSCRIPT: Clifton Waller Barrett Collection, University of Virginia.

1. By "City of Peace" is meant Salem, where Clara Crowninshield was then living. In a letter to Longfellow dated July 7, 1838, Eliza Potter mentions the fact that Clara had been spending some time in Sharon, Mass., with Mrs. Benjamin Ropes Nichols.

2. Zerah Colburn (1804–1840), a mathematical prodigy, had displayed his talent for calculation both here and abroad during his childhood years. At this time,

his unique faculty having disappeared, he was a professor of languages at Norwich University in Vermont.

3. Emerson delivered his Divinity School Address on July 15, 1838. Contrary to Longfellow's statement, he made no mention of Goethe.

4. Presumably Dr. David Humphreys Storer.

5. Clara Crowninshield had apparently not seen the Bryants since the autumn of 1836 when she, Mrs. Bryant, and her daughters Fanny and Julia had arrived in New York from Europe under Longfellow's protection.

6. Charlotte Elizabeth Peirce (1804–1888) was the daughter of Benjamin Peirce, librarian of Harvard College, 1826–1831, and Lydia Nichols Peirce, the sister of Clara's childhood guardian. Clara had boarded with the Peirce family after completing her formal schooling in 1827 (*Diary of Clara Crowninshield*, pp. xix–xx).

7. Longfellow had had an unfortunate experience in 1836 with a Heidelberg student named Schmincke, who had borrowed money from him and never repaid it (Clara Crowninshield to Longfellow, March 11, 1837 [MS, Longfellow House]). According to *Die Matrikel der Universität Heidelberg* (Fünfter Teil) there were two Schminckes in residence at the university in 1836: Heinrich Ferdinand Schmincke, aged 19, a medical student from Hessen-Cassel; and Ludwig Schmincke, aged 23, a law student from Nieder-Hessen. Longfellow mentions "the student Johannes Schminke" in *Hyperion* (*Works*, VIII, 267).

## 435. *To Samuel Ward*

CAMBRIDGE, July 30, 1838.

MY DEAR WARD:

On returning from Nahant, I hear that you have been in Boston, pushing through, as if it were an inconsiderable village not set down in the guide-books, and where you had no friends. I am sorry not to have seen you. That affair of the newspaper must be very thoroughly discussed and arranged before we begin. I fear that this library of Mr. Astor will so occupy Mr. Cogswell as entirely to remove him from journalizing. Moreover, Sparks takes the matter very coldly — says he cannot write much; does not wish to be a Proprietor, and fifty more conceits equally pleasant. You readily understand, therefore, that we have to begin anew, as it were; and must necessarily meet and reconsider the whole matter.[1] When and where shall this be? To-morrow I depart for Portland, where I shall remain till the twentieth of August, or thereabout, and after that date hold myself in readiness to meet you in Newport, or Cambridge, or Boston.

On Bowditch there is yet nothing to be had, worth having. Nothing has been published but the Eulogies of Young and White. The other matters which you mention have not yet dawned upon the world.[2] Therefore, I can think of no better plan, than that suggested in my letter from Nahant — namely, a pilgrimage to the library of the great translator, who has now translated (*Sartor Resartus*).[3]

That reminds me of Carlyle. Ticknor heard him lecture in London.

Thought him only *so-so-ish*. Another friend now in London has also heard him and writes: "I have heard Carlyle lecture. He is the Zerah Colburn of thought — dealing with the square-roots of ideas, and giving you any power you ask, in the twinkling of an eye."[4]

Carlyle's "Miscellanies" are just published. Commend the perusal of the chapter on Voltaire to Dr. Francis.[5] One thing I much like in this writer, which is his universal benevolence — the spirit of love, in which he sees all men and all things. And one thing I much dislike, which is the way he has of *ducking under* at the flash of every sharp-shooting inquiry. He does not come very boldly up to the encounter of difficult problems; but passes on saying; "Herein doubtless lies much significance; and more than most men will be likely to see at a glance," or some such phrase; which leaves the reader to infer, that he might say a great deal if he wanted.

This is a dissertation — and therefore, a *bore*, "though doubtless significant of much." Allow me to bore you with another instrument, and after the following fashion. Do you know any *young* Frenchman, who speaketh his native tongue pleasantly, and is a gentleman, and would be disposed to come to our College, and give *three* days in the week to instruction, remaining sole master of the other four — salary only $500 a year? The salary is certainly small, but the position good: an excellent *standpunkt* [station]. Will you do me the favor to think of this?

Did you ever know such red-hot weather? Say to Cogswell that not a whisper of the Library has fallen from my lips. The secret was not lisped by me.[6] "*I will apprize you when I go to Newport*" goeth [saith] the child of impulse; — but he did *not* apprize me.[7] With much regard to you all.

Truly yours,

LONGFELLOW.

MANUSCRIPT: unrecovered; text from "Letters to Samuel Ward, Part I," pp. 40–41.

1. Longfellow, Ward, Joseph Cogswell, and Jared Sparks were considering establishing a newspaper in New York, but the plan never got beyond the preliminary stages of discussion, primarily because Cogswell, who was their choice for editor, was completely occupied with the *New York Review* and with the development of the Astor Library. Thompson discusses the plan in *Young Longfellow*, pp. 288–290.

2. Ward was planning an essay on Nathaniel Bowditch and in a letter dated July 7, 1838, had asked Longfellow to send him information and materials on the subject. Two eulogies had already appeared: Alexander Young, *A Discourse on the Life and Character of the Hon. Nathaniel Bowditch, LL.D., F.R.S., delivered in the Church on Church Green, March 25, 1838* (Boston, 1838); and Daniel Appleton White, *An Eulogy on the Life and Character of Nathaniel Bowditch, LL.D., F.R.S., delivered at the Request of the Corporation of the City of Salem, May 24, 1838* (Salem, 1838). John Pickering's *Eulogy on Nathaniel Bowditch,*

*LL.D., President of the American Academy of Arts and Sciences; including an analysis of his scientific publications. Delivered before the Academy, May 29, 1838* (Boston, 1838) was apparently not yet available. Ward reviewed the three discourses in the *New York Review*, IV (April 1839), 308–323.

3. The letter from Nahant is unrecovered. The "great translator" may be a reference to Emerson (see note 5).

4. The friend in London was Charles Sumner. His description of Carlyle does not appear in any extant letter to Longfellow, but a comparison of Carlyle with Zerah Colburn is made by Sumner in a letter to George Hillard, June 14, 1838 (*Sumner Memoir and Letters*, I, 318–319).

5. Ralph Waldo Emerson had supervised the publication of the first two volumes of Carlyle's *Critical and Miscellaneous Essays* (Boston, 1838). John Wakefield Francis (1789–1861) was a physician in New York who had married Sam Ward's aunt; Poe included him among *The Literati.*

6. Cogswell's "secret" — his negotiations with John Jacob Astor to supervise the establishment of the Astor Library — was poorly kept. Astor was indecisive, and although Cogswell gave increasingly of his time to the scheme, he had to wait until 1842 before receiving a definite commitment (Orie W. Long, *Literary Pioneers* [Cambridge, 1935], pp. 105–106).

7. Longfellow took the quotation from Ward's letter of July 7, 1838.

## 436. *To Lewis Gaylord Clark*

[Portland, August 3, 1838] [1]

MY DEAR CLARK:

Will not this 'Psalm of Life' do well on the front and first page of your next number? [2] Is it not true? Has it not some spirit in it? If, however, you dislike it, into the *fire* with it. (Do you keep *fires* now?). . . How do you do, Mr. CLARK? How do you like the *Schloss Johannisberger Cabinet Wein* at the Waverley, that house 'to which a Philadelphian *may* go' — 'that *bore* to which to no traveller returns,' and to which I do not think WILLIS [Gaylord Clark] will return often: do you? Of all the Waverley Novels, that 'Tale of my Landlord' about the Johannisberger was the most decided failure. It was really too bad to try to impose on WILLIS, who in the warmth of his humane great heart, had done the man much service, and at that very moment was endeavoring to do him much more.[3] Commend me to 'Astoria'! [4]

After our 'quick farewell' we pursued our way up the North River. I had a very pleasant evening, sitting on deck with D—— [Dean] and Miss C—— [Curtis].[5] The steamer had a decided pulmonary complaint, and coughed all night. I thought it would raise blood before we reached Albany. Miss C—— [Curtis] was of the same opinion. We shared our fears, and made them double: and D—— [Dean] told a shocking adventure of his on one of the great lakes, in a burning sinking steamer, which raised our fears to the *fourth power.* During the night we ran into a sloop and then ran aground. . . . I have just had a glimpse of the KNICKERBOCKER: and thank you for the superb manner in which you *do the Anglo-Saxon.*[6]

MANUSCRIPT: unrecovered; text from *The Knickerbocker, or New-York Monthly Magazine,* LVII (February 1861), 228.

1. The date is established by Willis' reply of August 10, 1838 (*Clark Letters,* pp. 98–99).

2. The poem was first published in the *Knickerbocker,* XII (September 1838), 189.

3. This allusion is explained by Clark in a note accompanying his printing of this letter in the *Knickerbocker*: "Our host of the old New-York Waverley Hotel is no longer among us: so there can be 'no offence, no offence in the world,' in presenting this pleasant gossip touching a sham bottle of *Schloss Johannisberger Cabinet Wein,* which 'it was hoped might please,' but which *didn't* 'please' by a considerable, if not more.' "

4. Longfellow uses Irving's book title to refer, of course, to the Astor House in New York.

5. The supplied names are conjectural, but in his reply Clark mentions James T. Dean, a good friend and later business manager of the *Knickerbocker* (see 515.2), and remarks that his wife's sister, Miss Curtis, "has spoken of your politeness in grateful terms" (*Clark Letters,* pp. 98–99).

6. In reviewing the *North American Review* for July 1838, Clark had written of Longfellow's article on "Anglo-Saxon Literature": "We are not in error, we think, in tracing the paternity of this article to a pen which has been made familiar to our readers — that of Prof. Longfellow, of Harvard University, a fine poet, 'a scholar ripe and good,' and as a prose writer, second only to Washington Irving" (*Knickerbocker,* XII [July 1838], 78).

## 437. *To George Washington Greene*

Portland August 6. 1838

My dear George

Five or six days ago, just as I was leaving Camb. for this city, I received yr. very welcome letter of May 26. It delighted me with its warm sympathies, and vexed me with its brevity. You contrive to get so little into a sheet, that my morbid ravenous appetite to know about you and your surroundings, as is always the case, was left unappeased. I tell you, you must write me more in detail; and remember that a sheet of paper will hold a vast deal, if you only fill it full. The next time you write, tell me what you had for breakfast, and who visits you, and about your wife and her friends, and what Americans you see, and what you think of them, and what interesting Italians you know, and what new poet in putting his head above water, and about the Persianis, and the name of Julia's husband,[1] and his profession, and in one word, all the gossip of Rome. Make me also more in the living present about you. Where do you live? What kind of a home have you got? How does Cicognani[2] like you? How is his beauteous wife? O I should ask you fifty thousand questions if you were here beside me. Only imagine them and answer them. And write *small* — something after this fashion. I am conscious of having sinned much in the way you now sin, and you must do me the credit to say that though my letters have little enough in them, they have more than of old. I am reforming. In the first place, then, let me answer your last. I am sorry you did not get my letter touching Verazzano.[3] Yr. Article was excellent — that was the amount of it. The M.S. Letter was not sent to the *New York* Hist. Soc. so soon as to the *Rhode Island*, no good opportunity offering; nevertheless has been duly sent, care of Sam Ward.[4] Prescott's Ferdinand and Isabella is in three large 8vo volumes.[5] How the deuce can I send it? More easily by the way of Palermo than Paris. Be quiet: as soon as I can. Your Art. on Romance in Italy is the best thing I have seen of yours.[6] And in general let me say, you have made a great stride forward in point of style. You are simple, forcible and clear as noon-day. Felton agrees with me. So dont be nervous, and quarrel with the American literary public, which is as good as anybody's literary public; tho' the booksellers wont bite at Mr. Wilde, who seems to me a very loose and incorrect writer, in point of style. After all, what do we care about Tasso's amours. As a portion of his life all well and good; but two volumes! Pardon me, my friend; but confess, that there are so many more topics of living, inspiring, heart-cheering interest, that this is of very inferior consequence. I am far from saying it is of *no* consequence.[7]

But he might have given his mind a higher object in Italy.

On receiving your paper on Micali, I took pen and wrote you a few lines *instanter*.[8] I shall read the proofs. The M.S. is with the Dean [Palfrey]. He tells me he has not read it yet; because he cannot possibly get it into the October No. which has disappointed me, and will of course disappoint you. Editors are absolute individuals. The Dean makes up his Nos. to suit himself; and says he has two or three long Arts. already in type, which cannot be omitted.[9] The last No. (July) is a very good one. Art. I. *Fifty Years of Ohio.* Mr. Perkins of Cincinnati.[10] II. *Milton.* Mr. [Ralph Waldo] Emerson; very good. III. *Political Economy.* Mr. [Willard] Philips. IV. *Anglo-Saxon Literature.* H. W. L. V. *Indian History.* Sparks and Felton. VI. *Fashions in Dress.* H. R. Cleaveland, a good fellow, and one of our particular friends. VII. *Holmes's Prize Dissertations.* Author unknown, (and no matter).[11] VIII. *Voyages of the Zeni.* George Folsom, a young Lawyer in New York.[12] IX. *Romantic Poetry in Italy.* Mariotti; a very fine production. It is quite astounding that a foreigner should write such English. About this gent. I wrote you in my last, I think; a young man of genius, about yr. age, who will yet be heard of in Italy.

You desire a newspaper and shall have one soon. Mr. Cogswell, Sam Ward, Mr. Sparks and myself think of starting a new one in New York. The plan, however, is not yet ripe, and may come to nought: particularly as Cogswell will doubtless go to Europe again on the following most agreeable footing. Old Astor has given the City of New York 350 thousand dollars for a public Library; and Cogswell has the management of the matter, I believe, and will doubtless be librarian, and go forth to buy books. This may break up our plan, as he was to be editor. We shall see. Librarian and Editor both he cannot be; as I will not, for one, engage in any paper, the editor of which will not devote himself solely to it. Then yr. cousin Sam is *so* flighty! However, more of this, when I know more.

Felton is married, and safely *boxed* up in Cambridge, never probably to go abroad and smell the mortality of ruins in the Old World, which I, from my heart, regret. It would do him so much good. He is however perfectly happy, just like a child with both hands full of flowers. He lives in a pretty, new-built house, about as large as a fly-cage, which the students call *Mr. Felton's Box.* His wife is a *stoutish* woman of talent; as amiable as the month of June. I expect they will have twelve children — twelve apostles of their love. Indeed what a blessed thing it is to be married! What a miserable wretch you would be in your old Italy, were it not for the warm affection of yr. wife. Only think of it, and thank God everyday of your life, that you have a warm-hearted woman to be with you. Your prophetic dreams of *my* happiness are only dreams.[13] The *Madonna Francesca* affair is all dead and buried. My pride has written the *hic jacet* of that passion. I modestly think she made a mistake. But it was not her fault. She is a most noble and beautiful woman. God grant she may not love foolishly. After this I shall not be likely to see her equal in any woman. I knew her too well, not to suffer much. However it helps to complete the *circle of experiences,* which doubtless it is good for us to go through in Life. It makes men of us to suffer. On this point I refer you once more to my friend Chs. Sumner, who will be with you in the Spring probably. You will not fail *to make much of him,* as Nature has done before you; for he stands six feet, two, in his stockings. A *colossus* holding his burning heart in his hand, to light up the sea of Life. I am in earnest. He is a very lovely character; as you will find: — full of talent, with a most keen enjoyment of life; simple, energetic, hearty, good with a great deal of poetry and no nonsense in him. You will take infinite delight in his society; and in walking

Old Rome with him. And moreover he will tell you all things which I cannot write; and answer questions, which *letters* will not.

To come back again to yr. writings. The only fault I have to find with them is in the subjects you choose. Why dig up the ancient people of Italy; when *live* Italy is swarming all about you? Why struggle always to get out of the Present? Why devote so many days and nights to delving into old books, when such a *book* lies open before you? Write something on Art. Describe the works of Michel Angelo, or Raphael! And above all send us a paper on the social condition of the Italians, in vindication of their virtues against the furious onslaught of English Travellers. Such a paper would be interesting to all readers; whereas Verazzano and Micali can interest but few — very few indeed; and moreover may be written elsewhere as well as in Rome. If I were in your place, I would dedicate myself to the study of Art — to the Beautiful: and write such things as cannot be written out of Italy. I would learn Rome by heart: and be friends with all the statues and paintings; and the best Italian Poetry; — and under the inspiration of the climate write the Lives of the poets: and let the Etruscans rot in their old vases. This is particularly good advice; for Henry Tuckerman,[14] who has just returned from Italy tells me, that you buy old books, and absolutely wallow in them.

*Interesting items of intelligence, chiefly if not wholly, about myself.* I live in a great house, which looks like an Italian villa: have two large rooms opening into each other. They were once Gen. Washington's chambers. I breakfast at seven on tea and toast: and dine at five or six, generally in Boston. In the evening I walk on the Common with Hillard or alone; then go back to Cambridge on foot, drinking at every pump on the way — six in number. If not very late, I sit an hour with Felton or Sparks. If late, go to bed. For nearly two years I have not studied at night; — save now and then at intervals. Most of the time am alone — smoke a good deal. Wear a broad-brimmed black hat — black frock-coat — boots — trousers with straps — black cane. Molest no one. Dine out frequently. In Winter go much into Boston society. Into Cambridge society *almost never*. The last year have written a great deal: enough to make volumes. Have not read much. Have wasted much time on account of the *affaire du coeur*. Shall not go mad. Have a number of literary plans and projects, some of which will ripen before long, and be made known to you. Do not like this sedentary life. Want action — want to travel — am too excited — too tumultuous inwardly — and my health suffers from all this. My intimate friends are Felton; and Hillard, Mr. Sumner's partner in the Law, a brilliant youth, *married*; and Cleaveland, a scholar, living at ease in Brookline, having taken to himself an heiress. Vide *Sumner's* Reports. You see by the date of this, that I am now in Portland. It is vacation. I go to Brunswick tomorrow. I have not been there since my return. But at all times and in all places

Most truly your friend
Longfellow

P.S. My dear friend*ess* Maria,

This whole letter is to you, not to Greene; I direct it to him only to please him, and keep him quiet. Be assured that I keep the united memory of you both warm in my bosom, thinking of you often, and at times wishing much I [were] with you. Does it make you feel very dignified to be the wife of a Roman Consul? I trust you will answer my letter — my *long* letter very soon: and if George wants to write in it, dont let him. At most only a postscript. Tell me all about yourselves — and all the gossip of the town. I should have written you Boston gossip, but you have not been much in Boston, and it would have been dull to you. Dont be angry that this P.S. is so *spun out.*

Yrs. most truly
H. W. L.

All the family send kind regards to you both. Do you remember my sister Mary? She is *fiancéd* to a youth named Greenleaf; son of the Professor — and [a] merchant in Boston.[15]

MANUSCRIPT: Longfellow Trust Collection. ADDRESS: To/George W. Greene Esq./ Consul of the United States/Rome. Italy/via/New York: care of Welles & co/Paris. ANNOTATION (*by Longfellow*): paid POSTMARKS: PORTLAND ME AUG 7/NEW YORK AUG 10/PARIS SEPT 38 (60)/PARIS 8 SEPT (60)/PARIS 9 SEPT (60)/ROMA 20 SET 1838/PAYS D'OUTREMER PAR LE HAVRE/5e. Den./PAID ANNOTATION (*by Greene*): De Lannoy/Rue d'Anjou/St. Honoré No. 42

1. See 407.9.

2. Felice Cicognani, an Italian lawyer and Greene's predecessor as U. S. Consul in Rome, 1823–1837. His numerous dispatches as consul are included by Leo Francis Stock in *Consular Relations Between the United States and the Papal States* (Washington, D.C., 1945).

3. This letter is unrecovered, apparently not having reached Greene (Greene to Longfellow, May 26, 1838).

4. Greene's second copy of the Verazzano letter (405.1) was eventually published, with a translation by Joseph Cogswell, in the *Collections of the New-York Historical Society*, Second Series, I (1841), 37–67.

5. *History of the Reign of Ferdinand and Isabella the Catholic* (Boston, 1838).

6. *North American Review*, XLVI (April 1838), 325–340. The article is a review of *Raccolta di Romanzi Storici Originali Italiani* (Firenze, 1830).

7. In his letter to Longfellow of May 26, 1838, Greene complained of the difficulty of finding a publisher for Wilde's book on Tasso (407.1): "It is a disgrace to our reading public that every petty bubble that flows up from the impure work-

ings of corrupt society, should find a ready market and works of real merit, mould in manuscript for want of a publisher."

8. This letter is unrecovered.

9. Greene's essay, "Micali on the Ancient Italians," was published in the *North American Review*, XLVIII (January 1839), 1–63.

10. James Handasyd Perkins (1810–1849). See 482.2.

11. The author was Enoch Hale (1790–1848), nephew of Nathan Hale and a prominent Boston physician.

12. Folsom (1802–1869), a Harvard graduate of 1822, had practically abandoned the law profession in order to pursue his interest in historical writing. He was at this time librarian of the New-York Historical Society.

13. In response to Letter No. 407, Greene had written on May 26, 1838: "I cannot believe that the result [of Longfellow's courtship of Fanny Appleton] will be otherwise than what you wish. I look upon your present suffering as the prelude to long and pure enjoyment."

14. Henry Theodore Tuckerman (1813–1871), author of *The Italian Sketch-Book* (Philadelphia, 1835), was to enjoy a considerable reputation in polite literature.

15. Mary Longfellow became the wife of James Greenleaf, a commission merchant and son of Simon Greenleaf (1783–1853) of the Harvard Law School, on October 22, 1839.

## 438. *To George Stillman Hillard*

Portland August. 16. 1838.

My dear George,

For a few days we have had weather which October himself might envy. It makes one's pen dance in *one's* fingers, and *one* begins to feel as if *one* might write a letter to *one's* friend in Boston. I should have written you sooner, but have been away down East, — namely, at Brunswick where I found everybody and everything very much as I left them three years and a half ago; old Professors and all, save that Time — that is to say the twilight of old age begins to streak their heads with silver bars. The only reflection I made was, that I would not for all the world live again in that little world — so "remote unfriended, melancholy, slow." [1]

Do you know anything of Monsieur Picard a Frenchman? He has been here to see me about the vacant place at Cambridge. He is a bird-like individual, with no forehead and much beak; and is on the eve of publishing a Dictionary. Think of that, and tremble.[2] Another out-lander walked in yesterday morning without knocking. He proved to be an exiled Professor from Göttingen, by name Tellkampf,[3] with a letter from Judge Story. He passed the day with me. A very social, pleasant person — somewhat tinged with the *green vanity*, which every German *Privat-Docent* is clothed with, or tinged with. I gave him a note to you, as Editor of the Jurist,[4] he being desirous of inflicting an Article upon that journal; "*pensively adumbrative of much.*"

Cogswell is here, and remains a week longer. I shall go with him to Exeter to attend the *Abbot Jubilee*[5] next week. Therefore on Friday I shall be in your rocking-chair once more: after a vacation passed in utter idleness and sleep. I breakfast late and dine early; and after dinner smoke in the garden, under the plumb-trees. To-day I dine with Chs. Daveis. [John] Neal I have seen but once. He is growing political, and wishes to be run for Representative at Washington. Is not however nominated; and will not be.

Have you read *Buzz-fuzz's* Article on Steam in the London Quarterly?[6] Sumner wrote me a word thereupon some time since. You have doubtless heard from him (Sumner) since my letter — a fortnight ago. How gloriously the six-footer sails aloft in society, with his "*o'ertaking wings*"![7] Provincial Boston must look to him like a small luminous point on his map. I am right glad in my soul, that all this has been vouchsafed to him. As to its *spoiling* him, that is not to be thought of. There is no danger, though he may find it somewhat hard to put his Pegasus into a yoke hereafter.

Evening; and dinner over; and it is raining, and I got into the gutter with my french boots, and uttered several pious ejaculations, which I hope the recording angel has written down with a pencil only. I was altogether too *owly* to enjoy the dinner; and nobody seemed to be in the right dining mood. We needed you exceedingly. Why have you not come hitherward? It is now too late in the season; and too cold. Cogswell has a fire to sit by. (Seriously). There was a frost last night; so they say; though I did not see it, nor feel it. No matter. Snow once fell in Rome in the month of August. Why should not we have fire and frost?

John Neal is nominated as State Senator; Whig candidate from this district.[8]

*Poetry*

*Wer nie sein Brod mit Thränen ass*
*Wer nie die kummervollen Nächte*
*Weinend auf seinem Bette sass,*
*Er kennt euch nich[t], ihr himmli[s]chen Mächte.*
Göthe.[9]

Who ne'er his bread in sorrow ate,
Who ne'er the mournful midnight hours

Weeping upon his bed has sat,
He knows you not, ye heavenly powers.

*Advertisements.*

Ask Felton to have no more letters sent me after *monday next.* Important. Ask Cleaveland about *Sandau,* or whatever his name is — the Frenchman.[10]

We understand that Professor Longw. is expected in Boston on Friday next; and that he will dine at Tremont house with a number of citizens. We are glad to learn he has recovered from his late serious accident in Beacon Street.[11]

Yours truly
H. W. L.

MANUSCRIPT: Massachusetts Historical Society. ADDRESS: To/George S. Hillard Esq/Boston POSTMARK: PORTLAND ME. AUG 18

1. Goldsmith, *The Traveller,* l. 1.

2. Of Henri Picard's ten letters to Longfellow, 1838–1851, the one of November 14, 1838, best describes his melancholy situation: "I feel very grateful to you, my dear Sir, for consolations and encouragements which prove the kindness of your heart; but, unfortunately, they are offered to a man more than forty years old, and but too long acquainted with ill luck; a man absent for about eight years from his own country and relations, and almost without any hope of seeing them again!" With Longfellow's endorsement he obtained situations in schools at Sing Sing and Poughkeepsie but continued to yearn for the Harvard instructorship. His "dictionnaire des Gallicismes" was never published.

3. Johan Ludwig Tellkampf (1808–1876) spent several years in the U. S., four of them as professor of German at Columbia University, 1843–1847. He then returned to Germany as professor in Breslau and in 1871 was elected to the first German reichstag. See Letters No. 440 and 504.

4. *The American Jurist and Law Magazine* was edited at this time by Sumner, Hillard, and Luther Stearns Cushing (1803–1856), a jurist known for his works on parliamentary law.

5. This ceremony took place on August 23 in honor of Benjamin Abbot (1762–1849), who was retiring after fifty years as preceptor of Phillips Exeter Academy.

6. The epithet refers to Benjamin Bussey Thatcher (1809–1840), a Bowdoin graduate of 1826 and, during his short life, a voluminous author. His essay on "Atlantic Steam Navigation" appeared in the *Quarterly Review,* LXII (June 1838), 186–214.

7. Coleridge, "The Rime of the Ancient Mariner," I, xi, 3.

8. In his *Wandering Recollections of a Somewhat Busy Life* (Boston, 1869), Neal wrote: "I was mentioned, and fairly advertised, for the senate of Maine, I believe, the very year that Governor Kent [550.4] was elected; but nothing came of it. I never did run well, I never could, I never shall" (p. 344).

9. Modified slightly from *Wilhelm Meisters Lehrjahre,* Bk. II, Chap. 13. Longfellow used the translation as the motto of Book the First in *Hyperion.*

10. V. Cardon de Sandrau's seven letters to Longfellow, 1852–1865, indicate that he struggled for existence as a teacher of French and eventually returned to Paris.

Cleveland had suggested him as a candidate for the Harvard instructorship (see Letter No. 462).

11. A reference, of course, to his *affaire de coeur* with Fanny Appleton.

## 439. *To Stephen Longfellow*

Cambridge Aug. 28. 1838

My dear Father,

I am at length in Cambridge once more; and find that the Cra[i]gie house has been on fire during my absence and my Library narrowly escaped being destroyed. Fortunately the flames were extinguished, without much damage to any one, and none to me. Aunt Sally Lowell is quietly in possession of about 2/3rds of the house.[1] Some malicious person has told her that I was so much offended with her coming to the house, as to be on the point of leaving — in fact that I was going to leave. Funny folks — these Cambridge folks.

The Exeter affair was quite tedious to me, though in itself interesting; and to all the Alumni doubtless highly so. But the weather was intensely hot; and we were exposed to the sun, all the morning, and though we dined in a church, it was so very close and warm, that I was obliged to leave very soon after the speeches commenced; and thereby lost the best part of the entertainment. We started for Haverhill the same evening.

They began the order of exercises by Addresses in the Academy yard, so that people in general might have an opportunity of hearing. This was the most disagreeable and tedious part of the whole. Then in the church a part was divided off with rough boards, where the ladies were admitted to see through branches of fir and oak, the presentation of the *Silver Pitcher*, or as Mr. Webster unfortunately called it, *domestic utensil.* I did not think, that Webster's speech was very remarkable. He filled it full of Latin quotations. I never saw a man pump up so much Latin in one day, as he did. He seemed desperately bent upon being Classic. I was much more pleased with Edward Everett. Alex. Everett did not do so well. He talked too much about himself; and told how he had been abroad, and had the honor of shaking hands with the Duke of Wellington; &c in fine, showed his usual want of tact.[2]

I find no new applications for the French place. Only the single bird-like individual, whom you saw in Portland.[3] I do not think he will do. Since leaving you I have been a couple of days in Newport, and have had the Asiatic cholera, and fifty mortal diseases in the shape of cold, sore-throat &c. They boasted so much of the New Port air, that I thought one might do anything; and accordingly slept with the window open.

Sam. arrived this morning, and has gone to Boston again to dine with Mrs. [Hannah] Wells. He tells me you have been more unwell since I left you, which I am very sorry to hear. I trust you are now better. Almost everyone has been affected by the sudden changes of the weather.

I write these lines in haste. If I had written them with a pen of my own they would have been more legible; but I am writing at my friend Felton's, and I find it as difficult to make good pens out of other people's as they do out of mine.

I shall write again soon.

Yrs. truly
Henry W. Longfellow.

MANUSCRIPT: Longfellow Trust Collection. ADDRESS: To/Hon. S. Longfellow/ Portland. POSTMARK: CAMBRIDGE MS. AUG 29

1. Sarah Champney Lowell (1771–1851), James Russell Lowell's maiden aunt.

2. Daniel Webster and Edward Everett had both attended Exeter for brief periods, the latter when his brother Alexander was serving as an assistant instructor in 1807.

3. Henri Picard.

## 440. *To Stephen Longfellow*

Cambridge Sept. 2. 1838.

My dear father

The Commencement week is over; and things begin to assume their wonted course. It was very pleasant; and I should have enjoyed it much; had I not been unfortunate enough to take a bad cold in an excursion I made to Newport with Mr. Cogswell. The climate of Newport is famous for its mildness. I thought one might do anything there, with impunity; consequently exposed myself, and caught cold; and was unwell all last week. However, it is over now; and so is Commencement. The new order of things begins tomorrow. My German [1] is here; but I have not yet selected a Frenchman. I shall therefore take the French class, for the present, under my own charge.

The Phi Beta Oration was by Mr. Stetson, clergyman of Medford; [2] and was very good. He is somewhat of a Transcendentalist, and friend of Emerson. By the way, Mr. Emerson's sermon before the Theological class, which created such a sensation, has been published. I will send you a copy. A critique upon it, by Mr. Norton, has appeared in the Daily Advertiser; with answer and rejoinder.[3] You will see this controversy in your paper. This is the newest matter on foot; — and the most talked about.

Mr. Tellkampf is here, visiting his friend Dr. [Charles] Beck. He speaks of his day with us in Portland as one of the pleasantest he has passed in America. The coffee and cigars in the back yard he looks upon, as the most delicate attention he has received anywhere. He proposes to pass the Winter in Boston; and deliver a course of Lectures on the Various Schools of German Philosophy. I think the plan very good; as at the present moment the minds of the reading, lecture-going people in this quarter, are much excited on the subject.

Mons. Picard, also, proposes to lecture in Boston on French Literature, and in the French Language. I have encouraged him so to do. I think the plan an excellent one: there are so many, who would understand him, or like to have it thought they could. If he does well; it will be a great recommendation to him here.

These are the principal things which have transpired since my return. Alex will be disappointed about his coat. The first time I went to Earle, his shop was shut: and when I saw him he said he could not get the garment done before the middle of the week; but will send it by Thursday's boat.[4]

Yours in haste
Henry.

P.S. Alex must come to Boston, if he wishes to get a place. Arrangements will now be making for Winter's work. Let him not delay too long.

MANUSCRIPT: Longfellow Trust Collection. ADDRESS: To/Hon. S. Longfellow/ Portland. POSTMARK: CAMBRIDGE MS. SEP 3

1. Bernard Rölker (427.7).

2. Caleb Stetson (1793–1870), a graduate of the Harvard Divinity School in 1827, served as Unitarian minister in Medford, 1827–1848.

3. After Emerson's *Divinity School Address* appeared in print on August 25, 1838, the conservative Unitarian Andrews Norton made a vitriolic attack on it in the Boston *Daily Advertiser* for August 27. On August 30 Theophilus Parsons wrote a rejoinder in the *Advertiser*, in which he attempted to tone down Norton's denunciatory arguments. Norton replied on September 1, and a rebuttal by Parsons appeared on September 3. See William R. Hutchinson, *The Transcendental Ministers* (New Haven, 1959), pp. 69–72.

4. John Earle, Jr., Longfellow's tailor, kept a shop at 27 Washington Street, Boston.

441. *To Stephen Longfellow*

Cambridge Sept 11. 1838

My dear father,

I cannot let "young Jamie" depart without bearing a few lines of friendly remembrance to you.[1] Not a new thing, however, to tell you; save that I am afraid of "*dying of a Frenchman*" as Aunt Charity did, though in another way.[2] I have not yet found my man: but one by one they present themselves, and finally the right one will come, I doubt not. I find it tedious enough to go back to the first steps in instruction.

I passed a delightful day with the Commodore and Miss Henrietta;[3] and drove all about the environs of Boston. I did not know they were in this quarter of the world, till I received your letter. In the hurry of Commencement, Sam forgot to tell me they were in Portland. Hence in my last I sent no welcome to them and no greeting to Aunt Lucia, whom I want very much to see.

My new German, Mr Rölker, does very well. He has a popular talent, and is very much liked. Mr. Tellkampf proposes to lecture in Boston next Winter on Civil Law, and German Philosophy; and the little Frenchman, whom you saw in Portland, prepares to do likewise on French literature and in the French Language.

When Mary writes to Henrietta, she must not forget to inquire particularly about "*The individual in a White Hat,*" who figured so largely in her day in Boston, and assumed such graceful attitudes before her window; — affording thereby no little merriment to the company.

I hope ere this you are quite recovered and as well as I am. I have made a new arrangement about my board — living with Miss Lowell in close communion. She is only seventy two, and a good deal like [a] fly, brisk and buzzy. She is an excellent old lady; and everything is in the most genteel style. We breakfast at 8 and dine at 3; and I feel much more comfortable, than when I had to shoot my dinner on the wing, as it were. The arrangement is a mutual blessing — a mutual life-insurance company.

Love to you all.

Yours truly

Henry W. Longfellow

P.S. How does Alex like his frock-coat? Is the mulberry hue too vivid? Or does it please!

MANUSCRIPT: Longfellow Trust Collection. ADDRESS: To/Hon. Stephen Longfellow/Portland./["*Mr. Greenleaf*" *deleted*] POSTMARK: CAMBRIDGE MS. SEP 17

1. As the address cover reveals, Longfellow had intended to send this letter by James Greenleaf.

2. See Irving, *Salmagundi*, No. IX, Saturday, April 25, 1807.

3. Henrietta Henley, the daughter of Elizabeth Denison Henley (433.3), was Commodore Wadsworth's niece. Longfellow spent September 6 with them (MS Journal).

## 442. *To Pietro Bachi*[1]

Cambridge. Tuesday eve. September. 25. 1838

My dear Sir

I beg you to receive my best thanks for the copy of your Grammar, which you have had the goodness to send me. I have been looking into it this evening; and can fully appreciate the immense labor you have gone through in preparing the work. It certainly does you great honor; and puts into our hands a book at once comprehensive and clear, and wherein every rule is literally *shored up* with good authorities. This is the only way to write a Grammar; and when I say you have executed your self-appointed task in the most scholar-like manner, you will not think I say it as a matter of course, but receive it as the sincere opinion of your friend and well-wisher

Henry W. Longfellow

MANUSCRIPT: unrecovered; text from photostat, Longfellow Trust Collection.

1. The recent appearance of Bachi's *A Grammar of the Italian Language. A New Edition Revised and Improved* (Boston, 1838) suggests that he was Longfellow's correspondent.

## 443. *To Josiah Quincy*

[Cambridge] October 1. 1838.

My dear Sir,

I have at length found a person to take Mr. Surault's place in the French Language: and would thank you to lay the name of Mr. André Sary, before the Corporation at their next meeting, with the request, that he may be appointed to fill the vacancy.[1]

Very respectfully yours
Henry W. Longfellow

MANUSCRIPT: Harvard College Papers, IX, 98. PUBLISHED: *Professor Longfellow of Harvard*, p. 32.

1. Longfellow had no success with his recommendation of Sary, about whom nothing is known, and was instead asked by the Corporation to assume the duties of French instructor himself.

444. *To Stephen Longfellow*

Cambridge. October 5. 1838
Confidential

My dear Father

I suppose you think I am growing too negligent in my letter-writing. It is all owing to my being very much occupied. No French instructer has been appointed yet, nor do I think we shall have one this term. The gentlemen are very desirous that I should do this work; — and always take some active part in the instruction; with the understanding that my salary is to be increased in proportion to the number of students I instruct. I am not sure that I shall not enter into their views. I have been talking about it with the President this very evening. He seems very urgent to have me do it. And the plan in brief is to give me in addition to my present salary, eight dollars a year for each pupil; so that I might add to my income from five hundred to a thousand dollars. What do you think of it? I told the President I would consider of it, and give him an answer after he had again met the Corporation and they had said definitely what fees I should receive — the eight dollars being his proposition — but not sanctioned by them. I shall know in the course of a week. In the mean time, I hope you will find time to write me a line on the subject. It would occupy three whole days in the week. The other three, as now, would be mine. Therefore I think favorably of the plan: though I am not sure about it.[1]

I was very glad to see Alex. again. He is busily conversing with rail-road people though as yet with no great success. There is so little on foot at present and so many eager for employment, that it is very difficult to make one's self heard. However *nil desperandum.* Times will change.

Sam flourishes as usual. He seems to have set his heart upon a school; and has one already in view. I am glad of this. It is a good vocation in these days; and I think him well-fitted for such an occupation.

The first part of this letter is confidential. The matter is not yet settled; and therefore had better not be spoken of.

We are expecting the Commodore [A. S. Wadsworth] soon. I hope he will stop in Boston. I much desire to have one more day with him, as pleasant as the last.

Love to all at home and at the Judges [Barrett Potter].

Yours in haste
Henry W. Longfellow

I shall send a package to Anne by first opportunity.

MANUSCRIPT: Longfellow Trust Collection. ADDRESS: Hon. Stephen Longfellow/ Portland. POSTMARK: BOSTON OCT 9

1. Stephen Longfellow's reply is unrecovered, and his counsel in this matter is not known.

## 445. *To Joseph Bosworth*

Cambridge. Oct. 20. 1838

My dear Sir,

I write you this note in great haste; merely to say, that the copies of the Dictionary have arrived. Some weeks ago I sent you my review; which I trust reached you in safety; though, of course, as a veteran Saxon you will find nought in it new or wonderful. I meant it as a kind of Introduction to Anglo-Saxon Literature in this country. I herewith send you another Review of your work, by Mr. Greenough, a young man who took his degree at our College, a year ago. He is a young, but ardent scholar; and unfortunately not in good health; which for a time at least will render it necessary for him to close his books; and betake himself to a more active life than that of a student.[1] The New York Review is edited by Mr. Henry; a clergyman of the Episcopal Church:[2] and the Review was established to advance the cause of Church in our Country. A very good object, say I, though as you know, I belong to another parish.

Did I ever tell you, that I once wrote a book called "*Outre-Mer; or a Pilgrimage Beyond the Sea*"? It is a series of sketches, which I wrote many years ago, on returning from my first European Tour. It was published in London by Bentley; a few months before I first saw you. There are some parts of it, which I think would please Mrs. Bosworth — or at least [I] *hope* they would: and I am sorry I have not a copy to send you. If the book ever falls in your way pray give it a glance in remembrance of me: and the mournful past.

I think of nothing important to write you at this moment; but shall make up another package for you erelong. Meanwhile, I am on the look out for Reviews of you in the English Quarterlies. I think they are very negligent and behind hand.

My kindest regards to Mrs. Bosworth; and believe me very truly yours

Henry W. Longfellow

MANUSCRIPT: unrecovered; text from photostat, Longfellow Trust Collection.

1. See 416.1 and 416.2.

2. Caleb Sprague Henry (1804–1884) was one of the founders of the *New York Review* in 1837. He served as a professor of philosophy and history at New York University, 1839–1852.

## 446. *To George Washington Greene*

Cambridge October 22. 1838.
8 o'clock in the evening.

My dear George

An hour or two ago I had the pleasure — the great infrequent pleasure of receiving a letter from you (Aug. 25), who have the heart to answer my long letters, by little short things, which rather deserve the name of billets. You think that because you nearly cover three pages, and put a few last words aslant on the fourth, that you have done a genteel thing; when you have not. Write closer. *Serrez vos rangs* [close up]. Crowd the words. Dont write as if you lived next door; and then you may call yourself *model* and be d——d; — which is profane. And now open your great heart, and hold it open by the four corners, while I pour into it all thoughts, all passions, all desires,[1] which fill mine own. And first of the "*Dark Ladie,*" who holds my reason captive. As yet no sign of yielding. As stately and sublime, and beautiful as ever! While I likewise sail with the flag nailed to the mast, to sink or conquer. She has been in the country all Summer, and has atlength returned to town. But we seldom meet; never except by accident. I have given up society *entirely*: and live alone here, grim as Death, with only that one great thought in my mind. Meanwhile crowds are about her; and flatterers enough; and all the splendor of fashion, and suitors manifold. My hope and faith are firm planted in my righteous cause. If there be any difference between me and those about her — if our souls can understand each other — she will sooner or later find it so. If not — then I take this disappointment likewise by the hand; I bide my time. But my passion is mighty; *gigantic;* — or it would not have survived this. Meanwhile I labor and work right on with what heart and courage I may, and despise all sympathy; and am quite reasonably cool for a mad-man. I do a great deal in College; and devote all my hours to literature — morning, noon and night; "and by the Vision splendid, am on my way attended."[2] And as soon as I can bring my mind to bear upon a single point, with any effect, I mean to write something, that you shall hear of in distant Italy; — (if in no other way, by letter from me!) Thus endeth the first lesson; and the Second beginneth. This morning as I was sitting at breakfast, a gentleman on horseback sent up word that I should come down to him. It was Prescott, author of *Ferdinand.* He is an early riser, and rides about the country. There on his horse sat the *great author.* He is one of the best fellows in the world, and much my friend; — handsome, gay, and forty: — a great diner-out; — and fond of good wine — gentle, companionable, and modest, and quite astonished to find himself so famous all of a sudden. He will be much pleased when I tell him what you say, in your letter, about the Italian translation.[3] I should have sent you the book long ago; but how? tell me how to send it? There is the difficulty. Tomorrow I will make dilligent search in town for an opportunity, and write you when and how you may expect it, with Hawthorne's Tales.[4] I shall see Hawthorne tomorrow. He lives in Salem; and we are to meet and sup together tomorrow evening at Tremont house. Your health shall be remembered. He is a strange owl; a very peculiar individual, with a dash of originality about him, very pleasant to behold. How I wish you could be with us. By the way, in return for Prescott, send me no books, nor money, but some seven dollars worth of Italian wine — *in flasks* — Aliatico and Monte Pulciano, — ordered from Leghorn, to the care of any body in Boston. Can you not do this? You had better pay Felton in like manner. We will send you all the books in both our Libraries, if you will send us wine. But it must be *in flasks*! Ach; my beloved friend! when I one day sit with you in Italy again, and nothing on the snow-white table-cloth save bread still whiter, and fruit, and that most delicate wine; in "beakers full of the warm South"[5] will we pledge the happy present time, and those sorrows and disappointments, which are our schoolmasters; and it shall be no sinful pleasure nor riotous excess, but only an overflow of heart, under the light of evening lamps, which have so long beheld my countenance sorrowful and sad, that they know not how it looks when gay, but shall know, when *we* meet again. Sumner is the nearest and warmest thing I can send you. When you have him, you will think you have me. He can tell you so much of me and Madonna Francesca — and how beautiful she is — in fact I envy you the meeting, — and envy him still more! And thus endeth the second lesson. Your Article on Micali is printed, and makes some 60 pages.[6] The Dean did not send me the proof-sheets, as I requested he would of all your Arts. so I have not read the paper yet; but will get it and send to you as you direct without delay. It shall go with this letter by tomorrow's post. The last No. of N. A. Review (October) is heavy. Strange to say, I do not take this Review, tho' I write for it, now and then. So I have not the No. at hand to send you the Writers. Felton shall do it; who probably will not answer your letter so speedily as

I do. We went to the Post Office together this afternoon, and each had a letter from you. Why dont you *scatter* more? If his had come next week, it would have been like another to me. Dont you see? Take the hint. By the way, on receiving your Micali M.S. I wrote you a letter as long as this, without five minutes' delay.[7] Did you get it? You never condescend to mention dates; so one never knows. Moreover, last Summer I was in New York, and Clarke made you up a small[8] package of Magazines, Newspapers and things, which I gave to Ward, who promised to send them. Did they arrive? I shall send you a much larger one next Winter, when I again visit New York. Meanwhile let me say, that there is not much stirring in the Literary World. A huge satire in octavo, with copious learned notes has just appeared, elegant[l]y printed, with great parade of Greek and Latin erudition in the Notes, and all this to an[n]ihilate Col. *Stone* and Mr. King, two New York Editors. Nobody knows who wrote it; and what is most amusing nobody cares. "*The Vision of Rubeta*" is the title; this *Rubeta* being a nick-name for Col. Stone. The poetry is trash — an abortion of filth and fire. The book seems already forgotten, and is only a week old. Highly flattering to the author.[9] A new American Novelist has arisen. His name is Professor Ingraham; author of the "*Pirate of the Gulf*," (dedicated to me, but without permission, confound him) and "The Sieges." He is a tremendous ass!! really *tremendous*! I think he may say he has written the worst novels ever written by anybody. But they sell. He gets twelve hundred dollars apiece; but I think can never get much more. He is a terrific youth. I wish you could see him.[10] Dr. Bird is married, and writes no more.[11] People find his works too heavy, tho' he is a good fellow, as you know. *Kennedy*, author of "*Swallow-Barn*" and "*Horse-Shoe Robinson*" has a new novel in the press.[12] Nat Willis has bought a farm on the Susquehanna and writes plays for Miss Clifton, and Letters for the New York Mirror; and the Text to "*Views of American Scenery*" and gets well paid for all.[13] We do not correspond. I have no faith in him: tho' he is very pleasant, when we meet. In this quarter of the world *Lecturing* is the fashion. Mr. Combe the Scotch Phrenologist is in Boston — well attended; and English Mr. Buckingham the Egyptian traveller, lecturing on Egypt. He gets about three hundred dollars for each Lecture.[14] Also Mr. Emerson, a clergyman, with New Views of Life, Death and Immortality, author of "*Nature*" and friend of Carlyle. He is one of the finest lecturers I ever heard — with magnificent passages of true prose-poetry. *Ask Sumner*. But it is all *dreamery* after all. But for all these things I care not a straw; being wholly taken up with myself and my *sorrows-of-Werter* kind of Life. You ask about my Library. It improves slowly. I have not much money to spend upon it; or I should delight to send you a *carte blanche* for Italian Books. As to Dante, I should like to see the books you mention; and want very much to get the Florence edition in 5 large 8vo volumes. Have you seen [Gabriele] Rossetti's Work *"Sullo Spirito Antipapale dei Classici Antichi d'Italia. Londra. 1832"*?[15] Probably not. Such a book would make the earth quake in Italy. It is written in a grand, smashing style; but full of strange notions. I think it improves an Italian amazingly to breathe the air of England or America. If a blast or two of the North had breathed through the soul of milk-and-water Pellico, and aired his sentimentality, he would never have written that soft, sweet book.[16] There would have been some thunder, and not all tears. Have your own way about the Spielberg; and send me the M.S. on Dante.[17] Why dont you write some sketches of Rome for the Knickerbocker? You will get paid, and have your name in the Newspapers; and I should think it would be better fun than digging up dead Italians. You might, however, get into scrapes, being Consul. (How do [you] like the *Consulship*?) The only way would be to praise everything, and call the Italians the most moral people on the face of the earth, as Bennett, one of the New York editors, does the French.[18] Enough for to-night. Now I shall take a glass of Whiskey-punch and go to bed: for I am suffering dismally, and have been for a fortnight past, with tooth-ache and a swollen jaw. I have had one great grinder out, and it made me think of you and Naples, where I paid the tooth-drawer one dollar extra because his wife was a Spanish woman. Do you remember? He claimed it on that account. Good night.

*October* 23.

This is a most glorious autumnal morning, like the Winter mornings which used to shine into our parlor in Piazza Madama. What is the name of Julia's husband?[19] I intend to ask this question in every letter I write you, until I get an answer. In what part of Rome do you live? Tell me not the name of the street only, but describe the whereabout. If you can pick up that magnificent great plan of Rome by — Vasari? (is that the name?) I wish you would buy it for me.[20] One of them hangs in a friend's entry here; I never go into the house without stopping to look at it. I should like also the *Poeti Lirici Italiani*,[21] that new cheap book, which Goodwin brought home — a bound copy would be preferred. I never buy books unbound now-a-days. Am too poor. The binding costs more than the books, I find. You must have a glorious opportunity to buy a Library — and I give you this advice *gratis* about binding. The rest of this letter is to Maria.

My dear Maria, though I never write to you, I think of you often. The little *bronze chapel* with the *cerino* or taper, which in days long past you gave my wife as a souvenir, stands always on my table, and reminds me of the happy days, now gone forever. The time has come to me, which sooner or later comes to every one, to suffer and be silent, and so shall it be. I trust that in Rome you are very happy. I remember what a Roman Lady once said to me as we sat together at evening among the ruins of Caesar's palace and saw the sun set, with the Coliseum before us; "*How can any one live out of Rome? I should wish once a year to behold this scene. Else I should die!*" Does not that sound *Roman*-tic? Most decidedly so. I thought it very fine at the time. I only wish I could be enjoying Rome with you. I always liked the city, as Greene knows; and hope one day to see it again. But when, alas! when! Pray how do you employ your time? It was always a wonder to me what ladies did with their time. I hope George keeps in good spirits always. If ever his impatient spirit makes him restless and unhappy; tell him from me, that it is folly to vex himself about the future. Live in the present. I find no other way of keeping my nerves quiet than this: namely to do with all my might whatever I have to do, without thinking of the future, in which most people live. Dont blame me for preaching nor for writing you so short a note, here at the end of all things. It is only a forget-me-not.

Yours truly.

H. W. L.

*Things forgotten.* Dr. Howe is going along as usual: but he looks very ill — is thin and nervous. A new cant phrase is going the rounds, and a very good one; "*Does your anxious mother know you are out?*" as much as to say "you are a mere child yet." I was wrong about your Micali. It is not yet entirely printed — only a part of it. I have requested to have the remaining proofs sent to me. Mr. Folsom is scolding very much about your not writing out the names of places in their Latin form, but posing the Italian. He says English readers wont understand them. He wants you to be particular in these minutia in future, to write out all proper names and names of Places very clearly and distinctly.

Farewell.

Longfellow.

MANUSCRIPT: Longfellow Trust Collection. ADDRESS: To/George W. Greene Esq/ Consul of the United States/of America/at Rome/via Hâvre de Grace ANNOTATION (*by Longfellow*): Paid. 192. POSTAL ANNOTATION: via New York

POSTMARKS: CAMBRIDGE MS. OCT 24/NEW YORK OCT 27/PARIS 7 ||DEC|| 38/ ROMA 17 ||DIC 1838||/PAYS D'OUTREMER PAR LE HAVRE/PONT BEAUVOISIN/ PAID

1. Cf. Coleridge, "Love," l. 1.

2. Wordsworth, "Ode on the Intimations of Immortality," v, 73–74.

3. Greene had written on August 25, 1838: "I want to get it [*The History of the Reign of Ferdinand and Isabella*] translated for the honor of American literature, and mean to puff it in choice Italian in some Neapolitan or Milanese review."

4. In the same letter Greene had written that his desire to read *Twice-Told Tales* was stimulated by Longfellow's review of the book (371.3).

5. Keats, "Ode to a Nightingale," l. 15.

6. See 437.9.

7. This letter is unrecovered.

8. Longfellow first wrote "great" for "small."

9. *The Vision of Rubeta, an Epic Story of the Island of Manhattan. With Illustrations Done on Stone* (Boston, 1838), a poetic take-off on the *Awful Disclosures of Maria Monk* (New York, 1836) — a lurid account of supposed misconduct in a Montreal nunnery — was reviewed disparagingly in the November issue of the *Knickerbocker*: ". . . aside from a general mechanical ease of rhythm, and a few clever passages, it is remarkable for little else than acidity, indecency, and laborious, invincible dullness" (XII, 454). The author was Laughton Osborn (1809–1878), an eccentric New Yorker whose *Confessions of a Poet* (Philadelphia, 1835) had been harshly criticized by Col. William Leete Stone (1792–1844), editor of the New York *Commercial Advertiser.* Among other victims of Osborn's spleen were Wordsworth and Charles King (1789–1867), editor of the New York *American* and later president of Columbia, 1849–1864.

10. Joseph Holt Ingraham (1809–1860), a fellow Portlander, was at this time a professor at Jefferson College in Natchez, Mississippi. He wrote the highly successful novels *Lafitte: the Pirate of the Gulf* (New York, 1836) and *Burton; or, The Sieges* (New York, 1838). Upon later becoming an Episcopal clergyman, he turned his talents to the composition of epistolary romances with religious backgrounds.

11. Robert Montgomery Bird had married Mary Mayer (1809–1868), daughter of Rev. Philip Frederick Mayer of Philadelphia, in 1837. Because of a breakdown in health, he wrote no more novels after *The Adventures of Robin Day*, which appeared in 1839.

12. John Pendleton Kennedy, *Rob of the Bowl: a Legend of St. Inigoe's* (Philadelphia, 1838).

13. Willis had moved in the autumn of 1837 to Glenmary, a pastoral retreat on Owego Creek near its junction with the Susquehanna. Here he worked on *Bianca Visconti* (381.1), *The Betrothal*, and other plays for Josephine Clifton; wrote his "Letters from under a Bridge" for the New York *Mirror*; and completed the letterpress for *American Scenery* (London, 1840), a two-volume work featuring the drawings of William Henry Bartlett, the English artist.

14. George Combe (1788–1858), a founder of the Phrenological Society and of the *Phrenological Review*, delivered numerous lectures during a two-year sojourn in the U. S., 1838–1840. James Silk Buckingham (1786–1855), founder of the *Athenaeum*, lectured in America not only on his adventures in the Middle East but also on temperance and antislavery.

15. Longfellow's copy of this work is in the Harvard College Library.

16. In *Le Mie Prigioni* (Torino, 1832), Silvo Pellico (1789–1854), the Italian

dramatic poet, wrote an emotional account of his imprisonment in the Spielberg by the Austrians.

17. Greene had written on August 25: "By the way you are wrong about the Spielberg — it is a fortress situate on a hill — near but not in a town and the Italians always say sullo Spielberg." What precipitated the exchange is not known. The "M.S. on Dante" refers to an article by Greene, apparently unpublished.

18. James Gordon Bennett (1795–1872), whose predilection for the French was owing to his descent from them, founded the New York *Herald* in 1835.

19. See 407.9.

20. Presumably one of the folded maps prepared for Mariano Vasi's *Itinerario istruttivo di Roma,* a popular guidebook.

21. Greene did not mention this work in his reply of January 31, 1839. Longfellow may refer to a two-volume work entitled *Bibliotheca Portatile del Viaggiatore* (Firenze, 1835), a copy of which is in the Bowdoin College Library. The second volume, entitled *Raccolta di Lirici e Satirici Italiani,* bears the running title "Lirici Italiani."

## 447. *To Stephen Longfellow*

Cambridge October 25. 1838

My dear father,

The Commodore [A. S. Wadsworth] arrived safely: in my eagerness to see him I came very near not seeing him. I was in town early on Thursday morning; and breakfasted at Tremont House at the same table with him. We did not however see each other; though I must have passed near enough to him to have touched him. After breakfast I went into the parlor to sit a few moments; meaning then to go to the Pavillion,[1] as I did not see his name on the Book. He meanwhile had ordered a carriage to drive to Cambridge; and as he was stepping into it, thought he would ask at the bar, if I had been there. They told him I was somewhere in the house; and he then came into the parlor where I was. This was as curious as a Comedy; for if he had gone to Cambridge, I should have gone to the Pavillion, and not finding him, should have imagined that he had not come; and so have gone to Cambridge again, just as he, having found I was in Boston, was returning to town again. Quite an intricate adventure. It seems, that the letter Sam wrote on Sunday did not reach you till he had left. Otherwise he would have expected me in Boston. I should have written; but having so much tooth-ache did not feel exactly in trim. My face is somewhat better; though not entirely well. The rainy weather has been unfavorable to such pains. Otherwise I am quite well.

The Corporation have offered me eight dollars for each scholar, as I wrote you; provided the whole sum do not exceed five hundred. Therefore I have told them I would *not* take it; but in supplying the place of the French Instructer, would receive his pay, (five hundred) without regard to numbers. I dont like the principle of limitation; because it is opposed to the whole plan of remuneration *per cap.* This is as well — in fine, I think, better. I hope now to pay off my debts soon.

The Commodore purchased a beautiful piano-forte: rose-wood, with a most soft, and melodious tone. I think Aunt L[o]uisa will be delighted with it. If she is not, she must indeed be hard to please. Perhaps she has friends, who set themselves up for critics; and may think it necessary to find fault. He went at three o'clock in the Cars for Stonington.

There is nothing very new in Boston town. Mr. Buckingham, the traveller, is lecturing on Egypt; and Mr. Combe, the Phrenologist, on his Science. I have not heard either of them. Their lectures are spoken highly of, by those who attend.

I hope you have recovered, all of you, from your colds. How is Alex? Dont his *flamingo* coat improve upon acquaintance? It is not at all *outré* here.[2]

I write this in haste, at the close of day, with just light enough to see to sign my name Most truly, with much love to you all, and at the Judge's [Barrett Potter],

Henry W. Longfellow.

P.S. How does Aunt Lucia find Portland after the *Court* of Washington. It is a very long time, my dear Aunt, since we met. Patience till Thanksgiving.

MANUSCRIPT: Longfellow Trust Collection. ADDRESS: Hon. Stephen Longfellow/ Portland/Me POSTMARK: CAMBRIDGE MS. OCT 27

1. An hotel at 41 Tremont Street.

2. Longfellow's sophisticated taste in clothes had precipitated a family argument in Portland concerning Alexander's new coat. In a letter of September 17, 1838, Alexander explained the situation to his brother: "The frock from Earle arrived safely at last. Anne says I shall not wear such a color: *that* was your taste I suppose. Father says it will fade out and that the waist is too short — away up between the shoulders — and that he must take it back and make another — and so forth. For my own part I must confess it rather a *tight fit* and I fear it will not go on with winter flannels. I have therefore refrained from wearing the garment, some-what I confess from the apprehension that its usefulness, on the Da Capo principle in music, would *close with the first strains.* In this dilemma I have no judicious individual to assist my judgement of this 'light, visible expression of the spirit of the age' [Cf. *The Book of Common Prayer, The Catechism*]."

448. *To John Lord Hayes*[1]

Cambridge Nov. 8. 1838.

Dear Sir,

I have had the honor of receiving your letter of Oct. 25, with the request of the Board of Directors of the Portsmouth Lyceum. But as I could not, without much inconvenience to myself, accept their invitation to lecture, I beg you to present to them my thanks for the honor they have done me, and say that I respectfully decline.

Yours &c. &c.
Henry W. Longfellow

John L. Hayes. Esq.

MANUSCRIPT: Lehigh University Library. ENDORSEMENT: Geo. M. Longfellow [*sic*]/Nov. 1838

1. Hayes (1812–1887), a graduate of Dartmouth College in 1831, was practicing law in Portsmouth.

449. *To Stephen Longfellow*

Cambridge Nov. 11. 1838

My dear father,

Before going to bed I think I will write you a few lines, that you may not be disappointed on Tuesday morning at breakfast; for I imagine you expect to hear from me about this time. It certainly is not long since I last wrote; but time goes with speed now. Our long term is half over; and I hope to be with you at Thanksgiving, that is, in about a fortnight. I have no other news than this to send.

Owing to College duties I have had to change my way of life a little, and have got back to dining at one o'clock. I do not feel so well for it; but it is much more convenient. I dine at Mrs. Stearns's. The old gentleman no longer makes his appearance at table. I saw him to-day in the entry. He looks very feeble.[1]

What has become of John Nichols?[2] I have been expecting letters by him for some days. His fellow-students at Divinity Hall are few: *They say,* that Dr. Palfrey will soon leave us. He dislikes Cambridge; and the other day his father-in-law died, — (Mr [Samuel] Hammond) and left a large estate — perhaps eighty thousand to each of his seven children. The Dean will no doubt remove to Boston; and make the North American his chief care and occupation. However, this he does not yet say for himself; other people say it for him.[3]

I heard it whispered, too, the other day, that Professor Greenleaf would not probably remain here long, though I hardly believe the report. It is said he has had several advantageous offers of partnership in Boston, which strongly entice him. Have you heard anything of this?[4] James [Greenleaf] is well and flourishing. He comes to see me often; and says he shall soon go to Portland. He is a comely youth and tall. I like him exceedingly. Dont you, Mary?

I have not heard a word from the Commodore [A. S. Wadsworth] since he left. I presume he has written to you. I hope the beautiful piano reached Washington in safety.

What an atrocious Indian Summer we have had! Everybody has a cold or a fever. It is as damp and chill as March.

If Anne or anyone wants any Boston notions brought at Thanksgiving time, they must write in season.

Love to all

Yours most truly
Henry W. Longfellow.

MANUSCRIPT: Longfellow Trust Collection. ADDRESS: Hon. Stephen Longfellow/ Portland/Me. POSTMARK: CAMBRIDGE MS. NOV 12

1. The "old gentleman" was Asahel Stearns (382.3), whom Stephen Longfellow had known at Harvard. He died on February 5, 1839.

2. John Taylor Gilman Nichols (1817–1900), son of Rev. Ichabod Nichols, graduated from the Harvard Divinity School in 1842. He then served a pastorate of almost fifty years in Saco, Maine.

3. Palfrey resigned his professorship in 1839.

4. Contrary to the rumor, Professor Greenleaf did not retire from Harvard until 1848.

## 450. *To Samuel Ward*

[Cambridge] Saturday morning. Nov. 24. 1838.

"Ah! my dear Sam, why did you not send a letter with the books!" said I, as I looked into all four of the cream and molasses (*Milch und Blut*) covers of this beautiful *Molière*! It came, not five minutes ago. I stopped short in Book IV. chapter VI. of my Romance,[1] just where my heroine was going to speak "with a smile" (heroines always speak so) and have written the word *Molière,* right in the midst of an incipient love-scene, so as to remember the passage hereafter. But there was no letter to be found; and I remember, that I owe you one; which I commence with many thanks for your kindness in getting me the book, and acknowledging the obligation, to be paid when I see you in New York in January; as I intend to have that pleasure.

*Jan. 5. 1839.*

This was written more than a month ago, as you perceive by the date. I wanted to tell you what I was busy about; — and then I thought I had better keep my secret, as I have not told it to any friend here. I hate to say what I am doing. With some authors, as with money-diggers, when a word is spoken, the charm is broken, and the treasure sinks. I hope it will not be so in this case; though it has often happened to me before.

I was delighted to see Cogswell, though I had only a glimpse of him. He rode out from Boston one bitter cold morning, and found me in bed. My hours are abominable. Two bad habits I must break — smoking and late hours. Pray teach me how to do it. Matrimony might cure one — *which* one would depend upon circumstances. Are you still a "Peep-o'day" boy? Do you work in the morning; and go to bed at sun-set? I wish I had your temperament. My heart and head are both heavy: and sleep my great consoler.

Cogswell told me he had some leaves of your book; and had not time to say more. I wished much to see them; but did not know about it, till just as he was starting. Have you finished, or is only half the heavy task completed? [2] I devote what leisure I get from College *fagging* to my Romance, and between the Acts, sing Psalms, one of which perhaps you have seen.[3] There are some others coming soon. My poetry, however, is written seldom: the Muse being to me a chaste wife, not a Messalina, to be debauched in the public street. Your idea of mental *crystallization* is fine.[4]

The Newspaper-project has sunk down to the bottom of Time. I shall never dive for it again, that is certain.[5] I must write for some paper, where the remuneration will be certain, and not small; as my necessities point that way. This Cambridge is the dearest *nest* in the world. There never was anything like it. It is a den of thieves. So that I am forced to look for secure returns, and be thankful for them. With kind regards to all yr. family, including Mr Cogswell, who I trust reached New York safely,

truly yrs.

H. W. L.

MANUSCRIPT: Unrecovered; text from photostat, Longfellow Trust Collection.
PUBLISHED: "Letters to Samuel Ward, Part I," p. 41.

1. *Hyperion*, on which Longfellow had been at work for some weeks. The edition of Molière, was *Oeuvres de Molière précédées d'une notice sur sa vie et ses ouvrages par M. Sainte Beuve* (Paris, 1835–1836), 2 vols. The first volume bears the following inscription: "Amicus ad amicum./H W Longfellow/anno 1838/S Ward Jr" (Longfellow House).

2. In his reply of January 10, 1839, Ward wrote: "The book you heard of [a novel in French] is half-done and ended. You shall see it when you come amongst us. The day for publishing or finishing it has gone by and I am too much amid the dust of the money-race to touch it more."

3. "A Psalm of Life" (436.2).

4. Longfellow alludes to a sentence from Ward's letter of November 6, 1838: "Some will contrive to freeze their dreams and lo! the enchanted Castles are preserved with their every ornament and device — others neglect the crystalizing moment and suffer theirs to evaporate and become air-castles indeed."

5. After the plan to begin a newspaper in New York proved impractical (435.1), Longfellow weighed the possibility of transferring the project to Boston (*Young Longfellow*, pp. 289–290) but then abandoned it.

## 451. *To Stephen Longfellow*

[Cambridge] December 3. 1838

My dear father,

I shall write but a few lines, for the sun is setting, and it will soon be dark, and I must go. I arrived safely this morning; just in season for my classes. I was not alone in the stage with Mr. White; but had likewise the pleasure of passing a day in close confinement with Nat Knight and Charles Q. Clapp, two distinguished gentlemen of Portland.[1] I passed the night at Tremont house; and came out this morning.

Just think of my bringing the pipe-stems only! The remainder you will find laying their heads together in the back-room. Please send them by the first good opportunity, done up in cotton for fear of accident. It is quite a disappointment to me, after all my care and rejoicing, and expectation of future comfort.

I saw Mr. Greenleaf this afternoon; and the anxious maiden may know that all is well. The Higginsons are better.[2] The Doctor says they have the fever in its "*most beautiful form.*" No farther news.

H. W. L.[3]

MANUSCRIPT: Longfellow Trust Collection.

1. Nathaniel Knight and Charles Quincy Clapp, son of Asa Clapp (117.3), were Portland merchants. Mr. White is unidentified.

2. Louisa Storrow Higginson (1786–1864), widow of the philanthropist Stephen Higginson, lived with her large family in a house on Garden Street, Cambridge. Her youngest child, Thomas Wentworth Higginson, was a sophomore at Harvard.

3. A postscript by Samuel Longfellow follows.

## 452. *To Lewis Gaylord Clark*

Cambridge. Dec. 7. 1838

My dear Clark,

These lines I wrote yesterday morning, my heart moving me thereunto, and not without tears in my eyes. They may bring none into yours, perchance; and yet sitting lonely here and there in the world are sorrowing souls, who will not read them without feeling soothed.[1] Your letter came this morning, and this comes in quick return; rejoicing in yr. prosperity, concerning which you say but one dim word. What you say of Willis grieves me very much. I hope your fears are groundless. Tell him from me to be of good cheer. I hope to see you both in January; but before that time you must write the long letter you so much desire to write, and tell me what propitious star shines so brightly on yr. path.[2] Lend me a ray or two to cheer mine. The Psalm of Life seems to have found a response in many hearts. This was what I hoped; and I hope this Psalm of Death may. Tell Willis, that if he puffs me so hard he will puff my flickering life out; ungrateful individual, that I am, to thank him by saying *"Don't."*[3] My kindest remembrances to your wife. I see by the paper of this morning that Miss Haviland is dead.[4] The soft white hand is dust. Farewell.

Truly your friend in good report and mis-report

Longfellow

MANUSCRIPT: Clifton Waller Barrett Collection, University of Virginia. ADDRESS: To/Lewis G. Clark Esq/New York. POSTMARK: CAMBRIDGE MS. DEC 8

1. Clark printed "A Psalm of Death: The Reaper and the Flowers" in the *Knickerbocker*, XIII (January 1839), 13.

2. In his letter of December 3, 1838, Clark had mentioned "good personal news," which he left unexplained, and the ill health of Willis Gaylord Clark and his wife. On December 10, in response to this letter, he wrote that his brother's wife had died (366.2) and that his own good fortune involved the gift to him of a "beautiful, and well-finished and furnished dwelling" as well as an opportunity to add to his income by conducting "the correspondence of a large banking institution" (*Clark Letters*, p. 100).

3. Willis Clark had written a glowing tribute to Longfellow with special reference to "A Psalm of Life" in his *Philadelphia Gazette*, LXVII (Thursday, November 22, 1838), No. 15355.

4. According to an obituary notice in the *Evening Post*, Elizabeth F. Haviland died in New York City on December 4, 1838, aged 26. Longfellow had known her as early as 1834 and had on one occasion escorted her to an entertainment at Niblo's Gardens (Clark to Longfellow, November 2, 1834, and April 7, 1837, in *Clark Letters*, pp. 84 and 97).

## 453. *To the Harvard Corporation*

[Cambridge] December 28. 1838.

Gentlemen,

The vote passed at your last meeting in reference to the French Instruction in my department has been communicated to me by the President. As the new arrangement for increased remuneration, in proportion to the number of students taught, has not been introduced

PLATE I

Longfellow, 1839, by Wilhelm Hendrik Franquinet

Longfellow, 1840, by Wilhelm Hendrik Franquinet

Frances (right) and Mary Appleton, 1836, by Jean Baptiste Isabey

PLATE II

Frances Appleton, 1836, by Lorenzo Bartolini

PLATE III

PLATE IV

Samuel Ward, Jr., 1839,
by Wilhelm Hendrik Franquinet

George Washington Greene, 1839–1840,
by Thomas Crawford

into this Department, and perhaps could not be entirely, without difficulty, I should prefer, so long as I supply the place of the French Instructer, to receive the same remuneration, which he would, if here. Trusting that this arrangement will be acceptable to you,[1] I have the honor to be

Gentlemen, very respectfully yours
Henry W. Longfellow

MANUSCRIPT: Harvard College Papers, IX, 131. PUBLISHED: *Professor Longfellow of Harvard*, p. 33.

1. At its meeting the next day the Corporation voted that it was "not expedient to comply with this request" (*Professor Longfellow of Harvard*, p. 33).

## 454. *To William Abiah White*[1]

[Cambridge, 1838][2]

Dear Sir

I return your umbrella with many thanks. It saved me from a ducking.

Yours truly
H. W. Longfellow

MANUSCRIPT: O. O. Fisher Collection, Detroit. ADDRESS: Mr. W. A. White/ Present

1. White (1818–1856) was a member of the Harvard class of 1838.
2. The date is speculative. Records in the Harvard College Archives reveal that White had studied German under Longfellow during this year.

# PART SIX

# LITERARY SUCCESS

1839–1841

# LITERARY SUCCESS

## 1839–1841

THE publication of *Hyperion* and *Voices of the Night* in 1839 and of *Ballads and Other Poems* in 1841 caused Longfellow's literary reputation to rise steadily, while at the same time Frances Appleton's continued indifference to his suit caused him moments of despair, which he rationalized with complaints of real or imagined ill health. Few of the 198 recovered letters from this period (Longfellow wrote 280 known letters during 1839–1841) reflect the failure of his courtship. Indeed, the letters to his family in Portland make no mention of Miss Appleton and deal exclusively with the problems of his professorship, business and literary matters, and the details of his bachelor life. Even the letters to his intimate friends Greene and Ward are for the most part filled with literary and other gossip, bad puns and witticisms, and his own literary plans. On occasion, however, he revealed his troubled spirit to them, and it is clear that they (as well as the members of the Five of Clubs) were in his confidence.

With the publication of *Hyperion*, an autobiographical romance in the manner of Jean Paul, Longfellow displayed to the public his love for Frances Appleton (who recognized herself as the heroine, Mary Ashburton) and apparently destroyed any hope he had held that she would return the sentiment. The book was, in a sense, a means by which Longfellow purged himself of the emotional unhappiness caused by his wife's death and by Frances Appleton's disdain. In commenting on the failure of his publisher and the withdrawal of the book from the market, Longfellow revealed this intention: "No matter; I had the glorious satisfaction of writing it; and thereby gained a great victory, *not* over the 'dark Ladie' but over myself. I now once more rejoice in my freedom; and am no longer the thrall of anyone." But he was wrong, for his devotion remained, and Miss Appleton's disdain persisted.

The fact is that Longfellow had begun to experience the same kind of discontent that marked his years as a Bowdoin professor. As early as September 1839 he proposed to the Harvard Corporation that he be "wholly separated" from language instruction and be appointed to a professorship of belles lettres only. For this he was willing to relinquish half his salary and his prerogatives as a member of the faculty. To his father he wrote that his academic duties were intolerable: "unless they make some change, I will leave them, with or without anything to do. I will not consent to have my life crushed out of me so. I had rather live awhile on bread and water." The immediate cause of this imprudent proposal was a lost opportunity to accompany young John Jacob Astor III to Europe as companion and tutor, but the real reason must certainly have been more complex and compounded of a variety of ingredients: the monotony of classroom drill, the replacement of academic by literary enthusiasms, the nostalgic appeal of Europe as a therapy for unhappiness, his frustrated love for Frances Appleton, and of course his widower's loneliness. When the Corporation wisely refused to accept the proposal, Longfellow reluctantly adjusted to the situation, much to the relief of his father, who feared that he was being "allured by the visions of authorship" — a profession on which, according to his Yankee instincts, no reliance could be placed.

The virus of literary ambition, long recurrent in Longfellow and now nourished by the remarkable popular success of his poetry in the Boston, New York, and Philadelphia newspapers and journals, did indeed threaten to turn his life in the direction of authorship. Although he knew the dangers of relying on literature for a livelihood, he nevertheless chose to consider it an avocation that owed him support. His letters reveal that he drove hard bargains with his editors and publishers and that he measured literary success not only by fame but also by royalties. The money he earned with his pen was insignificant (which explains why he continued to cling to his academic lifeline), but his success as the author of "A Psalm of Life," "The Wreck of the Hesperus," "Excelsior," and "The Skeleton in Armor," among other poems of this period, paid him in the pleasant coin of fame and eased the pain of his rejection by Frances Appleton.

With the collection of his poems and translations in *Voices of the Night* and *Ballads and Other Poems*, Longfellow established himself as one of the leading poets of the day. Literary success, however, was not enough to cure him of the physical and emotional malaise that periodically afflicted him. In his search for the secret of well-being he developed an enthusiasm for the therapeutic powers of homeopathy and hydropathy. But not responding to medicine, the restorative element in creative work, or the encouragement of friends, he remained for the most part a lonely man, unfulfilled by his literary success and dissatisfied with the prospect of life before him.

## 455. *To Stephen Longfellow*

Cambridge January 3. 1839.

My dear Father,

I write only to wish you all a happy New Year; and to say that I am well, and very busy. Nothing new, nor wonderful has transpired since I last wrote you. The Term ends in about ten days; and I shall probably start at once for Washington.

The Bostonians have renewed the old-fashioned Assemblies. The first was held on the last night of the Year. Your friend Wm. Sullivan is head manager.[1] He figured in a white cravat and a *chapeau-bras,* with a black silk cockade. Daniel Webster shone conspicuous in tights; and Mrs. Richard Derby in the diamonds of her predecessor.[2] Old people danced, who had not danced before for years beyond the memory of man; and some looked like the stone figures in the french drama, which got up from the tombs one night in an old Cathedral, and danced the Old Year out — of countenance. The ball, however, was beautiful, and went off well. It makes some excitement in town, and those who cannot get in try to laugh at it and call it the Boston Almack's.[3]

I am very well, and very busy, — almost too busy. (Where are the Shaker pipes?) My love and good wishes to all at the Judges [Barrett Potter]. I will write again soon, but have no longer a moment now.

Most truly yours
Henry W. Longfellow

MANUSCRIPT: Longfellow Trust Collection.

1. William Sullivan (1774–1839), Boston lawyer, orator, and author. See 212.6.
2. After the death of Martha Coffin Derby (42.4), Richard Derby married Louisa Sophia Lear of Washington, D.C.
3. Almack's was a London club noted for its assembly rooms.

## 456. *To Samuel Ward*

Cambridge. Jan. 5. 1839

My dear Ward,

Think not it is without many self-reproaches that I have so long neglected to write to you. Many a correspondent, like many a lover, is "silent, when feeling most." As often as I have sat down to write you, some importunate care, or uninvited pleasure has taken the pen from my hand, and said, with the air of a master, "The hour is mine." Therefore do not feel hurt, my friend; nor blame one who already blames himself enough.

Boston is quite gay just now. They have got up a set of Assemblies, or *Papantis,* as they call them from the name of the Dancing master.[1] Cogswell saw No. 1. and from this you can judge of all. The last new book is Mr. Dwight's translations from Göthe and Schiller; which are too numerous and not literal enough. It is the third volume of the "Series of Foreign Literature" edited by Mr. Ripley. Menzel's Hist. of Germ. Lit. translated by Felton comes next. Sometime afterwards, a Life of Jean Paul, with Specimens, by me, if I cannot get rid of the task.[2] I believe I told you of this. I am sorry I made the engagement. I am very curious to see your handiwork. When will it be published?[3] You will show it to me when I come to New York: which will probably be between the fifteenth and twentieth of the month. *Vale.*

Yours very truly
Longfellow

P. S. As to the Miner's Journal I will make one more effort, if you still persist in saying the thing is to be found in the Boston Athenaeum.[4]

MANUSCRIPT: unrecovered; text from photostat, Longfellow Trust Collection. ADDRESS: To/Samuel Ward Jr. Esq/New York POSTMARK: CAMBRIDGE MS. JAN 7 PUBLISHED: "Letters to Samuel Ward, Part I," pp. 41–42.

1. Lorenzo Papanti (1799–1872), a former officer in the royal guard of the duke of Tuscany, had set up a dancing academy in 1827. His assemblies became a Boston institution.

2. In George Ripley's edition of *Specimens of Foreign Standard Literature*, 14 vols., Vol. III was entitled *Select Minor Poems, Translated from the German of Goethe and Schiller.* With Notes by John S. Dwight (Boston, 1839); and Vols. VII, VIII, and IX were entitled *German Literature. Translated from the German of Wolfgang Menzel.* By C. C. Felton (Boston, 1840). Longfellow's projected work on Jean Paul did not materialize.

3. See 450.2.

4. The *Mining Review*, published 1838–1840 as a supplement to the *Mining Journal* (London, 1835–1907). In connection with the abortive plan for a literary journal (435.1), Ward had written of the *Mining Review*, "Its form seemed to both Mr Cogswell and myself well suited for the *cadre* of our enterprise. When I wrote you about it [on October 24, 1838] — it was in order to make an estimate of the cost of the undertaking. I should still be glad to have my queries answered as I am sure some such publication exists at the Athenaeum" (Letter dated November 6, 1838).

## 457. *To Stephen Longfellow*

New York Saturday morning. Jany 26. '39

My dear Father,

I have got thus far on my way to Washington, and shall remain here three days longer. My New York friends are so very attentive, that I find it impossible to get away, so soon as I expected.

I dine with Mr. Higbee to-day. He stands very high here as a preacher. Some prefer him to Dr. Hawkes,[1] who has hitherto been their great *canon.* I mean to hear him preach tomorrow.

Last evening I was at a supper-party, at Mr. Steven[s]'s. Dr. Wainwright, Prof Mc.Vickar and Mr. Gallatin were there.[2] Gallatin is the funniest old gentleman I have seen for many a day; very antique in his dress, with a great nose, and a brown wig. He is seventy eight years old, and has not yet got rid of his French accent. I doubt if he ever will.

This evening I go to General Tallmadge's and afterwards to Chief Justice Jones's;[3] and dine there tomorrow; and have already engagements for Monday and Tuesday. You see I am very busy.

The Storers[4] I have seen two or three times. They are all well.

Love to all.

Most truly
Henry W. Longfellow

P. S. I shall write you again on Sunday, if I can — at all events soon. R. A. L. Codman, whom I met last night in the entry of Astor House offers to take this.

MANUSCRIPT: Longfellow Trust Collection.

1. Francis Lister Hawks (1798–1866), rector of St. Thomas in New York.

2. The host was presumably John Austin Stevens (54.4), a Yale graduate of 1813 and president of the New York Bank of Commerce, 1839–1866. The guests were Rev. Jonathan Wainwright, Professor John McVickar (1787–1868) of Columbia University, and the statesman Albert Gallatin, who was about to retire as president of the National Bank of New York.

3. General James Tallmadge (1778–1853), a New York lawyer and a founder of New York University, earned his title during the War of 1812. Samuel Jones (1769–1853) was chief justice of the Superior Court of New York City, 1828–1847.

4. The family of Ebenezer Storer (95.2).

## 458. *To William Henry Seward*[1]

New York. Jan. 30. 1839

Dear Sir.

Although I have not the honor of your acquaintance, I venture to address you in behalf of my friend Dr. [Ebenezer] Storer, who has applied for the situation of Health Officer of the port of New York. The Doctor was one of a little circle of friends, who passed the winter of 1827 together at Paris. [Pierre] Irving, [James] Berdan, and myself, were with him; and we had all the best opportunity of judging of Dr. Storer's character. Irving has already borne testimony to his many excellent traits; and were Berdan now alive, I am sure he would be among the most urgent petitioners to your Excellency in behalf of Dr. Storer. Indeed all of us can bear witness for him; that in addition to his professional acquirements, he possesses one of the most kind and humane spirits, that ever warmed a human breast. This seems to be almost as necessary as professional skill in the post he wishes to obtain; and I cannot doubt that it will be a point of great moment in determining your Excellency's decision.

I trust Sir, that the interest I take in a friend's success will excuse the liberty I have taken in addressing you.[2]

I have the honor to be

Your Obt. Ser[v]t.
Henry W. Longfellow
Professor in Harvard University

MANUSCRIPT: unrecovered; text from typewritten transcript, Longfellow Trust Collection (Longfellow House).

1. Governor of New York, 1839–1843.

2. Dr. Storer did not win the post. On February 14, 1840, Governor Seward appointed Dr. Augustus Sidney Doane (1808–1852), professor of physiology in New York University.

## 459. *To Samuel Ward*

Washington. Wednesday morning. [Feb. 6, 1839]

"Tasso, partito da Ferrara, e vicino
a Roma scorge il Campidoglio."[1]

My dear Sam,

I write you in great haste and some trepidation; for arriving here yesterday I indeed found the Campidoglio, and Preston[2] making a speech; but I found not a letter of Credit which Prest. Quincy promised to send me. Consequently the sinews of war begin to crack. In all friendly confidence I turn to you, instead of writing to him; as I fear I should be detained here longer than I wish, if I waited for an answer from Cambridge. If you will authorize me to draw on some house here for seventy-five or a hundred dollars, you will oblige me very much. The President should have been more considerate, than to put me into this awkward position. I shall refund to you, on reaching Cambridge.[3]

What shall I say of Washington after one day's experience? It looks like the Court of King Loafer. I never yet beheld anything which so strongly indicated equality of condition, as the appearance of this place. For instance, here is the Palace of a Foreign Minister, where I called yesterday.[4]

This I neither praise nor blame; but say merely that it surprises me. The weather, thus far, is of that kind, known among men by the name of *bleak*; *a hard, steely sunshine,* with a shrewd wind; and I begin to think, that if I were at home, I should be in a better place. However, all this will brighten, and warm soon, and I shall pass a week pleasantly enough, without doubt.

Now I go to present your sister's Epistle Dedicatory to the Vespucci.[5] When I next write you shall hear of her and others. To-night there are *Tableaux* at Señora Calderon's,[6] where I shall probably be.

I have already heard Preston and Benton,[7] in the Senate. To judge from this short specimen, the latter is much more of an Orator than the former: though perhaps the occasion was not great enough. Thompson[8] I have also heard in the House; and could not help thinking how *respectable Silence is*!

Write to the care of Comdre. Wadsworth, my much beloved Uncle, with whom I trust one of these days to sail up the Nile.

Kind regards to all yr. family. If my fingers were warmer I should write better.

Truly yours
Longfellow

MANUSCRIPT: unrecovered; text from photostat, Longfellow Trust Collection. ADDRESS: To/Samuel Ward Jr. Esq./New York POSTMARK: WASHINGTON CITY D.C. FEB 6

1. "Tasso, having left Ferrara, and nearing Rome, descries the Capitol." On March 15, 1828, in Rome, Longfellow implied in his MS Journal that this remark was part of the response of an Improvisatrice when the subject "Tasso" was "drawn from a silver vase by the auditors."

2. William Campbell Preston (1794–1860), intimate friend of Washington Irving and U.S. Senator from South Carolina. As an orator, Preston was considered the peer of his maternal uncle, Patrick Henry.

3. On February 8 Ward sent Longfellow a letter of credit accompanied by the statement: "I am happy to have a chance of serving you as above and said to myself just now, well! a business man may occasionally be useful after all."

4. Longfellow provides a sketch here of a very plain two-story house.

5. Late in 1838 a young Tuscan adventuress calling herself Marie Hélène America Vespucci arrived in the U. S. with a scheme for obtaining American citizenship and a grant of land by dramatizing herself as a descendant of the great navigator and as a victim of Austrian tyranny. The story of her petition to Congress, its failure, and her subsequent tour of the country can be found in Senate Document 264 (Washington, 1839), in numerous newspaper accounts of 1839, and in John Francis McDermott, "America Vespucci or Abroad in America," *Bulletin of the Missouri Historical Society*, XI (July 1955), 370–378. Ward, whose sister Julia presumably wrote the "Epistle Dedicatory," described her enthusiastically as "a fine creature," "*all Woman*," with "the finest shoulders on Earth" (MS letter, February 8, 1839); but Longfellow considered her a "magnificent humbug" (MS Journal, March 24, 1839), which in fact she was later discovered to be.

6. Frances Erskine Inglis (1804–1882), wife of Don Ángel Calderón de la Barca (1790–1861), Spanish minister to the U. S. and then Mexico. A Scotchwoman, Mme. Calderón had lived in Boston before her marriage in 1838 and was well known in social circles there. Longfellow may have met her through her friend William Hickling Prescott, the historian.

7. Thomas Hart Benton (1782–1858), U. S. Senator from Missouri.

8. There were two Thompsons in the House of Representatives at this time: Waddy Thompson (1798–1868), a Whig leader from South Carolina, and Jacob Thompson (1810–1885), Democrat of Mississippi.

## 460. *To Stephen Longfellow*

Washington. Feb. 9. 1839.

My dear Father,

I have been already two days in the City; and have seen and heard a great deal. The Commodore [A. S. Wadsworth] and his family are all well: and make me as comfortable and homelike as possible. In the Senate I have heard some of the best speakers; Preston, Clay and Benton and Calhoun. Yesterday Mr. Clay made a great speech on Abolition, which I shall not report, as you will see it reported in the papers.[1] It was highly interesting. Some tears were shed; a part of which, came from his own eyes. His voice reminded me of Dr. Channing. I heard also John Sargent[2] in the Supreme Court; and Mr. Webster told me he should argue a case there on Saturday. I think I have been very fortunate.

I called to see the President[3] last evening. The Commodore introduced me and a Bostonian. We found him sitting in his elegant parlor, with Mr. Wright,[4] one of the Kitchen Cabinet. We talked about the weather — the comparative expense of wood and coal, as fuel; and the probability that as the season advanced, it would grow milder. We staid fifteen minutes; the Commodore beginning to show symptoms of impatience at the end of ten. We took him home; and then called upon Judge Story; who recd. us very kindly, and sent for all the Judges of the Supreme Court to come down and see us. So down they came; and sat all in a row in front of the fire. I could hardly believe my eyes, when I beheld these men; so raw, and rusty! What an inferior looking set! and that one of these should have been put over Judge Story! Ye Gods, it doth amaze me![5]

I find it very pleasant here; and shall stay a week longer. That will be as long as I can possibly stay.

Yours truly
Henry W. Longfellow

P. S. Henrietta [Henley] sends her thanks to Alex for his present, and makes tender inquiries after the *cap.*

MANUSCRIPT: Longfellow Trust Collection. ADDRESS: Hon. S. Longfellow./Portland/Me. PUBLISHED: *Life*, I, 324–325.

1. In this speech, delivered on February 7, Clay urged the cessation of abolitionist activities and made an eloquent appeal for national unity (Richard Chambers, ed., *Speeches of the Honorable Henry Clay of the Congress of the United States* [Cincinnati, 1842], pp. 63–83).

2. John Sergeant (1779–1852), congressman from Pennsylvania and an eminent lawyer, had been the Whig candidate for Vice President on the ticket with Henry Clay in 1832.

3. President Van Buren.

4. Silas Wright (1795–1847), U. S. Senator from New York.

5. In 1836 President Jackson's nomination of Roger B. Taney, a Democrat, to succeed John Marshall as Chief Justice was confirmed by the Senate. Judge Story, a Federalist whose judicial views more closely paralleled Marshall's, was greatly disappointed. See 417.4.

## 461. *To Zilpah Longfellow*

Boston. Feb. 27. 1839

My dear Mother

I do not often trouble you with letters but at this season of the year, I am always more particularly reminded of you and your affection for me; so that in beginning this letter my pen has written Mother instead of Father.

You will see by the date that I have returned from Washington. I had a very delightful visit; never was more affectionately received and entertained, than by the Commodore [A. S. Wadsworth] and his wife; and was at home with them and the neighborhood in five minutes. I was delighted with the warm welcome and the warm weather; and passed fifteen days much to my satisfaction. We often wished we could take you from the cold Northern blasts, and let you breathe the Southern Sunshine. Aunt *Louisa* is a very lovely woman. She has bound me to her with cords of love: and moves on so gently and peacefully through this world of troubles, that one cannot be with her, and not feel something of the quiet influence. Little *Luly*[1] is more lovely than ever. They frequently asked me why Alexander did not make them a visit this Winter. He stands high in the good graces of the Washingtonians. I saw his friends the Roger*ses* frequently. They are very agreeable ladies.[2] Cousin Hen [Henrietta Henley], as they call her, is likewise very lovely; and so one has pleasant company enough in Franklin Row and the neighborhood.

And now the Vacation is over, and I am going to work again after all this play. When the steamboats begin to run I shall try to steal a day or two and make you a short visit; but cannot now.

Mr. Greenleaf tells me you are all well. I was sorry to find no letter from anyone on my return.

My love to you all and at the Judge's [Barrett Potter]

Most affectionately yours
Henry W. Longfellow

MANUSCRIPT: Longfellow Trust Collection. ADDRESS: Hon S. Longfellow/Portland POSTMARK: BOSTON Mas. FEB 28

1. Louisa Denison Wadsworth (b. 1833), Commodore Wadsworth's daughter.

2. The daughters of Mrs. Minerva Denison Rodgers (1784–1877), widow of Commodore John Rodgers, U.S.N. (1773–1838), and sister-in-law of Commodore Wadsworth.

## 462. *To Henry Russell Cleveland*

Cambridge March 5. 1839.

My dear Cleveland,

I was very sorry to pass so near you the other day without seeing you: but the temptation of the Railroad on the other side of the river direct from Philadelphia to New York, was too strong for me. So I rushed through, like a weaver's shuttle, to and fro. I think, however, that if I had received your letter in Washington, I should have returned by the way of Burlington. Unfortunately it did not reach me till yesterday, as I was sitting bolt upright in No 6. University Hall, where I should be happy to see M. de Sandrau in my place. I am sorry not to have had a glimpse of him. I shall insist upon having the vacant instructership filled before the next term. The salary, to be sure, is not large; but, you know, only three days in the week are occupied, and there are three months of vacation annually. Boston too, is a good field for one who has the ability to cultivate it. Would not Mr Sandrau do well there? Would he not be preferred to others, who now occupy the ground? I really think it would be worth his while to come on during the Summer and see for himself, what is likely to be done. He can take his own time for it. I shall be here till the middle of July.

Permit me to felicitate you on the birth of your daughter;[1] and thank God on your knees that it *is* a daughter, and no rantipole, care-bringing, forgetful, thankless son, as most of us are. I wish I were married and had a daughter, that I might experience the delight of seeing one human soul grow up under my care, not omitting

"the sweet benefit of time,
To clothe her age with angel-like perfection."[2]

But mine being a less joyful fate, allow me to sympathise with you in your happiness and that of your wife on seeing this ||faint|| shadow, or rather, this luminous outline of herself thrown upon the dark back-ground of the Future.

We are all of us well here, — both in body and mind, saving my sorrowful self, upon whom certain events have made too deep and lasting an impression. My kindest regards to your wife.

Very truly yrs.
Longfellow

MANUSCRIPT: Berg Collection, New York Public Library. ADDRESS: To/Henry R Cleveland Esq/Burlington/N.J. POSTMARK: CAMBRIDGE MS. MAR 6

1. Eliza Callahan Cleveland, born January 17, 1839, in Burlington, New Jersey.
2. *Two Gentlemen of Verona*, II, iv, 66–67.

## 463. *To Stephen Longfellow, Jr.*

Cambridge March 5. 1839

My dear Steve

Your letter of Feb. 18 did not reach me till yesterday, as I had left Washington before its arrival there. The rumor of war had already reached me; and the subject is now in everyone's mouth. For my part, I have not from the beginning felt any fear of a War: — a real *war* between England and this Country; nor do I now think it probable. It will not come to that. Nevertheless I have made search for such books as you mention; and thus far have not been able to find any. I will, however, inquire farther, and let you know the result, by sending anything I can lay my hands on.[1]

I cannot write you a very long letter this morning, because I have a great many things to do in the way of preparation for College work. My Washington visit was exceedingly pleasant; — one of the pleasantest you can imagine. Yet I feel very glad to get back again, liking this neighborhood better than any other. I find I have a great deal of work to do this term; and am obliged to be up before sunrise, which requires some resolution, in one of my habit of sitting up late. I shall write, as soon as I get time, a more full account of our friends in Washn. Meanwhile give my kindest regards to Marianne and all at home. Dont fight.

Very truly your affect[ionat]e brother
Henry.

P. S. I must tell you by way of amusement in yr. warlike occupations, that Dick Derby gives a Fancy Ball on Thursday next. One man is going in a regular antique suit of armor, if he can carry it. Dick himself is to sustain several characters; among which are a hack-driver and a clergyman. I *had* an idea of going as Faust; but think I shall not go at all. No doubt it will be vastly funny: almost too absurd for these serious times. See what a contrast! You all of you in alarm, and in earnest; and everybody here up to the neck in folly. Did you ever see Tom Motley? He is to play the part of the Bunker-Hill Monument — an unfinished structure. If you know him, the joke wont seem very bad.

MANUSCRIPT: Longfellow Trust Collection. ADDRESS: Stephen Longfellow Jr. Esq/Portland/Me. POSTMARK: CAMBRIDGE MS. MAR 6

1. The so-called "Aroostook War" was a dispute between Great Britain and the U. S. over the Maine-New Brunswick boundary, 1838–1839. Both sides sent troops to the scene, but General Winfield Scott, commander of the U. S. forces, managed to settle the issue without bloodshed, and an agreement was later ratified by the Webster-Ashburton Treaty. Longfellow's brother had written to request some books on partisan and guerrilla warfare so that he might be prepared "to speak or to write" on the dispute.

## 464. *To Samuel Ward*

Cambridge March. 11. 1839

My beloved Sam,

If this sheet perchance has in it an odour of the accursed weed, it will remind you only the more strongly of your absent friend and the morning cigar at the Astor House, with friendly conversation. It reminds *me,* that the vacation is over, and that I am no more an "idle truant, omitting the sweet benefit of Time."[1] Since my return, indeed, I have been so busy, that I have not found time to write you before to-day; or to send you word, that if you will call upon Goodhue & Co. you will find there the ducats you wot of, with no other interest than my thanks.[2] This is not a very business-like way of stating the case, but you will understand me.

Sparks received your amber mouth-piece with a radiant smile; and was very much pleased that you should thus remember him. He turned it over in his fingers, then put it into his mouth and blew through it, as if it were a child's whistle; and then laughed and said; "Sam is munificent; this is elegant"; and the like. He is to marry in April;[3] and inhabit a goodly home within bow-shot of the Colleges, where I trust you will see him in the Summer.

After all, Sam, Cambridge delighteth my heart exceedingly. I have fallen upon books, with a most voracious appetite; and have already devoured since my return, three or four Comedies of Molière, a strange work on the Millenium, "La Fa*meuse Comédienne*," twelve

Cantos of the Fairy Queen, a G[r]eek Tragedy, the Life of Cheverus, some Cantos of Dante, part of Nicholas Nicke[l]by, portions of Fairfax's Tasso (a grand book) and a good many of Göthe's minor poems.[4] There was once a man who took a fancy to see the quantity and quality of food he devoured in a day; and put into a milk-pan the same amount of the same things which he ate. The odd mixture — this *ambigu,* — rather startled him; and I am quite startled at this heterogeneous mass, which I have put into my brain-pan. What have you put into yours?

Tell Cogswell I have received his note; and sent the M.S. to Mr. Dehon, for Mr. Brooks.[5] I have had a letter from Greene, Rome. Dec 6. He is well, and in the best spirits imaginable. He has just written an Art. on the Social State of the Italians, which I think cannot fail to be interesting.[6] I hope he will write for the New York Review.

Nothing new in Boston; except an *old* painting of Allston, just brought to light, and for show. A beautiful fancy sketch; two girls, one from Titian; the other, his own *dreamerie.* They talk of getting up an Exhibition of all his paintings, for his benefit; he needs it: oh, ye Gods, how hard a fate! This old painting, which he loved and cherished as a child of his youth, and valued at fifteen hundred dollars, he has been obliged to part with for five hundred. Besides which his wife drops asleep in the evening over her knitting work.[7]

I hope your good father has quite recovered; and that Göthe and the Philosopher are quite well.[8] My kindest regards to your *gnädige Frau* and the fair *Fraüleins,*[9] and Cogswell, and to one and all, in fine and write me before shortly (avant peu).

Very truly yours,
Longfellow

P.S. Have I forgotten anything? I believe not. If I have, it must remain for my next. Anglo-Saxon Book and Music for yr. sister Julia, as soon as I can find an opportunity.

Liegt dir Gestern klar und offen,
Wirkst du heute kräftig frei,
Kannst auch auf ein Morgen hoffen
Das nicht minder glücklich sei. Göthe.[10]

MANUSCRIPT: Longfellow Trust Collection. ADDRESS: To/Samuel Ward Jr. Esq/ New York. POSTMARK: CAMBRIDGE MS. MAR 12

1. *Two Gentlemen of Verona,* II, iv, 65–66.
2. A reference to the money lent him by Ward (Letter No. 459).
3. Jared Sparks married Mary Crowninshield Silsbee (b. 1809), daughter of Senator Nathaniel Silsbee of Salem, on May 21, 1839.

4. Longfellow's journal entries for March 7–8 reveal that one of the Molière comedies was *Don Juan, ou le Festin de Pierre.* Among the other works were *A Treatise on the Millenium, shewing its near Approximation, especially by the Accomplishment of those Events which were to Precede it; the Second Advent or Coming of our Lord and Saviour Jesus Christ; and the Restoration of a State of Paradise upon Earth* (Boston, 1838); *La Fameuse Comédienne ou Histoire de la Guérin Auparavant femme et veuve de Molière* (Francfort, 1688); J. Huen-Dubourg, *The Life of Cardinal Cheverus, Archbishop of Bordeaux, and formerly Bishop of Boston, in Massachusetts.* Translated by E. Stewart (Boston, 1839); and an edition of *Godfrey of Bulloigne: or, The Recovery of Jerusalem. Done into English heroical verse, by Edward Fairfax, gent., together with the Life of the said Godfrey.*

5. Cogswell's letter of February 28, 1839, gave directions for delivering Richard Wilde's Tasso manuscript (407.1) to Sidney Brooks, who with Charles Augustus Davis (741.2) was a partner in the commission house of Davis & Brooks, 21 Broad, New York City. Theodore Dehon, Brooks's son-in-law, was also connected with the firm.

6. Longfellow misunderstood Greene who had stated specifically in his letter that he "did not dare to undertake so delicate and complicated a subject" as the social state of Italy and that he had written instead on the literary and intellectual pursuits of the Italians. His article appeared in the *North American Review,* L (April 1840), 301–336.

7. The painting by Washington Allston was "The Sisters," one figure of which was taken from Titian's "Girl Holding a Jewel Casket." Longfellow's dismay at Allston's poverty is perhaps overworked, for the painter's notation on the back of the picture, dated January 29, 1839, reveals that he received the full $1500 (Edgar Preston Richardson, *Washington Allston: A Study of the Romantic Artist in America* [Chicago, 1948], pp. 204–205). "The Sisters" was displayed in an exhibition of Allston's paintings at Harding's Gallery in School Street, Boston, April 1 — July 10, 1839.

8. Samuel Ward, Sr. (1786–1839), partner in the prominent banking firm of Prime, Ward, and King, was suffering from what his physician called "rheumatic gout." He died suddenly on November 27. See Letter No. 504. The reference to "Göthe" is obscure. The "Philosopher" was Dr. Henry M. Francis (1792–1842), a graduate of Columbia in 1808, brother of Dr. John W. Francis, and Sam Ward's intimate friend.

9. That is, Ward's sisters — Julia, Louisa, and Annie. Longfellow frequently misplaces the umlaut marks in "fräulein."

10. *Zahme Xenien,* IV, 92. "If yesterday was pure and truthful,/Today you'll labor strongly free,/If, too, you can expect a morrow/It will no less happy be."

## 465. *To Stephen Longfellow*

Cambridge March. 18. 1839

My dear Father,

I have postponed writing you from day to day because I am really very much occupied, and find every hour something which must be done without delay, and therefore whatever can be put off is left for tomorrow. I am working pretty hard in College. I have three Lectures a week, and recitations without number. Three days in the week I go into my class-room between seven and eight, and come out between three and four; with one hour's intermission. The other days are consumed in preparation, and in doing the usual small matters, which every man has to do; — the usual interruptions — and this, that and the other. However, I *like* it very well; and *am* very well, and very happy, — and have nothing in particular to annoy me. The season is opening beautifully and everything smiles.

Please tell Stephen I have found one little book on Partizan Warfare, — and only one — which I think will interest him. It is by Roger Stevenson — published in 1775; and went through the Revolution in the hands and pocket of Mr. Greenleaf's father.[1] It is a precious *relique,* and must be treated accordingly. Mr. Greenleaf says it is as precious to him, as his father's sword would be. I shall send it by James [Greenleaf] on Saturday next; as he proposes then to sail for Portland.

I have not seen Col. Fessenden yet, for Alexander; but wrote to him yesterday. He has removed to Salem. I shall try to get information from him soon.

As to Sketches of Washington, — I cannot think of putting such things on paper but will reserve them for pleasant conversations when we meet.

Sir Richard Derby's Fancy-ball went off brilliantly. I did not attend; not wishing to figure in fantastic robes. I am so busy here that I am obliged to give up Society for the present. Besides, I am quite too comfortable here in this *chateau* of a Cra[i]gie-house. My domestic arrangements are very complete. Breakfast at seven in my own room; dinner at three, with Miss Lowel[l]; tea at seven, with the same, a very remarkable old lady, with a heart full of goodness, and some little peculiarities which do not trouble me. It is an excellent arrangement for my comfort.

My love to all.

Affectionately yours
Henry W. Longfellow

MANUSCRIPT: Longfellow Trust Collection. ADDRESS: Hon. Stephen Longfellow/ Portland/Me POSTMARK: CAMBRIDGE MS. MAR 19

1. *Military Instructions for Officers Detached in the Field: Containing, a Scheme for Forming a Corps of a Partisan. Illustrated with Plans of the Manoeuvres Necessary in Carrying on the Petite Guerre* (Philadelphia: printed and sold by R. Aitken, printer and bookseller, opposite the London Coffee-House, Front-Street; 1775).

466. *To Stephen Longfellow*

Cambridge April 7. 1839

My dear Father

I was very glad to hear from you by James [Greenleaf], who returned safely, as I presume you have heard ere this; though what you say of your health, gives me pain. Everyone feels more or less the debilitating power of the Spring; which with us has been very warm, so that we already sit with open windows, though we have not yet given up fires. I never knew such a Spring in America. It is quite Italian; and makes one almost believe with Mr. Amos, that the Millenium is coming.[1]

How did Stephen like the book on partizan warfare, which I sent him? I am glad there is no probability of his having any use for it. The storm of war seems indeed already to have blown over; and people here think the affair will be peaceably settled. The Great Western is expected to-day; and we shall soon see what effect the warlike manifestations of Gov. Fairfield[2] have produced in England.

We have here a plague, which troubles us more than War, Pestilence or Famine; namely Canker-worms, which devour the largest trees. (I mean the leaves.) The fine elms round the Cra[i]gie house were entirely stripped last year, and the worms came swinging down on long threads, into all the windows. This year I am putting everything in operation to prevent their climbing. I have *Lynch'd* all the trees — that is tarred them, renewing it every night, and inspecting in the morning, to see that no rascally bug has escaped his impending doom. I hope next summer to be able to sit in the shade, with out being covered with creeping things, and brought daily like Martin Luther before a Diet of Worms. Are you plagued to death with these creatures? I do not remember seeing any in Portland.

Tell Aunt Lucia, that her friend Dick Derby has gone to Europe again. The Spring makes him frisky. Just before he went he wrote me a note requesting letters of introduction; and began thus "*Most amative Sir.*"

In College everything is quiet and tame enough; and the students very industrious. Sam is well, and keeps himself very busy and correct in everything, so that I have nothing to desire more.

My love to all. I shall certainly run down before vacation; though not immediately. I must wait till the Steamboat passages are sure, so as not to be detained.

Most affectionately yours
Henry W. Longfellow

MANUSCRIPT: Longfellow Trust Collection. ADDRESS: Hon Stephen Longfellow/ Portland/Me. POSTMARK: CAMBRIDGE MS. APR 8

1. See 464.4. This is the only indication that *A Treatise on the Millenium* was written by a man named Amos.

2. John Fairfield (1797–1847), a Democrat and the governor of Maine, 1839–1840, was being particularly aggressive in the Maine-New Brunswick boundary dispute. The *Great Western*, designed and constructed in 1838 by Isambard Kingdom Brunel (1806–1859), was the first steamship built especially for transatlantic voyages.

## 467. *To Stephen Longfellow*

Cambridge April. 14. 1839.

My dear Father,

I am learning to write with a steel pen, so as to be ready for the Millenium. This is a specimen. I dont think I shall stand very high. Mr. Greenleaf, who once had as great an aversion to steel pens as I have at this moment, has become a convert, and bought twenty gross, to begin with. It saves time; but spoils my hand, and makes me red with angry impatience as I write. However, having begun, I shall persevere to the end of this letter.

Since my last, I have had a visit from Mr. [John] Abbot.[1] He came at six o'clock in the morning, and breakfasted with me. He is brim full of what he has done and is going to do. The principal object of his visit however was to make me his Biographer. He wants me to begin now; for he says that as soon as he dies, everybody will be quarrelling to see who shall write his life; and I must do it. Next to this comes the establishment of a "School of Good Manners" at Waterford; and also an Insane Hospital. He says he has been appointed Commissioner for this purpose; and requested to reside a year at Charlestown and a year at Worcester to make inquiries. Thinks he shall. Then he means to be married. He is on the look out for a Widow. I asked him why he preferred a widow; and he said "Because you can never tell, till they have been tried, how people will turn out; whether they will be good breeders or not; and my principal object is to disappoint my heirs." He thinks he has hushed up the Eastern Boundary difficulties. He says the settlement is all owing to his exertions. Then he told me his sw[o]rd-cane story again: — and in fine seems to have failed a good deal since I last saw him; though he appears to be in good health.

I do not hear one word from Washington save through you. The Commodore [A. S. Wadsworth] has not answered my letter. He was never made for an author, so much does he dislike writing.

We have nothing new here; and I write this only to tell you I am well; and to show you what I can do with a steel pen. If the letter tries your patience as much as it has mine, I shall think the moral influence of steel pens very bad. Perhaps the fault lies in the paper. It seems to[o] soft and the pen cuts right in. I should write a very savage criticism with such a pen as this, and mean to reserve it for *cutting* remarks. After I have delivered fifteen more lectures, at the rate of three a week, I am coming down to see you. Probably about the first of June.

Give my *sharpest* regards to all, and believe me with the greatest hatred of cold steel in every shape,

yours affectionately
Henry W. Longfellow

MANUSCRIPT: Longfellow Trust Collection. ADDRESS: Hon. Stephen Longfellow/ Portland/Me POSTMARK: CAMBRIDGE MS. APR 15

1. See 44.1 and 401.1.

## 468. *To Willis Gaylord Clark*

Cambridge. April 21. 1839

My dear Clark,

Can it be possible, that I have not written you since my return? Too bad! But did you know all I have had to do, you would not blame me for ceasing to write letters. How are you? and how is small Aquarius, with his tea-pot? [1] And Becky and Jane, the handmaidens twain? Hints and glimpses now and then in the Gazette show, that you are stout again, and out again; which I am right glad to hear. Since my return I have been quite out of health and had such horrible *dissolving* colds, that I thought I should suffer the fate of that unfortunate individual, who blew himself out through his nose entirely, and left nothing but a hole in his handkerchief! However, I am now better; owing principally I believe to my ||bonhominy||.[2] This is *my last* joke; and I dare say ||you|| hope it may be my *last*. I think it ||better than|| the *grease-spot* joke. If good enough, mak||e use of|| it, as the fate of an *Eastern* General; su||ch will|| abuse so shockingly the *Maniacs* — the great Down-Easters one of which I am. My intimate friend Felton takes the same side you do, and has read yr. articles with great *gusto*. You are right. It was all *humbug*; but I have no doubt it has done great good; and will bring to a close the long neglected matter — long neglected by the culpable want of promptness of our Govt.[3]

I am very glad to read yr. eulogy on Frankenstein. He is a fine fellow, and a genius, and will go far.[4] How do I look when I am *dry*?

I was *moist* when I left you. Since my return I have thought often of you, and the hospitable reception you gave me in Phila; and the grand time I had with you, and so forth. I have been hard at work; and am sick of it, almost. Hyperion is nearly done; only two chaps. more, and I am free. I begin to feel lighter already. By the way — that Psalm of Life ||which I|| repeated to you one night, as we lay in ||the fire-ligh||t of yr. chamber, I have sent to LEWIS, ||and it will|| come out in the May Knickerbocker.[5]

||Have|| you any *autographs* of distinguished new ||authors you|| can spare? The *great* Bulwer for instance.[6] ||Can you c||ollect me any? Do so and oblige yrs. truly.

Upon reflection I have been sorry I did not stay longer in Philadelphia. I saw nothing of the Society there; nor the fair dames. Pity. Only the men; and the walls of Girard College. It was really going through town at too rapid a rate. You were kind enough to protest against it; but Orestes-like I stormed away both to and fro. I hope you wont do so when you come to Boston this Summer; but be calm as a Christian should be.

Do you know what would be a grand foot-journey? Why all through the western part of yr. state among the German towns and villages, among the Dutch Fraus and Fraüleins: and I have t||hought||[7] of it often. Nothing *sets a man on his feet,* like walking. It does one good for a whole year, — to walk a month.

What do you *really* think of Irving's lucubrations? I see that Park Benjamin is down upon them.[8] I pray you write me soon; and tell me whether the *Monster*[9] is going to travel beyond the sea, as they say he is. Farewell. My regards to Frankenstein.

Most truly yours
Longfellow

MANUSCRIPT: Longfellow Trust Collection. ADDRESS: To/Willis G. Clark Esq/ Philadelphia POSTMARK: CAMBRIDGE MS. APR 22

1. Possibly a reference to Willis Gaylord Clark, Jr., aged 2.

2. This word supplied from an incomplete text printed in the *Knickerbocker,* LVII (February 1861), 228.

3. In the March and April numbers of his *Philadelphia Gazette* Clark had printed several editorials attacking the independent conduct of the State of Maine in the Aroostook War (463.1). Longfellow refers specifically to a statement in the number for Saturday, March 9, 1839 (LXVIII, No. 15, 409): "As for the war-talk, that is all humbug, excited by that class of inffectual warriors, 'whose hearts are brimful of the ye[a]st of courage, and whose bosoms do work, and swell, and foam, with untried valor like a barrel of new cider, or a trainband captain, fresh from the hands of his tailor.' " The "*Eastern* General" was presumably Gov. Fairfield.

4. John Peter Frankenstein (c. 1816–1881), German-born artist, painted Long-

fellow's portrait in Philadelphia in late January or early February 1839. Unfortunately he did not fulfill his promise, and in 1864, unhappy with his limited reputation, he published a long poem entitled *American Art. Its Awful Attitude* and thereafter lived in New York as a poverty-stricken recluse. At his death a large amount of money was found in his squalid rooms, prompting an obituary in the *New York Times* entitled "The Miserable End of John Frankenstein Artist" (April 17, 1881).

5. "Voices of the Night. A Third Psalm of Life: By the Author of 'A Psalm of Death,'" *Knickerbocker*, XIII (May 1839), 376. The restored words in this sentence are from the *Knickerbocker* (n. 2, above).

6. The reference is barbed. When Longfellow was in London in 1835, he was disappointed in his reception by Bulwer Lytton, to whom he had a letter of introduction from Willis Clark. See Irving T. Richards, "Longfellow in England: Unpublished Extracts from His Journal," *Publications of the Modern Language Association of America*, LI (December 1936), 1129.

7. This word is from the *Knickerbocker* (n. 2, above).

8. Irving had begun a series in the *Knickerbocker* with an essay on "The Crayon Papers" in which he concluded, "I have much to say about what I have seen, heard, felt, and thought, through the course of a varied and rambling life, and some lucubrations, that have long been encumbering my portfolio" (XIII [March 1839], 210). "A Chronicle of Wolfert's Roost" appeared in the next number (XIII [April 1839], 318–328). Park Benjamin (1809–1864), the poet and journalist, edited the *New-Yorker* at this time, in association with Horace Greeley. After reprinting Irving's first essay (*New-Yorker*, VII [March 23, 1839], 6–7), he dismissed "Wolfert's Roost" as "tedious and dull," advised Irving against "running off any more such screeds of stupidity," and announced his decision to abandon the idea of reprinting the series (VII [April 13, 1839], 61).

9. Identified as Nicholas Biddle by Lewis Gaylord Clark in the *Knickerbocker* (n. 2, above). See also Letter No. 576. Biddle (1786–1844), statesman and financier, had recently retired as president of the United States Bank of Pennsylvania.

## 469. *To Samuel Ward*

Cambridge. Sunday afternoon. April 21. 1839

My dear Sam,

I *should* have answered yr. letter sooner, and thanked you for the Spanish Ballads[1] and for yr. excellent Address, which I read with very great pleasure, and should have thought a very clear and spirited description of the Long Island affair, if Park Benjamin had not stepped in with his great light of criticism and showed me I was all wrong. Are you thin-skinned? I trust not. I have one excellent remedy on all such occasions, which I commend likewise to you. I never read what is written against me. Therefore it is to me as if it had never been written; and I am saved the momentary pang, arising from abuse. I have had one or two occasions to try this during this last year; and find it perfectly successful. I mean to try it several times this year; so that any abuser may as well spare his ink, if he intends to disturb my equanimity. Try this, when you next hear your articles have been abused.

I trust I need not say, that I disagree with Benjamin about the Art. on Romance, likewise. The only fault I can find with it, is that it is not long enough; and it seems to me, you might have gone deeper into the discussion of Literature considered as an Art. However, you have made the beginning, and *Dimidium facti, qui coepit, habet.*[2]

You ask me to recommend an English *Boke.* Yes, my friend, one which I have just been reading with infinite delight; namely Spencer's Fairy Queen; and then after it Wieland's Oberon, to see how heaven-wide they stand apart; and how vastly superior Spencer is. I have just done this. As to Classics, Cogswell is a much better guide than I am. Still, if I may venture to advise. I should say take Horace — for fifty reasons, which you will please to imagine. He is the Latin Göthe — or rather (spirit of the Past forgive me!) Göthe is the German Horace. He is my favorite Classic; and whenever I quote Latin, which as you very well know, is not often, I quote him; because his phrases *stick.* What a beautiful affair, for instance, is the *Ad-Thaliarchum* Ode (I.IX.) which I beg you to read after dinner to Dr. Francis. It contains all Göthe's Philosophy — or nearly all: and half of what we now cry up as so wonderfully said by the German, was quite as well said some two thousand years ago by Horace.[3]

Is it true, that yr. sister Julia wrote the Rev. of Göthe and Schiller?[4] It is very good; and the figures of flowers very apt and true. There — the church bells begin to ring. Shall I go, or stay? Do you know I seldom stay at home from church, without thinking of that pretty little poem of Göthe, where he says a truant boy was chased over field and through forest by a church-bell![5] The confounded brazen-mouthed monitors seem to say to me, like Friar Bacon's brass head; "Time was — Time is — Time is past!"[6]

Farewell. Have I forgotten anything? Yes: the Spanish Drama. When you import from Paris, I should like to have it; *but not as a present.*[7] I shall feel no liberty of sending by you, if you always insist so on paying the bill.

With kind regards to all friends, and sympethiz[ing] for yr. indisposition (I was in the same condition ten days ago)

very truly yours
Henry W. Longfellow.

P.S. Can you give me some autographs of the French Novellists and others? Pray make me a small collection, and I will send by some friend for them.

2nd P.S. Please inquire if there is any young Parisien, who would be qualified to teach French here. I want some one to take charge of the classes: — a youth of spirit, and a gentleman, such as I have in German and Italian. If you can hear of such, please let me know.

MANUSCRIPT: Longfellow Trust Collection. ADDRESS: To/Samuel Ward Jr. Esq./ New York. POSTMARK: CAMBRIDGE MS. APR 22 ENDORSEMENT: Received and answered 25. April. 1839

1. An unidentified volume sent by Ward to Longfellow with a letter on April 3, 1839.

2. "He who has begun his task has half done it." Horace, *Epistles*, I, ii, 40. Ward had ventured into print twice during April: "Modern French Romance" appeared in the *New York Review*, IV (April 1839), 441–456; and "The Battle of Long-Island," an address delivered on February 7 before the New-York Historical Society, was published in the *Knickerbocker*, XIII (April 1839), 279–295. Benjamin dismissed the first article "as rather unworthy of a place in a periodical of the elevated character of the New-York Review" (*New-Yorker*, VII [April 6, 1839], 33). He denounced the *Knickerbocker* essay in more cutting terms: "The subject is important, and facts are usefully displayed; but the thoughts of the writer stalk along as awkwardly as country boobies in court dresses. In trying to be very fine and very dignified, they appear to be as slovenly, unmannered knaves as any in Christendom. They jostle each other in glorious confusion. The article is a specimen of what may be called 'the fuddled style,' each sentence seems to have taken a 'drop too much' " (*New-Yorker*, VII [April 13, 1839], 61).

3. That Horace's ode to Thaliarchus appealed to Longfellow is also evidenced by the similarity between its *carpe diem* theme and "A Psalm of Life."

4. Julia Ward had indeed written the review of Dwight's translations from Goethe and Schiller (456.2) that appeared in the *New York Review*, IV (April 1839), 393–400. See her *Reminiscences 1819–1899* (Boston and New York, 1899), p. 60.

5. A reference to Goethe's ballad "Die wandelnde Glocke."

6. See Robert Greene, *The Honourable History of Friar Bacon and Friar Bungay*, Scene XI.

7. Ward had offered to obtain for Longfellow a five-volume edition of the *Teatro Español* from his bookseller in Paris (Letter of April 3, 1839).

## 470. *To Richard Henry Dana*

Cambridge. April 30. 1839.

My dear Sir,

I take the liberty of sending you the passage in Dante, from which I quoted a line or two the other day in reference to Allston's Landscapes. Are not these paintings truly Dantesque in their beauty? The Poet and the Painter seem to have had the same kind of inspiration.

Very truly yours
Henry W. Longfellow.

Purgatory. Canto. XXVIII.

Longing already to search in and round
The heavenly forest, dense and living green,

Which to the eyes temper'd the new-born day;
   Withouten more delay I left the bank,
Taking my way field-inward, slowly, slowly,
Over the soil, that everywhere breathes fragrance.
   A sweetly-breathing air, that no mutation
Had in itself, smote me upon the forehead,
No heavier blow, than of a gentle breeze;
   Whereat the tremulous branches willingly
Did all of them bow downward to that side
Where its first shadow casts the Holy Mountain;
   Yet not from their true inclination toss'd,
So that the little birds upon their crests
Left off the practice of each tuneful art;
   But with full-throated joy, the hours of prime
Singing receiv'd they, in the midst of leaves
That made monotonous burden to their rhymes;
   Even as from branch to branch it gathering swells
Through the pine forest on the shore of Chiassi,
When Æolus lets loose the damp sirocco.
   Already my slow steps had led me on
Into the ancient wood so far, that I
Could see no more the place where I had enter'd.
   And lo! farther advance cut off a river
Which towards the left hand with its little waves
Bent down the grass, that on its margin grew.
   All waters, that on earth most limpid are
Would seem to have within themselves some mixture
Compar'd with this, which nothing doth conceal,
   Although it moves on with a brown, brown current
Under the shade perpetual, that never
Ray of the sun lets in nor of the moon.[1]

There — the effect on my mind in reading this and in looking at some of Allston's Landscapes is the same.

MANUSCRIPT: Longfellow Trust Collection. ADDRESS: To/Richard H. Dana Esq/ Boston. POSTMARK: CAMBRIDGE MS. MAY 1 POSTAL ANNOTATION (*by Longfellow*): PAID. 192

1. Longfellow's translation.

471. *To Margaret Potter*

[Cambridge, April, 1839][1]

My dear little Madge

I *did* forget that book in Philadelphia; and when I got yr. note felt very much mortified. I sent immediately for it; and it has not come. So I have sent a second time, and hope to be able to bring it to you, when I come in June, as I propose. Is there anything I can bring you from Boston? Do give me an opportunity to retrieve my character.

In great haste, with kindest regards to Eliza and yr. father

affect[ionatel]y yours

Henry W. Longw.

MANUSCRIPT: Longfellow Trust Collection. ADDRESS: To/Miss Margaret Potter/ Portland

1. The date is established by Margaret Potter's letter to Longfellow dated April 1, 1839, in which she asks about the book that is the subject of this note. See 476.3.

472. *Jørgen Bølling.*

Cambridge. *May 7. 1839.*

My dear Sir,

It is very curious, that your last letter should bear date *May 7. '38!* Just a year has elapsed since you wrote me. Meantime I have written you, telling you the reasons of this very long delay about the Books. The letter was sent by way of Hâvre de Grace. I hope it reached you safely.[1] The books I now send; and the bookseller, who packs them, will write you about the payment. I add a list of others, which may be useful, with the prices.

| | |
|---|---|
| Jefferson's Works. 4 vols. 8° . . . . . | $12.00 |
| Kent's Commentaries. 4 vols 8° . . . | 14.00 |
| Everett's Miscellaneous Writings. 8° . . | 3.00 |
| Webster's Speeches 2 vols. 8° . . . . | 4.00 |
| Tudor's Life of Otis. 8° . . . . . . | 2.50 |
| Irving. Life of Columbus. 2 vols. 8° . . | 4.25 |
| Life of Arthur Lee. 2 vols. 8° . . . | 2.00 |
| The Federalist (by Hamilton) 8° . . . | 2.00 |
| Pitkin's Hist. of U. States. 2 vols. 8° . . | 3.50[2] |

In return will you have the goodness to send me:

1. The *best* Icelandic Dictionary.

2. The *best* edition of the Prose Edda.
3. " " " " Poetic Edda, with translation, either in Danish or Latin.

Which work of Öhlenschläger's do you consider the best?[3] Write me about the present state of Poetry and Belles-Lettres in Denmark. In what esteem is held Wergeland's "*Skabelsen-Mennesket-Messias*"?

I beg you to present my best regards to Messrs. Rafn, Magnussen, and Riise. When shall we smoke a friendly pipe once more, among the old books! I have a Romance in Press, in two vols, entitled "*Hyperion*"; a copy of which I shall send you, as soon as it is published.

With great regard, very truly

Your friend
Henry W. Longfellow.

Write to me soon, by way of Hâvre. The price of the Icelandic books may be deducted from the bill, and I will refund it here.

MANUSCRIPT: Royal Library, Copenhagen. ADDRESS: To/A. Bölling Esq/Copenhagen. PUBLISHED: "Eight Unpublished Letters," pp. 175–176.

1. This letter is unrecovered.
2. *Memoir, Correspondence, and Miscellanies, from the Papers of Thomas Jefferson*, ed. Thomas Jefferson Randolph (Charlottesville, 1829); James Kent, *Commentaries on American Law* (New York, 1826–1830); Edward Everett, *Orations and Speeches on Various Occasions* (Boston, 1836); Daniel Webster, *Speeches and Forensic Arguments* (Boston, 1830–1835); William Tudor, *The Life of James Otis of Massachusetts* (Boston, 1823); Washington Irving, *A History of the Life and Voyages of Christopher Columbus* (New York, 1828); Richard Henry Lee, *Life of Arthur Lee* (Boston, 1829); Alexander Hamilton, James Madison, and John Jay, *The Federalist* (first collected in 1788); Timothy Pitkin, *A Political and Civil History of the United States of America* (New Haven, 1828).
3. For Longfellow's interest in Oehlenschläger, see *Longfellow and Scandinavia*, pp. 71–72.

## 473. *To Samuel Colman*

Cambridge May 20. 1839.

My dear Sir,

I should have answered your letter sooner, but have been confined to my bed by indisposition. I accept the terms proposed in regard to Hyperion; only they must be made more definite. You may print fifteen hundred copies of the work; in return for which you shall pay me $375.00, half at the end of three months from publication; and the remainder at the end of six months; in addition to which I am to have 25 copies of the work in sheets for distribution. If you accede to this I am ready to begin printing.[1]

Now for the "Boy's Wonder Horn." I object to the *square* child's book form. Duodecimo would please me most. I will have the first volume ready to print as soon as you may like; though it seems to me next Autumn would be soon enough. How large a book do you want? How many copies? and what terms? [2]

As to the Miscellany I can do nothing. I have written enough for Magazines; and have refused offers where I could charge my own price. It is all vanity and vexation of Spirit.[3]

My regards to Mellen and Cutter [4]

Yours truly
Henry W. Longfellow.

P. S. By the way, my friend Hawthorne wants to publish two vols of Tales in the same style with Hyperion; and would like the same terms you make with me. I think you would do well to take the work. Please write me a word on this subject in yr. next.[5] Hawthorne is a great favorite with the public, as you know, and a man, who is in future to stand very, *very* high in our literature. You ought to be his publisher.

MANUSCRIPT: Berg Collection, New York Public Library. ADDRESS: Samuel Colman Esq/8 Astor House/New York POSTMARK: CAMBRIDGE MS. MAY 21 POSTAL ANNOTATION: Single ENDORSEMENT: wrote 27 cd accept if Wells & co cd print

1. Colman agreed in a note dated May 27, 1839, and sent a "Memorandum of Agreement" dated June 1, 1839.

2. Longfellow and Hawthorne had discussed plans in March to collaborate on a children's book but had agreed shortly thereafter that Longfellow should develop the project alone (*Life*, I, 291–292; *Young Longfellow*, pp. 261, 403). Despite Colman's urging, he eventually abandoned the plan.

3. Longfellow had contributed a translation from the German, "Fragment of a Modern Ballad," to the first number of *Colman's Monthly Miscellany*, I (July 1839), 31–32. He later included his translation in *Voices of the Night* under the title of "The Happiest Land."

4. William Cutter (1801–1867), a Bowdoin graduate of 1821 and a biographer of Lafayette, edited the short-lived *Colman's Monthly Miscellany* with Grenville Mellen.

5. In his reply of May 27, Colman invited a correspondence on the subject of Hawthorne's tales, but his subsequent bankruptcy (Letter No. 511) prevented publication.

## 474. *To Stephen Longfellow*

Cambridge May 26. 1839

My dear Father,

I write to tell you, that I have got quite well again and am going out tomorrow. I have been laid up just a fortnight to-day, with I dont exactly know what, though one of the most unpleasant ingredients was ague. The weather has been very dull, cold and rainy; and altogether unfavorable. However to-day it brightens and I am going out.

This knocks in the head my visit to Portland. I have omitted all my classes for a fortnight, and cannot think of meeting them any more before the vacation. So I shall not have the pleasure of seeing you before the middle of July. I suppose Alex. told you I had finished a Romance lately. Colman will probably be the Publisher; if he agrees to my terms, the book will go to press immediately. I shall send it to you as soon as it is out: and I hope you will like it.

Speaking of Romances — does Stephen know that his friend Grattan, author of "High-ways and By-ways" is expected in Boston soon? He is appointed English Consul there. I shall be very happy to know him.[1]

I have no news to send you. My kindest regards at the Judges &c. Tell Margaret [Potter] I have not been able to get her book from Philadelphia; and Alex. that in looking over some old letters yesterday, I found one from him to Henrietta Henley which I suppose I was to take to Washn. last Winter. What shall I do with it?

Sunday evening.

I have been taking a long drive with James [Greenleaf] through Brighton and Brookline. The country is green and beautiful; and here and there a snug little white "cottage-for-one" peeps out from the thick foliage, like a fried egg in spinnage. You see my figures of speech are *hungry* — the figures of a convalescent man.

Much love to all

Very affectionately yours
Henry W. Longfellow

MANUSCRIPT: Longfellow Trust Collection. ADDRESS: Hon. Stephen Longfellow/ Portland POSTMARK: BOSTON MAY 27

1. Grattan (331.4) served as British consul in Boston, 1839–1853. One result of his residence was his *Civilized America* (London, 1859), a two-volume, ill-humored attack on American society and institutions.

## 475. *To Samuel Ward*

Cambridge May 30. 1839

My dear Sam

I should have written you sooner, but have been very unwell, confined to my chamber for a fortnight, and to my bed for several days. I know not what the deuce ails me. I have not been really *well* for a year past. I think I have overworked myself a little. This "*pulling by the head*," (as oxen do in some countries) is not conducive to health, I am persuaded.

How are *you*? What is the news with you? When does Moreton of Moreton Hope make its appearance? Do you know, I have this design. If I can get the sheets of the book, to write a notice for the July North American provided the book is to appear *before* July 1. and provided likewise I can praise it heartily and warmly. Why can't you see "the *Brothers*" and ask them diligently when the young child is to be born; and get me a copy for the above mentioned purpose; and say not a word to anyone about my reviewing it; because I have no idea of doing such a thing unless I can praise it with a relish. Then I will most gladly; for it would be a grateful welcome to a young author, to have *early* laudation. But *encore une fois*, dont mention it; for it would be awkward if I should not do it; you understand, as I am on very friendly terms with the author, and like him, and wish to do all I can to give him a fair start in the field.[1]

By the way, do you hear of any young Frenchman for me! Do not neglect to inquire, I beg of you; as the matter is one of great importance to me.

We have not begun to print Hyperion yet; but hope to get the first proofs next week. Useless delay, is all this; however, no matter. It will not take long to print.

Are we to have the pleasure of seeing you here soon? You threw out a hint to that effect in yr. last, which I eagerly caught up. I hope you will come. The Allston gallery and the Athenaeum Exhibition[2] will give you much pleasure.

Farewell. This letter is wretched because I am so. Give my best regards to Cogswell and yr. family.

Very truly yours
Longfellow

MANUSCRIPT: Longfellow Trust Collection. ADDRESS: To/Samuel Ward Jr. Esq./ New York POSTMARK: CAMBRIDGE MS. JUN 3

1. John Lathrop Motley's novel *Morton's Hope; or, The Memoirs of a Provincial* was published in New York by Harper Brothers in 1839. Longfellow did not write a review of the book, but a lukewarm notice appeared in the *North American Review*, L (January 1840), 295–296.

2. The Thirteenth Exhibition of Paintings, Athenaeum Gallery, whose catalog is dated May 27, 1839.

## 476. *To Anne Longfellow Pierce*

[Cambridge, May, 1839]

My dear Anna

I am very thankful for yr. note and the May-flowers, which are exceedingly sweet, and excite wonder and envy in the minds of the beholders; as such flowers do not grow here, and are not easily obtained.

I saw Pitt [Fessenden] last evening. He tells me you are all well, and that he has another son.[1] Why did I not hear of this before? He seemed quite surprised, that I should be ignorant of so great an event.

I have nothing new to write you; but hope to come and see you about the first of June. Senator Pierce[2] has been here lately; and desired his sincere regards to you and father. He laid so much emphasis upon the words, and said he wanted you *"to be persuaded they were not words of course,"* that I suppose you will best understand why.

I wish Anna dear, you would come to Cambridge. Will you return with me? It is truly pleasant here at this season of the year, and I want you, to bestow my sympathies upon.

Tell *Madge* [Potter] her book is not to be had; Bishop Manet's, I mean.[3] I have sent again for it, and if it comes will bring it with me.

Yours truly and aff[ectionatel]y.

Henry

MANUSCRIPT: Longfellow Trust Collection. ADDRESS: Mrs. Anna Pierce/Portland

1. Francis Fessenden (1839–1906), born on March 18, became a major general in the Civil War.
2. Franklin Pierce, 14th President of the U.S., had been an intimate friend of Anne Longfellow Pierce's husband. He served in the Senate, 1837–1842.
3. Richard Mant (1776–1848), an indefatigable English writer, was bishop of Down and Connor at this time. The book referred to here (and in Letters No. 471 and 474) is unidentified.

## 477. *To George William Welker and Solomon Saylor Middlekauff*[1]

Cambridge. June 15. 1839

To Messrs Geo. W. Welker and S. S. Middlekauff.

Gentlemen,

I have had the honor of receiving your letter of the 7th. informing me, that I have been elected an honorary member of the "Goethean Literary Society of Marshall College."

I beg you to express to the members of this Society, my thanks for this mark of their good-will, and my acceptance of the honor they have done me.

Wishing you much prosperity in your literary career,

very respectfully yours
Henry W. Longfellow.

MANUSCRIPT: Franklin and Marshall College Library. ADDRESS: To/Mr. George W. Welker/Marshall College/Mercersburg. Pa. POSTMARK: NEW-YORK JUL 30

1. Walker (1817–1869) and Middlekauff (1818–1845) were student officers of the Goethean Literary Society of Marshall College, in which Willis Gaylord Clark had proposed Longfellow's membership (*Clark Letters*, p. 50; *New Light on Longfellow*, pp. 66–67). The discrepancy between Longfellow's date and the postmark is unexplained; he may simply have forgotten to post the letter until his trip to New York late in July.

## 478. *To Stephen Longfellow*

Cambridge. June 16. 1839

My dear Father,

I certainly have not behaved very handsomely since my return; and the hint I received from you yesterday reminds me, that I promised to write you as soon as I reached Cambridge, and have let a whole fortnight elapse without fulfilling that promise.[1] I have not time to write; and have on hand a quantity of unanswered letters, quite awful to look at.

I have begun to print Hyperion, and have three men at work, setting type, upon it. I hope to have it out in about a month; and shall unless Colman delays. As to the *money* part of the business, I have him pretty closely bound up by papers signed. He is to pay me 375 dollars, by his notes, on the day of publication: said notes payable 187.50 in three months and the remainder in six months. So unless he *fails* before next Winter, I shall probably get my money. At all events I get the book very handsomely printed, and widely circulated; and this is a great point. As to its success, I am very sanguine. I look upon the work of my hands with a very complacent smile; and it will take a great deal of persuasion to convince me, that the book is not good. This is my candid opinion.

Mary [Longfellow] is very well, and seems to enjoy herself not a little; driving out in the paternal carryall, or talking sentimental on the sofa with Mrs. [Simon] Greenleaf, who is very powerful on the subject of old friendships, and such matters. I go to see her as often as I can; and people are busy calling, and inviting, and so forth; and thus the time passes away.

I had the pleasure last evening of receiving a long letter from Anne, which I shall answer soon, and a few lines from Alex. I know not how I can get the books he wants. Sumner has left England, and will not return there. However, I will bear it in mind, and if I have an opportunity, get them.[2]

*Tarring* the trees did not succeed with the canker-worms. On the ten magnificent elms which stand in front of my window, not one leaf is to be seen. All is as bare as in winter. We shall try again in Autumn. They are talking seriously here of forming a Society for the su[p]pression of Canker Worms; and making a regular crusade against them.

I have no news to send you at present, but hope to have some soon. With much love to you all, and hope of good results from Dr. Wood's skill,[3]

very truly yours
Henry W. Longfellow

P.S. My short visit in Portland did me much good; I have been much better since.

MANUSCRIPT: Longfellow Trust Collection. ADDRESS: Hon. S. Longfellow/Portland/Me POSTMARK: CAMBRIDGE MS. JUN 17

1. Longfellow had returned on June 4 from Portland.

2. In a letter of June 14, 1839, Alexander had asked his brother to obtain through Sumner the *Reports of the Commissioners appointed to consider and recommend a General System of Railways for Ireland. Presented to both Houses of Parliament by command of Her Majesty* (1838), which he had seen reviewed in the *Quarterly Review*, LXIII (January 1839), 1–60.

3. Stephen Longfellow had reported in a letter of June 13, 1839, "Dr. Wood has had me on my back for the last week, but whether for good or ill remains to be proved."

## 479. *To Charles Folsom*

[Cambridge, July 1, 1839]

My dear Sir,

Felton says we shall want hereafter a *Bowdler* to publish a *family* Edition of this work. As to the *blind beggary* on p. 106 he thinks they ought to be prosecuted for an indecent exposure of their persons. I have thrown a cloak over them.[1]

Yrs. truly
H. W. Longfellow

MANUSCRIPT: Boston Public Library. ENDORSEMENT: Rec'd 1 July, 1839.

1. *Hyperion* was being printed by Folsom's firm — Folsom, Wells, and Thurston. Since the bowdlerization was completed, the nature of the "indecent exposure" cannot be known.

480. *To Samuel Colman*

Cambridge. July 6. 1839.

My dear Sir,

In compliance with your wishes I have ordered 2200 copies of Hyperion to be printed. I do it with the understanding, that you will give your notes for $250 each, instead of the sums mentioned in the agreement; and that I shall be allowed 50 copies instead of 25 for distribution. This will leave you 150, which strikes me as a very large number.[1]

The first Vol. (212 pp.) will be done to-day: and the whole in a fortnight, I hope. It is *very* handsome; and those who praise you for publishing *handsome* books, will now have some reason for saying so.

Will you have the books, or any part of them done up here? and in the English style, uncut? Those for the Boston market I should think you would.

With best regards to Mellen and Cutter,

Very truly yours in haste
Longfellow

P. S. By the way; I was shocked yesterday to see in the New York Review that *Undine* was coming out in your Library of Romance. This is one of the Tales of the Wonderhorn. Have you forgotten?[2]

I intend to come to New York, as soon as I get through with printing Hyperion; and we will bring this design to an arrangement, and one more beside.[3]

MANUSCRIPT: Boston Public Library. ADDRESS: Samuel Colman Esq/VIII Astor House/New York. POSTMARK: CAMBRIDGE MS. JUL 8 ANNOTATION: Stop the L. Romance and put into the WonderHorn. PUBLISHED: Higginson, *Longfellow*, pp. 139–140.

1. The "Memorandum of Agreement" (see Letter No. 473), had been based on an edition of 1500 copies. Colman, however, wanted more copies for promotion purposes and on June 18 wrote, "I have concluded that if you do not object I should prefer to print 2000 besides those for Editors instead of 1500. It will of course be all the better for you." Longfellow here reveals his terms for the new proposal. There is no record of Colman's reaction, but publication apparently proceeded in accordance with this new arrangement.

2. See *North American Review*, V (July 1839), 249. Longfellow had apparently told Colman that he wished to include *Undine*, a fairy tale published in 1811 by the Baron de la Motte Fouqué, in his projected anthology for children (473.2). When the Wonderhorn plan fell through, *Undine* appeared later in the year as the second volume in Colman's Library of Romance, edited by Grenville Mellen.

3. The additional project is unknown.

481. *To Stephen Longfellow*

Cambridge July 9. 1839

My dear Father,

At length this long term draws to a close. I have nothing more, but my Examination next Monday. Need I say I quite rejoice. I am worn out; and in a few minutes start with Sam for Nahant to pass a day or two, and get revived.

The printing of Hyperion lags behind my wishes. Only the first Vol. is through the press. I am impatient, to have it out; as I dare say you are. I do not send you the sheets, because I think you will have more pleasure in reading it all at once.

The parts for Commencement are not assigned; but Sam stands well, and will have a good part, though not an Oration. He does not know yet, what his fate is to be and is quite restless about it. He comes out very honorably, and has improved his time to the utmost I think; and therefore we have every reason to be satisfied. He deserves great credit for his good conduct and attention through the whole course. I think very highly of his mind and his heart.

With much love to all

Very truly yours
Henry W. Longfellow

MANUSCRIPT: Longfellow Trust Collection. ADDRESS: Hon. Stephen Longfellow/ Portland/Me. POSTMARK: BOSTON MAS. JUL 10 ENDORSEMENT: Henry — Jun [*sic*] 9. 1839

482. *To Samuel Ward*

Cambridge. July. 13. 1839

My dear Sam,

It grieves me sore that I cannot meet you tomorrow at New-Port, and return with you to New York on Monday, as you propose in your last, which I received on returning from Nahant two days ago, and should have answered by the return post, had not pressing engagements prevented. It will not be in my power to leave Cambridge for a week or ten days. I cannot move an inch till Hyperion is out of press. We are now half through the Second Volume. I must bring you a copy with me. You will like it; because you will understand it with the *heart* as well as with the *brain*. I hope others will likewise; for if the book does not succeed will not the author, — as an *author,* — be *dished*?

Please tell Mr. Cogswell that his last No. is *excellent.* Motley has said the best thing on Faust (so far as it goes) that I have ever heard or read.[1] The French Revolution-paper (Perkins?) I like also exceedingly; even his placing Carlyle above Thiers as a historic scene-painter.[2] I have long believed with the Poet Wordsworth that there are

"Thoughts which lie too deep for *Thiers*."[3]

Who wrote the interesting paper on Claudius?[4] Capital; only no poetry, — none of those peculiar, racy, Charles-Lamb-like little pieces, — and those quaint fancies; — for example in the Happy Peasant, when he says; speaking of hay and harvests

"O he who never hath *seen* this,
He cannot *understand*;
One takes God in the very act,
With blessings in his hand."[5]

On Monday the 15th I shall be much less agreeably employed than in sailing down the Sound with you; namely in my College Examinations, which fall upon that day. So I must of necessity disappoint you. I will however come at the earliest moment. Doubt it not. And will write you in advance.

Have you fished me up a Frenchman yet? Dont forget; as I am in great need and shall hope to make the necessary arrangements during my visit.

My kindest regards to your family; — to *Goethe*; to Cogswell, and the Philosopher [Henry M. Francis], and yourself.

Very truly yours
Henry W Longfellow.

MANUSCRIPT: Clifton Waller Barrett Collection, University of Virginia. ADDRESS: To/Samuel Ward Jr. Esq/New York POSTMARK: CAMBRIDGE MS. JUL 15

1. A review of Goethe's *Werke und nachgelassene Werke* (Stuttgart and Tübingen, 1834) in the *New York Review*, V (July 1839), 1–48.

2. "The French Revolution," *New York Review*, V (July 1839), 109–135. The author was James Handasyd Perkins (437.10), a former pupil of Cogswell's at the Round Hill School, Northampton.

3. Longfellow's pun derives from the last line of "Intimations of Immortality": "Thoughts that do often lie too deep for tears."

4. "Matthias Claudius," *New York Review*, V (July 1839), 173–200. Ward did not answer Longfellow's query about the author.

5. A translation of Claudius, "Der glückliche Bauer," stanza 7.

483. *To Lewis Gaylord Clark*

Cambridge. Saturday. July. 20. 39

My dear Clark,

I had the pleasure of receiving your last, two days ago; and wish in this my answer I could fold you up a "Psalm or something" for your next No. But it may not be; as no "Psalm nor nothing" has sung itself through my lips of late. Since I *last wrote you* I have been ill. In fact, ever since I last saw you I have been so; — all the Spring, suffering, and finally obliged to give up all work, and get well; which I have not yet fully accomplished, though I am better. Next week I hope to see you. I shall be in N.Y. say on Wednesday or Thursday. You will find me at *Ward's*; with whom I am to pass a few days, in the absence of his family.

As you go down Broad Way tomorrow morning, just stop in at Colman's (No VIII! Astor House) and say to him, that Hyperion is printed and waiting his orders. I shall bring you a copy, when I come. I hope it will be in season for notice in [the] August No.[1] I hope the book will succeed. If it does not I shall be pushed to the verge of despair.

When does Willis sail? His going to Europe reminds me of the old Lady's dying. She used to call her family up every night to take a final leave: — got into a habit of doing it, and liked it. Willis does the same. Every now and then comes a note saying; "I'm off next week. Send letters of introduction. Dont fail. Good bye. God Bless you. Yours truly. *Willis G. Clark.*"

||One acts accordingly; sends letters in blank cover, addressed to Lewis in New York; and some three weeks afterwards finds out it is 'no go.' When I see him swung off I shall believe he has||[2] gone.

Felton was duly rebuked by yr. message, which I read to him; Laughed, then turned round and said: "When do you go to N. Y.?" "On thursday." "Well; I *will* send something by you." Perhaps he will send his regards.[3]

Notwithstanding my words about Psalm-singing I shall probably bring you a Poem from the German; merely because you like that one in Colman so much.[4] Dont have any *bad* poetry ||put in to fill up, will you? This is really good, but must be anonymous.||[2]

MANUSCRIPT: Longfellow Trust Collection. ADDRESS: To/Lewis G. Clark Esq/ New York. POSTMARK: CAMBRIDGE MS. JUL 22

1. Clark reviewed *Hyperion* in the September number of the *Knickerbocker* (XIV [1839], 277–280).

2. This restoration is supplied from an incomplete text printed in the *Knickerbocker*, LVII (February 1861), 229.

3. Felton had apparently promised a contribution to the *Knickerbocker* for some time. "Blücher's Ball," his translation from the German of August Follen, finally appeared in the December number (XIV [1839], 563). Longfellow reprinted it in *Poets and Poetry of Europe*, p. 348.

4. See 473.3. The German translation that he took to Clark was "Elegy. Written in the Ruins of an Old Castle" (364.1).

## 484. *To Clara Crowninshield*

[Cambridge] Saturday morning. [July 20, 1839]

My dear Clara.

Since I last saw you I have been seriously indisposed; — which is the reason of my not having been in Boston and of my not sending you the book. I forgot it. Have been a few days at Nahant; and next week go to New York; and then to Portland for the *remainder* of the Vacation.

Cambridge *kills* me. But now the Term and Hyperion are finished, and I am free for six weeks. Free! If you, who have nothing to do — whose *whole* time is your own, — did but know the sweet sound of that word to the *slave* (what am I but a slave?) you would know how delightfully to me sounded the Past Knell of that Chapel Bell. Free for six weeks! And then that book will be published shortly — and will make a noise in the world, (vanity and self-conceit!) and I shall be, like King Lear "*mightily abused*";[1] — but what care I? The *abuse* will not be read by me. I shall carefully avoid such indiscretion.

I send you the Vols. of Göthe. Also Dwight's Translation but not your copy; for Rölker has gone to N.Y.[2]

Can I do anything for you in N.Y.? I go on Wednesday or Thursday next.

Yours truly
H. W. L.

MANUSCRIPT: Brown University Library. ADDRESS: To/Miss Clara Crowninshield/ Hingham

1. *King Lear*, IV, vii, 53.

2. In a letter of July 14, 1839, Clara Crowninshield had asked Longfellow to send her the second volume of Goethe's autobiography and to have Bernard Rölker return her own copy of Dwight's translations from Goethe and Schiller (456.2). MS, Longfellow House.

## 485. *To George Washington Greene*

Cambridge. July 23. 1839

My dear Greene,

Yours of May 22 arrived two or three days ago. I was glad to get it although there was litterally nothing in it. Your "*turn*" to complain;

as if you ever did anything else but complain! Three pages of fault finding you call a letter. I dont. Hang such letters. Find fault to your heart's content! But be more concentrated. There you are in Rome; a central point, with all the world marching and countermarching before you, and you have no more to say than if you were in East Greenwich. And when I want particulars about yourself, you turn it into ridicule, laugh in my face, and then fill a whole page with "broken columns, moonlight and the Coliseum," as if I were a female cousin, and kept an album. This is not fair. I am regularly savage about it. The sheets of yr. articles shall be sent, as you request. The reason why I have not sent them before is absence from Camb. and then ill-health all the Spring and excessive labor in College and out, which led me to procrastinate and forget, for which you have just cause to complain; only be short. Let yr. venom be concentrated. In future they shall all be regularly sent. This I promise. Shall be mailed here as soon as published; and if they dont reach you, it is not my fault. I gave direction about yr. North American. Whether it *went,* and *goes* as directed, I know not. As to asking any human being to put these 8vo vols (Prescott's Hist. for instance) into his trunk, and take them through England, and France into Italy is what I will not do even for *you.* Every other means I tried in vain. Could find no opportunity. Atlength Prescott has sent you a *presentation* copy. I hope it will be translated into Italian under yr. eye. The Newspaper shall be sent regularly from next week, until you "cry hold! enough!" [1] It will be the "New Yorker" Edited by Park Benjamin. There is no paper in Boston worth sending. The New Yorker is good — the best, I think, for yr. purpose of any in the U.S. Now having disgorged this crude mass, let us pass to more important matters. Is not Sumner a glorious youth? with a *halo* round his head, as it were. His presence is beneficent; and we all await his return with fluttering impatience. A warm hearted manly fellow; and an ardent friend. I know you must have enjoyed his society. Of course he told you all about my *affaire du coeur* and of the Lady, sang the praises I trust till the Ruins of old Rome reëchoed the name. Since my last nothing has occurred *pro.* or *con.* You have probably smiled at the enthusiasm with which I have spoken of this thing in my letters, and said "O, he will get over it! He can get over it if he has a mind to!" Nevertheless, I have not got over it. I am as much in love as ever. Depend upon it my dear George, there are two mighty wills at work here; and as yet the victory hangs doubtful. The lady says she *will not*! I say she *shall*! It is not *pride,* but the madness of passion. I visit her; sometimes pass an evening alone with her. But not one word is ever spoken on a certain topic. No whining, — no beseeching, — but a steel-like silence. This *is* pride. So we both stand eyeing each other like lions. She is now absent in the country; gone with her sister, to pass the Summer. She thinks perhaps that during the long vacation I shall stroll that way. She is mistaken. Such are not my tactics. I move not a step toward that city.[2] But next week I shall fire off a rocket, which I trust will make a commotion in that citadel. Perhaps the garrison will capitulate; — perhaps the rocket may burst and kill me. You will know soon. I mean to say that I have written a Romance during the last year, into which I have put my feelings, — my hopes and sufferings for the last *three* years. Things are shadowed forth with distinctness enough to be understood; and yet so mingled with fiction in the events set down as to raise doubt, and perplexity. The *Feelings* of the book are true; — the *Events* of the story mostly fictitious. The heroine of course bears a resemblance to *the lady,* without being an exact portrait; so that the reader will say "It is! — no, it is not! And yet it must be!" Dont misunderstand me. There is no betrayal of confidence; — no real scenes described; — and the lady so painted (unless I much deceive myself) as to make her fall in love with her own sweet image in the book. Now I hardly need tell you that I look forward with intense interest to next week. The publication of the book will probably call down upon my head tremendous censure; and I trust also equal applause. As a literary work it far surpasses anything I have before written. How could it be otherwise, when you remember the circumstances of its origin. The book is a *reality*; not a shadow, or ghostly semblance of a book. My heart has been put into the printing-press and stamped on the pages. Whatever the public may think of it, it will always be valuable to me, and to my friends because it is a part of me. *I believe it*; therefore *some* others will believe it. They *must* be struck with the sincerity, with which things are said. *You* will be, for one; and will acknowledge, that the agony of soul which has found expression in this Romance, is not small, nor to be sneered at. So if any silly, Boston traveller passes your way anon and speaks slightingly of "*Hyperion*" set it not down against the book, but against the speaker. *I am in earnest*! I lay aside all sham modesty and speak to *my friend* as I really feel, having neither *time* nor *need* for apologizing because I speak what I think. "*Hyperion*" is the name of the *Book*, not of the *hero.* It merely indicates that here is the life of one, who likewise in his feelings and purposes is a "Son of Heaven and Earth" and though obscured by clouds yet "*moves on high.*" Farther than this the name has nothing to do with the book; and in fact is mentioned only once in the whole course of it. I expect to be mightily abused. People will say, that I am the hero of my own Romance, and compare myself to the Sun, to Hyperion Apollo. This is not so. I wish only to embody certain feelings, which are mine, not to magnify myself. I do not care for abuse if it is real, manly, *hearty* abuse. All that I fear is the "*laudatur et alget*"[3] — the damnation of faint praise. That I hope to avoid *this* time. And now, my dear George, just look one moment at the circumstances under which I have been at work upon this book — or rather under which the book has been at work on me. My wife's death — my meeting with this lady, — my return and a whole year's delirium of hope, before she came, during which my imagination had time to forge fetters as strong as the threads of life — then her return and the catastrophy — and an eighteen months' struggle, — humiliation — wounded pride, wounded affection, — derision, — conflicting feelings enough to drive one mad. Well, during the last year, and under this pressure the book has been produced. And if now and then there be a passage, which to a *well man*, in the light of sober reason may seem a little morbid, — is it any wonder! I fear, my dear Greene that I have been *very* near madness and even death, within the last few months. This disappointment and vexation ended in fever and a violent determination of blood to the head. And under all this I was working myself to death, having an *immense* deal to do in College, owing to the absence of my French instructer. Twice I have been obliged to give up all work, then rallied again, and finally brought the term to a close. I have been thus reeling and struggling along, like a wrecked ship, near stranding upon some tombstone, as on [a] sunken rock. Through the whole I have fought courageously, and am now better. The long summer vacation will, I trust, restore my health. Now I think you will understand "Hyperion"; and so far from its appearing extravagant to you, seen in this light, it will look absolutely tame. If so, attribute it [to] Felton, whom I have to thank for watching me very closely, and knocking in the head many very extravagant chapters and passages. And now we will dismiss the subject, and close by saying to your dear little wife, how much, how ardently I desire to sit at her table, and devour that "*piatto di strozzapreti* [dish of large noodles]" she promises me when I *do* come; and drink from the flask of Montefiasconi — the king of all wines — "il Re d'ogni Vino" as Redi sings.[4] By the way, you need not send the wine I wrote about. I have ordered some through the Consul, *Alessandro*,[5] who is now in Italy, or peradventure on his way back. He is to bring us sundry flagons in which you shall be kindly remembered. And now for American Literature. Hillhouse is publishing a new edition of his poems.[6] Prescott is writing a History of the

Conquest of Mexico. *Rufus Dawes* has pubd. a poem(?) called *Geraldine*, most rabid trash — trash with a tin-pail tied to its tail, — yet Nat Willis says in his "À l'Abri," that if "God ever made a poet, it was Rufus Dawes"!!! Willis's "A l'Abri" is a thin 12mo. collection of letters written from his country seat on the Susquehannah, and pubd. first in the "*Mirror*" as "Letters from Under a Bridge" — very racy, and beautiful![7] Willis is now in England. His father-in-law is just dead. Grenville Mellen has become Editor of a Magazine[8] which cannot live more than a year. His rhymes grow worse and worse. He is also Editor of Colman's Library of Romance; and has just been wofully cut up by Benjamin in the New Yorker.[9] I am sorry, upon the whole; though I do not like his "*poetry and things.*" Hillard has a new and beautiful Edition of Spencer in the press, with Preface and notes by himself.[10] Felton is busily at work upon a translation of Menzel's German Literature, which will be out in October next. He is doing it finely. This you knew before. Sam Ward has delivered and published a Lecture on the Battle of Long Island, likewise cut up by Aristarchus Benjamin; at which the said Samuel winced. (Sam and I are great friends. I am going to make him a visit next week.) Yr. "*poor relation*" notion is all nonsense. I suppose the package miscarried.[11] New York is becoming more and more literary. It will soon be the center of everything in this country; — the Great Metropolis. All young men of talent are looking that way; and new literary projects in the shape of Magazines and Weekly papers are constantly started, showing great activity, and zeal, and enterprise. They are becoming also a little less bigoted in their religious notions; and Mr. Brooks, ci-devant *Unitarian* (mark that) *clergyman* in Hingham, Mass. has been elected Professor of Botany (or something), in the New York University!!![12] Besides, they have at length got rid of that bob-tailed, striped bunting of a Chancellor, [James McFarlane] *Matthews.*[13] Do you remember him? Cooper (Novelist) is up to his arm-pits in lawsuits; — libel cases, against the Editors of newspapers for abusing him. If people dont praise his books, he prosecutes them for libel. Decidedly a disagreeable individual.[14] Bulwer*ism* is dying out. Marryat*ism* ditto. Boz, (Dickens) reigns supreme, as the *popular* writer. Bancroft has written a violent article against Göthe in the Christian Examiner.[15] The *Loco-focos* are organizing a new politico-literary system. They shout Hosanna to every *loco-foco* authorling, and speak coolly of, if they do not abuse, every other. They puff *Bryant* loud and long;[16] likewise my good friend *Hawthorne* of "*Twice-Told-Tales*"; also a Mr. O'Sullivan, once Editor of the "Democratic Review," — now Secretary of Legation at Paris; — a young man, with weak eyes, and green spectacles, who looks like you, and is a *Humbug* nevertheless and notwithstanding.[17] Washn. Irving is writing away like fury in the Knickerbocker; — he had better not; — old remnants — odds and ends, — about Sleepy Hollow, and Granada. What a pity. A *Miss* Fuller has pubd. a translation of "*flunky*" Eckermann's Conversations with Göthe.[18] (If you dont know what a flunky is ask the first Scot you meet.) Dr. Bird a new Novel which I have not read.[19] I like the Dr. exceedingly as a man, but cannot stand his books. Can you? Such, in brief, is the literary aspect of the time.

Mr. Ellis has arrived, bringing your Article. I have not seen him; do not know him, and do not want to know him.[20] Dr. Palfrey told me he had recd. the Article, but had not yet had time to read it. I suppose I shall not see it, till it is printed, as the Dr. choses to read his own proof sheets. *Micali* I read, and thought very highly of.[21] It seemed to me a masterly sketch; though the subject did not interest me; and of course, not having read the book, I knew very little of it. I thought it the best paper of yours I ever read — the most complete and elaborate.

Willis G. Clarke talks of visiting Europe this summer. If so you will see him in Rome. To-day, Mr. Bowen, one of our tutors, takes his departure for England.[22] He will be in Rome in the Spring. He is a friend of Felton's, who will give him a letter to you. What a bore it must be to you, to have so many querulous, self-sufficient Yankees to attend to! I dont think Bowen will bore you. You will be glad to see him for Felton's sake. By the way, Felton has a baby, which looks like me, they say. 'Tis well for us that we dont live in Paris.

Farewell. Where is Sumner? Gone. Well, I suppose he has; and left you once more all alone. My kindest regards to him, if he passes yr. way again. To yr. dear little wife, my most affectionate remembrance. Felton sends you a hearty salutation. You probably did not receive his last letter.

Very truly yours
Longfellow

P.S. The M.S. of Tasso's Love and Madness was duly sent to Davis and Brooks.[23]

Recd. yours of Jan. 31 }
May 22 }

MANUSCRIPT: Longfellow Trust Collection. ADDRESS: To/George W. Greene Esq./Consul of the United States./Rome./Italy./par le Hâvre. POSTMARKS: OUTRE-MER 26 AOUT 39 LE HAVRE/PARIS 27 AOUT (60)/VIA DI PT. BEAUVOISIN

1. Cf. *Macbeth*, V, vii, 63.

2. Fanny Appleton was spending the summer in Stockbridge.

3. Juvenal, *Satires,* I, 74.

4. In *Bacco in Toscano* Francesco Redi (1626–1694) refers to the wine not of Montefiasconi but of Montepulciano as "the king of all wines."

5. Pietro D'Allesandro, 23 Central Wharf, Boston, was consul for Sicily and Sardinia.

6. James Abraham Hillhouse, *Dramas, Discourses, and Other Pieces* (Boston, 1839), 2 vols.

7. Rufus Dawes, *Geraldine, Athenia of Damascus, and Miscellaneous Poems* (New York, 1839), had recently appeared as Vol. I of Samuel Colman's Library of American Poets. In *A L'Abri, or The Tent Pitch'd* (New York, 1839) Willis wrote an encomium on Dawes that Longfellow quotes inaccurately: "Rufus Dawes is a poet if God ever created one, and he *lives* his vocation as well as *imagines it* . . . He is our Coleridge, and his talk should have reverent listeners" (p. 119).

8. *Colman's Monthly Miscellany.* It survived for only three months — July–September, 1839.

9. In reviewing *Undine, a Miniature Romance* (480.2), Park Benjamin stated that Mellen was entitled to an auto-da-fé: "The fire should be built of his own poems and three volumes of the 'Library of Romance,' of which he is proclaimed the EDITOR!" *New-Yorker,* VII (July 20, 1839), 285.

10. George Stillman Hillard, ed., *The Poetical Works of Edmund Spenser.* With introductory observations on the Faerie Queene, and notes, by the editor (1st American edition, Boston, 1839), 5 vols.

11. In complaining that Ward had neglected to forward a parcel to him, Greene wrote, "Sam is a smart fellow, but is too rich and I am a *poor* relation" (Greene to Longfellow, January 31, 1839). For Benjamin's criticism of Ward's lecture, see 469.2.

12. Charles Brooks (1795–1872), a Harvard graduate of 1816, had served as pastor of the Third Congregational Church in Hingham, 1821–1838, after which he was appointed professor of natural history at New York University.

13. Longfellow's antagonism may be traced to the failure of his negotiations with Mathews (264.3) for a professorship at New York University. See Letter No. 274.

14. For Cooper's war with the press — which he carried on over the years by means of letters, articles, prefaces, and libel suits — see E. R. Outland, *The Effingham Libels on Cooper* (Madison, 1929). Cooper was particularly incensed at this time because his newspaper opponents were suggesting the creation of an "Effingham Libel Fund" to be used in their own defense. Longfellow's response to criticism was the antithesis of Cooper's, which accounts for his opinion here.

15. In a review of John S. Dwight's translations from Goethe and Schiller (456.2) in the *Christian Examiner,* XXVI (July 1839), 360–378.

16. This partiality is explained by the fact that the Loco-focos, or radical Democrats, had a voice for some years in Bryant's *New York Evening Post.*

17. John Louis O'Sullivan (1813–1895), a graduate of Columbia, 1831, published many of Hawthorne's tales during his editorship of the *Democratic Review.* In 1839 he applied for the position of secretary of legation in Paris, and his appointment was publicly but prematurely announced. Ambassador Lewis Cass preferred his son-in-law-to-be, Robert Ledyard, and O'Sullivan gracefully withdrew his application and published an explanation of the matter in a letter to the *Evening Post* dated August 30, 1839 (*Niles' National Register,* LVII [September 14, 1839], 45–46).

18. Sarah Margaret Fuller's *Conversations with Goethe in the Last Years of His*

*Life* (Boston, 1839) was a translation from the German of Johann Peter Eckermann (1792–1854), Goethe's secretary and editor of his posthumous works.

19. Robert Montgomery Bird, *The Adventures of Robin Day* (Philadelphia, 1839).

20. George Edward Ellis (1814–1894), a Harvard graduate of 1833, was returning to America after two years abroad to assume the pastorate of the Harvard Unitarian Church in Charlestown. Longfellow's reluctance to know him is unexplained. Ellis later served as professor of systematic theology at Harvard and wrote many books, sermons, and tracts. For Greene's manuscript, see 464.6.

21. See 437.9.

22. Francis Bowen (1811–1890) was the brother of Charles Bowen, one of Longfellow's publishers. He graduated from Harvard in 1833 and held an instructorship there in intellectual philosophy and political economy, 1835–1839. After his return from Europe he edited the *North American Review*, 1843–1853, and was then appointed Alford Professor of Natural Religion, Moral Philosophy, and Civil Polity at Harvard.

23. See 407.1. Having failed to place Wilde's manuscript in Boston, Longfellow carried out Greene's instruction in his letter of December 6, 1838, to forward it to the New York firm (464.5).

## 486. *To Stephen Longfellow*

Cambridge. July. 27 1839

My dear Father,

In a couple of hours I shall be on my way to New York. It requires some nerve to move Southward in such weather. I had much rather take the Portland steamer. But I must attend to my affairs with Colman; for fear he should fail; and I must get a French instructer for next year.

The book is finished. I expect some copies from the binder to-day. If they come I shall put one into the hands of James [Greenleaf] to be sent to you; though it must not go out of the family, before you see it advertised as published. It is a very handsome book. I hope you will like it; and think it better than Outre-Mer, as I do.

I do not know how long I shall be gone. I have an invitation from my friend Sam. Ward in the city: — another from his wife at Redhook on the Hudson;[1] and a third from Washington Irving at Sleepy Hollow. I think it doubtful, however, whether I go farther than the city. I shall do pretty much as the spirit prompts at the moment.

I hope to come back in better trim than I go. I am a martyr to tooth-ache; and for three months have not been free from it a day. It makes me feverish and uncomfortable. Yesterday I had two teeth out, and hope for a little rest.

When I come to Portland I trust I shall find you quite hale and robust. I have been thinking of a voyage for you, mother and myself; namely, to *Trinidad de Cuba,* next Winter; an affair of two months.

Will you go? Will *you,* mother? Yes. I have just been reading a book on the subject, which has inspired me with a desire to see this island. It will make a fine trip for us.

In haste truly and affectionately
Henry W. Longfellow.

P. S. Has Alex heard from Col. Fessenden? I wrote to him about a situation on the Eastern Rail-road.[2]

MANUSCRIPT: Longfellow Trust Collection. ADDRESS: Hon. S. Longfellow/Portland/Me. POSTMARK: CAMBRIDGE MS. JUL 27

1. Emily Astor Ward was spending the summer at "Rokeby," a stone mansion in Red Hook township built by her grandfather, General John Armstrong (1758–1843), and owned by her parents.

2. This letter is unrecovered.

## 487. *To Stephen Longfellow*

New York. August. 2. 1839

My dear father,

Instead of going out this morning, I will sit down quietly and write you a letter. I am enjoying myself highly in this red-hot city; being very cool and quiet in the home of my friend Ward. We are keeping bachelor's Hall, — the family having gone to New-Port; and Mr. Cogswell, my friend Sam and myself being the only persons left in this great palace of a dwelling. During the heat of the day, I sit at home in the cool large rooms; and stroll out in the evening. So you need not fear Cholera nor Yellow Fever, whatever the papers may say.

To-day I dine with Mr. Higbee. Mrs. Henly is there; — and Henrietta, and Miss Luce,[1] and Miss Rogers[2] has been. So in a call yesterday I saw half my Washington friends. The Commodore [A. S. Wadsworth] and his wife are not coming before September.

How do you like Hyperion? My friends here are very extravagant in their praises; and if the Public coincides with their judgement I shall be quite famous. It will be published next week.

By the way, I had yesterday the offer of a Professorship in the University of Alabama at Tuscaloosa. I declined and recommended Sam. Good Climate, and two-thousand dollars a year. My friend, who consulted me on the subject, and through whom the offer came, says he will write immediately, and thinks the place may be had. So Sam must not engage in a school, till he sees me or hears from me. This will be a grand situation for him, if he can get it; and make him quite indipendent. I shall not loose sight of it.[3]

Aug. 3.

I had a pleasant dinner at the Higbee's. They told me young Alexr. had just passed through town.[4] He is probably with you now.

I do not know when I shall leave New York. Not till I find a French Instructer and get my pay from Colman.

With much love to all.

Very truly yours
Henry W. Longfellow

MANUSCRIPT: Longfellow Trust Collection. ADDRESS: To/Hon. Stephen Longfellow./Portland./Me. POSTMARK: NEW-YORK AUG 5

1. Presumably a sister of Stephen Bleeker Luce (1827–1917), who subsequently married Mrs. Henley's daughter Eliza and rose to high rank in the U.S. Navy.

2. One of the daughters of Mrs. Minerva Denison Rodgers (461.2).

3. The chair of modern languages at the University of Alabama was vacant from 1836 to 1841. The university archives contain no record of an offer to Longfellow or of negotiations concerning him or his brother.

4. Alexander Scammell Wadsworth (1828–1862), son of Commodore Wadsworth. He passed through New York on his way from Washington to Portland to visit Longfellow's parents.

## 488. *To the Harvard Corporation*

Cambridge. August. 17. 1839

To the President and Corporation of Harvard University,
Gentlemen,

Feeling it important, that before the commencement of another term, the place of French Instructer should be filled, I take the liberty of recommending Mr. Chs. Hutet of New York, as a person qualified to fill the station. In accordance with your wishes I took charge of the French instruction during the past year; but am unwilling to do so longer. It seems to me of great importance, that the French should be taught by a Frenchman, as the other modern languages are by natives of the countries where spoken; and I therefore respectfully request, that Mr. Hutet may be appointed.[1]

Your Obt. Ser[v]t.
Henry W. Longfellow

MANUSCRIPT: Harvard College Papers, IX, 316. PUBLISHED: *Professor Longfellow of Harvard*, pp. 34–35.

1. Longfellow had apparently interviewed Hutet, about whom nothing is known, during his recent visit to New York. In a letter of August 31, 1839, Sam Ward wrote that Hutet had withdrawn his name from consideration.

489. *To Stephen Longfellow*

Cambridge Sept. 1. 1839

My dear Father,

I was to write you as soon as I had any news to send you. I am better than my promise, for I write you sooner. I have not yet heard from New York. Probably Mr. Astor is out of town, or my friend Ward, to whom I wrote; so that upon this point I am no wiser than when I left you.[1] In College, however, matters seem to be coming to a crisis. Since my return I have received the following Vote of the Corporation:

"At a Meeting of the President and Fellows of Harvard College held Aug. 19. '39 — A letter from Professor Longfellow recommending a French Instructer was read; whereupon — Voted — That it is not [*sic*] inexpedient to increase the Number of instructers in Modern Languages, and that the Smith Professor ought to continue to give all instruction required in the French Language."

Now the Smith Professor does not wish nor intend to do any such thing, if he can help it. At all events, if I stay I shall hit upon some way of shortening the time devoted in instruction in languages; or the labor will finish me before Winter. In all probability I shall have a letter from New York tomorrow; and if the proposals of Mr. Astor are as good as I expect they will be, I shall feel very much inclined to accept them. No doubt, if I could bring myself to give up all my time to the College, and not pursue any other study, I could get along very comfortably. But the idea of standing still, or of going backward is not to be entertained by such an ardent temper as mine. Tomorrow, or next day, I will write you again, if anything occurs.

We had a very good Commencement — the best we have had for a great many years; according to general consent. Sam performed very handsomely. Mr. Devereux, your Salem friend,[2] spoke to me in high terms of the performance; and desires his regards and compliments to you. Sam has had a new offer, and a more favorable one; namely to take charge of two boys in Bishop Doane's family at Burlington; board, lodging, and a salary of $500. I think he had better take it; though Doane is not much beloved in this quarter; being looked upon as a tyrannical personage.[3] I shall keep Sam here till we can hear from you. He is now in Boston. I have not seen him since the offer was made.

Stephen is well, and seems to enjoy his visit highly. I am persuading him to stay a few days longer; and shall keep him as long as I can.

With much love truly
Henry W. Longfellow.

MANUSCRIPT: Longfellow Trust Collection. ADDRESS: Hon. Stephen Longfellow/ Portland/Me POSTMARK: CAMBRIDGE MS. SEP 2

1. On August 21, 1839, Sam Ward wrote to Longfellow to inquire if he would consider accompanying his brother-in-law, John Jacob Astor III (1822–1890), as tutor and companion on a six-month educational tour of Europe. Asked to "say No at once" if his engagements precluded acceptance, Longfellow decided to apply for the position, although his answer to Ward has been lost.

2. Humphrey Devereux (1779–1867), whom Stephen Longfellow had known at Harvard, was the last survivor of the class of 1798.

3. George Washington Doane (1799–1859) was the Episcopal Bishop of New Jersey, 1832–1859, and a leading High Churchman. Two weeks later, on September 13, Stephen Longfellow replied that the offer to Sam had been withdrawn.

## 490. *To Stephen Longfellow*

Cambridge. Saturday morning. [Sept. 7, 1839]

My dear Father,

I write a few words by Stephen to say how much I have enjoyed his visit, and that he seems to have enjoyed it no less. He will tell you all, which I could write, of Commencement and Phi Beta Kappa.

Hyperion attracts great attention; and excites very strong and op[p]osite feelings. Some praise and others condemn in no measured terms; and the book sells with a rapidity far beyond my expectations. I hear that a new edition will soon be called for; which, if so, will be a triumph, considering the nature of the book. People seem to be much puzzled about the book, and some are quite angry because they cannot see through it, as easily as their A.b.c. But I have the approbation of those whose approbation I most desire; and of course do not much care how others curse and abuse. What delights me is that it calls forth very *strong* and decided opinions. I am free for once from the *laudatur et alget.*[1]

The New York affair remains suspended for the present. Old Mr. Astor[2] has taken a notion into his head, that the heir of his house, and inheritor of his name shall *not* go to Europe. When this caprice will pass away no one knows. However I have faith, that it will all come right at last; and that I shall go, and devote myself wholly to literature, without any breaks or interruptions. I shall then produce something which will live. Meanwhile, I have organized my classes and the term begins under very favorable circumstances, save the one you are aware of, namely no French Instructer.

With much love to all

Very affectionately yours
Henry W. Longfellow

MANUSCRIPT: Longfellow Trust Collection. ADDRESS: Hon. Stephen Longfellow/ Portland

1. See 485.3.
2. John Jacob Astor (1763–1848), the merchant prince and grandfather of the boy Longfellow hoped to accompany to Europe. For outcome, see Letter No. 494.

## 491. *To Willis Gaylord Clark*

Cambridge. Sept. 12. 1839

My dear Clark,

The thing uppermost in my mind, at this moment, is to find out why the devil you have stopped my paper![1] It has suddenly been discontinued, without any very apparent reason. Since my return to Cambridge, say three weeks ago, — I have not seen hide nor hair of it, and cannot imagine what the matter is. Can you? Pray inquire.

Likewise, some time last Summer came another bill from the Saturday Evening paper, which I used to take, but never paid for, because you objected to my doing so, saying you had settled the matter and had a receipt from Atkinson.[2] Dont you recollect, last Winter, you told me so "over the parcel gilt goblet"[3] in the quiet back parlor? But for this, I should have sent him the money, without troubling you. Have the goodness to look to this; for I do not wish to be published as a delinquent.

Have you had time to say anything about Hyperion? I have been expecting to get from you sundry newspapers with notices for and against. Please send any, which may fall in your way. The Book succeeds wonderfully well. I hope you have had time to read it, and that at times a responsive chord has sounded in your soul. Some abuse it and say it is not a Romance.[4] But these same persons raised no hue and cry when Byron called his Childe Harold, a *Romaunt,* which is as much as one should say, a Romance.

And now "*How are you*?" What put it in your head to go to Delaware Springs? I was in New York at the time; and had I known the way, might have been tempted to join you for a day or two. But it is too late now. Have you got quite well? Who has bought yr. paper? Are you still sole Editor?[5] I miss your semi-weekly visits much more than your humility would allow you to believe, were I to ||spell|| it out.

This short letter is not so short as yr. respectable last. It is only by way of a fresh start; just as people pour a pail-full of water into a pump *when it sucks.*

I hope this will find you in Phila. Dont fail to send me all notices of Hyperion, particularly the most abusive ones. By the way, what has become of Frankenstein, and my portrait? I wish he would send it to Care of "Sam Ward Jr. Esq" New York. Pray write soon, so that I may know in what frame of mind you are.

Very truly your friend as evermore
Longfellow.

MANUSCRIPT: Harvard College Library. ADDRESS: To/Willis G. Clark. Esq./ Philadelphia. POSTMARK: CAMBRIDGE MS. SEP 13

1. *Relf's Philadelphia Gazette*, of which Clark was editor.

2. Samuel Coate Atkinson, a Philadelphia journalist, had founded the *Saturday Evening Post* with Charles Alexander in 1821 (Frank Luther Mott, *American Journalism: A History of Newspapers in the United States Through 250 Years, 1690–1940* [New York, 1941], p. 205). His name disappears from the Philadelphia directories in 1845.

3. Cf. *King Henry IV, Part II*, II, i, 88.

4. That is, some critics thought of *Hyperion* as a thinly veiled autobiography or potpourri of anecdotes and criticisms rather than as a work of fiction conceived in idealistic terms and presenting the truth of the human heart. For Longfellow's definition of his romance, see Letter No. 485.

5. Clark was suffering from incipient tuberculosis, which took his life on June 12, 1841. Whether he sold the *Gazette* at this time is not known, but he remained its editor until his death.

## 492. *To Lewis Gaylord Clark*

Cambridge Sept. 18. 1839.

THE FIFTH PSALM.

A MIDNIGHT MASS FOR THE DYING YEAR.

I.

YES, the Year is growing old,
And his eye is pale and bleer'd;
Death, with frosty hand and cold,
Plucks the old man by the beard,
Sorely — sorely!

II.

The leaves are falling, falling,
Solemnly and slow;
Caw! caw! the rooks are calling!
It is a sound of wo,
A sound of wo!

III

Through woods and mountain passes,
The winds like anthems roll;

They are chanting solemn masses,
Saying, 'Pray for this poor soul,
Pray — pray!'

IV.

And the hooded clouds, like friars,
Tell their beads in drops of rain,
And patter their doleful prayers;
But it is all in vain,
All in vain!

V

There he stands in the foul weather,
The foolish, fond Old Year,
Crown'd with wild-flowers and with heather,
Like weak, despised Lear,
A King — a King!

VI

Then comes the Summer-like day,
Bids the old man rejoice;
His joy — his last! O the old man gray
Loveth her ever-soft voice,
Gentle and low.

VII

To the crimson woods he saith,
And the voice gentle and low
Of the soft air, like a daughter's breath,
'Pray, do not mock me so!
Do not laugh at me!'

VIII

And now the sweet day is dead;
Cold in his arms it lies;
No stain from its breath is spread
Over the glassy skies,
No mist nor stain!

IX

Then, too, the Old Year dieth,
And the forests utter a moan

Like the voice of one, who crieth
  In the Wilderness alone,
    Vex not his ghost!

X

Then comes, with an awful roar
  Gathering and sounding on,
The Storm-wind from Labrador,
  The wind Euroclydon,
    The Storm-wind!

XI

Howl! howl! and from the forest,
  The red leaves are swept away!
Would the sins, that thou abhorrest,
  O Soul! could so decay,
    And pass away!

XII.

For there shall come a mightier blast,
  There shall be a darker day,
And the stars from heaven down-cast
  Like red leaves be swept away!
    Kyrie Eleyson!
    Christe Eleyson!

HENRY W. LONGFELLOW.[1]

My dear Clark,

I here send you the best poem I ever wrote. It is wild, and wierd, and like the approaching season, which it sings. May you like it! Many thanks for yr. friendly notice of Hyperion. Why dont you send me some papers, that have notices for and against! By the way, when Mr. Edson makes up his accounts he must "*remember me.*" In your *admiration* for new friends, you must not forget the *old*, who have been with you from the first.[2]

Yours truly
Henry W. Longfellow.

MANUSCRIPT: Genealogical Society of Pennsylvania. ADDRESS: To/Lewis G. Clark Esq/Ed. Knickerbocker/New York. ANNOTATION (*by Longfellow*): single. POSTMARK: CAMBRIDGE MS. SEP 20

1. Longfellow's marginal note: "Send Proof to H.W.L./Cambridge." The poem appeared in the *Knickerbocker*, XIV (October 1839), 330–331.

2. Clement Massillon Edson (1811–1853) was Clark's partner on the *Knickerbocker* and had charge of its business affairs. In his reply of October 6, Clark pleaded inability to pay Longfellow for his contributions: "I must ask you, as we have Irving, and three or four of our oldest and best contributors, to indulge Mr. Edson, until more cheering times, with your *patience*" (*Clark Letters*, pp. 107–108).

## 493. *To the Harvard Corporation*

[Cambridge, September, 1839][1]

Gentlemen,

I respectfully beg leave to call your attention once more to the subject of my duties as Smith Professor in the University. You will recollect that when I entered upon my labors in the Department of Modern Languages, the special duties, which devolved upon me as Head of that Department, and Professor of Belles Lettres, were agreed upon by a Committee of the Corporation and myself. Native teachers having always been employed to instruct in the elements and pronunciation of the Modern Languages, the general supervision of the Department, instruction in some of the higher works of modern foreign literature, and certain courses of Lectures were assigned to me. This arrangement, so far as I know, proved satisfactory to all the parties concerned.

You will also recollect, that in the Summer of 1838, two gentlemen, namely the French and the German Instructers, for reason which it is unnecessary to specify, resigned. Another German teacher was immediately appointed; but as no suitable person occurred at the moment to fill the place of French Instructer, the appointment of one was postponed for a season, and I consented to take charge of the Classes in that language. I would respectfully remind you of the distinct understanding at the time, that this arrangement was to be only a temporary one, and to be given up as soon as a suitable appointment could be made. It so happened, however, that I continued to instruct in the French language during the whole year.

At the commencement of the present academic year, I proposed the name of a French gentleman; and this nomination was laid by the President before your honorable body. No appointment, however, was made; but to the contrary a vote was passed, requiring the Smith Professor to instruct all the French classes for the future.

I do not, of course, Gentlemen, call in question your right to modify the duties of my Professorship; and I have proceeded to organize the classes, and commence the instruction in the Elements of the French language agreeably to your vote. But I still entertain the hope that a different arrangement, and one more in harmony with the intent of a Professorship of Belles Lettres, and more advantageous to the University, may yet be made. The symmetry and completeness of the Department are at present destroyed. The organization introduced by Mr. Ticknor, and continued successfully, to the great honor of the University is broken up. The French language has no native teacher. And I submit to you, Gentlemen, whether depriving the Department of the services of such a teacher will not justly be regarded by the public as lessening the advantages of a residence at the University.

I have now under my charge 115 students in French, and 30 in German. Of course, with so many pupils my time is fully occupied. I can exercise but little superintendence over the Department; and have no leisure for the prosecution of those studies, which are absolutely requisite for the proper discharge of the duties originally prescribed to me. When the labor of mastering the Literature of even a single nation is considered, — the utter impossibility of my accomplishing anything, under the present arrangement, — in the various fields of Foreign Literature, over which my Professorship ranges, will be at once apparent. An object of greater importance is clearly sacrificed to one of less. I am required to withdraw from those literary studies and instructions, which had been originally marked out for me, and to devote my time to Elementary Instruction. Now if my labors are of any importance to the College it is to the former class of duties, that the importance belongs. The latter can be performed as well, perhaps better, by an instructer, employed and paid in the usual way. In point of fact, my office as Professor of Belles Lettres is almost annihilated, and I have become merely a teacher of French. To remedy this, Gentlemen, I make to you the following propositions:

I. That I should be wholly separated from the Department of Modern Languages, and be only Professor of Belles Lettres.

II. That I should reside, as now, in Cambridge.

III. That I should not be a member of the Faculty.

IV. That my duties be confined to lecturing during the Autumn Term; and the rest of the year be at my own disposal, as in the case of the Professor of History.

V. In consideration of which I relinquish one half of my present income from the College, and receive only one thousand dollars per annum.[2]

Respectfully submitted &c &c.
Henry W. Longfellow

MANUSCRIPT: Harvard College Papers, IX, 318 ff. PUBLISHED: Higginson, *Longfellow*, pp. 151–154.

1. Carl Johnson believes that Longfellow wrote this letter before September 21,

when in a letter to his father he threatened that "unless they [the members of the Corporation] make some change, I will leave them." In any event, he wrote the letter before September 28, at which time the Corporation met to consider it (*Professor Longfellow of Harvard*, pp. 35, 37).

2. The Corporation did not accept Longfellow's proposal, but his letter did win his release from elementary French instruction. On November 30 the Corporation voted "to provide a native instructer for the French language" (*Professor Longfellow of Harvard*, p. 37), and Longfellow's next recommendation for that position was accepted. See Letter No. 522.

## 494. *To Stephen Longfellow*

Cambridge. Sept. 21. 1839.

My dear Father,

If I had not been very busy, I should have written you sooner to say, that the European Tour is given up. They have concluded, that the young man shall have no travelling companion. Mr. Cogswell is going out with him, to see him comfortably established in Germany; and then leave him to sink or swim. I am very sorry; but as there is no remedy, I must forget it as soon as possible. But my work here grows quite intolerable; and unless they make some change, I will leave them, with or without anything to do. I will not consent to have my life crushed out of me so. I had rather live awhile on bread and water. I feel all the time, that I am doing wrong to stay here under such circumstances; though I know this is not *prudent*.

I was very sorry for Sam's disappointment. Very shabby conduct on the part of Bishop Doane; but just in character; just his sneaking, unprincipled way of acting. However, such a misunderstanding had better come *before,* than *after*; and if Sam can make up his mind to it, it is all well enough. If I were he, I would *not* write to Mr. Cleaveland, nor any one of the family for aid in finding a situation. I have not seen Cleaveland; but no doubt he feels badly enough about it. He is not to blame, in the slightest degree.[1]

This week I have written two more Psalms.[2] One of them you will have in the next Knickerbocker; and the other, I know not where. Moreover I am going to put to press a volume of Poems without delay.[3] All my last pieces; and a selection from the earlier ones; together with Translations.

Yr. letter to Stephen came the same afternoon, that he departed. It is lying here. What shall I do with it?

Much love to all. I hear that Professor Cleaveland is somewhere in these regions, but have not yet seen him. Prof Packard has been here. Did not see him. I am now going into town to see if I can find any of these gentlemen from the East.

Very affectionately yours
Henry W. Longfellow

P. S. Has anything been heard from Washington? When will the Com[modor]e be here? [4]

MANUSCRIPT: Longfellow Trust Collection. ADDRESS: Hon. Stephen Longfellow/ Portland/Me POSTMARK: CAMBRIDGE MS. SEP 21

1. Longfellow's impressions of Bishop Doane's character came from Sarah Perkins Cleveland (1818–1893), wife of Henry Cleveland, whose widowed mother had married the bishop in 1829. Sarah Cleveland's intense dislike of her stepfather is revealed in her letters to her cousin John Murray Forbes (Copies, Longfellow House). On February 29, 1836, for example, she wrote: "We certainly cannot be in Heaven with Doane — for surely his presence would convert it into a h——l . . . Oh! if we could only with a conscience void of offence — sprinkle a little arsenic into his tea — or help him to a dose of prussic acid — how pleasant it would be . . . It is strange how such fiends do live on and on — such specimens of longevity — then they get one foot in the grave and when you think they are just departing — with one desparate struggle they escape the Ring of Zenos and come with a new strength from the contest to begin again their work of wickedness."

2. "Midnight Mass for the Dying Year," composed on September 17, and "The Beleaguered City," completed on September 19.

3. *Voices of the Night*, published by John Owen in Cambridge, December, 1839.

4. Commodore Wadsworth and his family were expected in Portland for the marriage of Mary Longfellow to James Greenleaf on October 22, 1839.

## 495. *To George Washington Greene*

Cambridge. October 1. 1839

My dear Geordie,

I hope the great historian is not trying to persuade you to write a Life of your grandfather, is he? [1] I pray you do not think of it, but stick to *Literature*. On this point, no more at present. Having this single blank page, I must make the most of it. Sumner's letter from the Convent gave me a glimpse of you the other day. It revived the past rather too vividly. Likewise a Miss Hinkley [2] has lately returned from Italy and brought the story of my romantic passion for Madame Julia [Persiani] in days gone by. This, too, revived the past rather too vividly. I sometimes wish myself in Italy again. You have so much freedom there. I have been rending asunder some of the Boston cobwebs of prejudice and narrow-minded criticism by publishing a strange kind of a book, which I have the audacity to call a *Romance*. Most people think it is not, because there is no bloody hatchet in it. You will like it, *notwithstanding*. The Boston papers are very *savage*, and abuse me *shockingly*; for all which I am very glad; inasmuch as it proves to me, that the book is *good.*[3] I take all such things very calmly. If you were here you would be very angry; and would jump out of your skin, like the Danish ghost. I shall send you a copy of the book as soon as I can find an opportunity. It has had a fine run; and a large edition sold in a few weeks.[4] I have now in press a volume of poems, under title "Voices of the Night" — containing all I have written since my residence here — some of my earlier pieces, and some translations. This, too, you shall have by first opportunity. But, hang it, there are no opportunities here in Camb. *Hyperion* is as much a Romance, as Childe Harold or the *Roman de la Rose.* And now, Geordie, you can do me a *very* great favor; — namely by getting these books noticed in the foreign journals; — in Paris for instance, in the *Revue de deux Mondes* &c. You know what *cursed sheep* our countrymen are, and how they follow everything that comes from the other side of the sea. The fact that these books had been noticed in Italy, Germany or France would do me great good. I dont know that I shall need this, but I may; as the *opposition* seems to be *savage* and *strong.*

I went to visit your mother the other day; — "Veni *Newport* peramaenum, Ubi quaerens Georgium Greenum, Non inveni; sed in lignum Fixum reperi Georgii Signum,"[5] — that is to say your miniature, with a *flesh* waistcoast, a moustache and a crooked stick. Decidedly *tippy.* Your father and mother both well. *Nat* was not at home.[6] We talked of you and Maria beside the sounding sea-shore. It is a beautiful spot.

How is the beloved *cara sposa* [wife]? As fair as ever, and as gentle and witty. Some of the critiques upon her friend would amuse her. If I can I will send you some of them; so as to prejudice you against the book; for fear you should like it too well. By the way, what great work are you engaged upon, which is to take you twice as long as the Siege of Troy? You are right. Work on, with God's blessing: and success is inevitable.

Most truly and affectionately yours
Henry W. Longfellow.

N.B. This is only a note by the way — a visiting Card. I shall write you soon.

MANUSCRIPT: Henry E. Huntington Library. ADDRESS: George W. Greene. Esq./ Consul of U.S. America/Rome./par le Havre ANNOTATION (*by Longfellow*): Paid to N. York. 192. POSTMARKS: CAMBRIDGE MS. OCT 1/NEW-YORK OCT 4/OUTRE-MER [*date illegible*] ||LE HAV||RE/PARIS [*date illegible*] (60)/ROMA 18 [*remainder illegible*]/||VIA DI|| PT. BEAUVOISIN/PAID

1. On September 30, 1839, Jared Sparks wrote to Greene, disclaiming the rumor that he was preparing a biography of General Nathanael Greene and urging

Greene himself to take up the project. Sparks gave the letter to Longfellow, who added these remarks to it on the following day. See Letter No. 252 and n. 3.

2. Unidentified. The *Boston Directory* for 1839 yields several Hinckleys, but no Hinkley.

3. Longfellow had read a scathing review of *Hyperion* on the same day that he wrote this letter (Journal, October 1, 1839; *Life*, I, 344–345). The reviewer had concluded that it was "a mongrel mixture of description and criticism, travels and bibliography, common-places clad in purple, and follies 'with not a rag to cover them'" (*Boston Evening Mercantile Journal*, II [September 27, 1839], No. 2019).

4. Longfellow was mistaken on this point; only about half the edition had been sold (see Letter No. 511).

5. "I came to the very charming town of Newport where I asked for George Greene and did not find him; but I found a representation of George engraved in wood."

6. Greene's father was Nathanael Ray Greene (1780–1859). His brother Nat — Nathanael Greene (1809–1899) — was a physician and farmer.

## 496. *To Stephen Longfellow*

Cambridge. October 1. 1839

My dear Father,

I am much grieved to hear by your letter, that you are not so well as usual.[1] I trust that the Autumnal weather will revive you as it does me, and that when I next visit you I shall find you well again. I do not know when I shall come; for I am quite busy, as you know. I have addressed a letter to the Corporation, complaining of the duties imposed upon me, and showing how they were swerving from the original design of the Professorship in this &c; in brief, a statement of grievances. They have appointed a Committee to meet me, and agree upon some new plan. I have proposed to them to give me only one thousand per annum, and limit my duties to lecturing during one term, leaving me the remainder of the year at my disposal. We shall consider this, when the Committee is called together, which will be soon. I am determined to have some time for study, uninterrupted, and continuous; and what is wanting in salary will be made up in other ways. But *time* and *study*, I must and will have. I will write you as soon as anything is determined upon.[2]

Did I tell you in my last, that I had a volume of Poems in the Press? It is a collection of what I have already published; and will be divided into three parts; First, "Voices of the Night" which are the Psalms of Life, with two or three new ones, which you have not seen. Second, a selection from my earlier poems; — and third, Translations. Together they will make a small volume, in the Hyperion style. I shall have the first proof tomorrow, and will send you the sheets, as fast as they are struck off, if you wish. You may like to see the book in its growth.

Have the travellers returned?[3] Edward Davies[4] is quite unwell. I saw him Sunday and advised him to take [a] run down to Portland in the steamer. James [Greenleaf] was in last evening. Is well. The G——'s move to town this week.

Farewell well, and get well. With much love to all,

Very affectionately yours
Henry W. Longfellow.

P. S. If you will let me know how much I am in yr. debt, I will send the amount immediately.[5]

MANUSCRIPT: Longfellow Trust Collection. ADDRESS: Hon. Stephen Longfellow/ Portland/Me POSTMARK: CAMBRIDGE MS. OCT 2

1. Stephen Longfellow had for many years been subject to epileptic seizures. On September 22 he wrote: "I have had several attacks of late, and have just recovered from one. They are more violent than formerly, and are attended with utter insensibility, and I think my memory is much affected by them. These are admonitions that my powers will soon be destroyed. May we all be prepared for the will of Providence."

2. Longfellow's proposal to the Corporation produced an immediate response from his father: "Your letter received this morning gave us some anxiety. We regret that you should have made the Communication to the Corporation, as it will probably produce unfavorable results, by disturbing the harmony and confidence which has so happily existed. We cannot consider your plan of giving up half your salary, wise or prudent under present circumstances. It will be impossible for you [to] support yourself and pay your debts with the salary of $1000. The plan of making your professorship subservient to other less important objects, as it certainly will be on the principles proposed by you, we fear will prove ruinous in its consequences. Your present situation is a most eligible and respectable, and advantageous one, and should not [be] put in jeopardy by any considerations. We fear you are allured by the visions of authorship, from a more wise and prudent course. Of all employments authorship is the most uncertain in this country. No reliance can be placed upon it, and it should no[t] be permitted in any respect to affect the station you now enjoy" (Letter of October 4, 1839).

3. Longfellow's mother, his brother Alexander, and his five-year-old nephew Stephen Longfellow had gone to Hiram on September 21 (Stephen Longfellow to Longfellow, September 22, 1839).

4. Edward Henry Daveis (1818–1909), son of Charles S. Daveis of Portland, graduated from Bowdoin in 1838 and was attending the Harvard Law School.

5. In response, Stephen Longfellow listed his son's debits at $446.35 and credits at $175.00 and suggested that the balance be paid to Mary Longfellow after her marriage and move to Cambridge (Letter of October 13, 1839).

## 497. *To John Neal*

Cambridge. October 10. 1839

My dear Neal,

Your most friendly and warm-hearted letter reached me like "a beaker full of the warm South."[1] I am certainly very glad to have your good opinion. I have always known you frank, fearless and sincere; and therefore value your praise, as I ought to value the praise of such a friend, and will fain believe I have written a good book.[2]

Do you see the Boston papers? Some of them are quite savage against me; and have made ferocious onslaughts upon the book. But I hope I have got the start of them. If so, they may bark behind me, and welcome. I shall only speed the faster. Is it not so? You ought to know. For nobody except King Lear, was ever more *mightily abused*,[3] than you have been. But I could never find, that it hurt you in any way; but rather the contrary.

I have now in press a small volume of poems, with the title "Voices of the Night." They are the so-called Psalms and some others written lately; followed by a selection, from the earlier pieces, of such as I wish to preserve; and lastly some Translations. It will hardly be out before December. I will send you a copy as soon as it is ready.

What have you on the anvil now? Or do you still say to your Muse, as Moliere's clown to his mistress; "Adieu, rocher, caillou, pierre de taille, et tout ce qu'il y a de plus dur au monde!"[4] I see, that some one in the New York American ([Charles] King's paper) passing on his rambles through Portland pauses to sound a blast at your door.[5] Farewell.

Very sincerely yours
Henry W. Longfellow.

MANUSCRIPT: Clifton Waller Barrett Collection, University of Virginia. ADDRESS: To/John Neal./Portland. POSTMARK: CAMBRIDGE MS. OCT 10 ENDORSEMENT: HW. Longfellow/Oct 15/39

1. Keats, "Ode to a Nightingale," l. 15.

2. Neal had written to congratulate Longfellow on October 6: "I have just finished your Hyperion — and cannot resist the inclination I feel to say in a few words how much I like it. You have redeemed yourself — and though your book may not be popular in the popular sense of the word, that is, with the mere multitude, it will be a treasure with the few that know its value, not only now, but generations hence . . . Open where I may, I see nothing — absolutely nothing to remind me of your early timidity, watchfulness, wariness and evident self-distrust. All here is beauty, manly and beautiful — 'severe in youthful beauty.' In a word, you have published a book which is honorable not only to yourself, and to your country, but to the literature of the age."

3. *King Lear,* IV, vii, 53. Neal had invited journalistic abuse because of his hastily written novels and poems and his tempestuous literary criticism.

4. "Farewell, rock, flint, freestone, and everything that is hard in the world!" *George Dandin, ou le Mari confondu,* II, i.

5. An admixture of laudatory and adverse criticism of Neal, dated at Portland and signed "Rambler," appeared in the *New York American* for October 5, 1839.

498. *To Anne Longfellow Pierce*

Cambridge. October 15. 1839.

My dear Annie,

To tell the truth I was a little surprised to get so long a letter from you, knowing your various occupations. It does you the more credit; and I reply in an unusually short space of time, for me, as you will bear witness. The chief news I have to write are very disagreeable news to me; namely, that I am growing corpulent, (you know my amiable weakness) — and consequently unhappy. I have the most entire aversion to rotundity. You shall judge for yourself next week, as I intend to come; though, if possible I must know the day,[1] beforehand, so as to make the necessary arrangements.

I received a letter from Father and the bride this morning. I will make the necessary inquiries about the Grecian couches, though in my opinion they are a little worse than no furniture at all. They are very uncomfortable and to my eye very ugly things. A couple of Washington chairs are worth all the couches in the world. Do persuade Mary to change her mind and get something comfortable for me to sit down in, when I come to see her. A sofa is "not quite so worse"; as I heard a child say to-day. She need not be in a hurry, need she?[2]

At last, my dear Annie, I have got a tea-rose for you; but do not think I shall send it now, for fear of accident. I cannot bring it in the stage; and I am afraid to go by sea.

I hope the Commodore [A. S. Wadsworth] and his wife will arrive in Boston this week, so that we can *go down* together (not *sink* in the Steamer.)

The proof sheets[3] I cannot send yet; for the simple reason, that I have none to send. The book is nearly all in type; but the paper has not yet come from the mill. It is still rags; — and perhaps some of my future readers are now wearing it on their backs. John Owen[4] is the publisher; and he is a very slow coach.

Good night. I am tired. I have walked to town and back in a rainstorm to-day, for the fun of it; exercise and fresh sensations. Please say to Father, that the Committee have not yet held a meeting; and when they do, there is no great danger of their accepting my proposals. Love &c

Affectionately yours

Henry

MANUSCRIPT: Longfellow Trust Collection. ADDRESS: Mrs. Anne L. Pierce/Care of Hon. S. Longfellow/Portland. POSTMARK: CAMBRIDGE MS. OCT 18

1. That is, the day of Mary Longfellow's wedding to James Greenleaf — October 22, 1839.

2. In a postscript to Stephen Longfellow's letter of October 13, 1839, Mary had asked her brother to make inquiries about the cost and manufacture of some Grecian lounges she had seen in Cornelius Felton's drawing room.

3. Of *Voices of the Night.*

4. Owen (1805–1882), Longfellow's publisher at this time, was a member of the Bowdoin class of 1827. He remained a lifelong friend.

## 499. *To Stephen Longfellow*

Cambridge. November 10. 1839

My dear Father,

I sent you yesterday two proof-sheets of my poems, which will give you some idea of the size of the page &c. The book will be very handsomely got up. The paper is better than Hyperion; and when pressed looks finely. One thousand copies will be printed. I am to have half the profits. Bad arrangement; perhaps I can change a little for the better.

In College, nothing new. I have met a Committee of the Corporation, and stated my griefs and wishes. They have not yet reported; but keep post-poning, which vexes me. There seems no necessity for this; save that the gents. have so many other things to attend to. No matter.

Mary seems exceedingly happy in her house and home.[1] I see her almost every day. The new life has still the charm of novelty, and no day is too long, — no weather too dull — all sunshine.

We have had a wonderful performer on the piano-forte here; a German by the name of Rakemann; — a grand player! — the best in the Country.[2]

Likewise a Belgian painter, whose English was the strangest specimen of a language I ever heard. For instance; *fried oysters* he called *freed oosters*; and said to Miss Lowell; "Negs Zommer I zghall kom stay lit vid you iv you lige." (Next Summer I shall come and stay with you a little if you like.) He is the ugliest man alive; but has great skill in painting. He took my face, for friendship's sake, in crayon: exceedingly like. He has since used it as a decoy-duck in Boston, and has his hands full so striking do they find my likeness. His name is Franquinet; a magnificent specimen of the Philosophic Vagabond. He is fifty-five years old; and is now on his way to Mexico, and then to Spain! Only think of it! What a specimen of the *Verd antique.*[3]

Did the Tea *turn out* good? I hope so. Miss Lowell asked me, to-day, when I *supposed* the butter was coming. Hint.

With kindest regards all round,

affectionately yours
Henry W. Longfellow

MANUSCRIPT: Longfellow Trust Collection. ADDRESS: To/Hon. S. Longfellow/ Portland. POSTMARK: BOSTON MS. NOV 11

1. After her marriage Mary Longfellow Greenleaf lived in Cambridge almost continually until her death in 1902.

2. Ludwig Rakemann, a pianist from Bremen, gave his first concert in Boston on November 4, 1839 (*Daily Evening Transcript*). Despite his great reputation at the time, his name has not survived in the standard musical dictionaries.

3. Willem Hendrik Franquinet (1785–1854), portrait painter and lithographer from Maestricht, had emigrated to the U. S. in 1836. See Longfellow's journal entry for January 29, 1852 (*Life*, II, 230). For the crayon portrait, see Plate I.

## 500. *To Epes Sargent*[1]

Cambridge. Nov. 10. 1839

My dear Sir,

I have just received a letter from my friend Geo: W. Greene, American Consul in Rome, who tells me that he is writing a series of Letters on the Imperial City, and wishes to make some arrangement for their publication. It has struck me that you might like them for the Mirror. Greene is a good writer; as his Articles in the North American will testify. He has married an Italian woman; has resided many years in Florence and Rome, and has better opportunities for seeing Italian Society than any American ever had.

Will you have the goodness to speak with General Morris on this point and write me in the course of a few days. If you should not wish to make any arrangement with Greene, have the goodness to say a word to Benjamin — or Mrs. [Ann Sophia] Stephens; or in fine — to any one you might think of as likely to publish letters from Rome.

Are you at Work upon anything new? Have you found a new topic for a Tragedy?[2]

By the way — when you pass down Broadway this afternoon just stop in at Colman's and tell him I wish to know about the sales of Hyperion. I want him to write me.

I have in press *here* (John Owen is publisher) a volume of Poems, with title "Voices of the Night." It is a collection of the Psalms of Life — with some of the earlier pieces and some Translations. It will be out in a week or two.

With my regards to yr. brother[3] and Benjamin, very sincerely

Your friend
Henry W. Longfellow.

MANUSCRIPT: Clifton Waller Barrett Collection, University of Virginia. ADDRESS: To/Epes Sargent Esq/New York. ANNOTATION (*by Longfellow*): paid. 192. POSTMARK: CAMBRIDGE MS. NOV 11

1. Epes Sargent (1813–1880), assistant editor of the New York *Mirror*, was on the threshold of his long career as editor and author of poems, plays, novels, and miscellaneous works.

2. Sargent had written two successful tragedies, *The Bride of Genoa* and *Velasco*, both produced in 1837, and was in search of another theme. His reply to Longfellow's question was, "What with new speculations of various kinds — new acquaintances — the club — Delmonico's — and the Astor House, I find no time for the tragedy — have not even found a subject" (Letter misdated November 10 [1839]). His third and last dramatic tragedy, *The Priestess*, appeared in 1854.

3. John Osborne Sargent (1811–1891), associate editor of the New York *Courier and Enquirer*, 1838–1841. He subsequently became a lawyer of considerable repute. See 280.5.

## 501. *To Daniel Pierce Thompson* [1]

Cambridge Nov. 12. 1839

Dear Sir,

Not till a week ago did I receive your letter of October 16 with the copy of the "Green-Mountain Boys" you were so kind as to send. I have not yet had time to read your work; but have had too much curiosity not to look into it and read some chapters. Judging from these portions, I doubt not you have written a very stirring and interesting novel for such as love to contemplate the stern face of History reflected in the mirror of romance. I shall read it as soon as I have time to read it properly; — that is not too carelessly.

In regard to reviewing it, you must excuse me if I decline undertaking it. Since I have become an author myself, I feel exceedingly unwilling to play the part of critic. Do you not feel this yourself? You say; "a faithful critique, I should be gratified to see; that I might learn my faults as a writer, and correct them — my powers, if any I have, and improve them!" I am sorry to hear you say this. You know your powers better than any critic can tell them to you. The very impulse from *within*, urging you to write after the labors of the day — this restlessness to be *doing*, — is an evidence of power. Cho[o]se wisely how to direct it. From the *feeling within*, you must work — not from what the critics say. Why should you sacrifice your own opinion ||to that of anoth||er? I confess I have no great respect for critics, in reference to a *writer*. In reference to the effect upon *readers*, I have. They do much good ||for all||. But that is another point. I envy the position of those writers who lived, when they the authors *made* the taste of the public. Dante, for instance; — Spencer, Chauser m||ore than|| writers of these late days, have ||a better|| time of it in this particular.

Permit me to thank you ||for the|| book, and to send you in return a copy of "Voices of the ||Night,"|| a collection of Poems, which I will leave for you with Mr. Muzzy,[2] as soon as it is published.

Very respectfully yours
||Henry W. Longfellow.||

P. S. Excuse, also, my freedom in speaking to you thus of criticism; and allow me to ask if a copy of yr. book has been sent to the Editor of the N. A. Review.

MANUSCRIPT: Dartmouth College Library. ADDRESS: To/D.P. Thompson Esq/ Montpelier/Vt. POSTMARKS: CAMBRIDGE MS. NOV 13/PAID

1. Thompson (1793–1868), a Vermont lawyer and novelist, had just published *The Green Mountain Boys* (Montpelier, 1839), a historical romance about Ethan Allen.

2. Benjamin B. Mussey, bookseller at 29 Cornhill, Boston, and Thompson's literary agent.

## 502. *To Henry Russell Cleveland*

Cambridge. Nov. 13. 1839

My dear Cleveland

I was very sorry not to see you this morning; and particularly when Felton showed me Sumner's letter, where he urges you to take up the subject of English Literature, for an elaborate work. If you do, I fear we shall clash a little. English Poetry is a topic which I have already undertaken. I have been making the preparatory studies for some years past, in the languages of the North; and the Anglo-Saxon in particular. The paper on Anglo-Saxon lit. in the N. American is a sketch of the Introductory part of the work I proposed. My intention was to begin the work seriously this Autumn; and I should have done so if the Corporation of the College had provided me with a French teacher.

Now, how far this would interfere with your plan I cannot say. I had never any idea of including the English Prose-Writers; nor of touching upon prose at all, save when written by a poet, and then only incidentally, as a part of his works.

I have never spoken on this subject to anyone save Felton; because I have a great dislike to say what I am going to do. Nor did I mention it to him, even, till last Summer, when I thought myself on the eve of sitting down seriously to the work. I have revealed to you my secret; but beg of you not to speak of it to anyone — not even to Hillard, unless it be necessary.

The field is broad; and there will doubtless be room for us both, if we only start right, so as not to interfere too much. Indeed I think we may mutually assist each other.[1]

Very truly yours
Henry W. Longfellow

P. S. I saw it announced more than a year ago, that D'Israeli the elder, was engaged on a History of English Literature. Have you heard anything about it?[2]

MANUSCRIPT: Berg Collection, New York Public Library. ADDRESS: To/Henry R. Cleveland/Brookline

1. Longfellow abandoned this plan for a history of English poetry in favor of his anthology *The Poets and Poetry of Europe* (Philadelphia, 1845).
2. Three volumes of Isaac D'Israeli's projected history of English literature appeared in 1841 under the title *Amenities of Literature.*

## 503. *To Lewis Gaylord Clark*

[Cambridge, December 5, 1839][1]

As to the wind Euroclydon, it is blowing now a fearful blast through the night, here in Cambridge. What makes your friend imagine that this wind blows only in the Mediterranean? Because it was first called Euroclydon in those regions? The same may be said of *Boreas* and *Sirocco.* No; the word indicates a north-east wind, coming over the sea. Look into any good Greek lexicon, and you will find some such definition. The only place in which I have seen the word used before is in PAUL's shipwreck in the Acts. Just consult 'Robinson's Greek and English Lexicon of the New Testament.' To save you the trouble I copy out his definition for you: 'Εὐροκλύδων, *Euroclydon*, a tempestuous wind, Acts 27: 14; from Εὖρος, *Eurus* east-wind; and κλύδων, a wave.'

PASSOW, a great authority, defines it 'a violent storm-wind which throws up the waves of the sea.' I could give you some dozen authorities were it necessary. You may rely upon it, I knew what I was saying when I used the word.[2] . . . I AM sorry I have no psalms for your next number. I have been very much engaged of late in getting out my poems; a copy of which will be sent you in a day or two. How does MAGA flourish? . . . THE KNICKERBOCKER stands high in this quarter. It is infinitely superior to most of the Magazines, English or American.

MANUSCRIPT: unrecovered; text from *The Knickerbocker, or New-York Monthly Magazine*, LVII (February 1861), 229.

1. The date, provided by Henry Wadsworth Longfellow Dana, is approximate.

2. In the *Knickerbocker,* XIV (November 1839), 463, Clark had reported the objection of a reader to Longfellow's description of Euroclydon as a "storm-wind from Labrador" in "Midnight Mass for the Dying Year." This defense by Longfellow was printed almost verbatim in the next number of the magazine (XIV [December 1839], 560), but was identified as coming from a "Southern correspondent." The authorities cited are Edward Robinson, *A Greek and English Lexicon of the New Testament* (Boston, 1836), and Franz Ludwig Carl Friedrich Passow (1786–1833), German classical scholar.

## 504. *To Stephen Longfellow*

Cambridge Decr. 5. 1839

My dear Father,

It is so long since I wrote you last, that it seems as if I never did write you. Of late I have had many business letters to write, and have found my time taken up more than usual by company. Do you remember Dr. Tellkampf,[1] the German, who visited me last summer in Portland — no, the Summer before — and smoked under the trees after dinner? The same who was banished from Göttingen, because, as he said, the "King of Hanover wanted him to swallow his *oats*" (oaths) and he would not. He is now here on a visit. He is professor in Union College, Schenectady; and teaches there Civil Polity, French, Italian and German. I never see him, that he does not allude to the cigar and coffee after dinner, under the trees. It took him captive entirely. It was he says, *so* German!

Have you seen the last Knickerbocker? They are raising a slight breeze in it against the "*Wind Euroclydon.*" But I am right, notwithstanding. It means a storm-wind — or a North Easter, coming over the Sea; and is no more confined to the Mediterranean, than rude Boreas. Look into "Robinson's Lexicon of the Greek of the New Testament" — and you will find the whole explained.

The "Voices of the Night" will be out in a few days. It will succeed finely, I have no doubt. Having got this off my hands, I shall now get my Lectures ready for New York. They come on in January.[2] And this reminds me, that my friend Ward has just lost his father; —a most worthy, excellent man. He died suddenly last week of *Angina pectoris.*[3]

I have not yet given up, that Professorship for Sam. I think I stand some chance of getting it; though he must not hear of it, until I am certain. I shall have letters from Tuscaloosa before long.[4]

The Corporation have finally settled my case, by putting it on the old footing; I can now have a French instructer, when I see fit; which will be sometime in the course of the year.

Do you wish me to give any monies to Mary? or shall I pay away on the old Note? It is delightful to have Mary here. I see her every day; and have got quite well acquainted with her.

How are you all? Well I hope. The Wind Euroclydon is blowing tremendously, announcing Winter. Much love to all. How is young Harry?[5] Has he got his "*beaver up*"? — or his *Ebenezer*?

Very affectionately
H. W. L.

MANUSCRIPT: Longfellow Trust Collection. ADDRESS: Hon. Stephen Longfellow/ Portland/Me. POSTMARK: BOSTON MAS. DEC 5

1. See 438.3.
2. Longfellow had been invited to give three lectures before the New York Mercantile Library Association on January 24, 27, and 29, 1840. According to Thompson (*Young Longfellow*, p. 312) and Samuel Longfellow (*Life*, I, 357), his subjects were Dante and Jean Paul Richter, but Longfellow remarked as late as January 5 that he planned to lecture on Dante and Molière (Letter No. 516). His journal entry for September 18, 1839, reveals that he was to receive $200 for the three lectures (*Life*, I, 344).
3. See 464.8.
4. In the meantime, Sam Longfellow had taken a position as a school teacher in Elk Ridge, Maryland (*Samuel Longfellow: Memoir and Letters*, ed. Joseph May [Boston and New York, 1894], p. 14).
5. Henry Wadsworth Longfellow (1839–1874), son of Stephen Longfellow, Jr.

## 505. *To Willis Gaylord Clark*

Cambridge. Decr. 7. 1839.

My dear Ollopod,

I hope this letter will find you in better health, than when your last dateless epistle was written. You were then on the point of starting for New York and Albany. Have you got back again to Phil, or did you not go out of its lovely gates? I felt quite startled at the account you gave of your health. Why did you refuse to go to Santa Cruz? You could have taken Willie, or have left him with yr. brother. I think you were wrong. It would have been a delightful excursion. I hope you will think better of it and go, even now. You must see new scenes. It will not do for you to sit at home, and grieve your soul away.[1] Your Autumnal Dirge is one of the most sweetly solemn poems I ever read. There is the difference of writing from the *heart*, and from the *imagination* merely. In that poem I recognize my friend in his better hours. I got Clapp to publish it, with two or three lines introductory, in his paper. The piece is much admired here.[2]

I am glad you find something good in Hyperion; and trust you will likewise find something to like in the "Voices of the Night," which I shall send you next week, though there will be very little in the volume, which you have not seen before.

On the next page you will find two Literary Notices, which I wish you would publish, and send me a copy thereof. I think Menzel's book will delight you vastly. Take my word for it. Spenser you have probably heard of before![3]

Now, Clarke, dont let such an age pass before you write again. I never see your paper nor your handwriting now-a-days. I sometimes think you have taken offense at something; yet cannot really believe so; but have put it down to *multifariousness* and ill-health.

Very truly yours, as ever,
Henry Wad. Longfellow.

MANUSCRIPT: New York Public Library (A. W. Anthony Collection). PUBLISHED: Richard Henry Stoddard, *Henry Wadsworth Longfellow. A Medley in Prose and Verse* (New York, 1882), pp. 79–80.

1. Clark's doctors had ordered him to Santa Cruz for the winter in an effort to heal his lungs, but concern for his motherless son, Willis Gaylord, Jr. (1837–1853), prompted him to remain in Philadelphia (*Clark Letters*, p. 53).

2. "To Autumn" appeared in the *Knickerbocker*, XIV (October 1839), 367, and was reprinted in the *Boston Evening Gazette*, XXVII (November 2, 1839), 1, edited by William Warland Clapp (1783–1866).

3. Brief notices of Hillard's edition of Spenser (485.10) and Felton's translation of Menzel's German Literature (456.2) appeared in the *Philadelphia Gazette and Commercial Advertiser*, LIX, No. 15 (Wednesday, December 11, 1839), 648.

## 506. *To Andrews Norton*

[Cambridge] Sunday evening Decr. 8. '39

My dear Sir,

Permit me again to thank you for your Reply to Mr. R[ipley]. I have just been reading it, and find it written with all your customary strength, clearness and directness.[1]

I shall have the pleasure of reciprocating your kindness by sending Mrs. Norton a copy of my poems. I am waiting only to have a copy properly bound. I hope you will like them; as I look upon the publication of a volume of poems, though a small volume, as a serious matter.

Very sincerely yours
Henry W. Longfellow

MANUSCRIPT: Harvard College Library. ADDRESS: Rev. Andrews Norton/Cambridge.

1. Norton, a Unitarian conservative, had attacked the transcendental views of

Emerson in July 1839 in the address *Discourse on the Latest Form of Infidelity.* George Ripley's reply, *"The Latest Form of Infidelity" Examined*, brought forth the rejoinder by Norton to which Longfellow alludes: *Remarks on a Pamphlet Entitled " 'The Latest Form of Infidelity' Examined"* (Cambridge, 1839). Longfellow's Unitarian position lay between the extremes offered by Norton and Ripley. William R. Hutchinson analyzes the controversy in *The Transcendental Ministers* (New Haven, 1959), pp. 82 ff.

## 507. *To Josiah Quincy*

Cambridge. Decr. 8. 1839.

To President Quincy.
Dr. Sir,

I have no change to suggest in my Department, — except, that the Study of the Modern Languages begin with the Freshman year, instead of the Sophomore year as now; and be discontinued at the close of the First Term of the Senior year.[1]

Respectfully yours
Henry W. Longfellow

MANUSCRIPT: Josiah Quincy Papers, Harvard Archives. PUBLISHED: *Professor Longfellow of Harvard*, p. 40.

1. This letter was written in response to a faculty resolution of November 25, 1839, that "each Instructer be requested to propose any modifications which he may deem useful in the studies of the College generally, and of his department in particular" (*Professor Longfellow of Harvard*, p. 39).

## 508. *To Epes Sargent*

Cambridge Dec. 10 '39

My dear Sargent,

Permit me to present to yr. friendly attention Mr. Franquinet, an artist of very distinguished merit. His crayon-sketches are admirable; in proof of which, he will show you one he has taken of me. If you can, say a good word for Mr. F. in the papers.

He has also in his possession — or knows where there is — a m.s. translation of one of Paul de Kock's novels. I recommend him to the Harpers; and a line from you would be of service.[1]

Yours truly,
Henry W. Longfellow.

MANUSCRIPT: unrecovered; text from photostat, Longfellow Trust Collection. ADDRESS: To/Epes Sargent Esq/Mirror Office, 1 Barclay St./New York./Presenting/Mr. Franquinet.

1. Charles Paul de Kock (1793–1871) was a popular French novelist of Parisian life. This translation does not seem to have made its way into print.

## 509. *To Samuel Ward*

Cambridge. Decr. 10. 1839

My dear Sam,

I have just been writing a note of introduction to you for Mr. Franquinet, an artist of great merit; — but on the express condition, that he should not annoy you in any way at present, but only show you a crayon sketch, which he has taken of me, and then go on his way rejoicing Southward; which condition he promises to fulfil. Otherwise, believe me, I would not have given him the letter on any account. When he returns to New York, I hope you will let him sketch your beloved face. He will not return before Spring.

Of late, I have thought of you constantly; and in what a state of sorrow and excitement you must have been since my last. I have often wished I could be with you at this time; — or show you in some way, that I mourn with you for your loss.[1] I fear you must be harrassed to death, having so many cares in addition to your affliction. You must be careful; or you will yourself be ill.

I have no news to send you which may enliven or interest you. The only event which has made a stir here of late is Miss A——'s engagement to Mackintosh; upon which I have *no* opinion, being but slightly acquainted with the youth. He is taciturn, modest, and bald-headed; — three points worth considering in marriage. But then he is the Son of Sir James;[2] — "*enfin,*" as somebody says in the *Avare*, "*son père est son père*";[3] — which is also worth considering in marriage. By the way, what sent Jewett[4] spinning southward? Had it any connexion, think ye, with this affair? The marriage takes place anon; — and "débuter d'abord par le mariage, c'est prendre justement le roman par la queue [to begin with marriage is precisely to attack romance from the rear]." I have given her my benediction; and most sincerely hope, that all her hopes may be realised; — a common mode of speech, which translated into *Faust*-ese would be, "solve the great problem of existence — namely the reconciliation of the ideal with the real."

Did you happen to read a note in the Knickerbocker on the "Wind Euroclydon"? How utterly absurd. You might as well say that Boreas blows only in the Mediterranean, as this same Euroclydon. If you doubt, look into Robinson's Greek Lexicon of the New Testament; — or Passow, and you will doubt no longer.

Felton's Translation of Menzel will be out shortly. It is capitally executed;[5] and will delight you, I think, very much. "Voices of the Night" — next week.

My affectionate regards to you all.

Most truly yours
Longfellow.

MANUSCRIPT: Longfellow Trust Collection. ADDRESS: To/Samuel Ward Esq/ New York POSTMARK: CAMBRIDGE MS. DEC 11

1. See 464.8.

2. Mary Appleton was married to Robert James Mackintosh on Thursday, December 26 (Boston *Daily Evening Transcript*, Vol. X, No. 2889 [December 28, 1839]). Mackintosh (1806–1864), the son of the philosopher Sir James Mackintosh (1765–1832), edited his father's works and memoirs.

3. Longfellow misquotes Molière. Cf. *L'Avare*, IV, i: "Mais le mal que j'y trouve, c'est que votre père est votre père" (But the trouble I find is that your father is your father).

4. Isaac Appleton Jewett (1808–1853), a Harvard graduate of 1830, was Mary Appleton's cousin. Longfellow had first met him in Europe in 1836 (358.2).

5. Longfellow first wrote "translated" for "executed."

## 510. *To Luigi Mariotti*

Cambridge. Dec. 15. 1839.

My dear Sir,

Your short note of Oct. 16 gave me both pain and pleasure. I was very glad to hear from you, and very sorry to learn that the London Booksellers turned up their noses so at Hyperion.[1] Then again I was gratified with the praise of those who have read the book, and with the good opinion *implied* in the fact of your having read *it twice*; so that while reading your letter I was like Lady Blarney in the Vicar of Wakefield, by turns "greatly concerned" — and "extremely glad" — and "vastly sorry," and then "extremely glad again."[2] If the copy [Charles] Bowen gave you is still in your hands I wish you would send it to Professor Wilson, editor of Blackwood's Magazine,[3] in such a way that it should reach him without expense, of course; together with a volume of Poems, which I have just published, and a copy of which I beg you to accept from me as a souvenir of the Past, and a token of my good wishes for the Future. At the close of this letter you will find an order for six copies; which will be delivered to you in London. Keep one — send one to Wilson — one to Carlyle, one to Lockhart — one to Wordsworth — and the other to your friend Mrs. Jameson.[4] Say — will this give you too much trouble? I hope not. I wish, also, that if you ever pass through Red Lion Square, you would leave an order with O. Rich, to send me 12 copies of *Outre-Mer*. He knows me, and probably will not demur an account of payment, which I will make to his order in Boston or New York. Please say to him, that I cannot give more than *half* the original price.

There is nothing new in Cambridge. We go round and round like horses in a mill, grinding evermore. Last night *Signor Blitz*[5] performed *hocus-pocus,* with ventriloquism in the *Old Court House* [Cambridge]; — and the night before in the Unitarian Church was exhibited the *grand transparency* of the opening of the Seven Seals!! with explanatory remarks. The Exhibitor began by singing *alone*, and in *the dark, Old Hundred!*[6]

A Theological discussion is going on between Norton and Ripley of Boston, who undertakes (on a wager as it were) to get into Heaven with Spinoza on his shoulders![7] Felton has in press a translation of Menzel's History of German Literature. Mrs. Geo: Lee has written a Tale called *Rosana.*[8] Mr. Postmaster Greene has translated La Mennais' *Libre du peuple.*[9] My publisher Colman has failed,[10] and his creditors have seized my book (Hyperion) and half the edition (12 hundred copies) lies useless in sheets, and none in the market. Pleasant to me, as I have agreed not to publish a second edition before one year. Beside, I lost half of what he owed me for copy-right. So goes the world with us here. I am glad to hear from yr. letter to Mrs. King,[11] that it goes better with you. I feel sure of yr. success in London, if you have patience to *bide your time.* Meanwhile I remain

Sincerely your friend
Henry W. Longfellow.

MANUSCRIPT: Berg Collection, New York Public Library. ADDRESS: ||Prof. M||ariotti/||Mr. Pett||y Vaughan's/||70||Fenchurch street/London ANNOTATION (*by Longfellow*): paid to N. York/No. 192

1. Mariotti (422.3), who had gone to London and was writing for the periodical press, had tried in vain to find an English firm to republish *Hyperion.*

2. Chap. XI.

3. John Wilson (1785–1854) was not in fact the editor of *Blackwood's* but its principal writer. As Christopher North, he contributed most of its *Noctes Ambrosianae.* Longfellow presumably hoped that he would review *Hyperion.*

4. Anna Brownell Jameson (1794–1860), a popular English essayist on travel, art, and history. Mariotti had lent her a copy of *Hyperion* and reported in his letter that she was "not satisfied with reading it twice and would purchase it at any cost."

5. Antonio Blitz (1810–1877), prestidigitator and ventriloquist, had come to the U. S. from Europe in 1834. After performing throughout the country, he made his home in Philadelphia. The performance alluded to here took place on Friday, December 12 (Boston *Daily Evening Transcript,* No. 2875 [December 11, 1839]).

6. The "Old Hundred," a popular tune with early New England settlers, first appeared to the words of Psalm CXXXIV in Theodore de Beza's *Genevan Psalter* of 1554.

7. See 506.1. Ripley had defended Spinoza against Norton's accusation of infidelity.

8. Hannah Farnham Sawyer Lee, *Rosanna; or, Scenes in Boston: A Story* (Cambridge, 1839).

9. F. de La Mennais, *The People's Own Book*, trans. from the French by Nathaniel Greene (Boston, 1839).

10. Colman had been caught in the aftereffects of the Panic of 1837.

11. Sarah Worthington King (1800–1877), philanthropist and social leader, was the widow of a son of Rufus King, the Revolutionary statesman. In 1844 she married William Peter (1788–1853), British consul in Philadelphia.

## 511. *To Stephen Longfellow*

Cambridge. Decr. 22. 1839

My dear father,

I have no good news to write you, but rather the contrary. Colman has failed; an operation, by which I shall lose some three or four hundred dollars, if not five. Nor is this the worst of it. Hyperion has been out of the market for three months. I thought it all sold. But I find, this is not the case. Half the edition — about 12 hundred copies were seized by the Printers and Binders, as security for their notes; — and are lying under lock and key, till farther arrangements. It was very stupid in me not to get security of this kind on the notes. I am very sorry; as I was relying on the money to pay my debt; which will now linger still longer. Please say this to Judge Potter, whose patience must be somewhat tried by delay. It is very unfortunate.

Did you get the package of books, sent by water last week? I mean the poems. They are very successful; but I shall make no money upon them. The book is well printed is it not? I wished to have the copies bound more handsomely for you, but concluded not to wait.

We are now looking forward with pleasure to the close of the term. I shall go to New York immediately to deliver my lectures.

In the North American you will find a review of Hyperion, and of the Poems; and *probably* a review of the Poems in the New York Review.[1]

We are all well here; only too busy. Please say to Stephen, that I saw the Grattans two days ago, and they asked particularly after him and Mariane. Also, that I explained to Mrs. G's entire satisfaction, why her letter to Mariane has not been answered.

Good night. I feel quite tired, though it is Sunday. Tomorrow I have my last College Lecture for which, I desire to be duly thankful.

Affectionately yours
Henry W. Longfellow.

P. S. Tell Anne, if you please, that I dined with Mrs. Mason last Thursday, who made particular inquiries after her, and hoped to see her in Boston, now Mary had come. Mr. Mason[2] asked many questions about you, — yr. health &c

MANUSCRIPT: Longfellow Trust Collection. ADDRESS: To/Hon. Stephen Longfellow/Portland/Me. POSTMARK: BOSTON MS. DEC 23 ANNOTATION (*in Mary Longfellow Greenleaf's hand*): I have a letter partly written for home — all well — Love to all —

1. *North American Review*, L (January 1840), 145–161 and 266–269. A notice of *Voices of the Night* did not appear in the *New York Review* until July (VII, 268).

2. Jeremiah Mason (1768–1848), husband of Mary Means Mason (374.1). Mason was a U. S. Senator from New Hampshire, 1813–1817, and the legal opponent and friend of Daniel Webster. He had recently retired from active practice of the law.

## 512. *To Frances Sargent Osgood*[1]

Cambridge. Decr. 23 1839.

Dear Madam

May I beg your acceptance of this little volume, in return for that which you were so kind as to send me. I wish it were more worthy of your acceptance; but such as it is, I send it, hoping you may find something in it to please.

I understand there is to be a review of your poems in the next No. of the N. A. Review.[2] I had half a mind to write one, but thought it had better be done by some one else, as I was about publishing a volume, myself; and the double part of author and critic might not be well performed by the same individual.

Very respectfully your Obt. Ser[v]t.
Henry W. Longfellow

MANUSCRIPT: University of Washington Library.

1. Frances Sargent Osgood (1811–1850), whose sentimental verses earned her a conspicuous place among the female poets of the day, is remembered primarily for her friendship with Edgar Allan Poe.

2. A review of *A Wreath of Wild Flowers from New England* (London, 1838) appeared in the *North American Review*, L (January 1840), 269–272.

## 513. *To Stephen Longfellow*

Cambridge. Decr. 29. 1839

My dear Father,

You must have received my last at the very moment I was reading yours; and no very good news in either. I am very much grieved to see you are so low spirited. Believe me, what you attribute to your complaint — forgetfulness of names, and bad spelling happens to me and everybody else almost every day. I can seldom write a letter without a Dictionary at my elbow, unless I dodge all doubtful words; — can seldom remember a date, — and am sometimes so much in doubt as to my own age, that I have to begin at 1807 and count up.[1]

Christmass day I dined with Mr. W. Appleton.[2] Your friend and classmate Rich. Sullivan[3] was present. He said it always made him feel very old to see me; and made very particular inquiries after you. I mentioned to him these tricks of memory. He said it was precisely so with him; and Mr. Appleton exclaimed, "Why, I frequently have to ask Mr. Loring, my partner,[4] how to spell the most common words, and he is not always sure, till he writes them down; — and yesterday I introduced Mr. Mackintosh" (who married his niece two days ago) "as Mr. Mackenzie." You see the disorder is common; and I recollect perfectly well, when in Spain, that if any one asked Washington Irving a date, he would turn to his brother and say "When was that, Peter?" — and Peter always replied; "Well, Washington, I dont exactly recollect." So you must not think this a peculiarity in your own case. In which connexion I must say, I think Mr. R. Sullivan one of the most agreeable and pleasing gentlemen I meet with in Boston.

You do not know how grandly my *Voices* have succeeded. The publisher tells me he has only forty copies left on hand, out of nine hundred printed; and it is hardly a fortnight since the publication. In addition to which I get a good deal of praise, and constant applications to write for periodicals, at my own price. But of these offers, I am rather shy, just now. Colman writes me that he shall pay all his debts in the course of *fifteen months,* having put his property into the hands of Trustees for that purpose. We shall see.

My Lectures in New York are on the 24. 27. 28 of January; so that I cannot conveniently come to Portland till after that time; but shall as soon after that as possible.

Mary and James are well. We have had another violent blow, with rain. The town afloat, and ten pigs drowned between here and Boston, on Friday night.

The business part of your letter shall be attended to immediately.[5] With kind regards

Yrs. affectionately
Henry W. Longfellow.

MANUSCRIPT: Longfellow Trust Collection. ADDRESS: Hon. S. Longfellow/Portland/Me. POSTMARK: BOSTON ||Mas.|| DEC 29 ENDORSEMENT: HWLongfellow/*Decr. 29. 1839*/Jany 12. 1840

1. Stephen Longfellow's letter of December 15, 1839, had been interrupted by an epileptic seizure and was not finished until December 22. It gave a long account of his fit and concluded, "I am frequently at a loss to spell the most common words, in writing, and my recollection of names, times, and events, has almost faded away."

2. William Appleton (1786–1862), Boston merchant and financier and the cousin of Nathan Appleton, Fanny's father. See 367.2.

3. Richard B. Sullivan (1779–1861) was an overseer of Harvard College, 1821–1852.

4. Appleton does not seem to have had a business partner at this time. He may have been referring to Caleb Loring (1764–1850), a prominent merchant of the firm of Loring & Curtis, Boston.

5. In his letter of December 15 Stephen Longfellow had written regarding his son's debt: "I find that a Bill of some linnen, amounting to $17.86, should be added to the amount I sent you [see 496.5]. If convenient I wish you to pay $45 to Mr James Means of Boston and take his receipt." Means (1782–1850) was a Boston commission merchant and director of the Suffolk Bank.

## 514. *To John Gorham Palfrey*

[Cambridge] Friday morning [1839][1]

My dear Sir

I regret exceedingly that I cannot accept yr. very kind invitation to-day; but upon reflexion, I find that I cannot with propriety leave my classes.

Very truly yrs.
Henry W. Longfellow

MANUSCRIPT: Harvard College Library. ENDORSEMENT: 1839/H.W. Longfellow.

1. Year supplied by another hand.

## 515. *To Lewis Gaylord Clark*

[Cambridge] December, no January [2,] 1840.

My dear Clark,

I am chiefly occupied this evening in keeping two fires in full blaze, one in my bed room, and one in my study; for it is amazing cold, and I can hardly hold this pen in my rigid fingers. But I must thank you for your welcome letter, and the Knick. which came yesterday. Moreover there is a subject, which interests me much, because the interests of a dear friend are involved; and a voice within says "Write." I have just received a letter from Greene. He is *very* urgent about that *Letter* he sent you concerning Crawford, and wants to have it published as soon as possible. He says this; "Have you written to Clark about that Letter in the K. addressed to you? I am in great haste to have it out. *Much more than you are aware of depends upon that letter.* Pray urge him to attend to it *immediately,* and to send as I requested him, two copies to Rome, one to me and the other to Crawford, by *mail,* done up as newspapers. Now dont fail; and dont for God's sake delay for I say again, there is a vast *deal depending upon that letter*." Now there is evidently something *fearful* under this, for Greene never wrote so before; — nothing more nor less than the Life or Death of a poor Artist, whose cause Greene has warmly espoused. So I intreat you, publish the letter in the January No. if possible; and if not pray give it to Benjamin — state the case — and let us have it in the New World without delay.[1]

Furthermore — I have been urging Greene to write some "Letters from Rome" (*modern*) describing Life, Literature, Art, &c as they are around him. He consents; and wishes to make some definite arrangement with you for them, by which he can receive prompt pay, say every three months, or every Letter; for his means are small, and he is obliged to depend upon his writings for support in part, and of course any delay is to him exceedingly inconvenient. I most sincerely hope that your new arrangement with Deane,[2] will enable you to do this. I am sure that Greene's Letters will be good. Just reflect a moment. Rome is still the *heart* of Europe and all European life circulates through it. He has great opportunities for observation; and I am confident will give you sketches of Modern Italian Society, such as have not yet been drawn. Now what say you? What could you give him, per letter, or per page? Have the goodness to write me an immediate answer; that I may let him know.[3]

You ask my opinion of your December No. I have not yet had time to read it; have but glanced at the remarks of your *Southern* correspondent on Euroclydon (thank you) and at Felton's Ballad.[4] I am sorry I cannot send you something for January, but it is out of my power.

What has become of Lewis, (good) *Willis*, I mean? I wrote him, some four or five weeks ago, urging him to go to Cuba. No answer; but instead thereof his *mere effigies* on paper, all *creased* and dirty from the Post-office. Is he better? I trust so. I fear he is ashamed to write since *playing two pranks on one instrument.*[5]

I am very glad to hear of your junction with Deane. I think you will now go on magnificently. Give my regards to him; and to your wife my felicitations, and the good wishes of the season. To yourself the same.

Very truly yours
Henry W. Longfellow.

Cambridge. *Jan. 2. 1840.*

I want to *practice* on January 1840.

P.S. Since writing this letter I have been glancing over the Knick. It strikes me as being the best No. you ever published — a capital No. in truth. Go on and prosper.

MANUSCRIPT: Princeton University Library. ADDRESS: To/Lewis G. Clark Esq/ New York. ANNOTATION (*by Longfellow*): paid. *192*. POSTMARKS: CAMBRIDGE MS. JAN 3/PAID

1. In his reply on January 6, Clark wrote: "I have yours this moment before me; and hasten to say, that *I have never received a line from Mr. Greene, since he was in Rome* — not one; and such is my anxiety to serve him, that I have a great mind to write the letter he speaks of myself. But who is *Crawford*? Not knowing that, 'gives me pause' " (*Clark Letters*, p. 112). The matter was straightened out in time, and Greene's letter, addressed to Longfellow from Rome, October 1, 1839, appeared in the *Knickerbocker*, XV (June 1840), 488–496. It concerns the work of the classical sculptor Thomas Crawford (1814–1857) and is, in effect, a plea for his recognition and reward.

2. James T. Dean became business manager of the *Knickerbocker* after Clark bought out Edson late in December 1839 (*Clark Letters*, p. 121, n. 6).

3. Clark agreed to pay Greene $1.50 per page for his "Letters from Rome." Six of them, exclusive of the one concerning Crawford, appeared in the *Knickerbocker* in four installments: XVIII (November 1841), 371–378; XIX (April 1842), 293–301; XIX (May 1842), 412–415; and XX (July 1842), 11–14.

4. See 503.2. Felton's ballad was "Blücher's Ball" (483.3).

5. See Longfellow's MS Journal entry for December 14, 1839: "In Clarke's paper [*Philadelphia Gazette*], a notice I sent him of [Hillard's] Spenser, in which is this ludicrous misprint — 'playing two *pranks* at once on the same instrument,' instead of *parts*."

## 516. *To George Washington Greene*

Cambridge. January 2. 1840

Dearissimo George

It is now half-past nine at night. I have just been taking a solitary supper of Sardines, and wishing myself where they came from, namely in the Mediterranean. As this may not be, I will revenge myself on Fate by writing you a tremendous long letter, full of all that has happened since I last wrote in Spark[s]'s letter.[1] I am sorry for your eyes, as I write fine, having much to say. But first indulge me in a few preliminary observations.

Your letter of October 8 came safely. I wrote immediately to New York about your Letters from Rome,[2] but not to the Knickerbocker; because it has been in trouble, and not able to pay anybody. I wrote to Sargent, to negociate with whomsoever would pay best. After some delay I got an answer, showing that nobody pays now-a-days. He writes; "I have conferred with Morris in regard to the Letters from Rome. He is indisposed to have them if they cost anything. I am well acquainted with Greene's reputation, and should be happy to do anything in my power to serve him. I have spoken to Benjamin, but as he has given up the New Yorker, he tells me he is not in want of communications of this character. The Ladies' Companion pays for Tales and poetry, but I have made inquir[i]es, and learn that there is little chance for any higher composition. The fact is, that all our publishers *whether of books or of periodicals, are desperately poor at present. Money is not to be had.*" And this is very true. You have no idea of the state of things. So dont storm and pull your hair out; but take it coolly. My publisher has just failed. (Colman, New York). My loss on Hyperion $500 profit. Most publishers will not look at a book; and are working off the Obligations they had on hand. Yet dont despair. Clark writes me, that the Knickerbocker, that is the business part of it, will henceforth be in new hands. He complains of his former partner; and things look more prosperous. I have this very evening written him a long letter about Crawford and yr. correspondence from Rome; and shall have his answer in a few days. He has not paid me *for three years.* Poor fellow! He has had a hard time — and been almost desperate I fear. I presume the Crawford letter will be in the January No. which has not yet arrived.

The Dean [Palfrey], too, has not treated you as I wish. I do not like his delay; and have once or twice expressed my regret to him that your paper had not appeared. In vain. He has a fancy of doing things in his own way. I advise you to send part of your papers to Cogswell (New York Review.) But even here, something may be said for the Dean. *Mariotti* has been for three years past writing Arts. on Italian subjects; and has been dependent upon them for his support in part. This has given the N.A.R. so much Italian, that people begin to ask in the papers, "What makes the Editor so enthusiastic about Italy?" Both your papers and Mariotti['s] have been exceedingly liked and praised. But you can imagine that two able-minded writers working away on one theme might embarras[s] a man somewhat. So I advise a diversion to the New York Review now and then. Then you will have your hands full, and between both there will be no delay. Is this good advise? As to any criticising your style off here at this distance, it is quite absurd, except in generalities. You certainly go on from strength to strength; and this you must feel. When I see any marked defect, you will certainly hear of it. I am quite curious to see a specimen of what you call your *idiomatic* style.

Since my last letter I have published another book; — a volume of poems, with the title of "Voices of the Night." It contains the Psalms; — Manrique, and some of the Earlier Poems. Its success has been signal. It has not been out three weeks; and the publisher has not more than fifty copies left, out of nine hundred. This he told me four days ago. A copy is in the binder's hands for *Maria,* and will be sent with Hyperion and Outre Mer. Everyone praises the book. Even the Boston papers which so abused Hyperion, praise this highly. Hyperion they could not understand. This they *feel* more. So that I come out of my last six-months' literary campaign with flying colors. But see what ill-luck with Hyperion. Publisher fails. Half the edition (1200 copies. The whole number was 2200) seized by creditors and locked up. There they lie; and the book has been out of the market for four months. "Why dont you publish a new edition?" you ask. Because I agreed not to do so for the space of one year. This was my arrangement with my publisher. No matter; I had the glorious satisfaction of writing it; and thereby gained a great victory, *not* over the "dark Ladie" but over myself. I now once more rejoice in my freedom; and am no longer the thrall of anyone. I have great faith in one's writing himself clear from a passion — giving vent to the pent up fire. But George, George! It was a horrible thing; as my former letters must testify. I have an indistinct idea of raving on paper to a large amount. But it was all sincere. My mind was morbid. I have portrayed it all in the book; and how a man is to come out of it; not by shooting himself like Werter; but in a better way. In the present North American Felton has given a fine vindication of it as a Romance;[3] though he does not touch this point, which is *the* point. If I had called the book "Heart's Ease, or the Cure of a morbid mind" it would have been better understood. I called it *Hyperion,* because it *moves on high* among clouds and stars, and expresses the various aspirations of the soul of man. It is all modeled on this idea; style and all. In fine it contains my cherished thought for three years. Pardon my saying so much. In offset, I will send you the *"horrible dispraise"* I spoke of; though the papers that have uttered it have since nearly come round; — and have even praised some parts of it. *How victorious is Silence!*

I am sorry the New Yorker does not please you. You have only to say the word, and I will stop it. Benjamin is a good editor, but he left it you know. I thought you would like to know, as Consul, all that was going on in the political world. I have written to Benjamin to send you his new paper — the *New World* — a monstrous sheet full of all that is going on here — by far the best paper I see, tho' he republishes from the English — whole books even.[4] By the way, what is the postage of a paper from Havre to Rome? — and of a letter? I would keep up a constant fire of *papers and things,* if I did not fear the cost to you. This has constantly restrained me — *not in letters,* but in all things else. For instance the "Voices of the Night" is only

5 sheets (144 p.p.). I would tear off the covers and send it to you in less than no time, if I were not afraid of the terrible postage from Havre to Rome. Touch upon this point in your next. And whilst I think of it, let me say here for the one hundred and fiftieth time, *please acknowledge the receipt of our letters, naming the date,* a thing you have never yet been prevailed upon to do.

Jan. 5th.

I have not yet got an answer from New York, and think I will not wait, but dispatch this letter forthwith, and give the news which may arrive to Felton who will write you at the close of this week. Now for a few items in the *Laconic* vein. We are eagerly looking for Sumner, in the course of a month or two, and shall rejoice mightily at his return. We wish you were coming with him. I think he will make a sensation in Boston. The elder sister of the Dark Ladie is married to Mr. Mackintosh, son of Sir James. This happened a fortnight ago. Ticknor lives quite secluded; and goes little into society. Mr. Sam Ward of New York is dead. Instead of leaving millions, as it was supposed he would, he has left only thousands, at the outside not more than four hundred; some say two hundred and fifty. I had a *gaudiolum* [small party] here last evening, Hillard, Hawthorne, Felton, no more. We wished for you and Sumner. I go to New York in a fortnight to lecture on Dante and Molière. The *Lowell* Lectures (free, and the first free lectures in this country) commenced last week. Gov. Everett gave the Introductory.[5] And now for Literature. Felton's translation of Menzel is finished but not published. It is excellent. Seven hundred copies of Hillard's Spenser (5 vols 8vo.) sold. This is good. A Theological controversy is going on between Norton and Ripley, a young divine of the new school, who maintains that Spinoza was no atheist. *Hillhouse* has published two volumes of Poetry. The publishers say they have not sold a dozen copies! Ha! *Tappan's* poems — more *heart* than *brains. Calidore* a sprawling, puling thin octavo, called poetry, by Mr. Pabodie (not Peabody).[6] Since the poems, I have broken ground in a new field; namely, *Ballads*; begin[n]ing with the "*Wreck of the Schooner Hesperus on the Reef of Norman's Woe*," in the great storm a fortnight ago. It will be printed in a few days, and I shall send it in some newspaper. I think I shall write more. The *National Ballad* is a virgin soil here in New England; and there are good materials. Beside[s] I have a great notion of working upon *people's feelings*. I am going to have this printed on a sheet, and sold like *Varses,* with a coarse picture on it. I desire a new sensation, and a new set of critics. I wish you were sitting in this red arm-chair before me, that I might inflict it on you. Nat. Hawthorne is tickled to death with the idea. Felton laughs, and says "I wouldn't." [7] "Poets of America" with Illustrations by Chapman.[8] Some, good, others *very* bad; as for example one of my "*Indian Hunter,*" a strapping, shabby fellow holding on to a rock, and reminding you of "*Up the ragged rocks, the ragged rascal ran.*" The North American is out. The chief articles are "*Italy in the Middle Ages*" by Mariotti; "*Spenser's Works*" by Cleveland; "*Hyperion*" by Felton; "*Hillhouse's Poems*" by the Dean [Palfrey], highly laudatory.[9] I have not read any of them yet; save glancing over Hyperion; — a luminous *exposé* of the *why* and *wherefore* of its being called a Romance. But I forget; — I have told you this before. I understand there is a spicy article against me in the "*Boston Quarterly,*" a review you have never seen.[10] I shall get it as soon as I can; for strange as you may think it, these things give me no pain; but only show my shot has hit.

I am glad you are [at] work upon something. Keep your secret; I have great faith in this way of not saying much about a thing, until you can say "*I have done it.*" [11] It is often with authors as with money-diggers; — if a word is spoken, the treasure sinks. Only be sure you are not on the *wrong track.* Hillard's Spenser cost $17. I *believe.* He was very meanly paid for his work. The Printer here has a small bill of $8. against you for extra copies of Verazzano. Shall I pay it? I want the *Padua* edition of Dante in 5 large 8vo.[12] Would not the best way for us to send you books be by Trieste? Do you know the consul there?

Why dont you write me some of the gossip and scandal of Rome? How are the Persianis? Where is Fabio? Lorenzano? The Lante's — the mother, and that *hot* daughter, with the pale sister? — and old *Magrini,* who amuses every American he can get hold of with my *amour* with Julia.[13] No one returns now from Rome without *that* story. I am glad of it. How is Julia, do you hear? What did you say her name was? I shall be most happy to receive the *Dante* you speak of, and wish I had it now.

Give my most affectionate regards to yr. wife. Now, I will run over yr. letters again, to see that nothing remains unanswered; and then "*buona notte*"

Very truly yours
Henry W. Longfellow

MANUSCRIPT: Longfellow Trust Collection. ADDRESS: To/George W. Greene Esq/American Consul/Rome./Havre Packet ANNOTATION (*by Longfellow*): Paid to N. York. 192 POSTMARKS: CAMBRIDGE MS. JAN 6/NEW-YORK JAN 9/ OUTRE-MER FEVR 10 LE HAVRE/PARIS FEVR [*date illegible*] (60)/ROMA 15 FEB 1840/VIA DI PT. BEAUVOISIN/PAID

1. Letter No. 495.

2. Letter No. 500.

3. *North American Review*, L (January 1840), 145–161.

4. Park Benjamin's "Valedictory" appeared in the *New Yorker*, VIII, No. 5 (October 19, 1839), 77. He and Rufus Wilmot Griswold (1815–1857), the anthologist and literary executor of Edgar Allan Poe, began regular publication of the *New World* with an issue dated October 26, 1839.

5. The Lowell Institute had been endowed by John Lowell (1799–1836) as a center for adult education. On December 31, 1839, at the Odeon Theatre and Concert Hall, Governor Edward Everett gave a two-hour introductory lecture on Lowell and the aims of his Institute before two thousand people. Three days later he repeated his remarks before another capacity audience.

6. William Bingham Tappan, *The Poet's Tribute* (Boston, 1839), and William J. Pabodie, *Calidore; a Legendary Poem* (Boston, 1839). For works by Felton, Hillard, and Hillhouse, see Letter No. 485.

7. The "Wreck of the Hesperus" was still fresh in Longfellow's mind, having been written during the night of December 30 (*Life*, I, 350). He did not publish the ballad as a broadside, despite Hawthorne's promise that he would distribute copies "to every skipper of every craft he boards in his Custom-House duties; so as to hear the criticisms thereon" (MS Journal, January 4, 1840).

8. John Keese, ed., *The Poets of America. Illustrated by One of her Painters* (New York, 1840). John Gadsby Chapman (1808–1889), painter and illustrator, is remembered primarily for *The Baptism of Pocahontas* in the rotunda of the national Capitol.

9. See the *North American Review*, L (January 1840), 43–75, 174–206, 145–161, and 231–262.

10. *Boston Quarterly Review*, III (January 1840), 127–128. The "spicy article" is actually the first part of a dialogue between a "Professor Partridge" and the "Rev. Mr. Nightshade" entitled "Chat in Boston Bookstores — No. 1." Professor Partridge remarks that the reader of *Hyperion* is embarrassed by Longfellow's "extreme communicativeness, and wonder[s] that a man, who seems in other respects to have a mind of delicate texture, could write a letter about his private life to a public, on which he had as yet established no claim." The author of the dialogue was presumably Orestes Augustus Brownson (1803–1876), editor of the *Review*.

11. Longfellow's query in Letter No. 495 as to the "great work" Greene was engaged upon went unanswered in Greene's reply of November 9, 1839; hence this remark.

12. In his letter of March 21, 1840, Greene directed Longfellow to pay the bill for the Verrazzano pamphlets (405.1) and promised to balance the sum against the Dante volumes. The Padua edition of *La Divina Commedia*, ed. G. Campi, F. Federici, and G. Maffei, was published in 1822.

13. Greene replied, "Old Magrini is dead — the Lanti's [Lante della Rovere] I have never inquired after — Lorenzano is married and has a child — Fabio [Persiani] is a dandy" (Letter of March 21, 1840). Magrini and Lorenzano were acquaintances made in Rome in 1828.

## 517. *To Epes Sargent*

Cambridge. Jany. 2. 1840.

My dear Sargent,

Allow me to *bore* you. I want, if possible, $25 for this Ballad. Perhaps the General [George Pope Morris] would like it for one of the four pieces I was to furnish for the Mirror.[1] If you dont like it, send it to Mr. Snowden (Lady's Companion)[2] who has just made me a liberal offer for anything I will send. I shall be in New York in about three weeks. I have fished up a *plot* for you, out of a Spanish play "Life is a Dream," which I think capable of great effects.[3] I hope you have recd. "Voices of the Night"; if not you will find a copy for you, one for yr. brother, and one for Benjamin at Wiley & P's.

Yours truly
H.W.L.

THE
WRECK OF THE SCHOONER HESPERUS.
A Ballad[4]

It was the Schooner Hesperus,
That sailed the wintry sea;
And the Skipper had ta'en his little daughtér,
To bear him company.

Blue were her eyes as the fairy-flax,
Her cheeks like the dawn of day,
And her bosom sweet as the hawthorn buds,
That ope in the month of May.

The Skipper he stood beside the helm,
With his pipe in his mouth,
And watch'd how the veering flaw did blow
The smoke now West, now South.

Then up and spake an old Sailór,
Had sail'd the Spanish Main,
I pray thee, put into yonder port,
For I fear a hurricane.

Last night, the moon had a golden ring,
And to night no moon we see!
The Skipper, he blew a whiff from his pipe,
And a scornful laugh laugh'd he.

I would not put into yonder port,
Nor yet into yonder bay

Though it blew a gale, with fiery hail,
   As on the Judgment day![5]

Colder and louder blew the wind,
   A gale from the North-east;
The snow fell hissing in the brine,
   And the billows froth'd like yeast.

Down came the storm and smote amain
   The vessel in its strength;
She shudder'd and paus'd, like a frighted steed,
   Then leap'd her cable's length.

Come hither! come hither! my little daughtér,
   And do not tremble so;
For I can weather the roughest gale,
   That ever wind did blow.

He wrapp'd her warm in his seaman's coat
   Against the stinging blast;
He cut a rope from a broken spar,
   And bound her to the mast.

O father! I hear the church-bells ring,
   O say, what may it be!
'Tis a fog-bell on a rock-bound coast!
   And he steer'd for the open sea.

O father! I hear the sound of guns,
   O say, what may it be!
Some ship in distress, that cannot live
   In such an angry sea!

O father! I see a gleaming light,
   O say, what may it be!
But the father answer'd never a word,
   A frozen corpse was he.

Lash'd to the helm, all stiff and stark,
   With his face [turned] to the skies,
The lantern gleam'd through the gleaming snow
   On his fix'd and glassy eyes.

Then the maiden clasped her hands and prayed
  That savéd she might be;
And she thought of Christ, who still'd the wave
  On the Lake of Galilee.

And fast through the midnight dark and drear,
  Through the whistling sleet and snow,
Like a sheeted ghost the vessel swept
  Toward the reef of Norman's Woe[.]

And ever the fitful gusts between
  A sound came from the land;
It was the sound of the trampling surf,
  On the rocks and the hard sea-sand.

The breakers were right beneath her bows,
  She drifted a dreary wreck,
And a whooping billow swept the crew
  Like icicles from her deck.

She struck where the white and fleecy waves
  Look'd soft as carded wool,
But the cruel rocks, they gored her side
  Like the horns of an angry bull.

Her rattling shrouds, all sheath'd in ice,
  With the masts went by the board;
Like a vessel of glass, she stove and sank,
  Ho! ho! the breakers roar'd!

At day-break, on the bleak sea-beach,
  A fisherman stood aghast,
To see the form of a maiden fair,
  Lash'd close to a drifting mast.

The salt sea was frozen on her breast,
  The salt tears in her eyes;
And he saw her hair, like the brown sea-weed
  On the billows fall and rise.

Such was the wreck of the Hesperus,
  In the midnight and the snow!

Christ save us all from a death like this
On the reef of Norman's Woe!

Henry W. Longfellow.

MANUSCRIPT: Berg Collection, New York Public Library. ADDRESS: To/Epes Sargent Esq/New York ANNOTATION (*by Longfellow*): paid. 192. POSTMARKS: CAMBRIDGE MS. JAN 3/PAID

1. This letter found its way to Park Benjamin, who in a reply of January 7, 1840, accepted "The Wreck of the Hesperus" for the *New World* (Vol. I, No. 12 [Saturday, January 11, 1840]) and sent Longfellow the requested $25 (*Young Longfellow*, p. 310).

2. William W. Snowden (1812–1845) was editor and publisher of the *Ladies' Companion and Literary Expositor* and "a literary adventurer who knew more about circulation building than he did about literature" (Frank Luther Mott, *American Journalism*, p. 626).

3. A plot for Sargent's next dramatic tragedy (see 500.2). The Spanish play was *La Vida es Sueño* by Pedro Calderón de la Barca.

4. Benjamin, who used this manuscript for his printer's copy, added "(Written for the New World)" before the title and "by Henry W Longfellow/author of 'Voices of the Night,' 'Hyperion' and 'Outre Mer' " at the end of the title.

5. Longfellow crossed out this stanza, which does not appear in the printed versions of the ballad.

## 518. *To Stephen Longfellow*

Cambridge. January 16. 1840

My dear Father,

Your affectionate letter reached me yesterday; and I feel exceedingly glad, that my books find so much favor in your sight, and give my friends at home so much pleasure.

The vacation begins tomorrow; and I am now preparing in earnest for New York. I have not yet made up my mind when I shall go; it will depend on the weather and the boats. What a horrid accident the burning of the Lexington was! You will see the accounts in the papers. But I fear the whole truth will not be told. The boat was not sea-worthy. One fortnight ago Mr. Dana[1] (a friend of mine) went to New York in the same boat. He writes, that she took fire then also, but fortunately there was no cotton on board. The engine seemed much out of order then, and stopped six times during the night. Taking a deck-load of cotton, with 150 passengers, was intolerable. I have not heard any particulars, save that Dr. [Charles] Follen and wife were on board. Only three saved.[2]

Judge [Prentiss] Mellen and daughter arrived here last night. I have not yet seen them, but Mary [Longfellow Greenleaf] says the Judge called there this morning. I shall see him this evening.

I have paid Mr. Means as you requested.[3]

Jan. 17.

I met the Judge last evening at Mrs. [Sarah Worthington] King's — gay as a lark. He said you appeared to be very well this winter; and had lately "argued a case as well as ever you did in your life; — and a jury case, too." I was delighted to hear this; because it shows me that your fears have been groundless, in reference to the mental effect of your disorder.

To-day I have been idling away among my friends in Boston. It is quite a novel sensation for me to wake up in the morning and feel that I have nothing very particular to do.

I am now going down to call on Judge M. and take him to the Club at Judge Fay's.[4] And on my way shall take this letter to Mary, who perchance may have some message to send.

*Mrs.* Follen was *not* on board the Lexington; the *Dr.* was. He seemed to *fear* this boat, having been in her before, and had resolved never to go in her again; but was obliged to, on account of urgent necessity of his return. He said to one of his friends: "If anything happens to the Lexn. you need not be alarmed on my account, as I shall never go in her again."

Most affectionately yours
Henry W. Longfellow.[5]

MANUSCRIPT: Longfellow Trust Collection. ADDRESS: To/Hon. Stephen Longfellow/Portland. POSTMARK: BOSTON ||MAS.|| JAN 18

1. Richard Henry Dana, Sr. (1787–1879).

2. The steamboat *Lexington* had burned and sunk three nights before in Long Island Sound. The pilot, the second mate, a fireman, and one passenger were saved. Details may be found in *Proceedings of the Coroner in the Case of the Steamer Lexington, Lost by Fire, on the Thirteenth of January, 1840* (New York, 1840).

3. See 513.5.

4. Samuel Philips Prescott Fay (1778–1856), judge of probate, Middlesex County, 1821–1856, had been Stephen Longfellow's classmate at Harvard.

5. A postscript by Mary Longfellow Greenleaf follows.

## 519. *To Stephen Longfellow*

New York. Thursday Morning. Jan [23] 1840

My dear father,

Happening to find on the table here this half-sheet of paper, and pen and ink convenient, in the private parlor of the Astor-house, I sit down to send you word of my safe arrival in this city. I left Cambridge on Monday last and arrived here this morning at One o'clock, crowded to death in a Jersey wagon from New Haven — feet pinched with india-rubbers, and hat *pock-marked* with the rain, which was falling in torrents. I have just had breakfast; and the day looks bright. I am in haste to write you, that you may know I am alive having seen two days ago my name in the papers, as having been lost in the Lexington. Just before leaving Camb. I was at the Post-office with Felton, when he recd. a letter from New Haven, stating the same.[1]

My first lecture is on Friday evening (tomorrow) after which I shall write you again. Mr. Chs. [Francis] Adams (son of John Q) lectures to night. Mr. Dana is also delivering a course of Lectures in town. I have no news to send you. The British Queen is just coming up the harbor. I have not yet been out of the house. But it is a bright, warm day, like March; and the streets all afloat.

But here comes my friend Ward, so farewell

Most affectionately yours
Henry W. Longfellow.

MANUSCRIPT: Longfellow Trust Collection. ADDRESS: To/Hon. Stephen Longfellow/Portland/Me POSTMARK: NEW-YORK JAN 23

1. The rumor that Longfellow had perished in the Lexington disaster became widespread after several New York newspapers jumped to the conclusion that he had already left Cambridge for his lectures in New York. George Templeton Strong mentioned the rumor as early as January 16 (*Diary of George Templeton Strong*, ed. Nevins and Thomas [New York, 1952], I, 124), and it even crossed the Atlantic before finally dying out.

## 520. *To an Unidentified Correspondent*

Cambridge, Feb. 9, 1840[1]

I accept with great pleasure the invitation of the "Book Club" to become one of its members, and beg you to enroll my name accordingly. I should have written you sooner, but have been suffering from that

"tardiness in nature
Which often leaves the history unspoke
That it intends to do."[2]

Pardon this negligence, and believe me,

Yours truly,
Henry W. Longfellow

MANUSCRIPT: unrecovered; text from typewritten transcript, Longfellow Trust Collection (Longfellow House).

1. This date is probably in error since Longfellow did not arrive in Cambridge from New York until the next evening.

2. *King Lear*, I, i, 236–238.

## 521. *To Stephen Longfellow*

Cambridge. Jan.[1] 10. 1840

My dear Father,

I have just reached home, (8 o'clock Monday evening) having left Hartford this morning at five. I hoped to have been with you before this time; but have been delayed by the bad weather, and detained in New York longer than I anticipated.

Three weeks ago to-day I left Cambridge, hoping to take the boat from Stonington. There was none; and I was obliged to go by land, through Hartford and New Haven; and did not reach New York till Thursday morning. My Lectures went off very well; though I was quite ill with an influenza all the time; and I had very good audiences. On the whole, a pleasant visit, saving the unpleasant weather, snowing and thawing, and raining. On Saturday night the Sound being frozen as far as Hurl-gate, so as to prevent any steamer's going, — I started in the mail-stage, in a drizzling, foggy rain, the roads very bad, and everything afloat. We were on wheels; and about one o'clock the driver went off the road, and pitched us into a ditch four feet deep. There were three *insides* besides myself; and a dozen mail-bags. I was alone on the front seat, and in the upset, nothing came upon me but these bags. Only one passenger was hurt. When the coach tipped he cried out "We are going over!" and made a spring at the door, by which operation he got his head cut severely, and bruized himself not a little. The rest of us were unhurt. On a post-mortem examination of the carriage I found a pile of stones within a foot of where my head came down. Had there not been snow in the ditch I should have been severely hurt. We were more than an hour in getting the coach into the road again. We reached New Haven at noon the next day; having left the wounded passenger at a tavern, in bed and in the doctor's hands. After dinner I drove on to Hartford, sitting on top of the mail-bags, which were piled in an uncovered *pung*. The last eighteen miles it rained like fury, and I reached Hartford wet through. To-day's journey has been more lucky; and I hope to have a better one still to Portland, tho' it is raining again to-night.

I have not yet seen Mary, but shall stop in tomorrow-morning. I am now on my way to bed; but thought I would write these few lines to say that you may expect me on Thursday morning, or Friday at the latest.

With my best love to all

Affectionately yours
Henry W. Longfellow.

MANUSCRIPT: Longfellow Trust Collection. ADDRESS: Hon. Stephen Longfellow/ Portland/Me. POSTMARK: CAMBRIDGE MS. FEB 11

1. In error for "Feb."

## 522. *To Josiah Quincy*

Cambridge. Feb. 11. 1840

President Quincy.
Dear Sir

I have the honor to recommend as French Instructer in Harvard University, Mr. *A. de Goy*; now residing in New York, and to request you to lay this nomination before the Corporation at its next meeting.[1]

Very respectfully yours
Henry W. Longfellow

MANUSCRIPT: Harvard College Papers, X, 14. PUBLISHED: *Professor Longfellow of Harvard*, p. 96.

1. Anatole de Goy was a Parisian discovered for Longfellow in New York by Sam Ward. The Corporation voted his appointment on February 12 (*Professor Longfellow of Harvard*, p. 96). He resigned a year later.

## 523. *To Samuel Ward*

Portland Feb. 15. 1840

My dear Sam,

I write you from the extreme Down East; from the fair city, which gave birth to John Neal, Nat Willis and myself, and into which I entered triumphantly last evening, just as the town-sexton was ringing nine.

Did you receive a letter from me dated three days ago in Cambridge?[1] If so, I hope and trust you have not told Mr. de Goy what I there said. Be careful not to say anything to him which might embar[r]ass me, in making choice of any other person, who may offer, having superior qualifications. Indeed I think I have found such a person here in a Mr. Bouchette, who from long residence in Canada has the English language as perfectly at command as the French, and moreover understands the English c[h]aracter.[2] But this is *entre nous*. If you should see *De Goy*, therefore, do not tell him he has been nominated; as it may be advisable for me to withdraw the nomination.

How suddenly I have passed from New York into the retirement of a provincial Capital. The cries and carriage wheels of Broadway are still ringing in my ears. I can see the smoky light coming through the window curtain in the *Cadle* [Cradle?] attic; — I can hear your boots on the stairs, and hear you say *"Well, old gentleman!"* I have almost the filial impiety to wish I were still with you, and that we were to sit with Mersch[3] this evening, and drink Johannisberger. These things pass away; but they are the *aroma* in the *enameled* goblet of Life, whose rich perfume we perceive *before* and *after,* but not *while* drinking, the strong reality then overpowering both anticipation and remembrance.

When Major Douglas's books are sold, if there are any noted ones on Engineering which go cheap please purchase. I have a brother in that line, who would like them.[4]

And once more; — if De Goy comes prepare his mind for defeat, if necessary; but he must *not* imagine that it arises from what has been said to me of his youthful errors.[5] You need not seek him out, however, nor give yourself much trouble on the point; though I hate to disappoint him. It is not *certain* that I shall. What will be best for the College? is the only question I have a right to ask myself.

Very truly yours, my dear Sam,
H. W. L.

MANUSCRIPT: Longfellow Trust Collection. ADDRESS: To/Samuel Ward Esq/ New York. POSTMARK: PORTLAND Me. FEB 15

1. This letter is unrecovered.

2. Possibly a reference to Robert Shore Milnes Bouchette (1805–1879), a French-Canadian who had joined the rebellion of 1837 and been banished to Bermuda. He returned to Canada under the amnesty of 1844 and became commissioner of customs in 1851. Nothing came of Longfellow's maneuvering to obtain him as instructor.

3. Charles Fréderic Mersch (1820–1888), a native of Luxembourg, had become Sam Ward's intimate friend in Europe in the thirties; and Ward had helped finance his way to America. In 1849 the two men followed the Gold Rush to California, where Mersch became wealthy enough to be listed in *A "Pile," or A Glance at the Wealth of the Monied Men of San Francisco and Sacramento City* (San Francisco, 1851). He subsequently returned to Luxembourg to become a professor at the Athénée and a councillor of state.

4. Major David Bates Douglass (1790–1849), a Yale graduate of 1813 and an engineer of considerable repute, had served in the War of 1812. He had several academic positions during his lifetime and was presumably selling his books before leaving New York for Ohio, where he served as president of Kenyon College, 1840–1844.

5. The nature of these errors is not known. In a letter of February 14, 1840,

Sam Ward wrote, "It is at least a part of *our* philosophy to believe a man may atone for his past errors and so plain and sincere do this young fellow's intentions of reform appear that I have told him I should recommend him to you."

## 524. *To Samuel Ward*

Portland. Feb. 18 1840

"Well old gentleman,"

Your letter reached me this morning probably about the same moment that my last reached you. I can only hope that you have not seen *de Goy* a second time. I have written this morning to tell him, that the business is finally settled in his favor;[1] and write you now to say the same, that you may send him the cheering news, in case my letter should not reach him. I want him to be in Cambridge by the middle of next week, or as soon after as possible.

I am sorry that La Forêt and Guillet have met; as it will implicate me. I never, however, so much as mentioned Guillet's name in my interview with the Consul. However, it is of no consequence.[2]

I am going this afternoon to Brunswick, where so many laborious, happy years glided away, — and taught me to be tired of solitude. Yet then I was not so truly alone as now. Would I go back? No.

My brother told me yesterday that some paragraphs had appeared in some New York paper saying I stole the idea of the Midnight Mass from Tennison. Absurd. I did not even know that he had written a piece on this subject.[3]

Has anything new turned up since I left you? Dont fail to hear Emerson's lectures.[4] The difference between him and most other lecturers is this. From Emerson you go away and remember nothing, save that you have been much delighted, you have had a pleasant dream in which angelic voices spoke. From most other lecturers you go away and remember nothing save that you have been lamentably *bored,* you have had the *nightmare,* and heard her colts neigh. This is a true account; you shall yourself be judge.

My ink does not run smoothly to-day. Grim-visaged Winter has laid his hand upon the heart of the ink-stand, and curdled the black blood in its veins. Quills, likewise, split awry. And I, who am as much a descendant of the *Inkers* (Incas) as Garcilasso[5] ever was, resent the insult with many a half-suppressed half-uttered imprecation, which will never reach your ears.

Yesterday I read [Irving's] Astoria, shall I confess it? for the first time. It is a fascinating book. The venerable form of John Jacob stands erect there, like a statue of granite. A sublime enterprise.

Farewell. If you do not intend to read your four vols. of Spanish drama this spring, just throw them in with the other books, as I intend to take up that theme in earnest on my return to Camb.

Very truly yours
Henry W. Longfellow.

MANUSCRIPT: unrecovered; text from photostat, Longfellow Trust Collection. ADDRESS: To/Samuel Ward Esq/New York POSTMARK: PORTLAND ||ME.|| FEB 19 PUBLISHED: *Uncle Sam Ward and His Circle,* pp. 259–260.

1. Longfellow's letter to de Goy is unrecovered.

2. Charles-Adel Lacathon de La Forest (1784–1870), the French consul general in New York City, was apparently the sponsor of young de Goy (Sam Ward to Longfellow, February 14, 1840). Isadore Guillet, whom Longfellow had met in Paris in 1826 (Letter No. 110), was living in New York and participating in the search for the Harvard instructor. It was he, presumably, who had uncovered the story of de Goy's questionable background. In a letter of November 3, 1839, he wrote, "il [de Goy] a beaucoup d'esprit et assez d'instruction, mais on l'accuse de n'avoir pas de trés bon principes et de manquer entièrement de délicatesse" [he has a lot of intelligence and enough education, but it is imputed that he lacks high principles and is wholly deficient in manners]. Guillet's other letters to Longfellow concerning the French instructorship are dated September 19, 1839, and February 13, 1840.

3. This accusation was originally made by Edgar Allan Poe in a review of *Voices of the Night* in *Burton's Gentleman's Magazine,* VI (February 1840), 100–103. See 538.1.

4. Emerson lectured in New York before the Mercantile Library Association on "The Philosophy of History," March 10; "The Character of the Present Age," March 13; and "The Literature of the Present Age," March 17 (Ralph Rusk, *The Letters of Ralph Waldo Emerson* [New York, 1939], II, 260, n. 59).

5. Garcilaso de la Vega (c. 1535–1616), son of the Spanish conquistador Sebastián Garcilaso de la Vega and an Incan princess, was Peru's first native-born man of letters.

## 525. *To Zilpah Longfellow*

Cambridge. Feb. 27. 1840

My dear Mother,

This is *your* letter, it being to-day the 27. and I trust you will be glad to hear of my safe arrival. It was not so speedy as I imagined it would be. The roads were very rough and we did not reach Boston till half-past eight in the evening. Of course I passed the night in town; so I did the next day; and drove out with James [Greenleaf] in the afternoon. I found Mary perfectly well; and she has been busy all day reading her numerous letters.

Miss Lowell is moving to-day. I am very sorry for her. She has lost seven thousand dollars by her nephew's failure.[1] She is quite heroic about it *now*; but when there is no longer any glory attatched to this heroism, and she finds herself alone in her *cottage* (*half* a one-story house) I think she will suffer very much. I think she is wrong to move. I would not have done it, had I been in her place.

March 1.

I was interrupted in the midst of my letter, by business. Indeed I am now full of little occupations — arrangements with the new French Instructer, who has just arrived. There is a good deal of perplexity about new arrangements always.

As to household matters, I have made my plans to live where I am; and set up a kind of bachelor establishment for the present. Miss Lowell takes one of the servants, and the other remains here to provide me with necessary food. This is the only good plan. I could not go to a Boarding House; and Mary's dinner hour varies with James's movements, so that it will not answer my purposes.

The Higginsons remain in Cambridge, after all. Their friend Mrs. Channing[2] is to live with them. But these items of intelligence belong to Mary. I must not anticipate her.

It is a bright, breezy March day. The trees and the meadows look russet and the river blue. Everything is clothed with sunshine, and a quarter's salary due on Monday. I am consequently in very good spirits; and begin the new term under good auspices. I hope I shall be a better home-correspondent than I have been heretofore. But I do not know that I shall be able to reform my bad habits. I will try.

By the way — the "Portland Pie" came safe in the carpet bag. I have not yet cut down into it, not having had time to eat, and never feeling hungry at night, except in Portland.

Most affectionately
Henry W. Longfellow

MANUSCRIPT: Longfellow Trust Collection. ADDRESS: Hon. S. Longfellow/Portland/Me POSTMARK: CAMBRIDGE MS. FEB 29

1. After failing as a merchant during the Panic of 1837 (and losing as well a large part of his father's fortune, which he had been managing during his parents' absence abroad), Charles Russell Lowell (1807–1870), the brother of James Russell Lowell, devoted himself to the less competitive business of compiling the first card catalog of books in the Boston Athenaeum. He was the son of Rev. Charles Lowell, Miss Lowell's half-brother.

2. Mrs. Susan Cleveland Higginson Channing (1783–1865), the widow of William Ellery Channing's eldest son and the sister-in-law of Mrs. Louisa Storrow Higginson (451.2).

## 526. *To Stephen Longfellow*

[Cambridge] Sunday March 8. 1840

My dear Father

I have been wishing to write you since my return to Cambridge, and have at length found leisure. You know how much one finds to do at home after an absence, however short; — the greeting of friends — the visits — the unanswered letters lying on the table. These I have at last dispatched; and have arranged the classes for the term. The French Instructer, M. de Goy turns out to be just what I have so long wanted — young, gentlemanly, and well educated — with nothing about him to excite ridicule. I think he will succeed famously, and I feel that I have a great weight taken from my shoulders (as well as from my pocket). I begin my lectures on Dante tomorrow, with the first sentence of [Samuel Johnson's] Rasselas; "Ye who listen with credulity to the whispers of fancy; and pursue with eagerness the phantoms of hope"; &c. When I have finished Dante — say twelve lectures, or so, — I take up the Spanish Drama. I have one class in French — those farthest advanced; — and this occupies only two hours a day in the Lecture room. Judge, if I am in good spirits? Moreover, I have made a good arrangement here with Mrs. Craigie. I take another chamber and a kitchen of her; — one of Miss Lowell's servants remains, and I thus have everything comfortable — dine in my own room, as well as breakfast — and in fine, am the most independent man in town. I, therefore, promise myself a delightful summer.

Miss Lowell has retired to her cottage. It is a nice little place; and she has a talent for giving every place an air of elegance. She will be very comfortable, notwithstanding her loss; but is in great affliction on her brother's account, whose loss is much greater, and also on account of the disgrace. She says; "This is the first stain on the escutcheon of the Lowells!"

Mary is very busy in making her purchases. I paid her the money due, $244.21.[1] James took Mr. Mean's letter; and sent you the receipt, which I presume you received.

I have seen Mr. C. S. Daveis in Boston. He is probably now in Portland. I requested him to tell you I was well. He seemed to enjoy himself, and his dinner.[2]

Anne's package reached me this morning, and was welcomed warmly. I should like three pairs more, if convenient; though at her leisure; as I am not in immediate want thereof.

We have had soft, summer-like weather since my return. The

blue-birds begin to sing; and the south wind blows. But to-day was a wild, untamed Orson of a day, cold and surly. The canker-worms have begun their journey up the trees; and tomorrow I shall tar. I hope to abate this nuisance.

The Great Western has arrived and brings accounts of the Queen's marriage, and that she promised to *obey* her husband, as well as love and honor him. Prince Albert promised "to share with her all his goods," or bestow upon her all his property, or something to that effect.[3] You will see it in the papers.

Farewell.

Very truly
Henry W. Longfellow.

MANUSCRIPT: Longfellow Trust Collection. ADDRESS: Hon. S. Longfellow/Portland/Me POSTMARK: CAMBRIDGE MS. MAR 9

1. This discharged Longfellow's debt to his father.

2. According to his journal entry, Longfellow had dined with Daveis at George Ticknor's on March 4.

3. The marriage of Queen Victoria and Prince Albert occurred on February 10, 1840.

## 527. *To Stephen Longfellow*

Cambridge. March. 13. 1840

My dear Father,

Since my last no novelty has happened, either here or in the neighborhood, save the sudden death of Mr. John Lowell, which took place a few days ago. He was taken off by a stroke of apoplexy, on Thursday morning as he sat by the fire, reading a newspaper. Thus one affliction after another comes upon Miss Lowell.[1] But perhaps the worst of all is the misconduct of the nephew, which appears worse and worse, the more it is investigated; involving some moral delinquencies.

The Lowell lectures meanwhile are flourishing, and maintain the honor of the family. Mr. Nutall[2] commences next week on some branch of Science, I know not what; and I understand, that already *twelve thousand* tickets have been subscribed for. As only *twelve hundred* can be accom[m]odated in the lecture room, the question of who shall have tickets is decided by lot. Thus far the Lectures have been very good. They have been delivered at the Odeon; which in days gone by was the Federal street Theatre. The Boxes and Gallery remain, and the Pit, without much change. The Lecturer stands on the stage. The whole arrangement of lights &c. &c. produces quite a scenic effect; and thus many who would not for the world venture to a play, have here something of the same excitement, without any of the sin.

By the bye, when you have a good opportunity, please send me "Staples's Spanish-English Grammar,"[3] of which you have a copy, I believe. Likewise, when Alex. comes, the *board* for the Bull-Fight, which he will find behind the book-case in the back-room.

Affectionately yours
Henry W. Longfellow.

My dearly beloved Annie,

Permit me to thank you once more for those cotton articles (without a name.) They are just right; and very seasonable. The only change I have to suggest is to put two or three small buttons down in front. They will then be perfect.

Would you like a flower-pot from Italy in the style of an antique Vase? I have seen some lately, earthen-ware, *bronzed* with figures upon them in imitation of those found in Pompeii. I will get some for you if you have a taste for antiques.

Most truly yours
H. W. L.

MANUSCRIPT: Longfellow Trust Collection. ADDRESS: To/Hon Stephen Longfellow/Portland/Me POSTMARK: CAMBRIDGE ||MS.|| MAR 13

1. John Lowell (89.6), Miss Lowell's brother, was a Boston lawyer and ardent Federalist. He is remembered chiefly for his tract *Mr. Madison's War* (1812), an effective piece of political writing.

2. Thomas Nuttall (1786–1859), English botanist and ornithologist, noted for his scientific expeditions to the Mississippi and Missouri valleys and to the Pacific Coast.

3. Stephen M. Staples, *Gramática completa de la lengua inglesa, para uso de los españoles* (Philadelphia, 1825).

## 528. *To Stephen Longfellow*

[Cambridge] Sunday Evening March 22. '40

My dear Father,

I look upon myself as a very audacious letter-writer, inasmuch as I write you without any remorse, when I have nothing to say, which can bear the stamp of novelty or interest. But I consider it good news, when one can write without sending any bad news. This is just my case. Nothing has happened for a week; only one joke, and that not very good; merely a Canadian Frenchman dining with me the other day, on being asked to take Hock, handed his glass bottom upwards. It was so comical, that for the moment I was tempted to fill the bottom of the glass; but good-breeding got the better of fun, beside my being instinctively aware, that if *he* drank so, I should be obliged to do the same. What could I do? I took his glass, and gently turned it up. "Ah," said he, "I thought it went the other way." "Certainly, Sir, it goes both ways; but we *generally* use it in this way."[1]

The London papers have put my name on the list of the Lexington victims. Two letters from friends abroad lament my exit. Another from a bookseller, in four lines coolly asks me to let him know the fact, before sending a book ordered.

A second edition of the Poems will go to press soon. The success of the book is signal. I wish I could have sent you a letter, which was shown me, from a young man in Cincinnati, a few days ago; — very different from any notice you have seen, and showing the real *effect* of these little pieces, and how they *work* in some minds. He thinks them superior to anything that has been written in America; and as the letter was not intended for my eye, I take his opinion as sincere, and hope it may not be *too* exaggerated.[2] I have not written anything since my return to Cambridge; but trust the impulse and the happy moment will return again soon.

I am now at work on the Spanish Drama, reading and making notes for lectures, which commence as soon as I finish Dante — say a month hence. Besides which, as the warm weather advances, I have a prodigious deal of company, and Time has as many wings as the Angels on the Jewish arc.

Do you suppose it possible to kill worms on trees, by boring through the bark into the sap vessels, and introducing crude mercury into the hole? The *theory* is, that the mercury is taken up into the circulation, and salivates the little rascals. Can it be possible?

When is Alex. coming? I have a room for him.

Yours truly and affectionately
Henry W. Longfellow

MANUSCRIPT: Longfellow Trust Collection. ADDRESS: Hon. Stephen Longfellow/ Portland/Me POSTMARK: CAMBRIDGE MS. MAR 23

1. In his journal entry for March 12 Longfellow identifies his guest as "Mr Baillargeon of Quebec." Pierre Baillargeon (1812–1891) received his M.D. from Harvard in 1840.

2. "Mr. Sparks has sent me a letter to read from his friend Longworth of Cincinati, in which he speaks in most enthusiastic language of the effect my poems produce upon him. I am pleased thereat. Let me work thus in the hearts of the young" (MS Journal, March 3, 1840). Nicholas Longworth (1782–1863) was a lawyer and horticulturist of Cincinnati.

529. *To Stephen Longfellow*

Cambridge. April 12. 1840

My dear father,

Your very welcome letter of March 29 did not reach me till two days ago. I found it lying on my table with the Grammar. If Mr. Bowen [1] brought it, he forgot it; though it has finally reached me.

I trust that Mother is quite recovered long ere this. But how can anyone keep well in Spring? I cannot. I have a ferocious appetite; and yet feel the worse for eating. This is in truth, a tremendous climate; and I wonder we continue to live in it, and keep so well as we do.

You do not say one word about your own health; from which I draw only favorable inferences. Indeed from all I heard and saw when I was last with you, I was very much encouraged. Your attacks seem so much milder than they were formerly, that I hope they may go on diminishing in violence, and finally cease; a consummation devoutly to be wished.[2] I beg you, do not be disheartened.

I am glad Dr. Nichols likes the Ballad. It is generally liked. Yesterday I received an imitation of it, on the Burning of the Lexington, by Geo: W. Dixon, who has been in the State's Prison for slandering Dr. Hawkes of N. York! [3] It is not worth sending to you; and only shows, that the piece is felt.

The second edition of the Poems will go to press in a few days. We are only waiting for paper. There has been rather too much delay about [it] I think. John Owen is rather a slow coach.

Mr. Abbot came to see me, a day or two ago, with an attendant from the hospital. He brought me his miniature, sketched in pencil by young Flagg, (a nephew of Allston,) who has likewise been in the hospital for some months.[4] The old gentleman says he is treated worse than Baron Trenk [5] or General Lafayette, and seems consoled by comparing himself to these worthies. Yesterday he was eighty-one years old. He looks upon himself as the most remarkable man alive; and wants to walk to Washington on a wager against any man in a gig, with three changes of the best horses. In fine, there is no end to his boasting.

Thanks to Alex for his letter. I am sorry I cannot pay Earle's bill; but I am short of funds just now. I will speak to him, however, if necessary.[6]

Anne's flower pots I bought last Thursday, and James [Greenleaf] is to have them packed and sent. I suppose Anne will be disappointed at first sight; though afterwards she will confess they are very beautiful specimens of antique pottery.

In yesterday's New World there is an *exposé* of General Bratish, in reply to John Neal's Vindication. It makes some strong assertions, and strange disclosures. Neal had better have been quiet, so far as the General was concerned.[7] I do not take the New World, or I would send it to you.

Yrs very affectionately
Henry W. Longfellow

MANUSCRIPT: Longfellow Trust Collection. ADDRESS: Hon. S. Longfellow/Portland/Me POSTMARK: CAMBRIDGE MS. APR 13

1. *The Portland Directory and Register for 1841* lists both John Bowen and B. C. Bowen (a clothes dealer) as living at the Seamen's Boarding House at the corner of Fore and Willow Streets. One of them may be this Mr. Bowen.

2. *Hamlet*, III, i, 63–64.

3. George Washington Dixon (c. 1808–1861), a comic singer, was among the first to develop the Negro minstrel as a stage character. In 1839 in his short-lived New York weekly *Polyanthos* he became too specific about a rumor concerning Rev. Francis Lister Hawks and one of his young parishioners and consequently spent six months in prison for slander. His imitation of "The Wreck of the Hesperus" is not in the Longfellow Trust Collection.

4. Allston had two nephews named Flagg — George Whiting Flagg (1816–1897) and Jared Bradley Flagg (1820–1899) — both artists and the sons of his half-brother. Longfellow had seen the one referred to here when he visited John Abbot in the hospital on November 29, 1839 (MS Journal).

5. Friedrich, Freiherr von der Trenck (1726–1794), author of a celebrated autobiography, spent thirteen years in a Prussian prison for a supposed love affair with the sister of Frederick II and climaxed a colorful life by being guillotined in Paris as an Austrian spy during the Revolution.

6. On April 8, 1840, Alexander had asked Longfellow to pay a bill of $18 owed by him to John Earle, presumably for the "flamingo coat" delivered in September 1838. See 447.2.

7. Neal had swallowed the elaborate tales of a European imposter calling himself Gen. John Bratish Eliovich, Baron Fratelin (c. 1806–?), who claimed to have been an officer in the Polish, Spanish, Mexican, and other armies, as well as an envoy from Greece. Neal published a defense of him in the *New World*, Vol. I, No. 23 (Saturday, March 28, 1840). Shortly afterwards two Philadelphia lawyers named John Stille, Jr., and Henry McIlvaine answered Neal with the exposé referred to here (*New World*, Saturday, April 11, 1840), in which they called Bratish a swindler, liar, and rascal. Years later, in the article "A Mysterious Personage" in the *Atlantic Monthly*, XX (December 1867), 658–669, Neal admitted that he had been duped. See Irving T. Richards, *The Life and Works of John Neal* (Harvard dissertation, 1932), II, 950–962.

## 530. *To Stephen Longfellow*

Cambridge April 19. 1840

My dear Father,

Since I last wrote you, we have been very near being burned alive here in the Cra[i]gie house. About ten o'clock on Wednesday evening Mr. Rölker was sitting with me; when we heard an alarm of fire; but as the bell did not ring we went on with our conversation for five minutes or more. When finally Rölker grew uneasy, and looking out of the window, said the fire must be very near. It was nothing more nor less than the Gardiner's house on one side, and the barn on the other. Being both very old and dry they burst into a sheet of flame at once. Mrs. Cra[i]gie had not gone to bed. I knocked at her door, and told her what the matter was. She was quite calm and self-possessed notwithstanding an Irishwoman, who had penetrated into the house [and] set up a kind of funereal wail in the entry, which was responded to by the two Irish servants, upstairs in their night-caps. I then went out, and she locked all the outer doors, so as to protect the furniture from the exertions of indiscreet friends; a wise precaution, as the event proved; for not a thing was touched and no mud nor water brought into the house.

The fire burned magnificently; to the utter destruction of out-houses and the isolated gardiner's cottage. No great damage was done; *though* there were fifteen engines present. Fortunately there was not a breath of wind and the flames and sparks, and smoke rose up perpendicularly to a great height. Had there been a West wind, the spot where I sit writing, would now be some twenty feet up in the open air, without roof or floor. We could not have saved the house.

The scene was very splendid. The bright moon — the stars, and the red fire, and the crowd, made a fine show for those who were insured or indifferent. In the midst of all, I saw slowly riding under the elms on the green in front of the house, a figure on horse-back. It seemed like the ghost of Washington, directing the battle.

All the ladies in town (except Mary and Mrs. G.) [1] were on the spot; as spectators and condolers; and conspicuous among many, Aunt Sally, in her shoes and a sky-blue cloak, with nothing on her head but a muslin cap. It was a curious scene. Judge Fay, buttoned up to his chin in a brown surtout, — growling, and muttering now and then "It is all owing to the d——d democracy!" — and Judge Story gesticulating, shouting, and tramping this way and that, — mouth wide open, and the fire gleaming on his gold-spectacles; and ejaculating "We shall all have our houses burned down about our ears; and it is all because you wont hang the rascals, when you catch them!"

There is of course no doubt as to the origin of the fire. The only question is, *who* did the deed. As yet no suspicion has fixed itself upon any one; though it points to the late occupant of the garden house, who has lately been ejected; because he would not pay his rent.

Yours very truly
Henry W. Longfellow

Mary went into her house last night. So that she is now fairly under way, and will soon have her house in order.

MANUSCRIPT: Longfellow Trust Collection. ADDRESS: Hon. S. Longfellow/Portland. POSTMARK: BOSTON ||MAS.|| APR 2||0||

1. Mrs. Simon Greenleaf, Mary's mother-in-law.

## 531. *To Stephen Longfellow*

Cambridge May 2 1840

My dear Father,

I did not write on Sunday last, because I was interrupted by company, just as I had written the date, and was obliged to break off. Since then we have buried the old president Dr. Kirkland.[1] His death awakened the sympathies of the —

Here a rap at the door. Enter M. de Goy, dressed in black — gloves and cain. Takes a chair and begins to talk of Paris &c. &c. This continues for an hour. Another rap. Enter Mr. Soler[2] a Spanish Gent. from Majon: So now I am on the Pyrinees — that is between France and Spain. Talk — talk — talk. And now the clock strikes. It is twelve — noon; and the letter unwritten which I began soon after breakfast. This will give you some idea of how Time passes here.

I was going to say, that Dr. Kirkland died much lamented by all who had known him in his better days. A subscription is already on foot to erect a monument to his memory in Mount Auburn. Dr. Bowditch is soon to have a bronze statue there likewise.

In college there is nothing new. The term is about half over; and my health good — much better than last Spring. I keep out in the open air as much as possible; and take more exercise than heretofore.

Please say to Anne, that the Italian flower-pots had no saucers. The holes are to fasten them to a balcony or roof, with an iron spike.

In great haste, these few lines

Very truly yours
Henry W. Longfellow

MANUSCRIPT: Longfellow Trust Collection. ADDRESS: Hon. S. Longfellow/Portland POSTMARK: BOSTON MAS. MAY 5

1. President Kirkland was buried on April 28, 1840. In his MS Journal entry for that day Longfellow described the funeral ceremony: "Then to Dr. Kirkland's funeral; at the Church, where he once preached. Wretched funeral ceremony. No singing. Nothing but a dirge on the organ — and one interminable prayer, with passages from Scripture. Is *such* a man allowed to depart *thus*?"

2. Mariano Cubí y Soler (1801–1875), an author of Spanish grammars and textbooks.

532. *To Stephen Longfellow*

Cambridge May 16. 1840

My dear Father,

James [Greenleaf] has returned, bringing no letters save yours to Miss Lowell, which has caused great delight. I likewise saw Mrs. Rand[1] yesterday; so that I know you are all well, which is one great point.

I have not written you lately, having been very busy; a good deal of time being given to my friend Mr. Sumner, whose return gives us all great pleasure. He is full of life and excitement; and makes a sensation in our quiet circle, which is very agreeable. He is a man of superior talent, and will make a figure in the world.[2]

The Spring is in full blossom around us; and that pest, the canker-worm, has begun its devastations, to my great dismay. I wish Mrs. Craigie would take care of her trees. I[t] does not belong to me to defray the expenses, of keeping her grounds in order. She says; "Oh, Sir, it's because the world is so wicked! If people were more virtuous there would be no canker-worms!" There, there's a specimen of her reasoning on the subject. Her head is full of such notions. Either she or I must be a great sinner (or both) to be visited annually by such a plague. My opinion is, that tar, would be a better remedy than virtue.

{He (Sumner) and Felton came in and we have been talking for two hours about travelling &c. They have now gone down to see Judge Story, and I resume my letter.}

My second edition of Voices is nearly printed, and will be published in a few days. It will be precisely like the first; no additions having been made. I think this the best way.

I went to town yesterday to see Major Whistler on Alex's account; but found that both he and McNeal were on the road.[3] I think Alex had better forward to them a petition for a situation, or something to that effect, with due references. We will all do what we can. I hope he may succeed this time.

Sam has doubtless reached you safely, and you will have a pleasant visit from him.

Yours very affectionately
Henry W. Longfellow.

MANUSCRIPT: Longfellow Trust Collection. ADDRESS: Hon. Stephen Longfellow./ Portland./Me. POSTMARK: CAMBRIDGE MS. MAY 19

1. Caroline Doane Rand (b. 1816), Longfellow's second cousin, was the wife of John Rand, a graduate of Bowdoin in 1831 and a Portland attorney.

2. Charles Sumner's social successes abroad provided the standard subject of conversation among his friends for some weeks after his return to Boston. Long-

fellow's journal reveals that he saw him almost daily from May 7 to the time of this letter.

3. George Washington Whistler (1800–1849), father of the painter James Abbott McNeill Whistler, was a West Point-trained engineer, engaged at this time in the construction of the Boston and Albany Railroad. He later built the railroad between Moscow and St. Petersburg, for which in 1847 Czar Nicholas conferred upon him the Order of St. Anne. William Gibbs McNeill (1800–1853), Whistler's friend and fellow West Pointer, is generally considered one of the foremost railroad engineers of this period.

## 533. *To Stephen Longfellow*

Cambridge May 27. '40

My dear Father

We reached Boston yesterday morning between nine and ten o'clock; — night calm enough, and as pleasant as one could expect to pass in a bed-room with some hundred persons more or less. I found the carryall waiting; and sent by it to Cambridge my baggage and James's letters. I then went to Mr. Collins, (No 18 Centre street) [1] and paid the money. I have his receipt; and will send it by first good opportunity.

Nothing has happened in Cambridge during my short absence. Indeed, as I sit here this hot morning, and hear the birds sing, I do not seem to have been absent at all. Last evening I took tea at Mrs. Greenleaf's. They are all well. Mr. and Mrs. Fuller [2] are there.

I have ordered to go by the next boat four dozen bottles of soda-water; — or two dozen, in case he had not bottles enough for four. I think you will find it excellent with your dinner, instead of tea. It is only 50 cents per dozen, if the bottles are returned.

Affectionately yours
Henry W. Longfellow

MANUSCRIPT: Longfellow Trust Collection.

1. Probably Ebenezer Collins, a dry goods importer and jobber of 18 Central St., Boston.

2. Rev. Samuel Fuller (1802–1895) was Mrs. Greenleaf's son-in-law, having married Charlotte Kingman Greenleaf (b. 1809). The Fullers lived in Middletown, Conn.

## 534. *To George Washington Greene*

Cambridge May 28. 1840.

My dear George,

Yours of 21 March reached me about ten days ago. I begin my answer by showing you, that I have attended to your requests without any delay. I got yr. Article on the Campagna from Palfrey and sent it to Cogswell. I know that he received it, because he told me so with his own lips; and moreover said it was very good, without going into detail. I have not read it; but shall read it soon; as it will probably be in the July No. and I had rather read it in print than in M.S.[1] As to the North American Articles, here is the list thereof, with the number of pages in each.

| | | | | |
|---|---|---|---|---|
| No. 94. | Art IX. | Reformation in Italy. | 25 pages. | [XLIV, 153–178] |
| 96. | " VI. | European Libraries. | 32 " | [XLV, 116–149] |
| 97. | " II. | Verazzano . . | 19 " | [XLV, 293–311] |
| 99. | " I. | Italian Romance | 15 " | [XLVI, 325–340] |
| 102 | " I. | Micali. . . . | 62 " | [XLVIII, 1–63] |
| 107 | " I. | Italian Philosophers | 36 " | [L, 301–336] |

This last Article does you very great credit, and I hear it often praised. Gov. Everett has spoken to me twice about it. He likes it much, — and thinks it superior in point of style to yr. other papers. So do I. There is more life and elasticity in it; and seems to have been written more *con amore*. And now for the Volume of Lives you wish to publish. *Sparks* has sold his work to the Harpers, and has no longer any interest in it. I know not who the editor is; nor whether the work is to be continued. I will however make all needful endeavors to get yr. vol. in to this Library, or some other as good.[2]

Edward Everett leaves, with his family, for Europe in a few days. He will be in Italy next Autumn. Among his books will go a copy of the *Voices*, and one of Hyperion for you. You will not get them however before he reaches Italy. This will be no great matter, as I hear indirectly, that you have read both. I heard so last evening. Miss Davis, one of Minot's aunts told me she had seen Miss Greenbough, who had just received a letter from you, in which you spoke in high terms of Hyperion.[3] I am right glad, my dear George, that it pleases you; and that you sympathise with me in such moods of feeling, as those which produced this book. Here, the *poems* are much more generally liked, than Hyperion. With strange perversity, too many like the earlier poems best. This is because they understand them best. For my own part I should be very much mortified to think so; and maintain, that there is no kind of comparison between them. I trust you will agree with me. The poems have gone to a Second Edition, which is worth mentioning, as it does not often happen now-a-days, that a volume of poems runs through an edition so soon.

Clark has announced yr. letters; — and No. 1. is to come in the next Knickerbocker. I am very impatient to see it. I imagine it must be the Crawford letter.[4] I saw, too, the other day, an extract from some lady's correspondence (probably Miss Sedgwick) in which *your great secret* was revealed. This extract was in a newspaper. It stated, that you were engaged upon a history of Italy, and had heroically resolved to devote to it twenty five years of your life![5] I had been flattering myself all along, that you were engaged upon a History of Italian Literature; and I was not a little surprised to find my ||surmises|| wrong. When Sumner returned, I spoke to him on the subject, and told him how I had found out your secret. He smiled, and said it was strange. We then discussed the subject a little, and I did not conceal my regret, that you had chosen History instead of Literature. He then explained to me somewhat your reasons; and though I am not *convinced,* yet I have confidence enough in your judgment to *believe,* that you have done right in settling down upon Italian History. May God speed you in your labors, and the World reward with fame.

I see likewise that Wilde is writing a Life of Dante. I hope he does not mean to publish it. He cannot *write.* He can collect materials, but does not seem to me master enough of an English style to do justice to such a subject. But let him work on, and the Lord deliver us from evil.[6]

Since your last letter Sumner, Cogswell, and Nat. Willis have all returned safe and sound from foreign travel. Sumner is full of life, and soul, and anecdote, only a little too much *Anglo-mania* about him, which will wear off, I trust. Otherwise he seems to us all unchanged, save for the better. Of course they lionize him famously in Boston. Rather too much for my purpose, as I can never get a fair chance at him. Tomorrow I meet him at dinner at Prescott's, with Ticknor, and others. We shall probably have a good time. I wish you could be there. And this reminds me, Prescott spoke to me the other day in warm terms of what you were trying to do for him in Italy; and wished me to say to you, that if his History were translated into Italian, he would replace the copy, which you would necessarily furnish the translator by another presentation copy to yourself.

Cogswell was here a few days only. In good spirits, and vigorous, as a young man. He is as delightful in his way, as Sumner is. I wish he lived here instead of in New York. But the East Winds would kill him, in a week.

Nat. Willis I did not see. He was in Boston but one day. Of course I did not hear of his arrival, until he had departed. He had his wife, and his wife's sister with him; and has now gone to *Glen-Mary* for the Summer. This Glen-Mary you know, is his country-seat, in the Valley of the Susquehannah. He says he has made ten thousand dollars the last year by his writings. I wish I had made ten hundred. He has just published, or rather *re*published three plays, in London.[7] They are fine productions; — full of poetry; and do him honor. Those who read the modern English plays (which I do not) — for instance those of Bulwer, Knowles,[8] &c. give the preference to Willis; — say his are the best — decidedly the best; — which after all is not saying much, I fancy.

American Literature has taken a decidedly poetic turn of late. A Mr. Bacon of New Haven has published a large volume of very weak productions. A sophomore in our College, by name Shepherd has done the same foolish thing. *Congdon,* nephew of Dr. Wayland, who was in College here last year, has put out a thin volume, of a good deal of merit. Pierpont has a volume in Press. *Colvert* of Baltimore, translator of Schiller's Don Carlos, has just issued "Count Julian, a Tragedy" — and *Caribo,* a poem in the Don Juan style, neither of which I have read. Hillhouse has sent forth two volumes; — and Halleck *one,* containing Fanny, and the Croker poems, once so well known in New York.[9]

Felton's Translation ||of Menzel's|| History of German Literature will be published in a few days. ||He has|| had a laborious task, and has performed it well. I hope he will not fail of success. I think he cannot. The book will be very *à propos* just now, when everybody talks about German Literature and German Philosophy as if they knew something of them. I hope he will make money by the publication. *Fame* by such a work, of course he will not think of. It comes out in Ripley's Collection, as I have told you probably before, two or three times perhaps. Whether he (Ripley) means to reject Italian works I cannot say; not being intimate with him. But I believe he has an immense quantity on hand.

Now it is four o'clock p.m. and I go to dinner. O how I wish you were here to take the arm-chair on the opposite side of yonder round table, whereon await me a bottle of Italian wine, red-gleaming from its christal tower; — sardines in oil, and a ham; — with whatsoever may come after in the shapes of cake or custard. Alas! I must sit down alone. But I begin by pledging you and Maria in a goblet of iced Calabria. May you live a thousand years!

There — I have achieved that important action, — single-handed and have drunk your health, and am now smoking a pipe, and continuing the letter. In the volume I send you by Everett you will find a sketch of the house I live in. The situation is delightful; having fields, and trees, and flowers all about it. I will now draw you a plan of the interior; and if you will do the like in yr. next letter, you will do me a pleasure you little dream of, but which I dream of in drawing this.[10]

There you have a faithful picture of my whereabout[s] — all chambers. Where you see the black ✠ I am now sitting, facing Felton, who has just come in, and sits in the easy chair by the window. Dont fail to send me your bust by Crawford to adorn my dwelling with.[11]

Felton desires much love to you, and ||also to your|| wife. Write to me as soon as you can. Now your season of leisure is approaching; and your cares will cease for awhile. Sumner has told me all about you; and how infinitely and unmercifully you are bored by the *flats.* Never mind it; every man, who has to work for his living must be *bored* in one way or another.

You ask my advise about the Letters on Modern Rome. It depends solely upon how you manage the matter. I should think it a very rich field without compromising yourself as Consul. I would touch only on what is praiseworthy and agreeable; and whatever your heart prompts you to say, why say it. Tell us about the Modern Sculptors and modern painters of all nations — how they live and what they are doing. Give a ske[t]ch of low-life in Rome — the Minenti[12] — the popular songs — the ballads you buy in the street — and such matters. On this subject I have written you once before; so shall say no more on this chapter at present. My only advice is for you to do as *you* feel, not as *we* feel.

Did you receive a copy of Outre-Mer, which I had sent to you from London? The bookseller writes me, that he sent it according to my direction.

And now farewell. With most affectionate remembrances of you both, I remain

very truly yours
Henry W. Longfellow.

MANUSCRIPT: Longfellow Trust Collection. ADDRESS: George W. Greene Esq./ American Consul/Rome./Italy./Via New York/and Havre de Grace. ANNOTATION (*by Longfellow*): Paid to N.Y./No 192 POSTMARKS: CAMBRIDGE MS. MAY 29/OUTRE-MER JUIN &C LE HAVRE/ROMA 4 LUG 1840/VIA DI PT. BEAUVOISIN

1. The article on "The Country Around Rome, Its Climate, Culture, and Condition" appeared in the *New York Review,* VII (July 1840), 86–108.

2. Greene had indicated his interest in preparing "a volume or half volume of Lives of Italian discoverers in America" for Jared Sparks's *Library of American Biography* (Letter of March 21, 1840). Longfellow was unsuccessful in placing the projected volume.

3. It is clear from his answer of July 11, 1840, that Greene had written to a Miss Greenough, presumably one of the sisters of Horatio Greenough, with whom

he was on intimate terms. William Minot (1817–1894), a Harvard graduate of 1836, had made Greene's acquaintance while on a tour of Europe, 1839–1840. Of Minot's several Davis aunts, this one was most likely Miss Helen Davis, whom Longfellow mentions specifically in his MS Journal entry for May 10, 1838.

4. See 515.1 and 515.3.

5. Longfellow has added five years to the project. Miss Sedgwick had reported that Greene, "with frail health, has determined to devote twenty years to a history of Italy!" (*Letters from Abroad to Kindred at Home* [New York, 1841], II, 159). The history was never written.

6. Richard Henry Wilde's incomplete life of Dante remained in manuscript.

7. Willis republished not three but two plays abroad: *Two Ways of Dying for a Husband. I. Dying to Keep Him, or Tortesa the Usurer. II. Dying to Lose Him, or Bianca Visconti* (London, 1839).

8. James Sheridan Knowles (1784–1862), Irish actor and playwright, was the cousin of Richard Brinsley Sheridan.

9. William Thompson Bacon, *Poems* (New Haven, 1839); Isaac Fitzgerald Shepard, *Pebbles from Castalia* (Boston, 1840); Charles Taber Congdon, *Flowers Plucked By a Traveller on the Journey of Life* (Boston, 1840); John Pierpont, *Airs of Palestine, and Other Poems* (Boston, 1840); George Henry Calvert, *Count Julian; a Tragedy* (Baltimore, 1840) and *Cabiro. A Poem. Cantos I and II* (Baltimore, 1840); James Abraham Hillhouse, *Dramas, Discourses, and Other Pieces* (Boston, 1839); and Fitz-Greene Halleck, *Fanny, With Other Poems* (New York, 1839).

10. Longfellow's sketch of his rooms follows here. See Plate No. V.

11. Greene had offered the bust to Longfellow if he would pay the freight from Rome (Letter of March 21, 1840). It is now in the study of the Longfellow House. See Plate No. IV.

12. See 280.2.

## 535. *To Alexander Slidell Mackenzie*

Cambridge May 31. 1840

My dear Slidell

I almost blush, when I write your name; merely to think how I have neglected my promises to you since my return. The truth is, I have been disappointed in not procuring the information I hoped to find in regard to the Baron of Castine.[1] What I have found does not amount to much. This St. Castiens (so the name is sometimes written) or the Baron, as he was usually denominated, was an officer in the French Army in Canada in the last part of the Seventeenth Century. He commanded the Regiment of Carignan. After the peace of Breda, the army being disbanded, he went to Penobscot, on the shores of whose beautiful bay, he had a plantation with extensive gardens. He was a gentleman of fortune; and traded with the Indians, whose language he had learned in Canada. This I find in the History of Belfast, a town in the neighborhood of Castine. The history goes on to say; "The Baron opened a large trade in fish and furs, which he received in exchange for European merchandize. Naturally artful and insinuating, and being well informed, he soon rendered himself the idol and the oracle of the Indian tribes. Madocowando, the Sachem of Penoubscot, gave to the Baron his favorite daughter, to grace the circle of his Indian wives; and whenever the interests of his tribe were at hazard, took council with the Baron, whose secret influence was felt throughout all the settlements in New England. In some instances the Baron led the tribe to battle."[2]

The book then relates very briefly the storming of Gov. Andros's fort at Pemaquid point, and then drops Castine, without more ado. His references are to Abbé Raynal. Vol. 7. 219. and Houton's Voyages.[3]

To tell the truth, my heart rather misgives me about this subject. I do not want you to fall into Cooper's trail — or *wake*, I *should* say. People would cry out *imitation!* which heaven forfend. Your good genius will guide you to some good theme ere long; — where you will be master of something yet unattempted.

I was quite astonished at receiving only a week or two ago yrs. of *Feb.* 1840. I[t] came by the slow coach. As to the proof-sheets of Paul Jones, I will read them with the greatest pleasure. I am very glad to have it in my power to serve you in any way, and will make any suspicious looking sentence show his passport.[4]

In regard to the Piña de los Enamorados, I shall advise you not to publish it. The sack of Martos is very finely done, and the midnight scene in the Count's palace very striking. But still as a whole I do not think it would raise your reputation as an author. When you enter the realm of fiction, I want you to march in with a more lofty step.[5]

I am sorry that I cannot accept your invitation to visit you this summer; but I fear it will not be in [my] power. But if I can get as far south as New York, I will not fail to drive out and see you.

With my kindest regards to your wife

Very truly yours
H. W. Longfellow.

My volume of Poems has had the good luck to go to a second edition. I shall send you a copy by first opportunity. But to what address?

I asked the printer about Paul Jones a few days ago. He said he should commence upon it soon. As yet I have not received any of the proofs.

MANUSCRIPT: Massachusetts Historical Society. ADDRESS: Alex. Slidell Mackenzie Esq/New York. POSTMARK: CAMBRIDGE MS. JUN 2

1. Jean Vincent d'Abadie, Baron de St. Castin (1652–1707), French soldier and adventurer. See Longfellow's "The Baron of St. Castine" in *Tales of a Wayside Inn* (*Works*, IV, 179–188).

2. William White, *A History of Belfast, With Introductory Remarks on Acadia* (Belfast, 1827), p. 22.

3. Abbé Guillaume Thomas François Raynal, *Histoire philosophique et politique des établissemens et du commerce des Européens dans les deux Indes*; and Jacques Julien Houton de Labillardière, *Relation du voyage à la recherche de La Pérouse.*

4. Mackenzie's *The Life of Paul Jones* (Boston, 1841) was in the process of publication by Hilliard, Gray & Company.

5. Mackenzie appears to have taken Longfellow's advice and to have suppressed this abortive attempt at fiction.

## 536. *To Stephen Longfellow*

Cambridge June. 10. 1840

My dear father,

Since my last, the arrival of the steam-ship Unicorn has set Boston in motion for a couple of days. There was a public dinner in Faneuil Hall, at which I was present; and being called upon by the Mayor for a toast, was obliged to make a short speech, by way of introduction; in which I alluded to Mr. Friedrichsthal (read that, if you can) an Attaché of the Austrian Embassy, who was present, and gave as my toast "The steam-ships — the pillar of fire by night, and the pillar of cloud by day, which guide the wanderer through the wilderness of the sea." The connexion between Mr. Friedl. and this toast, is that the toast is a prose translation of a stanza from a German Poet of Vienna, the city Mr. F. comes from. This of course called him up. He is a curious looking individual with a horse's head, and mustachios, — and his English of the most decided foreign cut. The speech, therefore, was rather an amusing affair; and the more so, because the speaker kept his head bobbing about as if he were pulling hay out of a rack. Nevertheless it went off very well; and so in fine did the whole affair.[1]

I think the most amusing part of all was my speaking at a commercial dinner. Of course, I had no intention of doing so when I went; and was very much surprised when called upon. Being, however, used to speaking in public, I was not abashed, even on this occasion.[2] Several very good speeches were made. The best were the Mayor's and Hillard's.

In Cambridge there is nothing new. The Nichols's I did not see, save John,[3] for a moment, standing at Mary's door. Mary is well, tho' I have not seen her for a day or two; being very busy.

Mr. Felton's Translation of Menzel's German Literature will be out in a few days, and I have written a short review of it, which you will find in the next No. of the New York Review.[4] In the last No. of Knickerbocker, you will find a letter by Geo: W. Greene, addressed to me, on Mr. Crawford, an American Sculptor now in Rome. I think it will interest you.

I am glad to hear the soda pleased you, and will send you more, if you desire it. I find it was put up in small bottles of only one tumbler each. I have generally seen it in larger bottles.

Rakemann, the celebrated German Piano-forte player is here, and dines with me tomorrow. I wish you could be here to hear his exquisite music.

I saw Col. Fessenden two days ago. He has sent the letter Alex. wanted, and seems to think the chances of success favorable.

Yours very affectionately
Henry W. Longfellow.

MANUSCRIPT: Longfellow Trust Collection. ADDRESS: Hon. S. Longfellow/Portland. POSTMARK: CAMBRIDGE MS. JUN 10

1. The public dinner to celebrate the arrival of the *Unicorn*, a new Cunard steam packet, was held on June 5. The mayor was Jonathan Chapman (1807–1848), a Harvard graduate of 1825. Emanuel Ritter von Friedricksthal (1809–1842), whom Longfellow had met the day before (MS Journal, June 4, 1840), was an Austrian traveler and naturalist who had come to America on a study tour at his own expense. To support his research activities, the Austrian government had appointed him attaché to its legation in Washington, although his work was not of a political nature. He died in Vienna as a result of a fever contracted in Yukatan.

2. The *Daily Evening Transcript* reported, however, "Professor Longfellow, being called upon, made a few remarks which were not distinctly heard in all parts of the hall" (Vol. XI, No. 3026 [Saturday, June 6]).

3. Rev. and Mrs. Ichabod Nichols of Portland and their son, John Taylor Gilman Nichols.

4. Longfellow's announcement was premature. In a letter of June 12, 1840, Cogswell revealed his unhappiness with the review for the principal reason that it clashed with one of his own and asked Longfellow to modify it "as far as your conscience will allow." But on June 18 he wrote again, informing Longfellow that he had found the review too long and had sent it to Park Benjamin. Benjamin printed it in three installments in the folio *New World*, Vol. I, Nos. 35, 36, and 37 (June 20, 27, July 4, 1840). Cogswell subsequently reprinted an abridged version in the *New York Review*, VII (October 1840), 522–524.

## 537. *To Stephen Longfellow*

Cambridge June 22. 1840

My dear Father,

I was very sorry to hear by your last letter, that you had been more unwell than usual; and hope that the indisposition may be accounted for without supposing that your disorder has assumed any more unfavorable aspect. Mr. Whitney,[1] I did not see. I found he had been here to see his old acquaintance Mrs. Craigie, who handed me yr. letter.

During the last week I have had my friend Mr. Sumner with me. He has been lecturing in the Law School during the absence of Judge Story and Mr. Greenleaf. I have enjoyed his visit very much; and we have had rather a gay week, dining out, &c. &c. He left me on Saturday, and things have again resumed their wonted slow march.

I have been writing a Review of Menzel's German Literature for the N. York Review, as I think I mentioned in my last. Unfortunately I was too late for the July No. and have consequently directed to have it published in the New World; where the first part of it appeared on Saturday. This is rather unlucky; for the book reviewed is not yet published.

We are looking impatiently for Mother and Alex; and indulge even some faint ray of hope, that you may be induced to come with them. It might do you good, notwithstanding your repugnance to travelling.

On Wednesday next there is to be a festival in commemoration of the Invention of Printing. I have been invited to go and speak on the occasion; but shall not accept the invitation, having no ambition to figure in that way.

I am about getting out a new and fifth edition of my French Grammar. The Proverbes Dramatiques have just reached a third edition. I hope now to get these books into more general use, and make them profitable.

Farewell.

Yours affectionately
Henry W. Longfellow.

MANUSCRIPT: Longfellow Trust Collection. ADDRESS: Hon S. Longfellow/Portland. POSTMARK: CAMBRIDGE MS. JUN 24

1. William Clark Whitney (1765–1859), a wealthy businessman of Norway, Maine, and a friend of Stephen Longfellow (Stephen Longfellow to Longfellow, June 14, 1840).

538. *To Willis Gaylord Clark*

Cambridge. July 5. 1840

My dear Clark,

Your "business-hand" letter of the 20 June reached me safely. I knew it was from you before opening it. There is no mistaking that

W. though I cannot counterfit very elegantly. I was very glad to hear from you; though I had never argued from your silence, that you had taken offense or grown forgetful. I set it down to the right account; being mindful of my own great delinquencies in the same kind. Nevertheless I have often wondered what you were doing, and how you were faring. As I never see your paper now-a-days, I have been a stranger to your doings and sayings. But I have always had confidence in your friendly wishes; and that whatever I wrote would meet with more than justice at your hands.

Pray who is it that is attacking me so furiously in Philadelphia? [1] I have never seen the attacks, but occasionally I receive a newspaper with a defense of [my] writings, from which I learn there has been an attack. I thank you for what you have done for me; — for your good thoughts and good words.

What have you written lately? The last piece of yours which I have seen was that exceedingly beautiful Autumnal sketch, in which you painted in such moving words your feelings of loneliness and sorrow. It is one of the finest pieces, which have been written in this country. It is true pathos, and true poetry.[2]

Why did you not tell me where and how you are now living? and how little Willie flourishes? More about yourself — and your health, and your hopes, and intentions — in fine, an answer to all the questions I should ask if we were together?

For my part, I am still in the same spot — inhabiting the same chambers, — keeping the same Bachelor's Hall, as for the last three years past. No change; and apparently no nearer any, than when I last saw you. The Publisher of Hyperion stopped payment, and broke his engagements with me. A quantity of the books, seized by his creditors, is still in bondage. The *Voices* have gone to a second edition, which is already nearly half sold. I ordered a copy of the first edition to be sent you, which I trust you received. If not, I shall forthwith send you one. I am glad you like the "Hesperus." Did you read Green's Letter in the Knickerbocker about young Crawford? I think it the best thing I have seen from Green's pen.

The reason I did not inflict my brother upon you was, that he merely passed through Philadelphia; and being desirous of seeing the Library and that beautiful Chinese collection, I gave him a letter to our friend Smith.[3]

From Lewis I hear very seldom. I have not been able to write anything for the Knickerbocker of late; and in fact am getting out of writing for the periodicals; save now and then a notice of some book; as for instance Felton's Tr. of Menzel's German Literature.

I hope you will find time to read this work. It is good; and will interest you. Farewell. Let me hear from you soon.

Very truly yours
Henry W. Longfellow.

MANUSCRIPT: Clifton Waller Barrett Collection, University of Virginia. ADDRESS: Willias G. Clark Esq/Philadelphia POSTMARK: CAMBRIDGE MS JUL 6

1. Clark replied on July 18, 1840: "You ask me who attacks you here? The only ones I have seen against you, have been in *Burton's* Magazine — a vagrant from England, who has left a wife and offspring behind him there, and plays the bigamist in '*this*,' with another wife, and his whore besides; one who cannot write a paragraph in English to save his life" (*Clark Letters*, p. 58). The villain, according to Willis Clark, was William Evans Burton (1804–1860), an actor and the publisher of *Burton's Gentleman's Magazine*; but the attacks were actually written by Edgar Allan Poe in reviews of *Hyperion* and *Voices of the Night* (*Burton's Gentleman's Magazine*, V [October 1839], 227, and VI [February 1840], 100–103).

2. Longfellow had earlier expressed his admiration for this poem (Letter No. 505) and later printed it under the title "Dirge in Autumn" in his anthology *The Waif* (Boston, 1845), pp. 81–83.

3. John Jay Smith (1798–1881), librarian for the Library Company of Philadelphia.

## 539. *To Henry Russell Cleveland*

[Cambridge] Friday. July 10 [1840]

My dear Cleveland

Tomorrow I have the Club[1] to dine. I hope you have no engagement to prevent your coming. We are now free from care in Cambridge, — Term is over. I had my Examinations this morning. Tell your dear wife that Edward[2] acquitted himself very handsomely in his Translations from Tasso and Dante.

Sumner is here and Felton, having no household, dines with me, when he can do no better. Dont fail to come tomorrow.

Yours very truly
H. W. L.

MANUSCRIPT: Berg Collection, New York Public Library.

1. That is, the Five of Clubs — Longfellow, Sumner, Felton, Hillard, and Cleveland.

2. Edward Newton Perkins (1820–1899), Sarah Cleveland's brother.

## 540. *To Charles Folsom*

[Cambridge, July 13, 1840]

Mr. Folsom,

Dr. Sir,

In the Art. for N. A. R.[1] I intended that the extract on the *blueish* leaf should be a part of text, and not printed as a quotation. Please see that it is so made. Dr. Palfrey marked it to be in smaller type than text. The Art. is nearly all quotation; so that this must go into text with double commas.

Yrs. truly
H. W. Longfellow

MANUSCRIPT: Boston Public Library. ADDRESS: Mr Folsom/Camb./Folsom Wells & co ENDORSEMENT: Rec'd 13 July, 1840

1. "The French Language in England," *North American Review,* LI (October 1840), 285–308.

## 541. *To Josiah Quincy*

Cambridge. July. 1840

Harvard College to H. W. Longfellow Dr
To one Term's extra instruction
in French, to 26 students at
$4 each, from March to July, . . . $104.00
Cambridge. July. 15. 1840[1]

President Quincy,
Dear Sir,

The small note above is for the extra classes, and charged according to the provision made for such cases. May I take the liberty of asking, that it may be paid with my next quarter's salary.

Yours respectfully
Henry W. Longfellow

MANUSCRIPT: Harvard College Papers, X, 15. PUBLISHED: *Professor Longfellow of Harvard,* pp. 96–97.

1. Following this statement, President Quincy inserted an instruction to Levi Farwell, the college steward: "Mr. Farwell —/Please to pay the above as before in conformity with ye vote of ye Faculty./$104/J. Quincy."

## 542. *To John Vaughan*

Cambridge. July 15. 1840.

To John Vaughan Esq
Dear Sir,

Knowing the lively interest you take in all young men of character and talent, I take pleasure in presenting to you the bearer of this Mr. Stallknecht, a Dane.[1] He is now a member of our college; and during his short stay in your city is desirous of seeing all that is most interesting there. May I ask you to show him the Library &c of the

Am. Phil. Soc. and also to give him a note to Mr. [John Jay] Smith of the City Library, and the Chinese Collection.

Very respectfully yours
Henry W. Longfellow

MANUSCRIPT: American Philosophical Society.

1. Frederick Stoud Stallknecht (d. 1875) was a member of the Harvard class of 1843 but did not actually receive his degree until 1872.

## 543. *To the Harvard Corporation*

Harvard College August 3. 1840.

To the Corporation of Harvard College.
Gentlemen,

I take this occasion respectfully to inform you that some farther provision for instruction in French will be necessary before the commencement of next Term. By the new arrangement of studies, the French has been made a part of the regular and required College Course. The result has been to crowd the Sections in this language; so that instead of twelve in a section we have now from twenty to thirty. At the Commencement of next term an entire new class (the Freshman) will be added to the number; and we shall consequently have in French the whole of the Freshman Sophomore and Junior classes, together with a section from the Senior class, not yet ready for examination.

Of course it will be impossible for one instructer to take charge of so many pupils; and I consequently would request you to make such provision for them, as you may deem proper.[1]

Respectfully yours
Henry W. Longfellow
Smith Professor &c.

MANUSCRIPT: Harvard College Papers, X, 87. PUBLISHED: *Professor Longfellow of Harvard,* p. 41.

1. When Longfellow's recommendation in Letter No. 507 that the study of modern languages begin in the freshman year was accepted, the Corporation specified that the language be French. For details of the academic imbroglio that followed, see *Professor Longfellow of Harvard,* pp. 40–42.

## 544. *To Charles Sumner*

Portland. August. 12. 1840

My dear Charles,

I found this morning on the breakfast table your very interesting letter from Lancaster. It leaves me nothing to wish, save that you had yourself been the bearer thereof. I hope you mean to come. If you will, I promise to return with you next week. Only a fortnight of the vacation remains. It is astonishing how the broken-winded steeds of Time get over the ground; — how *fast,* I mean. I have not corrected any of my bad habits yet. I smoke as much as ever; and when I look down at my corporeal dimensions, like Falstaff I exclaim "O my womb! my womb! my womb!"[1] I fear that in spite of diet, I shall have to give it up, and be "a short, fat man."

You did not say which of the three fair sisters of my friend *was going to Kirk.* I do not think my little Anna would have been led astray; and on the whole I am glad it is neither, as your P.S. informs me.[2] I am sorry not to see Lieber. I like him much, and only stand in mortal fear of his letters.[3] With Mrs. Otis I shall be most happy to renew my acquaintance; and am glad she has chosen Cambridge for her residence.[4]

I must not forget to thank you for your most friendly notice in the Athenaeum. I thought it yours before you sent the paper with your initials.[5] In return I send you a paragraph to-day, out of which you will draw some mirth.[6] The original to which this is but a reply, I have not seen. Perhaps you have. The sting is in its tail, where the rascal says, that some of my friends are intimate *friends of his.* The author is, I believe, Mr. George Dixon of Penetentiary renown.[7] Pray confine it to the club. It ought not to have been noticed at all.

It is a great pity you should have missed seeing Miss Arnold. I have a strong curiosity to know her.[8] Has Miss Barker arrived?[9] The *women* here are very fair; and among them one whose *responsive* nature would lead you captive, — a *Creole,* with the softest black eyes imaginable. Besides, there is a dangerous young widow, and sundry girls, who would chase from your heart the daughters of "*Old G.*" By the way, how could you resist going to Newport with Lieber. I am fearful he may imagine himself your ambassador, and set the lady's imagination at work to your annoy.[10]

One word to Felton. If the Proctors are not yet appointed for next year, I should like to have my younger brother Sam numbered among them; as he means to pass next year at Cambridge as a resident graduate. Have the goodness to think of this.

Most affectionately yours
Henry W. Longfellow

MANUSCRIPT: Longfellow Trust Collection. ADDRESS: Charles Sumner Esq/Boston POSTMARK: PORTLAND ME. AUG 14

1. *Henry the Fourth, Part Two,* IV, iii, 22.

2. Longfellow's pun concerns Edward Norris Kirk (1802–1874), a New York minister described by Sumner as "fiery, Parisian, well-dressed, [and] orthodox"

(Letter to Longfellow of Sunday, August 9, 1840). According to Maud Howe Elliott, Kirk was engaged for a brief period to Julia Ward (*Uncle Sam Ward and His Circle*, p. 208). The Anna referred to was Anne Eliza, youngest of the three Ward sisters.

3. Francis Lieber (1800–1872), German-American political philosopher and at this time professor of history and political economy at South Carolina College. Longfellow's fear of inviting correspondence with him seems justified not only by his reputation for voluminosity but also by the 52 letters Lieber wrote to him, 1844–1872 (Longfellow Trust Collection).

4. Eliza Henderson Bordman Otis (1796–1873), widow of Harrison Gray Otis, Jr. (1793–1827), was a prominent Boston social leader. Having recently returned from Europe, she was moving to Cambridge for the sake of educating her three sons.

5. Sumner's review of *Voices of the Night* appeared in the London *Athenaeum*, No. 569 (Saturday, June 13, 1840), pp. 472–473.

6. This paragraph, presumably a newspaper clipping, is unrecovered.

7. See 529.3.

8. Sumner's letter of August 9 refers obliquely to the notoriety involving Miss Elizabeth Rotch Arnold (1809–1860) of New Bedford — her seduction in 1830 by a relative — which apparently made her interesting to Longfellow. See "The Great Rotch Scandal" in John M. Bullard, *The Rotches* (New Bedford, 1947), pp. 159–165.

9. Presumably Anna Hazard Barker (1813–1900), daughter of Jacob Barker, a prominent lawyer, politician, and entrepreneur of New York and New Orleans. She married Samuel Gray Ward of Boston on October 3, 1840.

10. Sumner was much interested in Miss Elizabeth Wadsworth (1815–1851), the beautiful daughter of James Wadsworth (1768–1844), a well-to-do land proprietor of Geneseo, New York (she was thus one of the "daughters of *'Old G.'* "). That Miss Wadsworth dashed his hopes seems clear from Letter No. 546. A year later Sam Ward asked Longfellow, "Does he [Sumner] dream of Miss Wadsworth still?" (Letter of September 17, 1841).

## 545. *To Stephen Longfellow*

Cambridge August 24. 1840

My dear Father,

You must have been amused to hear by Mary's letter, that I abandoned my New York visit. My night on-board the Bangor gave me such a disgust to steamers, that even the pleasure I promised myself in seeing my N. York friends could not seduce me into two more nights on board the steam-boats.

I have got three pupils for Sam, and though no terms are yet agreed upon, I presume they will pay him enough for his support during the year. I think therefore, that I shall not apply for a Proctorship, as he expressed himself against any such office, when I last saw him. If however, in bringing the matter of remuneration for pupils to a close, I find it will not be sufficient for his expenses, I will put in the claim for a Proctorship. The pupils are the three sons of Mrs.

Otis, who comes to reside in Cambridge, in order to educate them. They are not yet ready for College. I am going to town to-day to arrange this business as far as possible. My friend Sumner has it in hand; as Mrs. Otis applied to him to procure an instructer.

Mary is very well. James *not* very well. The weather has been excessively warm, here. Last night a violent rain, and to-day bright and cool.

In haste, very affectionately yours
Henry W. Longfellow.

P.S. Portland Transcript does not come to me.[1]

MANUSCRIPT: Longfellow Trust Collection. ADDRESS: Hon. S. Longfellow/Portland. POSTMARK: BOSTON ||MAS.|| AUG 25

1. A postscript by Mary Longfellow Greenleaf follows.

546. *To Charles Sumner*

[Cambridge] August. 29. 1840

Dearly beloved Charles,

Both Felton and myself condole with you most sincerely in your disappointment. Two such women[1] do not exist on the face of the earth. But never mind. Such things have happened before. It is told by Camoens in his Lusiad that when the Giant Adamastor tried to embrace the sea-nymph Thetis, she slipped away, and he embraced the shaggy Cape of Good-hope. Your fate is like his. Sam Ward

"colla bella sua barca
*Se ne va!*"[2]

and you remain embracing Egg-Rock.[3]

Felton with tears in his eyes, has just opened Theocritus to find some consolation for you; and I therefore give room for him to repeat a few words of condolence.[4]

Mournfully your sympathizing friend
H. W. L.

MANUSCRIPT: Longfellow Trust Collection. ADDRESS [*by Felton*]: C. Sumner, Esq./COURT Street/Boston

1. Presumably Elizabeth Wadsworth and a friend.
2. Sam Ward "with his beautiful boat/is going away!"
3. A small rock island off Nahant.
4. The letter is continued by Felton, with quotations from Theocritus.

547. *To George Washington Greene*

Cambridge September 4. 1840

My dear George

Pleasant in the soul is the voice of an absent friend! Your delightful letter of July 11. reached me this afternoon, and irradiated the walls of my lecture room. I must answer it before going to bed; — night being favorable to monologues and long letters. What a strange crochet you have got in your brain, that because you do not receive things, *therefore* they were never sent. Not so. Your last Art. *was* sent.[1] I put it into the post-office with my own hands. *Micali* [*on the Ancient Italians*] I did not send, because when that came out you had not asked me to send any; and furthermore I then supposed you received the [North American] Review. I will attend to this tomorrow; and insist upon having the Review sent. Your most praise-worthy performance is the *Campagna.*[2] This is beyond comparison the finest thing I have seen from your pen. It is beautifully written, and interesting in the highest degree. It is alive; and one sees that your heart was in it, when you wrote. That is the way to do things. I can find but few bad sentences in it; and those come in before you have fairly got under way. It has been a good deal copied in the newspapers. The paper on Manzoni is now printing.[3] You will be disappointed to hear that I do not take a great fancy to it. I agree with you only in your *censure.* Sumner will take up the other side and subscribe to your lavish encomiums; as he has been bitten by "*I Promessi Sposi*" and has the disorder very bad. I shall send you the sheets of the Art. in a few days; — tomorrow, if they are out of press. By the way, do write your *proper* names more carefully. Neither Palfrey, nor Folsom, nor I can make out one of the names in your *title,* and it will probably be printed wrong. Tomma*sio's* (is that right?) Dante has not yet arrived, for which I am exceeding sorry.[4] You did not say how it was sent. [Edward] Everett will make Florence his head quarters. Minot[5] does *not* go back to Italy. His father wants him in the Law; to which hard fate he goes with eyes shut, unless he is lucky enough to be taken sick again. Thus have I answered all your questions in the letter of July 11. Anon I will answer some things in yours of May 5. which reached me just as I [was] going to Portland to pass the vacation, and could not then be replied to for want of the necessary information. But first let me dip my pen in midnight, and ask you why you imagine, that after having spoken to you *à coeur ouvert* [unreservedly] so many times concerning the lady, whom I *loved,* I should now be trying to play off upon you an *agreeable surprise* — the most *dis*agreeable thing on earth to me. No. The brazen lips of Fate have said that "Time is *past!*" [6] We now move wholly in separate orbs, and hardly see each others faces once a year. The passion is dead; and can revive no more. Though on this account I lead a maimed life; yet it is better thus, than merely to have gained her consent — her cold consent — even if it could have been done. So of this no more — no more — for evermore! For though I feel deeply what it is *not* to have gained the love of such a woman, — I have long ceased to think of it; — and remember it only, when I see that my elasticity is nigh gone, and my temples are as white as snow. Three of the best years of my life were melted down in that fiery crucible. Yet I like to feel deep emotions. The next best thing to *complete success* is *complete failure.* Misery lies half way between. But you have thrown me into a reverie, with your *query*, and I can write no more to night. I shall smoke, and then to bed. I must contrive to send you *Hyperion* which is the *Apology* for my madness.

September 5.

Evening again. I have been to town, to bring some matters to a close for you, as few as possible. I saw the Agent of the North American. He says it has been sent to you regularly; and showed me his books with the address I gave, according to your direction "*Renoward, Paris*, to be forwarded to *Viessieux Florence.*" That was the order you sent, and he assures me it has been punctually attended to. I then went for the prices of certain books you spoke of. Spencer costs $7.00 — Burke $18.00, and Shakespeare $12.00. There is no *good* American edition of either Clarendon, Swift or Dryden. Next I proceeded to bring to a close some arrangement about yr volume of Biographies of Italian Discoveries in America, or whatever you choose to call the book. I had a conversation with Dr. *Webb,* of the firm of Marsh, Capen & Lion. You know the Dr., at all events he knows you. Their house is publishing a Common School Library, for which Sparks, Story, Irving and others have furnished books.[7] All books which form a part of this Library must be approved by a Committee. Webb has faith in you, and though he will not promise to accept the book unconditionally (for he cannot) he says there is no reasonable doubt but it would be accepted. In this I coincide. He will publish an edition of fifteen hundred copies; giving you, what he gives Judge Story and others, namely, ten per cent on the retail price of all published, in semi-annual payments, beginning six months after publication; which would give you, for the first edition of one volume, $112.00 and no more; and for all other editions at the same rate. The volume must contain at least 350 pages; and the pages contain nearly as much as those of the North American — the type being the same, the size of page a trifle smaller. The remuneration is very small, but there is no risk. Moreover, you will have your name carried into every village in New England, and it will grow up with the rising generation. How much this may weigh with you I know not. I think it weighs something with Story, Irving &c. &c. When the Library was started I was applied to to write some volumes for it. I declined having anything to do with it. I would not write a book on such terms. Nor would advise you to do it. The same number of pages in the Reviews would give you three times the profit. The only plan worth thinking of is to publish first in the Reviews and then collect your papers for a volume in the Library. But it will take a great many articles to make a volume of 350 pages. Dont waste the youth and beauty of your mind in such things. It draws you away from the great work you have before you. Whatever you write, ought to play into this. Make a rush at it. Take any epoch you please. Take Leo X for instance; — write it in a condensed form — then take the best parts of it and put into a Review, with Roscoe's Leo X[8] for a title. In this way you will imperceptibly make great progress. I look upon your *Campagna,* and your *Micali* and Macchiavelli[9] papers as portions of your book, as I suppose you do. I have come round to your opinion, that an entire History of Italy will be better than a Literary History. But for the sake of Posterity *condense* — condense! I have a vision before me of Sismondi['s] Sixteen octavoes on the Italian Republics[10] — and cry *Beware.* It is a glorious theme; and you will execute it nobly. You are gathering strength daily. As to the other book on Italian Literature (Present State of) you are much mistaken in thinking you even mentioned it to me before.[11] I heard of it for the first time by your letter last night. I must say frankly, I do not approve the plan. You would make out a very feeble case for our beloved Italy. Indeed what has she to show, compared with France, England and Germany? What names can you put beside those of Balzac, George Sand and Victor Hugo; — Heine, Uhland, and Auersperg; — Carlyle, Dickens, Campbell and Wordsworth? Your greatest hero would be *Manzoni!* and — *Scusatemi* [Excuse me] — saving the *Cinque Maggio,* which is one of the finest productions of our age, — I should not care, for my part, whether I ever saw another line of his to the end of my days. No, barren as the east-wind — barren as the east-wind, *in all that feeds and nourishes thought and the soul.* Now, frankly, is not this the case with the modern Italian writers? Ugo Foscolo,[12] even, does he stir your soul to word and deed in the same *way* (I do not say *degree*) in the *same*

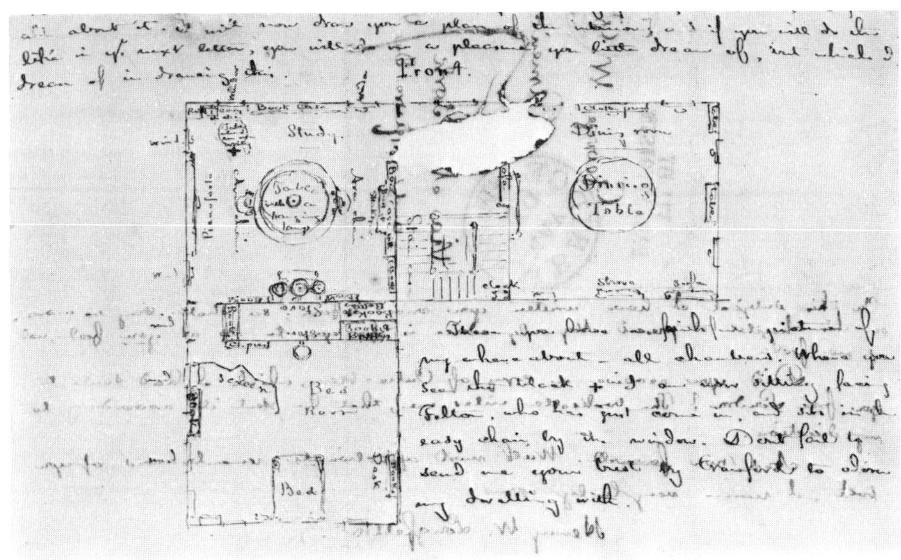

all about it. I will now draw you a plan of the interior; and if you will do the like in your next letter, you will do me a pleasure you little dream of, and which I dream of in drawing this.

Front

Study. Table. Pianoforte. Dining room. Dining Table. Stove. Sofa. Clock. Bed Room. Bed. Desk.

[illegible] pipes, books [illegible] pictures of my chums about — all characters. When you see the black print [illegible] sitting, facing [illegible] fellow, who has just come in, and sits in the easy chair by the window. Don't fail to send me your bust by Crawford to adorn my dwelling with.

Henry W. Longfellow

Sketch by Longfellow, Letter No. 534

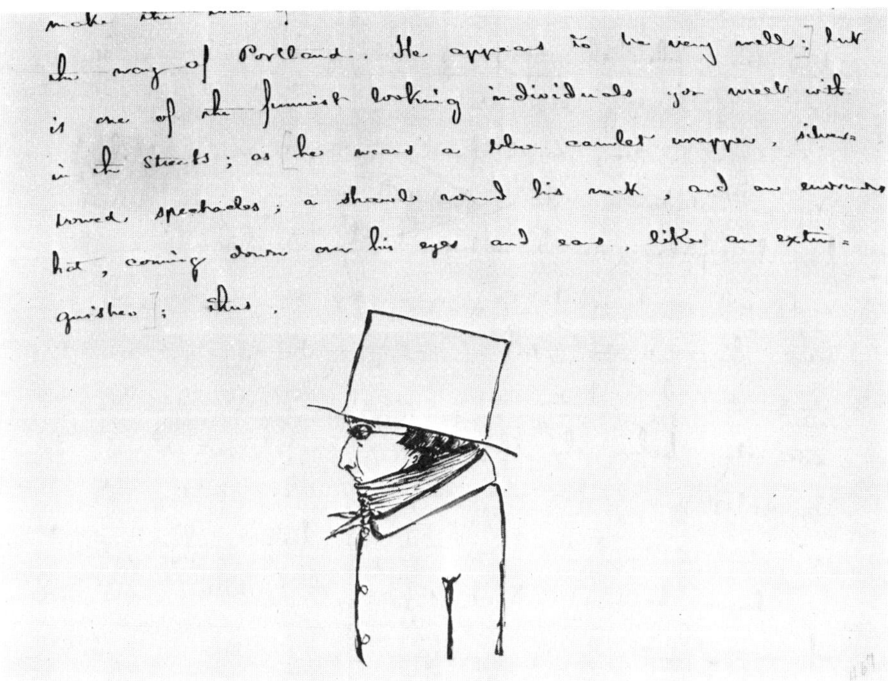

make the [illegible]

the way of Portland. He appears to be very well: but is one of the funniest looking individuals you meet with in the streets; as he wears a blue camlet wrapper, silver-bowed spectacles; a shawl round his neck, and an enormous hat, coming down over his eyes and ears, like an extinguisher; thus.

Sketch by Longfellow, Letter No. 573

Longfellow, 1840, Cephas Giovanni Thompson

PLATE VI

Longfellow, c. 1840, by Joseph Alexander Ames

PLATE VII

Longfellow, 1841, by Auguste Edouart

*way even* that Dante does? But enough. I am getting very prosy; and you very angry; and we had better part.

Greene — this writing of letters is often all a *very* unsatisfactory way of communing with an absent friend. Here I have been working away for a full hour, writing as fast as my pen can move — and have not been able to set down, what I could have told you in two minutes; — not to mention what affection and overflowing of the heart, I should have thrown into the bargain, by look, gesture and tone of voice had you been sitting in the red arm-chair yonder; — or had I been sitting between you and Maria in that Roman Palazzo of yours. Send me a sketch of the rooms you *occupy* no matter about the rest. Sumner gives me a fascinating description of your study, with its books and busts; and [Francis] Bowen, who got back last week, a fascinating description of Maria, with whom he was vastly delighted. I know now how she dresses and wears her hair; — not differing much from the olden time — the *golden* time I should say of our acquaintance.

Sept. 6.

Bowen was exceedingly pleased with Italy — particularly with Florence, whither he says he would straightway turn his steps, were he free, and make it his home for some years.

I wish you would let me have all you pick up about *Dante* that is worth sending, particularly Balbo's life of him. I have read Balbo's *Quattro Novella.* They are rather (not very) meagre and weak; but, O God, how beautiful is his dedication; — "A te, dolce compagna mia, che questa Storia del maestro di Scuola udisti meco nella solitudine dove me facevi così felice del tuo amore, tu felice del mio." [13]

And now my love to Maria, in which Sumner and Bowen join. I told them yesterday I was writing to you. Sumner scolds a little at you [for] not writing to him.

Affectionately yours
H.W.L.

Why dont you write often to your mother? She wrote me a few days ago asking news of you; and saying she had not heard from you since last Spring. You ought to write her once a month.

The Italian books I shall not take as *a present.* Let me know what they cost and I will join it to what the Dean [Palfrey] pays you.

Though absent from us you are present in our thoughts. We seldom meet without remembering you, and conversing of you.

MANUSCRIPT: Mrs. Brenton Greene Meader, Providence, R.I. ADDRESS: To/ George W. Greene Esq/American Consul/Rome/Itale./par le Hâvre ANNO-

TATION (*by Longfellow*): Paid to New York./No. 192 POSTMARKS: CAMBRIDGE MS. SEPT 7/NEW-YORK SEP 9/LE HAVRE [*date illegible*]/OUT 21 OCT 40/ROMA [*date illegible*]/VIA DI PT. BEAUVOISIN/PAID

1. See 464.6.
2. The article in the *New York Review* (534.1).
3. Greene's essay on Alessandro Manzoni (1785–1873), the Italian poet and novelist, appeared in the *North American Review*, LI (October 1840), 337–362.
4. Greene had sent Longfellow the three volumes of *La Commedia di Dante Allighieri col comento di N. Tommaseo* (Venezia, 1837), inscribed: "Al E. W. Longfellow/pegno d'affetto/dal suo GWG/Roma li 5. Maggio 1840 [To E. W. Longfellow/token of affection/from his GWG/ Rome, May 5, 1840]." They are now in the Longfellow House.
5. See 534.3.
6. Robert Greene, *The Honourable History of Friar Bacon and Friar Bungay*, Scene XI.
7. Thomas Hopkins Webb (1801–1866), a Brown graduate of 1821, had attended the Harvard Medical School and is listed as a physician in the *Boston Directory* for 1839. He was also a member of the firm of Marsh, Capen, Lyon & Webb, stationers, 109 Washington St., Boston. In 1839 the firm published three volumes of *The School Library*, which comprised the *Lives of Eminent Individuals, Celebrated in American History*. Nothing came of Longfellow's attempt to have Greene's work included in the series, which seems, in fact, not to have been continued.
8. William Roscoe, *Life and Pontificate of Leo X* (Liverpool, 1805).
9. See 350.4.
10. J. C. L. Simonde de Sismondi, *Histoire des républiques italiennes du moyen âge* (Paris, 1809–1818), 16 vols.
11. This is in response to Greene's letter of July 11: "I should like too, as I have already said, to write a small volume on the present state of Italian literature . . . But of this you say nothing."
12. Niccolò Ugo Foscolo (1778–1827), Italian poet and patriot.
13. "To you, my sweet companion, who have heard with me this story of the schoolmaster in the solitude where you, happy with my love, have made me so happy with yours." Cesare Balbo (1789–1853), Italian writer and statesman, was the author of *Quattro novelle narrate da un maestro di Scuolo* (Livorno, 1829) and *Vita di Dante* (Torino, 1839).

## 548. *To Stephen Longfellow*

Cambridge. Sept. 18. 1840

My dear Father,

I was very glad to receive your letter yesterday, and to hear such good accounts of you all by James [Greenleaf], who came up last evening. Mary I have not yet seen, being laid up with a bad cold. She has promised however to come up this morning; and whilst waiting for her I write you this. The reason of my late long silence has been the unusual confusion in Boston of late; and the number of strangers calling and to be called upon, together with a great deal to do in College. Of course I was in town on Thursday, the day of the procession. I had a good station on a balcony in Beacon Street; and when the Maine Delegation passed I heard a well-known voice exclaim, "Delegation from Maine! three cheers for the Ladies!" and looking down I beheld the Colonel [Samuel Stephenson] on horseback, at the head of his troops. In the afternoon I saw John Neal completely drenched, yet looking very courageous. This is all I have to add to the descriptions you have in the papers.[1]

I am both surprised and delighted at the result of your elections. It is very lucky for Pitt;[2] for I think defeat has a very bad effect on young men; by destroying their confidence in themselves. I think he will now go on successfully, and triumphantly.

I have not written to Sam, because I had nothing in particular to say to him. I have not spoken with Mrs. Otis on the subject. Sumner has the matter in his hand and the details are not yet arranged, the lady not having yet come to Cambridge. This part can be better done when Sam arrives. She requested Sumner to find her an instructer for her boys, and he found Sam, and thus the matter stands, or at least did stand when I last saw him. I shall see him again tomorrow and will try to have things put into the best possible shape.

Mary thinks it probable that Aunt Lucia will return with the Commodore [A. S. Wadsworth] next week. I hope she will; and here join my intreaties with Mary's, that she would come and make us a visit in Cambridge.

Present my felicitations to Pitt, and to all my kind remembrances,

Very affectionately yours
Henry W. Longfellow.

P. S. Many thanks to Anne for the cranberries. They are very good and very acceptable.

Sep. 20.

I saw Sumner yesterday. The only thing that remains to be settled with Mrs. Otis is the amount of remuneration; which I shall converse with Felton about; and which of course will depend upon what she wishes the Tutor to do.

MANUSCRIPT: Longfellow Trust Collection. ADDRESS: Hon. Stephen Longfellow/ Portland/Me. POSTMARK: BOSTON ||Mas.|| SEP 21

1. The "unusual confusion in Boston" was caused by a five-day fair to raise money to complete the Bunker Hill Monument, climaxed by the Bunker Hill Convention on Thursday, September 10. "The procession, which was formed on the Common and passed through many of our principal streets to Bunker Hill, was composed of over 25,000 delegates. Its banners, emblems, and badges, were numerous and beautiful beyond precedent, and the enthusiasm of those composing

and those beholding it, made it a most animated scene. A heavy rain came on in the afternoon as the procession was about returning, wetting many to the skin, without even damping their ardor" ("Events in Boston During the Year 1840" in S. N. Dickinson, *The Boston Almanac for the Year 1841*, I, No. 6, 35).

2. William Pitt Fessenden, a Whig, had just been elected to his first term in Congress.

## 549. *To Julie Hepp*[1]

*Cambridge.* den 28ten Sept. 1840

Meine liebe Freundin!

Der Überbringer dieses ist der Herr Shaw aus Boston. Er wird den Winter in Heidelberg zubringen; und ich weiss Ihm kein grösseres Vergnügen dort zu verschaffen als Ihre Bekanntschaft. Er ist von einer sehr ansehnlichen Familie; hat viel Talent, und einem milden, schönen Charakter. Ich bin überzeugt dass Er Ihnen gefallen wird.[2]

Ich danke Ihnen recht sehr für Ihren lieben Brief des 26 Feb. Immer mit Freude denk' ich mich in Heidelberg zurück; und wahrscheinlich werden wir uns noch einmal dort treffen. Das wird aber nicht diesen Winter geschehen; also schick' ich Ihnen diesen jungen Freund um meinen Platz in Ihren Herzen und in den Whist Parthien zu behalten bis ich wiederkomme. Unterdessen rede ich mit Ihnen in den *Stimmen der Nacht* die ich Ihnen hinüber schicken als ein Hauch von meiner Seele.

Adé! liebes Fräulein! Meine schönsten Empfehlungen an die Frau Mutter, Evchen, und Eduard. *Clara* [Crowninshield] ist in Portland, dreissig Meilen von hier; immer wohl, und immer geheimnisvoll wie die Heldin eines französischen Romans.

Und so, gute Nacht! Mit treuer Anhänglichkeit

Ihr ganz ergebener
Wilhelm Meister.

MANUSCRIPT: Clifton Waller Barrett Collection, University of Virginia. PUBLISHED: Henry A. Pochman, *German Culture in America 1600–1900* (Madison, Wisc., 1957), pp. 420–421.

TRANSLATION:

*Cambridge.* the 28th Sept. 1840

My Dear Friend,

The bearer of this letter is Mr. Shaw of Boston. He will spend the winter in Heidelberg; and I know of no greater pleasure to arrange for him there than your acquaintance. He is from a very respectable family; has much talent, and a gentle, fine character. I am convinced that he will delight you.[2]

I thank you very much for your charming letter of the 26th of Feb. I always think back on Heidelberg with pleasure; and probably we will meet there again sometime. It will not happen this winter, however; I therefore send you this young friend to take my place in your hearts and in the whist parties until I return. Meanwhile I speak with you in *Voices of the Night* which I send over to you as a breath of my soul.

Farewell, dear girl! My warmest respects to your mother, to little Eva, and to Edward. *Clara* [Crowninshield] is in Portland, thirty [German] miles from here; always well, and always as mysterious as the heroine of a French novel.

And so, good night! With true devotion

Yours faithfully
Wilhelm Meister.

1. Daughter of Frau Hepp of Heidelberg (374.5).
2. Joseph Coolidge Shaw (1821–1851), son of a prominent Boston merchant, wrote Longfellow from Heidelberg on May 25, 1841, "With the Hepps I have long felt 'at home.'" Shaw's brother, Robert Gould Shaw (1837–1863), was the Civil War hero who died leading the first regiment of Negro troops from the North.

## 550. *To Stephen Longfellow*

Cambridge. October 4. 1840.

My dear Father,

I begin my letter with the names of the writers in the N. A. Review. They are Art. I. H.W.L. II. John Pickering. III. C. Adams. IV. Geo: W. Greene. V. Dr. Palfrey. VI. Unknown [Willard Phillips]. VII. Gov. Cass. VIII. Prof. Felton. IX. Prof. Felton. X. Dr. Palfrey.[1] I have not yet read the No. and therefore cannot tell you how good it is. Probably an average No.

We have nothing new here, save Fanny Elssler the dancing girl, who is a beauty, and an admirable dancer.[2] She has excited great enthusiasm among the Bostonians. Her Spanish dances are exquisite; and remind me strongly of days gone by. She has five hundred dollars a night; — consequently makes with her heels in one week just what I make with my head in one year. She gave one thousand dollars to the Bunker Hill monument; — that is to say, she danced one night for the benefit thereof, and the sum collected was about one thousand dollars. But this you have seen in the papers.

The negociation with Mrs. Otis remains *in status quo*; because she is now moving into her Cambridge house, and no good opportunity has offered to settle the matter. Meanwhile I have sent Sam to Virginia, to look [at] a vacant Professorial Chair at the University of Virginia. If he can get this place, it will be better than all the Otis children in the world. It is the Professorship of Modern Languages. The late incumbent, a German by the name of Blättermann has been turned out for beating his wife, and such matters.[3] The salary is one thousand dollars and perquisites; together with a house, I believe. It is a good situation; and if he gets it, he will be lucky. I shall set in motion without delay all the machinery within my reach; and if there are not two Professors in the family before the year forty-one, it will not be my fault.

We have been trembling here a little about the Maine election; but there seems to be no longer any doubt of Kent's[4] success, at which we rejoice greatly. You must present my congratulations to Pitt [Fessenden] on his triumph, when you next see him.

For the last fortnight I have been almost sick with an influenza, which has been making us wretched in this quarter. I did not see the Commodore [A. S. Wadsworth] on his return. Thanks to Annie for her short letter, and its very amusing Appendix, which is a gem in its way.[5]

I am glad to hear Clara [Crowninshield] reached Portland in safety, and hope she will enjoy her visit. Kind regards to her, and to all at the judge's [Barrett Potter].

Most truly yours
Henry W. Longfellow

P. S. Did I tell you the second edition of my poems is nearly sold; and probably we shall have a third published before the close of the year.

When Alex. finishes the volumes he has from the College Library, I should like to have them sent by private hand, that I may return them.

MANUSCRIPT: Longfellow Trust Collection. ADDRESS: Hon. Stephen Longfellow/ Portland/Me POSTMARK: CAMBRIDGE MS. OCT 5

1. The reference is to Vol. LI (October 1840). Longfellow's article is "The French Language in England," pp. 285–308. The author of Art. III was Charles Francis Adams (1807–1886), son of John Quincy Adams. For the author of Art. VI, see Letter No. 552 and n. 1.

2. Fanny Elssler (1810–1884), the Austrian ballet dancer, was on a triumphant tour of the U.S. Famed for her beauty and for her sensuous dancing, particularly of the Spanish cachucha, she amassed a fortune and retired in 1845. Longfellow modeled Preciosa, the heroine of *The Spanish Student*, after her.

3. George Blaettermann had been recommended to the University of Virginia by George Ticknor and others, but his constant ill-temper made his tenure there a precarious one. The public cowhiding of his wife that caused his dismissal on September 14, 1840, was merely the last in a series of eccentricities, which included delivering inflammatory lectures and building smokehouses on the campus (Philip Alexander Bruce, *History of the University of Virginia, 1819–1919* [New York, 1920], pp. 157–160). Nothing came of Samuel Longfellow's effort to succeed him, and the professorship went to Charles Kraitsir (1804–1860), a wandering Hungarian philologist.

4. The re-election of Edward Kent (1802–1877) as governor of Maine gave

rise to a well-known political rallying cry, "Have you heard the news from Maine," and was the first indication of the nationwide Democratic defeat in 1840.

5. Anne Pierce wrote to her brother on October 1 for the express purpose of sending him a verbatim copy of a letter to Zilpah Longfellow, dated September 5, 1840, from Emeline Benson of the village of Gray, Maine. Miss Benson, who had formerly worked for the Longfellows, regretfully declined a position in the Longfellow household because she was "under engagements for [a] considerable length of time which I am not at liberty to disregard."

## 551. *To Henry Elijah Parker*[1] *and Others*

Cambridge October 10. 1840

To the Committees of
The Social Friends; and
The Literary Fraternity.
Gentlemen,

I have had the honor of receiving your letter of the 6th inst. and send you an immediate reply. I am sorry that I cannot accept your very polite invitation; but my plans for next Summer are such as to render it impossible.

I beg you, Gentlemen, to accept my thanks for the honor you have done me, and my regrets at not being able to meet your wishes.

Very respectfully yours
Henry W. Longfellow

MANUSCRIPT: Longfellow Trust Collection. ADDRESS: Mr. Henry E. Parker/ Dartmouth College/Hanover POSTMARK: CAMBRIDGE MS. OCT 12

1. Parker (1820–1896), a member of the Dartmouth class of 1841, was president of the Social Friends, a literary fraternity in the college. He became professor of the Latin language and literature at Dartmouth in 1866.

## 552. *To Stephen Longfellow*

Cambridge. October 11. 1840

My dear Father,

In my last letter I gave you the names of the writers in the last North American, with one sole exception, which I now supply. The article on Bentham is by Willard Phillips.[1] The Review is getting into a contest with the New York Review on the subject of Prof. Anthon's school Books. Thus far the Knickerbocker has replied to the North American; But in the last number of the N. Y. Review there is a severe article, which I suppose will call forth an answer. I do not take much interest in the business; but think the North American has the advantage.[2] Dr. Palfrey is likely to have another quarrel on his hands. The family and friends of Dr. Bowditch have taken great offence at a passage in Dr. Palfrey's Eulogy on Pres. Kirkland; and have written a letter upon the subject, which I suppose will see the light before long. This will bring out Palfrey and Kirkland's friends; and I fear a general *mêlée* will follow; as there is much feeling on both sides. It will be a pity; though as there has been a beginning there had better be an end, and settle the matter once and forever.[3]

Mary and James dined with me yesterday; and in the evening I was at Mr. Greenleaf's. I saw also Anne Smith southward bound in search of matrimony.[4] So that yesterday was decidedly a Portland day with me. Anne Smith brought a letter which I did not see; but as she said you were all well, and told us much news from the East, I went away satisfied.

{Before the steam-boats stop running I want you to send me a firkin of butter. What I get here is too intolerable. This by way of parenthesis.}

Have you read Dana's "Two Years before the mast"?[5] It is a very interesting book, written in a simple style, which I think will please you. It reminds one of Robinson Crusoe; and has the advantage of being a record of real adventure. Dana is now a lawyer in Boston; and will turn his ship-knowledge to advantage in sailor-practice, to which branch of the profession he means particularly to devote himself. I suppose he will be employed in all cases of mutiny, piracy &c.

Have you ever read the *Dial*? the organ of the Transcendentalists? I am sure it would amuse you; — its affectation, — its beauty, its wisdom and folly, make a strange mixture. No. 2 has made its appearance; and is as strange as No. 1.[6]

In College no news, and no news from Sam. I expect a letter every day, and hope he will not miss the University of Virginia; for though far from home, it is a situation much better adapted to Sam's mind and character than any profession, usually so called.

With much love, truly yours
Henry W. Longfellow.

P. S. For Alex[ande]r. Your note and book have arrived safely. You did not keep it too long. All is right. Do you want any more?

MANUSCRIPT: Longfellow Trust Collection. ADDRESS: Hon. Stephen Longfellow/ Portland. POSTMARK: CAMBRIDGE MS. OCT 11

1. *North American Review*, LI (October 1840), 384–396.

2. In a harsh treatment of Frederic Jacobs, *The Greek Reader*, A New Edition, with English Notes, Critical and Explanatory, by Charles Anthon (New York, 1840), a writer in the *North American Review*, LI (July 1840), 213–225, charged Anthon with plagiarism and other editorial crimes. Answering broadsides soon followed from New York, where Anthon was professor of Greek and Latin at

Columbia. The controversy developed through a six-month succession of articles: *Knickerbocker*, XVI (August 1840), 166–176; *New York Review*, VII (October 1840), 501–513; *North American Review*, LI (October 1840), 492–500; *Knickerbocker*, XVI (November 1840), 431–439; *North American Review*, LII (January 1841), 238–248.

3. In *A Discourse on the Life and Character of the Reverend John Thornton Kirkland, D.D., LL.D., Late President of Harvard College; Pronounced on Thursday, June 5, 1840, in the New South Church in Boston, Before the Pupils of President Kirkland, and the Government and Students of the University* (Cambridge, 1840), Palfrey alluded to a widely circulated rumor that Nathaniel Bowditch had precipitated Kirkland's resignation as president of Harvard by an intemperate outburst against him at a meeting of the college corporation. Bowditch's sons denied the rumor and challenged Palfrey in a "Letter Annexed to the Second Edition of the Memoir of Nathaniel Bowditch," datelined Boston, October 1840. This elicited Palfrey's rejoinder in an "Appendix to the Second Edition of the Rev. Dr. Palfrey's Eulogy on President Kirkland." The Bowditch sons enjoyed a last word in a "Reply to Remarks Contained in Dr. Palfrey's Appendix." The materials of the controversy were collected in the pamphlet *Remarks Concerning the Late Dr. Bowditch, by the Rev. Dr. Palfrey, with the Replies of Dr. Bowditch's Children* (Boston, 1840).

4. Possibly a Miss Anne C. Smith (d. 1845) of Topsham, who according to papers in the archives of the Maine Historical Society, had been a client of Stephen Longfellow in 1831–1832. The notice of her death in the *Vital Records of Topsham, Maine, to the Year 1892*. ed. Mary Pelham Hill (Concord, 1929) indicates that she married a man named Washburn. Or it may have been Anna Smith Prentiss (555.1) of Portland, who in 1843 married Rev. Jonathan French Stearns (1808–1889) of Newburyport.

5. Recently published by Harper Brothers, New York.

6. *The Dial: A Magazine for Literature, Philosophy, and Religion* was edited by Margaret Fuller. The first two numbers of Vol. I are dated July and October 1840.

## 553. *To Samuel Ward*

Cambridge October 11. 1840

My dear Sam,

Since I last wrote you I have been reading your magnetic paper in the New York Review;[1] with all the interest which friendship lends me for all you write, and with that ignorance, which mars my pleasure in all scientific conversations and writings. It seems to me an able paper; and I am only sorry for an oversight, by which you have done an unintentional injustice to our College. I refer to the paragraph on p. 493, beginning "Hitherto no part has been taken among us in these observations." This is a grave error, my dear Sam. We have here "a complete collection of the apparatus," — an observatory sufficient for the purpose; — and observations have been made for a year past in exact conformity with Gauss's plan, by W. W. Pierce, Lovering and Bond.[2] This has been acknowledged in one at least of the foreign journals; and I am sorry you did not know the fact sooner, as it is of some importance.

But this *en passant.* The principal object of my letter is in reference to the Lectures of the Mercantile Library Association. My friend Cleveland, who is a capital lecturer, and a capital fellow likewise, after delivering a course here before the *Diffusion of Useful Knowledge* Society goes to Burlington to pass the Winter at Bishop Doane's. While there he would like to run up to New York and deliver the same lectures before the Library, if an arrangement to that effect can be made. Cogswell knows him; and perhaps you and he can bring the matter about. Moreover, *Marion*[3] who knows Cleveland well, will tell you what kind of a fellow he is, and what a pleasant companion you will gain for an evening now and then. I want *you* to know Cleveland, and want him to know you. Perhaps Marion would take charge of the whole negociation.

It is a rainy sunday. I am writing on the small round table near the window. Behind me, in an arm chair, sits Sumner, reading the Sketch Book, and exclaiming "I wish I knew Irving! How shall I get acquainted with him?" I reply, "By means of Sam Ward." Then he asks, "When is Ward coming here?" I ask the same question. Let the answer come soon — and you with it, *old gentleman.* Sumner is *bivouacking* with me for a day or two. Another exclamation from him "What a *beautiful* writer Irving is." Felton is also sitting by the stove reading an article on Greece in the Democratic Review.[4] What would I not give if I could now hear the tramp of your boots on the stairs, and your inspiriting voice singing "Was kommt dort von der Höhe? [What comes there from on high?]" The truth is, you must come here for a few days. We have been separated too long; and though passage of letters — though the *mail* keeps the grass from growing on the road between us, yet the *rail road* of speech would do it more effectually. I shall return the visit with interest in the winter.

Shall you lecture this winter? I shall not. I have refused all invitations to that effect — three in number. I mean to hold my vacations sacred, and free from ordinary cares. They are my reconciliations with the world, after long seclusion. The next one I hope to enjoy much; and partly in your society. Though that horrible winter passage on the sound terrifies me in advance. Kindest regards to your wife.

Most truly yours
H. W. L.

P. S. I hear that Cogswell is coming here next week. I hope it is true.

MANUSCRIPT: unrecovered; text from photostat, Longfellow Trust Collection. ADDRESS: Samuel Ward Esq/New York POSTMARK: CAMBRIDGE MS. OCT 12 PUBLISHED: *Uncle Sam Ward and His Circle*, pp. 272–273.

1. "Terrestrial Magnetism," *New York Review*, VII (October 1840), 475–501.

2. Karl Friedrich Gauss (1777–1855), German mathematician, was the inventor of several magnetic instruments. The three Harvard scientists were Benjamin Peirce (1809–1880), professor of mathematics and natural philosophy (Longfellow's version of the name is certainly an inadvertency); Joseph Lovering (1813–1892), Hollis Professor of Mathematics and Natural Philosophy; and William Cranch Bond (1789–1859), director of the Harvard Observatory.

3. Francis Marion Ward (1820–1847), Sam Ward's youngest brother, was at this time a student at Harvard, where he received his M.A. in 1841.

4. George Sumner, "The Present Condition of Greece," *The United States Magazine and Democratic Review*, VIII (September 1840), 204–226.

## 554. *To Stephen Longfellow*

Cambridge. Oct. 18. 1840.

My dear Father,

Since I last wrote you, sundry novelties have appeared in this quarter of the world, which you may see hinted at in the papers. They are among the moral reforms of the day; and have at once something serious and something comic about them. You probably have heard of the Non-Resistance Society in Boston, who wish to follow out literally the injunction; "if a man strike you on one cheek" &c and "if a man take away your cloak" &c. One of the chief men of this society is Mr. Edmund Quincy, second son of our President. They have now called a convention, inviting people of all creeds and denominations to attend, and discuss the great questions "What is the Church, — the Sabbath, — and Religion?"[1] Not long ago there was a similar convention held in Groton. The first resolution was "Voted, that we are not sectarian!" whereupon discussion arose as to what constituted a sect, which discussion lasted for three days, when the convention adjourned. Not long after came up from Cape Cod a new Sect called the *"Out-and-Outers,"*[2] who formed a holy alliance with the Transcendentalists. Out of this fermentation of mind has sprung up a new plan; namely to form a new community, to be called "The Practical Christians." Each individual is to subscribe two hundred dollars, and each family one thousand; a farm is to be bought near Boston; cottages to be built; and there the community goes to work. Every member is to labor three hours a day; the remainder of the time is to be at his own disposal. There is no farther community of goods than this. The three hours labor it is thought will feed, clothe and lodge them all; and the rest of the time is to be devoted to the Fine Arts — music, drawing &c. &c. I hear that the Rev. Geo. Ripley, Mr. Emerson, Miss [Margaret] Fuller, and other prominent Transcendentalists are going to this land of Promise.

Likewise Mr. Allcot, the author of "*Orphic Sayings*" in the Dial;[3] though I fear he will be an unprofitable farmer; for being a great Grahamite,[4] he refuses to put manure on the land he now cultivates in Concord, thinking it too stimulating! What will be the final result of all these movements it is impossible to foresee; some good end, I trust, for they are sincere men, and have a good intent.[5]

Our President met with an accident a few days ago, which came near leaving the College headless. He was driving down Park-street in a gig, with one of his daughters in law, when by the strain upon the shafts they (the shafts) were both broken short off, and the gig pitched forward onto the horse. Mrs. Q. was thrown out upon the pavement, and somewhat bruised tho' not badly; but the President was caught like a rat in a trap, the top of the gig resting on the horse's crouper. Thus they went bumping down the hill; the horse being an old family nag, whose sole defect, according to his owner, is that "when he once stops you cannot make him go, and when he once goes you cannot make him stop." Luckily some one seized the rein; or in all probability the President would have been dashed to pieces. The only amusing part of the affair is, that when he went down in town about half an hour afterward, in telling the story he could not for his life tell *which Mrs. Q. it was!*[6] Nor will you be astonished at this, when I tell you that not long ago he drove into town to announce his daughter's engagement, and when they asked *which* daughter he said "Why really I dont recollect, but I believe it is Abby." It was Anna — the younger sister.[7]

And so we go on in this mad world.

John Neal called yesterday. But I was out, and did not see him. Mrs. [Nancy Doane] McLellan I have not yet seen. From Sam no news; but we now expect him daily. Mary is well; James, laid up with a cold.

With much love, very truly yours
Henry W. Longfellow.

MANUSCRIPT: Longfellow Trust Collection. ADDRESS: Hon. Stephen Longfellow/ Portland. POSTMARK: CAMBRIDGE MS. OCT 19

1. Edmund Quincy (1808–1877), son of Josiah Quincy and an ardent abolitionist, was president of the New England Non-Resistance Society. William Lloyd Garrison was secretary.

2. Longfellow's term is incorrect. The "Come-Outers" — who took their name from the injunction in Rev. 18:4 to leave Babylon — were religious zealots whose philosophy was rooted in abolitionism. Their fanaticism is indicated in the following statement by Stephen Symonds Foster (1809–1881), a leader in the movement: "I said at your meeting, among other things, that the American church and clergy, as a body, were thieves, adulterers, man-stealers, pirates, and murderers;

that the Methodist Episcopal church was more corrupt and profligate than any house of ill-fame in the city of New York; that the Southern ministers of that body were desirous of perpetrating slavery for the purpose of supplying themselves with concubines from among its hapless victims; and that many of our clergymen were guilty of enormities that would disgrace an Algerian pirate!!" (*The Brotherhood of Thieves; or a True Picture of the American Church and Clergy: A Letter to Nathaniel Barney of Nantucket* [Boston: Anti-Slavery Office n.d.], pp. 7–8.

3. *The Dial: A Magazine for Literature, Philosophy, and Religion*, I (July 1840), 85–98. The author of "Orphic Sayings" was Amos Bronson Alcott (1799–1888).

4. A follower of Sylvester Graham (1794–1851), the vegetarian and reformer.

5. This paragraph, written during the early discussions that led to the organization of Brook Farm, is one of the first descriptions of that experiment. There is no evidence, however, to support Longfellow's statement that Brook Farm sprang from an alliance between the Transcendentalists and the Come-Outers.

6. Whether it was Mrs. Josiah Quincy, Jr., or Mrs. Edmund Quincy.

7. Anna Cabot Lowell Quincy married Rev. Robert C. Waterston in March 1840. Abigail Phillips Quincy, President Quincy's second daughter, remained a spinster.

## 555. *To Stephen Longfellow*

Cambridge October 25. 1840.

My dear Father,

I was very happy to hear from you a few days ago; though you must not feel obliged to answer all my scrawls, and write only when you feel in the humor, and have leisure. Miss Prentiss[1] arrived yesterday and brought us news of you; and mother's letter to Mary gives the pleasing intelligence that the offerings to the household gods in the shape of eggs and butter are on the way, for which we duly thank you. I should like some eggs likewise.

I am glad you found anything interesting in the French Article. To most people it must be very dull. It is the result of some studies I made formerly in Brunswick; and which probably at the present moment I should not have either time or inclination to make. Having the materials ready at hand, I thought it worth while to work them up. Duponceau of Philadelphia has read it; and wrote to Mr. Pickering to say, that he liked it, and that I had taken the true ground. My pen has not been very prolific of late; only a little poetry has trickled from it. There will be a kind of Ballad on a Blacksmith in the next Knickerbocker, which you may consider, if you please, as a song in praise of your ancestors at Newbury.[2] The third edition of the Voices is now in press; and the publisher, John Owen, has so lively a faith in the continued sale of the work, that he is stereotyping it.

If the New York Review falls in your way I wish you would read an Article headed "Brisbane's Social Destiny of Man." It will serve as a comment on my last letter; and show you how far the same notions have been already carried in France and England. I am thankful I am too old to have any of Brisbane's experiments tried on me. As for example; "A correct ear for music will also be given" (*that is to babies*) "by singing trios and quartettes, three or four times a day, in the nurseries, and by teaching those who are old enough to march to the sound of instruments." And again; "The cradles can be moved by a mechanical contrivance, so that twenty can be rocked at once." At two years old, the children are set to work; thus for instance; "Two children between three and four years of age, are seated at the upper side; (of *an inclined table*) they pod the peas, which roll to the lower side, where three *little commencers* of the ages of twenty five, thirty, and thirty-five months, are seated, who have merely to separate the smaller from the larger peas"; &c — after the peas have passed through all these little hands, they are ready for cooking, and the Lord have mercy upon the eaters thereof. There is more matter of this kind, which will amuse you. I commend it also to Anne's consideration.[3]

We are expecting Sam daily. His visit to Charlottesville, I begin to fear, will not bring about the desired result; at least, I judge so from the tone of his last letter to Mary. Still I am glad he went; being in that part of the country.

With much love,

very truly yours
Henry W. Longfellow.

MANUSCRIPT: Longfellow Trust Collection. ADDRESS: Hon Stephen Longfellow/ Portland. POSTMARK: BOSTON MAS. OCT 26

1. One of the three Prentiss sisters of Portland, each of whom was acquainted with the Longfellow family: Abby Lewis Prentiss (1814–1847), Anna Smith Prentiss (1818–1869), and Mary Smith Prentiss (1821–1881).

2. "The Village Blacksmith," composed on October 5 according to Longfellow's journal entry, appeared in the *Knickerbocker*, XVI (November 1840), 419. The first Stephen Longfellow (1685–1764) was a blacksmith of Newbury.

3. An unsympathetic review of Albert Brisbane, *Social Destiny of Man; or, Association and Reorganization of Industry* (Philadelphia, 1840), appeared in the *New York Review*, VII (October 1840), 525–529. Brisbane (1809–1890), an admirer of Charles Fourier, had written his book to project and defend the theory of a socialized community.

## 556. *To Stephen Longfellow*

Cambridge. November 3. 1840

My dear Father,

Sam has atlength made his appearance and takes the boat to night for Portland. I send by him;

1. All the news.
2. A rose-bush for Anne.
3. Several small packages for different persons.
4. Several Catalogues; among them one for Doctor Weed, to supply him materials for conversation; and to bring to his mind *that* story, beginning "*You know Fargues!*"[1]
5. Two small volumes for Mr. Bowen;[2] to be sent to him with my thanks, and apologies for keeping them so long.

Affectionately yours
Henry W. Longfellow.

MANUSCRIPT: Longfellow Trust Collection. ADDRESS: Hon. Stephen Longfellow/ Portland.

1. Longfellow's MS Journal entry for August 2, 1846, makes it clear that Dr. Weed (3.2), a member of the Harvard class of 1800, habitually used this expression to begin his college reminiscences. Thomas Fargues (1780–1847), class of 1797, practiced medicine at this time in Quebec.
2. See 529.1.

## 557. *To Anne Longfellow Pierce*

Cambridge November 5 1840

My dear Annie

I hope the rose-bush reached you in safety, and that you will not be disappointed. It was the best I could find in Cambridge; and besides is a mixture of your two wishes, namely the tea-rose and monthly. There were several buds on it when it left, which I trust will soon enliven your parlour with roses and fragrance. At all events, if this is not so beautiful a bush as you expected, I can send you another, though if you take the Brunswick rose for a standard, it will be difficult to find one like it.

Tell Sam that Mrs. Otis accepts his proposition without a murmur; and consequently that I shall engage the rooms for him at Deacon Munroe's.[1] I saw Mrs. Otis last evening at Miss Lowell's. The rooms were as hot as an oven; and we all looked and crawled about like lobsters. You would doubtless like to know something about Mrs Otis. You shall have her portrait drawn by Margaret my Irish girl, who was at the party last night, handing round tea. When she brought up breakfast this morning she said;

"That's the first time I ever saw Mrs. Otis!"

"Well, what do you think of her?"

"O, she's a fine and social lady, with a great and large talk!"

Now it is utterly impossible to convey by words a more complete definition of her ladyship; and if you compare it with what Mary and Miss Prentiss write you will see how exact it is.

Did you ever hear of Mrs. Peck?[2] Mary and Miss P. are in a gale about her. She had them to tea, and with them Tutor Wheeler,[3] whom she had invited expressly to meet Miss. P. So she kept him seated by her side all the evening, and when he once got up to speak to some one else, up ran Mrs. Peck exclaiming:

"Tutor Wheeler, there is a vacant chair by Miss Prentiss. Wont you sit down by Miss Prentiss?"

Good bye, my dear child. I cannot write any more, I am so tired. It is now half-past one o'clock; and I have been writing letters ever since breakfast; and must bring this to a close instanter, or my head will drop off my shoulders, and make a great blot, right here. But I must tell you first, however, that a few days ago I was at Mrs. [Jeremiah] Mason's and saw your screen. It is very beautiful; and the good old lady seems to set great store by it; — and hopes you will come to Boston soon, and asks if I do not think you will; and wants to see you and des[4]

MANUSCRIPT: Longfellow Trust Collection. ADDRESS: Mrs. Anne L. Pierce/Care of S. Longfellow Esq/Portland/Me POSTMARK: CAMBRIDGE MS. NOV 6

1. James Munroe (1775–1848), a blacksmith who lived on James St., was deacon of the First Church, Cambridge, 1818–1848.

2. Possibly Harriot Hilliard Peck (b. 1788), the widow of William Dandridge Peck (1763–1822), professor of natural history at Harvard, 1805–1822.

3. Charles Stearns Wheeler (1816–1843), a classics scholar, graduated from Harvard in 1837 and served as tutor there, 1838–1842. He died while studying in Leipzig.

4. The letter ends abruptly here with an ink blot that has been shaped by Longfellow to represent his head.

## 558. *To Stephen Longfellow*

[Cambridge] November 15. 1840.

My dear Father,

It is raining again to-day; and so dark that I can hardly see here by the window. I think we had but three bright days for the last three weeks. For my own part I care very little about it — except the mud. But Mary and Miss Prentiss mourn over it, as it keeps them for the most part in-doors. Perhaps this rain on Monday last, our election day was fortunate. It kept both parties cool; and everything passed off quietly — though gloriously for us, in the State. But alas! in this district a Loco-foco representative has been elected by some half-dozen votes, it is said, unless we can detect some fraud, which is suspected.[1]

After making the arrangement with Mrs. Otis, I thought it best to secure Sam's rooms, which I did, fearing he might lose them, as new Law Students are constantly coming in. I did not however take them for any specified time. And that part of the business he can settle when he comes.

Being in town yesterday, I stepped in with my friend Sumner to take a glass of soda; and the thought struck me, that a few more bottles might be acceptable to you. Accordingly I ordered six or eight dozen to be packed up and sent by next steamer, as a Christmass present. The number of dozen will depend on the number of bottles the apothecary happens to have on hand.

The third edition of my poems is finished, and will be out in a few days, and I shall bring you a copy when I come down at Thanksgiving. The second edition is all sold; which considering the hard times is very well. The publisher is confident it will continue to sell, and, as I believe I wrote you, has accordingly stereotyped it.

I believe I have several small matters to get for Anne; but have only an indistinct recollection of what they are, the commission being a verbal one last Summer. If anything is wanting she must write me in the course of next week.

I thought of you the other evening at a party, where four Tyrolese musicians were singing. Their music would have delighted you. There were four voices, two male, and two female; — a tenor, a treble, a counter and a bass — one of the softest and yet most powerful I ever heard. Their harmony was perfect; and their national songs well sung, and delightful. This having minstrels at parties is a new idea, and a very good one.

Monday morning [November 16].

It is bright and cool, and the storm seems finally over, which I do not regret. When is Sam coming? I thought he was to be here last week. I saw his pupils last evening. They are good little fellows.

Farewell.

Yours truly

Henry W. Longfellow

MANUSCRIPT: Longfellow Trust Collection. ADDRESS: Hon Stephen Longfellow/ Portland POSTMARK: CAMBRIDGE MS. NOV 16

1. In the election of November 9, 1840, the Whigs, whom Longfellow favored, swept into office in Massachusetts with the national landslide that elected William Henry Harrison over Van Buren. Longfellow uses "Loco-foco" as an epithet for a radical Democrat, the Loco-foco party having by this time been absorbed by the Democrats.

## 559. *To Edward Everett*

[Cambridge] November 19. [1840]

My dear Sir,

I return with many thanks Mr. Milne's note which I was glad to read. For a poet, how absorbed he seems to be in politics. Indeed is not his life more political than poetical throughout? [1]

We had very pleasant letters from Mrs. Mackintosh. She is still in the country; but moves to London after Christmas. She sends kind remembrances to you and your family. Mackintosh is in Scotland.

Very truly yours
Henry W. Longfellow

MANUSCRIPT: Massachusetts Historical Society. ENDORSEMENT: 19 Nov. 1840/ Prof. Longfellow

1. Richard Monckton Milnes (1809–1885), a friend of Everett, had published *Poems of Many Years* in 1838. He was a Member of Parliament at this time and in 1863 through the influence of Palmerston became a peer (1st Baron Houghton). Longfellow became acquainted with him later.

## 560. *To Stephen Longfellow*

Cambridge Nov. 22. 1840

My dear Father,

I write you a short letter to-day to say that you may expect me in Portland on Wednesday evening; and that Miss Prentiss is coming under my wing. I fear we shall have deep snow to wade through, which is disagreeable. I never knew such an Autumn. To-day is as dismal as a dungeon; and the air feels like snow. But the rail-road inspires courage.

Sam begins tomorrow. I think he has no fancy for Virginia; and particularly since yesterday, when we saw in the southern papers the news of Professor Davis's death. He was shot by a student in a mask — literally murdered in an attempt to quell some disturbance. I do not know the particulars of this tragedy; but a man will think twice before taking a Professor's chair in such a University. Davis was Professor in the Law department; and acting as President of the Institution.[1]

Braham, — or what remains of him — the once celebrated vocalist is here, giving concerts. I have not heard him. People are greatly disappointed. But he is between sixty and seventy years of age; and cannot be expected to sing as he did at twenty. People seem, however, to think, that if he ventures to sing at all, he ought to sing well.[2]

We are in for it. While I write the snow is beginning to fall, and who knows when it will cease. You probably are enjoying the same spectacle. I hope Alex. has finished his survey. Tell him that the English rail-road Reports are on the way; but have not yet arrived. Perhaps the next steamer will bring them.[3] On receiving his note I went immediately to see Mr. Reed,[4] but did not find him. James [Greenleaf] has now that affair in hand, and will not neglect it.

Yours truly
Henry W. Longfellow

MANUSCRIPT: Longfellow Trust Collection. ADDRESS: Hon S. Longfellow/Portland. POSTMARK: CAMBRIDGE MS. NOV 23

1. Prof. John A. G. Davis (1801–1840) was fatally wounded on November 12 when he attempted to remove the mask from a student rioter. His murderer, Joseph E. Semmes, forfeited $25,000 bail and was never brought to trial. Philip Alexander Bruce, *History of the University of Virginia, 1819–1919* (New York, 1920), pp. 309–311.

2. John Abraham or Braham (1774–1856), an English tenor, enjoyed a considerable success on the English stage from 1787 to 1830, but his American tour in 1840 was not fortunate.

3. See 478.2.

4. Benjamin Tyler Reed (c. 1796–1874) of Boston was president of the Shawmut Bank and treasurer of the Eastern Railroad Corporation.

## 561. *To Evert Augustus Duyckinck*

Cambridge Nov 24 1840

My dear Sir,

You will think I am very long in answering the friendly letter you wrote me, with the Prospectus of your new Periodical, and the copy of Mr. Mathews' Comedy.[1] The truth is the package did not reach [me] so soon as it should have done, by a week.

I like very much the plan of your work, and its title; and I feel confident that it will be a very gentlemanly and scholar-like affair. But as to the poem, you speak of, I cannot promise it; because I rely somewhat on my pen to stretch out the ends of my moderate income. You shall, however, find my name among your subscribers, and I will do what I can here to advance your interests.

Hawthorne has just written a book for children, called "Grandfather's Chair," which will be out in a few days. I have not seen it; but from the description he has given me of his plan, and the stories in this first part (for he means to continue it) I venture to say it will be a capital work.[2] You will agree with me in my expectations, as you do in my admiration of Hawthorne.

I beg you to present my thanks to Mr. Mathews for his courtesy in sending me a copy of the Politicians. He has great wit and vivacity;

though the subject he has here chosen to display them upon, is not one which tickles the imagination.

I hope your Arcturus may indeed be "a fixed star of the first magnitude" as defined by astronomers. Here's a motto for you, if you want a classic one.

Μεσονυκτίοις ποθ' ὥραις
Στρέφεται ὅτ' [ἤ]Αρκτος ἤδη
Κατὰ χεῖρα τὴν Βοώτου,
Μερόπων δὲ φῦλα πάντα
Κέαται κόπῳ δαμέντα.

Anacreon. Ode γ'.[3]

— alluding of course to your midnight lucubrations.

With sincere regard

very truly yours
Henry W. Longfellow.

MANUSCRIPT: New York Public Library (E. A. Duyckinck Papers). ADDRESS: Evert A. Duyckinck Esq/New York. POSTMARK: CAMBRIDGE MS. NOV 25 PUBLISHED: *Bulletin of the New York Public Library*, I, No. 9 (1897), 245.

1. Duyckinck (431.2) and Cornelius Mathews (1817–1889) founded and edited the critical magazine *Arcturus: a Journal of Books and Opinion*, 1840–1842. On November 14 Duyckinck had sent Longfellow a prospectus of the new journal, a copy of Mathews' *The Politicians, a Comedy, in Five Acts* (New York, 1840), and a request for a contribution.

2. *Grandfather's Chair. A History for Youth* was published in 1841, but Hawthorne dated his preface from Boston, November 1840. It was followed by *Famous Old People. Being the Second Epoch of Grandfather's Chair* (Boston, 1841) and *Liberty Tree. With the Last Words of Grandfather's Chair* (Boston, 1841).

3. "At the midnight hour/When the Bear is already circling/In the hand of Bootes,/And all the tribes of mortal men/Lie overcome by exhaustion." *Anacreontea*, No. 31, ll. 1–5. Duyckinck used this motto on the title page of *Arcturus*, I (December 1840–May 1841).

## 562. *To Charles Sumner*

Portland Nov. 25 [1840]

Carissimo Carlo,

Passing through Boston on Tuesday I called at your office; but found no one. You had not returned; and Hillard as I afterward heard, was sick with a cold.

I shall be back on Saturday and desire your company to Cambridge. So make your bundle, putting in "*Esmeralda*"[1] and "*Herman und Dorothea*"; — and take which Buss you please. You will either find me in my room; or I shall not be long in coming. You will find a fire, and Margaret; so that you can have yr. tea.

I came down here by land; rather a rough journey. Travelling companions of the usual interesting stamp. I shall return by boat tomorrow night, if the weather is fair.

Yours truly and affect[ionatel]y, between daylight and dark, Thanksgiving afternoon.

H. W. Longfellow

MANUSCRIPT: Longfellow Trust Collection.

1. The play by Victor Hugo.

563. *To Stephen Longfellow*

Cambridge Decr. 1. 1840

My dear Father,

I arrived safely — Persian water-pipe and all. We were only eleven hours on the way, — reaching Boston, and the Cambridge hourly office at two o'clock. The morning I left you was cold; but I did not feel it. The two outside passengers felt it so much, that we took them in; and part of the way had *eleven insides.* Among them was Russel, the American vocalist;[1] whom I found good-natured, and a pleasant travelling companion; and a Mr. Morse, from some back town in Maine, — a stout fellow with whiskers, — who could not feel cold, — and whose conversation consisted chiefly of the phrases "*Jess so!*" — and "*I shouldn't wonder!*" The rest were not characters. The roads were good, and we went over the ground pretty fast, reaching Portsmouth in season for the eleven o'clock train, or *trail,* as Mr. Morse called it.

I found Mary and James [Greenleaf] very well — and nothing new save a half-dozen letters to answer. I have not yet got my studying gear in order; but am chiefly occupied in sleeping, to restore the equilibrium, which was disturbed by travelling at improper hours. My ideas begin, however, to assume their wonted march, to the sound of the tall clock in the corner; and when I wake up in the morning I know where I am.

I find Sam going on famously with his pupils; and thus far the most friendly relations exist. His cold is better, though not yet quite gone. He will get over it soon.

I write you these few lines in haste to let you know of my safe arrival without cold or inconvenience. With love to all,

Yours very affectionately
Henry W. Longfellow.

MANUSCRIPT: Longfellow Trust Collection. ADDRESS: Hon Stephen Longfellow/ Portland. POSTMARK: BOSTON MAS. DEC 1

1. Henry Russell (1812–1900) was in fact an English vocalist and composer, who had enjoyed an extended American tour and was about to return to London. He was known particularly for his musical recitals of the soliloquies from *Hamlet, Macbeth,* and *Richard III,* as well as his popular songs, including "A Life on the Ocean Wave," "Cheer, Boys, Cheer," and "Woodman, Spare That Tree."

## 564. *To Samuel Ward*

[Cambridge] December 1, 1840.

. . . Why can't you come here for a day or two? I want to see you very much, and have a great many things to show you in the literary way. I will read you the 'Skeleton in Armor,' which is too long to copy; and something still longer, which as yet no eye but mine has seen, and which I wish to read to you first.[1] . . . At present, my dear friend, my soul is wrapped up in poetry. The scales fell from my eyes suddenly, and I beheld before me a beautiful landscape, with figures, which I have transferred to paper almost without an effort, and with a celerity of which I did not think myself capable. Since my return from Portland I am almost afraid to look at it, for fear its colors should have faded out. And this is the reason why I do not describe the work to you more particularly. I am not sure it is worth it. You shall yourself see and judge before long.

Mr. Coxe, in the notes to his poems, speaks of the "pantheism of Cambridge."[2] This is too gross. Why, there is in all Cambridge only one Transcendentalist, — and he a tutor![3] In the Theological School there is none of it; the infected class is gone. The students are now inclining to rigid *Puseyism*.[4] You New Yorkers are altogether mistaken in your notions about Cambridge. Take my word for it, you are.

MANUSCRIPT: unrecovered; text from *Life,* I, 378.

1. *The Spanish Student.*

2. In his *Christian Ballads* (New York, 1840), p. 101, Arthur Cleveland Coxe remarked: "the Congregationalist schism of New-England, is the father of *American Socinianism,* and the modern Pantheism of Harvard University; a college which, though founded with Puritan money, in common with hundreds of congregations throughout New-England, 'denies the Lord that bought them.' Is there nothing fearful in this?" Coxe (1818–1896), a graduate of New York University in 1838, became an Episcopal bishop.

3. Presumably Charles Stearns Wheeler (557.3), a friend of Emerson and member of the Transcendental Club.

4. A term applied by its opponents to the religious philosophy generally known as the Oxford Movement, of which Edward Bouverie Pusey (1800–1882), the English clergyman, was a leading figure. Pusey emphasized in particular the observance of ritual.

565. *To Stephen Longfellow*

Cambridge Decr. 13 1840

My dear Father,

I let last Sunday slip by without writing you, because I had a visit from my friend Ward of New York, who came to pass the day and night with me; — and Sunday having gone by, I found it very difficult to find a moment during the week. I never knew a week pass so rapidly; and can hardly believe it is Sunday again. I have been hard at work; and hardly taken note of time, till I remember'd yesterday, how long it was that I had not written to you. I have been for the most part wrapped up in my own dreams; — have written a tra[n]slation of a German Ballad;[1] — and prepared for the press another original Ballad, which has been lying by me some time. It is called "*The Skeleton in Armor,*" and is connected with the old Round Tower at Newport. This Skeleton in Armor really exists. It was dug up near Fall River, where I saw it some two years ago. I suppose it to be the remains of one of the old Northern Sea-rovers, who came to this country in the Tenth Century. Of course, I make the Tradition myself; and I think I have succeeded in giving the whole a Northern air. You shall judge soon; as it will probably be in the next Knickerbocker;[2] and it is altogether too long to copy in a letter. I hope it may be successful; though I fear, that those who only glance at it, will not fully comprehend me; and I must say to the benevolent reader, as Rudbeck says in the Preface of his *Atlantica,* (a work of *only* 2500 folio pages) "If thou hast not leisure to *study it through ten times,* then do not read it once, especially if thou wilt utter thy censure thereof."[3] A modest request.

So much for myself, during the past week. On Saturday, (a week ago,) I dined with Gilman Daveis[4] at Mr. Ticknor's. His father will be pleased to know, that Gilman is studying with great zeal and enthusiasm, surgery and *auscultation.* He had that day been to visit a patient with a disease of the heart; and exclaimed with a kind of rapture, "I was never so happy in my life, as I was when I heard the *bellows'-sound* of her heart!" We all cried out against his barbarous enthusiasm; and for my part, I laughed aloud.

Sam has got well again; and Mary, James, and all the Greenleafs are well. I have not been able to give any attention during the last week to Alexander's business; but will endeavor to do so, early this week.

On Christmass day I dine with your old friend and political comrade Harrison Gray Otis; as he has been so polite as to invite me. I anticipate a very pleasant dinner.

If the copy-right of a book is taken out in the publisher's name, and there is no written contract between him and the author, is not the book, in the eye of the law, the property of the publisher? This is the position of some of my books; and if the publishers are not very honest men, I shall find it difficult to prove property.[5]

With much love to all,

very truly yours,
Henry W. Longfellow

P. S. The soda-water was not sent for want of bottles. Shall I have some sent by stage; or does *Murray's* Magnesia answer the purpose?[6]

MANUSCRIPT: Longfellow Trust Collection. ADDRESS: Hon S. Longfellow/Portland. POSTMARK: BOSTON ||MAS.|| DEC ||14?||

1. "The Luck of Edenhall" (*Works*, VI, 273–275).
2. "The Skeleton in Armor" was published with marginal notes in the style of "The Rime of the Ancient Mariner" in the *Knickerbocker*, XVII (January 1841), 52–54.
3. Olaus Rudbeck (1630–1702), professor at Upsala University, published his *Atland, eller Manheim* in four parts, 1679–1702.
4. John Taylor Gilman Daveis (1816–1873), son of Charles Stewart Daveis, received his M.D. from the University of Pennsylvania in 1837, studied in Boston, and thereafter practiced medicine in Portland.
5. Stephen Longfellow's reply to this query, dated December 21, 1840, is unrecovered, but see Letter No. 570 and n. 3.
6. A postscript by Mary Longfellow Greenleaf follows.

## 566. *To Sarah Perkins Cleveland*

Camb. Dec. 14. 1840

My dear Mrs. Cleveland,

I accept with the greatest pleasure your kind invitation for Thursday next. Luckily I have no engagement for that day; but if I had I think I should excuse myself from it to dine with you.

With my kindest regards to Heinrich,

Very truly yours
Henry W. Longfellow.

MANUSCRIPT: Berg Collection, New York Public Library.

## 567. *To Samuel Ward*

Cambridge. Decr 18. 1840.

My dear Hypolito,[1]

I here send you a translation of the Organist, not having the patience to copy the original, and finding this ready made. It was executed by young Story, son of the Judge, and a former pupil of mine.[2] And here I hear you exclaim, like M. Jourdain (all my epistolary illustrations are drawn from Molière) "Oui; mais il ne falloit pas faire faire cela par un écolier; et vous n'étiez pas trop bon vous-même pour cette besogno-là." To which I reply, like the *Maître de Musique*; "Il ne faut pas [, monsieur] que le nom d'écolier vous abuse; Ces sortes d'écoliers en savent autant que les plus grande maîtres."[3] And in truth you will find the translation a good one. Much good may it do you.

I drove over to dine at Cleveland's yesterday, with the young Nortons.[4] I happened to speak of Rakemann, as we passed the house he lived in last summer; and in that connexion mentioned your Lecture, with his musical illustrations. They both exclaimed, with the enthusiasm of young girls "Oh, how delightful! I wish we could hear it!" I therefore do not hesitate to say that the plan is excellent; and I should put it in execution without fear or doubt. Hang what people may say! You must not act in reference to that; but in reference to your own tastes.

Lacon; or
Many Things in Few Words.

Hold fast the "Luck of Edenhall" until I see you.

Give Clarke the Skeleton for $25.

*Champion* is a better word than *Warrior,* because it is Saxon, and Northern. The old Danish warriors were called *Kaemper. Cempa* is the Saxon.

Your objection about *was* and *were,* is not I think well-founded. I think I can persuade you that the verse is well as it stands. Let it pass; and if you persuade me I am wrong, we will change it in the *Illustrated edition.*[5]

I am very much pleased with Halleck's[6] commendation of the poem. But what did he say against it?

I thanked you for the French papers in my last,[7] and now thank you again. I like the little ones best. Have you any more *Echoes*? The *heavy* ones, I do not read. I like French fun, better than French wisdom.

Preciosa reads the Song. It commences Act II. thus. "Scene 1. Preciosa's chamber. Morning. The sun shining in at the window. A bird in its cage. Preciosa stands among the flowers on the balcony reading," — and what she reads is the song; which comes from Victorian of course.[8]

Received yrs. of Saturday 12. and Wednesday 16th. The latter arrived just in season to dine with me to-day. I answer both in one.

Tomorrow, (Saturday) I dine with Dean Palfrey, to meet Felton, Sumner, and Hillard. Would you could be there! Sumner said he was "very much *mortified* not to know you were in town" that day.

Where is the box of saw-dust? [9]

I have seen Ticknor in regard to Graeter.[10] He says he knows of no book worth translating; and turns up his nose (I should like to see him turn it *down*) at Menzel's Hist. of Germany. My own choice would be Jean Paul's *Titan* — at least, I thought so, till I had written it down here, — and now I recollect the awful fate of the lovely heroine, and doubt. He might throw a gauze veil over that one night, in which her "virtue fell in ashes." Let him cho[o]se Thibaut's book on Music.[11] That is good; and would do good. Let him take that; and then try his teeth on Titan.

I have been talking with De Goy this evening about *domestic felicity,* and the necessity of being married. I see it coming. I shall have another infernal love scrape before long. What is a poet without a passion! A pipe without fire. I have made up my mind. I renounce the vanities of life — and hence forth devote myself to the love of song and the love of woman.

How gloriously I should live here! Lapped in dreams elysean. But alas! who will ever love me? Thus ends the song. Good night, my dear.

Yours very, *very* truly,
H. W. L.

P. S. I shall put this into the Boston Post-office with my own hand. Everyone recognizes your bust,[12] and says, "How striking."

MANUSCRIPT: unrecovered; text from photostat, Longfellow Trust Collection. ADDRESS: Samuel Ward Esq/New York. POSTMARK: BOSTON MAS. DEC 19 PUBLISHED: *Uncle Sam Ward and His Circle,* pp. 279–281.

1. During the next several months Ward assumed this sobriquet and addressed Longfellow as Victorian. Hypolito and Victorian were the two students of Alcalá in Longfellow's *The Spanish Student.*

2. William Wetmore Story (1819–1895) graduated from Harvard in 1838, practiced law for several years, and eventually devoted himself to sculpture, achieving great popular success. "The Organist," a translation from the German of Theodore Well, ultimately appeared in *Graham's Magazine,* XXIV (October 1843), 191, and was apparently used by Ward in a lecture on music, with illustrations by the pianist Rakemann, which he was to deliver on February 11 (Ward to Longfellow, January 20, 1841).

3. "Yes; but it was not necessary to leave this to a pupil; and you were not too good yourself for this work." "It is not necessary, sir, to let the name of pupil deceive you; these kinds of pupil know as much as the greatest masters." *Le Bourgeois Gentilhomme,* I, ii.

4. Louisa (b. 1823) and Jane Norton (1824–1877), the daughters of Andrews Norton.

5. In a letter of December 16, 1840, Ward had suggested revisions in stanzas 6 and 11 of "The Skeleton in Armor." See *Uncle Sam Ward and His Circle*, p. 278.

6. Fitz-Greene Halleck (1790–1867), the New York poet.

7. Dated December 14, 1840, and unrecovered. In a letter of December 10, 1840, Ward had written: "Now I send you today a bundle of French Papers I just received. Let me know if they afford you a pleasure equal to the cost of postage. One of these read every day after dinner systematically keeps a man *au-courant* of the Parisian World."

8. In the final version of *The Spanish Student* this episode introduces Act II, scene iv.

9. The box in which Crawford's bust of Greene (534.11) was packed. Ward had taken it through the New York customs and was arranging its shipment to Cambridge.

10. In a letter of November 25, 1840, Ward had explained Graeter's situation: "Your friend Graeter is here in great poverty. I have been feeding him and his for a month. He would like to translate Menzel's Geschichte der Deutschen — or any other Book from the German. Can you not get him employment of that kind." Then in a letter of December 10, having obtained a tentative promise of help from Harper Brothers, Ward had asked Longfellow to consult Ticknor about an appropriate book for Graeter to translate.

11. *Über Reinheit der Tonkunst* (Heidelberg, 1825).

12. Sent to Longfellow by Ward the previous summer.

## 568. *To Stephen Longfellow*

Cambridge Decr. 20. 1840.

My dear Father,

I was in town yesterday, and saw Mr. Reed on the subject of the rail-road. He says that the affairs are not yet organized, nor so far advanced as the papers say; but that next week he is going to Saco to have matters brought to a point as far as possible. He farther said that Fessenden had spoken to him about Alexander; — and that his name was on the list, and should not be forgotten, though he did not make any promise of a place. Alex's plan now must be to send his recommendations to his friend Batchelder[1] in Saco; or go on and present them. I do not see that anything more can be done.

My Third Edition is published, and is quite superb. I shall send you a copy by first opportunity. The Fourth is now printing; the Third, or large paper edition being only two hundred and fifty. In the Brother Jonathan of last week you will find a favorable notice, written by [Nathaniel Parker] Willis.[2] The Ballad of the "*Skeleton in Armor*" will appear in the January No. of Knickerbocker. There will be various opinions as to its merit. My friend Ward, to whom I sent it, is very enthusiastic about it; which I am not, though I am very well satisfied with it. You will be amused to see how my friend's heart and head take fire and blaze away together. He writes,

"I could not forbear reading it to *Halleck* (the poet) this morning. His bright eyes glistened like diamonds, and he read it through aloud himself with delight. He thanked me warmly for the pleasure it had afforded him — said it placed you extremely high, and [was] superior to any of your previous efforts. His laudation flowed from the heart. I am going to see whether Miss Hall [3] will not engage to make designs for it in case *we* publish an edition *à la Gray's Elegy*. It will spread like wildfire over the country, and richly reward you. Halleck remarked there was nothing like it in the Language!" [4]

In order not to be led away by this, you ought to know the glowing and sanguine temperament of my friend. You must not expect to find the poem so fine as he does. He has associations with Newport, which make him invest it with a charm, which it will not have in the eyes of others. I think, however, that it is striking, and in its conception, perhaps, unique, at least in our Country. It is a National Ballad, as the "Wreck of the Hesperus" is.

I have also written a much longer and more difficult poem, called "The Spanish Student" — a Drama in Five Acts; on the success of which I rely with some self-complacency. But this is a great secret; — and must not go beyond the immediate family circle; as I do not intend to publish it, until the glow of composition has passed away, and I can look upon it coolly, and critically. I will tell you more of this, bye and bye.

I hope you will not think me self-conceited because I parade all these things before you. I remember that I am writing to my father; and that my letters do not go beyond the family.

The Otis boys are delighted with Sam, and go on well in their studies. He is pretty well; tho' not wholly rid of his cold.

Yours very affectionately
Henry W. Longfellow.

MANUSCRIPT: Longfellow Trust Collection. ADDRESS: Hon. S. Longfellow/Portland.

1. John Montgomery Batchelder (1811–1892), engineer and inventor. He had studied civil engineering with Professor James Hayward of Harvard, possibly with Alexander Longfellow. See 371.6.

2. This unsigned notice, in which Longfellow is praised as a "rational" poet, appeared in the folio *Brother Jonathan* for December 19, 1840.

3. Anne Hall (1792–1863), an artist who excelled at miniature painting on ivory, was the first woman to become a member of the National Academy of Art. Her sister, Mrs. Henry Ward, was Sam Ward's sister-in-law.

4. Quoted, with minor emendations, from Ward's letter of December 16, 1840.

## 569. *To Josiah Quincy*

Cambridge Dec 24 1840

Dear Sir,

Upon examining my Record of studies I find that my account with the College stands as follows.

*Spring Term* 1840. Thirty pupils in French at $4. each. . . . $120.

From this no deduction should be made; because this instruction did not prevent my attendance at the recitations of the Instructers, as required by vote of the Corporation.

*Autumn Term* 1840. Eighty-nine pupils in French at $4. each. . . . $356.

All the Modern Language hours being occupied by me with these classes I did not attend the recitations of the Instructer. The time given by me was two thirds more, than it would have been, without these French classes.

So that if the Corporation wish to measure the service rendered, by the time employed, it will [be] right to make a deduction of one third. I would state, however, that I think this difference more than made up by giving to a section of the Senior Class, three oral lectures, or recitations per week instead of one, which is required by Law; — and for which I have made no charge.

On account of the great difficulty attending the arrangement of hours, (with which you are well acquainted,) it is not always practicable to carry out, to the letter, the requisitions of the Law. But you may rest assured, that what is from necessity omitted in one place and time, will be fully made up by more attention in another.[1]

Very respectfully yours
Henry W. Longfellow.

MANUSCRIPT: Harvard College Papers, X, 154. PUBLISHED: *Professor Longfellow of Harvard,* p. 97.

1. On January 1, 1841, the Corporation voted Longfellow the sum of $300 as extra compensation, with the understanding that a precedent was not being established (*Professor Longfellow of Harvard,* p. 98).

## 570. *To Stephen Longfellow*

Cambridge. Dec. 27. 1840

My dear Father

I had the pleasure of receiving yours of the 21st. about the time that my last must have reached you, so that neither was an answer to the other. I am glad to hear that Dr. Nichols gave you so good an Address. I communicated the fact to John, whom I happened to meet in the street a few moments after reading the letter; whereat he seemed highly delighted.

The President's History of the College is atlength published in two very large octavo volumes.[1] As yet I have only glanced over a few pages. I think it will prove a very interesting work. If you have not subscribed for it, I will send you my copy this winter, which will save you the expense of buying it. Each volume contains over 700 pages; and it seems to be a pretty complete History of the College in all its departments. The President has been engaged in it between four and five years.

I cannot answer your question in regard to what money I received from you while I was in Europe, because I cannot this evening lay my hand on my note-book. I have put it away so carefully, that I cannot find [it]. I will make more diligent search among my papers by day-light, and let you know.

The Reports on the Railroads in Ireland have arrived — a quantity of them with some large maps. I shall send them to Alex, as a New Year's present, by first opportunity.[2]

On Christmass day I dined with Mr. Otis. There were about a dozen guests; and the dinner was very good, and served with elegance. Mr. Otis asked very particularly after you, and desired his remembrance to you. He looks pretty hale; but suffers so much from gout, that his fingers are all crooked, and his knuckles stick out like knobs. It was a pleasant party. We sat down at half past six; and left the table at half-past nine; when we went into the drawing room, and took tea. Mr. Otis appeared in pumps, and a crimson velvet waistcoat.

I have no news to send you of Mary nor of Sam; except that they are as well as usual. I have not seen them for a day or two, having been in town; and the bad weather to-day has kept me in doors. I have likewise my friend Sumner passing Sunday with me, as he does once in a while.

I shall attend immediately to all my Copy-Rights, and have neglected it too long already. In future I mean to have everything done by written contract; for these things promise henceforth to be of some value to me. With the Harpers I have no contract. When they published Outre Mer, they gave me $300 in advance, and no contract was drawn up. I gave them the right of printing one edition. The copyright stands in their name. If they claim the entire property in the book, must they prove their right to it, or must I prove mine? That is the question. There are no written papers, nor signature of either party; — except mine for the money received. I do not know that they will claim the book as theirs; but there is a possibility of it; and I wish to guard against it.[3]

Yours very truly
Henry W. Longfellow.

MANUSCRIPT: Longfellow Trust Collection. ADDRESS: Hon. S. Longfellow/Portland POSTMARK: CAMBRIDGE MS. DEC 28

1. Josiah Quincy, *The History of Harvard University* (Boston, 1840).

2. See 478.2.

3. Stephen Longfellow replied on January 10, 1841: "I do not see how the Harpers could have taken the Copy right of Outre Mer unless you gave them a conveyance in writing, which may be contained in your receipt for the $300. You had better ascertain how this is, and whether the right extended beyond one edition, for delays in these things are dangerous. If they have no transfer of the Book, I do not see how they can claim the Copy right. But you will probably find, on examination, that they have some letter, receipt, or other paper, which will amount to transfer of the work, in a right to print one edition." There is no evidence that Longfellow pursued this matter with the Harper Brothers.

## 571. *To George Roberts*[1]

Cambridge Dec. 29 1840.

Dear Sir,

I have had the honor of receiving your letter and paper this evening, and regret that it is not in my power to send you such an answer as you request. But at this moment I have nothing on hand, which I am willing to print; and am so much occupied that I could not conveniently turn my thoughts that way. Under these circumstances I do not feel at liberty to accept your kind offer of sending me your paper free of charge; but shall be very glad to become a subscriber, if you will be so good as to put my name on your list.

Respectfully yours
Henry W. Longfellow

MANUSCRIPT: unrecovered; text from typewritten transcript, Longfellow Trust Collection (Longfellow House).

1. Publisher of the *Boston Daily Times* (1836–1855) and of the *Boston Notion*, with offices at 5 State St. This letter is in response to a request that Longfellow contribute to the *Notion*. See Letter No. 585.

## 572. *To Richard Bentley*

[Cambridge, 1840]

Dear Sir

Perhaps you would like these for your Miscellany. It is but right to tell you that they have been published here but not in a volume.[1]

Yrs. &c
Henry W. Longfellow

MANUSCRIPT: Clifton Waller Barrett Collection, University of Virginia. ADDRESS: Richard Bentley Esq./London.

1. Longfellow reprinted eight poems in *Bentley's Miscellany*, 1839–1842, the first two from *Voices of the Night* (1839): "The Reaper and the Flowers," VI (November 1839), 482; "The Voices of the Night," VIII (July 1840), 78; "The Wreck of the Hesperus," VIII (August 1840), 152; "The Village Blacksmith," IX (January 1841), 53; "It is not Always May," IX (February 1841), 196; "The Rainy Day," X (December 1841), 626; "Endymion," XI (January 1842), 16; and "Excelsior," XII (July 1842), 36. The poems referred to in this letter must be those that appeared in the magazine before the publication of *Ballads and Other Poems* (1841), which would restrict the date to 1840 or early 1841.

## 573. *To Stephen Longfellow*

Cambridge Jan 3. 1841.

My dear Father.

I met yesterday in a bookstore in Boston your old friend Dr. [William Ellery] Channing. He inquired very particularly after you; said you used to be intimate in former times; that he had not seen you for many years; but hoped to see you next Summer, as he intended to make the tour of the White Mountains, and return by the way of Portland. He appears to be very well; but is one of the funniest looking individuals you meet with in the streets; as he wears a blue camlet wrapper, silver-bowed spectacles; a shawl round his neck, and an enormous hat, coming down over his eyes and ears, like an extinguisher; thus,[1]

In Boston the year 1840 ended with an Assembly, not political, but fashionable. Being among the invited guests, I was there. As I never dance, my duty on such occasions is to console those, who not wishing, or not being asked to dance, perform that respectable part of female duty in a ball-room, known under the name of "*sustaining the walls*"; — (*botanicà,* wall flowers — the only kind of flowers I cultivate.) It was a very pleasant evening; and we staid till the morning of the New Year, when the company wishing each other a Happy future, gradually separated.

De Goy sailed for Europe yesterday in the Steamer Caledonia. The night before he received letters from his father, (as I understand, for I did not see him,) and not waiting to say good bye to any one, off he went, the next day before noon; making no more ado about it, than I should in going to Portland. He will return the beginning of next term; though I do not suppose he will remain in the country. It was some misunderstanding with his father, which made him leave home; and I suppose their letters were letters of reconciliation.

Did Alex. receive his Irish Rail-Road Reports?[2] I sent them down to Mary's for Edward Davies [Daveis] to take; but it is ten to one he did not take them, owing to their bulk. Had it not been for this, I should have sent by him some other small matters.

The North American[3] is a good No. I do not know all the writers yet. Art IV. Bancroft's History is by W. H. Prescott. Art. VI. Congressional Eloquence, by Dr. Palfrey, and very amusing. Art VIII. Irish in America, by Grattan.

Last night I went to hear *"The Song of the Bell,"* performed at the Odeon; — words by Schiller, translated by Mr. Eliot — music by Romberg.[4] The singers will not compare with the Portland singers — not one of them, but the instrumental performers are much superior.

Finally, a Happy New Year to you all, and much love from

Yours very affectionately
Henry W. Longfellow.

P. S. To Annie. Your note paper &c is all ready and will come soon, my dear.

MANUSCRIPT: Longfellow Trust Collection. ADDRESS: Hon. S. Longfellow/Portland. POSTMARK: BOSTON Mas. JAN 4

1. Longfellow's sketch of Channing follows. See Plate No. V.

2. See 478.2.

3. Vol. LII (January 1841).

4. *Schiller's Song of the Bell,* trans. for the Boston Academy of Music by S. A. Eliot (Boston, 1837), was reprinted by Longfellow in *Poets and Poetry of Europe,* pp. 309–312. The choral music was by Andreas Jakob Romberg (1767–1821), German violinist and composer.

## 574. *To Stephen Longfellow*

Cambridge Jan. 10 1841

My dear Father,

I forgot to send you in my last letter the account I promised; and did not think of it until I had sealed the letter. I therefore postponed it. In brief it stands thus; in my account book

| | |
|---|---|
| In Spanish Dollars | 650.00 |
| Francs 13.000 — | 2566.80 |
| Calculating the franc at .93 cents. | $3.216.80 |

In my Note Book I have all the dates, with the amount of each separate draft. I had also a sum in gold, though I have forgotten how much, which I took out with me. If you wish, I will send you the Book.

I have got through the labor of the Term. I had my examinations on Friday last. They were very satisfactory to the Committee. The Department is in a flourishing condition; and the number of students in it greater than it ever was before.

Tomorrow I go to work again on my Drama, to retouch some of the scenes, and get the whole copied out fairly. I have great confidence in its success. But I do not mean to publish it before the Summer.

The Ballad of the Skeleton in Armor made its appearance in the Knickerbocker yesterday. I will send it to you in a few days. I have not the slightest idea what I shall write next; and am much more curious to know, than anybody else can be.

I hope the New Year begins as pleasantly with you, as it does with me. I feel very happy, and very well contented with the present state of things.

Mary and James are well; likewise Samuel.

Very truly yours
Henry W. Longfellow.

MANUSCRIPT: Longfellow Trust Collection. ADDRESS: Hon S. Longfellow/Portland. POSTMARK: BOSTON ||MAS.|| JAN 11 [?] ENDORSEMENT: Henry Jany 10 1841 —/Statement of Advancements

575. *To Joseph Reed Ingersoll*[1]

[Philadelphia] Jan. 30. 1841.

My dear Sir,

Both Mr. Sumner and myself feel very sensible to your kindness in procuring for us the invitations to dine with the Directors of the Mercantile Library Association; and regret that our present engagement with Mr. Peters[2] has forced us to decline that honor; which we have just done by our notes.

Mr. Jackson,[3] who dines with us at Mr. Peter[s]'s, has made arrangements to take us after dinner to the Opera from which we go with him to Mr. Bache's,[4] which will deprive us of the pleasure of waiting upon you at your house, and meeting Mr. Kennedy,[5] which we are both anxious to do.

The invitation to breakfast we most gladly accept, and thanking you again for your repeated courtesies,

I remain, very truly yours,
Henry W. Longfellow.

MANUSCRIPT: unrecovered; text from typewritten transcript, Longfellow Trust Collection (Longfellow House).

1. According to a letter from Sumner to Hillard, January 24, 1841 (*Sumner Memoir and Letters*, II, 172), Longfellow arrived in New York on January 23. He spent approximately two weeks there and in Philadelphia. Ingersoll (1786–1868), a Philadelphia lawyer, was a member of Congress, 1835–1837 and 1843–1849, and minister to England, 1852–1853. His letter to Longfellow of January 30, 1841, establishes him as the correspondent.

2. Richard Peters (1780–1848), Philadelphia jurist and intimate friend of Justice Story, through whom Sumner had made his acquaintance.

3. Isaac Rand Jackson (d. 1842). See 716.2.

4. Presumably Alexander Dallas Bache (1806–1867), great grandson of Benjamin Franklin. An educator and physicist, he was at this time principal of the Central High School of Philadelphia.

5. Possibly John Pendleton Kennedy (1795–1870), the author and a member of Congress from Maryland.

## 576. *To Stephen Longfellow*

New York. Feb. 3. 1841

My dear Father,

I have been exceedingly negligent in not writing you sooner, since leaving Boston; but I have been so constantly on the move that I have not until now found leisure. I have got back this far homeward. My friend Sumner is with me; and next week I shall be in Portland. We have been as far as Philadelphia where we passed a week; and saw many agreeable people, among them Judge Hopkinson;[1] — Mr. Ingersoll; Mr. Binney,[2] Mr. Biddle (the "*Monster*")[3] and many more. We were received with the utmost cordiality and kindness; — dined, and breakfasted, and supped; — and seldom went to less than three parties in an evening. All this is very agreeable for a while; but a week satiated me; and I have come back to this place in hope of being a little more quiet. But alas! fallacious hope! I have already received six invitations to dinner; and I know not how many to parties and Concerts &c. In fine, for the sake of change, I have turned my habits of life upside down; and do nothing but run to and fro from morning till night and from night till morning. It grows very tiresome; and the effect is to make me cling more closely to Cambridge and the life of a student.

When in Philadelphia, I was very much tempted to go to Washington to see the Captain[4] and his wife, but time and money wait for no man, and I gave up the design.

"The Skeleton in Armor" I find very successful. Everybody speaks to me about it; and we are thinking of publishing an edition with illustrations, like Gray's Elegy. Mr. Graeter, a german, has already made some designs; which he brought to me this morning. They are very spirited. I am not, however, sure that the expense will not prevent a publisher's undertaking the work.[5]

The weather has been of all kinds; during our short journey; rain, snow, and sunshine jumbled together in great confusion. But in Philadelphia it was so mild as to require no fire. Old John Vaughan was very ill. At his door a Bulletin of his health was placed every morning, and those who called left their names on a list. It is not probable he will recover.[6]

But I am interrupted; so farewell

Yours very affectionately.
Henry W. Longfellow

MANUSCRIPT: Longfellow Trust Collection. ADDRESS: Hon. S. Longfellow/Portland/Maine POSTMARK: BOSTON Mas. FEB 6

1. Joseph Hopkinson (1770–1842), U. S. judge for the eastern district of Pennsylvania and author of the patriotic song "Hail Columbia" (1798).

2. Horace Binney (1780–1875) of Philadelphia, one of the country's leading lawyers.

3. Nicholas Biddle (468.9) was called "The Monster of Chestnut Street" by his Jacksonian political enemies.

4. Commodore Wadsworth's permanent rank was Captain.

5. Longfellow wrote to Samuel Colman on February 17, 1841, proposing a special edition of this poem (letter unrecovered). James P. Giffing, answering for Colman on March 3, 1841, declined the proposal.

6. Vaughan lived another year and died on January 2, 1842.

## 577. *To John Forsyth*[1]

[Cambridge, February 10, 1841]

Dear Sir,

I am induced to address you this note in vindication of the character of my friend George W. Greene Esq, Consul at Rome, from the aspersions of Mr. Austin of Boston, contained in a letter from him to you.[2]

I have known Mr. Greene intimately for many years. He is a young man, who has devoted his life to Literature and the Arts; and is one of the most promising scholars, that this country has produced. He is moreover one, who by his gentlemanly deportment and unusual attainments has done the country honor in the position he occupies. This I hear from various quarters.

I am not personally acquainted with Mr. Austin; but I am satisfied, that he had no just cause to complain of Mr. Greene. The whole tone of his letter is that of a man bent upon revenging himself for some imagined wrong; and it convinces me, that by his want of regard to

Greene's feelings, and his violence of language, he forced him to treat him as he did.[3]

Having seen Mr. Austin's letter I cannot forbear troubling you with these few lines of protest against his whole conduct.

I have the honor to be, Sir, very respectfully

Your Obt. Ser[v]t.
Henry W. Longfellow.

Hon. John Forsyth &c &c

MANUSCRIPT: National Archives, Washington, D.C. ENDORSEMENT: Rec. 15 Feby[1841]/Mr Ringgold[4] ANNOTATION: Recd. with Mr. Sumner's letter of Feb 10. PUBLISHED: *Consular Relations Between the United States and the Papal States,* ed. Leo Francis Stock (Washington, D.C., 1945), p. 79.

1. A former U. S. Senator and governor of Georgia, Forsyth (1780–1841) served as secretary of state under Jackson and Van Buren.

2. On July 29, 1840, Arthur W. Austin, a Boston lawyer, had written to Secretary Forsyth complaining in bitter terms of Greene's practice of charging American tourists $4 for visaing their passports and demanding his removal from office on the grounds of extortion. For his defense, Greene enlisted the support of Charles Sumner as a character witness. Sumner wrote to the Secretary and forwarded to him, in addition to this letter from Longfellow, separate testimonials from George Ticknor, William H. Prescott, and C. C. Felton. All manuscripts relating to the controversy are included in the "Despatches from United States Consuls in Rome" in the National Archives. Greene retained his office until 1846 when the Polk administration summarily removed him.

3. When, according to Greene, Austin had become abusive during the argument about the visa, he had turned him out of his office (Greene to Forsyth, October 30, 1840, in the National Archives).

4. James S. Ringgold of Maryland (d. 1844) was a clerk in the Department of State (State Department Records, National Archives).

## 578. *To Parker Cleaveland*

Portland. Feb. 13. 1841

My dear Sir,

I send you a pipe-full of German Tobacco; hoping it may please you, being mild and fragrant. If you like it, I will send you a larger quantity, and then come and smoke some of it with you; — though not this Winter.

I have only time to send with it my kindest regards to your family, as Mr. Smith[1] is waiting for this note.

Very truly yours
Henry W. Longfellow

MANUSCRIPT: Brown University Library. ADDRESS: Professor Cleaveland/Brunswick.

1. Possibly Benjamin Smith (1814–1858), a member of the Bowdoin class of 1841.

579. *To George Washington Greene*

Portland. Feb 22. 1841

My dear George Doubleyou,

On returning to Cambridge a few days ago from an excursion to Philadelphia, I found your very welcome letter of December 17. which I have brought with me here to the regions of perpetual snow, in order to answer it without delay. I found also your bust for which accept my warmest thanks.[1] It is a beautiful thing; and shall stand in the Halls of Washington.[2] You are somewhat *idealized* by the artist; but on that account I like it all the better. That is a great power in an artist; to paint or model the *soul that is in a man. A propos* of Crawford; the Orpheus is exquisite, delicious, lovely; and the necessary funds will shortly be raised in Boston.[3] The New Yorkers too have taken fire at the idea; and are getting up an order for this or some other work by the same hand. I suppose you have heard of Allston's warm and cordial admiration. I was present when he first saw the engraving. He said it was very beautiful; and in reply to the objection made by some, that it resembled the Apollo; he replied "It no more resembles the Apollo than Orpheus himself resembled Apollo"; which is a good justification of Crawford against Cavillers. The two great masters of the Lyre should have something in common. But I will not say much on this topic for fear of forestalling or imitating Sumner.

Mr. Austin's attack upon you was plebian in the lowest degree. But when I saw among the names of your accusers that of *Ashton,*[4] the seller of toys and perfumery in Washington Street, I laughed aloud. We all wrote to Mr. Forsyth on the subject, and as we do not hear that you have been turned out of Office, we presume he is satisfied, that the assault was a malicious one.

I am glad you like the poems.[5] They have already reached the fourth edition. I did not send Hyperion because I had no copy to send. As I told you sometime ago, two months after publication, all the copies unsold were seized by the Publisher's creditors; and have, very unwisely, I think been kept out of the market since then. Colman told me a few days ago that he had redeemed them; and I shall now be able to send you a copy, which I will do in a few days. I will likewise send the sheets of Micali *if I can get them.* The Dante arrived safely.[6] I am very much obliged to you for it; the brevity of the Comment is delightful after the *trash! trash!! trash!!!* of most of the Commentators. (Is *trash* too strong a word?) I agree with you, it is a pity so much was said about yr. Italian History. Nobody is to blame but yourself. You told your secret to a woman (not your wife). Still I would not let it annoy me. It is precisely so with Prescott's "Conquest of Mexico." One of the newspapers last Summer announced that it would be out in the Autumn; but the fact, very well known to his friends, is, that he has only completed the *Introduction* and that the work will not appear for some years. I will see [Thomas Hopkins] Webb for you, but the books you speak of will cost you more than he will give you for your Grandfather's Life.

In Philadelphia I saw some of our old friends; *Rush* (author of Hamlet) [7] *Smith (John)* and [Willis Gaylord] *Clark,* who has been a most disinterested friend of yours, and taken every occasion to say a good word for you in his paper. Poor fellow! He lost his wife two years ago; and is now apparently in the last stages of consumption. You will behold his face no more.

In New York I saw all your friends; and had many a consultation with Mr. John Ward,[8] as to the probability of getting you a better place under the new administration. But there is such a rush for offices that it seems next to impossible to do anything, and my own opinion is that we shall not succeed in making your condition more tolerable. You may be assured, however, that we shall make a trial, if there is any prospect of success. By the way, how would you like a Professorship in the University of Virginia, at *Charlottes*ville? (a lucky name for you). The Chair of Modern Langs. is now vacant. Salary and fees amounting to $3000, together with a house. This is worth thinking about; as the climate is good, and would not destroy your lungs and nerves. The vacancy will be filled next Summer; so that if you wish for the place let us know in season, and we will put in your claims. Meanwhile you must dip into *Anglo-Saxon,* as that is required.

Wilde was in New York during *our* visit there; by *our,* I mean Felton, Sumner, and myself. He is a glorious fellow. I like him exceedingly; and look forward with curiosity to his Life of Dante. Cogswell thinks he can *now* get a publisher for the Tasso Papers. I hope he may. We had right pleasant intellectual festivals in the den of Mammon; as for instance when at Sumner's brother's dinner table were united; Felton, Sumner, Willis, Cogswell, Wilde, Stephens (*author of Travels*) [9] and one or two more.

Sam Ward has met with a great calamity; namely, the death of his wife. She died on the 18th inst. in child-bed. I left them but two days before. He had no fears; as her health was good, and her first *accouchement* had been an easy one. She died very suddenly, a few hours after the birth of a son.

Your letter on Crawford is excellent; only in one or two sentences you *soar a little.* I have no doubt it has done great good, and prepared the minds of people for what has since been said; (which in praise *transcended* even you.) The wind blows fair for him; and most cordially do I, with so many more, wish him complete success.

Sumner and Felton are both rejoicing in their youth and strength. Sumner writes me that he and Cleveland (another of our mutual friends) were to dine with Felton on Saturday, to examine the beautiful Shield of Achilles.[10] I go back to them tomorrow, rather tired of six weeks of idleness. I shall probably find, that both Sumner and Felton have written you. Felton's Translation of Menzel's German Litr. in 3 vols. has been very successful. Since I last wrote you I have written another book, though a small one; — a Drama in 3 acts, blank verse, called *"The Student of Alcalá."*[11] It will not be published before Summer. I have also made lately a successful hit in a long ballad; called *"The Skeleton in Armor"*; being the story of an armed knight, (dug up two or three years ago at Fall River,) and of the Round Tower at Newport. In my next I will send you all the literary news of the last year. I did not think of it soon enough for this letter. Meanwhile, fare you well, Sir Traveller. Give my love to Carlotta, and thanks for her commendation of my poems. I beg you also to go to the *Persiani* and tender them my kind regards and remembrances and good wishes. I beg you, dont forget this. Yours very truly, with friendly greeting from my father's family,

H.W.L.

My mother and sisters (Mrs. Pierce) send their particular regards to yr. dear wife, who has left behind her in all hearts *"the odor of sanctity."*[12]

MANUSCRIPT: Mrs. Brenton Greene Meader, Providence, R. I. ADDRESS: George W. Greene Esq/Consul of the United States/at Rome/Italy/par le Hâvre ANNOTATION (*by Longfellow*): Paid to N. York/No 192 POSTMARKS: PAID 17 MR 17 1841/ANGL||?||/19 MARS 41 CALAIS/DIREZIONE DI ROMA [*date illegible*]/||DA GENOVA CORRISP*a* EST*a*||/VIA DI PT. BEAUVOISIN

1. See 534.11.

2. Longfellow refers to the fact that Gen. Washington once made the Craigie House his headquarters.

3. A drive to raise $2500 for a marble copy of Crawford's "Orpheus" for the Boston Athenaeum succeeded largely through the efforts of Charles Sumner. The sculpture arrived in Boston in September 1843. See *Sumner Memoir and Letters,* II, 230–232.

4. Elisha V. Ashton, a dealer in imported fancy goods, 117 Washington St., Boston.

5. *Voices of the Night.*

6. See 547.4.

7. James Rush (1786–1869), a physician and psychologist of Philadelphia and son of the patriot Benjamin Rush, wrote *Hamlet, A Dramatic Prelude in Five Acts* (Philadelphia, 1834).

8. John Ward (1797–1866), financier and uncle of Sam Ward, was president of the New York Stock Exchange for many years.

9. John Lloyd Stephens (1805–1852), traveler, had written several volumes describing his experiences in the Near East, Russia, and Central America. See 610.5.

10. The allusion is partly explained by Sumner's letter to Thomas Crawford, March 31, 1841: "We all admire the 'Shield of Achilles,' which is the chief ornament of Felton's house. Tell Greene he must write us the history of that. How did he come by it?" (*Sumner Memoir and Letters*, II, 176).

11. *The Spanish Student.*

12. Longfellow's image is unusual in this context. The expression "odor of sanctity" derives from the balsamic odor supposedly exhaled by saintly persons at their death.

## 580. *To Stephen Longfellow*

Cambridge Feb. 28. 1841.

My dear Father,

The day I left you proved very fine; and I reached Boston at a good hour, without suffering cold or inconvenience. I remained in Boston until Thursday afternoon, in order to despatch the few visits I had to make there; and then came out to Cambridge. I find all well here; though on calling at Mrs. Well's door in Boston, I was told she was very low.

The three days that I have been here I have kept my chamber; having discarded and taken off my hair. You cannot imagine how it changes me. It looks worse than the *old scratch.* And I am so annoyed, that I cannot help looking in the glass, and thinking what a fool I have been. Time alone can heal my mortification.[1]

Please say to Alex. that his list of matters wanting in the Railroad Surveys, goes tomorrow by the Britannia; but I cannot answer for the result. He must hope for the best.[2]

I here send an exact account of monies drawn by me during my first visit to Europe.

| | | | | | |
|---|---|---|---|---|---|
| 1826. *Paris.* | | | *Marseilles.* 1827 | | |
| | October | 500 francs. | | December | 500 francs |
| | November | 300 | 1828 } | January | 600 |
| | December | 500 | *Florence* } | February | 500 |
| 1827 | January | 500 | *Naples.* | April | 1000 |
| | February | 500 | *Rome.* | May | 500 |
| *At Bayonne.* | do | 200 | | June | 500 |
| | | | | July | 500 |
| | | | | October | 500 |
| | | | | do | 500 |

| | | | | | | |
|---|---|---|---|---|---|---|
| *Madrid. 1827* | | | *Venice* | December | 500 | |
| | March | $ 50 | | | | |
| | April | 100 | 1829 | | | |
| | May | 50 | *Vienna.* | January | 500 | francs |
| | June | 100 | *Dresden.* | February | 500 | |
| | July | 50 | *Göttingen* | March | 500 | |
| | August | 50 | | April | 1000 | |
| *Seville* | do | 50 | | May | 500 | |
| *Gibraltar.* | October | 200 | *Rotterdam* | do | 500 | |
| | | | *Göttingen* | June | 500 | |
| | | | " | do | 1200 | |
| | | | *Paris* | do | 500 [3] | |

I here send you places, dates, and amounts drawn, though I have not reduced the *francs* to dollars.

As Sam is waiting for this letter, I close in haste.

Very truly yours
Henry W. Longfellow.

MANUSCRIPT: Longfellow Trust Collection. ADDRESS: Hon. S. Longfellow/Portland

1. Longfellow had shorn his hair in favor of a wig, but the experiment proved unsuccessful.

2. In a letter dated January 7 and 11, 1841, Alexander had acknowleged the receipt of two series of English Railway Reports (see 478.2) and asked Longfellow to send for additional material.

3. The totals are 13,800 francs and 650 dollars.

## 581. *To Clara Crowninshield*

[Cambridge] *Monday* morning [February 29, 1841][1]

My dear Clara

I herewith send you

1. Lavy and Hughes's Letter.[2]

2. A curious letter from Lady Bulwer to Wikoff, (the Man who stays with Fanny Elssler).[3]

Both which I beg you to return as soon as convenient, as I wish to answer the first, and show the second.

If you have finished *that* volume of Göthe, you may send it out.

Yrs. very truly
H. W. L.[4]

P.S. I want you to come to Cambridge as soon as possible to see a beautiful bust of my friend Greene by *Crawford*, and a fine Portrait of Nat Willis.

MANUSCRIPT: Royal Library, Copenhagen.

1. Longfellow did not receive Crawford's bust of Greene mentioned in the postscript until mid-February (Letter No. 579), from which fact the date is conjectured.

2. Charles Lavy's letter is dated September 21, 1840, and contains a long postscript by Christopher Hughes.

3. Rosina Doyle Wheeler (1802–1882), an Irish beauty, married Bulwer-Lytton in 1827 and became legally separated from him in 1836. Her letter (unrecovered) was addressed to Henry Wikoff (1813–1884), American dilettante and chronicler of his social, political, and amatory adventures on two continents. He was Fanny Elssler's manager during her American tour.

4. The instruction "Over" follows the signature.

## 582. *To John Gorham Palfrey*

[Cambridge] March. 1. 1841.

My dear Dr.

I have just received your note, and will write the notice you speak of, with the greatest pleasure.[1] I shall have to trouble you, however, for a copy of the book, as mine is lent (how often *that* happens!)

I owe you an apology for not answering your note, which came at the beginning of the Vacation.[2] But the truth is, in the hurry-scurry of departure, (I may as well out with it) I forgot it; probably owing to the impossibility of my doing the Danish Ballads, or anything else in Vacation.

I hope to see you *here* soon, as I cannot see you *there,* because I have lately been *scalped,* and *it is mortifying.* If you dont comprehend this, any friend, who has seen me within these days, will tell you, that I look as if just returned from the Florida War.[3]

I hope Mrs. P. and yr. daughters are well. My regards to them, if you please

Very truly
Henry W. Longfellow

P.S. In looking again at your note I see you have beat me this time in *hand-writing*; but the next time, I shall send something superb in that line.

MANUSCRIPT: Harvard College Library. ADDRESS: Dr. Palfrey/Boston.

1. Palfrey's note is unrecovered, but the notice was presumably of *A New Spanish Grammar, Adapted to Every Class of Learners,* by Mariano Cubí i Soler (6th ed., Baltimore, 1840). Longfellow's remarks concerning it were printed in the *North American Review,* LII (April 1841), 516–518.

2. Palfrey had written, "You must without fail let me have your Danish Ballads or Modern Drama for the April number" (Letter of January 11, 1841). Neither article was ever published.

3. See 580.1.

583. *To Stephen Longfellow*

Cambridge March. 14. 1841.

My dear Father,

We have at length got fairly at work in College; and things go on in the usual, jog-trot, commonplace style; — grind, grind, grind; I have been in town but once since the Term began; and consequently know nothing that is going on in the world.

When you next see Colonel Stephenson, you may say to him, that I have made inquiries about the report of Webster's intemperance, and find that it is not admitted by his friends, but contradicted. He may have been merry once or twice at dinner, which would be enough to set such reports on foot. And I believe he has made one or more brilliant speeches after dinner, when the excitement was attributed, by his enemies, to brandy. On one occasion in Virginia, someone in the crowd cried out "If you will only speak like that, drink brandy like H——ll!" The Colonel may put his heart at rest.

Did Annie receive her blank book safely? I shall soon send her another, with the seal, and a box of Cologne water. How did Alex look in the black pants? Did they fit? I see by the papers, that the Ball began with a tragedy. I think those who witnessed it must have danced with heavy hearts.[1]

Mary and Sam and all your friends here are perfectly well, though shivering in a perpetual East Wind. Horrible month of March! I hope it is not so bad with you, as it is here. I feel it in every bone. Mrs. Craigie, too, is groaning with pains in her joints; and has been so ill, that we begin to fear she will not live long. She sees no Doctor; having a great contempt for Doctors and medicine.

Judge Story has returned from Washington. He is well and merry; and has as usual a good deal to say for himself. He says, among other things, that John Quincy Adams's argument in favor of the Amistad negroes did not come near the points of Law in question, but was a tirade against individuals, consisting chiefly of a thorough examination of the Correspondence, which passed between the several Ministers on the subject, and filled with what the Judge calls "*scorching sarcasm*," a phrase which he has stolen from the Washington Letter-writers. He did not manage the case in a lawyer-like manner, but oratorically.[2]

With kind regards

Very truly yours

Henry W. Longfellow.

MANUSCRIPT: Longfellow Trust Collection. ADDRESS: Hon. S. Longfellow/Portland. POSTMARK: CAMBRIDGE MS. MAR 15

1. The Boston *Daily Evening Transcript*, XII (Monday, March 8, 1841), No. 3257, reports: "At the Inauguration Ball at Portland, on Thursday evening [March 4, 1841, for President Harrison], Mr. William Parker, of that city, had just led out his partner for a dance, when he fell dead upon the floor."

2. In 1839 a group of African slaves being transported between Cuban ports aboard the Spanish ship *Amistad* successfully revolted and were subsequently captured by a U. S. warship and brought to New London. A long litigation developed, which found its way finally to the U. S. Supreme Court. Adams, counsel for the Negroes, delivered two four-hour arguments on February 24 and March 1. The court's decision, reached on March 9 and delivered by Justice Story, freed the Negroes and directed that they be returned to Africa. See *Memoirs of John Quincy Adams*, ed. Charles Francis Adams (Philadelphia, 1876), X, 427–437.

## 584. *To Stephen Longfellow*

Cambridge. March 21. 1841

My dear Father,

We have such a celestial, delightfully pleasant day, that I am enjoying it by the open window. The blue river runs in front, and the wind roars loud in the trees, and it is all Spring-like. We deserve this for the purgatory of snow, mud and rain we have just passed through. My friend Sumner is passing the Sunday with me; and lies stretched in all his majestic length upon the sopha reading Poliziano, the Italian poet.[1] It is delicious to get one's window open again; — and breathe freely, as in Summer. But I think Spring is a most restless season. I cannot possibly sit still. Change of place seems almost indispensable; yet being chained I can only move in thought.

This Term I have an easier time than usual in College; and am occupied on three days, only four hours each; I have no Lectures; which relieves me much; and the recitations of classes is a thing very easily managed, and needing no preparation. So that I have a great deal of time to myself, and do not find it disagreeable.

You have of course heard of Mrs. [Hannah] Wells's death.[2] She was buried on Tuesday; a cold, blustering, gloomy day. After the prayer was said, and the procession was forming, Chs. Wells rushed into the room, where the body lay, sobbing and weeping bitterly, and stood for some time gazing his last on the face of his mother. It was an affecting scene; and exhibited a grief uncontrolled by what form and ceremonies prescribe, and forbid. Mrs. Wells was much beloved, and is much lamented; though the concourse at her funeral was not great, owing I suppose to the inclemency of the weather.

On Thursday I dined with Mary; and on Friday took tea with the Greenleafs; (or Green*leaves*?) They are well, and flourishing. To-day I dine with Felton; — as I did yesterday. And so the days wear away, in doing the self-same things over and over again. We have very little variety here. Only occasionally a stranger, as last evening at the President's, Mr. Silliman,[3] who is now lecturing in Boston. He looks so much like Joe McKeen[4] of Brunswick, that I find it hard for me to think him a great man. A distinguished man he certainly is; and his lectures are so crowded, he is obliged to repeat the Course.

In Literature there is nothing new, save Mr. Emerson's Essays, which have just appeared full of sublime prose-poetry, magnificent absurdities, and simple truths.[5] It is a striking book; but as it is impossible to see any connexion in the ideas, I do not think it would please you much, and I shall not send it.

I shall send shortly a small box of trifles to Annie; as soon as the steamers begin to run; perhaps sooner.

With much love &c

Yours very truly
Henry W. Longfellow.

MANUSCRIPT: Longfellow Trust Collection. ADDRESS: Hon. S. Longfellow./Portland. POSTMARK: BOSTON ||MAS.|| MAR 22

1. Angelo Poliziano (1454–1492).
2. On March 13.
3. Benjamin Silliman (1779–1864), professor of chemistry and natural history at Yale.
4. Joseph McKeen (1787–1865), Brunswick merchant and banker, was treasurer and ex-officio trustee of Bowdoin College, 1829–1865.
5. This was the first publication of *Essays, First Series* (Boston, 1841).

## 585. *To George Roberts*

[Cambridge] March 28. 1841

Dear Sir,

Yours of the 23rd. with the $15. was duly recd. and is perfectly satisfactory.

I send you a very amusing sketch to-day; but for particular reasons, *I wish it to be published anonymously.*[1]

Yours truly
Henry W. Longfellow.

MANUSCRIPT: unrecovered; text from photostat, Longfellow Trust Collection. ADDRESS: George Roberts Esq/Boston. ENDORSEMENT: Professor Longfellow/March 28, 1841/No. 17

1. This sketch has not been identified. Roberts' letter of March 23 reveals that the $15 was in payment of Longfellow's translations from Jean Paul (367.3).

## 586. *To John Gorham Palfrey*

[Cambridge, March, 1841]

My dear Dr.

*"Eccolo,"* [Here it is] in *Cubic* measure.[1] If not exactly what you want, I will make any changes, or you may add and take from it what you please.

Yours truly
H. W. L.

MANUSCRIPT: Harvard College Library. ADDRESS: Rev. Dr. Palfrey/Boston. ENDORSEMENT: ||Mar|| 1841/H. W. Longfellow.

1. A punning reference to his critical notice for the *North American Review* (582.1).

## 587. *To Stephen Longfellow*

Cambridge April 1. 1841.

My dear Father,

Last evening I had the pleasure of receiving a letter from Dr. Nichols in reference to an Instructer for the Academy.[1] Please say to him, that I shall give immediate attention to it; and will write him upon the subject in the course of a day or two; that is, as soon as I can make the necessary inquiries, and find some suitable person, to recommend, which will be easy or difficult, as chance favors.

I hope you have had as delightful weather as we have, for the last week. It has been truly delicious. The Winter seems fairly over. Yesterday I was in town, and saw Caroline Doane. She seems very much broken down by her sister's death; and very sorry, that Mrs. [Nancy Doane] McLellan had not come on. During her last days Mrs. Wells was delirious. She thought they had taken her from home; and was constantly entreating to be carried back.

Mrs. Craigie has the same disease; and in all probab[il]ity will not live long. Some days she is confined to her bed; then again rallies. She will have neither Doctor nor Nurse; — and has nobody to attend her but her cook, who is lame. She says her system is *not adapted to medicine,* and that it always makes her worse; and she is determined to die as she has lived, — pretty much in her own way, without regard to the opinions of others.

In the mean time my friend and fellow lodger Mr. [Joseph Emerson] Worcester is about making a rush into the Elysian Fields of matrimony; thereby illustrating the great doctrine of the Perseverance of the Saints. He has been for six years looking over that fence with longing eyes; — and has at last cleared the ditch at a leap, and to all appearances is revelling in clover.[2]

As to Alexander's getting a place on the Rail-Road, I hardly know, what to think. I do not think it will be of any use for me to see Mr. Reed again. I have already said to him, all that I could well say; and if he cannot, or will not bring the appointment about, there is nothing more to be said. Nor, in fact, do I know how much power he has in the matter. I hope, however, that matters will work well; and that Alex. will get what he wants. I am inclined to think that enough has been done by way of solicitation.

I have no news to send you this week. On Friday evening I met Miss Jane Mason at Mr. Ticknor's. She inquired after Anne; and I told her we were expecting her here — as soon as the rail-road is finished.

We are all well.

Yours very truly.
Henry W. Longfellow.

MANUSCRIPT: Longfellow Trust Collection. ADDRESS: Hon. Stephen Longfellow/ Portland. POSTMARK: CAMBRIDGE MS. MAR 29

1. The Portland Academy, which Longfellow had attended as a child.

2. Worcester (392.7) married Amy Elizabeth McKean, daughter of Professor Joseph McKean of Harvard, on June 29, 1841.

## 588. *To Stephen Longfellow*

Cambridge April 4. 1841

My dear Father,

I had the pleasure of receiving your letter last evening; and am sorry to hear you have been more unwell than usual. I think it must be in part the Spring weather, which has more or less influence on every one.

I wrote to Dr. Nichols on the subject of the Schoolmaster, recommending Mr. Sanger;[1] — a relative of the Greenleafs. If you can get him, you will get somebody worth having. But I fear the Salary is too small to command his services for a very long time, unless he have an opportunity of increasing his income *indefinitely* by the tuition. This is the case, is it not? The Instructer has all the tuition, has he not? I hope you will be able to secure Sanger; for I agree with you in thinking it very important to have a good school in Portland. When I look back upon the years I wasted within those gloomy brick walls, I feel ready to cry about it. It was too bad; but *the milk is spilt,* and there is no remedy but to milk the cow over again.

I have the pleasure of informing you that the *fifth* edition of the *Voices* will go to press as soon as paper can be made or bought, suitable for the purpose. I am very agreeably surprised at the success of this work.

Has the *E[c]lectic Review*, pubd. in New York ever reached you in Portland? I am going to publish in it a "Syllabus of the History of German Literature during the Middle Ages"; — an account of all the works, — what editions have been published, and where extracts may be found of such as have not been published. It is a kind of guide-book for the student in German literature, and I hope may prove useful. As soon as it appears, I will send you a copy.[2]

The North American for April[3] is out. I have nothing in it but a brief notice of a Spanish Grammar.

The writers are:

I. Unknown [Sidney Willard]
II. Wm. Minot (a young Bostonian)
III. Mr. S. Elliot.[4]
IV. Dr. Palfrey.
V. Mr. Wharton (Philadelphia Lawyer)[5]
VI. Mr. Pickering.
VII Chs. Adams. (Son of J. Q.)
VIII. Mr. Hillard.
IX. Dr. Palfrey
X. Mr. Felton.

Nothing new here.

Yours very truly
Henry W. Longfellow.

P. S. Dr. Comb has pubd. his Tour in America; and gives an extract from his wife's Journal — a glowing description of Cape Cottage.[6]

MANUSCRIPT: Longfellow Trust Collection. ADDRESS: Hon S. Longfellow/Portland POSTMARK: BOSTON MS. APR 5

1. Longfellow presumably recommended George Partridge Sanger (1819–1890) for the Portland Academy position, but this cannot be verified since his letter to Rev. Nichols is unrecovered. Sanger, a Harvard graduate of 1840, served as tutor there, 1843–1846, and subsequently became an editor of legal works.

2. If Longfellow published such a syllabus, it has not been located; nor has a New York journal called the *Eclectic Review* for 1841. See Letter No. 344 and n. 1.

3. Vol. LII.

4. Samuel Atkins Eliot (1798–1862), mayor of Boston, 1837–1839, and father of Charles William Eliot (1834–1926), president of Harvard, 1869–1909. See 573.4.

5. Thomas Isaac Wharton (1791–1856).

6. George Combe returned to Great Britain in June 1840 after a successful lecture tour in America and published his *Notes on the United States of North America* the following year. His wife, Cecilia Siddons, was the daughter of the actress, Mrs. Sarah Kemble Siddons. Cape Cottage lies some three miles from Portland near the Portland Head Light.

## 589. *To Stephen Longfellow*

Cambridge April 11. 1841.

My dear Father,

Inclosed are half a dozen seeds of the large Spanish sweet Pepper, which I wish you to try in the garden. It is a delicious vegetable, and cooked with the Tomato makes a favorite Spanish dish, which (if these thrive) we will taste next Summer.

Since I last wrote, De Goy has concluded to resign his place here, and I have written to Mr. Bonneville,[1] offering it to him. For fear my letter may have miscarried, I wish Alexander would see Bonneville, and tell him such a letter has been directed to him in Portland, and requesting him to come on as soon as convenient.

The offer to Sam seems to stagger him. He dreads the responsibility, and tells me to-day that he has declined.[2] I have been trying to inspire him with a little courage, which is all he wants. Though I do not see how he could go before the middle of July; on account of the Otis boys, for whom he could not get a good instructer probably till that time, when a new class leaves college. I doubt whether he will make up his mind to take the place; though I wish it might remain open for a day or two, that he may have time to reflect.

Tell Annie I am very much obliged to her for her kind letter, which I shall answer in due course of time.

I hear of a person who has been cured of fits like those you suffer, by the use of emetics. If you have never tried this I wish you would do so, when you feel your next attack approaching. So simple a remedy is worth trying; for it could not injure you, even if it should fail to produce the desired effect.

We are all well.

Very truly yours
Henry W. Longfellow

MANUSCRIPT: Longfellow Trust Collection. ADDRESS: Hon. S. Longfellow./Portland. POSTMARK: BOSTON MAS. APR 12

1. Louis C. H. de Bonneville is listed in the Harvard catalog as instructor in French, 1841–1842. He resigned to embark on a "Mesmeric tour" of America, motivated by religious fervor and confidence in the Mesmeric therapy (Letter to Longfellow, August 20, 1843).

2. Samuel Longfellow had been offered the preceptorship of the Portland Acad-

emy. He declined the position in a formal letter to his father (one of the trustees) on April 10, 1841 (MS, Longfellow House).

## 590. *To Theodore Sedgwick Fay*[1]

Cambridge, April 14, 1841.

MY DEAR SIR,

This will be handed you by Mr. Welch[2] of Boston, who will pass a week or two in Berlin, and is desirous of making your acquaintance. As Mr. Welch is a scholar, and visits Germany for the purpose of studying its language and literature, you will have at least one bond of sympathy, and should you have it in your power to further his views in any way, I shall feel much obliged to you for it.

Yours very truly,

HENRY W. LONGFELLOW

P.S. A week or two ago I sent by way of London (or rather Sumner did for me) a small package for *you.* I hope it reached you safely.

MANUSCRIPT: Formerly in the Deutsche Staatsbibliothek, Berlin, and now missing; text from "Some Unpublished Longfellow Letters," p. 185.

1. Fay (1807–1898), formerly an editor of the *New York Mirror* and author of *Norman Leslie: A Tale of the Times* (New York, 1835) and other works, served as secretary of legation in Berlin, 1837–1853. Longfellow may not have known him personally at this time, but they had a common friend in Sumner. Fay's reply of September 15, 1841, establishes him as Longfellow's correspondent.

2. Possibly Edward Holker Welch (1822–1904), a Harvard graduate of 1840 who later became professor of French and German at Georgetown University.

## 591. *To Josiah Quincy*

[Cambridge] April 15. 1841

Dear Sir,

Mr. de Goy having signified his intention of resigning the place he now holds as Instructer in French in Harvard College, I propose in his stead Mr. L. de Bonneville, who is ready to enter upon the duties of the office.[1]

Yours &c &c

Henry W. Longfellow.

Harvard College.
Hon. President Quincy.

MANUSCRIPT: Harvard College Papers, X, 216. PUBLISHED: *Professor Longfellow of Harvard,* p. 98.

1. Bonneville was appointed by the Corporation on April 24 (*Professor Longfellow of Harvard,* p. 98).

592. *To Stephen Longfellow*

Cambridge. April [May] 2. 1841

My dear Father,

I was prevented by accident from writing you last Sunday; and so the week slipped away without it; as I had nothing of importance to write you. Nor have I now, save the safe arrival of Mr. and Mrs. Thacher.[1] I saw them yesterday in the street; and to-day have been in to town to see them at Mr. [Robert] Storer's. Margaret looks very well; and so does St. Peter. They go to Philadelphia on Thursday next; and are very busy in paying visits and *shopping*. Margaret does not seem very gay; but cheerful and quiet. Clara [Crowninshield] goes with them as far as New York; at least such is the present plan.

Since I last wrote you Mrs. Craigie has grown worse and worse. She is now lying at the point of death; and I should not be surprised at any moment to hear she was dead. She is very calm and untroubled. The last time I saw her, she said in rather a gay manner; — "You will never be married again, for you see how ugly an old woman looks in bed." This is very characteristic.

What is to become of me, when she dies, I know not. There are four heirs, and the estate is undivided. If possible I shall remain here. It must however depend upon accident. I shall be very sorry if I have to change my lodgings; and am quite at a loss which way to look for a home. As usual, I hope for the best; and trust that the old house will fall into Mr. Worcester's hands; and that I shall keep my foothold in it.

I have not written anything lately, save the Translation of a German Ballad, called "The Luck of Eden Hall," and published in The Boston Notion.[2] If you have not seen it I will send it to you. It is pretty good.

Mr. Bonneville does very well in College. He is laborious and careful, and very much liked by the students. I have no doubt he will do very well.

With much love, affectionately yours
Henry W. Longfellow.

MANUSCRIPT: Longfellow Trust Collection. ADDRESS: Hon. S. Longfellow/Portland/Me. POSTMARK: BOSTON ||MAS.|| MAY 4

1. Margaret Louisa Potter, Longfellow's sister-in-law, married Peter Thacher (1810–1894) on April 26, 1841. Thacher, a member of the Bowdoin class of 1831, was a lawyer in Machias, Maine.

2. II, No. 3 (April 24, 1841), 1. The original, by Johan Ludwig Uhland, was "Das Glück von Edenhall."

593. *To Charles Timothy Brooks*[1]

Cambridge. May. 5. 1841

Dear Sir,

I had the pleasure of receiving your letter yesterday, and in answer would say that it will not be possible for me to make any new translations for your volume, nor have I any on hand which have not been published. You are however perfectly welcome to anything among those published pieces which will suit your purpose. The only pieces I have translated from Uhland are "The Castle by the Sea" "The Black Knight" and the "Luck of Edenhall."

Felton wishes me to say to you that he has received your letter and will prepare something for the volume very soon.

Did you ever see Matthisson's Anthologie? some sixteen volumes of selections from the German Poets.[2] There are many things in it you cannot easily find elsewhere; and a vast quantity of trash. I own a copy, which is at your service, if you wish to look it over.

Yours very truly
Henry W. Longfellow.

MANUSCRIPT: Historical Society of Pennsylvania. ADDRESS: Chs. T. Brooks/Newport./R I [*in another hand*] POSTMARK: CAMBRIDGE MS. MAY 6

1. Brooks (1813–1883), pastor of the Unitarian Church in Newport, was preparing *Songs and Ballads; Translated from Uhland, Körner, Bürger, and Other German Lyric Poets* (Boston, 1842).

2. *Lyrische Anthologie,* ed. Friedrich Matthisson (Zürich, 1803–1805).

594. *To Catherine Jane Norton*

Cambridge. May 7. 1841

My dear Jane,

I send you a volume of Vasari in which I have marked the lives of *Cimabue* and of *Giotto* his pupil, with whom the History of painting in Italy begins.[1] These two lives I want you to read; and I would also copy their portraits.

Next week I will bring you another volume and thus by reading the lives of the best painters you will get an idea of the history of Painting in Italy, as well as preserve your *Italian.*

Very truly yours
H. W. L.

MANUSCRIPT: Harvard College Library. ADDRESS: Miss Jane Norton.

1. *Vite de' piu' Eccellenti Pittori Scultori e Architetti scritte da Giorgio Vasari pittore e architetto aretino* (Milano, 1807–1811), II, 147–164, 267–323.

595. *To Stephen Longfellow*

Cambridge. May 9. 1841.

My dear Father,

During the last week we have had rather a mournful time here. Mrs. Craigie's death [1] makes the house gloomy; and renders the future rather uncertain. Her disease was supposed to be some complaint of the heart; but an examination after death discovered a cancer in the breast, which was the cause of her death. She must have suffered great pain; but she died calmly.

What disposition will be made of the estate is not yet known; and consequently I do not know, whether I shall be permitted to remain in the house or not. If this portion should come into the hands of Mr. Worcester, I may keep my rooms yet a while longer. If not, I shall doub[t]less have to beat a retreat; in which case, I have made up my mind to go into College, where I can have rooms rent free. I feel, therefore, no uneasiness upon the subject; and do not care what happens, provided it does not happen too soon, that is to say, before vacation. Sooner than that it would be inconvenient to move.

This is literally all [2] the only news I have to send you; save that being in town yesterday I saw Mrs. McLellan; who, as usual, was full of plans for other people; as for example, the absolute necessity of Judge Potter's getting married!

The weather has suddenly grown very warm and I find it almost too warm sitting here with the window open all day.

We are all well.

Very truly yours
Henry W. Longfellow

MANUSCRIPT: Longfellow Trust Collection. ADDRESS: Hon. Stephen Longfellow/ Portland POSTMARK: BOSTON M||a||s, MAY 11

1. On May 6.
2. This word was inserted after the sentence was written.

596. *To Anne Longfellow Pierce*

[Cambridge, May 9, 1841.]

My dear Annie,

I was very much pleased on coming home last evening and lighting my lamp, to find beneath it a large bunch of May-flowers, fresh and blooming, and your kind note, equally so. I ran over, without delay, to present Miss Lowell her bouquet, with which she was much gratified. Poor soul! She was sitting doleful and alone, meditating upon Mrs. Craigie's departure, with some dismal forebodings about her own. So your present came just in season; and your remembrance of her, together with the sweet odor of the flowers, revived her drooping spirits.

If you wish to see my beautiful rooms you must come quick; as I am doomed soon to take leave of them; — at least, so people say. I, however, have hope and faith (not to say charity) that I shall remain here through the Summer at least. Then come what may, I am resigned to any fate.

Margaret and Don Pedro [Thacher] have gone to Philadelphia. I believe Clara [Crowninshield] went with them as far as New York. Margaret looks very well; and Don Pedro is radiant, as he should be.

What shall I send you, dear Annie, by the next opportunity? Any paper, or perfumes wanting? I mean to run down in June if possible.

Most affectionately yours
H. W. L.

P. S. The Butter has arrived safe and is very welcome.

MANUSCRIPT: Longfellow Trust Collection; written at end of Letter No. 595.

## 597. *To Catherine Jane Norton*

[Cambridge] Saturday morning [May 15, 1841][1]

My dear Jane,

I send you two volumes with a Life in each. *Buffalmacco* will amuse you; but *Frate Angelico* will *delight* you.[2] It is the life of a monk, who painted only Saints and holy subjects; never took his pencil in hand without a prayer, nor drew a crucifix without shedding tears. His life is as interesting as that Tale of the Organist, who was so absorbed in music.

You need be in no haste about the books. Read at yr leisure. See what a fine head for a sketch there is on p. 219 of Vol. 5. and what a beauty on p. 239.[3]

Very truly yours
H. W. L.

MANUSCRIPT: Harvard College Library. ADDRESS: Miss Jane Norton.

1. The date is questionable, but on May 7 (Letter No. 594) Longfellow wrote, "Next week I will bring you another volume [of Vasari]." The date, therefore, is not inconsistent with this remark.

2. The life of Buonamico Buffalmacco appears in Vasari, III, 69–102; that of Fra Giovanni [Angelico] da Fiesole in V, 31–54.

3. The heads of Antonio Rossellino and Mino da Fiesole.

598. *To Edgar Allan Poe*

[Cambridge] May 19, 1841.

Your favor of the 3d inst.,[1] with the two numbers of the Magazine, reached me only a day or two ago.

I am much obliged to you for your kind expressions of regard, and to Mr. Graham[2] for his very generous offer, of which I should gladly avail myself under other circumstances. But I am so much occupied at present that I could not do it with any satisfaction either to you or to myself. I must therefore respectfully decline his proposition.

You are mistaken in supposing that you are not "favorably known to me." On the contrary, all that I have read from your pen has inspired me with a high idea of your power; and I think you are destined to stand among the first romance-writers of the country, if such be your aim.

MANUSCRIPT: unrecovered; text from *Life*, I, 390–391.

1. For Poe's letter, see John Ward Ostrom, ed., *The Letters of Edgar Allan Poe* (Cambridge, Mass., 1948), I, 158–159. In it he asked Longfellow for contributions to *Graham's Magazine*, of which he was editor, and offered carte blanche with respect to terms.

2. George Rex Graham (1813–1894), proprietor of *Graham's Magazine*, whose April and May numbers Poe had forwarded to Longfellow.

599. *To Stephen Longfellow*

Cambridge May 31. 1841.

My dear Father,

For the last week this house has been a scene of confusion and desolation, such as I hope never to see again. The sale of Mrs. Craigie's furniture began on Tuesday and continued two days, and the delivery after the sale, and clearing the house continued till Saturday. But at length all is quiet again. Mr. Worcester takes the house for one year; and I keep my rooms. I should dislike to move; and had it come to that should have gone into College; an arrangement, which on the whole, I should not be very well satisfied with.

Everything goes on here in its usual monotonous train. As the Spring opens I keep out in the air as much as possible; and have taken to riding on horseback for exercise and recreation. I like it very well — though I have to run for luck as to horses; which is not so agreeable.

We had a very pleasant visit from Alex; — and little Stephen;[1] who made a large circle of acquaintances in a very short time. I am glad Alexr. has a place for the Summer.[2] I should like to join the expedition myself, if I had time. It would be a grand thing for my health. You will however miss Alex a good deal; and so shall I when I come on in the Summer. I mean to pass as much of the vacation with you as possible.

In literature, nothing new. I hear that Hyperion has been republished in London, though I have not received a copy of it.[3] The fifth Edition of the Voices has been sometime printed, though it is not yet out of the binder's hands. Shall send you one as soon as it is ready.

We have had delicious weather here till yesterday; when there came a fearful change. This evening is like October; a bright moon out of doors, and a bright fire in-doors.

Mary and James [Greenleaf] are well. I saw them wending their way to church to-day. They go to Portland on Thursday next.

Good night. With much love

Yours very truly
Henry W. Longfellow.

MANUSCRIPT: Longfellow Trust Collection. ADDRESS: Hon. S. Longfellow/Portland. POSTMARK: BOSTON ||MAS.|| MAY 31

1. Longfellow's nephew Stephen Longfellow (1834–1905).
2. With the Northeast Boundary Survey.
3. *Hyperion. A Romance* (London: John Cunningham, Crown-Court, Fleet Street, 1840), the first English edition of the book, was unauthorized.

## 600. *To Samuel Ward*

Cambridge June 2. 1841.

Most amiable and beloved Sam,

Pardon me for not answering instantly your affectionate letter of May 26; but I have been knocked up with a cold for some days past, with hardly sunlight enough within me to see by; *plus* sundry and almost continual interruptions. In fine enough to prevent me from taking the gray goose-quill in hand, until this morning.

In regard to the Dalmatian, my judgment approves your decision. I submit, and she takes her place among the bright Ideals.[1]

Like a pure lily on some river floating,
So floats she on the river of my thoughts.[2]
Finis!

Your visit was delightful to me, — and to all your friends here; only, alas! too short. Such meetings are the wine of life; — the "*golden-seal Johannisberger*" — 1841-Cabinet-Wein; — I am glad you enjoyed it, also. It is wise as well as pleasant to sit down once in a while on the mile-stones of Life's journey; and compare Notes of

Travel; — these same mile-stones being mostly grave-stones either of a friend or of a Hope. We were all much pleased to see in you so much strength of nerve; such a cheerful, courageous bearing, after your many sufferings.[3] May you always rise thus triumphant over the pains of life.

I hope to set to work in a few days upon the Student of Alcalá [*The Spanish Student*], to re-write some parts of it, and cleanse it of dross and all impurities. It shall come out of the crucible pure and bright; as you shall see anon.

As to Frithiof's Saga, both you and Felton are wrong. There are already *four* English Translations of the work. Nevertheless I shall not lightly throw away the advice of such good friends, but give due consideration to what you say.[4]

Sumner is well. I drove with him last evening to Pine-Bank. Cleveland is quite ill, with a kind of slow-fever. Bishop Doane sailed yesterday for England in the Steamer, to the great joy of Ned and Charley,[5] who make no secret of their utter detestation of the Prelate.

A good pun. Someone seeing a bass-viol in the Choir of a church on Sunday said it was a *bass-viol-ation* of the Sabbath. Very clever; and with that I close my letter, being obliged to go down to College and lecture on Lafontaine. I shall take that opportunity to slip my letter into the P. O. By the way, is there no way by which I can send my letters, as you do yours? Are there no return-packages in which I can smuggle them free?

Mr. [Joshua] Bates is here, and the people do him sufficient hommage. Tom Ward gives him a party tomorrow evening.

Very truly and affectionately yours
Henry W. Longfellow.

MANUSCRIPT: unrecovered; text from photostat, Longfellow Trust Collection. ADDRESS: Mr. Samuel Ward/New York POSTMARK: CAMBRIDGE MS. JUN 3 PUBLISHED: "Letters to Samuel Ward, Part II," p. 166.

1. It is unfortunate that this allusion is inexplicable, particularly in view of Ward's cryptic remarks in his letter of May 26: "The more I ponder upon a certain scheme which you unfolded to me the more I am constrained to say, I find it impracticable for the reasons then mentioned. Banish the thought from a mind so triumphantly tranquil and philosophical as yours now is. A certain man was well, would be better, took physic and died. Believe me life is too short to run such risks."

2. Cf. *The Spanish Student*, II, iii, 44–45.

3. Ward's brother, wife, and infant son had all died within the year.

4. Ward had written: "I regretted anew with Felton your unwillingness to translate Frithiof. It would be a noble and successful undertaking. Think of it again. I question if, having such a superb gift as you possess, a man has a right to refuse to impart to others a portion thereof" (Letter of May 26, 1841). For more on Longfellow and Tegnér, see *Longfellow and Scandinavia*, pp. 47–66.

5. Charles Callahan Perkins (1823–1886), brother of Edward Perkins and Mrs. Cleveland, was a student at Harvard. He became an art critic of note.

## 601. *To Catherine Jane Norton*

[Cambridge] Saturday morning June 5. [1841]

My dear Jane

I am delighted to see how much interest you take in the lives of these Painters. We shall soon come down to names more famous. Perhaps you will find nothing very attractive in Pietro Perugine. He is mainly known as the teacher of Rafaella; and on that account if on no other, his Life is worth reading. The renowned Lionardo da Vinci follows next.[1]

Would you like an *Olean*[*d*]*er*,* a very fine and healthy plant, which will be in bloom about the time the *Travellers* [2] return?

Yours truly
H. W. L.

* It is one of Mrs. Craigies, which has come into my possession. I think it would flourish better under your care than under mine.

MANUSCRIPT: Harvard College Library. ADDRESS: Miss Jane Norton.

1. Vasari, VI, 275–311; VII, 33–97.
2. Presumably the other members of the Norton family.

## 602. *To Alexander Wadsworth Longfellow*

Cambridge June 6. 1841.

My dear Alex,

James [Greenleaf] took charge of some Railroad Plans and Reports, which have just arrived from England for your special behoof. I trust they reached you safely and gave you pleasure. I hear they are quite magnificent. You are endebted for them to Mr. Sumner, who obtained them from his friend Mr. Ingham member of Parliament for South Shields.[1] Mr. Ingham has been very kind, and taken no little trouble to get them as you will perceive by the following extracts from his Letters.

"3rd May 1841. I hope by the next month's Packet to send you out *many* of the parliamentary papers, which Mr. Longfellow's brother wishes for, — if not all. Some of them are not papers printed by *Order of the Commissioners* but presented to the Members of both houses, by order of the Crown, being Reports of Royal Commissioners, and there is generally a less quantity of them in store. My copies of the plans &c had been given to the Mechanic's Institution of South Shields. Blackett[2] believes that his are at Oakwood in Northumberland, and he will have much pleasure in sending out to you any that are there."

From another letter of May 15th.

"I have sent to Mr. Hillard all I believe of the Parliamentary Plans &c on Irish Railways, which Mr. Longfellow wished for. Blackett sent them up to me, and is very happy in having the opportunity of sending you anything acceptable. I cannot send the *first Report* of the Commissioners. They tell me at the Parliamentary Paper office, that it is out of print, and that it was merely an Essay, of a few leaves, without any maps. I have substituted the last report of the Commissioners for Railway communication between London and Edinburgh."

So you see, my dear Sandro, that Mr. Ingham has been very attentive and very expeditious. I trust you will be duly gratified and thankful

Yours very truly
Henry W. Longfellow.

MANUSCRIPT: Longfellow Trust Collection. ADDRESS: Alexander W. Longfellow/ Portland POSTMARK: BOSTON ||MAS.|| JUN 6

1. Robert Ingham (1793–1875), MP for South Shields, 1832–1841 and 1852–1868.
2. Christopher Blackett (1788–1866) of Wylam, MP for South Northumberland, 1837–1841.

603. *To George Washington Greene*

Cambridge. June 10. 1841.

My dear George,

Looking into the morning's paper I see a vessel up for Genoa; and most eagerly do I avail myself of the opportunity to send you *Hyperion*. If this chance fails, and the book does not reach you, I will send another copy by mail, as you directed; and which I have not done sooner, because it is only a day or two ago that a few copies fell into my hands.

I hope you will like Hyperion. It is a *sincere* book; showing the passage of a morbid mind into a purer and healthier state.

In the same package I send you two copies of the Voices of the Night. You will see it is the fifth edition; and this within eighteen months of its first appearance; which is more like success than anything I have hitherto experienced. One copy is for your friend Crawford; — the other for Manzoni. Have the goodness to send it, with a couple of lines from yourself; as you will perceive I have only written his name in it.

Kind regards to Crawford. He is a true man of Genius. The country will be very proud of him. His bust of you is exquisite. How many times must I tell you this. Often as I look at [it] my eyes grow moist with feeling. Every one is delighted with it. Indeed you seem to be in the midst of us here; and not long ago in the middle of dinner, Sumner cried aloud: "My God! What a bust that is! How like Greene!"

With much love to your dear wife,

most truly and affectionately yours
Henry W. Longfellow

P.S. The third copy of the Voices is for you. The other copy of Hyperion for Crawford.

Sumner, Felton, and Howe dine with me to-day. We will crown your bust with flowers.

George W. Greene
Rome.

MANUSCRIPT: Longfellow Trust Collection.

604. *To Edward Curtis*[1]

Cambridge June 13 1841

My dear Sir,

It is with the greatest pleasure that I bear my testimony in favour of Mr. Graeter. I have known him for many years. He has always been regarded here and in Boston as a man of most distinguished abilities; and I feel great confidence in his power to discharge fully and faithfully all the duties of Translator of the Custom House should he obtain that place.[2]

Henry W. Longfellow

MANUSCRIPT: Longfellow Trust Collection.

1. Curtis (1801–1856) was collector of customs in New York during the Harrison-Tyler administration. He had previously spent two terms in the House of Representatives, 1837–1841.

2. This letter seems to have been ineffectual, since the Bureau of Customs in New York contains no record of Graeter's employment.

## 605. *To Samuel Ward*

[Cambridge, June 14, 1841]

My dear Sam,

I have shown your last letter to Felton and Sumner; and though we desire as much as you do, that Graeter should obtain the office of Translator in the Custom House, yet we do not agree with you as to the mode of obtaining it. Webster has nothing to do with the appointment; and therefore should not be molested. All lies in the hands of the Collector, Mr. Curtis. We have thought it better, therefore, to send you such documents as we can in favor of Graeter; tho' feeling at the same time that one word from you and your friends in N. York would have more influence there than all Cambridge, — crying till Doomsday. Sumner promised me he would write to you.

How did you find my *cousin*? [1]

Katzenberger would not do in English. It is too *dirty*. The sale of Menzel is not sufficient to give the Translator anything like compensation for his labor. Have confidence in me, dear Sam; I know what I am about.[2]

Tell Cogswell I had a strange dream about him last night. I thought he kept a Mad-house for dogs. I went to visit his establishment; and was all the time in the greatest terror. He had the dogs, however, in perfect subjection. It was a horrible night-mare, as you may imagine. I had been dining with Ticknor, Prescott and Allston. A very pleasant dinner. Dont forget his *cigars*. You could not do him a greater pleasure.

Thanks for the hints on the *Student*. They shall not be lost. I no longer intend it for the stage.[3]

Very affectionately yours
Henry W. Longfellow.

MANUSCRIPT: Longfellow Trust Collection. ADDRESS: Samuel Ward/New York. POSTMARK: CAMBRIDGE MS. JUN 14

1. In a letter of May 12, 1841, Ward identified this "cousin" as a Mrs. Greenough. Her relationship to Longfellow is obscure, but it is clear that she lived with her family in or near Brooklyn.

2. Ward had written on June 6, 1841: "Why abandon Katzenberger? If you want money, such books — which a man like you is alone capable of rendering — will sell like bread. Let your honest publisher have the *exploitation* of it — and it will bring you income. See how Menzel sells." The reference is presumably to Jean Paul Richter, *Doktor Katzenbergers Badereise* (Heidelberg, 1809), 2 vols.

3. Ward's letter of June 6 began with a page of critical comment on *The Spanish Student*. Among other things he wrote: "If there be a defect in the structure it lies in the personages who may be a thought too ideal for the stage which is condensed and active reality. They are beautiful and interesting with perhaps too much

of inward soul courtliness to suit the pit and galleries upon whose verdict you will agree with me the dramatic reputation of a play depends."

## 606. *To Samuel Ward*

[Cambridge]
Thursday night. 10 1/2 June 24 [1841]

The Two Locks of Hair.

A youth light-hearted and content
  I wander through the world; —
There Arab-like is pitch'd my tent,
  And straight again is furl'd.

Yet oft I dream, that once a wife
  Close in my heart was lock'd,
And in the sweet repose of life
  A blessed child I rock'd.

I wake! Away, that dream, away!
  Too long did it remain!
So long, that both by night and day
  It ever comes again!

The end lies even in my thought!
  To the grave so cold and deep,
The mother beautiful was brought; —
  Then dropt the child asleep.

And now the dream is wholly o'er,
  I bathe mine eyes, and see,
And wander through the world once more,
  A youth so light and free.

Two locks, — and they are wondrous fair, —
  Left me that Vision mild;
The brown is from the mother's hair,
  The blond is from the child.

And when I see that lock of gold,
  Pale grows the evening-red!
And when the dark lock I behold,
  I wish that I were dead.

Sitting sad and sorrowful, my dear Sam, the other morning, I felt the mood come over me of turning into English those sweet lines of *Pfizer*, which, when you asked me to do it, I said I could not. You have now the piece entire. But I beg of you do not give it to anyone to print, as I have given it to my friend Hillard for a book, of which he is Editor, and which is now in press.[1]

On Tuesday I drove over with Sumner to see your sweet sisters. They are all well, rejoicing in delicious coolness, and the green of the country. We passed a couple of delightful hours with them; and have only to regret they are so far off.

When shall we look for you? Good night. I can write no more, having a dire tooth-ache.

Affectionately yours
Henry W. Longfellow.

MANUSCRIPT: Clifton Waller Barrett Collection, University of Virginia. ADDRESS: Samuel Ward/New York. POSTMARK: CAMBRIDGE MS. JUN 25

1. Longfellow's translation of Gustav Pfizer's "Der Junggesell" was first printed in *The Token and Atlantic Souvenir* (Boston, 1842), pp. 22–23.

## 607. *To Stephen Longfellow*

Cambridge June 27. 1841

My dear Father,

There is nothing in our green and flourishing Cambridge, worthy of record. One quiet day succeeds another, and leaves no trace. Each finds us well, and leaves us well; and so we go on. I am glad to hear by James [Greenleaf], that it [is] pretty much the same with you. We are looking, however, with anxiety toward Washington. Things seem to be going on very badly there; — as badly as under the last administration. *Colonel Todd*, one of Harrison's old friend[s] is to go as Minister to Spain; — to enable him to pay off a mortgage of twenty thousand on his farm.[1] *Jennifer* is nominated for Austria.[2] Now neither of these men know anything about Courts, or foreign policy, or foreign languages. These are the reports of the day. Other bad news you will see in the papers. We fear the Whig Administration will be a failure; and that instead of setting a noble example in its appointment of worthy men to places of honor and trust, the party which came in professedly as a Reform Party will close its career with ignominy, after having perpetuated the evil courses of its adversary.

Speaking of Washington, has the Commodore [A. S. Wadsworth] arrived? I hope he will be in Portland when I arrive. But Annie must not [let] Little Red Ridinghood go before I see it. I fancy it must be very beautiful.[3]

Will you not come to Cambridge when Mary returns? The journey is now a mere trifle by the steamer and rail-road. Do think of it.

I intended, when I sat down, to write you a long letter, to atone for past delinquencies; but I have been interrupted; and the clock has struck midnight. Good night

Yours ever affectionately
Henry W. Longfellow

MANUSCRIPT: Longfellow Trust Collection. ADDRESS: Hon. S. Longfellow/Portland. POSTMARK: BOSTON ||MAS.|| JUN 28

1. Col. Charles Scott Todd (1791–1871), owner of an estate in Shelby County, Kentucky, was appointed minister to Russia, not Spain, in 1841 by President Tyler.

2. Daniel Jenifer (1791–1855) of Maryland served as minister to Austria, 1841–1845. He had been a Whig member of Congress.

3. See 378.3.

## 608. *To Catherine Jane Norton*

[Cambridge, June 1841][1]

My dear Jane

In this volume there are three lives; Lionardo the Magnificent; — Correggio, and Raffaellino; — the last a rather melancholy story of a man who grew worse instead of improving, — all his life long.[2] It is not particularly remarkable, saving for this circumstance.

When shall we begin the Purgatorio? I hope your mother will be persuaded to assent; and I have no doubt she will waive her objections.[3]

You are all very happy to-day of course. I sympathize with you most sincerely.[4]

Yours very truly
H. W. L.

MANUSCRIPT: Harvard College Library. ADDRESS: Miss Jane Norton

1. The exact date is problematical, but inasmuch as this letter accompanied the volume containing Vasari's life of Leonardo da Vinci — which Longfellow mentioned in Letter No. 601 would come next to Miss Norton — it must have been written after June 5.

2. Vasari, VI, 33–97, 141–163, 165–184, 285–293.

3. Mrs. Norton's objection to her daughter's reading Dante with Longfellow may have been related to her husband's conservative Unitarianism.

4. Possibly an allusion to the return of "the *Travellers*" mentioned in Letter No. 601.

608a. *To Catherine Eliot Norton*

[Cambridge] July 2, 1841

My dear Mrs. Norton

Inclosed is a little poem,[1] which I have just translated from the German. It is a good illustration of our conversation last night on the effect of prose-like simplicity in verse, and the power it has of awakening in us images of the highest poetic beauty. I hope the poem will please you, and that you will think it worth reading twice.

Very truly yours
Henry W. Longfellow

P.S. Pray do not forget that Washington's first Letter from Cambridge is dated July 4. — Sunday next.[2]

MANUSCRIPT: Harvard College Library.

1. "The Two Locks of Hair." The poem accompanies the manuscript. See 625.1.
2. For this letter to the Provincial Congress of Massachusetts, see *The Writings of George Washington,* ed. Jared Sparks (Boston, 1837), III, 14–15.

609. *To Stephen Longfellow*

Cambridge July 5 1841

My dear Father,

You have probably seen by the papers that we have had a rebellion in College. It lasted, however, only two days. All is again quiet, and orderly. There was never a more silly and boyish out-break; nor one with less cause. Two students have been expelled, and six dismissed from College. Luckily the term is nearly over, and Vacation will soon intervene, giving time for hot-headed youth to cool. Dislike to one of the Tutors was the reason given for this uproar; and a determination not to attend to the College exercises while he remained here the plan of operations. The result was what it always is on such occasions. The weaker party must yield.[1]

I began yesterday to read Washington's Letters from Cambridge; as yesterday was the date of the first of them. He came to Cambridge July 2nd. 1775; — took command of the Army on the 3rd and wrote his first letter on the 4th. It will be very pleasant to read here in Head-Quarters the Letters he wrote sixty-six years ago, perhaps in this very room; certainly in this very house.

Sumner is passing a day or two with me; and I must close my letter suddenly, for I am expecting Mr. Halleck, the Poet,[2] and some other gentlemen to breakfast this morning.

Very truly yours
Henry W. Longfellow

MANUSCRIPT: Longfellow Trust Collection. ADDRESS: Hon. S. Longfellow/Portland. POSTMARK: CAMBRIDGE MS. JUL 7 PUBLISHED: *Life*, I, 394.

1. The rebellion began with the burning of several fences in the College Yard, endangering Harvard Hall and the library. On June 28 there was a "riotous meeting" in the Yard, which resulted in the suspension of several students. Thereafter a boycott of recitations was attempted but broken with more suspensions. The identity of the unpopular tutor is not known. Faculty Records, Harvard College, XII, 45 ff.

2. See 567.6. Several days later, Sam Ward wrote to Longfellow, "Halleck was enchanted with his reception at the Craigie House" (Letter of June [July] 11, 1841).

## 610. *To Samuel Ward*

Cambridge July 7. 1841.

My dear Sam,

Your welcome letter of the 2nd reached me on Saturday, on my return from a drive to South Boston with your sisters. We had been to see the Institution for the Blind.[1] They seemed much pleased with the visit; and I rejoiced in their enjoyment. They all seem very well; — inhaling the cool New England, *native* air; — for you are all of you New Englanders. I told them I should write you on Sunday; but I was prevented from putting my threat into execution, by company.

I had the pleasure of seeing Halleck at breakfast with me on Monday, with Sumner, Felton &c. I did not know he was in these regions until Sunday evening. He is a glorious fellow certainly. He staid too short a time here; — merely long enough to shake a few friends by the hand, and then off again. This is not right. How can you show a man any civilities, if he will not stay long enough to receive them?

We have had a little uproar in College, but all is again quiet. The honors of the Institution will be distributed in a few days; — I mean the performances for Commencement. Hoffman, of your city, and a fine fellow by the way, carries off one of the first parts.[2]

Much obliged for the American, which is very welcome.[3] It serves as a kind of link between me and you, through which the electric spark may pass daily. If two lovers gaze at the same moon, at the same hour, *by appointment,* why may not two friends read the same Newspaper &c. &c.? I take it for granted, that those Letters from England are by Armstrong.[4] I think them excellent; and trust they are to be continued. I have *not* bought a copy of Stephens's Book;[5] and if you have a spare one, I shall not refuse it. In the same package (or trunk) put the long-promised

☞ 1. Ritterwesen! ☜
2. Mönchwesen![6]

You cannot forget this time.

Who are the writers in the July No. of the New York Review? It has not yet reached Cambridge, but I see the Contents in the American. It looks like an interesting No. The writers in the *Old North* are Art. 1. Francis Bowen. 2. Chs. [Francis] Adams. 3. Lieut. Davis.[7] 4. (*Good*) Francis Bowen. 5. Hillard. 6. Dr. Colman (*not Sammy*).[8] 7. Dr. Frothingham.[9] 8. Prof. Emerson (to me an unknown quantity = x).[10] 9. Capt. Whiting, who once wrote a poem called *Ontwa*.[11]

When shall I have your bed made at Head-quarters? Julia [Ward] pretended that you are to stay with them at Dorchester; but I corrected that error. Come soon, Patroclus, and we will fight for your body. My vacation has commenced; and I am tugging at the *painter*, like a boat when the wind and tide are rising.

Most affectionately yours
Henry W. Longfellow

MANUSCRIPT: unrecovered; text from photostat, Longfellow Trust Collection. ADDRESS: Samuel Ward/New York POSTMARK: CAMBRIDGE MS. JUL 8 PUBLISHED: "Letters to Samuel Ward, Part II," p. 168.

1. The Perkins Institution and Massachusetts Asylum, chartered in 1829 and opened in 1832, was under the direction of Samuel Gridley Howe, whose success with the blind deaf-mute Laura Bridgman had attracted great attention. Julia Ward Howe, who met her future husband on this occasion, described the visit in her *Reminiscences 1819–1899* (Boston and New York, 1899), pp. 81–82.

2. Wickham Hoffman (1821–1900), son of Murray Hoffman, the assistant vice-chancellor of Columbia University, became a diplomat and served briefly as minister to Denmark, 1883–1885.

3. Ward had presented Longfellow with a year's subscription to the *New York American* (Letter of July 2, 1841).

4. James Kosciusko Armstrong (1800–1868), son of Gen. John Armstrong, was Ward's good friend and the uncle of his wife. He does not seem to have written the four letters from England (*American*, Vol. XXIII, Nos. 4876, 4879, 4884, 4885 [June 21, 24, 30; July 1, 1841]), all of which bear the initials "H. N."

5. John Lloyd Stephens, *Incidents of Travel in Central America, Chiapas, and Yucatan* (New York, 1841), which Ward had offered to send Longfellow.

6. An undated letter by Ward to Longfellow mentions these volumes on chivalry and monasticism but does not identify them more closely.

7. Charles Henry Davis (1807–1877), lieutenant, later rear admiral, U.S. Navy.

8. Not Samuel Colman, the publisher, but Henry Colman (1785–1849), who had been both a Congregational and a Unitarian minister and was an agricultural expert.

9. Nathaniel Langdon Frothingham (1793–1870), pastor of the First Congregational Church, Boston.

10. Caleb Emerson (1779–1853), a lawyer, editor, Baptist minister of Marietta, Ohio, and a trustee of Marietta College.

11. Henry Whiting (c. 1790–1851), brevetted brigadier general in the U.S.

Army for gallantry in the Battle of Buena Vista (1847), was the author of *Ontway, the Son of the Forest: a Poem* (New York, 1822).

## 611. *To Stephen Longfellow*

Cambridge July 22. 1841

My dear Father,

I intended to have been in Portland long before this, but have been detained some days by a visit from my friend Ward of New York. I mean, however to start soon; and shall be in P. on Wednesday or Thursday next, without fail. The books for Anne I will bring with me if I can find them.

It has been excessively hot here for a few days past; but to-day we have a cool East-wind.[1]

MANUSCRIPT: Longfellow Trust Collection.

1. The rest of the manuscript is missing.

## 612. *To William Pitt Fessenden*

Portland. July 31 1841

My dear Pitt,

I have been in this land of Romance three days, and my organ of *amor patriae* begins already to "*cave in.*" Your absence is severely felt. I was at your house for a few moments last evening, and found your wife well. The children not visible, owing to the measles. Deblois[1] is still in Boston. Two nights ago your friend Mr. Little[2] had a very nice affair in the way of a party, where I saw the Belles of Portland, and likewise Nat Deering, who has just returned from a cruise in the Cutter, during which he saw as many lighthouses as the Skipper in his Ballad.[3] This is a faithful account of what I have seen and heard since my arrival; and I hope you [it?] will so warm your heart, that you will lend a favorable ear to what follows.

It is proposed to give the Consul at Rome, George W. Greene, a salary instead of fees. Sumner, at Mr. Webster's request, has drawn up a *Memorial* upon the subject, a copy of which will be sent to Choate and others, and which I wish you to read, that you may get at the facts of the case. Hitherto Greene has been obliged to take the fees allowed by law for signing Passports, having no other means of support; which has very much exasperated the "gentlemen travellers"; and his duties being rather diplomatic than commercial it seems adviseable if possible to obtain a salary for him and thus remove any cause of complaint against a very excellent fellow.

I hope you will find time to read Sumner's memorial, and will think so favorably of it as to give it your cordial support, and if possible obtain Mr. Evans's.[4] I should say more on the subject, did I not think you would read the paper referred [to], wherein you will find the necessary details to form your judgment of the merits of the case.

Anne sends her thanks for the paper with Frank Pierce's speech, and in return begs you to accept the inclosed solemn warning.[5]

Very truly yours,
Henry W. Longfellow.

MANUSCRIPT: unrecovered; text from typewritten transcript, Longfellow Trust Collection (Longfellow House).

1. Thomas Amory Deblois (1794–1867), a partner in the law firm of Samuel Fessenden and Deblois, Portland. William Pitt Fessenden had once been associated with this firm.

2. Presumably Josiah Stover Little, Longfellow's classmate at Bowdoin and, like Fessenden, an active Whig in politics.

3. Deering's ballad, entitled "The Wreck of the Two Polleys" and signed "Professor Shortfellow," was a burlesque of "The Wreck of the Hesperus." It contains the following explanatory stanza:

A plague on all our Congressmen!
Lighthouses so thick I see —
Odd's bloods! on such a darksome night
They bother exceedingly.

L. B. Chaplin, *The Life and Works of Nathaniel Deering* (Orono, Maine, 1934), p. 150.

4. George Evans (1797–1867), U.S. Senator from Maine, 1841–1847.

5. A newspaper clipping, annotated by the warning "Beware," accompanied the letter: "Washington City. — Mr. [James Silk] Buckingham, the traveller, gives a revolting description of the moral atmosphere at Washington. According to his account, it is exceedingly noisome and corrupt. — He says that in Washington, the Capital of this Republic, 'the total absence of all restraint upon the actions of men, either legal or moral, occasions such open and unblushing displays of recklessness and profligacy as hardly would be credited, if mentioned in detail. Unhappily, too, the influence of this is more or less felt in the deteriorated characters of almost all persons who come often to Washington, or live for a long period there. Gentlemen *from the northern and eastern States,* who, before they left their homes, were accounted moral, and *even pious men,* undergo such a change at Washington, by a removal of all restraint, that they very often come back, very altered characters, and while they are at Washington, contract habits, the very mention of which, is quite revolting to chaste and unpolluted ears.'

"This is surely a vile story to get abroad — and what is worse, we fear that, although it may be 'embellished,' it is not *altogether* untrue. — Boston Mercantile Journal."

613. *To Samuel Ward*

Portland, August 5, 1841.

My dear Sam,

I have just received your note of Aug. 3, payable at sight; and after the first pleasing emotions at seeing your hand-writing have subsided, what emotions do you suppose take their place? Fear, apprehension, — despair; lest in your letter to Kach[1] you forgot to write in large letters "*Johannisberger 1834*." I have an awful presentiment, that by some demoniac shuffling of the cards (corks) it will turn out "*Rudesheimer*"; which will be equal to 500 bottles [of] pure vinegar. Don't be angry. I only say this to vex you. When it arrives we will have a *Symposium,* and drain that green Luck of Edenhall which stands on your mantel. *Hoch! Es lebe die Rosamunda* [Long live Rosamond]!

If you found my chambers Paradise why did you stay so short a while? For my part, when I think of it, I wonder we did not prolong a pleasure, which occurs so seldom. To me it was delightful. It was almost like travelling. We were free from care; almost joyous; the sunshine only subdued and broken by some long, sharp shadows from the Past. Come again, soon, dear Sam; and if possible I will run on and pass a couple of days with you before the vacation closes, in your *Purgatorio!* (What? please repeat that last word.) If I come, will you consent to pass a Sunday at Katskill instead of going up to Red Hook? I have not yet seen that glorious landscape.

I have just been asked if I would deliver a Poem in New York before the New England Society, to which I have said No.[2] You who know my plans and ways of thinking will not be surprised at this.

I have been here already one week; and shall remain two more. Then to Nahant for a day or so. I cannot work. My brain is asleep; and the best thing I can do (next to mending this pen) is not to fash myself about it, but consider it as so much ammunition saved for more vigorous operations in Autumn.

There is a sister of *James* the Novelist now residing here.[3] I dined with her a few days ago. She is a woman of very decided talent, great vivacity, and easy manners. But what think you? After dinner by way of *chasse-cousin* (there was no coffee) she read me her own poetry for two hours; then a prose-tragedy in three acts; — and began another in five. At the end of the first Act, (excuse the vulgarism) I *bolted.*

I beg you to write me soon. My days here pass slowly, and solitary. With kind regards to Mersch, Cogswell, and the good Doctor.[4]

Yours very truly,
H. W. L.

P.S. The books may be sent to Cambridge at yr convenience.

MANUSCRIPT: unrecovered; text from "Letters to Samuel Ward, Part II," p. 169.

1. Presumably a German wine dealer. Ward spelled the name Koch (Letter of August 3, 1841).

2. See Letter No. 616.

3. Mrs. Joshua Webb (see Letter No. 614). She was apparently the sister of the English historical novelist George Payne Rainsford James (1799–1860). Her poetical effusions appeared occasionally in the *Portland Advertiser* during this period.

4. Dr. John Wakefield Francis.

## 614. *To Alexander Wadsworth Longfellow*

Portland. August 7. 1841

My dear Alejandro,

They tell me that if I mean to write you, now is my chance; and as the days are short here, owing to the hours of rising and going to bed, I begin *immediately* after breakfast, and *soon* after ten o'clock. I have been in town about ten days, and miss you very much. I am constantly reminded of you by the pipes; and you have left so much drowsiness and so many foolish dreams in your pillow, that they haunt me every morning, mistaking me for you. I am lodged in the sleep-haunted chamber, you perceive, at whose door everybody knocks in the morning, and says "Come, get up! It is after nine!"

The town is decidedly dull. I have however seen the lovely Fanny [Elssler]. Gilman [Daveis] is busy. He has just performed two surgical operations with great success. One for *Strabismus*; very successful.[1] The other was for club-foot; John Neal present as amateur, who exclaims "What a pity this discovery was not made before Byron's time! It would have made a very different man of him."

Business is dull. Reuel Shaw[2] sits all the afternoon on a chair under Preble's elms, watching his shop-door on the other side of the street. I bought at Little's Auction Room a Holy Family by Hannibal Carracci,[3] for *eight dollars!* John Neal says it is an undoubted original; he never doubts, you know. Mr. Sinclair (father of Mrs. Forrest)[4] has been giving Concerts here; and thinks of "taking up his residence among us," as the Advertiser says. I have made a new acquaintance in the person of Mrs. Josh Webb, a Scotch widow, married to the aforesaid Joshua. I dined at her house on Sunday last; and after dinner she read her own poetry to me for two hours; satires, hymns, reminiscences, letters to Grenville Mellen and impromptus to "*that rascal's whiskers*" (meaning her husband's.) She then asked me to read a play of hers, and give her *my candid opinion* of it. I declined the honor; whereupon she read the whole play to me, three acts, in prose; and then began another in five acts; but at the close of the first act I pleaded an engagement, and withdrew. She has talent; but this was too much for one sitting. I am to dine with her again to-day; could not contrive to get off. I fear I am booked for another Tragedy.

The family are pretty well, not very. Some trouble has been produced by the miscarriage of your package of cigars &c. I hope it will finally reach you. How do you like the wild woods? Have you a pleasant set? Kinsman says he had a jovial dinner with you and the Officers; that you were well, but looked as savage as a young *Orson.* After leaving you, on his way home the Marshal[5] was attacked in the woods by a — violent colic, which obliged him to dismount and roll in the grass for two hours, and came near putting an inglorious end to his career. But he survived to tell the tale.

Judge Potter's nigger says "this hot weather tans her so, that her folks tell her she aint a bit her natural color." The Judge and Eliza [Potter] start on Monday for a "*tower*" to the West, namely Connecticut River. Ned Preble has joined the Washington Temperance Society. With all kinds of remembrance from everybody,

yours very truly
Henry W. Longfellow

P. S. I shall remain here only a week longer. So your answer must go to Cambridge.

Stephen has returned from his Cruise in the Cutter, in good health and spirits; and threatens to write you before long.

MANUSCRIPT: Longfellow Trust Collection. ADDRESS: Mr. Alexander W. Longfellow/attached to the North Eastern/Boundary survey/Houlton [Me.]. POSTMARK: PORTLAND Me. AUG 8 ENDORSEMENT: H.W. Longfellow. Portland/ August 7. 1841/Recd. Camp 5. Augt. 18/Ansd. Camp 5. Sept. 18

1. Longfellow drew two sketches here, entitled "Before." and "After." See Plate IX.

2. A Portland grocer.

3. Italian painter (1560–1609) of the Bolognese school.

4. John Sinclair (1791–1857), Scottish tenor, was the father of Catherine Sinclair (1817–1891), an actress who had married Edwin Forrest in 1837 and whose divorce suit in 1852 became a *cause célèbre.*

5. John Dafforne Kinsman (7.1) had recently been appointed U.S. marshal for Maine.

615. *To Charles Sumner*

Portland — Thursday. Aug. [12] 1841

My dear Charley,

I shall be back on Saturday; and pray you to go down to the Eastern Railroad *Dépôt,* on the arrival of the evening train; about six I think; otherwise I shall not see you until monday, as I shall go at once to Cambridge.

I have not written you, because I have not been in the mood; — rather too sombre a tint for epistolary diversions.

Ever yours
Longfellow.

MANUSCRIPT: Brown University Library. ADDRESS: Chs. Sumner Esq/Boston POSTMARK: PORTLAND ||ME.|| AUG 12

616. *To Edward Sherman Gould*[1]

Cambridge August 15. 1841

Dear Sir,

I have had the honor of receiving yours of July 30, and regret that I cannot accept the Poem you offer, at your next anniversary. I have a great aversion to appearing on such occasions; and you will easily find persons near you, who will do you much greater honor, than I should.

With many thanks for your kind consideration,

Very truly yours
Henry W. Longfellow.

Edward S. Gould Esq
for the Committee of the
New England Society.

MANUSCRIPT: University of Washington Library. ADDRESS: Edward S. Gould Esq/New York. POSTMARK: CAMBRIDGE MS. AUG 16

1. Gould (1805–1885), author and translator, had achieved notoriety in 1836 with a series of lectures before the Mercantile Library Association of New York on "American Criticism of American Literature," his thesis being the inadequacy of American when compared with English literature.

617. *To John Gorham Palfrey*

[Cambridge] Thursday eve[nin]g. [August 19, 1841][1]

My dear Dr.

I found the accompanying Article on my table this evening, and send it without a moment's delay, hoping it may reach you in season for the October No.

I returned two days since from Portland, and hope to have the pleasure of seeing you soon.

With kind regards to Mrs. Palfrey

Very truly yours
Henry W. Longfellow

MANUSCRIPT: Harvard College Library.

1. Date provided by H. W. L. Dana. The article referred to is unidentified.

## 618. *To Stephen Longfellow*

Cambridge Aug. 21. 1841

My dear Father,

Sam has just dropt in on his way to Portland; and I write you a couple of lines to say that I arrived safely, and having passed a few days at Nahant very pleasantly am now quietly seated here at home. There is nothing new, save the Veto; which people do not seem to care much about, now the first effervescence is over.[1] Mary has gone to Cohasset beach, to pass a few days. She returns on Tuesday next, I believe. She and James are well. Mrs. Greenleaf has gone to Dover to see a sister, who is very ill. The weather is of the hottest kind; and next week bids fair to be very tiresome.

Yours very truly in haste
Henry W. Longfellow.

MANUSCRIPT: Longfellow Trust Collection. ADDRESS: Stephen Longfellow Esq/ Portland.

1. On August 16 President Tyler had vetoed a Whig bill to establish a Fiscal Bank of the United States. If adopted, it would have meant the revival of a government bank.

## 619. *To Samuel Ward*

Cambridge August 21. 1841.

My dear Sam,

Yours of the 13th reached me last evening, via Portland. How could you deceive that lady so, by saying I was *not* "a tall thin man, quite emaciated"? I will never forgive you for telling her I am "round as a barrel"; and I will tell the next woman, who inquires about you, that you are only five feet, three; with a white swelling on your knee, and the erysipelas in your face; and if she does not say "*Dear me!*" to that, then *dear-mes* have risen.[1]

Nevertheless, I *am* melancholy, and I *did* write you from Portland. Did you not receive an *illustrated* epistle, the East-Greenwich ghost, clearing a stone-fence, with "the trailing garments of the night" behind him? — namely, yourself and trousers?[2] If that letter has gone to Washington it will puzzle the Clerks in the Dead Letter office.

I had the pleasure of seeing the Astors yesterday; and John Astor[3] dines with me to-day. He has taken rooms at Mrs. Newel's;[4] and if he gives himself up to books I am sure he will like Cambridge; though not otherwise. Mr. Astor[5] was kind enough to ask me to go back to N. York with him, and run up river to Red Hook. I was obliged to decline, for reasons stated in my last; and I find by your note that I have again missed seeing Armstrong under your roof, which I regret exceedingly. You must come to Cambridge with him this Autumn. You can strike across from Rokeby by the rail-road some Monday morning instead of going down river. I remember *that Landing*; having waited there some hours for the boat, in the month of May 1826 — before you were born. I was on my way to Europe.[6] With what different feelings and reflections should I wait there now!

I had a very pleasant visit at Nahant, and the sand and the hazy sea still gleam silver-white in my imagination. To be sung to sleep by the perpetual lulaby of the surge, is delightful. Boating is the fashion there this season. Bill Wadsworth[7] gave a pick-nick on a "*dissolute island.*" Among the guests was Legaré,[8] who probably went on *Schwesterlein's* [little sister's] account; but *Schwesterlein* did not go. There was probably a "*deep expression*" in his eyes, and several still deeper on his tongue, when he found the beloved bait was left behind, and himself kidnapped, and carried away like another Sampson to amuse the Philistines. However, this is mere surmise, mere fancy-work. For my own part, I did not have an invitation; nor should I have gone under any circumstances; being always sick on such excursions.

Chs. Amory has a pleasant cottage at Nahant not far from Prescott's. Bancroft, Sparks and Grattan are at the Hotel, called the *Hôtel Diable* in contradistinction to the *hôtel Dieu.* I should like to pass a day or two there with you. Where is Lieber? Have you seen him? I was sorry to miss him here. He departed the day I came. Farewell.

Most sincerely yours
Henry W. Longfellow.

MANUSCRIPT: Longfellow Trust Collection. ADDRESS: Samuel Ward Esq/New York. POSTMARK: CAMBRIDGE MS. AUG 23

1. The deceived lady's repeated response to Ward's outrageous remarks was, "Dear me!" For Ward's letter, see *Uncle Sam Ward and His Circle*, pp. 299–300.

2. The "illustrated epistle" is unrecovered. Ward explains the allusion to the "East-Greenwich ghost" in his letter of August 9: "I omitted to add [in the letter

to the wine-merchant Koch] what a fearful attack of cholera mortus drove me at 2 oclock that night out of my kinsman's house, into the open fields with a pair of pantaloons *under my arm* and not a string of Beads on. Fancy me scudding over stone walls holding on to said breeches — under the powerful simultaneous actions of the principles of vomitive and purgative! It must have been the potatoes I ate at Parker's." This event occurred during Ward's visit to Cambridge in late July.

3. John Jacob Astor III was attending the Harvard Law School.

4. Possibly the wife of Rev. William Newell (1804–1881), minister of the First Parish Church, Cambridge.

5. William Backhouse Astor (1792–1875), son of the patriarch and father of John Jacob Astor III and Emily Astor Ward.

6. See Letter No. 91.

7. William Walcott Wadsworth (1810–1852), brother of the captivating Miss Elizabeth Wadsworth, who is referred to here as "Schwesterlein."

8. Hugh Swinton Legaré (331.6) was a confidant of President Tyler and on September 13 became attorney general of the U.S.

## 620. *To Samuel Ward*

Cambridge Aug 24. 1841

My dear Sam,

(Permit me to call your attention to the elegance of that new, favorite S. and pray dont mistake it for a German H. and make Ham of yourself).[1] Your two letters, (they were German certainly, that is to say *brief*, — a very bad pun, but let it go at that) reached me yesterday afternoon. I assure you again, I *did* write you a long epistle, a few days before leaving Portland, touching on all the one hundred and ninety nine topics of your Geneseo-Farmer-Prince project, and sundry others. It may be a good one, but I think you would get tired of it in a year.[2] I shall think you in earnest, when you have first established your Magnetic Observatory at Miliwaukie. I will discuss the matter with you, to your heart's content, when we next meet.

*John Astor* came to dine, as I told you in my last. I like him much. He is amiable and intelligent, as you know; and I trust he has resources in himself sufficient to make Cambridge pleasant.

Did I write you from Portland about Lady Isabella Graham,[3] the lady who read so much poetry to me, together with prose in any quantity?

*Infant Phenomenon.* Cleveland's little girl, (you remember her), as she lay musing in her cradle saw a *father-long-legs* crawl over her pillow, and cried out to her mother; "O ma! here's Mr. Longfellow in here!"

*Dear-mes* are looking up.

Felton has returned from Niagara. He enjoyed his journey highly;

making friends of whole families — with room enough for more in his capacious heart. He was particularly intimate with a family of Schuyler's in Jersey-city, whom he found at the Fales.[4] He intended to drop down the Hudson for the purpose of seeing you, but time failed.

Dr. Woods has returned. My compliments to Mersch, and inform him of the fact. I saw Pierce[5] a few moments ago. He was wishing that Woods *"would only publish that Oration on Science!* Only let him print, that is all!" "Why Pierce, you are like a ravenous shark, swimming round a vessel and saying to the Captain, *only* jump overboard, that's all."

But good bye. I am off to dine with Cleveland. Willard's[6] gig will be at the door in a few moments. *I shall have it charged to you!*

Most truly yours
Henry W. Longfellow.

MANUSCRIPT: Longfellow Trust Collection. ADDRESS: Samuel Ward Esq/New York. POSTMARK: BOSTON||MAS.|| AUG 24

1. Longfellow's *S* resembles the *H* in German script.

2. In his letters of August 9 and 11, Ward had revealed his dream of becoming a country squire in the Genesee Valley and invited Longfellow's comment. Longfellow's answering letter, presumably the "illustrated epistle" mentioned in Letter No. 619, is unrecovered.

3. Isabella Graham (1742–1814) was a Scottish-born pioneer in the organization of relief societies in New York City and the headmistress of a fashionable boarding school attended by Sam Ward's grandmother, Julia Cutler. Longfellow's identification of her with Mrs. Joshua Webb (Letters No. 613 and 614) is inexplicable.

4. The references are possibly to the family of J. Rutsen Schuyler, merchant, of Jersey City and New York City; and certainly to the family of Samuel Fales (1775–1848), Boston merchant and president of the Union Bank.

5. Presumably Professor Benjamin Peirce.

6. A Cambridge hotel.

## 621. *To Stephen Longfellow*

Cambridge September 1. 1841

My dear Father,

Commencement week passed off pleasantly. Mr. Hedge's Oration before the Phi Beta Kappa was in the main good, and in parts brilliant; though rather deep, and oracular.[1] Mr. Ingersoll's Poem was a kind of Prose run mad; but full of jests and puns; — more amusing than dignified.[2] I did not attend the dinner. To some it was pleasant, to others unpleasant. Judge Story is no longer President of the Society. Josiah Quincy Jr. has taken his place.[3] On the whole the week went off as well as usual.

And now the Term has begun. Nor am I sorry for it. I gave my first Lecture yesterday. I never commenced a Term in better health and spirits; and I think everything will go on vigorously and harmoniously.

I was at Mary's this morning. Anne Sophia [Longfellow] is better for the Cambridge air; though she hardly knows whether to attribute her improvement to this, or to the society of James and Mary! Sam is busy in arranging his College room; and I hope he may have a quiet reign. Indeed, I think he will. I do not believe there will be any trouble this year. The outbreak at the close of last term is enough for a twelve-month.[4]

I enjoyed my trip to Nahant very much. I found a great many of my friends and acquaintances there, and three days were soon passed. Sparks, Prescott and Bancroft were there; — Legaré, from South Carolina; — the Wadsworths of Geneseo; — and the Eliots and Lowells and many others.

The painting arrived safely. I fear I gave you a great deal of trouble about it. It now hangs in my bed-room, there being no place for it in the study.[5]

We were disappointed not to see mother with Sam; though it is perhaps lucky for her that she did not come; as we had a North-east storm for three days, and have not seen the sun for a week.

Have you read Pitt Fessenden's Speech on the Bankrupt Bill? It seems to be direct and forcible; and I think will please his constituents.[6]

Deblois is still in this neighborhood. He was at Cambridge at the Phi Beta Oration; and figured extensively.

Love to all.

Yours very truly
Henry W. Longfellow

MANUSCRIPT: Longfellow Trust Collection. ADDRESS: Hon. Stephen Longfellow/ Portland/Me POSTMARK: CAMBRIDGE MS. SEP 1

1. Frederick Henry Hedge (1805–1890), son of Levi Hedge and a founder of the Transcendental Club, was at this time pastor of the Unitarian Church in Bangor, Maine. The commencement had been held on August 26.

2. George Goldthwait Ingersoll (1796–1863) was a member of the Harvard class of 1815. His poem, "The Present is the Golden Age," apparently does not survive.

3. President Quincy's eldest son (1802–1882) graduated from Harvard in 1821 and was mayor of Boston, 1845–1849.

4. See 609.1.

5. See Letter No. 614.

6. On August 11 Fessenden had delivered a speech in the House of Representatives in support of a bill to establish a uniform bankruptcy law.

622. *To Sarah Perkins Cleveland*

[Cambridge] Sunday morng. Sept. 5. [1841]

My dear Mrs. Cleveland

As soon as I received your note last evening I went to see the President, but was not fortunate enough to find him. I will see him tomorrow and make the best arrangements for Charles [Perkins] that the case admits of. I think Frank Cunningham[1] would be a very good person to take charge of his studies; though I know not what others may think.[2]

In regard to "jumping the *year* to come," I should think it hardly possible, tho' I know of nothing in the Laws to prevent. Could Charles go over in *six* months the studies which in College occupy *eighteen*? I should think it inadvisable to try; for the examination would necessarily be rigid, and failure disheartening.

I will ride over to see you as soon as I can and we will talk more at large upon the subject. I hope you hear good news from Henry and Ned [Edward Perkins]; but what dismal weather they have had for riding!

With kind regard to your mother,[3]

Very sincerely yours
Henry W. Longfellow

MANUSCRIPT: Berg Collection, New York Public Library.

1. Francis Cunningham (1804–1867), a graduate of Harvard in 1825, had been pastor of the Third Parish Church, Dorchester, and was now devoting himself to literary pursuits at his home in Milton Hill.

2. On August 27 Perkins had been "suspended from College until Saturday after Thanksgiving, for leaving at end of term without passing exams, after permission so to absent himself was refused" (Faculty Records, Harvard College, XII, 70).

3. Mrs. Eliza Perkins Doane, wife of Bishop George Washington Doane.

623. *To Samuel Ward*

[Cambridge] Monday. Sept. 6. 1841.

"Der Tod [das] ist die kühle Nacht,
Das Leben ist der schwüle Tag!
Es dunkelt schon; — mich schläfert; —
Der Tag hat mich müde gemacht."[1]

Dearly beloved brother,

You will find this text recorded in the Gospel according to Heinrich Heine, first volume, second page. And again in another chapter, these words:

"Ich hab' im Traum geweinet;
 Mir träumte, du lägest im Grab'.
Ich wachte auf und die Thräne
 Floss noch von der Wange herab.

Ich hab' im Traum' geweinet,
 Mir träumt', du verliessest mich,
Ich wachte auf, und ich weinte
 Noch lange bitterlich." [2]

My dear Sam, your two last letters lie still unanswered; — the one witty the other sad — the one a light, the other a shadow; but the shadow is more beautiful than the light. What a frantic old *Rabelais* the Philosopher has become to jest so upon such a theme! [3] But at times the river of life must rush through *such* wild *Lurley Felsen* [4] also, with mad whirlpools and loud, demoniac laughter! — $(x + y = \frac{\text{Carlyle.}}{2})$

I had two or three very pleasant interviews with Marion [Ward], during his short stay in Boston. From what he says, you seem really to have thought in good earnest of the plan of a Geneseo Farm. You must look *twice* before you leap there. You ask my opinion; but of course I cannot give it without knowing more about your private affairs than I now do.

Pray send me Ritterwesen and Mönchwesen by earliest opportunity.[5] Why did you not slip them into Marion's trunk, O most forgetful of men? If you can find at any of your book-sellers the edition of Molière, by L. Aimé-Martin, forming part of the Bib. d'Auteurs Classiques, have the goodness to buy it for me, and send by Harnden.[6] I cannot get it here; and it is incomparably the best edition I have ever seen, on account of its notes. Let me know in your next, whither it can be had in N.Y.

Did you think to pay my bill for Arcturus? If not, I beg you to do so, as I am in doubt about it, and do not wish to pay the Boston Agent for fear of paying twice. This, and the Molière shall be instantly repaid to your order. And while I am in this business paragraph, I will ask some information about Colman. Can I rely on getting anything from him before January next?

Excuse this Bore.[7]

I will not close this letter yet; for I imagine I shall find a note or a Newspaper at the Office, when I go down. By the way, I have arrived at the honor of a caricature, in a Newspaper,[8] "Illustrations of Longfellow's Voices of the Night." A tall, desperate looking individual, with wild hair and eyes, — hat knocked off by branch of a dead tree, — rushing through a dismal swamp at m||idnight, — ||a heavy mist everywhere about, — dim wo||ods in|| the back-ground, — frogs and owls — &c. I will send it to you, as soon as I get ||another, — ||very coarse and poor.

Half-past-One o'clock, and no letter. I have however a copy of the "Voices," which I send by to day's mail. Show it to Dr. Francis.

In haste, very truly yours
Henry W. Longfellow

P.S. Do take the trouble to see Colman, and appeal to his sense of Justice — *or shame.*[9]

MANUSCRIPT: Longfellow Trust Collection. ADDRESS: Samuel Ward Esq/New York. POSTMARK: CAMBRIDGE MS. SEP 6 PUBLISHED: "Letters to Samuel Ward, Part II," p. 170.

1. "Death is the cool night,/Life is the sultry day!/Dusk is falling; — I drowse; —/Day has tired me." Heine, "Der Tod, das ist die kühle Nacht," stanza 1.

2. "I have wept in a dream;/Dreaming you lay in a grave./I awoke and a tear/Still ran from my cheek.//I have wept in a dream,/Dreaming you left me,/I awoke, and I wept/A long while bitterly." Heine, "Ich hab' im Traum geweinet," stanzas 1 and 2.

3. In a letter of August 27, 1841 — presumably the "shadow" letter — Ward had devoted two pages to an effusion on the advantages of dreams over reality. In the same letter he reported a dinner-table conversation with Henry Francis ("the Philosopher"; see 464.8) as follows: "He said the papal chair was the only office on Earth he would accept. I asked him if he would be liberal of *indulgences.* No replied he I shall want them all myself. I will worship the holy Virgin in all her representatives on Earth. Have a Maria (Ave Marie) shall be my motto. Yes said I and many would be born to call you *Pater Noster.*"

4. The rocks of the Lurlei (Lorelei) above the Rhine.

5. See 610.6.

6. William Frederick Harnden (1813–1845) began the first express service between Boston and New York in 1839. The work requested was *Œuvres de Molière, avec les notes de tous les commentateurs,* 2nd edition, published by L. Aimé-Martin (Paris, 1837), 4 vols.

7. Longfellow's sketch of an auger follows.

8. Unidentified.

9. Another sketch of an auger concludes the letter.

## 624. *To Sarah Perkins Cleveland*

Cambridge Sept. 10. 1841

My dear Mrs. Cleveland,

I hoped to have the pleasure of seeing you at Pine Bank before this, and the opportunity of explaining to you why your wishes in regard to Charles could not be complied with. The President had already written to Dr. Robbins,[1] and made the present arrangement, before I saw him. I proposed Cunningham in vain. The Faculty preferred Lancaster to Milton, and approved the President's decision.

Upon reflection, I am inclined to think that you will acquiesce in this decision, and find it, upon the whole, the better one, though you will not have Charles's pleasant society so often at Pine Bank.

With kind remembrances to your mother,

Very truly yours
Henry W. Longfellow

MANUSCRIPT: Berg Collection, New York Public Library.

1. Presumably Rev. Chandler Robbins (1810–1882), pastor of the Second Church, Boston. He maintained a summer residence in Lancaster.

625. *To Catherine Eliot Norton* [1]

[Cambridge] September 14. 1841

My dear Mrs. Norton,

Inclosed is a poem I wrote by the light of the last moon. It came into my mind, (or as the *Stranger in Ireland* would say "It found its way into my pocket-book") [2] in part as I walked down your avenue, and in part as I looked out of my own window. I hope you will not think it *all* moonshine; but if so, confess at least that it is *real* moonshine, and "Myself the man i' the moon do seem to be." [3]

When Jane's birth-day comes round, (when is it?) will you permit me so far to express my good wishes as to send her a copy of the *Voices*? I hope you will not refuse this request; for I shall feel the sincerest pleasure in being admitted, so far as this, to join with you in celebrating her *fête*.

Very truly yours
Henry W. Longfellow

Endymion.

The rising moon has hid the stars.
Her level rays, like golden bars,
Lie on the landscape green,
With shadows brown between.

And silver white the river gleams,
As if Diana, in her dreams,
Had dropt her silver bow
Upon the meadows low.

## LITERARY SUCCESS

On such a tranquil night as this,
She woke Endymion with a kiss,
    When sleeping in the grove
    He dream'd not of her love.

Like Dian's kiss, unask'd, unsought,
Love gives itself, but is not bought,
    Nor voice, nor sound betrays
    Its deep impassion'd gaze.

It comes, — the beautiful, the free,
The crown of all humanity, —
    In silence and alone
    To seek the elected one.

It lifts the boughs, whose shadows deep
Are Life's oblivion, the soul's sleep,
    And kisses the clos'd eyes
    Of him, who slumbering lies.

O weary hearts! O slumbering eyes!
O drooping souls, whose destinies
    Are fraught with fear and pain,
    Ye shall be lov'd again!

No one is so accurs'd by fate,
No one so wholly desolate,
    But some heart, though unknown,
    Responds unto his own.

Responds, as if, with unseen wings,
An angel swept its quivering strings;
    And whispers in its song,
    "Where hast thou staid so long."

MANUSCRIPT: Clifton Waller Barrett Collection, University of Virginia.

1. Catherine Eliot Norton (1793–1879) had married Andrews Norton in 1821. Her thirty letters to Longfellow, 1838–1868, in the Longfellow Trust Collection, suggest a friendship of some intimacy.

2. Edward DuBois, *My Pocket Book; or Hints for "A Ryghte Merrie and Conceitede" Tour, in Quarto; to be called, "The Stranger in Ireland," in 1805, by a Knight Errant* (New York, 1807), p. 17. See also Irving's *Salmagundi,* No. IV, Tuesday, February 24, 1807.

3. *A Midsummer Night's Dream,* V, i, 243.

626. *To Samuel Ward*

[Cambridge] September 17. 1841.

My dear Sam,

I had no sooner sealed and sent my last,[1] with Endymion asleep under its leaves, than who should come in but Park Benjamin himself. I told him what I had done, whereat he expressed great grief; and to console him, I promised to write you, and cry "Stop that poem!" If therefore it is not already in the hands (*paws*?) of Arcturus or the claws of *Old Knick*, you may send it to Benjamin, without saying a word about the price, as we settled that matter beforehand.[2]

It is a long while (that is three days) since I heard from you. I am glad to know by your last (Sept 11.) that you like Lieber better on knowing him more. He is a strong man; and one whose conversation, like some tumultuous mountain brook, sets your wheels all in motion, and a "*demnition grind*" begins. He it is, who has made you restless. Sing, then, with old Göthe;

The Wanderer's Night-Song.

Der du von dem Himmel bist
Alles Leid und Schmerzen stillest,
Den, der doppelt elend ist
Doppelt mit Erquickung füllest, —

Ach! Ich bin des Treibens müde!
Was soll all der Schmerz, die Lust!
   Süsser Friede,
Komm, ach komm in meine Brust!

Thou, that from the realms of bliss
All our care and sorrow stillest, —
Him, who doubly wretched is
Doubly with refreshment fillest, —

O! I'm weary of contending!
Why this sorrow, this unrest!
   Peace, descending
Come, O come into my breast.[3]

But before this reaches you, you will have changed your mood, and be very likely to say, "I wonder what he means?"

This Term begins beautifully with me. My Lectures come in the afternoon, so that I have all these golden Autumnal mornings to myself. Believe me, I both enjoy, and improve them. I have fairly cast anchor here, as in a safe harbor, — *drying my sails,* — and occasionally, (as now for instance,) *dropping a line* out of the cabin windows, to catch a friend. Life is sanctified by its uses.

I have two or three literary projects, foremost among which are the *Student* and the *Skeleton.* I have been thinking this morning, which I shall bring out first. The Skeleton, with the few other pieces I have on hand, will it is true, make but a meagre volume.[4] But what then? It is important to bring all my guns to bear now; and though they are small ones, the shot may take effect. Through the breach thus made the Student may enter the citadel in triumph. In fine, such are my thoughts this morning.

Washington Alston has a book in press; — a tale, written *twenty years ago!* Scene in Italy; — title and subject unknown.[5]

Yours very truly
Henry W. Longfellow

MANUSCRIPT: Longfellow Trust Collection. ADDRESS: Samuel Ward Esq/(Prime Ward & King)/New York. POSTMARK: CAMBRIDGE MS. SEP 17 PUBLISHED: *Life,* I, 398–400.

1. This letter is unrecovered.
2. The poem appeared in Benjamin's *The New World,* III, No. 13 (September 25, 1841), 193.
3. Longfellow's revision of this translation of Goethe's "Wanderers Nachtlied" first appeared in "A Handful of Translations," *Atlantic Monthly,* XXVI (September 1870), 362.
4. *Ballads and Other Poems,* published by John Owen in December 1841. Longfellow originally planned to call it *The Skeleton in Armor* (see Letter No. 635).
5. Allston's Gothic tale *Monaldi* (Boston, 1841).

## 627. *To Stephen Longfellow*

Cambridge September. 26. 1841

My dear Father,

I have not written to you for a long while, partly on account of the dearth of news, and partly because I have been busy in various ways. I am going to put to press soon another volume of poems. It will be very small; not more than fifty or sixty pages. Still I think it important to bring it out now, and not to wait till a larger number of pieces are ready. Blow upon blow, is the word; and not let the iron cool.

College affairs go on smoothly. Rölker has moved into town; and is now sick of a bilious fever. Sam is to take his classes till his recovery. He begins tomorrow, and I think will do very well.

Mother and Mary are well. We think of going to Lowell tomorrow or next day, to see the wonders there; particularly the manufactory of carpets.

Annie's Little Red Riding Hood [1] is much admired; and we are all looking forward with pleasure to her visit here, which we think promised, and mean to claim. Her books (Bishop Mant and Mrs. Fry) [2] have arrived from London and will be sent by first opportunity. Also a book for you; — a Treatise on the Water-Brash — so profound that I cannot see far into it; perhaps you and Dr. Wood may be more successful.[3]

The weather has not been fine since mother came. It has rained a good deal; and to day the wind blows a hurricane. I wonder how Alex weathers it in his camp. We have not heard from him lately. I have written him only once; but every week I send him a newspaper, which I suppose he does not receive. If so, they count for nothing.

Have you tried the Homœopathic system yet? I sincerely think it is worth while; and hope you will conclude to give it a trial, even if you condemn it afterwards. It cannot possibly harm you, and it may do you great good. No matter what the Doctors may say about it. It remains to be seen which is right, the old or the new method.

Please say to Stephen, that I beg fifty pardons for not sending his shoes sooner. They are lying ready for an opportunity; and several chances have missed fire. They shall go by first opportunity, without fail. Anne's boots went yesterday, I hear. I hope they fitted.

Have you read John Quincy Adams's speech on the McLeod affair? [4] If you have not, pray read it. It will amuse you.

The Judge and Eliza [Potter] are probably safe in Free Street before this. They were to leave Boston yesterday.

Yours very truly
Henry W. Longfellow.

MANUSCRIPT: Longfellow Trust Collection. ADDRESS: Hon. Stephen Longfellow./ Portland./Me. POSTMARK: BOSTON MAS. SEP 27

1. See 378.3.

2. See 476.3. Mrs. Elizabeth Gurney Fry (1780–1845), the English prison reformer, wrote *Observations on the Visiting, Superintendence and Government of Female Prisoners* (London, 1827).

3. This book is unidentified but was probably a treatise on the homeopathic therapy for water-brash (pyrosis). See Letter No. 631.

4. *Speech of Mr. John Quincy Adams, on the Case of Alexander McLeod. Delivered in the House of Representatives, September 4, 1841* (Washington, 1841). McLeod, a Canadian, was about to be tried in Utica, New York, for murder and arson in connection with the burning of the steamboat *Caroline* above Niagara

Falls on the night of December 29, 1837. This incident of the Canadian Rebellion of 1837 created a tension between the U. S. and Britain that was relieved only with McLeod's acquittal. See Alastair Watt, "The Case of Alexander McLeod," *Canadian Historical Review,* XII (June 1931), 145–167. Adams, whose speech advocated conciliation toward the British, took the opportunity to direct a satirical barrage against Andrew Stevenson (1784–1857), an old political adversary and U.S. minister to England, 1836–1841.

## 628. *To George Stillman Hillard*

[Cambridge] Wednesday eve. [September 29, 1841][1]

Dear George,

Will you be kind enough to present the inclosed for payment, and send me the money at your leisure. I hope you will be out soon. I have two or three new poems to read to you; which may have the same effect upon you as the Vicar of Wakefield's *old boots* had upon his relations.[2]

Yours truly
H. W. L.

MANUSCRIPT: Clifton Waller Barrett Collection, University of Virginia.

1. The date is conjectural. The poem referred to in the text may be "Excelsior," which Hillard is known to have sent to Park Benjamin for publication and payment (see 632.1), and "Excelsior" was written on September 28 (*Works,* I, 79).

2. See *The Vicar of Wakefield,* Chap. I. The Vicar's relations never returned to deliver the boots he had lent them.

## 629. *To Samuel Ward*

Cambridge, Sept. 30, 1841.

My dear Excelsior,

Many thanks for "Ritter-Wesen" and your letters. I am glad you liked "Endymion," for sympathy is sweet. But today I send you something much better; indeed one of the best things, if not the best, that I have written.[1] The other night, about one o'clock, as I was smoking a cigar preparatory to going to bed, it came into my mind; but, as it was late, I thought I would not write it out until morning. Accordingly, I went to bed, but I could not sleep. That *voice* kept ringing in my ears; and finally I jumped out of my bed, lighted my lamp and set to work. The result was this poem and a dreadful cold and rheumatism, which have confined me to my chamber for two days. The idea of the poem is the Life of Genius. This you will comprehend at a glance. Many people will not comprehend it at all. I send it to you because I know you will like it. No one has seen it but Felton who found less than usual to criticise. Don't give it to anyone; but keep it quietly to yourself.[2]

I am in such great bodily pain that I cannot write a word more, and must shuffle this off upon you as a letter.

Yours very truly,
Henry W. Longfellow.

MANUSCRIPT: unrecovered; text from *Uncle Sam Ward and His Circle,* p. 305.

1. The accompanying poem was "Excelsior."

2. Maud Howe Elliott interpolated at this point: "[Here follows 'Excelsior,' the entire poem]."

## 630. *To Charles Sumner*

[Cambridge] Thursday morning. [October 21, 1841][1]

*Stop that steamer!* After you left me last evening, I *dragged* the *River Charles,* and got out all the stones that ruffled the smooth-flowing current. The *celestial* emendations I wish to introduce into Bentley's copy.[2] Therefore if not too late, keep back the letters, and bring them out with you on Saturday. You *must* come. It is very important to tread with iron heal upon the last pieces of my new volume[3] and winnow out the chaff.

Love to Hillard.

Yours evermore
H. W. L.

P.S. Do not forget the Luck of Edenhall.

MANUSCRIPT: Longfellow Trust Collection. ADDRESS: Charles Sumner Esq./ Boston. PUBLISHED: *Life,* I, 402–403.

1. The date is approximate but agrees with Longfellow's statement on October 24 (Letter No. 632) that he wrote "the other evening a Song to the River Charles."

2. Longfellow apparently intended to send "To the River Charles" to *Bentley's Miscellany* in London, using Sumner as his intermediary; but the poem did not appear there. The "*celestial* emendations" probably referred to the phraseology of stanza 6.

3. *Ballads and Other Poems.*

## 631. *To Stephen Longfellow*

[Cambridge] October 23 1841.

My dear Father

I write you a few lines to show you I am better; though, to tell the truth, it is still rather an unpleasant operation. I have in fact nearly recovered; and should be entirely well were it not for some obstinate trouble in the stomach. I have not yet the least appetite; and unluckily the weather is so bad I cannot go out to find one.

Annie's short visit has helped to revive me. But she vanishes like the dew. She seems hardly to have arrived, and is away again. I wish I could accompany [her] back to Portland.

I trust the *Learned Book*[1] did you no harm; and that you have made up your mind to try Homœopathy. There is certainly no danger in chronic complaints; and if the old practice has failed year after year, it really seems worth while to think of this.

Thanking you for your kind letter, and with much love to all

Very truly yours
Henry W. Longfellow.

MANUSCRIPT: Longfellow Trust Collection.

1. An allusion, perhaps, to the treatise on the water-brash mentioned in Letter No. 627.

## 632. *To Samuel Ward*

Cambridge October 24. 1841

My dear Sam,

I am quite mortified at the fate of *Excelsior.* I would rather have paid the price of it, than have it go into that milk-pan, the Ladies' Companion.[1] *Ay de mi Alhama!*[2] But you are all wrong in your criticism. Strange that [Andrews] Norton should have started it; and that so many should have listened. *Excelsior* is correct. "An *adjective* qualifying the substantive is sometimes used instead of an *adverb,* modifying the verb." Beck's Syntax p. 53.[3] Moreover I asked the learned Feltonius; whereupon he quoted from his full head this line from Virgil.

"Tu ne cede malis, sed contra *audentior* ito."[4]
Aeneid VI. 95.

And followed it up with another from Ovid;

"Ecce venit Telamon *properus.*"
Again "In medio *tutissima* ibis." (seldom quoted!)[5]

There, dear Sam, that is erudition enough for Sunday. Now let me thank you for your letters, which always give me great satisfaction and consolation. I am glad you think better of Wesselhoeft and the Wasser-Cur.[6] (Water-dog.) That will be my pool of Bethesda. I shall never get well till my good Angel troubles the water for me.[7] More of this anon. But send me Graeter's book as soon as it comes out. I am curious to see it. I have faith, myself, but wish to strengthen the faith of others.[8]

How strange! While you are urging me to translate *Nattvardsbarnen,* comes a letter from Bishop Tegnér himself, saying that of all the Translations he has seen of Frithiof, my fragments are the only attempts "that have *fully* satisfied him." "The only fault" he says, "that I can find with your Translation is, that it is not complete; I take the liberty of urging you to complete the task, that I may be able to say that Frithiof has been *translated* into at least *one* language." Highly complimentary is the Bishop, to my humble endeavor. He is about publishing his complete works in some twenty volumes, Prose and Poetry, and promises me a copy, hoping I shall find something therein to translate. After this kind letter can I do less than *overset* the Nattvardsbarnen?[9]

Your late visit to Cambridge was as delightful

"as the sigh
Of Summer winds, that breathe and die."[10]

But you left a deeper imprint of yourself upon the minds of your friends. I am delighted to hear the words of praise that spring to the lips of Hillard and Felton, when they speak of you; — such epithets, for instance, as *"noble, generous, — large-hearted"* &c.

Lord Morpeth was kind enough to drive out to see me with Sumner, the evening of his arrival. He is a very simple, cordial man, — *mezzo cammin* [middle-aged] — with a red face and white hair, — a live coal with white ashes on it. A very unostentatious, friendly *man.*[11]

I wrote the other evening a Song to the River Charles; — quite successful; though as it is local, I think it had better appear first in the volume, not in any magazine. Also, last night a funereal chant called *"God's-Acre,"* full of ghastly images, which I shall not publish at all, as I hate grave-yards, and would like to be *burned,* not *buried.*[12]

Would you not like to know how I am? I dined to-day on cold chicken and a glass of Burgundy, and feel stupid and strong.

Kind regards &c.

Yours mostruly.
H. W. L.

P.S. Much obliged for George Sand, tho' I have not had time to read a line in *her.*[13]

P.S. This evening I have added twenty six lines to the nine I translated for you in Nattvardsbarnen — notwithstanding my stomach.

MANUSCRIPT: Longfellow Trust Collection. ADDRESS: Samuel Ward Esq/(Prime Ward & King)/New York. POSTMARK: CAMBRIDGE MS. OCT 25

1. Longfellow had hoped to have $25 for "Excelsior" and had sent the poem, through Hillard, to Park Benjamin for the *New World*; but Benjamin sold it to William Snowden of the *Ladies' Companion* for $15. Longfellow eventually had to return the money when "Excelsior" appeared in *Ballads and Other Poems* before Snowden could publish it in his journal.

2. "Woe is me, Alhama!" Refrain from the anonymous "Romance muy doloroso del sitio y toma de Alhama." Longfellow printed Byron's translation of this ballad in *Poets and Poetry of Europe*, pp. 651–652.

3. Charles Beck, *Latin Syntax* (Boston, 1838). Longfellow later "explained *excelsior* as the last word of the phrase *Scopus meus est excelsior*" (*Works*, I, 80).

4. "Yield not to misfortunes, but go more bravely against them."

5. "Here comes Telamon *quickly*"; "you will go *safest* in the middle." Cf. *Metamorphoses*, VII, 647; II, 137. The proper form — "tutissimus" — has been provided in pencil.

6. Dr. Robert Wesselhoeft (1797–1852), a German immigrant in 1840, practiced medicine in Cambridge for five years before establishing a hydropathic resort in Brattleboro, Vermont, in May 1845. For an account of this popular Water-Cure, see Mary R. Cabot, *Annals of Brattleboro 1681–1895* (Brattleboro, 1922), II, 564–584. See also 798.6.

7. A reference to Fanny Appleton's coolness toward him.

8. That is, of his father. Francis Graeter's book was *Hydriatics; or, Manual of the Water Cure, Especially as Practised by V. Priessnitz in Graefenberg*, compiled and translated from the writings of C. Munde, Dr. Oestel, Dr. B. Hirschel, and other eyewitnesses and practitioners (New York, 1842).

9. Tegnér's letter of July 10, 1841, is printed in his *Samlade Skrifer*, ed. Wrangel and Böök (Stockholm, 1918–1925), IX, 422; and a translation appears in *Life*, I, 394–396. For the details of Longfellow's translation of "Nattvardsbarnen," ("The Children of the Lord's Supper") see *Longfellow and Scandinavia*, pp. 54–58, and John Leighly, "Inaccuracies in Longfellow's Translation of Tegnér's 'Nattvardsbarnen,'" *Scandinavian Studies*, XXI (November 1949), 171–180.

10. Cf. stanza 5 of "The Land of the Blest" by William Bourn Oliver Peabody (1799–1847), Unitarian clergyman of Springfield, Mass.

11. George William Frederick, Viscount Morpeth (1802–1864), whom Sumner had met in England, was on a tour of the U.S. He became 7th Earl of Carlisle upon the death of his father in 1848 and served as lord-lieutenant of Ireland, 1855–1858 and 1859–1864.

12. "To the River Charles" appeared first in the *Ladies' Companion*, XVI (January 1842), 115; "God's Acre" in the *Democratic Review*, IX (December 1841), 597. Both poems were included in *Ballads and Other Poems.*

13. Ward had sent Longfellow a copy of George Sand, *Le Compagnon du tour de France* (Letter of October 21, 1841).

633. *To Samuel Ward*

[Cambridge] October 29. 1841.

God's Acre.

I like that ancient Saxon phrase, which calls
The burial-ground, God's Acre! It is just; —
It consecrates each grave within its walls,
And breathes a benizon [1] o'er the sleeping dust.

God's Acre! Yes; that blessed name imparts
Comfort to those, who in the grave have sown
The seed, that they had garner'd in their hearts,
Their bread of life, alas! no more their own.

Into its furrows shall we all be cast,
In the sure faith, that we shall rise again
At the great harvest, when the Archangel's blast
Shall winnow, like a fan, the chaff and grain.

Then shall the good stand in perpetual bloom,
In the fair gardens of that second birth,
And each bright blossom mingle its perfume
With that of flowers, which never bloomed on earth.

With thy rude ploughshare, Death, turn up the sod,
And spread the furrow for the seed we sow!
This is the field and Acre of our God,
This is the place, where human harvests grow.

To the River Charles.

River! that in silence windest
Through the meadows bright and free
Till at length thy rest thou findest
In the bosom of the sea!

Four long years of mingled feeling,
Half in rest and half in strife,
I have seen thy waters stealing
Onward, like the stream of life.

Thou hast taught me, Silent River,
   Many a lesson deep and long;
Thou hast been a generous giver,
   I can give thee but a song.

Oft in sadness and in illness
   I have watched thy current glide,
Till the beauty of its stillness
   Overflowed me, like a tide.

And in better hours and brighter
   When I saw thy waters gleam
I have felt my heart beat lighter
   And leap onward with thy stream.

Not for this alone I love thee,
   Nor because thy waves of blue
From celestial seas above thee
   Take their own celestial hue.

Where yon shadowy woodland hides thee
   And thy waters disappear,
Friends I love have dwelt beside thee
   And have made thy margin dear.

More than this; thy name reminds me
   Of three friends, all true and tried,
And that name like magic binds me
   Closer, closer to thy side.

My dear Sam,

At your request, received this afternoon, I send "God's-Acre." Sumner thinks it very striking; and I hope you may like it. The Song to the River Charles is, however, better liked. If O'Sullivan would like either or both, let him have them, on your own terms; but with this caution, that they must both appear in December or the volume will be out before them. Perhaps he could exchange one of them for *Excelsior*. Would that it were possible! — and get the Prophet's Breaches (the banner) from under the petticoats of the Ladies' Companion.

Thanks for your letter and the poem of Count Auersberg,[2] next to Uhland the best living Poet of Germany — for me. But dont urge me to translate. I am heartily vexed with you every day, for having laid at my door that basket full of babies the "Children of the Lord's Supper." They are so beautiful, that they draw me away from everything else and woe to the Student of Alcalá, who knocks in vain at my heart; though this evening I *will* write a few lines for *him.*

I was at College to-day, for the first time.

Armstrong's joke was a Joseph Miller; — if one stove saved half the cost of fire-wood, two would save all, and with them you would make money. Where and how is Armstrong? I shall be delighted to see his designs.[3] Kind regards all. Where is Cogswell?

*Yours ardently,*
H. W. L.

I have recd. a letter from the Agent of the Brooklyn Lyceum, which I cannot answer, because I cannot read his name. It looks like *Reed* or *Need.* Who can it be? [4]

MANUSCRIPT: Longfellow Trust Collection. ADDRESS: Samuel Ward Esq/(Prime Ward & King)/New York. POSTMARK: CAMBRIDGE MS. OCT 30

1. Corrected to "benison" in pencil.
2. Anton Alexander von Auersperg (1806–1876), Austrian poet, wrote under the pseudonym of Anastasius Grün. Ward had sent Longfellow a copy of Auersperg's "Mannesträne" with the hope that he would translate it (Letter of Thursday, October, 1841).
3. Sam Ward's letters do not clarify this allusion.
4. See Letter No. 634.

## 634. *John Keese*[1]

Cambridge Nov. 3. 1841

My dear Sir,

I am very sorry that my plans for the winter will not allow of my acceding to your proposition in regard to the Brooklyn Lyceum. I have a good deal of work to do, and unfortunately my health is not very good; and so far from being able to lecture in New York this Winter, I fear I shall not be able to visit you, even for recreation. Please express to the Committee of the Lyceum my thanks and regrets.

I take this opportunity of saying a few words in regard to my own affairs. I have in press here a small volume of "Ballads and Other Poems" — about p.p. 100. which will be out before January. Poetry has its Laws, and Law has its Poetry, — but whether Law-Books and Poems will pull together in the same yoke, is another question. Perhaps they may; and you may have it in your power to promote the sale of my volume. I should be much pleased if you and Mr. Owen could make it mutually advantageous to interchange your books, which

I suppose not impossible, considering the Law School here — &c. &c. Have the goodness to give this a thought. These new Poems will be uniform in size and appearance with the "Voices of the Night"; and on many accounts the volume will be more valuable. Mr. Owen of this place is the Publisher.

I take the liberty of calling to your mind the drawings you were kind enough to promise me, not "in the Dolphin chamber, at the round table, by a sea-coal fire, upon Wednesday in Wheeson-week,"[2] — but in *this* chamber, and at *this* round table, where I am now writing, — and on a Sunday in the Summer-time.

Fields[3] I have not seen for a long time; having been imprisoned here in my chamber for the last month, with a fever. They have in press a handsome edition of Motherwell's poems.[4]

Yours very truly
Henry W. Longfellow

MANUSCRIPT: Clifton Waller Barrett Collection, University of Virginia. ADDRESS: Jno. Keese Esq/New York. POSTMARK: CAMBRIDGE MS. NOV 4

1. Keese (1805–1856), editor, book auctioneer, and wit, was at this time a partner in the publishing firm of Collins, Keese and Company, which was primarily concerned with publishing legal works. He had written Longfellow on October 26, inviting him to lecture before the Brooklyn Lyceum.

2. *King Henry IV, Part II,* II, i, 97. The drawings are not identified.

3. James T. Fields (1817–1881) was associated with the publishing house of William D. Ticknor, where he ultimately became a partner. He later became one of Longfellow's most voluminous correspondents.

4. William Motherwell, *Poems, Narrative and Lyrical* (Boston, 1841). See Letter No. 642 and n. 2.

## 635. *To Samuel Ward*

Cambridge Nov. 3. 1841

Blind Bartimeus.

Blind Bartimeus at the gates
Of Jerico in darkness waits.
He hears the crowd; he hears a breath
Say, "It is Christ of Nazareth!"
And calls, in tones of agony,
Ἰησοῦ, ἐλέησόν με!

The thronging multitudes increase;
Blind Bartimeus, hold thy peace!
But still amid the noisy crowd

The beggar's cry is shrill and loud;
Until they say; "He calleth thee!"
Θάρσει, ἔγειραι, φωνεῖ σε!

Then saith the Christ, as silent stands
The crowd; "What wilt thou at my hands?"
And he replies; "O give me light!
Rabbi, restore the blind man's sight!"
And Jesus answers; Ὕπαγε.
Ἡ πίστις σου σέσωκέ σε!

Ye who have eyes, yet cannot see!
In darkness and in misery,
Recall those mighty Voices Three,
Ἰησοῦ, ἐλέ[η]σόν με!
Θαρσει, ἔγε[ι]ραι, Ὕπαγε!
Ἡ πίστις σου σέσωκέ σε!

Dearest of Sams,

I was reading this morning, just after breakfast, the Tenth chapter of Mark in Greek, the last seven verses of which contain the story of Blind Bartimeus, and always seemed to me very remarkable for their beauty. At once the whole scene presented itself to my mind in lively colors; — the walls of Jerico, the cold wind through the gate-way, the ragged, blind beggar, his shrill cry, the tumultuous crowd, the serene Christ, the miracle; — and these things took the form I have given them above, where perforce I have retained the striking Greek expressions of entreaty, comfort and healing; — though I am well aware that Greek was not spoken at Jerico. The poem is for your private eye; and is not to be sold at any price. It must see the light first in the volume, which is going bravely on. I think I shall add to the title "Supposed to be written by a Monk of the Middle Ages"; as it is in the Legend style.[1]

I had the pleasure of receiving yrs. of yesterday this afternoon — *one day on the way*. Why are mine five? Your sister Julia's "Imprisoned Angel" is a *very, very* beautiful poem, both in design and execution. Only in the third Stanza the line "And gently o'er its fetters sweeps" mars the symmetry of the piece. Though the line in itself is beautiful, I should reject it without mercy.[2]

Also a letter from Benjamin to-day. He wants two poems, (orders two pairs of boots!) and offers twenty dollars each. If you have not disposed of *Charles River*, send it to him. If you have, send one of the others. I shall send him a new poem, called simply "*Fennel*," which I do not copy here on account of its length. It is as good perhaps as *Excelsior*. Hawthorne, who is passing the night with me, likes it better. But what about *Fennel*? *Chew upon it*, till you see the plant nod its yellow flowers in the New World.[3] Thanks for the *Illustrations* (?) of *Excelsior*. Hawthorne laughed mightily at them; and says "the absurdity of ambition is now rendered obvious to him, by seeing this figure carrying the huge log of wood up the Alps, with as much fervor as if the safety of the world depended upon it." They *are* funny.

When shall I look for you here? I am delighted to hear you are coming. But is it *my* visit, or Ticknor's? At all events come *alone*; for I shall have the "Children" to show you. The work is more than half done; and goes into the volume of "Ballads and Other Poems"; for *Skeleton in Armor* is no longer an appropriate title, the volume being now more than one hundred pages.

I told Felton of your riding ten miles before breakfast. His only comment was: "*Poor fellow*!" You know he has the *Hippophobia*. I have much, *much* more to say, but alas! where is the Time?

Evermore and more yours
H. W. L.

MANUSCRIPT: Longfellow Trust Collection. ADDRESS: Samuel Ward Esq/(Prime, Ward & King)/New York. POSTMARK: CAMBRIDGE MS NOV 4

1. "Blind Bartimeus" was first printed in *Arcturus*, III (December 7, 1841), 65, and collected in *Ballads and Other Poems*.

2. Ward may have sent Longfellow a copy of his sister's poem, but the manuscript does not survive, nor was it collected in any of Julia Ward Howe's published works.

3. Longfellow later changed the title to "The Goblet of Life" and changed his mind about who should get it. It appeared first in *Graham's Magazine*, XX (January 1842), 5; but Benjamin reprinted it in the *New World*, IV (January 8, 1842), 23.

## 636. *To Anne Longfellow Pierce*

Cambridge Nov. 5. 1841

My dearest Annie,

I have not till now found a moment's leisure to thank you for your note, and the very welcome firkin of sundry household matters. They were all very acceptable and well-timed; and the jelly has enlivened and sweetened many a solitary supper.

I am happy to tell you, that I have been out a week. I am not yet very *strong*; but I am very *busy*, which is *not* precisely the same thing. The return of pleasant weather has brought a good deal of company with it; and I have a volume in the press, as you know; and college affairs; and two or three letters to write every day; and in fine, my hands *so* full, that I postpone too long, perhaps, writing to those, who will excuse my delay; as yourself, for instance.

I was very much pleased and delighted, on Monday, returning from College in the afternoon to find the Commodore and Margaret[1] waiting in my rooms. They were not *gay*; for the Commodore was evidently homesick; and Margaret had the weight of household cares upon her, and Peter's absence. Since then he has arrived; but has not been in Cambridge; nor have I been to Boston to see him; being still rather too weak to undertake the thousand and one calls I shall have to make, when I once set foot on the pavement of the city.

Did you enjoy your visit here, dear Annie? It was *short* enough to be *sweet*; but there is a difference between *shortening* and *sweetening*.

I hear from James and Mary [Greenleaf], that Stephen has purchased for me that picture of Copley in the Museum of Antiques. Tell him I am exceedingly obliged to him; But how can he send it? As the painting is old, I am afraid it would crack if taken out of the frame and rolled. Perhaps he had better ask *Cole* about it.[2]

Love to all.

Most affectionately your
*"Blushing friend Henry."*

P. S. Has she gone? Will it be safe for me to come to Portland?[3] Has father begun the Homœopathic cure yet? Dont forget my payment in advance for the Portland Transcript, $2. — for 1841–42 — 1840–41 was paid in August '40.

MANUSCRIPT: Longfellow Trust Collection. ADDRESS: Mrs. A. L. Pierce/Care of Hon. S. Longfellow/Portland POSTMARK: CAMBRIDGE MS. NOV 6

1. Commodore Alexander Wadsworth and Margaret Potter Thacher.

2. Samuel Longfellow remarked on the painting: "This fine old picture is a full-length of a boy and girl, — the grandchildren of Sir William Pepperell, of Louisburg fame. It is believed to have been painted by [Mather] Brown, a fellow-pupil of Copley. It was found, a very dilapidated canvas, at the sale of the old 'Portland Museum,' among a rubbish of wax-works, Indian weapons, stuffed animals, etc., was bought for a trifle, and, after being carefully restored, was hung in the drawing-room of Craigie House, which it still adorns" (*Life,* I, 410 n.). Charles Octavius Cole (b. 1814), a portrait painter, was living in Portland.

3. Possibly a reference to Mrs. Joshua Webb.

## 637. *To Samuel Ward*

Cambridge Nov. 6. 1841

My dear Sam,

It is Saturday night, and eight by the village clock. I have just finished the Translation of the Children of the Lord's Supper; and with the very ink that wrote the last words of it, I commence this letter to you. That it is with the same pen, too, this chirography sufficiently makes manifest. With your permission I will mend that.

The poem is indeed very beautiful; and in parts so touching, that more than once in translating it I was blinded with tears. Perhaps my weakness makes the Poet strong. You shall soon judge; for as I told you in my last, this poem goes into the forth-coming volume; and with many — with all you Episcopalians — will make the most attractive part of it. I hope the Monk's Hymn, (Blind Bartimeus,) pleased your fancy. As to the other pieces, now in your hands, pray give yourself no trouble about them. Turn the Charles River into Benjamin's Office, and like another Peneus let it wash away the filth of the three thousand oxen! Ye gods, what a figure! He deserves it for so captiously abusing me at times. What a funny name Augias Benjamin would be! [1]

Sumner is passing the night and Sunday with me. He has just returned from New Haven, the "City of Elms," — where he has been for a week on business. While I write, he has run down to Judge Story's; but will be back in a minute and send his love to you. From your short note, which reached me this afternoon, I read him the story of the *"lady's work-bag."* He seemed to think it a "lady's *ridicule,"* (as some pronounce it).[2]

Speaking of *Stories* (not the Judge nor the lady's) the best things for Gräter to translate from are *Zschokke's* [3] Tales. What a magnificent name that is; — six consonants and two vowels; reminding one of Leonora's bridal bed,

"*Sechs* Bretter und *zwey* Brettchen"; — [4]

(which an unfortunate wight in College the other day translated, "Six chains and two tables.") But to return to Zschokke. His tales I think would please. So would some parts of Hoffman's *Serapions Brüder.*[5] In fine, almost anything but Tieck.

Nagel [6] I have not yet had the pleasure of seeing; not being yet strong enough to go into town. His *supernaculum,* or *Nagel-probe,* comes off to-night at the Tremont Theatre. I have no doubt he will have a good house; and I hope there will be no *Nagel-schneider* [Nail-cutter] present, to dispute his claims to applause. I make these unpleasant puns upon his name to revenge myself upon human nature for the crime of my forefathers in perpetuating such a name as mine; and because instead of sending me your letter of introduction in an envelope, with his card or address, he sealed it with a gross red *lawyer's* wafer, and threw it into the Boston Post-office, without any hint as to where he hangs up his violin.

I much desire to hear him, when he *bow-strings* that "Imprisoned Spirit,"[7] (nothing sacred to-night.) and draws forth sighs and sweet laments.

The title of "*Fennel*" has been discarded for that of "*The Goblet of Life.*"

Yours very truly
Henry W. Longfellow.

Two days ago a pleasant call from Wilde.

MANUSCRIPT: Longfellow Trust Collection. ADDRESS: Samuel Ward Esq/(Prime Ward & King)/New York POSTMARK: BOSTON ||MAS. NOV|| 6

1. Longfellow's classical geography is confused. Herakles diverted the river Alpheus, not the Peneus, to cleanse the Augean stables. For the reason that Longfellow felt he had been abused, see 632.1. "To the River Charles" appeared in Benjamin's *New World,* IV (January 1, 1842), 14, after it had been printed in the *Ladies' Companion* (632.12).

2. Ward had written: "A little lady told another the other day who was sounding Sumner's praises, that she would look, if she were to take his arm, like a ladies workbag hanging upon it" (Letter of November 5, 1841).

3. Johann Heinrich Daniel Zschokke (1771–1848), a German-Swiss author.

4. "Six planks and two boards," that is, "a coffin." Gottfried August Bürger (1747–1794), "Lenore," stanza 18, line 4.

5. The German romantic novelist Ernst Theodor Amadeus Hoffman (1776–1822) published *Die Serapionsbrüder,* a collection of supernatural tales and personal reminiscences in 4 vols. (1819–1821).

6. Johan Jacob Nagel (1807–1885), a violinist and composer born in Moravia, had been since 1830 a member of the Royal Swedish Orchestra. He spent two years on tour in the U. S., 1841–1843, and then returned to his position in Stockholm. He was said to have been a pupil of Paganini.

7. Possibly an allusion to Julia Ward's poem "Imprisoned Angel" (635.2).

## 638. *To Evert Augustus Duyckinck*

Cambridge Nov. 9. 1841

My dear Sir,

I send you the foregoing lines for Arcturus.[1] You will see at a glance, that it is a piece not to be bought and sold, but to be given where it will be understood. I beg you to accept it as a slight token of my personal regard for yourself, and of my good wishes for Arcturus.

I shall soon send you a whole volume of poems; among which you will find a translation of the "Children of the Lord's Supper," from the Swedish of Bishop Tegnér; one of the most remarkable men of this age.

Yours very truly
Henry W. Longfellow.

P.S. If you could send me a copy of Arcturus No. 3. without breaking a set, I should be much obliged. Mine is lost, and I wish to have the work entire.

MANUSCRIPT: New York Public Library (E. A. Duyckinck Papers). ADDRESS: Evert A. Duyckinck, Esq/New York POSTMARK: CAMBRIDGE MS. NOV 9 PUBLISHED: *Bulletin of the New York Public Library*, I, No. 9 (1897), 246.

1. A manuscript copy of "Blind Bartimeus" precedes the letter. For a similar copy, see Letter No. 635.

639. *To Stephen Longfellow*

Cambridge Nov. 14. 1841.

My dear Father,

Since my last nothing strange nor new has transpired; only Mary's departure[1] had made a slight break in some of my usual visits, and Mrs. Greenleaf mourns not a little. My new book comes on bravely; being all stereotyped, save about forty pages, upon which they are now at work. It will be uniform with the Voices, and nearly as large, though not quite; and will contain a long poem, translated from the Swedish, and a good many pieces never published. It will be about equal in merit to the other volume; in some things better, and in others not so good.

Have you thought anything more about Homœopathy? Anxious as I am to have you try it, I am not anxious to have you put yourself under the hands of one of the new beginners in Portland. I want that you should come here and consult Dr. Wesselhoeft, or let me bring him to Portland. The Germans, who have been familiar with the practice for many years, understand the matter better, than our American doctors do. I feel very confident that if you are not entirely cured; you will be very much relieved; and that in a short time. May I bring Dr. W. with me at Thanksgiving time? You have given the old system, a trial of twenty years or more; — and had the advice of the best physicians in the country; and now I want you to try for a few months this new system, which in its operation is so gentle, and so sure in its effects. Mr. Felton, who began by scoffing, has become a convert; not by my persuasion; but because on trial he found more relief in a week from the "*little pills*," than he had before for five years from all the plasters, blisters, bleedings and purgings of Allopathy. You cannot do better, than see Dr. Wesselhœft. (Pronounce Vessel-heft). Shall I bring him?[2]

Unless I am mistaken Thanksgiving-day is the 27th; and I intend to be with you, if nothing prevents.

Cary and Hart of Philadelphia are having my portrait by Thompson, (said to be very good) engraved by Cheney, the best American engraver. It is to go with Bryant's, Halleck's, and Willis's into a "Selection of American Poets." [3]

I received yesterday by mail a package, with my address upon it, and in addition these words; "Missent to Athens; there is no such man in these diggings."

Yours very truly
Henry W. Longfellow.

P. S. Health rather delicate. Think I shall make a *voyage* in Spring, to cure me of all ills.[4]

P. S. Did Annie receive a letter from me the other day? [5]

MANUSCRIPT: Longfellow Trust Collection. ADDRESS: Hon. S. Longfellow/Portland. POSTMARK: CAMBRIDGE MS. NOV 15

1. For New Orleans, where her husband was engaged in business as a cotton broker for the next several years.

2. There is no extant letter from Stephen Longfellow answering this query.

3. The original portrait of Longfellow by the American artist Cephas Giovanni Thompson (1809–1888) now hangs in the Longfellow House. See Plate VI. The engraving by John Cheney (1801–1885), with a decorative frame by R. W. Dodson, shared the frontispiece with the elder Dana, Bryant, Sprague, and Halleck in Rufus W. Griswold's anthology *The Poets and Poetry of America* (Philadelphia, 1842). See Letter No. 680.

4. This is the first indication in the letters that Longfellow was planning a third trip abroad for the purpose of undergoing the German water-cure treatment.

5. This letter is unrecovered.

## 640. *To Samuel Ward*

Cambridge. Nov. 14. 1841.
For a good specimen of *cock-crowing* see p.s. on next page.

Quotations.

"I have seen Benjamin and promised him the Song to the River Charles." Pandemonium. Tuesday [November 9, 1841]

"The River Charles shall be sent to Benjamin on Monday. The other poem is for O'Sullivan." Saturday Nov. 6.

"O'Sullivan threatens to require the Charles River at my hands. I shall send Benjamin the God's-Acre, in case I am obliged to comply with the Democrat's desire." Nov. 11th.

I beg you, my dear Sam, to do no such thing, as hinted at in the last Quotation. As Benjamin had the promise, he must have the poem. Moreover, he has made me a generous offer, and I think it ought to be met as generously, with the best pieces I have. He should certainly take precedence of O'Sullivan in this matter.

Blind Bartimeus I have sent as a Christmas Present to Duykinck, because I like him, and his Arcturus. The Greek — those musical sweet organ-stops at the close of each stanza, — may however prevent him from *performing* the piece; that is, publishing it.

I am rejoiced at Sparks's warm welcome in New York. Your Notice of his first Lecture I had already sent to Mrs. Sparks, before your letter and paper arrived.[1] I called to see her yesterday, and informed her of the authorship of the article; whereupon she expressed herself duly grateful. Please inform General Washington, that his "Dear Patsy" is in good health and spirits.

Thanks for your *Ballad-hints*,[2] which reached me last evening. I fear, however, that I shall not be able to make use of them. The wild legend from Cotton Mather's *Magnalia* (By the way, how could you suspect a New Englander to be so ignorant of the book?) has been used by Irving as a Tale, and a Ballad has been written on the subject by Professor Upham of Bowdoin College. As to the Newport ship, the same thing happened on the shores of Marblehead, with an additional horror; namely, in the cabin of the "Deserted Ship," — on a table was a coffin, with a corpse in it. And a few evenings ago I read an English Ballad on a ship in the Bay of Biscay, floating about at the will of the wind, with a dead crew! I never loved the horrible; and am not *Monk-Lewisy* enough to write upon these themes.[3]

Have you read Monaldi?

Munde's book on the water-cure I have seen. It is very dull and poorly written. You would rather go through the *Cure* itself, than his description of it. The other work by Hirschell I shall be much pleased to see.[4] *Palestrina* came safely.[5]

In answer to your kind inquiries after my health, what shall I say? I think there is no immediate danger of my entering "the Green Gate of Paradise"; [6] — but I am all unstrung, eating only bread and meat, — which, all things considered, one may content one's-self withal. Not a glass of wine — not a drop of coffee — not a whiff of tobacco. No agile limbs like yours, — no slapping stalwart health, like Sumner, but a meek, Moses-like state of being, not without its charms. This reminds me that Dr. Palfrey has discovered, that the Hebrew word usually translated *meek* in connection with Moses, does not mean *meek*, but *miserable*; and we should read "Now Moses was the most miserable of men"; [7] — which makes much better sense than the old reading.

But dont let me deter you from coming on at your earliest leisure; always excepting Thanksgiving week when I shall be away. Come of a Friday, so as to reach Cambridge Saturday morning by the *Hourly,* without the trouble of stopping at Tremont house. I am sorry you ever promised Ticknor; for I want my roof to shelter you whenever you are within sight of it. Come as soon as you can; and meantime write like the very Devil.

Yours truly
H. W. L.

P. S. If O'Sullivan does not like God's Acre, pray send it to [Lewis Gaylord] Clark. I suppose he is hard-beset for money. Let him have it, for old acquaintance sake, and the love of our kind. I have not the heart to press him.

P.S. continued . . .

"Der flüchtige Vorsatz wird nie eingeholdt,
Geht nicht die That gleich mit."

Göthe,[8] and of course not to be doubted. I have a right to say this to you; for three weeks ago you asked me to translate *Nattvardsbarnen,* and I have done it. Two years ago, I *urged* you to translate *Palestrina* and — you know the rest.

If you have the 2nd part of Munde's book, please send it. Also "Richter. Versuch einer wissenschaftlicher Begründung des Wasserheilkund."[9]

Into your next package put *Mönch-Wesen* or bring it with you — that is better.

MANUSCRIPT: Clifton Waller Barrett Collection, University of Virginia. ADDRESS: Samuel Ward Esq/Prime Ward & King/New York POSTMARK: CAMBRIDGE MS. NOV 15 PUBLISHED: "Letters to Samuel Ward, Part II," pp. 170–171.

1. With his letter of November 6 Ward had sent a copy of the New York *American* for the same date, which contained his brief notice of Sparks' lecture in New York on the evening of November 5.

2. Contained in Ward's letter of November 12, 1841.

3. Despite his disclaimers, Longfellow had long been interested in the Flying Dutchman theme. He may first have met with it in "The Storm-Ship," a reworking of the legend by Irving, which appears in "Dolph Heyliger" in *Bracebridge Hall.* On April 11, 1838, he wrote: "Copied from an old New York Mirror a ballad of the Phantom Ship; good. I wonder who wrote it!" (MS Journal). The author may have been Upham, whose ballad is otherwise unidentified. Finally, some nine years after Ward's "*Ballad-hints,*" Longfellow went to the college library, looked up the "wild legend" described by Mather in *Magnalia* (I, vi), and composed his own ballad, "The Phantom Ship" (MS Journal, October 11, 1850; *Life,* II, 191).

4. Karl Munde had written two books on the water-cure that were available to Longfellow at this time: *Genaue Beschreibung der Gräfenberger Wasserheilanstalt und der Priessnitzische Curmethode* (Leipzig, 1837; 2nd ed., 1841) and *Hydro-*

*therapie, oder die Kunst, die Krankheiten des menschl. körpers, ohne Hülfe von Arzneien, durch Diät, Wasser, Schwitzen, Luft und Bewegung zu heilen . . . Ein Handbuch für Nichtärzte* (Dresden and Leipzig, 1841). Bernhard Hirschel wrote *Hydriatica, oder Begründung der Wasserheilkunde auf wissenschaftl. Principien* (Leipzig, 1840).

5. Ward's letter of November 21, 1839, reveals that this work was written by Anton Friedrich Justus Thibaut of Heidelberg, an authority on Palestrina, although no work of that title is listed in his bibliography. Ward had borrowed the book from Professor Charles Beck and was now returning it.

6. From a concluding stanza, later omitted, of "God's Acre." See Letter No. 641.

7. Cf. Num. 12:3.

8. Longfellow's ascription is incorrect. Cf. Schiller's translation of *Macbeth,* IV, i, 145–146 (the German reference is IV, v, 14–15): "Der flücht'ge Vorsatz ist nicht einzuholen,/Es gehe denn die rasche That gleich mit" ("The flighty purpose never is o'ertook/Unless the deed go with it").

9. C. A. W. Richter, *Versuch zur wissenschaftlichen Begründung der Wasserkuren* (Friedland, Neubrandenburg, 1838).

## 641. *To Samuel Ward*

Cambridge Nov. 17. 1841

*Quotations, continued from my last.*

"O'Sullivan is to have the God's Acre." Your letter of Nov. 16.

That is right, my dear Sam; and now all will doubtless flow on harmoniously. Benjamin has probably been in some perplexity, between my negociations with him and yours; in a misty dubious frame of mind, like Fibel's father, when the bird and baby came together, and grasping one and looking at the other, he exclaimed; "Hab' ich ihn? [Do I have it?]" Charles River and God's Acre performing respectively the parts of Fibel and the Finch; ("*Fibel und der Finke schrieen erbärmlich, und jeder anders.*" 1 Judas-Capitel.) [1] And to make matters in all respects equal on each side I here add a concluding stanza for God's Acre, which I think improves the piece, and rounds it off more perfectly than before; the thought no longer resting on the cold farrow, but on the waving harvest beyond.

Green Gate of Paradise! let in the sun!
  Unclose thy portals, that we may behold
Those fields elysian, where bright rivers run,
  And waving harvests bend like seas of gold.[2]

I handed the last sheets of my new volume to the printer this morning; the proofs will soon be read, and the book in your hands. I am now free to think of my next movement, which undoubtedly will be sea-ward. In truth I hate to go. On many accounts it is inconvenient; and particularly on account of *Don Dinero,* — the *monies,*

> "quas, qui possidet, ille
> Clarus erit, fortis, justus, sapiens, etiam et rex
> Et quidquid volet," [3]

and I am neither, being worth only a *mite,* which commentators have shown, in the case of the Widow, to be only the seventh part of a brass farthing. You are very kind to make me offers in this respect; but how far can you trust me? For what amount would you allow me to draw upon you, in case of need? [4]

My present plan is to sail for London, that is *England,* in January; pass a few weeks there, and be in *Germany* in March; and if the Water-dog's bark is not *better* than his bite, to return in August, hale and hearty.

I hope you will drop in suddenly upon me next Saturday. It would delight my weary heart exceedingly. Pray come soon. Next week I go to Portland on Wednesday, and return on Saturday; so that you may be sure of being in season, come when you will, save on those three days of absence.

You complain of my letters being long on the road. The *American* of Monday has just reached me, Thursday evening — fresh as a rose. I wish you would put a paragraph into the paper, complaining of this delay somewhere. I think it is in the Boston Post-office. Something is out of joint likewise in the Magazine line. If you chance to meet Duykinck, and think of it, say to him that Arcturus for November has not yet made its appearance in Cambridge.

I am truly glad to learn, that Sparks's Lectures are so successful. *Viva la Storia* [Long live History]!

Please remember, dearest Sam, that all the story of my ills, and my intentions of foreign travel and German Baths is a secret. I do not want one word said about [it], until I am fairly on the waving main.

Yours most truly
Henry W. Longfellow.

P.S. I regret that I could not show Nagel any more attention. I wrote to him, begging him to come to Camb. and went to see him; but could do no more.

There is a beautiful *aurora borealis* to-night; an arch in the North.

MANUSCRIPT: Longfellow Trust Collection. ADDRESS: Samuel Ward Esq/(Prime Ward & King)/New York POSTMARK: CAMBRIDGE MS. NOV 19

1. "Fibel and the finch cried pitifully, and each differently." Jean Paul Richter, *Leben Fibels*, Chap. I.

2. This stanza was included with the version in the *Democratic Review* (631.12) but omitted in *Ballads and Other Poems*.

3. "which, whoever has it [money], he/shall be illustrious, brave, wise, even a king,/and whatever he desires." Cf. Horace, *Sermones*, II, iii, 96–98.

4. Ward had written: "When the time comes for your decision as to the contemplated journey — if take it you must — I stand ready to contribute my share of what aid you may require" (Letter of November 11, 1841). In answer to Longfellow's query, he promised him "a credit of Frs. 2500 upon Paris" (Letter of November 22, 1841). Whether Longfellow took advantage of this offer is not known. See Letter No. 643.

## 642. *To Samuel Ward*

Cambridge Nov. 20. 1841.

My dear Sam,

Yesterday afternoon I walked from the Post-office triumphantly to my Lecture room, waving like banners three letters from you; and chaunting that immortal stave from the "Sword Song of Thorstein Raudi" (? *rowdy.*)

"[But] Thy metal's as true
  As its polish is bright;
When ills wax in number,
  Thy love will not slumber,
But, star-like, burns fiercer
  The darker the night.
*Heart-Gladdener!* I kiss thee!"[1]

The plan of foreign travel is taking shape and forming itself, from a possibility to a probability. Since I wrote you I have had a conversation with Dr. [James] Walker, one of the College Corporation; and he espouses my cause, and thinks, that without doubt on application, I shall have leave of absence. It seems best, however, not to go before May; as by remaining till then I can finish my Course of Lectures for the Spring term; and go with a lighter heart. The secret is a secret still.

I send you by Harnden a Volume of Poems by Motherwell, of very great and distinguished power; though in parts rather *unruly.* "The Battle Flag of Sigurd" is a noble production. It is just from the press; edited by Dr. Cole, of Baltimore; now surgeon at the Navy yard Charlestown.[2]

My volume will be out in a few days. You are very good to offer a Review.[3] Pray dont wait for the book; you know it by heart already; all except the *Nattvardsbarnen,* and though that is all in type I think I shall suppress it, for the present, at least, if not forever. There have been such desperate failures in English Hexameters, and by such men as Sir Philip Sidney, and Robert Southey, that I begin to look wild, like a horse without blinkers. The translation is imperfect in melody. It wants revision. I must let the profits of my book go to pay the *pots cassés* [piper], and suppress this part of it; — murder the Children in the tower; they will rise again hereafter. Besides, there is some pleasure in having your own way, — *and paying for it*; you feel sure then that it *is your own.*

You are right in your surmise touching Monaldi. There is a coarse kind of horror in it; adapted to the taste of the times, when it was written; the times when Monk Lewis and Mrs. Radcliffe danced the Carmagnole together in grave-yards, and the dead clapped their bony hands, and cried with dusty lips, "*Encore!*"

There is a book of Voyages in press here by Richard Cleveland, (*our* Cleveland's father) which for wild adventure bids fair to rival Robinson Crusoe. I have looked over a few pages of it with great delight.[4]

You need not trouble yourself about the November No. of Arcturus. It has come at last, rumpled and tumbled, like a chamber-maid, coming out of a batchelor's room at the *Hôtel des Princes.*[5]

Very bad { Conundrum. Why is *Nagel* like a *Nagekäfer* [Gnawing beetle]?
Answer. Because he is a *hum-bug.*

Much worse { Another. Why is *Herwig*[6] no *true* musician?
Answer. Because he is only *false 'air.* (hair.)

I wish, dear Sam, you would go to Germany with me in May? Will you? Steamer to London; cross over to Antwerp; and plunge into the German forests. My kind regards to *Moses.* When will he make his Water-book run from the rocky hearts of the Harpers?[7]

Most truly yours
Henry W. Longfellow.

P. S. What is the price of the illustrated Nibelungen Lied?[8]
Cleveland, and Felton "*the hater of horses*" dine with me to-day. We will drink your health in a deluge of water.

Did you take a bill from *Willard* for horse-hire last Summer? If so please send it to me, to compare dates with mine.

MANUSCRIPT: Berg Collection, New York Public Library. ADDRESS: Samuel Ward Esq/(Prime Ward & King)/New York POSTMARK: CAMBRIDGE MS. NOV 20

1. From "The Sword Chant of Thorstein Raudi" in William Motherwell's *Poems Narrative and Lyrical* (Boston, 1841), pp. 41–42.

2. This statement constitutes the only evidence that William Edward Coale (1816–1865) of Maryland, an assistant surgeon in the Navy, 1837–1843, edited the Boston volume of Motherwell's poems.

3. In a letter of November 16, 1841, Ward had indicated his desire to write a review of *Ballads and Other Poems,* which Longfellow assumed would be printed in the *New York Review.* But after a laudatory notice appeared in the *Review* (X [January 1842], 240–245), Longfellow attributed it first to Cogswell and then revealed his uncertainty as to the author (Letter No. 655). It is not clear, therefore, who in fact wrote the review.

4. Richard Jeffry Cleveland, *A Narrative of Voyages and Commercial Enterprises* (Cambridge, 1842). See Letter No. 736.

5. Sam Ward stayed in this hotel on first landing in Paris in 1832 (*Uncle Sam Ward and His Circle*, p. 47).

6. Leopold Herwig, a German-born violinist, gave his first Boston concert at the Melodeon on October 16, 1841 (*Daily Evening Transcript*). He performed in Boston for several years as a soloist, co-soloist, and conductor of the symphony orchestra.

7. A reference to Graeter and his book on the water-cure (632.8). It was published not by Harpers but by William Radde, New York.

8. Ward responded, "The *Nibelungenlied* was published at Leipsic — by subscription — to commemorate the 4th Saecular Feier of the Buch-drucker-Kunst. It is not for sale" (Letter of November 24, 1841). The reference is to *Der Nibelunge Lied.* Abdruck der Handschrift des Freiherrn J. von Lassberg. Mit Holzschnitten nach Originalzeichnungen von E. Bendemann und J. Hübner (Leipzig, 1840).

## 643. *To Samuel Ward*

Craigie House. Nov. 30. 1841.

My dear Sam,

I have just returned from Portland, where I had the satisfaction of receiving your charming domestic Novel of "Write like the Devil" chapter X.[1] I did not write you, as you requested, on account of the inconveniences attending the operation, and the little leisure I had. Besides which, I expected to be back sooner; and consequently to have dated this, Nov. 28 and not Nov. 30. Enough. He who excuses himself, accuses himself.

I came back from Portland in the stage-coach, eleven inside, including two babies and a fat boy, who amused himself by eating chestnuts, crying, fighting, kicking, and finally discharging the aforesaid chestnuts from their stomachic repository upon my cloak. After this, upon the consideration of his having made such great exertions to entertain the company, he was pensioned off with a corner in the coach, and suffered to sleep on his laurels. In fine, the journey was long and tedious. On reaching home I found yours of *Sunday* 22; — received a week and a day after it was written. This reminds me of the oft-complained-of delay between Cambridge and New York. I have made representations thereof, through a third person, to the Boston Post-master, who promises reform. And this in turn reminds me of another reform, which you might easily introduce into [Charles] King's Paper; — namely, that of separating the Booksellers' advertisements from the rest, and giving them a fixed place in a corner. At present one has to look through the whole paper to find the lists of new books. And what a medley! For example, in the last No. of the American; —

"American Harp — India-Rubber — Guizot's Éloise and Abailard — Sharp's Liniment, partly in verse,

> "What angel, O Sharp! inspired thee to invent
> Thy wondrous pain-killing Cerates and liniment!"

Gems for Travellers — Rail-road Iron — Westphalia Ham — Cook wanted —Illustrated and Standard Works—Pitch, 150 barrels superior — (*Das ist Pech* [How annoying]!)" and so on to any amount.

Among the books advertised are two I want you to bring me when you come, next Friday; — "*Chorazzin,*" by D. E. Ford; and "The Neutral French" by Mrs. Williams; both pubd. by Dodd, Brick Church Chapel opposite City Hall.[2] Into your other pocket put *Mönchwesen.*

Lieber made a good speculation by translating the *Conversation Lexicon;*[3] why would it not be a good plan for Gräter to translate the Continuation of it now publishing in Germany, containing the Present, living Authors &c. I think he might do it to advantage. Or why not set him to work upon Palestrina? if you abandon it. Then follows a secret.

Wesselhoeft has translated Monaldi into German, to be pubd. by *Brockhaus,* Leipzig.[4] He has also translated some of my poems; as for instance, "Footsteps of Angels," under the title of "*Es gehen Engel durch das Zimmer,*" — the beautiful Proverb. You shall see it when you come; as likewise "*The Children*"; upon reading which you will acknowledge that I am very pious — on paper. I have concluded to print it — having gone so far.

Many, *many* thanks, dear Sam, for your ready, generous offer. It is more than I should have ventured to ask, had I named the sum; and will be ample for my plans and purposes. You understand, however, that I shall not touch a farthing of it, unless it is perfectly convenient for you to advance it; for I know the many demands you have upon your purse.[5]

Dont forget that you are coming here — on Friday or Saturday — make it Friday, if possible.

Yours evermore
H. W. Longfellow

If you have room in your trunk, put into it that *rowdy* portrait of me, which you have, in oils.[6]

MANUSCRIPT: Longfellow Trust Collection. ADDRESS: Samuel Ward Esq/(Prime, Ward & King)/New York. POSTMARK: CAMBRIDGE MS. DEC 1 PUBLISHED: "Letters to Samuel Ward, Part II," p. 166.

1. Heeding Longfellow's admonition in Letter No. 640 to "write like the very Devil," Ward began to embellish his letters with a series of chapters under the heading "Write Like the Devil." Chap. X described in detail his dinner party for Lord Morpeth. See *Uncle Sam Ward and His Circle,* pp. 318–319.

2. David Everard Ford, *Chorazin: or, an Appeal to the Child of Many Prayers on Questions Concerning the Great Salvation* (London, 1841); Mrs. Catherine Read Williams, *The Neutral French; or, the Exiles of Nova Scotia* (Providence, 1841).

3. Lieber's translations of the Brockhaus *Conversations-Lexikon* became, with the inclusion of much original material, the *Encyclopedia Americana* (1829–1833).

4. The entry in Kayser's *Bücher-Lexicon* reads: *Monaldi. Eine Erzählung.* Aus dem Engl. übers. von . . . Kahldorf (Leipzig, 1843, Brockhaus).

5. See 641.4.

6. Apparently the portrait by Frankenstein (468.4). See 711.15.

## 644. *To Rufus Wilmot Griswold*

[Cambridge, November 1841][1]

Born in Portland Feb. 27. 1807.
Entered Bowdoin College in 1821
Took my Batchelor's degree 1825
Went to Europe in Summer of 1826 making long residence in France, Spain, Italy and Germany; studied at Göttingen; passed through England on my return. See [Slidell's] Year in Spain. Ch. IX.
Reached home in the Summer of 1829. Appointed Professor of Modern Languages in Bowdoin College. 1829. Married in 1831.
Resigned this place in the Spring of 1835; and sailed for England. Passed the Summer in Denmark and Sweden; my Wife died in Rotterdam autumn of 1835. The Winter following in Germany. Summer of 1836 in Tyrol and Switzerland. Returned home in October; and entered upon my duties as Professor of French and Spanish Literature in Harvard College, Cambridge.

While a student in College wrote for the Literary Gazette.
While Professor at Brunswick wrote for the N. A. Review.
In 1835 published Outre Mer.
In 1839 Hyperion.
In 1840 Voices of the Night.
In 1842 Ballads and other Poems.[2]

MANUSCRIPT: Clifton Waller Barrett Collection, University of Virginia. ADDRESS: Rev. Rufus Griswold/Philadelphia

1. The date is approximate. The information provided here, presumably in response to an unrecovered request from Griswold, appeared in the notice of Longfellow and his poetry in *The Poets and Poetry of America* (Philadelphia, 1842), p. 297. The accompanying letter to Griswold, if there was one, has been lost.

2. This line has been added at a later date and apparently by another hand.

## 645. *To Stephen Longfellow*

Cambridge. Decr. 5. 1841.

My dear Father,

I have been too busy, since my return, to write sooner than to-day. The homeward journey was long and tedious. All day Saturday we dragged along through mud and snow; and did not reach Portsmouth till after six in the evening; and consequently too late for the cars that night. I did not reach Cambridge till Sunday morning; and have been almost sick with a violent cold, taken on the way. The stage was crowded; *eleven* inside, including two babies and a fat-boy, who amused the company by slapping his mother, kicking, crying, eating apples and chestnuts, and finally discharging them again from his bodily tenement upon my cloak, and a lady's, who sat near. However, the pains and inconveniences of the journey are now forgotten, and I remember only its pleasures.

The Painting has arrived safely;[1] but *not* the butter. What has become of *that*, I know not; but have ordered diligent search to be made for it; and am not without hopes of recovering it.

Nothing new in Cambridge. Sam arrived last night. Thanks for Annie's note, and the apples; and the information in regard to the "*Unblushing-One.*" Her malediction upon Portland is published in the "*Transcript*";[2] and is not calculated to increase her popularity in Portland. Upon the whole, she is to be pitied. Her feelings seemed to have become exasperated; and she is uncomfortable in herself and to others.

The Volume of Poems is working its way, through furnaces and plaster moulds, and all the furniture of the Stereotyper's workshop. It will be ready in a few days; and shall be sent to you immediately.

I have given letters of introduction to Mr. Farnham, who intends to establish a school in Portland. I think you will be much pleased with him; and I hope he will succeed with his school; as he evidently has a strong taste for the profession of a teacher.[3]

With much love to all

Yours affectionately
Henry W. Longfellow.

MANUSCRIPT: Longfellow Trust Collection. ADDRESS: Hon. S. Longfellow/Portland. POSTMARK: BOSTON MS. DEC 6

1. See 636.2.

2. In the poem "My Bark is on the Wave," published in the *Portland Transcript,* V, No. 34 (Saturday, December 4, 1841), 267, Mrs. Joshua Webb reveals her pleasure in leaving Portland, where "kindness finds a grave" and the "heart is fashion's slave."

3. Luther Farnham (1816–1897) was a graduate of Dartmouth, 1837, and of the Andover Theological Seminary, 1841. After his trip to Portland he decided against establishing a school (Samuel Longfellow to Anne Longfellow Pierce, December 30, 1841 [MS, Longfellow House]).

## 646. *To Samuel Ward*

Cambridge Decr. 5. 1841.

O for shame, my dear Sam! How could you for a moment entertain such an unworthy suspicion of me! I have burned your letter that no record thereof may exist. The flame has gone up to help make a draft of air, to turn the weather-cocks up there, and left no vestige behind it here upon earth.

My last letter, written before this *condemned scroll,* must have persuaded you of the vanity of your fear. I fully comprehend your position; and the demands that must constantly be made upon you; and should have thought you right in refusing my request altogether, if it were not convenient to grant it. You know me thoroughly, dear Sam; and have never known me *sulky,* or in ill humor with you. Therefore, fear not.[1]

But where are you? I fully expected you this morning. Come soon. In great haste,

Yours truly
H. W. L.

P.S. It is after midnight, or I should not palm off so short a letter upon you. I close, because otherwise you will have to wait a day longer for my *nouvelles* [news]; and my object in writing is to eradicate from your sensitive mind any doubt, suspicion, or shadow.

MANUSCRIPT: Longfellow Trust Collection. ADDRESS: Samuel Ward Esq/(Prime Ward & King)/New York. POSTMARK: BOSTON ||MS|| DEC 6

1. Ward seems to have concluded rather hastily that Longfellow's failure to reply sooner to his letter of November 22, in which he offered 2500 francs toward the expenses of the proposed European trip, was evidence of his friend's disappointment and perhaps anger that the sum was not larger. This is made clear by Ward's letter of December 3, 1841: "The long agony is over. Your letter of the 30th Ulto reached me this mor[nin]g and broke a long long pause. I hasten to say that you must consider my letter of the 1st as *non avenue* [void]. It was unworthy to think such a consideration as the one referred to could influence one whom I have found so uniformly delicate and disinterested as yourself. Sometimes we feel out of tune if not disappointed and delay writing until our mood has mended. It will be convenient to me to go to the extent named and you may rely upon it."

## 647. *To Stephen Longfellow*

Cambridge Decr. 18. 1841.

My dear Father,

To my great sor[r]ow the firkin of butter has never arrived. There seem to be some rogues connected with that steamboat, who are bent on robbing me. This is the second time. If anything of the kind happens again, I mean to have the whole business investigated; and I would now, if the weather were not so cold.

Mrs. Greenleaf had a long letter from James and Mary yesterday. They were both well; and *very* comfortable at the St. Charles Hotel in N. Orleans; — weather mild; trees in leaf, and *roses* full blown in the open air. (*Here* it is *noses.*) Mrs. Greenleaf is in a rapture of delight whenever she gets a letter; and thus far the children have been very good to write as often as possible.

The Ballads &c will be published tomorrow. I shall send you a copy by the earliest opportunity. I hope you will like it as much as you expect. I think the last two pieces the best; — perhaps as good as anything I have written.[1]

We have had a deligh[t]ful musician here; a Miss Sloman; a pianiste of great talent, and only seventeen years old. I wish you could hear her; for to wonderful execution she unites the greatest delicacy of touch imaginable.[2] She and *Old Braham*[3] are filling Boston with music.

The time spared from these is taken up in feeding Lord Morpeth; who is so much in demand, that he is no more to be had. The modern German critics have proved from the Iliad that Ulysses accepted three dinner invitations on one day. I doubt whether his Lordship is up to that; though he certainly can do a good deal in that way. I gave him a small dinner, on my friend Sumner's account; and had

Mr. Prescott, Mr. Norton and one or two more pleasant people; — we dined from 5 o'clock till 10; and had a pleasant time.

I find I can have the old picture entirely restored.[4] It will make a brilliant affair.

Much love to all,
||Henry W. Longfellow||

P. S. I dined yesterday at Harrison G. Otis's. He inquired particularly after you. He is a curious old gentleman.

MANUSCRIPT: Longfellow Trust Collection. ADDRESS: Hon. S. Longfellow/Portland. POSTMARK: CAMBRIDGE MS. DEC 20

1. "Maidenhood" and "Excelsior."

2. Jane Sloman gave six concerts at the Melodeon, November 6 — December 2, 1841 (Boston *Daily Evening Transcript*). The precocious daughter of itinerant English actors, she became a favorite with Boston audiences and returned for later triumphs.

3. See 560.2.

4. See 636.2.

## 648. *To George Roberts*

[Cambridge] Saturday. Decr. 18. 1841.

My dear Sir

If you could make it convenient to send me soon what is due for the Luck of Edenhall, and the prose translation I furnished for the Notion, it would oblige me.[1] This is a small matter; and I suppose in the multiplicity of your engagements has slipped your memory. You will excuse me for reminding you of it. But you know, at the close of the year bills numberless shower down upon us, and we are obliged to call in as well as pay out.

Yours truly
Henry W. Longfellow

MANUSCRIPT: Hispanic Society of America. ADDRESS: George Roberts Esq./Boston.

1. For "The Luck of Edenhall," see 592.2. Longfellow's "Passages from Jean Paul" appeared in the *Boston Notion*, II, No. 24 (March 13, 1841), 1.

## 649. *To Samuel Ward*

Cambridge. Decr. 22. 1841

My dear Sam,

I was wrong in saying that the Fund of the Nat. Hist. Professorship amounted to only 27.000. It is by the last Report 28.763; so that to complete it we want only 1.237; — a considerable abatement in your favor.

I have had another interview with the President. There has never been a Professor on this foundation; your nomination will be the first.

Write me more particularly about Mersch; and his credentials. Also about your Library; the number of Vols; and its value. If you had not *ticknorized* so much when you were here, we might have brought matters to a point. In yr. answer tell me definitely what you will do and so far as the Corporation is concerned the whole matter may be arranged in a very short time. The approval of the Board of Overseers may take more time; there may be opposition there; and more fight shown by friends of rival candidates.

Tell me all about Mersch's studies with dates; all in the smallest possible compass.[1]

The Ballads come out tomorrow. This goes in your package. Thanks for the "Master of Life." I promised you *Outre Mer* without looking to see if I had a copy to give you. I find I have not; but will try to get you one from England. I am glad you relish "Maidenhood."[2]

Saturday, Christmass, I dine with the Ticknors; I wish you were to be there. Why not come? They were delighted with your visit; and I look upon myself as an abused individual, cheated out of my friend.

I had a letter from Clark to-day; a kind of half-way, lame apology for his foolish epistle, while you were here. But he says he has seen you, and persuaded you "that everything he *could* do, has been done"; and that is precisely what I am afraid of.[3]

Good night. It is a glorious night, and near its noon; and I am transgressing my rules of going to bed early.

Yours very affectionately
Henry W. Longfellow.

— I do not send you a copy of Ballads; — waiting for the large paper edition.

MANUSCRIPT: Longfellow Trust Collection. ADDRESS: Samuel Ward Esq/(Prime Ward & King)/New York.

1. The professorship of astronomy and mathematics referred to here and in subsequent letters to Ward went in 1842 to Benjamin Peirce, who had been professor of mathematics and natural philosophy at Harvard since 1833. Ward hoped to obtain the chair for Charles Mersch and considered several plans of subsidy — including a gift of money and the donation of his valuable library of scientific books — to persuade the Corporation to appoint his friend. Longfellow did what he could as Ward's intermediary but apparently had no real influence. When it became obvious that only a substantial endowment of the chair could effect Mersch's appointment, Ward quietly withdrew his tentative offers of subsidy.

2. Ward had written: " 'Maidenhood' is excessively admired here and the new vol looked for with impatience" (Letter of December 17, 1841). A copy of Cornelius Mathews, *Wakondah; The Master of Life. A Poem* (New York, 1841), in the Harvard Library is inscribed: "Henry W. Longfellow/from S. W. N Y. 18 Decr 1841."

3. Lewis Gaylord Clark's "foolish epistle" is unrecovered, but his letter of lame apology, dated December 21, 1841, is printed in *Clark Letters*, pp. 115–116. Longfellow's irritation was caused by Clark's failure to pay him for his contributions to the *Knickerbocker*.

## 650. *To Stephen Longfellow*

Cambridge Decr. 26 1841

My dear Father,

My Ballads &c are at length published; and some copies are on the way to you. The first edition was small; only about four hundred, and went off immediately. The second, of five hundred, came out yesterday. It is neater, than the first, the paper being smoother. A large-paper edition will be in readiness soon; it being already printed and in the binder's hands. I send you the second edition, not wishing to keep you waiting. I hope you will like these poems as well as the last.

I dined yesterday, Christmass Day, with Mr. Ticknor. Mr. Prescott, Frank Gray, Sumner, [Andrews] Norton &c were the other guests; and Lord Morpeth, for whom the dinner was given. He is a very pleasant, jolly, sociable, red-faced man, with gray hair, blue coat and red waistcoat; — A laughing bachelor of forty. He is the oldest son of the Earl of Carlisle; has been for many years Secretary for Ireland; and in all probability, when the Whigs come into power again will be Prime Minister. He seems to be enjoying himself in Boston; but leaves for Washington on Tuesday.

We have a very mild, open Winter here; as yet no snow, that remains on the ground; and the weather Spring-like.

I have found a man in Boston who can restore *the great painting*, so that you would not know it had been injured. I have seen some of his work; and shall put it into his hands. Every crack and hole can be completely filled, so that the eye cannot detect any defect. It will make a magnificent picture. I consider it worth five hundred dollars, at least.

Have you seen Mr. Farnham, to whom I gave letters of introduction? I hope he may succeed; for he seems to be very ambitious to excel; and very worthy of success. As I have not heard of his return to Boston I presume he has made up his mind to remain in Portland.

With best wishes for a Merry Christmass and Happy New Year,

Affectionately yours
Henry W. Longfellow.

MANUSCRIPT: Longfellow Trust Collection. ADDRESS: Hon. S. Longfellow/Portland. POSTMARK: CAMBRIDGE MS. DEC 27

## 651. *To Samuel Ward*

Cambridge Decr. 26. 1841

My dear Sam,

Your few, brief, but expressive lines of the 23rd reached me on Friday, and yesterday I looked for a "Merry Christmas" salutation in the promised letter, which *should* have come but did not. I have nothing new to communicate on the subject; saving an answer to one of your questions in regard to the time of commencing operations in the new Professorship. This will certainly not be before Spring; perhaps not so soon. Meanwhile I pray the plan may not break through; and hope you will not let anyone else meddle with it, for fear of interrupting the good train things are now in. As soon as I get yr. letter about Mersch and the Library, no. of vols. &c I will see Judge Story and some other influential men in the Corporation; and I feel confident that I can carry the matter through.

This will be a great thing for Mersch, because it places him at once on a vantage ground; and his *avenir* [future] will be such as he chooses to make it. *Science* is just commencing her career in America. He may do much for her. Particularly *here* are they disposed just now to make exertions in this department, and *Pierce* is to have here a Mathematical and Scientific Journal.[1] In fine, *Es tagt*; day breaks.

The second edition of the *Ballads* is out. It looks better than the first, the paper being smoother, and the whole getting up neater. The large paper edition will be ready during the week; and then you shall have a New Year's Present.

I dined yesterday with the Ticknors, Lord Morpeth, Prescott, Mr. and Mrs. Norton, Frank Gray and Sumner being the other guests. It was a pleasant Christmas dinner. His Lordship wore that flaming red waistcoat you wot of ("quite jolly") and was gay as a lark. So was Prescott. His Lordship told us he was to dine with you on Tuesday; and I sent my *regards* by him. By the way, you have made a conquest of Mrs. Ticknor. She says there is no resisting your *winning ways*; from which I infer, *that all your cards are trumps.*

Frank Gray amused me with a[n] account of his *Wassercur* experiences in Marienburg, near Boppart, the very place I had fixed upon for my Summer residence.

I hope you continue to like *Maidenhood.* Sumner says "I do not like that piece!" To me, it is one of the best. I have not yet got the key to his taste. He rejects Motherwell with a sneer, and praises Milnes, for which Ticknor laughs in his face.[2]

Yours affectionately
Henry W. Longfellow.

P. S. Recollect to send me *facts* about Mersch; not praise of him; I can make that here. Note what he has written since his residence with you.

MANUSCRIPT: Clifton Waller Barrett Collection, University of Virginia. ADDRESS: Samuel Ward Esq/(Prime Ward & King)/New York POSTMARK: CAMBRIDGE MS. DEC 27 PUBLISHED: "Letters to Samuel Ward, Part II," p. 171.

1. Benjamin Peirce's *Cambridge Miscellany of Mathematics, Physics, and Astonomy* survived for four numbers of Vol. I, April 1842 — January 1843.

2. Ward commented on Sumner's taste in his reply of December 27: "What you say of Sumner does not surprise me. You know there are some people who have no ear for music, others who have no eye for colors &c — so he has no taste for maidenhood."

# PART SEVEN

# EUROPE

# 1842

# EUROPE

## 1842

In 1841 Emerson had announced that "Traveling is a fool's paradise," but Longfellow, dissatisfied with his situation, worried about his health, and caught up emotionally in the tangles of a seemingly one-sided love affair, saw in travel the only escape from the frustrations of his life in Cambridge. As early as November 17, 1841, he had revealed to Sam Ward his intention of going to Germany to test the therapeutic effects of the Water-Cure. He did not confide in his father, however, presumably because he wished to avoid until later what he suspected would be his disapproval of the plan. The presence of Charles Dickens in Boston in January did much to stimulate Longfellow's desire to escape to Europe again, and on January 30 he finally informed Stephen Longfellow in a casual postscript of his decision to make the voyage. On January 24 he had been more direct and explicit in a letter to the Harvard Corporation: "I am reluctantly compelled by the state of my health to ask leave of absence from College for six months from the first of May next. In this time I propose to visit Germany, to try the effect of certain baths, by means of which, as well as by the relaxation and the sea-voyage, I hope to re-establish my health."

Longfellow left Cambridge on April 23 and arrived in New York the next day. Sam Ward, who had arranged his sailing accommodations, was his host in the city, where he spent four pleasant days before boarding the packet *Ville de Lyon* on April 27. With the help of his letters and journals of the period, an itinerary of his third European experience can be constructed as follows:

*May 19–21*: Arrival, Le Havre. En route Paris.

*May 22–25*: Paris.

*May 26—June 3*: En route Boppard via Brussels (May 28–31, excursion to Antwerp, Ghent, Bruges), Aix-la-Chapelle, Liège, Cologne.

*June 4—September 17*: Wasser-Heil-Anstalt Marienberg, Boppard (July 25–28, excursion to Rolandseck, Königswinter, Bonn, Cologne; September 10–14, excursion to Bonn, Brühl, Coblenz).

*September 18–29*: Excursion to Bingen, Mainz, Frankfort, Würzburg, Nuremberg; return to St. Goar via Würzburg, Heidelberg, Mannheim, Frankfort.

*September 30—October 4*: En route London via Cologne, Malines, Bruges, Ostend.

*October 5–20*: London.

*October 21–22*: En route Bristol via Bath.

*October 23—November 6*: En route New York.

*November 7*: Arrival, Cambridge.

Although Longfellow's three months at the Wasser-Heil-Anstalt Marienberg took his mind off his troubles from time to time, hydropathy was not noticeably effective in restoring his health — either physical or emotional. With a good deal of time on his hands, he devoted himself conscientiously to correspondence, writing at least 55 letters from Europe, of which 43 are available for publication (out of a total of 86 recovered from some 116 written during the year 1842). These letters reveal his fluctuations in mood as he shifted from dissatisfaction with his progress as a patient to a sense of well-being when gripped by the spell of the Rhineland scenery or when immersed in water, or conversation, with his fellow-sufferers. With one exception, he did not concern himself with writing poetry. "I have not had time since I [c]am[e] here to write a verse or a line," he wrote to Charles Sumner on August 8. "There is no inspiration in dressing and undressing. Hunger and thirst figure too largely here, to leave room for poetical figures." But on August 25 he found inspiration in his restlessness and composed "Mezzo Cammin," a sonnet that clearly reflected his mood of melancholy and unsatisfied ambition.

> Half of my life is gone, and I have let
> The years slip from me and have not fulfilled
> The aspiration of my youth, to build
> Some tower of song with lofty parapet.
> Not indolence, nor pleasure, nor the fret
> Of restless passions that would not be stilled,
> But sorrow, and a care that almost killed,
> Kept me from what I may accomplish yet;
> Though, half-way up the hill, I see the Past
> Lying beneath me with its sounds and sights, —
> A city in the twilight dim and vast,
> With smoking roofs, soft bells, and gleaming lights, —
> And hear above me on the autumnal blast
> The cataract of Death far thundering from the heights.

The most significant reward of Longfellow's third sojourn in Germany was the friendship he formed with the German poet Ferdinand Freiligrath, whom he met shortly after his arrival at the Marienberg baths. Freiligrath, who was spending the summer at St. Goar (eight miles upriver from Boppard), liked Longfellow immediately. He introduced him to his small circle of literati and friends and whetted his appetite for German literature. With his wife Ida and their guest Fräulein von Gall, a young writer of romantic tales, Freiligrath provided Longfellow with delightful moments of social relaxation, which contrasted with the institutional disciplines of the hydropathic establishment. Although this one brief summer was the only time they were ever together, it stimulated a correspondence that lasted until Freiligrath's death in 1876.

Longfellow left Germany after concluding that the Harvard Corporation would not take kindly to the idea of extending his leave. He was, of course, in no position to cut off his support from that source. Besides, he was homesick. After a crowded two weeks in London as the guest of Charles Dickens, he sailed from Bristol on the *Great Western*, to undergo his customary discomfort at sea and, in calmer moments, to compose drafts for his *Poems on Slavery*. After arriving in Cambridge, he wrote to his father that on many accounts he was glad to be back. "On other accounts," he continued, "I ought to have staid longer in Germany. The cold water was doing me so much good, that it was a pity to break off before getting thoroughly well. But Fate has so decreed, and here I am, determined to make the best of it." Thus determined, he settled back into the same routines of mind and body that had precipitated his flight to Europe in the spring.

## 652. *To Samuel Ward*

Cambridge Jan. 2. 1842.

My dear Sam,

Pray do not be vexed at my most ungracious way of receiving your New Year's Present — the "*Yellow Book*." You know I feel your kindness in sending it; but as I have neither interest in, nor respect for the author, I thought I would be frank enough to say so.[1] Besides, every thing in my last letter, was abrupt to the last degree; as I wrote in great haste, and with a guest sitting at my elbow. *One thing* you shall give me credit for; that is for walking to Boston to put the letter into the office in order to prevent delay. Last week was rather a busy and anxious week with me, on account of the College Examinations; but it is over; and my boys appeared gloriously, both in French and German; so that Prescott and the rest of the Committee said, they had never attended so good an examination.

I wish from the bottom of my heart, that I could have a long conversation with you on this subject of the Professorship. One cannot write, — (at least I cannot) — one tenth of what one has to say. I want to know fully your feelings and thoughts, — to hold a heart to heart talk, — a combining with you and for you, — a strong *tug* together for our friend — a concert of means to persuade the older heads that our praise of Mersch is not the effect of one-sided, partial, much-forgiving friendship, — in fine to make them see with our young eyes. At all events we have now time to meditate. Far be [it] from me, my dear Sam, to hurry you into any act, that you could *possibly* regret. You must think *maturely* on the subject. Do you not prefer this last plan, — with the increased salary to the other? [2] It is vastly better in my opinion.

You *must* see Judge Story, when he passes through New York; — you *must* have a talk with him, — a regular discussion of the whole subject and whole ground of proceeding — the *pros.* and *cons.* He will be there on *Thursday* or *Saturday* — depending somewhat upon the weather. If you do not see him — I pray you write to him in Washington. He said he should be happy to hear from you about Mersch, and that he thought you "a man of judgment." You made an impression on *him,* too.

As to the detail of the appointment, that would, I think, be easily arranged. I do not think they would care about Mersch's beginning his duties before Autumn, if he wished to pass the Summer at the *Jardin des Plantes.*

My book has won me "golden opinions" [3] here; and I shall send you by first opportunity a large-paper copy. This edition is beautiful. I am glad there is to be a notice of it in the New York Review.[4] Tell O'Sullivan, that *God's-Acre* is liked by more persons than any other piece in the volume.

Sumner is passing Sunday with me. He and Felton have just gone down to Beck's, leaving their best wishes for a Happy New Year to be folded up with mine, and sent you, in this note. Many and many happy years to [you] [5] and yours is the sincere prayer of your friend

Henry W. Longfellow.

Recd. yours of the 24. 29. and 31st. No doubt you had a delightful dinner. The story of the "*Madman of Hexenheim*" is excellent. I wish I had an Aunt, who could tell such stories! [6]

Cambridge. Jan. 2. 1842.

My Dear Benjamin,[7]

Please pay to Saml. Ward or his order forty dollars; and accept my thanks, and best wishes for a Happy New Year to the New World. Yours truly Henry W. Longfellow.[8]

P.S. I wish you could see my *Copeley* — or did you see it? It will turn out one of the most beautiful paintings of that artist.

P.S. Upon reflection you need not send the draft to Benjn. I will wait a few days. He will probably send the money of his own accord.

MANUSCRIPT: Longfellow Trust Collection. ADDRESS: Samuel Ward Esq/(Prime Ward & King.)/New York [*in another hand*] POSTMARK: BOSTON Mas. JAN 3

1. In a letter of December 28, 1841, Ward identified this book as *Arthur Carryl, a novel. By the author of The Vision of Rubeta* [Laughton Osborn]. *Cantos first and second. Odes; Epistles to Milton, Pope, Juvenal and the Devil; Epigrams; Parodies of Horace; England as she is; and other minor poems. By the same* (New York, 1841). See 446.9. Longfellow's letter of December 29, in which he gave a frank opinion of Ward's gift, is unrecovered.
2. That is, a plan for Mersch to receive an annual salary of $2000 if Ward would present Harvard with $10,000 (Ward to Longfellow, December 31, 1841).
3. *Macbeth,* I, vii, 33.
4. See 642.3.
5. Longfellow wrote "to to" instead of "to you."
6. Ward had described a dinner party for Lord Morpeth and his aunt's tale of the "Madman of Hexenheim" in his letter of December 29, an abridged version of which appears in *Uncle Sam Ward and His Circle,* pp. 323–324.
7. The figure "$40.—" appears to the left of the salutation.
8. Park Benjamin owed Longfellow $20 each for "The Goblet of Life" and "To the River Charles," which he had rejected for the *New World* and sold to *Graham's Magazine* and the *Ladies' Companion* respectively. See his letter to Longfellow, December 4, 1841 (*Life,* I, 408–409).

## 653. *To Stephen Longfellow*

Cambridge. Jan 4. 1842.

My dear Father,

I was very much surprised on going to the Bookseller's yesterday to find, that the copies of *Ballads* I had done up and directed to you more than a week ago, he had forgotten to send. They go to-day; or rather he promises they shall.

The book has succeeded wonderfully well. Three editions on small paper, of 500 copies each, on an average, have been printed, and one edition on large paper, of 250 copies.

I inclose you a couple of letters on the subject, which I should like to have sent back, when you have read them. One is from Judge Story, the other from W. H. Prescott. The Judge is particularly struck with the Hesperus, being a Marblehead man, and acquainted with the scene of Norman's Woe. He told Sumner the other day, that "he did not think I knew so much about *skippers*."

I throw in also a note from Mrs. Otis. She is an enthusiastic individual. Miss Lowell is afraid she will do me more harm than good in the opinion of others by *over-praising me!*[1]

Many thanks for your kind letter of the 26. Decr. Two days ago Mrs. Greenleaf had letters from Mary. She was *well and warm*; writing by an open window, and no fire. Delightful climate.

With many Happy-New Years to you all,

Very affectionately
Henry W. Longfellow.

P.S. When is Alex coming this way? He can have board and lodging here for any length of time, and moreover a warm welcome.

MANUSCRIPT: Longfellow Trust Collection. ADDRESS: Hon. S. Longfellow/Portland/Me.

1. Mrs. Otis' letter is dated January 1, 1842; those of Judge Story and W. H. Prescott (*Life*, I, 411–412) are dated January 3, 1842, and December 30, 1841.

## 654. *To Samuel Ward*

Cambridge. Jan 6. 1842.

My dear Sam,

The sexton has just rung nine at night, and I have had so much of my own society this evening, that I would fain have a friendly crack with you. Why are you so far away? And why am I so dull?

Did you get letters from Mrs. Ticknor and me on Tuesday? I went to town and put mine into the post-office there. I saw Mrs. Ticknor and your beautiful New Year's present; which stood sentinel on the centre-table, keeping guard over fifty other gifts, and filling the hearts of all beholders with delight. Rakemann was giving Miss Anna a lesson. I had heard him play a few nights before very beautifully. The term is over, and I am *raking* it a little. Last night I was at Mrs. Guild's; tomorrow night, go to Mrs. Ticknor who begins her Winter *Friday-Evenings*. They are very pleasant. You must run on, during the winter, and charm her again with your presence.

I am impatient to see your notice of the Ballads in the New York Review.[1] The book pleases far beyond my expectations. I have received several pleasant letters, which I should like to show you; — from Prescott, Judge Story &c. Only one poor dog of an Editor in Boston has "lifted up his leg against me, and passed on, as if nothing especial had happened."

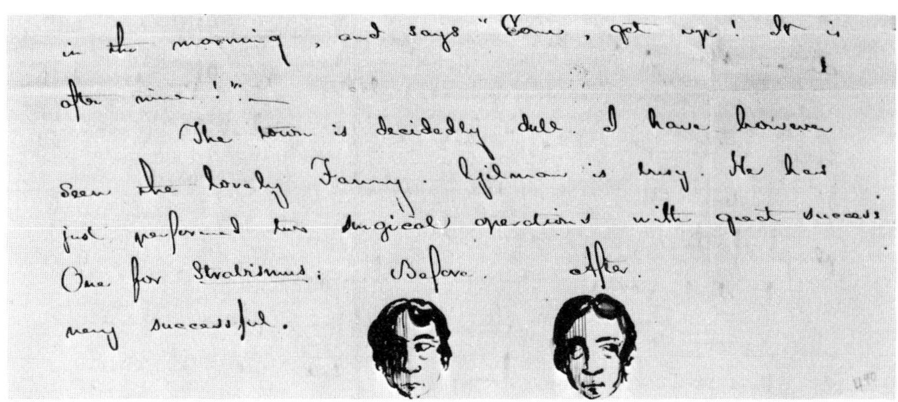

in the morning, and says "Come, get up! It is after nine!"—

The town is decidedly dull. I have however seen the lovely Fanny. Gilman is busy. He has just performed two surgical operations with great success. One for Strabismus; Before. After. very successful.

Sketch by Longfellow, Letter No. 614

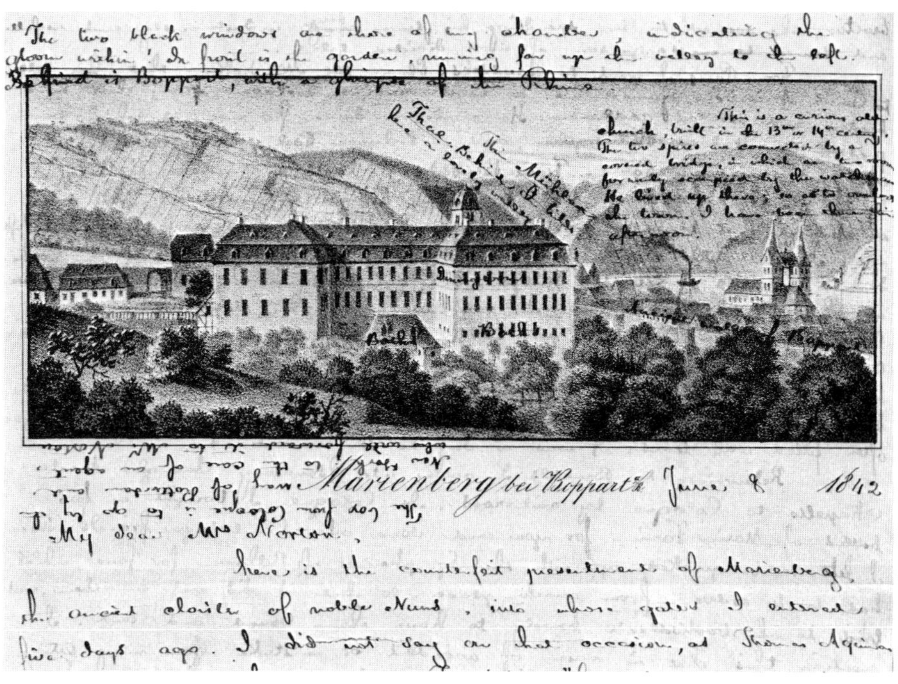

"The two black windows are those of my chamber, indicating the gloom within.' In front is the garden, running far up the valley to the left. Behind is Boppard, with a glimpse of the Rhine.

This is a curious old church, built in the 13th or 14th century. The two spires are connected by a covered bridge,

Marienberg bei Boppart June 8 1842

My dear Mrs Norton,

here is the counterfeit presentment of Marienberg, the ancient cloister of noble Nuns, into whose gates I entered, five days ago. I did not say on that occasion, as Thomas Aquinas

Marienberg bei Boppard am Rhein, 1842, Letter No. 690

PLATE IX

Longfellow, c. 1841, by Charles Octavius Cole

PLATE X

Longfellow, 1843, by Seth Wells Cheney

PLATE XII

Craigie House, 1843

I hope you will see Judge Story on his transit through New York. I think it necessary, that upon a subject so important, as the one in hand,[2] you should have a long and friendly conversation with some one of the Corporation. And Judge Story is the one of all others I should like to have you see. It would be more satisfactory to you, and to all concerned.

This has been an excessively dull and stupid day with me; — one of those stagnant days, on which that intellectual mud-puddle the brain, reflects no bright images. What a hateful feeling! Besides, I have lying before me *twelve* unpaid Bills, and my purse is as empty as the Treasury of Uncle Sam. *Hinc* [hence] the following draft, which I hope will not be of air only.

Write me as soon as you can. I am starving for *your news,* — pardon the Gallicism. Mrs. T. was much delighted with Julia's poems; but agrees with me, in what I once said to you in regard to publishing.

Yours very truly
Henry W. Longfellow.

If Benjamin pays, please send me an order or draft on some Boston banker as soon as you conveniently can.

Yours of the || . . . || am putting th|| . . . || [3]

MANUSCRIPT: Longfellow Trust Collection. ADDRESS: Samuel Ward Esq/(Prime Ward & King)/New York. POSTMARK: CAMBRIDGE ||MS.|| JAN [*date illegible*] PUBLISHED: *Uncle Sam Ward and His Circle,* pp. 325–326.

1. See 642.3.
2. Mersch's appointment as professor at Harvard.
3. About six words are missing.

## 655. *To Samuel Ward*

Cambridge, Jan. 14th, 1842.

My dear Sam,

Two days ago, on receiving yours of the 10th and 11th, I sat down and wrote you a long letter in reply, which alas! I forgot to put into the post office, and consequently shall now put into the fire, as being old. You shall have a new one. And it shall begin, by saying that I told you as plainly as pen could write the words, the first time I spoke of Judge Story, — that he would stop at the Astor House if he stopped at all.[1] And there let it end.

The Review has at length reached me, but I have not yet had time to read Mersch's Article. Thank Cogswell for his notice of me. He handles me almost too daintily; and I half envy W. Lester, who comes next, the vivid satisfaction of being fired into with broken bottles.[2]

Who emitted that asinine bray against Harvard College on page 221? I mean in the notice of *The Method of Nature.*[3] Cogswell should be above petty ill-humor and unfairness. Which *Method of Nature* do you prefer, Van Zandt's or Emerson's? Out of revenge I had an Episcopal clergyman to dine with me on Wednesday. I did not ask him to say grace.[4] Just as we were finishing dinner, Knoop came in with your letter, and accompanied by Hening [Herwig].[5] I gave them a cordial reception; and made their hearts merry with Johannisberg, coffee and cigars. They sat an hour and were *quite* jolly! ("*Hast du vor'm rother Womms nicht mehr Respect?*")[6] He — that is Knoop, not Morpeth (nor Mephisto) gives a concert soon, and I am all impatience to hear your "connecting link with another world." (Do you mean the *Old* World or the *Next* World?) — .

I intended to send you the large-paper edition of the ballads by John Astor; but he slipped through my fingers. I shall not encourage Har[n]den; his charges being too enormous, but will send you the books some *beau matin,* together with the new edition of Hawthorne's "Twice Told Tales" which is just out, in two volumes.

Have you read Sumner's article on the Right of Search, in the Boston Daily Advertiser?[7] It is a very able, diplomatic paper. I will send you a copy by this mail, for fear you may not have seen it.

As to the *Student of Alcalá,* I have no longer any courage to look at it. Neither you, nor Sumner, nor Ticknor, nor Felton likes it; and I am so weary, that I cannot nerve my mind to the task of connecting it. I shall probably throw it into the fire.

Farewell. Ever thine,
Henry W. Longfellow.

P.S. I shall not tell you how I like the notice of my poems, until you tell me who wrote it.[8]

MANUSCRIPT: unrecovered; text from "Letters to Samuel Ward, Part III," pp. 301–302.

1. In a letter of January 10, Ward had written: "I like your way of begging me to call on Judge Story, without letting me know where the Old Boy puts up. Mr. Astor and myself have been ransacking the Hotels since Thursday and, finding him no where, we have concluded he must have passed through the air on a broomstick."

2. Mersch had contributed Article VI, a review of Roswell Park's *Pantology* (Philadelphia, 1841), to the *New York Review,* X (January 1842), 152–169. The same number contained the laudatory notice of *Ballads and Other Poems* (642.3), followed by a condemnation of C. Edwards Lester's *The Glory and the Shame of England* (New York, 1841).

3. The unidentified and unsympathetic reviewer of Emerson's *The Method of Nature. An Oration, delivered before the Society of the Adelphi, in Waterville Col-*

*lege, Maine, August 11th, 1841* (Boston, 1841) referred to the Harvard Divinity School on p. 221 as "the seat of rigid Calvinistic orthodoxy."

4. Ward could not have failed to appreciate Longfellow's sly allusions here, for the public was currently enthralled by newspaper reports of the trial of Rev. Washington Van Zandt (1807–1868), rector of Grace Church in Rochester, New York, for the seduction of Miss Sophia Murdock, "a young and beautiful member of his church." According to the published *Report of the Trial . . .* (Philadelphia, 1842), Rev. Van Zandt's employment of the "method of nature" lost him, among other things, $3125 in damages.

5. George Knoop, a German-born cellist who advertised himself in America as "Concert-Meister of the late King of England, William IV" (George C. D. Odell, *Annals of the New York Stage* [New York, 1927–1949], IV, 591), appeared in his first Boston concert on January 22, 1842. The *Daily Evening Transcript* reported on January 12 that he had "arrived in this city, in company with the universal favorite, Herwig, and they intend to give a series of concerts, which will probably excel in splendor anything of the kind ever before exhibited here" (Vol. XIII, No. 3516).

6. "Have you no longer any respect for the fiery waistcoat?" The owner of the "fiery waistcoat" was Lord Morpeth. See Letter No. 663.

7. For January 4, 1842.

8. See 642.3.

## 656. *To George Tyler Bigelow and Others*[1]

[Cambridge, January 18, 1842][2]

Gentlemen,

I have had the honor of receiving your invitation to the Dickens' Dinner, which I accept with the greatest pleasure.

Very truly yours
Henry W. Longfellow

George T. Bigelow and others
Committee of Invitation

MANUSCRIPT: Longfellow Trust Collection.

1. Bigelow (1810–1878), later chief justice of the Massachusetts Supreme Court, was a member of the committee on arrangements (with Nathan Hale, Jr., Jonathan Barrett, Theodore W. Crocket, and William Wetmore Story) for the famous Boz Dinner held at Papanti's Hall on February 1. Dickens arrived in Boston on January 22. For accounts of his visit and the dinner, see *Dickens Days in Boston,* pp. 3–136, and H. W. L. Dana, "Longfellow and Dickens: The Story of a Transatlantic Friendship," *Cambridge Historical Society Publications,* XXVIII (1942), 55–68.

2. The date is approximate. Longfellow had received the invitation on January 17 (Dana, p. 57).

## 657. *To Samuel Ward*[1]

[Cambridge, January 19, 1842]

My dear Sam

Your last with Benjamin's money received. I shall write you soon. Vide Cogswell. A lovely day this. I am *raking* it in town, for the sake of my health. There is a sweet Spanish woman here, playing the guitar, La Señora de Goñy,[2] — delicious.

Yours truly,
H. W. L.

MANUSCRIPT: unrecovered; text from *Uncle Sam Ward and His Circle,* p. 332.

1. This letter is a postscript to Charles Sumner's letter to Sam Ward of the same date.

2. Dolores Nevares de Goni played her first public concert in Boston on January 22, 1842, on the same program with the cellist Knoop (*Daily Evening Transcript*).

## 658. *To Samuel Ward*

Cambridge. Jan. 21. 1842.

My dear Sam,

I have been leading so wild a life in town this last week, that I have not been able to write to anyone — not even to your dear self. I have dined in town every day; and been to one [or] two parties every night, — and reaching home at midnight tired and sleepy, have felt no nerve for writing even that indefinite quantity, — a few lines. This week I have devoted entirely to gayety, — and two days more remain. After that, I propose to *subside within my banks,* like a subsiding stream, after an overflow. To-day I dine with Chs. Amory, and pass the evening at Ticknor's; and tomorrow comes Knoop's first concert. His wonder-working instrument I have heard already several times in private. It utters exquisitely sweet and plaintive notes. But there is with him a Spanish Lady — *La Señora De Goñy,* whose guitar *delights* me more, perhaps because it awakens sweet remembrances of early youth and Spain; — perhaps because a woman plays it, and the *devil is in it.*

Speaking of *notes of hand,* Owen gave me his note a day or two ago, which Sumner endorsed and Hillard took to the Globe Bank to have it discounted. Owen is not know[n] at this bank. Sprague, the Poet is Cashier — a friend of Hillard. Hillard said to him;

"Mr. Sprague, I want you to discount this note, for a brother poet, whose notes are good on Parnassus, and the Banks of Helicon and I hope may be equally good at the Globe Bank."

Mr. Sprague read the face of the Note — "pay to H. W. Longfellow &c &c &c. John Owen." — and said

"I dont know any such persons!"

The President of the bank inquired, who the endorser was.

"Mr. Sumner."

"Mr. *Charles* Sumner?"

"Yes."

"O pay it — pay it instantly!"

Moral. — the decided advantage to a *person of retired habits* having a friend known on Change.

Cogswell made too short a visit. He did not get so far as Cambridge; but I saw him in town several times, and we discussed the matter of the Professorship.[1] He will tell you the substance of our conversation.

A new edition of the Voices goes to press immediately. This is the sixth. The *Ballads* have given their elder brother a new start.

Your brief analysis of Sumner and myself, which I read to him, is skilfully sketched, and shows a good deal of insight.[2]

Your sister Julia is very well. I met her last evening at Mrs. Wm. Appleton's — the evening before at Mrs. Eliot's — neither of them parties — only a chance medley of friends and, — strangers. I wish you would come to Boston now. She would enjoy herself much more if you were here. Better come.

Dissipation does not suit me. I get tired of it in a week. It kills all better thought and is in itself unsatisfactory; and to be taken not as daily food, but as a medicine, to purge away dull care and melancholy.

If I had the same conveniences for sending letters that you have, I would write as often as you do. But I cannot burden you with too great a bill for postage.

I have a beautiful little poem to show you written by a young damsel of Portland; — and quite remarkable for its Germanic coloring. For my own part I am doing literally nothing, but am nevertheless

very affectionately yours

H. W. Longfellow.

MANUSCRIPT: Longfellow Trust Collection. ADDRESS: Samuel Ward Esq/(Prime Ward & King)/New York. POSTMARK: BOSTON MAS. JAN 22 PUBLISHED: *Uncle Sam Ward and His Circle*, pp. 332–334.

1. For Mersch. See 649.1.

2. In a letter of January 14 Ward had written: "I often think of him [Sumner] and imagine he will never abstract himself enough from his abstraction to fall in love. There is something of the Isaac Newton about him. If he fell violently in love,

however, he would go it very strong at the expense of every thing else. What a study he would make of his wife's heart and character. I think a woman would have hard work to please him — and easy work to please you. He is like the Sultan in the Arabian tale who sent a mirror out to reflect the face of an unsullied virgin. He requires nevertheless that he should be master — superior in intellect. It seems to me, that the character of your companion wd have the greatest influence upon your own and much less wd that of Sumner's have upon his."

## 659. *To the Harvard Corporation*

Harvard University January. 24. 1842

Gentlemen,

I am reluctantly compelled by the state of my health to ask leave of absence from the College for six months from the first of May next. In this time I propose to visit Germany, to try the effect of certain baths, by means of which, as well as by the relaxation and the sea-voyage, I hope to reestablish my health. My medical attendant advises this course as more efficatious, than any treatment I can receive at home.

I shall be able, before leaving, to deliver all the lectures of the Spring Term; and on my return in November, those of the Autumn Term before its close;[1] and it is in reference to the necessary arrangements for this, that I make thus early my application for leave of absence. The general supervision of the Department will be undertaken by Professor Felton, without any charge to the College; — the classes will lose none of their lectures; — and I trust the interests of the College will not suffer.

I would repeat in conclusion that the state of my health is the sole reason of my making this request.

I am, Gentlemen, Your Obt. Ser[v]t.
Henry W. Longfellow

To the President and Fellows of Harvard University

MANUSCRIPT: Harvard College Papers, X, 363. PUBLISHED: Higginson, *Longfellow*, pp. 155–156.

1. By concentrating the lectures at the beginning of the spring term, which began about March 1 and lasted until late July, and at the end of the autumn term, which began about September 1 and ended in mid-January.

## 660. *To Stephen Longfellow*

Cambridge Jan 30 1842[1]

My dear Father,

Many thanks for your kind letters, which I should have answered long ago. I cannot plead business as my excuse, but idleness. The weather for ten days past has been so delicious and summer-like, that I have not been able to keep in doors. I am trying, though I am sorry to say with little success, the effect of air and exercise. To-day I have walked ten miles. I am disappointed in not getting well.

You see by the papers that Dickens has arrived. He is a glorious fellow; and the greatest possible enthusiasm exists among all classes. He has not a moment's rest; — calls innumerable — invitations innumerable; — and is engaged three deep for the remainder of his stay, in the way of dinners and parties. He is a gay, free and easy character; — a fine bright face; blue eyes, long dark hair, and withal a slight dash of the Dick Swiveller about him. He went with Sumner and me to hear father Taylor[2] preach this morning; and then we took him to Copp's Hill, and to Bunker's Hill. The other evening he was at the Theatre; and was received with nine cheers, and forced to come forward in the box and make a bow. On Tuesday has a public dinner — and leaves town on Saturday for Worcester, where he passes Sunday with the Governor.[3] There on Monday he is to be met by a committee of Young Men from Springfield, who take him on to dine. At Springfield he passes into the hands of another Committee, who take him to Hartford for the same purpose; — and so on through New Haven to New York. Luckily he is young — only thirty, next month, — and has a good constitution, and likes the fun of the thing. His wife is with him,

"To share the triumph and partake the gale."[4]

She is a good-natured — mild, rosy young woman — not beautiful, but amiable.

I shall come to Portland as soon as possible though probably not before next week. I do not intend, however, to lecture before the Lyceum, not being fond of such exhibitions.

We have just got out a new edition of the *Voices.* — the sixth. I make no changes. The *Ballads* are also very successful; and I am glad they find favor in your eyes.

With much love to all,
||Henry W. Longfellow||

P. S. In the Spring I intend to make a voyage to Europe — say about the first of May — to be gone through the Summer.

MANUSCRIPT: Longfellow Trust Collection. ADDRESS: Hon ||S. Lo||ngfellow/Portland/Me. POSTMARK: CAMBRIDGE MS. JAN 31

1. Longfellow inadvertently wrote "1840." The correction is in another hand.
2. Edward Thompson Taylor (1793–1871) had been a seaman before his con-

version to the Methodist Episcopal faith. In 1830 he became minister of the Bethel Church in North Square, where his pulpit style, flavored with nautical terms, attracted wide attention, including Melville's, whose Father Mapple in *Moby Dick* delivers a characteristic Taylor sermon. Dickens described his visit to the church in his *American Notes.* See also *Dickens Days in Boston,* pp. 72–77.

3. "Honest John" Davis (1787–1854), governor of Massachusetts in 1842, entertained Dickens at his mansion in Worcester (*Dickens Days in Boston,* pp. 132–134).

4. Cf. Pope, *An Essay on Man,* Ep. iv, l. 386. "Kate" Dickens (1815–1879) had come to America reluctantly (Edgar Johnson, *Charles Dickens: His Tragedy and Triumph* [New York, 1952], I, 358–359).

## 661. *To Samuel Ward*

Cambridge. Jan. 30 1842.

My dear Sam,

I am much obliged to Mr. King for showing Armstrong his *béjaune* [mistake] in regard to that stanza; and in return for Halleck's criticism on the "falling Star," ask him what he means by

"One of the few, the *immortal* names,
*That were not born to die.*"

Things *immortal* are not generally born to die, are they? Put that in your pipe.[1]

To-day I have walked ten miles; namely, *to* town, *through* town, and *out* of town to Charlestown, (Bunker Hill) and back again. I went to hear Father Taylor preach, with Dickens and Sumner, and then we made a pilgrimage through North End, over Copp's Hill to Bunker's. Dickens is a glorious fellow. You will be delighted with him; and I have promissed him a letter to you, and want you to see him first, on his arrival in New York, — before anyone has laid hands upon him. He will reach New York on Saturday week — that is Feb. 12. I beg you, have him and his wife to dine that day, with Irving, Halleck and Dr. Francis. And in order to secure to yourself the great pleasure of introducing to each other two such men as Irving and Dickens, write an invitation to Dickens, and inclose it to me, and I and Sumner will arrange the whole matter before hand, if you like the plan.[2]

When shall you be here? Dickens breakfasts with me on Friday. Will you come? Let me know beforehand; for every place at table is precious; — but I shall count upon you.[3]

How do you like the parody on Excelsior? The *idea* is good, — but the execution execrable. The builder of that rhyme is no artist.[4]

Well — in May I go into exile on the Rhine. I presented my request to the Corporation yesterday, and it was allowed forthwith, and I cross the great sea again. I hope I shall return with a sound body and mind.

Julia is enjoying herself much in Boston, and making many friends and admirers. Felton is in love with her; and in speaking of her uses the superlative degree only. Park Street was never more brilliant than now.

Good night; my great lamp is going out and darkness falling on the sheet. Nevertheless, "while the lamp holds out to burn,"[5] and long afterwards,

Yours very truly
H. W. Longfellow.

P. S. I shall take this to the office tomorrow morning before breakfast. It must be in your hands on Tuesday.

In the next No. — the March No — of Graham's Magazine, you will find a short Article by me on Heine, which I want you to glance at.[6] Graham pays me $50 per paper — without regard to length.

MANUSCRIPT: Berg Collection, New York Public Library. ADDRESS: Samuel Ward Esq/(Prime Ward & King)/New York. POSTMARK: CAMBRIDGE MS. JAN 31 PUBLISHED: "Letters to Samuel Ward, Part III," p. 302.

1. Ward had written in his letter of January 24: "Halleck made this criticism upon the last stanza of *Excelsior*, 'a voice fell like a falling star.' What is a falling star? said he, a lump of stone and iron — an *aerolith* such as Silliman picks up and analyzes. Charles King dined with me on Friday and spoke enthusiastically of your poems. He argued at length with Armstrong the vexed stanza of the Psalm of Life

'Footsteps that perhaps another
Sailing o'er life's solemn main'

and not only beat him — but convinced him of its beauty and fitness — adding that the 2d line is not surpassed in any poem in our language." The lines of Halleck's are from the poem "Marco Bozzaris."

2. This plan could not be carried out because of Dickens' full schedule in New York. The letter of introduction to Ward is unrecovered.

3. Longfellow's breakfast for Dickens on February 4 is described in *Dickens Days in Boston*, pp. 122–127. His other guests were Felton and Andrews Norton.

4. This parody appeared in the *Boston Morning Post*, XXI, No. 22 (January 26, 1842), 1. The author was Frederick Octavius Prince (1818–1899), a member of the Harvard class of 1836 and a Boston lawyer. It is printed in "Letters to Samuel Ward, Part III," p. 302.

5. Isaac Watts, *Hymns and Spiritual Songs*, Bk. I, Hymn 88.

6. *Graham's Magazine*, XX (March 1842), 134–137. See 400.2.

## 662. *To William Pitt Fessenden*

Portland. Feb. 15. 1842

My dear Pitt,

I write as usual on business. On the first of May I sail for Europe; and it has passed through my mind, that possibly I might have the good luck to be made Bearer of Despatches to London or Paris. Sumner has written to Choate upon the subject; pray speak with him; and perhaps you can lend me a helping hand.[1] My chief object in going is my health. I have leave of absence for six months.

I saw your wife this evening. She is well. Mrs. Deblois[2] was with her; and Nat Deering dropped in during the visit. No particular communications.

I am glad to see you are coming out on the Slavery petitions. All good people in these regions are disgusted with Southern bullying on this subject. How could such a *Rule,* as you propose to repeal, have ever passed? Is it not directly contrary to the First Amendment of the Constitution?[3]

Farewell. I shall be in Cambridge next week, where I hope soon to have a line from you.

Yours very truly
Henry W. Longfellow.

MANUSCRIPT: unrecovered; text from photostat, Longfellow Trust Collection. ADDRESS: Hon. Wm. P. Fessenden/M.C./Washington/D.C. POSTMARKS: PORTLAND ME. FEB 16/FREE

1. There is no indication that Longfellow was successful in this petition.

2. The former Dorcas Deering (1794–1872), sister of Nathaniel Deering and wife of Thomas Amory Deblois.

3. The "gag rule" was used in Congress to suppress discussion of the slavery issue. Fessenden had informed the House that "he would on the first opportunity offer a resolution to repeal the twenty-first rule (the 'gag rule'); but he never got the opportunity" (Francis Fessenden, *Life and Public Services of William Pitt Fessenden* [Boston and New York, 1907], I, 26).

## 663. *To Charles Sumner*

Portland Feb. 15 1842.

My dear Charles,

Your parting injunction, as we stood shaking hands under the dim street lamp at twelve the other night, and you looked over your shoulder to see that no one was listening to your éloge upon the beer barrel, — your parting injunction was "Write." At day-break the next morning I was on my way Eastward, saw the sun rise from the sea, which you never did, — and rolled on rapidly to Portsmouth.

There we took the stage-coach, and bumped it to *Goose Creek,* running into a wagon on the way, and knocking a woman in a red plaid-cloack out of the said wagon into the mud. At Goose Creek we took the cars for Portland, and my arrival was celebrated by six small boys, imitating the steam whistle. Carriages were in waiting; and in an incredibly short space of time we were — to borrow the elegant expression of a fellow-traveller, — *"ticketed through the depot"* — pronouncing the last word so as to rhyme with *tea-pot.*

Such was my triumphal entry into the city of my nativity. I have not yet been honored with a public dinner; but a portrait-painter has *Alexandered* me,[1] which occupies several hours of the mornings, and will send me down to posterity with a face as red as Lord Morpeth's fiery waistcoat. This painter's name is [Charles Octavius] Cole; — a good fellow; who has made me a present of a painting of great merit; — a portrait of Mrs. Wright — the renowned maker of wax-work figures — (*the original Jarley*).[2] This painting is probably by West[3] — and though unfinished is striking and valuable. It came from London. For an account of Mrs. Wright see Mrs. Adams's Letters p. 228.[4]

I have seen John Neal. He thinks the Bostonians have made fools of themselves in the Dickens affair. I half agree with him. Tom Deblois said he looked eagerly for your speech at the Dinner, and wanted to know why you did not make one. Everybody here thinks Hillard's speech the best made on the occasion, which shows their taste.

What do you think I did to-day? I looked into the Boston Daily Advertiser (that great *Historical Work* as Mary Dwight[5] calls it) for *something to amuse me!* Pray write me a line or two, that I may know what is going on in Boston and Cambridge.

I have just written to Fessenden about the *Bearer of Despatches.*[6] I hope you did not forget to mention the subject to Choate, for possibly something may come out of it.

It is near midnight — so farewell and to bed — perchance to dream some blessed dream, that shall perfume the night, and give me fragrant thoughts for a week.

Such dreams be yours. Good night.

Ever affectionately yours
H. W. L.

MANUSCRIPT: Longfellow Trust Collection. ADDRESS: Charles Sumner Esq/ Boston. POSTMARK: PORTLAND||Me||. FEB 16

1. An allusion to Francis Alexander (1800–1880), Boston portrait, genre, and still-life painter.

2. Mrs. Patience Lovell Wright (1725–1786), American modeler in wax, is said to have served as a spy in England during the Revolution (*Dictionary of Ameri-*

*can Biography*, XX, 562). Mrs. Jarley was the proprietor of "Jarley's Wax Work Show" in Dickens's *Old Curiosity Shop*. For Cole's portrait of Longfellow, see Plate X.

3. Benjamin West (1738–1820). There is no record of his having painted a portrait of Mrs. Wright.

4. *Letters of Mrs. [Abigail] Adams, the Wife of John Adams. With an Introductory Memoir by her Grandson, Charles Francis Adams* (Boston, 1840), pp. 228–230.

5. Mary Eliot Dwight (b. 1821), daughter of Edmund Dwight (1780–1849), a merchant prince of Boston, and the former Mary Harrison Eliot (1788–1846). She married Dr. Samuel Parkman (1815–1855) in 1849.

6. Letter No. 662.

## 664. *To Samuel Ward*

Cambridge, Feb 24, 1842.

Best of Sams,

The night before I left Portland my sister said to me, "It is very strange! You have been here a fortnight and have not received a single letter from Mr. Ward!" Nor was the mystery explained till last night, when on my arrival at lonely Castle Craigie my eyes were gladdened by your two letters. I am exceedingly sorry that Boz disappointed your young ladies; and no doubt he was sorrier than they.[1]

I regret, too, that I did not write you from Portland; since you seem to have been looking for a letter. But deuce take it, when I am [away] from this round table I forget that there are such things as pens, ink and letter paper.

Felton has not yet returned. You fascinate him so entirely in New York, that he cannot break away from you. Pray send him back to his disconsolate family, who will "pay all charges and no questions asked." I long to hear his glowing account of your hospitalities, as he turns his heart inside out, and lets the golden medals fall.

I am in great haste this morning, eager to see the faces of some friends, and have therefore only time to enclose the letter you request, and which I assure you I am very glad to give.[2]

I shall set about "The Spanish Student" immediately. Graham offers me $150 to let him publish it in his magazine. What do you say to that?[3]

Please let me know what I am sure of getting out of Coleman this spring, and when I shall get it.[4]

Expect a long letter from me in a day or two and remember me,

Ever affectionately yours,
Henry W. Longfellow.[5]

MANUSCRIPT: unrecovered; text from *Uncle Sam Ward and His Circle*, pp. 338–339.

1. Ward had hoped to entertain Dickens for his sisters' sake, among other reasons. See Ward to Longfellow, February 22, 1842 (*Uncle Sam Ward and His Circle*, p. 337).

2. On February 18 Ward had requested Longfellow to write a letter recommending Charles Mersch — who had now abandoned hope of a Harvard professorship — for a chair in German literature just established at Columbia. Longfellow's letter is unrecovered.

3. Ward had admonished him: "And now I want you to lose no time in taking up *the Spanish Student.* Purify it and publish it as a dramatic poem and it will sell like bread. See what pleasure the Children of the Lord's Supper gives and the Rainy day which I was almost alone in approving. Remember the Skeleton — and set at once about *Preciosa.* Let me have one peep under her — before you let the veil fall away, and the drapery, and expose the modest and lovely ideal to the public gaze. But let her postures and those of personages grouped around her be decent and let no lecherous Satyr mar the delicacy of the *tableau*" (Letter of February 22, 1842). For the publishing of *The Spanish Student,* see Lawrance Thompson, "Longfellow Sells *The Spanish Student,*" *American Literature,* VI (May 1934), 141–150.

4. See Letter No. 668.

5. A postscript by Sumner follows (*Uncle Sam Ward and His Circle*, pp. 339–340).

## 665. *To Stephen Longfellow*

Cambridge Feb. 27. 1842.

My dear Father,

I had a very pleasant time up on Wednesday, and reached Cambridge before eight o'clock in the evening. I find a new family has moved into the vacant rooms of Castle Craigie; and the old pile has an air of unwonted animation about; not to say anything of unusual noises and peals of laughter. I found Miss. Lowell in great distress at the death of her cat, killed the day before, by two ruffian dogs. She had the body put in a shroud and decently buried. Mother's note delighted her; and I find she is now in better spirits.

My friend Felton has just returned from New York. He brings me a note from Dickens; a copy of which I send you, that you may see what a cordial person he is.

"My dear Longfellow

You are coming to England, you know. Now listen to me. When you return to London, I shall be there, please God. Write me from the continent, and tell me when to expect you. We live quietly — not uncomfortably — and among people whom I am sure you would like to know; as much as they would like to know you. Have no home but mine — see nothing in town on your way towards Germany, and let me be your London host and cicerone. Is this a bargain?

Always faithfully your friend
Charles Dickens"[1]

So hearty an invitation as this I shall not hesitate to accept, if he is in London when I am there. It will render my visit very agreeable.

The Greenleafs are well. They have had sundry long and pleasant letters from James and Mary; and Mrs. Greenleaf begins to count the days between now and their return.

My Lectures begin tomorrow; I have three hours, in the afternoons of Monday, Wednesday and Friday.

With much love to all

Very affectionately
Henry W. Longfellow.

MANUSCRIPT: Longfellow Trust Collection. ADDRESS: Hon S. Longfellow/Portland. POSTMARK: BOSTON MAS. FEB 28

1. Letter datelined "Carlton House./Twenty Third February 1842." MS, Longfellow Trust Collection.

666. *To Samuel Ward*

Cambridge, Feb. 27, 1842.

My dear Sam,

I trust you duly received my letter, written some three days ago, with a few words for Mersch. I now send the other documents,[1] and most sincerely hope they may prove effectual in securing the Professorial Chair you have in view. As to the Bussey bequest, it does not operate upon the College until it has killed three old women, and how long that will be, is not known.[2] I hope Mersch may finally be placed in those fair domains. Keep an eye upon that.

Felton has returned from New York radiant and rejoicing. Yesterday Willis, Sumner, Hillard and he dined with me, together with a younger brother of Willis.[3] Felton entertained us with his New York experiences — his "*roistering and oystering*" as Hillard calls it. He must have had a merry time. You have given him new youth and beauty. He brought me a note from Dickens, containing a very cordial invitation to stay with him in London — "have no home but his house, and make him my host and cicerone." Inclosed is the answer: which I beg you to hand to him, if he has not left N. York; and if he has, give it to David C. Colden, who is his agent — or what not.[4]

I am making my arrangements for a start on the first of May. What ship sails for Havre on that day? and how long in advance should I secure my berth? I am decidedly of your opinion, that a Packet ship is better than a steamer. The steamer of the 4th is not yet in. Great fears are entertained for her safety.[5]

I begin my Lectures tomorrow. Two months will soon be over; and I shall pass a few brief days with you — and away. O that you were going with me!

I have not yet read the *Compagnon*; but will give my first leisure to it. I hope I shall see Geo. Sand. How can I bring it about? Can you put me in the way of making her acquaintance through *Janin*?[6]

Thank you for Schmeide's Novellen. Are they good? Who is Schmeide?[7]

I saw the Ticknors a day or two ago. They are well; and Anna rejoices exceedingly in the Symphonies you sent her. She is *at play* upon them; and finds them delightful.

This is my birth-day. I am thirty-five. Do you not wish you were as old, my dear? We have snow today; a quiet fall of snow. Sumner is passing the Sunday with me; we wish you were here. He is at this present moment down at Felton's. They both desire their kindest remembrances to you.

Ever most truly yours,
Henry W. Longfellow.

MANUSCRIPT: unrecovered; text from "Letters to Samuel Ward, Part III," p. 303.

1. Ward had requested Longfellow to arrange the return of the various documents sent to President Quincy to support Mersch's candidacy for the Harvard professorship (Letter of February 22, 1842).

2. Benjamin Bussey (1757–1842) had died on January 13, leaving a long and complicated will with six women among the principal legatees. The "three old women" were presumably Judith Bussey (his wife), Lucy Bussey (his sister-in-law), and Mrs. Mary Blasland (his first cousin). Harvard University was the residuary legatee, and in 1871 the estate was used to endow the Bussey Institution, an undergraduate school of agriculture at Jamaica Plain.

3. Richard Storrs Willis (1819–1900), a Yale graduate of 1841, later became a composer and editor of musical publications.

4. This letter is unrecovered. David Cadwallader Colden (1797–1850), grandson of Cadwallader Colden, the colonial scholar and political leader of New York, had known Dickens in London. Longfellow may have met him late in January when Colden came to Boston as a special envoy to invite Dickens to the Boz Ball in New York.

5. It was not known until March 11 that the steamer Caledonia, on the seventh day out from Liverpool, had been driven back to Cork by a storm (S. N. Dickinson, *The Boston Almanac for the Year 1843*, I, No. 8, 127).

6. Jules Gabriel Janin (1804–1874), the French novelist and drama critic, whom Ward had known in Paris in 1836. Longfellow called on him in May with Ward's letter of introduction, but Janin had quarreled recently with George Sand

and was unwilling to act as intermediary. See Letter No. 688 and the reminiscence reported by James T. Fields (*Life*, III, 368).

7. Since Ward did not answer this query in his reply of March 1, 1842, and since there seems to have been no author of *novellen* named Schmeide, the transcription is probably incorrect.

## 667. *To William Henry Duncan*[1]

Cambridge March 2. 1842.

Dear Sir,

I have had the honor of receiving your favor of Feb. 8.[2] and regret, that it will not be in my power to accept the Poem, as therein proposed. In a few weeks I sail for Europe, and shall be absent at the time of your anniversary.

Please express my thanks to the Society for the compliment they pay me by their invitation.

Yours very truly
Henry W. Longfellow.

Wm H. Duncan Esq.

MANUSCRIPT: Dartmouth College Library. ADDRESS: Wm H. Duncan Esq/Hanover/N.H.

1. Duncan (1807–1883), a lawyer and member of the Dartmouth class of 1830, had invited Longfellow to Hanover to deliver the Phi Beta Kappa poem on July 27.

2. Duncan's letter was actually written on the 28th.

## 668. *To Samuel Ward*

Cambridge March 5. 1842

My dear Sam,

I have three letters from you, making all together five pages. I have to thank you for comparing me to [Goethe's] Prince Egmont with his *santé désespérante* [desperate health]; and to say that I will attend to Amory's Wine at the earliest moment.[1]

I see by the papers that the *Ville de Lyon* sails for Hâvre on the 24th of April — and is a very large ship. I think I must go in her. I shall gain a week, and *Ich habe mein Herz darauf gestellt* [I have my heart set on it]. This will be better than the Utica will it not?[2] I have an idea that the Ville de Lyon is what one may call a splendid ship. How long beforehand ought I to secure my passage in order to get a good berth?

You speak of Colman's note soon due, as being the last. How can that be? He has not yet paid $300. All I have received from him is $72.50. Then there was the $250 due to you, of which I paid $50.

In reality he has paid only $272 out of $500; and 15 copies of the book. I am curious to see what price he will put upon those. I do not want you to give yourself any trouble about this; but when you see the Broker, who has the notes in his hands, please ask him about it. I should like, if possible, to make a final settlement with Coleman before sailing.[3]

Dr. Tellkampf, a German Professor — one of the unlucky Göttingen Exiles was here a few days ago on his way to New York. He is to leave some letters of Introduction with you for me. So, if a package comes to hand addressed to me, keep it till I come.

Evening.

Felton and myself have been dining with Cleveland. On my way down I took from the office another *page* from you. Let Hunt[4] have 50 bottles of Felton's; and I will tell Sumner to write to his brother[5] in regard to his. They ought each, — that is Felton and Sumner, — to keep 50. If the wine is up to its reputation and the care it has cost, it will never come amiss. However, if you know persons who would like it in New York, it would save trouble to let them take it all. I will get Amory's directions for you as soon as I can.

March. 6.

A stormy Sunday. I have been to Church, and heard a dull sermon which edified me about as much as St. Anthony's did the fishes, as described by Abraham a Santa Clara, in his uncouth Rhyme.[6] Now, having no special vocation nor urgent need for writing, I will dip into *Ritterwesen.*

Very affectionately
Henry W. Longfellow.

P.S. I look forward with the greatest pleasure to my short visit with you. You must so manage it, that I can be under your roof. I can sleep on a sofa in the library — "*wisely,* if not *too well.*"[7] By hook or by crook we can arrange it. Then it will be a visit to you; otherwise I shall not come to New York till the day the ship sails.

MANUSCRIPT: Longfellow Trust Collection. ADDRESS: Samuel Ward Esq/(Prime Ward & King)/New York. POSTMARK: CAMBRIDGE MS. MAR 7 PUBLISHED: "Letters to Samuel Ward, Part III," p. 303.

1. In an exuberant moment in the summer of 1841 Longfellow, Ward, Sumner, Felton, and Charles Amory had ordered 500 bottles of Rhenish wine from Germany (see Letter No. 613). After its arrival in New York the news of its cost — $631.50 according to Ward's letter to Longfellow of February 16, 1842 — caused some sober reflection. Ward sold Longfellow's share for him, and in this letter Longfellow promises to send instructions as to the disposal of the other shares.

Only Amory and Ward, of the original purchasers, seem to have finally enjoyed the product of their indiscretion.

2. Ward's answer of March 9, 1842, was not enthusiastic: "You know she [the *Ville de Lyon*] has a *cracked,* from having had a *crack,* reputation. It is now 2 years since she was blown into the Bermudas by a gale and the passengers exposed to many perils were brought by another vessel to Charleston whence they found their way to New York considerably damaged. I do not doubt she has been fully repaired but think it my duty to mention this fact to you." Longfellow nevertheless took the ship.

3. Ward had written on February 25 that Colman's "last note of $70— falls due on the 4th April and I believe it will be paid." Longfellow seems to have felt that he could hold Colman, despite his bankruptcy, to his contract regarding *Hyperion.* The terms of the final settlement are not known.

4. Freeman Hunt (1804–1858), editor, publisher, and minor author, was engaged at this time in editing the *Merchants Magazine and Commercial Review* of New York.

5. Albert Sumner (1812–1856) of New York.

6. Longfellow later included "Saint Anthony's Sermon to the Fishes," an anonymous selection from *Judas, der Erzschelm* by Abraham a Sancta Clara (1644–1709), in *Poets and Poetry of Europe,* pp. 241–242.

7. Cf. *Othello,* V, ii, 343.

## 669. *To Anne Longfellow Pierce*

Cambridge March 6. 1842

My dearest Annie,

I am much obliged to you for your note and to the *Wonderment*[1] for the shirts, which seem to be very good in material and very charmingly made. Some slight variation and shadow of change they must however undergo; but that can be done here, without giving you any farther trouble. Upon the whole, I think I will not have any more made at present; but will content myself with these. It would hardly be possible to get any made (as I want them), before my departure, which wind and weather permitting will be on the 24th of April; or sometime between the 20th and 30th. If I need a farther supply I can get it in New York before sailing. Therefore you need not engage any more.

There is nothing new here in Cambridge excepting the arrival of Mr. Cleveland and his family, particular friends of mine, who have moved to Cambridge for a year or two, in order to take care of younger brothers,[2] who are in College. This makes Cambridge pleasanter than ever; and makes me more reluctant to leave it; but I shall not change my plans on that account, as my health is no better; and I am *determined* not to linger along in this way any longer, if it can be prevented by any action of my own. I mention the 24th of April as the day of sailing, because a fine ship leaves New York on that day; and unless something new turns up, I shall take passage in her.

Your friends here are all well. Aunt Sally [Lowell] has determined not to "shut herself up so any longer," but is coming out again; — with which movement I fear the mud and mire and bad weather may somewhat interfere for the present. She says she has a mortal disease upon her, and sat up the other night till five o'clock in the morning, reading Barnaby Rudge, totally unconscious of the passage of time.

Thank you for the little poem. It is very beautiful; more so on a second and third reading. It will be a gem in my collection. I received, a few days ago, a very pretty poem, in a female hand — addressed to me — but anonymous. I will send it to you by first opportunity; for I think you will like it.[3]

Yours very affectionately
H. W. L.

P. S. How comes on the frame of my picture?

MANUSCRIPT: Longfellow Trust Collection. ADDRESS: Mrs. A. L. Pierce/Care of S. Longfellow Esq/Portland. POSTMARK: CAMBRIDGE MS. MAR 7

1. Anne Pierce's note is lost and the allusion is cryptic; perhaps Longfellow refers to a Portland tailoring establishment.

2. Sarah Cleveland's brothers, Charles and Edward Perkins.

3. See Letter No. 675. Neither poem is recovered.

## 670. *To John Tomlin*[1]

Cambridge, March 17, 1842.

My Dear Sir. —

Your favor of February 28th ult. did not reach me till yesterday. I beg you to accept my thanks for your expressions of regard. I feel sincerely happy when I hear that anything I have written from my own heart finds a response in another's. I feel this to be the best reward an author can receive; as his highest privilege is to speak words of sincerity to those who in sincerity will hear them.

Reciprocating your good wishes,

Very truly yours,
Henry W. Longfellow.

MANUSCRIPT: unrecovered; text from *Holden's Dollar Magazine,* II (December 1848), 717.

1. Tomlin (1806–1850), minor poet and periodical writer, was at this time postmaster of Jackson, Tennessee. Elizabeth C. Phillips has accumulated the details of his life and literary career in an unpublished dissertation, "The Literary Life of John Tomlin, Friend of Poe," University of Tennessee (1953).

671. *To Stephen Longfellow*

Cambridge March. 27. 1842

My dear Father,

My conscience smites me, when I think how long it is, that I have not written to you. I neither know *how* nor *why* it has so happened; but I have been remiss in my correspondence with every one of late.

I had a very pleasant little visit from Alexander. He left me on Tuesday last, in the midst of a snow-storm, to start with the Commodore [A. S. Wadsworth] for New York. You have probably heard from him since that time. The Commodore I hardly saw. He was very busy; and had not time to come out to Cambridge; much less to go to Portland, which he seemed to regret very much; particularly, as I told him, you would all be disappointed in not seeing him before his return to Washington.

There is nothing particularly new here at present; save the account of the invasion of Texas by the Mexicans; which came in the Extra daily papers this afternoon.[1]

Dr. Channing has in press a pamphlet on the Creole case. He takes ground against Mr. Webster in his instructions to Mr. Edward Everett in London. I understand the book is very eloquently written.[2]

Dr. [Ichabod] Nichols is still here. I met him at tea last evening at Mr. Worcester's, — (my landlord.) He seems well; and is so, saving a neuralgic affection in the face. I prescribed homœopathy.

For more than a fortnight my dear friend Felton has been very ill with a rheumatic fever; suffering great agony, and stupified with opium. In an evil hour he abandoned homœopathy for the old practice; and is paying the penalty. He is however better; and I hope may have no relapse.

Incendiaries are busy here again. The old house opposite to us, belonging to Mr. Batchelder[3] was set on fire a few days ago, in broad day-light; but was saved, with some considerable damage. Two barns have been consumed within the week; and a suspicious individual was found lurking round our premises a few nights ago, between the hours of one and two, probably with no friendly intentions. I do not feel much alarmed; being insured — I mean my books and furniture.

Sam as well as usual.

With much love to all,
||Henry W. Longfellow||

MANUSCRIPT: Longfellow Trust Collection. ADDRESS: Hon. S. Longfellow/Portland. POSTMARK: BOSTON MS. MAR 29

1. On March 5, 1842, General Rafael Vasquez occupied San Antonio in a

maneuver to demonstrate Mexican rights in Texas. His force left on March 7, having accomplished little more than to excite the Texans.

2. In November, 1841, a cargo of slaves being carried from Hampton Roads to New Orleans aboard the brig *Creole* took possession of the ship by force and sailed her to Nassau. The British authorities held the leaders of the mutiny on criminal charges but freed the rest. The case then became a *cause célèbre,* with Secretary of State Webster demanding the return of all the slaves for trial in the U. S. and Channing and others using the incident to enlarge on their antislavery sentiments. Channing's pamphlet was *The Duty of the Free States; or, Remarks Suggested by the Case of the* Creole (Boston, 1842).

3. Samuel Batchelder (1784–1879), inventor and businessman, was prominent in the cotton manufactory of New England.

## 672. *To Joseph Bosworth*

Cambridge March 30 1842.

My dear Sir,

I have to thank you for two very kind and welcome letters, of October 6th. and Jany. 13th. The first of these I should have answered long ago; had not indisposition and absence prevented me. I had a fever in the Autumn, which confined me for many weeks; and afterward went to visit my parents in Portland.

I am rejoiced to hear that a new edition of your dictionary in a condensed form is about to appear.[1] It is a noble work; and merits the success it has met with.

My own literary labors have been slight. I have published only a second volume of Poems; a copy of which I put into the hands of Little &co for you. It contains a translation of Tegnér's *Nattwardsbarnen,* which I trust you will find time to read. In the same package is a copy for the Vicar of Southwick. Many thanks to you for the copy of his Sanscrit Grammar; which is indeed a great literary curiosity.[2]

I shall be in Europe almost as soon as this letter; but alas! not in England. I am going to the Continent for my health; and shall pass the Summer at *Marienberg bei Boppard am Rhein,* where I hope to hear from you. I go to make use of the water, having much faith in the *Wassercur.* If in the Autumn I do not go to Italy, I shall return home through England; and if the thing is possible, will run down to Nottingham expressly to see you and Mrs. Bosworth to whom present my best regards.[3]

The package I will direct to your publishers — that *long* firm of Longman and five others.[4] I hope it may reach you without charge; a consideration which always makes me pause when about sending a package to England; for fear the game should not be worth the candle.

Very truly and affectionately yours.
Henry W. Longfellow

P. S. I had a letter a few weeks ago from Bishop Tegnér. He urges me to translate Frithiofs Saga. Instead thereof I have prefer[r]ed the shorter poem, — the Children of the Lord's Supper, — which I hope you will like.

MANUSCRIPT: Pierpont Morgan Library. ENDORSEMENT: Longfellow Prof/Recd. April 22d 1842/Ansd. July 23d. 1842.

1. This abridgment, entitled *A Compendious Anglo-Saxon and English Dictionary* and published in London by J. R. Smith, did not appear until 1848.

2. Thomas Richard Brown (1791–1875), vicar of Southwick, wrote *The Essentials of Sanscrit Grammar, With Examples of Parsing* (Southwick, 1841).

3. Bosworth had left Holland in 1841 because of his wife's ill health and was residing at Carrington, near Nottingham.

4. Longman, Hurst, Rees, Orme, Brown & Green.

## 673. *To Stephen Longfellow*

Cambridge April 5 1842

My dear Father,

I have pretty much made up my mind to go on the 24th in the Ville de Lyon, one of the Havre Packets. It is a ship of 800 tons; one of the best in the line. From Havre I shall go to Antwerp by steamboat; and thence by rail-road to Cologne. At least such is my present plan. I begin to grow rather impatient; and want to get away. I promise myself great pleasure in the tour; and am confident I shall return in perfect health.

There is nothing new here. The writers in the North American Review, I will send you as soon as I can get them from the Editor. I know but a few of them now.

I send by to-day's mail to Judge Potter a draft for the money I still owed him; and yesterday, I paid the remainder of the Howard note,[1] which you had endorsed. So these old scores are entirely wiped off.

April 6th.

I have just received Anne's note and package by Jno: Owen, for which many thanks to her, and the promise of writing soon.

In haste,

Very affectionately yours
Henry W. Longfellow.

MANUSCRIPT: Longfellow Trust Collection. ADDRESS: Hon. S. Longfellow/Portland

1. Presumably held by Dr. John Clark Howard (212.1).

## 674. *To Samuel Ward*

Cambridge, April 5, 1842.

My dear Sam,

I received your last on Saturday evening. I had just come from town where I had seen Ticknor who told me of Cogswell's destiny as a great secret. On leaving the house, I took a stroll down Beacon Street with Prescott. He told me the same story. "But it is a great secret, Ticknor says," quoth I. "Yes, a very great secret" said Ferdinand, "it is in all the New York papers." On reaching home I found your letter confirming the news. I am both glad and sorry. I hoped to have Cogswell as a fellow-passenger in the *Ville de Lyon,* and I think he would have enjoyed a short residence at the Court of Spain.[1]

My plans are now pretty clearly defined. I shall sail for Havre in the *Ville de Lyon*: — and I shall want you to go to the ship and select me a stateroom; put my name on the lower berth, and that of Richard S. Willis on the upper. This is a younger brother of Nat. P. Willis. We go together.[2] If the agent wants the money he may draw upon me and Willis separately at sight: tho' I don't think it worth while unless he is very hungry for money. Upon the whole this seems the best arrangement we can make: for I fear the vessels direct to Antwerp will not be very good: and I like a little comfort at sea. The *Ville de Lyon* is advertised for April 24th which is Sunday. Will she sail on that day or Saturday? or Monday?

Willis is going to pass three or four years in Germany to study music. He already composes with a good deal of skill; and has several pieces full of feeling and fancy which I should like to have you hear. One of them is "Spring," with the gushing of waters, waving of boughs, singing of birds, etc. Another is "Undine," the flowing of a stream in shadow and sunshine — very beautiful. His music is like his brother's poetry.

I hope your mind is at length serene. What has the matter been? You have made known to me nothing. I hope there has been no serious trouble: — nothing worse than navigating the ship of commerce through breakers and icebergs.

For my own part, I begin to tug and pull, like a vessel whose sails are spread, but whose anchor is not yet up.

Felton is much better, "sitting clothed and in his right mind."[3]

Cleveland is now living in Cambridge: and the place is pleasanter than ever. His pleasant house is a great resource to me.

Yours ever truly,
H. W. L.

MANUSCRIPT: unrecovered; text from "Letters to Samuel Ward, Part III," p. 304.

1. See 435.6. Because of John Jacob Astor's procrastination in the matter of the Astor Library, Cogswell had accepted a position as secretary of legation under Irving in Spain. This move prompted Astor to reach a decision. He induced Cogswell to resign the secretaryship by promising to make the endowment for the library and by guaranteeing him the librarianship.

2. Willis (666.3) studied music in Frankfurt-am-Main and Leipzig.

3. Mark 5:15.

## 675. *To Anne Longfellow Pierce*

[Cambridge] April 6th 1842

My dearest Annie,

I hear of a good opportunity of sending to Portland; and avail myself of it to write you a line, and send the poem you desire. I think it very pretty, more than pretty. But after all, is this || . . . ||?

|| . . . || for the package of || . . . ||.[1] I am rather in a hurry; but certainly have time to write to you, dear Annie; time enough, at least to acknowledge your letters. I have done as you desired me to do in regard to the Judge [Barrett Potter], though not quite so promptly as I could have wished; owing to the difficulty of making my debtors pay me. But now the whole matter is arranged.

Your surmise about the College Tutor, (namely, that his appointment was "merely a movement to prevent Sam from applying") is unfounded. The person nominated is Parker, son of the late Dr. Parker of Portsmouth, and a very good scholar. &c.[2] Sam did not apply soon enough; and after knowing of Parker's nomination, it would be ungraceful in him to become his rival.

With much love to all,
||Henry W. Longfellow||

P.S. I am quite ignorant of the authoress of this poem. It came to me in a blank cover.

MANUSCRIPT: Longfellow Trust Collection. ADDRESS: Mrs. Anne Pierce/Portland

1. When the signature was cut out of this letter, about six or eight words were lost where indicated.

2. Francis Edward Parker (1821–1886), a member of the Harvard class of 1841, subsequently withdrew as a candidate, and the tutorship went to Evangelinus Apostolides Sophocles (1807–1883), later professor of Greek, 1860–1883. Parker was the son of Rev. Nathan Parker (1782–1833), tutor at Bowdoin, 1805–1807, and pastor of the South Parish Church in Portsmouth for many years.

676. *To an Unidentified Correspondent*

Cambridge. April 14. 1842.

Mr. Howorth[1] has cleaned and repaired for me a large Painting by Copely. It was in a very bad state; the canvass being cut and broken in several places. It is now in fine condition; and I am perfectly satisfied with the skilful manner of the reparations.

Henry W. Longfellow

MANUSCRIPT: Bowdoin College Library.

1. The *Boston Directory* for 1842 lists "George Howorth, Restorer of old paintings, 1 Bradford Place." See 636.2 and Letter No. 650.

677. *To Stephen Longfellow*

Cambridge. April 17. 1842.

My dear Father,

I was very glad to get your letter a few days ago; but am sorry to perceive that you feel so gloomily about my going away. It is only lengthening the vacation a little; and you will see me back again, well and in good spirits, before you feel that I [have] gone. The undertaking gives me no more trouble or anxiety, than if I were going to New York only; and the anticipation of renewed health makes the whole affair rather a gay one. I wish you could be induced to take as decided a step in regard to your own health. At all events, I think you ought to try Homœopathy; indeed I cannot urge it upon you too strongly. Here is Hillard, sitting by my side, who in his own family within the last few months has had cured by it, Typhus fever, rheumatic fever, lung fever, and a case of chronic sick-headache — of many years' standing, which had entirely baffled the other doctors. I most sincerely hope that you will consult a Homœopathist, and when you feel another fit coming on, take the remedies he prescribes; and I feel confident you will find great relief.

I promised to send you the writers in the N. A. Review. Here are all the names I have been able to get

Art. I. Professor Felton.
II. Mr. Schoolcraft.[1]
III. Unknown[2]
IV. Wm. H. Prescott Esq
V. Mr. Charles Bowen.
VI. Prof. Felton

VII. Mrs. Robinson (a German lady)[3]
VIII. Lieut. H. Davis (son of Sollicitor)[4]
IX. Geo: S. Hillard Esq
X. Unknown [Henry Colman].

With regard to the picture,[5] pray do not trouble yourself. It had better remain in Portland until my return.

I shall sail from New York on Monday the 25th in the Ville de Lyon; a fine ship, with her cabin on deck. I shall probably leave Cambridge as early as Thursday next. I shall write again from New York.

With much love to all,

Very affectionately yours
Henry W. Longfellow.

MANUSCRIPT: Longfellow Trust Collection. ADDRESS: Hon. S. Longfellow/Portland POSTMARK: CAMBRIDGE MS. APR 19

1. Henry Roe Schoolcraft (1793–1864), the ethnologist.

2. Joshua Forman (1777–1848), founder of Syracuse, New York, and promoter of the Erie Canal.

3. Therese Albertina Louise von Jacob (1797–1869), linguist, translator, and author of considerable talent. She was the wife of Edward Robinson, the biblical scholar and professor in the Union Theological Seminary, New York City.

4. Lieutenant Davis (610.7), son of Daniel Davis (1762–1835), solicitor general of Massachusetts, 1800–1832.

5. Apparently the Cole portrait mentioned in Letter No. 663.

## 678. *To Henry Russell Cleveland*

New York. April 24. 1842

My dear Cleveland,

Allow me to present to your friendly attention Mr. Charles Kentgen of Berlin, who means to pass a few days or weeks in Cambridge. I am desirous, of course that he should see you. He is a traveller: has been in Mexico and the West Indies; and is now giving some time to the United States, to satisfy his curiosity.[1]

Yours very truly
H. W. Longfellow

MANUSCRIPT: Berg Collection, New York Public Library. ADDRESS: Henry R. Cleveland Esq/Cambridge

1. Kentgen arrived in Cambridge shortly after May 1, filled with misconceptions about life in America. Cleveland's amused description of his odd notions in a letter of June 15, 1842, brought forth the exclamation by Longfellow: "How could he be such a *boob*" (Letter No. 701).

679. *To Stephen Longfellow*

New York. April 24. 1842.

My dear Father,

I arrived here yesterday and am very comfortably quartered upon my friend Ward. The Ville de Lyons does not sail until Tuesday 26th. so that I have leisure to see my friends here.

April 25.

I was interrupted yesterday just as I began to write you, by my friend, who took me out to walk. We dined at Mr. [William Backhouse] Astor's; and the evening I passed with the Bryants.

The weather to-day is delightful; and everything promises a good beginning of our voyage. We shall doubtless have a calm and rather long one; but perhaps I shall not be very sick. I have a notion I shall enjoy it upon the whole; and am confident I shall be the better for it. At all events I shall return quite well; which I beg you to bear in mind, and to consider it an ample recompense for the trouble and inconvenience of a sea-voyage.

I have been on board our ship. She is a large, fine ship; but the accommodations are not very good. The state-rooms are small; but in return, they are on deck, and can be well ventilated. We have twenty six passengers. Consequently we shall not be crowded. I am quite impatient to sail; and hope there will be no farther delay; though I should not be much surprized to hear tomorrow morning, that we are to wait a day or two longer. On Saturday hardly any of her cargo had been taken on board. In the same state-room with myself is Willis, — not the Poet, but his younger brother, who is going to Germany to study music. He means to be gone for four years. I like him very much; — he is amiable and I hope a good sailor, as I wish to monopolise all the sea-sickness of our state-room.

But good night, and good bye. It is now very near midnight; and I have another letter to write.

Much love to you all.

Very truly yours
Henry W. Longfellow.

MANUSCRIPT: Longfellow Trust Collection. ADDRESS: Hon. S. Longfellow/Portland/Me POSTMARK: BOSTON ||MS|| APR 28 [1]

1. Longfellow presumably forwarded this letter to George Hillard for posting in Boston. See 683.4.

## 680. *To Alexander Wadsworth Longfellow*

New York. April 26. 1842.

My dear Alex,

I am much obliged to you for your long and welcome letter, which I found here on my arrival; and would send you one as long in return, had I time. But the sands run fast. And moreover I have a thousand last things to do, which would have remained undone, had we sailed on our regular day, which was Sunday. We have been detained here, first, by not having our cargo on board; and secondly by a head wind, which set in this morning. The first favorable blast, will waft us out into the deep.

The portraits in Griswold's book are certainly unhappy specimens. I think, however, that I am the best of the set. If I look as though I had stolen a sheep, the others look as though they were going to be hanged for it. It is a bad business; but how is it to be helped.[1]

I hope you are enjoying yourself in Washington. Remember me most kindly to Aunt Louisa; and tell her I will get the Music she wants from Germany, and anything else. I will select such pieces as seem to me to lie within the reach of Louly's fingers, and some which do not, as a provision for the future. I doubt however whether I shall be able to send them before my return. That will depend upon accident.

I am sorry you did not see more of the Wards when you were here. Sam says you mistook the hour of taking tea with him. You came at six instead of seven, and he was out with his sisters. He regrets he did not see more of you; and so do I. No matter; it will be for another time.

When you return, step in some evening to the Olympic Theatre, near Niblo's Garden in Broadway. You will there see some clever burlesques; and a very good comic actor by the name of Mitchel.[2] I was there last night to see *Boz*; an imitation of Dickens's reception in New York. Dickens was represented very well by Horncastle[3] who looks like him, and has caught his manner and way of speaking very well. It is rather an absurd affair; with some good jokes; as for instance, the invitation from the firemen to see a fire, with a request to know, whether it should be a single house or a whole block; — and another to see a steamer burst her boiler! But perhaps you saw the piece when you were here.

I hope you will write to me when I am in Europe. I shall be delighted to hear from you; though I cannot promise to be a good correspondent, having so many letters to write. My address will be *Marien-*

*berg bey Boppart am Rhein*; and you can send by the Hâvre Packets, by paying to New York.

Good bye. With kindest regards to Aunt, Mrs Greenhow[4] and my other Washington friends,

Very truly yours
Henry W. Longfellow.

MANUSCRIPT: University of Washington Library. ADDRESS: Mr. Alexander W. Longfellow/Care of Commodore Wadsworth/Washington. ANNOTATION (*by Longfellow*): Paid POSTMARKS: NEW-YORK APR 27/PAID

1. Alexander Longfellow had written on April 21, 1842: "I cant tell you how much disappointed I am in Thompson's portrait of you from which they are engraving the head in Philadelphia. I grieve that it is to be perpetuated. It has a sneaking, downcast and sinister expression, which belongs to any body sooner than to yourself. You look, on that canvass, as if you had been stealing sheep, which I am confident you never did." See 639.3.

2. William Mitchell (1798–1856), English actor and stage manager, ran the Olympic Theatre, 1839–1850. "This house was frequented by the wits and men-about-town, and became popular for the performance of operas in miniature, farces, and burlesques, in which the manager usually performed the leading parts" (*Appleton's Cyclopedia of American Biography*, IV, 348).

3. Henry Horncastle (1802–1869), an English actor. The "quizzical and satirical extravaganza" called "Boz" is described in George C. D. Odell, *Annals of the New York Stage* (New York, 1927–1949), IV, 579.

4. Rose O'Neal Greenhow (d. 1864), who lived near the Wadsworths at 4 Franklin Row, Washington, was the wife of Robert Greenhow (1800–1854), physician, historian, linguist, and at this time translator in the Department of State. An impassioned Southerner, Mrs. Greenhow became a leader in Washington society and, during the Civil War, a notorious Confederate spy. See Margaret Leech, *Reveille in Washington 1860–1865* (New York and London, 1941), *passim.*

## 681. *To Charles Sumner*

New York. April 26. 1842

My dear Charles,

Your letter reached me this afternoon, and made my heart swell into my throat. But I have determined to put away all doubts and fears, and half-formed, vain regrets, and all the gloomy forebodings which are wont to haunt the imaginations of the outward-bound. I send you back, therefore, none of the darkness, which as you can easily imagine, (you, who know so well how truly I love my friends) — at times usurps the empire of my thoughts; but a parting gleam of sunshine, as a last farewell and benediction. Meanwhile I treasure up your kind, parting words in my inmost soul; and will read your letter over again far out at sea, and hear in it friendly voices from the shore.[1]

I have passed three days very pleasantly here; though my impatience hardly brooks any delay, and I am restless to begin my pilgrimage. The Wards are all well; and little Annie smiles meek and childlike still as when you saw her. Julia thinks you might have called a second time to see them. I think so likewise; for she is certainly a remarkable person, and worth a half-dozen calls, at least. Louisa you will see in Boston on Friday next. Sam is as multifarious as usual; in the morning reads Livy an hour before breakfast with Mersch; — then hurries down to his business; — rides on horseback *before* dinner, and sings Italian duets *after*. Of the other individuals I have seen, my letter to Felton will inform you.[2] Cogswell tells me, that McCrackan did not write the article on *Petrarca*.[3] Wilde wrote it! Mc. wrote one in which he called Laura a humbug, and Petrarca a fool; but Cogswell would not print it. I have seen to-day John O. Sargent and Epes. John O. says he is doing a good deal of business, and Epes is writing children's books for the Harpers; — and a Tragedy for Forrest.[4]

I have been this evening to see a play called *Boz*. It is a caricature on Dickens's reception here. Dickens is very well represented by Horncastle. The best joke in the piece is the invitation from the members of an Engine Company to see a fire, and the accompanying request to know, whether he will have a single house burnt, or a whole block. He is also invited to see a steamer burst her boiler on the North River! I tried exceedingly hard to amuse myself; but found it rather dull.

But one of my candles is sinking in its socket. It is nearly one o'clock; and I am the only person up, in the house. So you see, I devote my last moments and last thoughts to you. Think of me often and long. My kindest remembrances to Hillard, Cleveland and Howe, and farewells to all my friends. You hardly know what it costs me to leave you all. But I see the beckoning hand, and follow trustingly.

Once more *Benedicte!* When this reaches you I shall be rocking on the broad sea; and thinking of you all through many long hours.

Ever affectionately yours
Henry W. Longfellow

P.S. At this very moment two voices not the most melodious are singing under the window *"Thou thou reignest in this bosom!"* A serenade to — which of the three? If to Julia they will not gain much by the transaction. They sing too horribly out of tune.

They have now got to "Oft in the Stilly Night!" and [it] is quite intolerable. I expect Sam or Uncle John to interfere; if they do not, I shall.

MANUSCRIPT: Longfellow Trust Collection. ADDRESS: Charles Sumner Esq/Boston./Mass [*in another hand*]

1. Sumner's letter, dated April 23, 1842, is printed in *Sumner Memoir and Letters,* II, 205–206.
2. This letter is unrecovered.
3. J. L. H. McCracken (c. 1813–1853) was a New York merchant and literary amateur whose chef d'oeuvre, the five-act comedy *Earning a Living,* was printed in six installments in the *United States Magazine and Democratic Review,* XXV and XXVI (1849–1850). The article on Petrarch appeared in the *New York Review,* X (April 1842), 294–330.
4. Epes Sargent wrote several juvenile works for Harper Brothers, the best-known being *Wealth and Worth* (New York, 1840) and *What's To Be Done, or The Will and the Way* (New York, 1841). The tragedy for Edwin Forrest did not materialize.

## 682. *To Henry Russell Cleveland*

[New York]
Wednesday morning [April 27, 1842]

My dear Henry,

(This looks to me as if I were writing to myself — and I came near inditing my whole signature). I write you this last word between the shrimp and the ground, or to speak more correctly between land and water. I am off in ten minutes; and contrive to stuff these last letters in between now and my departure, as we hastily stuff the last things into a carpet bag.

Never was a fairer morning for a start. With such a wind we shall reach Newfoundland in a very short time. Shall I send you another dog, or another fog?

Addio, carissimo

Yours ever
H. W. L.

MANUSCRIPT: Berg Collection, New York Public Library.

## 683. *To George Stillman Hillard*

Marienberg bey Boppart am Rhein
Wednesday. April 27. 1842.

My dear George,

I reached this delightful spot on Saturday last, by water. Dr. Schmit[1] received me with a very cordial, pump-handle shake of the hand; and took my measure for a tub. I have already made several acquaintances, and find the women very interesting *à douchanter* [while taking showers]. I shall —

And here my dream closed. I awoke in New York, and heard a chimney-sweeper sing Excelsior. I saw the sun shining bright, and from sundry chimneys the blue smoke streaming east-ward, like the pennons from the masts of ships. Every-thing indicates, that we sail to-day; and before putting the last packages into my trunk, (pray relieve Sumner's mind by informing him, that I have bought a new one of proper dimensions.) I will write a few words to you.

And first of all, — I wish to have the Spanish Student published as soon as possible. If Owen does not want it, or cannot pay for it, let Little and Brown have it. You need not wait to hear from Graham. The terms, *twelve cents* on each copy printed to be paid on the day of publication. The style of getting out, like the other books.

I want, likewise, to have the picture at Dogget's sold for three hundred dollars, or as much more as possible. Why wont you get Franklin Dexter's opinion on the subject and that of some other; — *Davis* of the Athenaeum for instance.[2] In fine, get it sold for the most you can; and if it falls short of my price, why no matter.

And so once more farewell. Prescott I hear arrived last night. I am going down to see him now. In a few hours I shall be in that floating castle, buffeting the waves. I read your poem yesterday in the newspaper with a moist eye.[3] Good bye, — good bye.

Ever very truly yours
Henry W. Longfellow

P.S. Please send the inclosed [4] as soon as possible.

I could not find Prescott. I shall be off in a few minutes, with a lovely west-wind and fine spirits.

MANUSCRIPT: The Carl H. Pforzheimer Library, New York. ADDRESS: George S. Hillard Esq/Boston. ANNOTATION (*by Sam Ward*): L —— sailed yesterday (27th Apl) Wednesday — a[t] 1/2 past 12.A.M. SW.

1. Dr. Franz Josef Schmitz (1803–1847), owner, manager and chief physician of the Badanstalt Marienberg, the spa that Longfellow had chosen for his treatments.

2. Longfellow had apparently left his "Copley" painting (636.2) at John Doggett & Company, 37 Tremont Row, to be framed. Isaac P. Davis (1771–1855), a trustee of the Boston Athenaeum, was much interested in art.

3. Hillard's poem, "Lines Addressed to the Ship Ville de Lyon, Which Sails from New York for Havre, Tomorrow, April 24th," appeared in the Boston *Daily Advertiser and Patriot* on April 23, 1842. See *Life,* I, 417–418.

4. Presumably letters that Longfellow wanted Hillard to forward.

684. *To Catherine Eliot Norton*

[New York]
Wednesday morning. [April 27, 1842]

My dear Mrs. Norton,

As I have five minutes before the carriage comes to take me to the boat, I cannot forbear writing two words to take leave of you once more. We have been detained here by head-winds and foul weather; but this morning literally laughs with sunshine; and all the clouds and flags and vanes point sea-ward.

The air is fresh and jubilant; and to this my own heart responds. Indeed I almost reproach myself for not being more sad.

Farewell, once more. I take with me such bright images of you all, that they alone would make sunshine in a shadier place than my heart.

Ever very truly yours
Henry W. Longfellow

MANUSCRIPT: Harvard College Library.

685. *To Stephen Longfellow*

Ville de Lyon 17 May. 1842

My dear Father,

Here we are, beating about in the British Channel, between the Lizard and Casket Lights. We have made a glorious voyage, till within the last few days. In seventeen days we had crossed sea, and made the southern shore of England, at the entrance of the Channel. Since then we have had head-winds, and make but little progress. We are within a day's sail of Havre, but cannot reach our harbour. The Pilot came on board to-day; and I write you these few lines in the hope of having a chance to send them as soon as we arrive.

The passage has been a pleasant one though cold; and we have dashed on frequently at the rate of two hundred and fifty miles a day. My fellow passengers are a worthy set; French, German, Spanish and American. There is on board a Dr. Durbin, President of the Weslyian College at Carlyle (Penn.)[1] with four hobbledehoys under his wing, all quite green; some half-dozen Frenchmen with dogs and moustachios; a fat Flemish merchant, with a beard like a goat; a retired dealer in ready-made clothes from Charleston, the but[t] of the ship, and who for a long time believed that the Prince de Joinville[2] was on b[o]ard disguised in woman's clothes; a German woman; two French women; and an American girl, in love with one of the Frenchmen, but on whose cheeks "the pale livery of sea-sickness has succeeded to the *red regimentals* of the tender passion."

May 18.

We are working slowly around toward Havre; and expect to be in tomorrow morning to breakfast. It is now after nine at night; and the Frenchmen are drinking punch and singing merrily. I hasten to finish this note; to slip it into the Post tomorrow. Two of the Frenchmen have had a quarrel; and one of them is now waiting with his cane to give the other a threshing. We shall doubtless have a noisy night of it. It will soon be over; and we shall set foot on *terra firma* again.

The voyage has done me good. I am in good spirits and have a good appetite.

With much love to you all

Very affectionately yours
Henry W. Longfellow.

P. S. I wish Annie would write a line to Miss Lowell to let her know of my safe arrival; as I have not time.

MANUSCRIPT: Longfellow Trust Collection. ADDRESS: Hon. S. Longfellow/Portland./Me/U.S.America./Per Great Western/Steamer. POSTMARKS: HAVRE (74) 19 MAI/LONDON SHIP LETTER PAID [*month and day illegible*] 1842/NEW-YORK SHIP JUN 5/PD

1. Longfellow's facts are twisted. John Price Durbin (1800–1876), a minister of the Methodist Episcopal Church, had been professor of natural science in Wesleyan University and was at this time president of Dickinson College, Carlisle.

2. François Ferdinand Philippe Louis Marie (1818–1900), prince de Joinville and third son of King Louis Philippe.

## 686. *To John Owen*

Paris May 26. 1842

My dear Owen,

Please send *immediately* to Hector Bossange [1]

12 Voices of the Night
12 Ballads &c

the small edition, and put down to my account. Send these as soon as possible. If you publish the Spanish Student.[2]

I start to day for Brussels. Kind remembrances to all my Cambridge friends.

Yours very truly
Henry W. Longfellow

MANUSCRIPT: Yale University Library.

1. Bossange (b. 1795) was a well-known bookseller in Paris, whose father had established the firm.

2. This sentence was not completed.

## 687. *To Henry Russell Cleveland, Cornelius Conway Felton, George Stillman Hillard, and Charles Sumner*

Paris. May 26. 1842.

My dear *Children*

I have been here four or five days; and leave the gayeties of Paris for the dreams of Germany in the course of a few hours. There was no steamer from Havre to Antwerp; and the Rotterdam boat had departed the day before our arrival; and the next boat did not start for five days. Hence I am here.

I have found your brother,[1] my dear Charley — and scrawl this in his rooms [in the] *Hotel Favart.* You remember the old Dutch Landlady.

Much love to all *four* of you; and kind remembrances to the Ticknors, Nortons, Howe, Miss Lowell, the Guilds

&c &c &c.

H. W. L.

MANUSCRIPT: Longfellow Trust Collection. ADDRESS: Charles Sumner Esq/ Boston

1. George Sumner (1817–1863), political economist and writer, was in the fourth year of a fourteen-year residence abroad, during which he traveled extensively in Europe, Asia, and Africa.

## 688. *To Samuel Ward*

Marienberg bei Boppart, June 5, 1842.

My dear Sam,

I have just received yours of the 13th May. Many, many thanks. This is your second, since I left you. The first reached me in a most amusing way. We were landing at Havre in a little boat, not being able to come quite up to the quai in our own ship; when abreast of us, running along the wharf, and waving a paper in his hand appeared an individual, who as soon as he was near enough to be heard, shouted my name with sundry fantastic gestures. At first I thought it must be a sheriff with a writ; but upon landing I found it to be a messenger from Hollings [Hottinguers] [1] with your letter. I leave you to imagine how glad I was to meet the grasp of your hand, on reaching

Havre; and I should have answered your most welcome salutation with an immediate reply, had I not been too much in haste to set forward on my journey hitherward.

There was no steamer for Antwerp; and the boat for Rotterdam sailed the day before we reached Havre; and went but once a week. I at once concluded, therefore, to go to Paris; and so on by land; and took the first Diligence for Paris.

Our passage was twenty-two days; not an unpleasant one, on the contrary, very pleasant, till we were becalmed four days in the Channel. I liked the Captain much. He is a very good fellow. A brother of Kasowski, the musician,[2] was on board. He suffered exceedingly; so much that he was obliged to stop in Havre to recruit. Of the other passengers I shall say nothing.

In Paris I stopped at the Hôtel de Paris, which I think was your hotel. Of course, I saw Jules Janin. He is living in the Rue Vaugirard, opposite one of the gates of the Luxembourg gardens. His apartment is *au quatrième.* I was shown through his library, up a narrow winding staircase, through a bathing room, into a drawing room, where sat the redoubtable Jules under the barber's hands. He was sitting in an arm chair, his shirt-sleeves rolled up; his feet thrust into a pair of high shoes, and his *ventresaillant* [protruding belly], as the Charivari calls it, arrayed in a pair of brown linen trowsers without straps and not reaching to the tops of his stockings. He read your letter, said I was welcome to his house; and asked a great many questions about you; all of which I answered to the best of my ability. He is a curious character. He has quarrelled with Geo. Sand, Victor Hugo and Alexandre Dumas; — in fine with all the literary characters. He says he does not like them and does not visit any of them. He then washed his face with a huge sponge; shook his ambrosial locks, and invited me to dinner for that evening (Sunday). I accepted the invitation and went. Saw his wife, a very pretty woman, rather a spoiled child; and her mother, who wears green spectacles. There was also at table a rough, silent lawyer, a friend of the family, to whom I was introduced, and did not wish to be. We had a nice little dinner; and after dinner played whist. I left them at ten; upon the whole not very much delighted with Janin. He is not a well-bred man; and is altogether too selfish. He seems to be very happy in his marriage; is desperately in love with his wife; and she with him; — even to caressing and kissing each other at the card-table! He has lately picked a house and garden at Passy, where he means to pass the rest of his days — so he says. As a critic, he still maintains his sway; and there is an amusing caricature of him sitting in a car, drawn by dramatic authorlings.

I was four days in Paris; and then started for Bruxelles; took a run upon the rail-road to Antwerp, Ghent, Bruges; then back to Bruxelles, and on through Aix-la-Chapelle, and Cologne, up the Rhine to this ancient cloister, which embosomed in high hills overlooks the town of Boppard, or Boppart, as it is sometimes written. I reached here Friday evening, June 3rd, on Saturday had a consultation with the doctor; and tomorrow make my first plunge. Today is a holiday, and no bathing except in extreme cases. In the view of Marienberg I have blackened my windows, so that you may see where I am.[3] They look down into the garden, and a wooded valley, with glimpses of the Rhine. It is all exceedingly pleasant thus far, though I am impatient to commence my baths. At present there are only about thirty patients here. My next neighbor at table is an Englishman by the name of Garney, an elderly man, with a moustache. I think he has been an officer in the army.[4] He has gone down the Rhine today to purchased the island and cloister of Nonnenwerth near Bonn, it being for sale; and the prettiest place on the Rhine. Of the other guests hereafter.

As to writing a book upon Germany; I answer I have no such intention. You mistake altogether my position. I am here for my health; and am in retirement among the hills of the Rhine. I shall have little time for study and little opportunity for observation. Besides the elasticity of my mind is gone; and until I get well I shall do nothing but meditate. Thus far the objects that have most delighted me are the Cathedral at Antwerp and the Paintings of Rubens there.[5] These are glorious indeed.

I forgot to tell you that I met De Goy one day on the Boulevard des Italiens. I went home with him to dine; — and where do you think he lives? At Mme. Michu's, No. 7 Rue de Tournain [Tournon]![6] Your memory was as fresh and green there as the peas we had for dinner. I almost expected to see you come in at the door and *manger votre soupe* with us. So strong is the illusion, when we visit a place once inhabited by a friend. Mme. Michu was particular in her inquiries after you, and you have left the odor of sanctity behind you in that habitation.

Do you know the poems of Freiligrath?[7] I bought a copy in Köln. Some of them are striking. He is decidedly the most popular of the young poets. He is expected here tomorrow, and I hope will come.

This is my first letter from Marienberg. When I next write you shall know more of the Wasserkur. Meanwhile remember me to all my friends in New York and Boston; and sweet dreams haunt your brain to-night and forever.

Yours truly,
Henry W. Longfellow.

P.S. What will the Harpers give for the Play,[8] on condition of having it printed in Cambridge uniformly with the other poems?

MANUSCRIPT: unrecovered; text from "Letters to Samuel Ward, Part III," pp. 304–306.

1. Messrs. Hottinguer et Cie, the banking firm of Paris.

2. Little is known of Kossowski, a Polish pianist who played his first concert in Boston on March 7, 1840 (*Daily Evening Transcript*). He is mentioned as having "fire and energy" and "inspiration, as well as skill in his performances" in *The Dial: A Magazine for Literature, Philosophy, and Religion,* I (July 1840), 129.

3. Longfellow's stationery bore an engraving of the Wasserheil-Anstalt Marienberg bei Boppard.

4. In his journal entry for July 1, 1842, Longfellow describes him as "Mr Gurney, a stout gentleman, of some fifty years, pleasant and worldly-wise"; he may therefore have been a member of the English banking family of that name. However, he is also listed as "Herr Garney, Rentner aus England" in the *Zweite Kur-Liste. Mai und Juni 1842* of the Wasser-Heil-Anstalt Marienberg (Longfellow Trust Collection).

5. The Rubens collection in the Cathedral of Notre Dame includes his masterpiece "The Descent from the Cross."

6. Where Ward had once boarded.

7. Longfellow's first mention of Ferdinand Freiligrath (1810–1876), whose *Gedichte* (Stuttgart and Tübingen, 1838) he had purchased on June 2.

8. *The Spanish Student.* Ward's answer is unrecovered.

## 689. *To Julie Hepp*

Marienberg bey Boppard am Rhein [June 8, 1842]

Liebe Freundinn,

Hier bin ich wieder in Deutschland. Seit drei Jahren finde ich mich nicht ganz wohl; und was ich von der Wassercur gehört und gelesen habe, hat mich so sehr eingenommen, dass ich mich entschlossen habe den Versuch zu machen. Heute habe ich das erste Bad genommen. Wie lange die Cur dauern wird, kann ich nicht voraus sagen; aber so bald als möglich komme ich nach Heidelberg um Sie zu besuchen.[1]

Die zwei Briefe, die ich Ihnen schicke, sind, wie sie bemerken werden, schon aufgemacht worden. Es geschah des Gesetzes wegen in *Hâvre de Grace.*[2]

Darf ich um eine Antwort bitten, um mich zu versichern, dass Sie alle wohl sind?

Mit schönsten Grüssen &c &c &c

Henry W. Longfellow.

MANUSCRIPT: University of Washington Library. ADDRESS: Dem Fräulein Julie Hepp/in Heidelberg. ANNOTATION (*by Longfellow*): franco POSTMARKS: BOPPARD $\frac{8}{6}$/WASSERHEIL ANSTALT MARIENBERG BEI BOPPARD A.R/HEIDELBERG 9 JUN 42/WP

TRANSLATION:

Marienberg, near Boppard, on the Rhine

Dear friend,

Here I am again in Germany. For three years I have not been very well; and I have become so enthusiastic about what I have heard and read concerning the Water Cure that I have determined to give it a trial. Today I have taken the first bath. How long the Cure will last, I cannot predict; but as soon as possible I will come to Heidelberg to visit you.

As you will notice, the two letters that I am sending you have already been opened. This happened because of the authorities in *Hâvre de Grace.*

May I request an answer so that I may be assured that you are all well?

With fondest greetings &c &c &c
Henry W. Longfellow.

1. According to his journal, Longfellow visited the Hepps in Heidelberg on September 27.

2. Longfellow presumably carried letters to the Hepps from Clara Crowninshield, who had boarded with them during the winter of 1835–1836.

## 690. *To Catherine Eliot Norton*

[Marienberg bei Boppart a/R] June 8 [18]42 [1]

My dear Mrs Norton,

Here is the counterfeit presentment of Marienberg,[2] the ancient cloister of noble Nuns, into whose gates I entered five days ago. I did not say on that occasion, as Thomas Aquinas did on entering the convent at Terracina, "here let me rest in peace forevermore"; but the quiet of the place delighted me, and prophecied at once a pleasant summer. But first let me tell you how I got here.

We had a three weeks passage to Havre. Finding no steamer there for Antwerp, and none for Rotterdam without waiting five days, I took the diligence for Paris; loitered there three or four days, hoping but in vain, to meet Sam Eliot and Ned Perkins, and reviving some old associations and acquaintances. Among others was the Countess de Sailly, whom I knew very well of old; a very interesting woman and sister of Berryer the distinguished orator.[3] General Cass[4] I did not see; but I saw with perfect delight Mlle Rachel[5] the actress, in Racine's Mithridate, and discovered, for the first time in my life, that one of Racine's plays could be made interesting. The play seemed to me admirable, as well as the performance of the two principal parts. The rest was the poorest declamation imaginable. I saw likewise Sumner's brother [George], who seemed to be spending his time very industriously and usefully and is a person of most decided talent.

From Paris I went to Brussels. Please tell Mr. Ticknor that his letter to Count Arrivabene gained me a most cordial welcome from that kind-hearted and excellent gentleman. He made a dinner for me, at which were present an Italian Philosopher, and a Belgian Poet. Unfortunately the Acconati [Arconati] were in Paris.[6] From Brussels I took a run through Belgium by the railroad, visiting Malines, Ghent, Bruges and Antwerp. The day at Antwerp was beyond comparison the happiest I have passed since I left you. It was filled with exciting thoughts. The glorious spire of the Cathedral; — the Well of Quintin Metsys,[7] his paintings in the gallery; his grave at the church door, with the remembrance of his struggles and his *success*; — and the noble paintings of Rubens, scattered in such profusion over the whole city, — the antique streets — the chiming bells, — touched me deeply. Had you passed that sunday there, you would have wept with emotion many times. I confess to having my eyes often filled with tears. It was a day to be remembered.

Returning to Brussels I came into Germany through Aix-la-Chapelle to Cologne by rail-road. In Cologne I bought a few bottles of *Maria Farina* for you and some other Cambridge friends. These I left to be packed up with the Symphonies of Bethoven for Jane, which had to be ordered from another place, so that I did not see them, and trust to the bookseller's honesty to have them bound and sent. I mention this, that in case of accident or mistake you may let me know before my return. From Cologne I came up the Rhine to this place in a steamer. Out of forty passengers, thirty were English. There was a lady with four daughters, each with a little straw hat without any trimming whatever; — and each with a sketch-book, and paint-box. They *worked* their passage up the Rhine, sketching with untiring energy. We dined very pleasantly on deck under an awning. Beside me sat another English family — man, wife and child, with whom I was exceedingly amused. Here is a brief specimen of the man's conversation. "Now, Ernestine, (his wife) look at that castle. (Her back was towards it). That's *Harmersteen* (Hammerstein). Remember there's a long tale to that. Jemmy, if you want your plate changed tell the servant. There, the man's right behind you. Do look at Harmer-*steen,* my dear. That's where the man was swallowed up by rats! (The scene of this event is some fifty miles higher up). Pay attention. Here come ducks and roast mutton. We have had our plates changed at least a dozen times. O do look at that castle! Beautiful! *charmant.*" &c &c

I landed at Boppard; and came up at once to Marienberg whose walls almost touch the old walls of the town. I was shown to a chamber without delay; and on throwing open the window, (one of the first things a traveller does, as you will remember) I beheld right beneath it — *a great well,* around whose brink were growing bright blue flowers; and instantly came to my mind the lines of Tasso; "*Così all'egro fanciul porgiamo aspersi — Gli orli del vaso, di soave licore.*"[8] This was five days ago. I find Marienberg a delightful place. It stands on the hill-side overlooking Boppard and the Rhine. Behind is a large garden or park running up the valley, and still farther back high hills lording it over all. The house was once a nunnery of noble ladies. In the cloisters their grave-stones are still standing. Here is one of the inscriptions — "Anno 1553: 6 Septembris. Obijt illustrissima ac religiosa Virgo Odilia Rheni Comitissa et Bavatia [*sic*] Ducissa. Cuius anima requiescat in pace."[9] The whole day is occupied in walking and bathing; and so far from having any tedious idle hours, I cannot find time to write a letter.

Monday. June 12.

Yesterday was a holiday in Marienberg, as every Sunday is. There is no bathing, after the morning bath; and various excursions are made in the neighborhood to change the scene. Yesterday I went with a party up the river to St. Goar. On board the steamer I saw the first beautiful woman I have seen in Germany. She looked so much like Mrs. Mills,[10] that had there not been a table between us to check the impulse, I should have been guilty of some indiscretion. At St. Goar I scaled two ancient ruins, and sitting alone amid solitary walls, indulged myself with a little romance. I likewise made the acquaintance of a poet, one of the best if not the best of the young poets of Germany. His name is Freiligrath. I found him writing in a very pleasant room *overlooking the Rhine* (I wonder how many times I shall use that phrase before I return home?) and near him, writing a letter, sat his pale wife. They are exceedingly agreeable people; though I do not think the outward man of the poet would find favor in your eyes. Imagine Dr. Follen, with thick, long black hair, and a moustache and whiskers flowing into each other, like the Mosel and the Rhine, — and behold Ferdinand Freiligrath! But his inward man I am sure would please you. His poetry is fresh and *virtuous*. He is a great admirer of Mrs. Hemans, and has translated her Forest Sanctuary and enough of her miscellaneous poems to make a volume, which will be published in a few months.[11] I think you will find a notice of his poems and some specimens in one of the last English Reviews.[12] I have an impression of having seen it just as I was leaving New York. Another young poet, Nikolaus Becker by name, has acquired *fame* among his countrymen by a single piece. It is a patriotic song on the Rhine, which appeared a year or two ago when a war was anticipated between France and Germany, and begins "Sie sollen ihn nicht haben, Den freien deutschen Rhein! [They shall not have it, The free German Rhine!]" The author received sundry silver pitchers from cities on the Rhine, and a thousand Thalers from the King of Prussia, and an office under government, — literally *for a song.*[13] One whisper more about literature and I have done. One or two evenings ago I saw in a Berlin paper [Francis] Bowen's Article on Locke and Cousin[14] highly praised and most of it translated, in four successive nos. I have written to Berlin for them, and will send them to him.

I have just received a letter from Cologne, saying that the Music (two volumes) and the Cologne-water are despatched. I hope they will reach you safely. There are seven large flasks of the water, — the best Maria Farina; and it is indeed *very* good. You, Louisa, Jane, Mrs. Cleveland, Mrs. Felton, Miss Lowell, and my sister Mrs. Greenleaf have each one; so that I hope to remain in good odor with you all until my return. Meanwhile pray think of me as walking in pleasant gardens, through valleys, and vineyards, and ruins, on steep hills, and thinking often of you. Indeed I cannot tell you how often we walk together through these scenes, how often I shake hands with you and say "Good morning," and "Good night," and long to see you again in reality. There are so many things that recall the absent! — the fragrance of a flower, a strain of music, any casual resemblance in voice, manner, or features — in fine, a thousand little things without a name, which suddenly startle me from my dream, and make my pulses beat quicker.

I ought to have told you more about Marienberg; but have found no room for it. I shall say more in a letter to Felton; — I will turn the river through his grounds. He would be in his element here. I enjoy the baths very much. I think I am growing a little web-footed; which is not wonderful, as I take four cold baths a day; beside an occasional swim in the Rhine. I have had letters from Hillard and Sumner, which I shall answer as soon as possible. But I am obliged to be out of doors all day long, constant exercise in the open air being as much insisted on as the baths. I have heard also from Sam Eliot. They[15] are all in Paris; and expect to pass up the Rhine about the middle of next month; when I shall see them.

With most affectionate regards to you all, and entreaties that you will write to me soon, to tell me you are well, very sincerely yours,

Henry W. Longfellow.

*Particular remembrances to all my friends.*

The box from Cologne is to go by the way of Rotterdam and New York: to the care of an agent, who will forward it to Mr. Norton.

MANUSCRIPT: Harvard College Library. ADDRESS: Mrs. C. E. Norton/Cambridge/ near Boston ANNOTATION (*by Longfellow*): par Le Hâvre et New York/ franco. POSTMARKS: BOPPARD 17/6/PRUSSE FORBACH 21 JUIN 42/BUREAU MARITIME (HAVRE) 22 JUIN 1842/NEW-YORK SHIP AUG 15/P.P.

1. The bracketed material comes from the letterhead.

2. Longfellow annotated the engraving of Marienberg on the letterhead with the following comments: "Ancient walls of Boppard"; "The *Mühlen Thal.* Behind the hills here a lovely valley"; "The two black windows are those of my chamber, indicating the gloom within! In front is the garden, running far up the valley to the left. Behind is Boppard, with a glimpse of the Rhine"; and "This is a curious old church, built in the 13th or 14th century. The two spires are connected by a covered bridge, in which are two rooms formerly occupied by the watchman. He lived up there; so as to overlook the town. I have been there this afternoon." He also identified the dining room and the apartments containing the baths. See Plate IX.

3. Pierre-Antoine Berryer (1790–1868), one of the most prominent French Legitimists.

4. Lewis Cass (1782–1866), U. S. minister to France, 1836–1842. According to Longfellow's journal entry, General Cass had tried to call on him on May 23 but he was out.

5. Stage name of Elizabeth Félix (1821–1858), Swiss-born queen of the French theater at this time. Matthew Arnold commemorated her death with a sonnet sequence. Longfellow's journal entry reveals that he saw her perform at the Theâtre Française on the evening of May 24.

6. Count Giovanni Arrivabene (1787–1881), a political writer, had lived for many years in Brussels in the ménage of the Marquis Giuseppe Arconati (1797–1883), a fellow exile from Italy who possessed a large fortune beyond the reach of the Austrian authorities. Ticknor had first met them in 1835 (George S. Hillard, ed., *Life, Letters, and Journals of George Ticknor* [Boston, 1876], I, 450–451). Count Arrivabene gave his dinner on May 31. In his journal Longfellow identifies the Italian philosopher as Vincenzo Geoberti (1801–1852) and the Belgian poet as Andre Henri Constant van Hasselt (1806–1874).

7. A statue of Salvius Brabo surmounting a 15th-century well in the Marché aux Gants was considered to be the work of the Flemish painter Quentin Metsys (1466–1530).

8. "Just as to the sick youth we proffer the brims of the glass, coated with sweet liquor." Cf. *Gerusalemme Liberata,* I, iii.

9. "In the year 1553, on September 6, there died the most illustrious and devout virgin, Odilia, countess of the Rhine and duchess of Bavatia."

10. Anna Cabot Lowell Dwight (b. 1818), sister of Mary Eliot Dwight and niece of Mrs. Norton, had married Charles Henry Mills (1812–1872), a Boston merchant, in 1839.

11. Freiligrath did not publish these translations for several years. They first appeared in *Englische Gedichte aus neuerer Zeit. Nach Felicia Hemans, L. E. Landon, Robert Southey, Alfred Tennyson, Henry W. Longfellow u.a.* (Stuttgart, 1846). Eventually he published them separately under the title *Das Waldheiligtum, nach Felicia Hemans* (Stuttgart, 1871).

12. Unidentified.

13. Becker (1809–1845), whose *Gedichte* (Köln, 1841) was his only volume, published his Rhine song in 1840.

14. *North American Review,* LIII (July 1841), 1–40.

15. That is, the Eliot family: Mrs. Margaret Boies Eliot, her two sons, Samuel

**and William, and her daughter Margaret. Samuel had been in Europe for some months, traveling with his friend Edward Perkins, and the rest of the family had just joined him.**

## 691. *To Samuel Eliot*

[Marienberg bei Boppart a/R] June 12 [18]42[1]

My dear Sam,

I was exceedingly delighted this morning at receiving your warm-hearted letter. My heart beat at least ten beats a minute quicker. It was put into my hands just as I was stepping on board a steamer with a party up the Rhine to St. Goar to pass the day; for Sunday is a holiday here, and we poor wet devils are hung out to dry. I have just returned after a delightful day; and before going to bed send back your kind greetings, with my most cordial congratulations on your mother's pleasant passage out and your meeting, and your future bright prospects for the year to come.

This Marienberg is a very charming place. It is an old Convent; and the tombstones of the noble nuns are still standing in the cloisters, which makes it very lively and cheerful for the sick! A garden, or Park stretches up the valley behind the house; and fountains are flowing in every nook and corner. The society is very agreeable and the women excessively ugly; — probably the German peasant women are as ugly as anything can be "in this imperfect state of existence." Badinage apart; — it is truly a delightful place, and delighted am I that you are all coming here. I feel quite confident the baths would do you good;[2] at least in my own case I have great confidence. Still this is too delicate a point for even a friend to urge. Come and judge for yourself. At all events it is the most elegant cold-water establishment in Germany. This everyone allows. It is in due proportion the most expensive; and yet not very expensive. Board, lodging and baths cost from 8 Prussian Thaler to 15 a week, according to the goodness of your room. A Thaler is about 75 cents. I pay 11 and something more; — medium price, about $8. a week. Then there are some little extras, such as Physician's fees &c. &c. which depend upon the length of time you stay. But I will not go into particulars; for you will certainly find me here when you come. I do not expect to get away before the end of August; as I have to take things gradually. I am most agreeably disappointed in the baths. After the first plunge one really likes them. Some of them, the *Douche* for instance and the *sitz-bad,* are delicious. The system is not half [as] barbarous as it sounds. Come and see the operation of it, and you can then better judge. William

[Eliot] ought not to be allowed to escape without a course of these cold baths. I think it would entirely remove his nervous irritability.

Do not pass through Belgium without going to Antwerp. Delicious place! with *that* cathedral and those glorious — o most glorious paintings of Rubens. Leave your trunks &c at the Hotel in Brussels, and take the rail-road for Antwerp; then to Ghent and Bruges, and so back; — the affair of three or four days. You then take the rail-road to Liége; — diligence to Aix-la-Chapelle; — rail-road to Cologne, — one day. At Cologne you will stop to buy some eau-de-Cologne — and see that magnificent beginning of a Cathedral — in comparison with which all others in the world are child's playthings. From Cologne steamer to Boppard; — start at 7 in the morning, reach Boppard at 5 in the afternoon. Write me from Brussels or Cologne, and I will be at the landing to receive you. Marienberg is a pistol-shot above the town, as you see by the engraving.

As to studying French, there can be but one opinion. It should be done in France. But I will not go into detail about that now. German you can study here. Bring with you *Ollendorf's Grammar.*[3] All these matters we will discuss when we meet; and it is now late for a water-drinking Saint in Paradise, like myself, who daily lays a wager with the morning, which will be up first.

With kindest regards to you all, and to Ned[4] when you write

Ever very truly your friend
Henry W. Longfellow.

*Hotels.*

Brussels. Hotel de Flandre.
Antwerp. " St. Antoine.
Ghent. " de la Poste.
Bruges. " de la Fleur de Blé.
Cologne. Rheinberg.

Boppard (in case I should be out of the way) Rheinischer Hof, close by the landing. Or if you have made up your mind to try the *Wassercur,* directly to Marienberg, which consists solely of this one house.

P. S. I must repeat, by way of caution, that Marienberg is the most expensive establishment of the kind in Germany. Should you dislike it, close by, not ten minutes walk is another on a smaller scale; a new house, with nice rooms, looking out upon the Rhine. There is still a third near Coblenz; where all expenses inclusive the Dr's fees, are 10 German Thaler p. week.

One word more, and good-bye. The Wassercur requires the greatest possible patience. I expect to be at least three months here, from the beginning. Day after day elapses with very slight results — nothing to be noticed.

MANUSCRIPT: Boston Athenaeum. ADDRESS: Mr. Samuel Eliot/Care of J. B. Greene & co/Paris ANNOTATION (*in another hand*): Hotel Meurice POSTMARKS: BOPPARD $\frac{14}{6}$ /WASSERHEIL ||ANSTALT|| MARIENBERG ||BEI BOPPARD A.R||/PRUSSE FORBACH 17 JUIN 42

1. The bracketed material is printed beneath the engraving of Marienberg on the letterhead.

2. Eliot was in poor health, but the exact nature of his complaint is not known.

3. Presumably an edition of Heinrich Gottfried Ollendorf, *A New Method of Learning to Read, Write, and Speak a Language in Six Months, Adapted to the German* (London, 1838). Mark Twain referred to Ollendorff (d. 1865) as "the party who has inflicted so much suffering on the world with his wretched foreign grammars, with their interminable repetitions of questions which never have occurred and are never likely to occur in any conversation among human beings" (*Roughing It*, Chap. XXX).

4. According to Eliot's letter to Longfellow of June 8, 1842, he had left Ned Perkins in Milan.

## 692. *To Ferdinand Freiligrath*

Marienberg June 13. 1842.

My dear Sir,

I here send you the books, which I hope you will find time and patience to read. To the Poems I have added a Prose work, Hyperion, which is also by me.

We reached home safely last evening just after sunset. I passed a delightful day yesterday at St. Goar; and for a great part of the pleasure I enjoyed was indebted to you and your fair wife, to whom I beg my kindest remembrance.

In haste, very truly yours
Henry W. Longfellow

MANUSCRIPT: Harvard College Library.

## 693. *To Stephen Longfellow*

[Marienberg bei Boppart a/R] June 21 [1842][1]

My dear Father,

I wrote you about three weeks ago, from Paris informing you of my safe arrival there, and of my plan for reaching Germany by the way of Belgium, which plan I put into execution.[2] I had a very pleasant journey through Belgium, visiting Bruges, Ghent, Antwerp, and Brussels; and then coming to this place by the way of Aix-la-Chapelle and Cologne. I was particularly delighted with Antwerp; — its magnificent Cathedral, and the paintings of Rubens, which are scattered through all the churches and galleries in the richest profusion.

The Rhine looks very much as in former days. Half a dozen steamers ply up and down its yellow waters; and cockney tourists infest its towns. Boppard is a very ancient place, — an old Roman town. Parts of the Roman walls are still standing. The church, whose roof and spires you see above, is as old as the thirteenth century. The spires are connected by a covered bridge in which are two rooms, a bed room and a kitchen. The watchman formerly lived up there. Marienberg is just above the town. It is a fine old building, once a convent of noble nuns. The cloisters still remain, with the tomb-stones of the nuns in the wall. Behind the house is a large garden and park; from which walks run up the several valleys and hills in the neighborhood. It is a very beautiful establishment. I have a window towards the garden; as you see by the mark.[3]

At present there are about sixty persons here, going through what is called the *water-cure*. Among them are some very agreeable persons. The process of cure varies of course somewhat with the nature of the disease; but in general it is this. About four o'clock in the morning a servant comes in and wraps you in a blanket, then covers you up in a mass of bed-quilts. There you lie for ||an h||our or more, until you perspire freely. You are then wheeled in an arm-chair to the bathing room, where you plunge into a large bath of running water, and remain a couple of minutes, splashing and rubbing. You then dress and walk an hour in the garden, drinking at intervals at the fountains; to the amount of four or five glasses. Next follows breakfast, which consists of bread, butter and milk, and sometimes strawberries. After breakfast another walk; (or a letter, as to-day). At eleven o'clock a *douche*; which is nothing more nor less than standing under a spout. The *douches* vary from 18 to thirty-five feet in height; and are perhaps the pleasantest baths, the force of the water making you warm in an instant. The water from the hills is brought into the bathing rooms by pipes, under which you place yourself for three or four minutes. You then take another walk for an hour; then a *fliessandes Sitsbad,* or flowing bath; in which you sit for half an hour, the water flowing through continually. Then walk till one o'clock. At one dinner; very frugal, without wine or spice of any kind. After dinner, sit or walk or play billiards till five. At five another *sitsbad* as at 12; and then a long walk up the hills to the neighboring villages, till supper; which is on the table from 7 1/2 to 9; and is the same as the breakfast; at 10 to bed.

Such is a day in Marienberg; where one day is like another; saving Sunday, when we rest from our bathing. You will think the treatment quite barbarous; but it is not half so much so as it seems. To me, indeed, it is extremely pleasant. I delight in the cold baths; and have great faith in their efficacy. I have been here now a fortnight; and enjoy myself much. I like particularly the long walks we take at sunset, to the neighboring valleys and up the neighboring hills. From morning till night we are in the open air. Indeed I can hardly find time, once a week to write a letter. This part of the treatment, and the diet I think you will approve; and there are here some striking proofs of the efficacy of the *Water-cure.* But I will not go into details.

I hoped to receive letters from home before this to hear that you are all well. I cannot help thinking how much you would be benefitted by such a course of cold-baths; though I suppose nothing could prevail upon you to try them, if they were within your reach. Still I hope erelong that we shall have some such establishment in America. The White Hills would be a capital place; having a great abundance of cold water, and plenty of high hills to climb.

I beg you to give my kindest regards to all my friends in Portland; and my love to all the family. Annie must write to me. I sent you my address, just before leaving Boston; — *Marienberg bey Boppart am Rhein.*

Good bye, for the present. I shall write again as soon as I can find time.

Most affectionately yours
Henry W. Longfellow.

MANUSCRIPT: Longfellow Trust Collection. ADDRESS: Hon. S. Longfellow/Portland/Me POSTMARK: BOSTON MS. AUG 20

1. The bracketed material is printed beneath the engraving of Marienberg on the letterhead.

2. This letter is unrecovered.

3. On the letterhead engraving.

## 694. *To Charles Sumner*

MARIENBERG, June 24, 1842.

MY DEAR CHARLEY,

I am not in a very gay mood this morning, yet I must write you a few lines or I shall lose the chance of the Moselle.[1] The water begins to work upon my nerves. I had a dream last night, in which I saw you. You mentioned a certain person's name, whereupon, like the patriarchs in the Old Testament, I fell on your neck and wept, exclaiming

"I am very unhappy." The most amusing part of the dream was that we were in bed together, and you were buried up to your neck in tan [tar?], which absorbed my tears. Then the scene suddenly changed. I was walking in Cambridge with Felton and Cleveland, just at daybreak, wrapped in a blanket. By way of showing his agility Cleveland jumped into a pond of water, and performed several difficult movements, at which Felton laughed and I awoke!

Awoke to be literally wrapped in a blanket and plunged afterwards into a cold bath, in which I executed as well as I could the difficult movements which Cleveland had executed in the dream. And so began another day; the twentieth since my arrival here.

Need I tell you how delighted I was to find your letters, yours and Hillard's, — waiting for me?[2] I wish that I could answer them by letters as long and full, and as grateful to the receiver. But at present I cannot. We have no time for reading and writing here. Bathing and walking in the open air, climbing mountains, and the like. As to the poems you speak of, it is alas! quite impossible to write them, much as I desire to do so.[3] My ideas leap horizontally like frogs. We are a drowsy, unintellectual set here. The Doctor says I am better; I say, I am not. I do not perceive the slightest change. *He* says I shall not get away before the end of September. *I* say, perhaps I shall.

This Marienberg is a lovely place. Unluckily there are six English people here; and still more unluckily I sit between two of them at table; so that I have my native language ringing in both ears all day long. If I could hear of a place, where there is no Englishman, I would pack up my trunk and go there. There were between twenty and thirty on board the steamer, which brought me up the Rhine. Another thing that is annoying here is the trivial tone of thought prevailing among the patients; the mean wants, and never-ending complaints, the querulous frame of mind — of which this letter, now that I think of it, is no bad specimen.

I am very sorry to hear of Owen's conduct.[4] I expected better things from him. Please see the President and Judge Story.[5]

MANUSCRIPT: unrecovered; text from "Letters to Samuel Ward, Part III," p. 306.

1. The ship *Moselle.*

2. An emasculated version of Sumner's letter, dated May 14–15, 1842, is printed in *Sumner Memoir and Letters*, II, 207–208. The original is in the Longfellow Trust Collection.

3. Sumner had written: "What red-hot staves has your mind thrown up? What ideas have been started by the voyage? A poem on the sea? Oh! I long for those verses on slavery. Write some stirring words that shall move the whole land. Send them home and we'll publish them. Let us know how you occupy yourself with

that heavenly gift of invention." Longfellow wrote the poems on slavery on his return voyage.

4. John Owen was involved with Longfellow and Sumner in a somewhat complicated financial arrangement. In his letter Sumner had written: "You remember the note for $247 signed by him and endorsed by you and me, expressly to enable him to take up at the bank his old note and to pay you $60. It seems that he succeeded in raising the money needed for the old note without using the 2nd note. I had supposed therefore, that the latter note was destroyed; but to my astonishment found a week after you left that he had passed it to Cleveland as *collative security* (!!) for borrowed money. This was wrong, as the note was not given for any such purpose, and it was making you and me liable for this sum, *without any consideration therefore*; so that if he had failed, you would have lost by him the $60 he now owes you, [and] the face of this note besides. I told Owen that I thought he had not acted properly; and Hillard joined me and said that, as your *legal Attorney*, he should forbid his using the note further. Owen at our office talked very earnestly, and when Hillard had left, and he had me alone, told me that he thought my conduct 'unjust and ungentlemanly.' I was not much disturbed by this. Perhaps, we have made too much of this; but I cannot but think that his whole course about these notes shows a want of business tact and knowledge at least. I fear also, a departure from the strictest integrity. So ends this story, about which you need not concern yourself, as we are sufficient to cope with Owen!" This misunderstanding seems to have been resolved, for Owen continued as Longfellow's publisher and as both his and Sumner's friend.

5. Concerning a continuation of his leave of absence.

## 695. *To George Stillman Hillard*

Marienberg. June 26. 1842

My dear George,

I had not been here half an hour before the servant told me there were two letters waiting for me, and had been received several days before. Accordingly he brought in yours and Sumner's. They perfumed the room. I opened and read them with eager delight; and did you know with what skill you throw the *lasso* round my wild and runaway heart, you would exercise your skill very often, as I trust you will, now I have told you of it.

In regard to the rooms, you have done exactly right; though should I stay in Europe a year longer, it would be as well to give them up, when anyone offers to take them, with the remaining rooms. I pray you thank Mr. Worcester for his disinterested kindness in this matter. If he remains in the house another year, I shall remain with him; at all events I will not leave him in the lurch.[1]

I am astonished at Owen's conduct; and cannot understand it. He broke his written contract with me, without expressing any regret. He must pay the money he now owes me, ($60.) and publish no more editions unless he is ready to comply with our agreement.[2] In regard to the Play,[3] I want it to appear in a uniform shape with the others; and you may sell the copy-right for two years, dating from January next; — that is, if you can!

As to Homœopathy, I can find out nothing more than this; that in Berlin it is in the ascendant, because the King has espoused its cause. It is admitted here, even by allopathic doctors that the experiment in the Hospital at Leipzig was not a fair one, as it was tried by a person avowedly at enmity with Homœopathy.[4]

But the *Wassercur* is delightful. I wish, with my whole heart, you were here to undergo it. I often say to myself, "what shall I do when I have to give up these pleasant baths?" The *Douche,* and the *fliessendes Sitzbad* are great inventions. In truth I am never happy now, except under water. I am disappointed only in the slowness of the process. Put that down to natural impatience.

Excuse this brief epistle. We are not allowed time to read and write; and I have staid at home to-day in stead of sailing on the Rhine, to write this and half-a-dozen more notes like it to my friends at home. The most I can do is to assure them of my never-ceasing remembrance.

As soon as I return I shall have a private water-establishment for you. I am sure it would benefit you. The White Mountains shall be the scene of it.

Ever, with kind regards to your wife, yours most sincerely.

H.W.L.

MANUSCRIPT: Longfellow Trust Collection. ADDRESS: George S. Hillard Esq/ Boston.

1. In his letter of May 16, 1842, Hillard had reported that Joseph Worcester, the leaseholder of Craigie House, had been offered $350 per year for one-half the house (including Longfellow's rooms) by Mrs. Greenough, mother of the sculptor. When Hillard revealed reluctance to meet this offer on his friend's behalf, Worcester replied that he was "willing to make some pecuniary sacrifice" and proposed that Longfellow take half the house for $250 per year. Hillard agreed to this and asked for confirmation from Longfellow, which he here receives.

2. See above, 694.4.

3. *The Spanish Student.* Hillard had written that Graham, to whom the play had been sent, had not been heard from and that Little, Brown & Company had decided against publishing it.

4. "A homoeopathic hospital was established about this time (January 1833) in Leipzig, but there was such constant wrangling among the physicians connected with it that its sphere of usefulness was curtailed, and it was finally converted into a dispensary" (*Encyclopedia Britannica,* 11th edition, XIII, 647).

## 696. *To Catherine Eliot Norton*

Marienberg. June 26 1842

My dear Mrs. Norton,

I am sending home a small package of letters to-day, and I cannot bear to have it go without bearing a friendly greeting to you and yours. By the last Havre packet I sent you a letter;[1] and by the way of Rotterdam, a box from Cologne; and this goes direct to Boston by a transient ship. So there are three chances of your being reminded of me, by note or by rote, in the course of July.

The season is growing more and more lovely here every day. The cherry trees, which line the public roads and overshadow every field and garden, are bending with rich fruit; we breakfast daily on strawberries; and the air is perfumed with the odor of the vine-blossom. You see how bent I am upon making this out to be a pleasant place. I do it to compensate me for the golden morning hours in Cambridge, from whose light I am shut out. But you all enjoy them, and are all well, I trust; and in this thought I rejoice.

Please tell Charles, that I am making him a collection of coins, as I promised. I have already the Belgian and Prussian smaller coins; — about a dozen in all; and whenever I find a new coinage, I will remember him.

I fear you would smile or shake your head if I should tell you I am delighted with the cold baths. But nevertheless it is really the case. I *am* delighted with them; and am constantly asking for more; being impatient to get well with all speed.

Farewell once more. With kind remembrances to the Ticknors and Guilds &c.

Very truly yours
Henry W. Longfellow.

MANUSCRIPT: Harvard College Library. ADDRESS: Mrs. Norton/Cambridge.

1. Letter No. 690.

## 697. *To Charles Sumner*

[Marienberg] Sunday. June 26. 1842.

My dear Charles,

I have just had a letter from Fay, in which he says; "I am delighted to hear from Sumner" — (in my letter to him,[1] he means) "I dont know how far you have been enlightened on the affair he is moving in, and therefore will not bore you with it. But Sumner has behaved in it like a frank, high-hearted fellow as he is, and I shall esteem and love him for it as long as I live." [2]

Take care of the inclosed.[3]

Yours most truly
Henry W. Longfellow.

MANUSCRIPT: Longfellow Trust Collection. ADDRESS: Charles Sumner Esq. No. 4 Court Street/Boston./America [*in another hand*]/Care of Messrs G[*remainder of word illegible*] & co/Hâvre/To go by the Moselle. ANNOTATION (*by Longfellow*): franco. RETURN ADDRESS: H. W. Longfellow./Marienberg am Rhein. POSTMARKS: BOPPARD $\frac{26}{6}$/PRUSSE FORBACH 29 JUIN 42/BUREAU MARITIME (HAVRE) 30 JUIN 1842/BUREAU MARITIME 12 JUIL 1842/6 [*rest of postmark illegible*]/P.P.

1. This letter is unrecovered.
2. Sumner, who had met Fay in Berlin in 1839, had recently intervened with Daniel Webster, the secretary of state, to save his post as secretary of legation after it had been threatened by an intrigue (*Sumner Memoir and Letters,* II, 120, n. 2, and Letter No. 706).
3. This was the covering letter for Letters No. 693, 694, 695, and 696.

## 698. *To George Washington Greene*

Marienberg bey Boppard am Rhein. June 28. 1842

My dear George,

I will not let another hour pass without writing to you, to tell you that the Atlantic is no longer between us. I am once more in Europe, and unless I am absolutely obliged to return in October, I shall accomplish the long desired visit to you in Rome! What a delightful prospect to me! But of that more anon.

In Paris I saw Prentiss,[1] who was fresh from Italy. He said you knew I was coming to Europe. How did you find it out? I have come on account of my health; having quite run down. I am trying the *Wassercur*; that is taking five cold baths a day; and walking between whiles in the open air, climbing mountains, &c. &c. This leaves me hardly a moment unoccupied; and has prevented me (together with the letters I have been obliged to write to America) from writing to you sooner. Therefore I beg you do not reproach me; but take for granted that I have said to myself, all that you could say on that subject.

I left all your friends well, both in Boston and New York; and since my arrival here have had letters from Sumner; in which he says; (May 14) "The packet that carries this letter, will carry a credit on the Barings in favor of Crawford for $2000." [2]

Your last letter I received in the Autumn; and did not answer it because I was then suffering under a fever which confined me to the chamber for a month. The Play, you inquired about is not yet published. Instead thereof I have published a second volume of poems,[3] which has been as successful as the first. You shall, of course, have a copy as soon as I can get one to you.

How is Crawford? How is Maria? How are you? You cannot imagine how I long to see you again. As soon as this reaches you, sit down and write me ten lines to say you are well, and want to see me as much as I want to see you. I *dare* you to say that. Direct as above, Marienberg &c.

If I do not return in October, I shall remain in Europe a year longer; and mean to revisit not only Italy, but Spain. I trust I shall not be disappointed. The whole depends upon my getting a longer leave of absence from the college; which in turn will depend upon how they get on in my department without me.

Felton, too, has been very ill this Spring. He had a violent rheumatic fever; which made us tremble for him; but thanks to a robust constitution he got well in spite of the doctors. Still I should not be surprised if he were obliged to visit Europe for his health particularly, as he very much desires so to do. All the Wards are well. The report in regard to Miss Julia and myself has not, and never has had the slightest foundation in fact; nor did I ever hear of it, till I received yr. letter.[4]

Good bye. Much love to Maria.

Yours ever affectionately
Henry W. Longfellow.

MANUSCRIPT: Mrs. Brenton Greene Meader, Providence, Rhode Island. ADDRESS: à Monsieur/Monsieur George W. Greene/Consul des États Unis d'Amérique/ Rome. ANNOTATION (*in another hand*): franco frontière POSTMARKS: BOPPARD $\frac{29}{6}$/ASCHAFFENBURG $\frac{30}{6}$/DIREZONE DI ROMA 9 LIG 42

1. George Lewis Prentiss (1816–1903), Bowdoin, 1835, had gone to Europe in 1839 to study theology at Halle and Berlin. Upon his return to America he entered the ministry, and in 1845 he married Elizabeth Payson (1818–1878), author of juvenile and religious fiction. He was the brother of the Miss Prentiss mentioned in Letters No. 555, 557, 558, and 560.

2. See 579.3.

3. *Ballads and Other Poems.*

4. Greene had written in his letter of October 24, 1841: "A few weeks ago I had a letter from Sam Ward who gives a jovial account of you all. They (i.e.) vox populi tell me that you are in love with his sister Julia. Is it true?"

699. *To Ferdinand Freiligrath*

[Marienberg] July 2. 1842.

My dear Freiligrath,

I owe you a thousand apologies for not having sent you a more speedy reply to your very friendly note with the books.[1] The truth is, I was very busily engaged at the time in writing letters to go by a chance opportunity direct from Havre to Boston; and moreover hoped to have the pleasure of thanking you face to face for the many kind things you say of my poems. But to-night I *will* write you two or three lines before going to bed, by the dim light of this solitary *Wasserheil-Anstalt* candle, which burns, as if it had just taken a *vollbad* [plunge bath].

I am very much pleased that you should find so many things to like in my volume. You are a very amiable critic; and as you are pleased with the translations, I have only to regret, that I had not sooner been acquainted with your poems, that I might have added some to my collection.

This morning came your second letter, with the admirable translation of Excelsior.[2] You have been perfectly successful and it would be sheer affectation in me to pretend not to be exceedingly gratified. I showed it to the Landrath,[3] who thinks it a fine translation. The poem, which Wesselhoeft put into German was a different one. I send it to you with this. I also send you the "Poets and Poetry of America," which will be of great use to you if you go on with the *American Anthology*.

Meanwhile, I have been reading your own original poems over and over with new delight. They are fresh, vigorous and striking in the highest degree. I have neither time nor room to particularize; not even to tell you which have delighted me most; for it is now late at night, and at half past three tomorrow morning I am to be waked to *execution!* Still I must not forget to thank you again for sending Nodnagel's book,[4] which though somewhat pretentious and pedantic, has interested me much.

With kindest salutations to your wife,

Very sincerely yours
H. W. Longfellow

MANUSCRIPT: Harvard College Library; tipped into Rufus Griswold's *Poets and Poetry of America* (Philadelphia, 1842) with this inscription: "Ferdinand Freiligrath/with the kind regards of/Henry W. Longfellow/July 2. 1842."

1. For this letter, datelined St. Goar, June 22, 1842, see "Longfellow-Freiligrath Correspondence," pp. 1226–1227.

2. Freiligrath's translation accompanied a letter dated July 1, 1842 ("Longfellow-Freiligrath Correspondence," pp. 1227–1228). See 704.2.

3. Hans Carl Heuberger (1790–1883), a patient at the baths and perhaps Longfellow's most intimate friend at Marienberg, was the subprefect of the St. Goar district. On Sunday, June 12, he had taken Longfellow to meet Freiligrath at St. Goar (MS Journal). For a comment on Heuberger, see *New Light on Longfellow*, pp. 89–90.

4. *Deutsche Dichter der Gegenwart, erläutert von August Nodnagel* (Darmstadt, 1842) contains a discussion of Freiligrath and his poetry.

## 700. *To Ferdinand Freiligrath*

Marienberg. Wednesday. [July 6, 1842]

My dear Freiligrath,

I had the pleasure, or rather I should say the *sorrow,* of receiving your note this morning.[1] We regret very much, that you cannot come tomorrow, but will fain wait another week in hope, that no untoward accident nor friendly visit will then prevent your coming.

I am sorry also that I cannot accept your invitation for tomorrow. I should like much to know Mr. Howitt;[2] and would *not* fail to come, if I could do so without interrupting my baths. But this would not be possible; and I must therefore forego the pleasure of ascending the *Mouse*[3] with you.

The Landrath [Heuberger] sends his regards. He was at St. Goar yesterday, and his rosy-cheeked daughter was here. Like John Gilpin and his wife, they missed each other on the road.[4]

Begging you not to forget your umbrella, and to excuse the *Birch-Pfeiffery*[5] nature of this note,

With kind regards to your wife and your guest,[6]

Very truly yours

H. W. L.

MANUSCRIPT: Longfellow Trust Collection. ADDRESS: Herre Freiligrath/Wohlgeboren/St. Goar ANNOTATION (*by Longfellow*): frei POSTMARKS: BOPPARD $\frac{7}{7}$/N $\frac{7}{7}$ I

1. See "Longfellow-Freiligrath Correspondence," p. 1229.

2. William Howitt (1792–1879), English poet and miscellaneous writer. He and his wife, Mary Howitt (1799–1888), were to visit the Freiligraths at St. Goar on July 7.

3. The ruins of the Thurnberg, which command a fine view toward St. Goar. The counts of Katzenelnbogen called this stronghold the Mouse in contrast to their own fortress of Neu-Katzenelnbogen — the Cat.

4. See William Cowper, "The Diverting History of John Gilpin, Showing How He Went Further than He Intended and Came Safe Home Again."

5. Commenting on a trip by steamer from Coblenz to Marienberg with Freiligrath, Longfellow wrote in his journal entry for July 4: "On board was a fat, ugly and vulgar woman, whom he pointed out to me as Fräulein Charlotte Birch-Pfeiffer,

a tragic actress and authoress of horrid robber plays, so bad that the verb *Birchpfeiffern* has been invented to express this kind of writing." Charlotte Birch-Pfeiffer (1800–1868) managed the Zürich theater at this time.

6. Louise von Gall (1815–1855), a young, beautiful, and talented poetess from Darmstadt who had a room in Freiligrath's house in St. Goar for the summer.

## 701. *To Henry Russell Cleveland*

Marienberg. July 10. 1842.

My dearest Hal,

You are now just sitting down to dinner, and I am looking bed-ward; it being three o'clock with you, and nine at night with me. (*Now I lay me. &c*). But first a few words to thank you for your welcome and amusing letter of June 15. which reached me on the 3rd of July. with other letters, to the great astonishment of all the Dutchmen here, who have but faint ideas of the power of steam. Your letter was indeed a magic mirror. I looked and lo! not "a maiden with a dulcimer" but a lady with a *lily*,[1] a child playing in the sunshine, and the river, and the blue hills; — and within doors a handsome young man with dark whiskers, writing a letter to me. And the Lady with the Lily said "Remember me." And I repeated her words a thousand times, till the ruins of the Rhine learned English and answered without accent, "Remember me."

What you say of Kentgen amused me exceedingly. How could he be such a *boob*. He evidently knows nothing of good society; and I shall be wary in presenting his letters of introduction.[2] I cannot tell you how glad I am, you miss me in Cambridge. I consider it a great pleasure to give such kind of pain. Your father's book, too, so successful! Make my congratulations to him on his fortunate *début*.[3] It must be a source of the highest gratification to you all; and I rejoice with you.

For my part, I have few tidings of any kind to send in addition to what I have written to Sumner and Felton. Two of the English have gone — the best of them. The regular *bête noire* remains; — a vulgar, disagreeable Cockney, by whose help I am cultivating such a dislike to the English in general, that I think seriously of returning home without going to England. My most agreeable and intimate acquaintance left Marienberg two days ago. He has got *better*. It was the Landrath Heuberger; a jovial little man; who was *toujours gai*, and ready for a long walk, and always carried an umbrella. He has left me to the tender mercies of Graf Hohenthal, a hypochondriac.[4] I know not for what cause, but he seems to rely upon me for sympathy, and breathes into my ear all his sorrows. The poor man fears he is going crazy, and by meditating on the subject is already half what he fears to be. He is tormented to death about the merest trifles, as for example, what coat he shall put on in the morning, and whether he had better eat his strawberries at 4 o'clock in the afternoon, or keep them for supper! "Good morning, Herr Graf. How are you to-day?" "Ach Gott! ach Gott!" (holding up his hands to a level with his ears and dangling the fingers downward, as if he were ringing little bells,) "just as bad as ever! (two groans.) I was awake in the night tormenting myself as usual. I have been here eleven weeks; and have drunk only 15 glasses of water a day. And I was thinking in the night, that perhaps I had retarded my cure by drinking too little. I ought to have drunk 16. That would have made a great difference." And so on. I generally succeed in calming him in a few minutes; and in the course of the day he grows gradually better. I pity him from my heart. Such disorders are terrible.

There are likewise here, General *Peroffskji* (I need not say of what nation), — the same who led that disastrous expedition to [the] Caucasas, in which an army of ten thousand was frozen to death;[5] — another Russian, who is sweated twice a day, till the perspiration runs through to the floor, and then plunges into the cold bath and remains there 15 minutes; — a Dr. Mayo, from London, distinguished as a surgeon and head of I know not what College;[6] — half a dozen students from Bonn; — a huge, old Dutch General, who looks like some condemned hulk in a Navy Yard;[7] — a son of Murat, retired and gentlemanly;[8] — a Belgian who cannot walk without dancing,[9] and another who cannot walk at all.[10] And so on to the number of a hundred or more.

As to any results of the *Wassercur* I cannot yet speak decidedly. I can say that thus far I like it; and am decidedly better. If it succeeds with me, you must make up your mind to try it for a month or so, when you come to Europe. It would invigorate you very much; and be a good preparation for the enervating climate of Italy. Think of this.

I had a letter a few days ago from Sam Eliot, Paris. He was just starting for Switzerland to join Ned [Perkins]; and his mother had taken up her abode at St. Germain where she meant to pass the summer, unless tempted away to Boulogne-sur-Mer, by the Thorndikes.[11]

And now, to close this letter, I wish I had some pleasing intelligence to communicate; some lovely little gossip about persons you know. But alas! I have not. And my thoughts revert to you and yours. My heart untravelled still returns to Cambridge; — Jerusalem, my happy home.[12] (Excuse these numerous quotations from the poets.)

I look forward with the greatest delight to the time, when from the omnibus window, I shall first catch a glimpse of your chimney-tops. Meanwhile I shall enjoy all I can; and most of all a scamper across the country as soon as I am *wrung out and dried.* Can I do anything for you in Germany? If so, write, write, write.

When this note reaches you, you will have returned from your Summer journey. Was it pleasant? A great deal of love to Sarah and the Nortons, and keep a warm corner for me in your heart.

Most truly
H. W. Longfellow.

P. S. Willis is at Frankfort; and seems to be delighted with his position there. He is an amiable, gentle creature; with a good deal of his brother Nat's *laissez aller.*

Liszt is now in Paris; but is coming to the Rhine during the Summer, to live on the island of Nonnenwerth, near Cologne. I hope I shall see him, and hear him.[13] His fame is great in the land. He is by birth a Hungarian; and there is a letter of his to Heine in one of the papers I shall send to Bowen, which will interest you. Some of Sebastian Bach's church music has been lately published. I shall bring it with me; together with Ring's *Choral-Buch,* or Book of Chaunts.[14] Do you know it?

My last letters, — to Mrs. Norton, Hillard, Sumner &c. must have been a long time in reaching Cambridge. I sent them by the way of Paris and Havre; not knowing how to get them through England. I very foolishly forgot to take Hillard's address. I believe it is *Coates &co.*[15] If it is not "Farewell, then O Luck of Edenhall!" This letter and Corny's[16] will never see the light of your evening lamps; and my all-hail! from afar will waste itself on vacant winds.

I hope to have letters from Cambridge soon again. I tell the portboy Jacob, every day, to bring me more letters; whereat he smiles and says "ja! ja!" Last week I received five in two days! Think what a jubilee for a single gentleman, in a foreign country.

But I *must* stop, and go to bed, for tomorrow morning at half past three o'clock the hinges of yonder door will creak, and I shall leap out of bed like a man in a nightmare. And that reminds me of Willis again. Did you know he is a Somnambulist? I found it out at sea. He slept in the berth above me; and one night he leaped out of bed, and rushed for the deck, with a tremendous scream. I pursued and saved him. He repeated this several times during the voyage. I would be waked by a distressing scream, and out would come Willis with a flying leap, knocking over the chairs and making a furious din.

Luckily no mischief happened; but I was seriously alarmed. He says it is nothing; — he is used to it, being in the habit of getting up in his sleep and riding horse-back on third-story windows.

I never had any great talent for jumping out of bed, but a very great talent — I think I may say a *genius* for jumping in. So give me your hand and once more *good night.* The gentleman in the next room has just knocked the ashes out of his pipe, and blowed through the stem, signifying that he has finished smoking, and is going to bed. He cries to me from his dormitory; "*Schlafen Sie schon, mein lieber Nachbar?* [Sleep well, dear neighbor?]" While the gentleman on the other side of me, a paralytic Professor from Ghent, has already ploughed a deep furrow in the Land of Nod, — a land worth cultivating. From each of these neighbors I am divided by antique carved doors; not quite equal to those of the Baptistry of Florence.[17] I hope that to-night they will prove the Ivory Gate of Dreams, and admit only pleasing visions and the forms of those I love; and through them will I send towards you many a fond thought and many a good wish, too ethereal to clothe itself in words; and too delicate to be pinned into a letter, like a rice-paper butterfly in a lady's album. Once more, good night.

H. W. L.

MANUSCRIPT: Berg Collection, New York Public Library. ADDRESS: Henry R. Cleveland Esq/Cambridge, Mass/U. S. America. ANNOTATION (*on cover*): London July 18th/42 Recd and forwarded by/John Hillard

1. Longfellow approximates Coleridge's line, "A damsel with a dulcimer" ("Kubla Khan"), and alludes to Sarah Cleveland and her daughter Lily.

2. See 678.1.

3. See 642.4. Cleveland had written: "The book has received overwhelming applause, and sells finely" (Letter dated June 15, 1842).

4. Graf Peter Carl von Hohenthal (1784–1856) is identified in the *Erste Kur-Liste. Januar bis Mai 1842* of the Wasser-Heil-Anstalt Marienberg as a Royal District Prefect of Saxony, retired, and a landed proprietor of Dobernitz.

5. In November 1839, General of Cavalry and Adjutant General Count Vasilii Alekseevich Perovsky (1794–1857), military governor of Orenburg, led an expedition of 4000 men and 20 guns against the marauding nomads of the steppe. His force survived with little loss an attack by 2000 Khivans on December 18, but subsequently encountered severe weather and began a retreat on February 4, 1840, that did not reach Orenburg until June 2. The expedition suffered 2200 casualties, including 1000 dead. Despite Longfellow's exaggeration, the general's desire to seek his health in Marienberg is therefore understandable.

6. Dr. Herbert Mayo (1796–1852), founder of the medical school at Middlesex Hospital, London, had gone to Germany to seek relief from rheumatic gout. Having resigned his post in England, he progressed from patient to physician at the Wasser-Heil-Anstalt Marienberg. He moved later to the hydropathic establishment at Bad Weilbach. See the *Dictionary of National Biography,* XIII, 172–173.

7. Theophile Briatte (1775–1844), a retired Dutch lieutenant general, is listed

in the *Dritte Kur-Liste. July und August 1842.* Longfellow makes him an admiral in Letter No. 715.

8. Identified in the *Zweite Kur-Liste. Mai und Juni 1842* merely as Herr Murat, a former Deputy of Paris. He does not, however, seem to have been a son of Marshal Murat.

9. Identified in Longfellow's journal entry for June 20 as "Mr. Pierrepont, a Belgian landed-proprietor, who figures here in a blue blouse; an agreeable man." He is listed as "Hr. de Pierpont, Gutsbesitzer aus Sethan" in the *Erste Kur-Liste. Januar bis Mai 1842.*

10. Identified from the *Erste Kur-Liste* as Dr. Phillippe Houdet (1799–1851), professor of surgery in the University of Ghent.

11. Augustus Thorndike (1797–1858), son of the Boston merchant Israel Thorndike, and his wife, Henrietta Steuart Thorndike (b. 1801).

12. Longfellow combines line 7 of Goldsmith's "The Traveller" with line 1 of "The New Jerusalem," an anonymous translation of "Urbs beata Hierusalem."

13. There is no evidence that Longfellow met Franz Liszt at this time.

14. Apparently a work by Johann Christian Heinrich Rinck (1770–1846), German organist, composer, and author of two *choralbücher.*

15. George Hillard's brother, John Hillard, was connected with the firm of Coates & Company, 13 Bread Street, London. Longfellow's later letters to America were forwarded through him.

16. Longfellow's letter to Cornelius Felton, July 12, 1842, is unrecovered.

17. The celebrated bronze doors of the Church of San Giovanni Battista, where all children born in Florence were baptized.

## 702. *To Ferdinand Freiligrath*

Marienberg July. 20. [1842]

Many thanks, my dear Freiligrath for your letter, and the superb translation.[1] It must have been a hard nut to crack; but you have dispatched it in the style of the most successful *Nussknacker.* The old Berserk seems now to speak his native tongue. The changes are not important, and sometimes improvements; as for example

"Ungestüm warb ich dann,
Warte, wer warten kann."[2]

In the stanza of the "gusty skaw" there seems to be a little confusion. It is the Berserk's ship that is struck by the flaw, and driven back upon Hildebrand's. Finding his sails flapping in this head flaw, the old Viking puts about, and runs down before the wind right into his pursuer, and sinks him.

I reached home safely on Monday. The pale gentleman in spectacles, who rejoices in the name of Langewiesche, was very polite; and gave me a copy of his "*Sagen-und Märchenwald im Blütenschmuck* [*A Forest of Legends and Tales in Floral Decor*](!) which title is certainly indicative of the book and its author.[3] I feel perfectly sure of this. Am I not right?

I hope no untoward accident will prevent my coming to St. Goar on Friday. A clergyman once announced to his congregation, that there would be a collection for the poor on the next Sunday, *God willing*; and on the Sunday after *whether or no.* I shall not go so far as this, but will come to St. Goar if I can; for I say with your friend Simrock;

Zieht nicht vorbei an St. Goar,
Der Stadt, die allzeit gastlich war,
Nicht mit dem Dampfer vorüber fahrt,
Grüsst erst den Dichter Freiligrath,
Verzehret den heiligen Kirchenkuchen;
Werdet umsonst seinen gleichen suchen.[4]

It seemed very strange to me to lie snugly in bed on Monday morning, instead of being waked from my slumbers by a servant. But on Tuesday, I began again in the old course; and my first consciousness in the morning was the *striped* Mathias, who like the executioner in one of Shakespeare's plays, entered with his "Master Bernardino! Master Bernardino! Wake up and be hanged!"[5] (*drowned*). But habit — habit — every thing depends upon that.

Friendly salutations to the ladies and to the Heubergers.

Very truly yours
H. W. Longfellow.

MANUSCRIPT: Longfellow Trust Collection. PUBLISHED: "Longfellow-Freiligrath Correspondence," pp. 1229–1230.

1. Of "The Skeleton in Armor."

2. "Impatient I courted then,/Let him wait who can." This is apparently a free version of lines 65–66.

3. According to his journal, Longfellow had met Wilhelm Langewiesche (1807–1884), poet, dramatist, and book publisher of Barmen, when returning on the steamer from St. Goar to Boppard on July 18. Langewiesche had published his *Sagen-und Mährchen-wald im Blüthenschmuck* (Barmen, 1841–1842) under the pseudonym L. Wiese.

4. *Translation:*

"Go not by St. Goar,
That ever hospitable town,
Travel not by on the steamer,
Greet first the poet Freiligrath,
Eat the holy church wafer;
You will seek in vain its equal.

Longfellow quotes the first two and amends the next four lines of the poem "St. Goar," which he had read in Karl Joseph Simrock, *Rheinsagen aus dem Munde des Volkes und deutscher Dichter* (Bonn, 1837). Simrock (1802–1876), poet, man of letters, and friend of Freiligrath, became a professor at Bonn in 1850.

5. Cf. *Measure for Measure,* IV, iii, 21–22.

703. *To Anne Longfellow Pierce*

Marienberg. July 20. 1842

My dearly beloved Annie,

Your letter of June 15 reached me in eighteen days, to the great wonderment of all Dutchmen. I was delighted to hear from you and to know you are so well and lively in Portland; and I should have sent you an answer by the last steamer, if I had had leisure. You surprised me very much by your account of Miss Lowell. So far from telling her I should not write to her, I expressly promised to write to her. I accordingly wrote from New York; and again on arriving here.[1] The whole mischief lies in her not sending to the Post office. The reason I wanted you to write was that she might have the earliest intelligence of my arrival. I am sorry she torments herself so, without cause. But she cannot help it; it is her nature.

And now, my dear Annie, I have the satisfaction to announce to you that I am better. The course of treatment agrees with me. I take now six cold baths a-day. Think of a human being dressing and undressing six times in the course of as many hours! Between whiles I walk; climb mountains. &c. &c. The early hours; the water; the diet; the air; the exercise; all these together work the cure; and the time flies rapidly by, without giving one much leisure for thinking. The number of persons now here is about one hundred; so that the house is quite full. How long I shall remain is uncertain; but I do not intend to leave before the end of August; if so soon. I shall try the treatment thoroughly.

The neighborhood of Boppard is very delightful. The beautiful green Rhine is always a pleasant object; and the valleys extending in all directions, with the ruins on the hills give occasion for various agreeable excursions. About six miles up the river is the little town of St. Goar where I have some friends, the Freiligraths. He is a youth of about my own age, and the best of the young poets of Germany. His wife is a very genteel person, and quite American in her manner and looks. They are very agreeable people and are a great resource to me. He has translated a good many of my poems into German; which I shall not copy here, as they would not benefit you much. We make excursions together to old castles and ruins. He is good-humored and stout, like my friend Felton, though of a more restless nature.

I need not tell you, however, that no new friends can make good the absence of the old; and that I often grow impatient of restraint; and long for motion and change of place. I want to see you all again, though I have been so short a time absent; and should like to take a run through Italy and Spain; and then come home. You may rely upon it; I shall be very glad to get back.

July 24th.

Mr. Colvert and his wife from Baltimore arrived here yesterday, to pass the rest of the summer.[2] They are exceedingly agreeable people, and not entire strangers to me. It is very pleasant to have one or two countrymen here and we are daily expecting Sam Eliot, whose health is poor, and who would certainly be benefitted by a course of cold baths. Mrs. Eliot is passing the Summer at St. Germain near Paris. From Greene I have heard nothing. In Paris I saw Prentiss, who was looking remarkably well. I saw also De Goy, whom you probably recollect. As yet I have met no other friends of yours.

Tomorrow I am going to make an excursion down the river as far as Cologne with the Freiligraths, to buy some Cologne-water for you, and to try a change of air, and a suspension of the baths for a day or two, which is thought to be advantageous.

I beg you to write me as soon as this reaches you. There are so many little matters that will interest me, that you have always at hand abundant materials for long letters. Let not my short ones be a model for yours; but remember how many I have to write; and how little leisure I have to write them in.

Give my best love to all, and remember me as ever most affectionately your brother

Henry.

P. S. I wish father could have the benefit of some of these baths. I think they would work wonders upon him by giving him strength, and good digestion. If an establishment of the kind should be set up in America, as before long there will be, I think he would be induced to try the cold bathing.

When you write to Aunt Louisa [Wadsworth] tell her I have not forgotten her commission for music; but shall execute it tomorrow in Bonn, where is a large establishment of music of all kinds.

I am very glad to hear that Mary [Longfellow Greenleaf] is so comfortably settled in Boston. Summer Street is a very pleasant street. Pray has she the house my friend Mrs. Eliot once lived in? If so my footsteps are no strangers to the door; — but wherever she may be they will easily find the way to her.

I hope Marianne [Longfellow] enjoyed her visit in the red-hot city of New York. It is delightful on the Island in Summer. I have been there.

For my own part, I wish I had a little of the warmth of an American

Summer. It is so cold here that I am obliged to wear my winter clothing; and though to-day is a bright sunny day, and I am wrapped in a thick wadded dressing gown (you know it) I find it rather uncomfortably cool sitting with the window open. Consequently I am obliged to take a great deal of exercise. Indeed I am on my feet from five in the morning till ten at night; and am so much strengthened by the baths as to feel no fatigue. These are good results.

MANUSCRIPT: Longfellow Trust Collection. ADDRESS: Mrs. Anne L. Pierce/Care of S. Longfellow Esq/Portland.

1. These letters are unrecovered.

2. George Henry Calvert (1803–1889), Harvard, 1823, was known to Longfellow (who seems to have consistently misspelled his name) through several of his literary works. See 534.9. His wife was Elizabeth Steuart Calvert (1803–1897), sister of Mrs. Augustus Thorndike (701.11). Calvert described and defended the water-cure in his *Scenes and Thoughts in Europe* (New York, 1846), pp. 40–55.

## 704. *To Ferdinand Freiligrath*

Marienberg. Saturday July. 22. 1842.[1]

My dear Freiligrath,

I was very agreeably surprised this morning by your package of papers and letters. Many, many thanks for such repeated marks of your kindness and regard. Your introductory notice is just the friendly word I expected from what you told me last Sunday, and the translation of Excelsior exceedingly fine.[2]

I was sorry not to see you on Friday. I wanted to tell you among other things, which I had not time to write, how much I liked the Ballad of the Spieler von Ebernburg. It gave me very sincere gratification; and I rejoice with you, that it *broke the bank*. It must be a subject of honest pride and self-congratulation with you to know, that the poem took effect in the hearts of your readers. I know of no greater pleasure than that of producing such effects.

This morning, at six o'clock, in the Cloisters of our Convent, I read to three admiring Nuns, yr. delightful poem of Der Blumen Rache. And I wished, that invisible yourself, you could have witnessed their eager attention and heard their applause. One fair hand is now copying the poem into a book.

A countryman of mine, Mr. Colvert of Baltimore, arrived here yesterday with his wife. I want them to know you and Mrs. Freiligrath, and that you should know them. He is a young man of fortune and an author, having published a translation of Schiller's Don Carlos.[3]

I shall join you on Monday, on board the earliest Cölner Dampschiff; promising myself great pleasure from the tour, and hoping that your friends will not be annoyed by the addition of a stranger to the party.[4]

With kind regard &c

Yours very truly
Henry W. Longfellow

P.S. You need not take any staff for your journey; as I shall bring one for you.

MANUSCRIPT: Longfellow Trust Collection. PUBLISHED: "Longfellow-Freiligrath Correspondence," pp. 1232–1233.

1. The date is incorrect, since Saturday was the 23rd.

2. Freiligrath's translation of "Excelsior," with introductory remarks on Longfellow, had appeared in the Stuttgart *Morgenblatt für gebildete Leser* on July 11, 1842. For the contents of the package sent by Freiligrath, see his letter of July 22, 1842 ("Longfellow-Freiligrath Correspondence," p. 1231).

3. Friedrich Schiller, *Don Carlos; A Dramatic Poem* (Baltimore, 1834).

4. On July 25 Longfellow joined an excursion that took him down the Rhine to Rolandseck, Königswinter (where he climbed the Drachenfels), Bonn, and Cologne, with brief overland visits to Löwenburg and Godesberg. He returned to Boppard on the 28th. The traveling party included the Freiligraths; Fräulein von Gall; Karl Simrock; Justizrat Karl Buchner (1800–1872), a minor poet and dramatist from Darmstadt; his wife; Karl Schlickum (1808–1869), a landscape painter; Karl Krah (1803–1873), burgomaster of Brohl; and his sister. See Longfellow's MS Journal entries for July 25–28 and Käthe Freiligrath-Kroeker, "Ein Rhein-Idyll," *Deutsche Revue*, XXVI (April bis Juni 1901), 30–31.

## 705. *To George Stillman Hillard*

Marienberg July 22. 1842.

My dearest George,

Yours of the 2nd [July] has just been put into my hands by the melancholy Count [Hohenthal], who took it from the post-boy, that he might have the pleasure of handing it to me himself. My sympathy has brought its reward. (See Cleveland's letter.)[1] Of course, it is a jubilee with me, whenever a letter arrives; and yours are always doubly welcome. I am delighted to hear of you all; and of the several moves on the checker-board of life. And how provoking, that my letters should have been so long in reaching you! It is wholly owing to my own stupidity. I forgot your brother's address in London; so that all my first letters went by the way of Havre. Letters from you and Sumner I answered by the ship *Moselle* direct to Boston from Havre. But now I have your brother's address; and there shall be no break. I will write as often as I can.

Your notions of the water-cure are quite preposterous. Those foolish books have led you astray. Believe me, there is no miraculous Pool of Bethesda here; and the accounts we have had are the exaggerations of speculation.[2] Clairidge, for instance, and Munde, both of them wrote to get up an excitement, intending to establish Water-institutions themselves.[3] The effects of cold-bathing are gradual; and the greatest *patience* is necessary, not to say a fixed *will,* to enable one to wait for the good results anticipated.

Mr. Colvert and his wife arrived here this morng. They are Baltimorians, you know. I am very glad they have come; for they are exceedingly agreeable people. He is not well; and means to *take to the water*; which he tried with success last Summer, but not long enough. They know a great many Boston people, and we shall have some sympathies in common, which I do not find to be the case with me and the English. I feel there is a partition wall between us; and sympathize more with all other nations. How I differ in this particular from Charley [Sumner]! They tell me — the Colverts — that they saw a good deal of Eliot and Perkins in Switzerland. Sam is very feeble, and intends to come here; probably in a few days. They tell me also that everyone speaks in the highest terms of our friend Greene, the Consul; and that a petition has been sent home signed by all the Americans in Rome, urging that he may have a salary. Has Sumner heard of Crawford lately? The Colverts were not in Rome, but they said Sam Eliot is very enthusiastic in his praises.

I must revisit Italy. One week would bring me there. You and Sumner must help me. Judge Story was inclined to have me purchase books for the College before I came away. I spoke with him on the subject. You think I should not make good bargains; but having a certain facility in the various tongues, I should not be so easily imposed upon by the booksellers as many others. I want to have the matter settled; and to know whether I am to return in October or remain another year. Now pray you put it in such a light with the President as that I can stay. Let my salary continue, give me leave of absence till next Summer, and I require no more; — no percentage, which any other person would of course require — (and at least ten per. cent.).[4] I do not make this proposition, but you can state it, if they have any doubts or fears, or uncertainties.

There is an Englishman here with two daughters, the one a widow, the other a maid. Yesterday as I was walking through the cloisters of this Convent with the maiden, she said to me; "I dont like the *vollbad* [plunge bath] it makes my *legs so cold!*" Whereupon I told her a story I had just heard of a lady, who had her leg cut off at the hip joint; and that the doctor said it was a *very pretty* operation;

which the maiden doubted. She evidently wanted to astonish me with the coolness and freedom of manner with which an English girl can speak of her legs, having no doubt read Madam Trollop.[5] How do you like such a *sans-culotte* style of conversation for a damsel?

I observe here many vulgarisms generally called Americanisms; as for example eating with the knife; and *one* which is most decidedly *not* American; namely, holding up a dirty silk handkerchief over the table and *spitting against it.* Picking the teeth with a fork prevails to some extent. But pardon me; I am growing scandalous; and noting down things quite unworthy of notice.

Excuse this shabby letter, my dear George, in answer to your excellent epistle; and remember the will and not the deed. You did exactly right in the case of Griswold and the play.[6] Will you ask Owen if he got a note from me in Paris, and if he has sent the books to Hector Bossange.[7] If he has not, ask him to send me 10 copies of my poems, the small edition, and the last N. A. Review to the above address, H. Bossange, Paris. If you can get any money from him please send it to yr. brother [John Hillard], as likewise that of Griswold in case I do not return in October.

I am sorry Mrs. Mills has been so ill.[8] A child was cured of the same disease here two days ago, by wrapping it in a wet sheet, and changing this wet sheet every half hour. (Pool of Bethesda!) I think *the judicious*[9] would make an excellent wife for Howe. She is a brilliant creature, certainly, and such a character as Howe's would have a capital influence upon hers. She would become a glorious woman. Felton's plan of marrying *the rest of the club* and Howe to the three sisters is amusing. Tell him I have no objection if he will do the wooing.[10]

I am not surprised at what you say of Worcester. I always thought him precocious.[11] Tell Bowen I have his article on Paley tr. into German, for him.[12] My regards to Rölker and *Scroffels.*[13] I am often reminded of them here in Germany. Remember me very particularly to Charles Amory. The Colverts desire also their kindest remembrance to him and his wife. And finally, farewell for a season. I wish you were here to inhale health with the morning air, and drink strength from these fountains. With kind regards to your wife.

Affectionately yours
H. W. L.

Particular remembrances to Nat. Hawthorne.

MANUSCRIPT: Longfellow Trust Collection.

1. Letter No. 701.
2. In his letter of July 2, Hillard had expressed a conviction that the baths would

cure Longfellow and had indulged in fantasy: "Sometimes we see you, stooping down and receiving between your shoulders the douche-bad (is that the way they spell it) and setting your teeth hard to bear the cold and crushing blow; again we have you in the mind's eye, soaking in a sitz bad, like a bundle of hemp, water rotting (pray pardon my simile) and anon some bodiless hand comes and sees you and pops you in the midst of two feather beds; where you lie, like a slice of ham, in a sandwich, between two pieces of bread and butter."

3. Capt. R. T. Claridge, an English water-cure enthusiast, had written *Hydropathy; or, The Cold Water Cure, as Practised by Vincent Priessnitz, at Graefenberg, Silesia, Austria* (London, 1842). For Munde's book, see 640.4.

4. That is, no percentage of his salary, which would have to be used to provide the college with a replacement. See Letter No. 717.

5. In her *Domestic Manners of the Americans* (1832), Frances Trollope (1780–1863) had ridiculed the affected delicacy of Americans. The English girl who tried to embarrass Longfellow was Miss Gyde, who is entered with her father and her sister, Mrs. Grey, in the *Zweite Kur-Liste. Mai und Juni 1842* of the Wasser-Heil-Anstalt Marienberg. In his MS Journal entry for July 1, 1842, Longfellow wrote, "There is a Mr Gyde here with his two daughters; one a young widow, the other a young maiden, rather striking in her appearance. English; and very proud."

6. After Rufus Griswold had succeeded Poe as editor of *Graham's Magazine,* Hillard accepted his proposal to purchase *The Spanish Student* for $150. He informed Longfellow of this fact in his letter, assuring him that he had also reserved the right to publish the play in a volume after it had appeared in the magazine (Lawrance Thompson, "Longfellow Sells *The Spanish Student,*" *American Literature,* VI [May 1934], 147–149). Griswold printed the play in three installments (*Graham's Magazine,* XXI [September, October, November 1842], 109–113, 176–180, 229–234).

7. See Letter No. 686.

8. Hillard had reported that she was "quite ill with a lung fever."

9. Julia Ward.

10. In a letter to Longfellow of June 15, 1842, Felton had written: "By Jupiter, Longfellow, you are the most insensible block in existence not to fall in love with one of those incomparable sisters — and Charles is as bad. Julia is the most remarkable person I ever knew. Every time I see her, some new power or attraction strikes me; and I am astounded that all the unmarried men are not piled up at her feet. If the three destinies could bring matters into such a train as to divide that band of Graces between you and Charles and Howe, I should proudly exclaim, 'nunc dimittis domine.' Pray think of it. Hydropathy, I hope, will bring you to a proper frame of mind."

11. Hillard had written: "I must inform you that it is currently reported that Mr. Worcester, with the assistance of his wife is about to give to the world a work unlike any of which he has been before the compiler or author, an instance of reproductive vigor late in life which has no parallel since the days of Abraham and Sarah." This rumor of Worcester's accomplishment was untrue.

12. The article had appeared in the *North American Review,* LIV (January 1842), 102–141.

13. Possibly a reference to Herman Bokum, Rölker's predecessor as instructor in German at Harvard.

## 706. *To Charles Sumner*

Marienberg. July 22. 1842.

My dearest Charles,

I make you but a poor beggarly return for your kind letters which come winged with blessings from my distant home, and laden as deep with little spicy facts, as ships from Araby with aromatic gums. You must be contented to be repaid in thanks and benedictions. And now, therefore, before stepping into bed, to sleep a few short hours, and then to be waked by red-bearded Mathias crying like the hangman of Shakespeare, "Master Barnadino! wake up and be hanged!" [1] (*drowned*) — I fill the sails of this note with sighs, and prayers and blessings.

Within a fortnight my heart has been made glad by letters from you, Hillard, Felton and Cleveland — the whole club. From all of them I gather that the bright arrows of Julia's wit have hit that one vulnerable point in Howe's bosom not dipped in the dragon's blood. I hope it is so. Corny is eloquent upon the subject and writes; "if the three destinies could bring matters into such a train as to divide that band of Graces between you, Charles and Howe, I should piously exclaim '*nunc dimittis domine.*' " [2]

I have just recd. a letter from Fay on the subject of his troubles. His health is quite restored; and his hopes revived. He says "You will be glad to hear, that th[r]ough the *noble* conduct of Sumner a most unworthy intrigue to displace me is likely to end in a total failure." [3] From Greene I cannot get a line. What can the matter be? I hear the most favorable accounts of him. His countrymen begin to appreciate him. Crawford too wins golden opinions still. Greenough is in Paris making a bust of Washington Irving. Mrs. Eliot has given up the idea of going to Italy, — at least for the present; and Sam and Ned Perkins are expected here in a day or two. For my own part, I am going tomorrow to Bonn and the glorious Drachenfels, with my new friend Freiligrath, the young poet; a capital fellow, fatter than Corny, and almost as funny; we are to pick up one or two other poets on the way, and expect to set the river on fire.[4] Half my bathing being done, I stop for a day or two, better to judge of the effect. I promise myself great pleasure; but not a drop of wine — not one cigar! By the way, smoking is allowed here; and am I not a virtuous man to resist my ruling passion? I give you notice, however, that on my return I shall resume this amiable accomplishment.

A translation in German of the Skeleton in Armor lies before me.[5] I wish I could read it to you; for it is striking; and copy it I cannot, for it is too long. This and many more you shall see all in good season.

Am I to return in October or not? The fine frenzy of travelling in Italy begins to stir within my [heart]. I am so near! The sunny land beckons me with all its soft allurements. Pray see the President, and let me know. Lay before him, as you well know how, the advantages of having books purchased for the College Library by some one here; — the opportunities of purchase infrequently presenting themselves. &c. &c. &c. In fine, get me leave of absence till next Summer.

If in any of my letters to any of you I am out of humor or make ill-natured remarks, or say what I ought not to say, charge it to my nerves; — to the excitement of the gigantic *douche,* that scourges me daily into a rather sensitive state. Of course, I write as I feel at the moment and you can well pardon a few contradictions, provided I contradict myself only. Allow me to abuse the English a little; I will praise the amiable Germans all the more. In fine, allow me any amount of absurdity I choose; and rebuke me not.

Good night. It is nearly eleven o'clock. I have not been up so late before since I arrived here. It is a lovely night. The full moon has hid the stars, so that it would take some time to find them. "The air is cool, and it darkles; And peacefully flows the Rhine." How expressive is that little poem of Heine's![6] It is the best of all the *Rheinsagen.* Do you remember it? Night is the most propitious season for writing to one's friends. I feel now as if I could sit for hours and pour into your heart in one continuous flow the hopes, fears, passions, purposes, that agitate my own. I look back upon Cambridge as if I were still there; and this body and the soul that animates me were another's. From this distance I see so distinctly the position of us each and all. Ah! would that you could look with my eyes! What a cheering sight it would be to you! How it would inspire you with cheerful courage, and serene confidence. Dear Charles, let us *never despair of the Future.* The wave that has borne us thus far, will return with new force to bear us farther, and farther. At this moment you are probably sitting with Howe, looking upon the fluctuating sea, and moralizing on the wayward course of events in the life of man. "Look not mournfully into the Past."[7] Farewell for a season.

Ever yours
H. W. L.

Remember me particularly to Howe.

MANUSCRIPT: Longfellow Trust Collection.

1. Cf. *Measure for Measure,* IV, iii, 21–22.
2. See 705.10.
3. Fay's letter is dated July 15, 1842.

4. See 704.4.
5. Presumably by Freiligrath (see Letter No. 702).
6. "Lorelei."
7. A sentiment from *Hyperion* (*Works*, VIII, 275).

## 707. *To Catherine Eliot Norton*

Marienberg. July 24. [1842]

My dear Mrs. Norton,

I write you this morning — this bright Sunday morning, — merely to tell you of a misfortune which has happened to me, and of which you will have a presentiment before you open this letter. My beautiful Excelsior ring is lost.[1] It dropped from my finger in the *Douche* a few days ago, and was swept away beyond recovery by the force of the water. So much cold bathing had made my fingers too small, and my beautiful talisman is gone forever. Everyone who saw it here admired it, and I wore it with pride and pleasure, as a constant memento of you. I assure you, I am grieved beyond measure at my loss; and know not how to excuse myself, or express to you my regret. Forgive me this apparent carelessness; — for really it was *not* carelessness; — and let the poem itself plead for me in the German tongue.[2]

I had a letter yesterday from Pfizer the author of "The Two Locks of Hair."[3] He writes me that the poem was not written with reference to his own condition but that of a friend. Since writing it he has married; and for a long time was haunted with the prophetic fear of its proving true in his own case; but is at length ransomed from this fear by the birth of a second child.

The translation I send you is by Freiligrath. He has also translated The Skeleton in Armor, and is at work upon the Hesperus and several others. He no longer reminds me of Dr. Follen, but of Felton; being constantly so merry and laughter-loving. We are going tomorrow down the Rhine to Bonn and the romantic region of the Siebengebirge which lies opposite.

Yesterday arrived here Mr. Colvert and wife of Baltimore. I knew them some years ago at Newport. They are exceedingly pleasant people; and it is delightful to grasp once more an American hand. She is a sister of Mrs. Aug. Thorndike; and knows all my Boston friends; so that we have a great many sympathies in common. They left Sam Eliot and Ned Perkins in Switzerland; and speak in high terms of both. (Please give Mrs. Cleveland her part of this.) Last Winter they were in France; and have come away *inspired* with Powers' Statue of Eve.[4] It must be a very great work of art; for there seems to be but one voice about it, and that of enthusiastic eulogy. "It is more beautiful than the Venus, and Thorwaldsen, the Dane, says that Powers has produced a new era in Art." He wants five thousand dollars for it. Could that sum be raised by subscription in Boston? or have the Bostonians enough with Crawford's Orpheus?[5]

Sam Eliot is coming to Marienberg; with half a mind to take the cold baths. He complains of being still very weak; and in that case would find them of the greatest use; for I have become very strong; and so patient of fatigue that I am all day long on foot without any sense of weariness. I hope he will try the waters here; though I shall not urge him, against his will. Mrs. Eliot, as you probably know, is at St. Germain with the Thorndikes.

It is now half past ten in the morning here; and with you about half past five. The birds are just waking you from pleasant dreams; and the sun shines bright on those eastern windows. You will soon hear that symphony of distant and low-toned bells to which I used to listen with such delight every Sunday morning. Then remember me. I awake in the morning just in time to bid you good night as you go to bed; and if you and my other Cambridge friends think of me half as often as I think of you we shall bridge the Atlantic with affectionate remembrances, and there will be no hour in the day, when some friendly thought is not taking wing hither or thither, like a carrier-pigeon.

And so, Good morning. My kindest regards to you all. Kiss little Grace[6] for me; tell Charles the purse of coin increases; and beg Louisa and Jane to tell Miss Lowell I have written to her twice; and a third time by to-day's mail.[7]

Ever yours
H. W. L.

P. S. I wrote you last by the *Moselle,* direct from Havre to Boston.[8] I wrote last week to Cleveland and Felton.[9]

MANUSCRIPT: Harvard College Library.

1. Before Longfellow departed for Europe, his Cambridge friends had presented him with a seal ring, engraved with the motto "Excelsior." According to his journal, he lost it on July 6. It was later replaced (see 743.13).

2. A printed copy of Freiligrath's translation of "Excelsior" from the Stuttgart *Morgenblatt* (704.2) follows at this point.

3. Gustav Pfizer (1807–1890), a minor German poet and translator, was editor of the Stuttgart *Morgenblatt für gebildete Leser.* His letter to Longfellow, dated July 10, 1842, is printed in Maria Applemann, *H. W. Longfellows Beziehungen zu Ferdinand Freiligrath* (Münster, 1915), pp. 16–17. For Longfellow's translation of Pfizer's "Der Junggesell," see Letter No. 606.

4. Hiram Powers (1805–1873), Vermont-born neoclassical sculptor, resided

in Florence, where the Calverts had visited him in his studio. Calvert described the "Eve" in his *Scenes and Thoughts in Europe* (New York, 1846), pp. 93–96. It is now in the Cincinnati Art Museum.

5. See 579.3.

6. Youngest of the Norton children (b. 1834).

7. These letters are unrecovered.

8. See Letter No. 696.

9. For the letter to Cleveland, see No. 701. The letter to Felton, written on July 12 (MS Journal), is unrecovered.

## 708. *To Ferdinand Freiligrath*

Marienberg July 30. 1842[1]

My dear Freiligrath,

I send the inclosed with many thanks. The pipe and I arrived safely; and the former excited the admiration of the multitude, being formally introduced after supper, as children generally are after dinner.[2]

Meanwhile I hope no accident happened to you and your friends. I suppose they have now left you; and that you will be able to come to our Ball tomorrow evening. To repeat the invitation is one reason why I now write. You must *all* come; and close this delightful week with a dance. If you see the Landrath, pray tell him, we all expect him, and his family.[3]

I find the trip down river has really done me good. I confessed my sins to Dr. Schmitz, and the gracious and pleasant manner with which he received the intelligence of my flirtation with the Maitrank[4] made me regret that I had not been more ardent and assiduous in my devotion.

I close this here, for fear of missing the post. And so good bye, till Saturday evening. With kind regards to Helena and Andromache, I remain, my dear Hector,

Ever yours
Nestor.[5]

MANUSCRIPT: Longfellow Trust Collection.

1. Although Longfellow dated this letter July 30, the reference in the second paragraph to "our Ball tomorrow evening" makes it clear that it was written on the 29th (see n. 3).

2. The "inclosed" refers possibly to money borrowed from Freiligrath during the Rhine tour. The pipe was a "beautiful Meerschaum," purchased by Longfellow in Cologne on July 27, according to his journal.

3. Longfellow's MS Journal entry for Saturday, July 30, gives details of the Marienberg ball: "A grand ball by the company here. Very gay: and swift-footed dancing. The Germans dance the Walz well, in the quadrille they do not excel. We did not break up till half past one. At the close the servants young and old

had a dance. Freiligrath did not accept the invitation to what he called our *Sitzbad-dansant.*"

4. A wine flavored with woodruff.

5. The Homeric names refer to Fräulein von Gall, Ida Freiligrath, Freiligrath, and Longfellow. They were adopted when one of the group dubbed Freiligrath's house "Ihlium" (after the landlord, a man named Ihl). See *New Light on Longfellow,* pp. 91–92.

## 709. *To Joseph Bosworth*

Marienberg. 31 July 1842

My dear friend,

I received this morning with great pleasure and still greater pain yours of the 23rd. Most deeply and most sincerely do I sympathize with you in your bereavement;[1] and recall the time when I was afflected and you the consoler. I know but too well what a dreadful blow this must be to you; and how poor is that consolation, which the words of others can inspire. I will not, then, intrude upon your grief with any attempt to make it less, saving so far as the expression of my sympathy with you may do it. From your own heart, from dear recollections of the departed — and from that stream, by whose waters you have sat so long, will flow serenity and peace.

I fear, however, that so sudden a blow will affect your health even more than you may at first imagine; and am glad your physician has recommended travel. Shall you come to the Continent? If so I beg of you to come this way. I have been here already seven weeks, taking the usual course of cold baths; and find my health and strength improved. Should you feel the need of something of the kind pray remember Marienberg, where I shall remain till the end of August, and where I should be delighted to see you.

I am rejoiced to hear, that my little volume of poems found favor in your sight. I confess the sin of being pleased when my friends tell me I have given them pleasure; and you will agree with me, that there is a certain satisfaction in finding, that one's words have found an echo here and there in another heart.

Have you published the new edition of your Dictionary yet?[2] Within the last few years, I have not heard of many new publications in Anglo-Saxon. What are Mr. Thorpe and Mr. Kemble doing?[3] The former has a step-daughter in America. She lived some time in Cambridge; — a very intelligent young woman.

I hope before returning to America to visit England. But *when,* is still uncertain. I may return home in October; I may remain in Europe another year; in which case I should visit Italy again, and perhaps Constantinople.

I shall hope to hear from you again, as soon as you have leisure and spirits to write; and meanwhile remain

Very sincerely and affect[ionatel]y
Henry W. Longfellow

MANUSCRIPT: Pierpont Morgan Library.

1. Mrs. Bosworth had died of a heart attack on July 6 (Bosworth to Longfellow, July 23, 1842).

2. See 672.1

3. Benjamin Thorpe (1782–1870) and John Mitchell Kemble (1807–1857), philologists and Anglo-Saxon scholars. Kemble was the nephew of Mrs. Siddons and the son of Charles Kemble, the actor.

## 710. *To George Washington Greene*

Marienberg. Aug. 2. 1842.

My dear George,

I was on the point of writing to you again, fearing that my first had miscarried, when your answer arrived. I need not tell you how glad I was to hear from you. But the air wafted from Rome in your letter; — the air, that has stirred the pines in the Villa Borghese, and cooled its wings in the Fontana di Trevi, makes my cheek flush with impatience to see once more the streets of Rome, and take you and your wife by the hand. You have struck your spurs deep into my already excited imagination; and were I not afraid of marring instead of making our mutual happiness, I would start tomorrow for Milan, and reach Rome as soon as this letter will. But any precipitate step would disturb a well regulated plan. I must wait patiently until I receive letters from Cambridge authorizing my longer absence; and then I may be able to pass two months in Rome instead of two days.

I am sorry to see you in so mournful a state of mind as your letter indicates. I think you do your friends at home a good deal of injustice. The Wards were very much interested in your case; particularly Mr Richard Ward.[1] We talked the matter over and over again; and tried to derive some method of bringing about the result desired. I wrote one or two letters to Members of Congress on the subject; and Sumner watched every opportunity to bring the matter forward without being intrusive. One member of the house I saw personally and urged the matter upon him. In fine all that could be decently done by us, was done. I had a letter a few days ago from Hillard, in which he says that Sumner was at that moment writing you; and I hope before this, that his letter has reached you, with some good tidings. So much for the main business. As to other matters, I cannot reproach myself much. I have always written you very, *very* long letters; and if your last was not answered, it was owing to severe illness in the Autumn, and the hurry of preparation for departure afterwards. I have sent you repeatedly, and *by post as you requested,* pamphlets, newspapers and books, and have not heard of one of them reaching you. I sent you all the sheets of my last volume of poems, in this way; and find by your letter that they never came to hand. I can send,—but to make things reach you safely, that is not in my power. I have sent by post, by private hand, by transient vessels; and it would seem that the only thing that ever went straight to the mark, was the volume of poems taken to you by Mr. [Edward] Everett.

But I beg of you, do not despond at such trifles. Have confidence in your friends, and believe me, you are never forgotten by them. Mr. and Mrs. Calvert, who passed the winter in Florence, are now here. They give me glowing accounts of you, taken from the lips of others. It would seem, indeed, as if the conduct of that poor Mr. Austin had turned the hearts of his countrymen towards you, without an exception.[2] So do not bate one jot of courage, but walk forward to success.

I long to talk with you about your History of Italy.[3] I long ago came over to the opinion, that this was better than a mere literary history; particularly as you can weave in the literary history through the whole. Of course you have times and seasons when you cannot write. Everyone has. I have not written anything since last November. I often have weeks of mental inactivity;—weeks?—no, months. But what of that? I know, and you know from experience, that after such seasons of repose comes a harvest. The greater part of my last volume, was written in October and November last, and out of that time deduct three weeks of fever, when I could not hold a pen.

You see, my dear George, that I have as hard a time of it as you do; but my temperament is not so desponding. Still, I sometimes feel as if my mind never would resume its activity; and then lo! *quelque beau matin* [some beautiful morning], a poem rains down upon me, like manna in the desert; and I revive again. You see, therefore, that your case is not peculiar. But enough of this. We will discuss these matters when we meet.

My dear Carlotta,

It is a shame to answer your kind note thus, on the back of your husband's letter; but you must remember that I am a poor invalid here at the baths, and that it is a great effort for me to write a letter of any kind. I am trying to get well with all possible speed, so as to visit you the sooner (*whether I can or not*) and stay the longer with you. I long most ardently to see you and Italy once more; and as soon as the cords that bind me fall, I shall start like a race-horse in the Corso at Carnival,

Yours as ever very truly
H. W. L.

And now, my dear George, good bye. I must go to my bath — my *fifth* to-day, with a sixth still *in petto*. Patience — patience. Remember me most particularly to Crawford and thank him again and again from me for the delight unceasing he has given me by his admirable bust of you. Write again as soon as you can; for I hope in my next to send you something more definite in regard to my visit to you.

Till then, ever yours
Henry W. Longfellow.

Pray send me in your next the name of *Julia's* husband, and their address in Paris.[4] I want to see once more my *antiqua flamma.*

Ticknor has not yet pubd. any part of his History of Spanish Literature.[5] He is working at it in a gentlemanly way, — and with none of that speed "which mars all decency of action."[6]

MANUSCRIPT: Mrs. Brenton Greene Meader, Providence, Rhode Island. ADDRESS: George W. Greene, Esq/Consul of the United States/Rome./Italia POSTMARKS: BOPPARD $\frac{3}{8}$/ASCHAFFENBURG $\frac{3}{8}$/DIREZIONE DE ROMA 15 AGO 42

1. Richard Ray Ward (1795–1873), New York lawyer and uncle of Sam Ward. In his letter of July 17, 1842, Greene had included a querulous paragraph on the subject of his consular salary: "From Sumner I have heard nothing but by letters of introduction for a year. He has never told me the result of his efforts in favor of my salary and I have been left to conjecture it from the tone of the newspapers and the silence of my friends. Had some of my relations seen fit to exert themselves upon that occasion, the thing would have succeeded — or at least, they could have got me a better berth. A friend of mine who called upon the Wards to ask their concurrence in an effort he was making, found them so indifferent or rather so ill desposed that he left them in disgust. I know that by proper steps the thing might have been accomplished — but a man who has lived abroad seven years, must make up his mind to be forgotten however hard the lesson be to learn."

2. See 577.2.

3. An abortive project.

4. Greene answered: "You will find Julia here with all her family. The old lady is dead: the girls still unmarried and with precious little chance of ever getting husbands, unless their faces should change or some old codger leave them an attractive dowry" (Letter of August 16, 1842).

5. The three volumes were published in 1849.

6. *Divine Comedy,* "Purgatory," III, 11.

711. *To Samuel Ward*

Marienberg August 6 1842

My dear Sam,

I have received two letters from you since my arrival here. The first I answered as promptly as I could;[1] and the second I am now answering. I should have written you sooner; but my time is very much occupied; as you will perceive anon. I have been here now exactly two months; and have gone on *crescendo* in the number of my baths. I have now six a day; with long walks between; and if you will look at the matter dispassionately, you will see, that I have very little leisure. You will not therefore be astonished nor surprised that I write so seldom; particularly when I tell you that in addition to yourself I have ten other correspondents not including chance shots every now and then. To all these I have written at least twice; and yet by some unlucky *Windstoss des Schicksals* [windstorm of Fate], my letters seem to have been scattered to the four corners of the heavens. A letter from Sumner two days ago says that nothing has been heard from me, and upbraids me for my silence. Now I beg of you, if at any time you feel disposed to chide me for neglect, that you will duly consider what I can do and what I cannot. I have been here sixty days and have written at least thirty letters; and I consider this very well for a sick-man, who is wrapped in a wet sheet every morning at half past three, — walks and bathes all day long; and goes to bed at nine, with a wet towel round his throat. When you write to Sumner, tell him of this; and tell him likewise that I have written him by the steamer that brings you this.[2]

Your account of Felton's carpet bag trying to elope with Dickens's was very amusing.[3] Felton enjoys himself exceedingly in New York. He has written me about his visit there with Howe. His admiration of your sisters is beyond all bounds. Among other things he says; "Julia is the most remarkable person I ever knew. Every time I see her, some new power or attraction strikes me; and I am astounded, that all the unmarried men are not *piled up at her feet*!"[4] That is a compliment worth sending across the Atlantic. I am glad you like Howe so much. He is one of the noblest characters in the world. Are they not a glorious set of Friends, Sumner, Hillard, Howe, Felton, Cleveland?

I had a letter a day or two ago from Greene in Rome. He feels that his friends in America neglect him, and that we might have done more about his salary as Consul, or a better place for him. If any stone can still be turned pray have it done. I hear the best accounts of Greene from the Calverts of Baltimore, who are here. They passed last Winter in Italy; and give me delightful tidings of his popularity among his countrymen, and their exertions to obtain him a better place or a salary. The[y] also speak in glowing terms of the Eve of Powers; — likewise of Crawford and Clevenger.[5] The American Artists stand high. Greenough is now in Paris. He is making a bust of Washington Irving.

Inclosed is a translation of Excelsior, by Freiligrath. It was published first in the *Morgenblatt,* of which Pfizer is the editor. I had a letter from Pfizer touching my translation of his Jungesell or "The Two Locks of Hair." It is singular; — it was not his own personal experience, but was written for a friend, to whom it was applicable; and I translated it for a friend to whom it was equally so.[6] Freiligrath has also translated the Skeleton in Armor. It will appear in a few days in the Morgenblatt; and I will send it to you as soon as possible.

I have been giving as much attention as possible to the young poets. Freiligrath stands at the head of them all and at present attracts more notice than any living poet, save Uhland. Nikolaus Becker has published a volume, remarkable only for one song on the Rhine, which procured the author a place under government, and a great deal of reputation.[7] Herwegh[8] is another poet, who has won a hearing by his political (radical) songs. They are full of fire and energy. *Geisel,*[9] a young man of Lübeck imitates Freiligrath, but is a poet of promise. Lenau[10] and Auersperg stand high, of course. *Young Germany* is rather quiet just now. Heine has injured himself exceedingly by a book against Börne, which I have not read.[11] Three remarkable novels have appeared within as many years. *Münchhausen* by Immerman, who died lately; — a work in six volumes, satyric and idylic; — William's Dichten u. Trachten (meaning Will. Shakespeare —) by H. König; — an imaginary romance of his youth and manhood; — and Blasedow, by Gutzkow.[12] Sedlitz, author of the *Nächtliche Heerschau* is writing a long poem in the style of the *Minnesängers.*[13] He passed down the Rhine the other day; so did Uhland;[14] — I was not fortunate enough to see either of them.

I am vexed with you for giving away my portrait. In the first place, it was not yours to give; — in the second place, if it had been you should not have given it away; — and in the third place it is a mere caricature, and ought to have been destroyed.[15]

And how is the Summer passing with you? I imagine you toiling through the red-hot days in Wall street; and at nightfall mounting your steed, and trotting out to woo the sea-breeze and your sisters at Hell gate. Pray tell Mr. Astor that Mr. Rumpff[16] is here, trying the *Wasserkur*. What a mild, beneficent expression of countenance he has! How is Cogswell? Is it true that the New York Review has been discontinued?[17]

The "Spanish Student" apears in Graham's Mag. for September. Send me a copy straightway, I beg you; or rather drop a line to Mr. Griswold, Editor of the Mag. requesting him to send me a copy of all the sheets, *as soon as printed*, care of "Coates &co. 13 Bread Street Cheapside London."[18]

Farewell my dear Sam. Half my time of absence has expired and more than half. I shall soon be with you again; sitting once more by the fire-side — by the old Dutch tiles in Castle Craigie. Home is pleasanter than this wandering alone over the world. If I come back well! — *if* — ah, that is the worst thought; for I am not well yet; but fluctuating between the same and better.

Brentano, Bettina's brother and editor of the Wunderhorn is dead.[19] A copy of Dr. Francis's Address has been sent to Humboldt.[20] Freiligrath has another. He likes it very much, and promises such a notice as a poet can write. Send your next letters to the care of Coates &co. London. Graeter's book on the *Wasserkur*[21] pleases people here very much. Give my kindest regards to your sisters three and to all my friends in New York.

Ever affectionately yours
Henry W. Longfellow

P.S. I intended to give you some account of the baths here; but had not room.

This will be a great year for wine; — equal they think to 1834.

MANUSCRIPT: Longfellow Trust Collection. ADDRESS: Samuel Ward Esq/(Prime Ward & King.)/New York./Care of Coates &co/No 13 Bread Street/London [*all after "New York" deleted*] POSTMARKS: B/PAID AUG 1842/BOSTON [*remainder illegible*]

1. Letter No. 688.
2. Letter No. 712.
3. "On board the packet ship [in New York harbor] Felton accidentally met with his carpet bag which, it seems, had taken a liking to Dickens' luggage and bewitched the porter who had been charged to carry it on board the Providence steamer, into placing it along with the 'Boz baggage' " (Ward to Longfellow, June 15, 1842).
4. See 705.10.
5. Shobal Vail Clevenger (1812–1843), Ohio-born sculptor, had lived in Rome since 1840. His sculpture "North American Indian" was attracting considerable attention.
6. The "friend" was Ward himself. See Letter No. 606.
7. See 690.13.
8. Georg Herwegh (1817–1875), revolutionary poet and author of *Gedichtes eines Lebendigen* (Zurich and Winterthur, 1841).

9. Emanuel Geibel (1815–1884), whose first book of poems, *Zeitstimmen,* appeared in 1841.

10. Nikolaus Lenau, pseudonym of Nikolaus Niembsch von Strehlenau (1802–1850), Austrian poet.

11. In *Heinrich Heine über Ludwig Börne* (Hamburg, 1840) Heine permitted himself to indulge in personal animosity against his enemies. He was attacked severely for the book. Both Heine and Börne (1786–1837) had been leaders in Young Germany, a literary movement with liberal and revolutionary ideals.

12. Karl Leberecht Immermann, *Münchhausen. Eine Geschichte in Arabesken* (Düsseldorf, 1838–1839), appeared in 4 vols., not 6 (second edition, 1841). The other two novels were Heinrich Joseph König, *Williams Dichten und Trachten. Ein Roman* (Hanau, 1839), and Karl Ferdinand Gutzkow, *Blasedow und seine Söhne. Komischer Roman* (Stuttgart, 1838), 3 vols.

13. "Die nächtliche Heerschau," a celebrated ballad by Joseph Christian Freiherr von Zedlitz (1790–1862), concerns Napoleon's review of his fallen heroes. The "long poem" is presumably a reference to von Zedlitz's *Waldfräulein. Ein Mährchen in 18 Abentheuern* (Stuttgart, 1843).

14. Johan Ludwig Uhland (1787–1862), whose "Das Schloss am Meere," "Der schwarze Ritter," and "Das Glück von Edenhall" had been translated by Longfellow (*Works,* VI, 268–269, 269–271, and 273–275).

15. Ward had written: "Your picture has passed into the hands of a young lady — one of your ardent admirers — as her *cultus* of Frankenstein's red and white applications of paint to canvas sufficiently shows. So that your visage will soon live in another heart."

16. Vincent R. Rumpff (1789–1867), minister-resident in Paris of the free cities of Hamburg, Lübeck, Bremen, and Frankfort. He had been the husband of John Jacob Astor's youngest daughter, Eliza Astor Rumpff (1801–1838).

17. The *New York Review* had ceased publication in April 1842.

18. Longfellow deleted this paragraph and inserted the following note: "You need not execute this commission." See 705.6.

19. Clemens Brentano (1778–1842), German poet, was the brother of Bettina von Arnim (1785–1859), romantic authoress and correspondent of Goethe. Brentano and his brother-in-law, Ludwig Joachim von Arnim (1781–1831), published *Des Knaben Wunderhorn* (Heidelberg, 1806–1808).

20. Baron Alexander von Humboldt (1769–1859), naturalist and traveler. The "Address" was presumably *A Discourse: Delivered upon the Opening of the New Hall of the New-York Lyceum of Natural History,* by John W. Francis, M.D. (New York, 1841).

21. See 632.8.

## 712. *To Charles Sumner*

Marienberg, August 8, 1842.

My dear Charles,

Pray look upon this as a Psalm Penitential and pardon my sins. Yours of the 15th of July reached me in seventeen days and filled my soul with dismay. None of my letters received! But how could you for a moment imagine that I had not written? Learn then that I have written to you twice before this, twice to Felton, twice to Hillard, twice to Sam Ward, twice to Miss Lowell, twice to Mrs. Norton, twice to my father, and once to Cleveland.[1] The difficulty was I had forgotten [John] Hillard's address in London, and was obliged to send by the way of Havre. I rue my negligence most bitterly, for I have fallen under the reproaches of my friends.

And now must I imagine these letters all lost? Must I begin again, and tell you how often I lay on the deck of our ship at night, and gazed up at Charles' Wain, and the rocking of "marble sails"[2] overhead? Must I tell you again how I reached the Rhineland? How many baths I take a day; and in fine go through the details of my insignificant life once more? No, I will trust to my stars. Those letters have all reached you ere this and your wrath is appeased.

And now, my dear Charles, I wish I could pour out into your heart in one overwhelming douche all the thoughts that fill and agitate my own. This I dare not do, for I know that other eyes than yours will read this letter, and though they are the eyes of my best friends yet the letter is no longer tête-à-tête. I cannot speak to six together as I could to each. Rather let me seem dull and commonplace.

It is now afternoon of a hot day. A legion of flies from the garden into which my window looks, are buzzing about my head, and I have just hit a wasp a whack with a book which sent him reeling across the room. On such days cold baths are delicious, and I am looking forward with a certain inward satisfaction to the one that awaits me. But I have resolved to say nothing of baths in this letter, so I turn to something else. As you may imagine, I never lose an opportunity of making excursions in the neighborhood. I have been to Rolandseck, and the Drachenfels, to Bonn, Cologne, Coblentz and Ems. I have climbed every ruin within ten miles, and some more distant. I shall know the Rhine well before my return. When is that to be? Have you seen the President about the books?[3] I am quite in doubt as to my future destiny. I should like to take a run to Italy, and Spain, and I should like to return home. — What annoys me is the slowness of the Wasserkur. It does not operate with one-half the speed and vigor I imagined it would. After two months I do not find the decided advantage I anticipated. But two months are a very short time. There is an Englishman here who has been at Graefenberg three years, and is not yet well. This however does not shake my confidence. I hope in one month more to feel a very great change for the better.

I had a letter from Greene a few days ago. He complains of us all for not writing to him oftener, and seems to be hurt by supposed neglect of his friends at home. I consoled him in my answer as well as I could, explaining a letter was on the way from you, which fact

Hillard mentioned in his last. Greene urges me very strongly to come to Rome. I need no urging. By the way, Mr. Calvert who is here fresh from Italy, gives excellent accounts of Greene and says among other things that he is much beloved by all Americans, and that they have all signed a petition about his salary.

I have already told you of the Freiligraths at St. Goar and my intimacy with them. I almost imagine Felton translated into German with scraps of a mustache, and one of his front teeth knocked out. I send you in this a translation of Excelsior by him, and will soon send you the Skeleton, the Blacksmith and Endymion. Freiligrath is the best of the young poets of Germany. He is not one of the Gutzkow school; — not one of young Germany.[4]

Let me say with pride and thankfulness — even here upon the glorious Rhine, I think with longing of Boston and its beautiful environs; and the pleasant drives through Brookline. In my imagination the whole landscape floats in sunshine, and you all — my friends — are the Saints walking the terrestrial Paradise. I envy myself my beautiful home in Cambridge so well adapted to enjoyment and to labor. — I shall return even from Italy with a zest.

I have not yet fully made up my mind when I shall be in England, probably not before the first of October — I mean in case I return this Autumn. As soon, however, as you can get a copy of the "Spanish Student" send it to the care of Coates & Co. to be kept by them until I come to England.[5]

I have not had time since I am here to write a verse or a line. There is no inspiration in dressing and undressing. Hunger and thirst figure too largely here, to leave room for poetical figures.

I am expecting daily Eliot & Perkins. Sam is not well yet; and I think it possible he may stay here awhile. I am confident it would do him good.

Kind regards to my friends in Boston and Cambridge. When you see Charley Norton tell him I have 68 Roman coins for him — time-worn, rusty old Caesars dug up here under the walls of Boppard. And now for fear of losing the next steamer *Finis*!

Yours ever affectionately,
Henry W. Longfellow.

I have written to Sam Ward by this post.[6]

MANUSCRIPT: unrecovered; text from "Letters to Samuel Ward," Part III, pp. 306–307.

1. With the exception of those to Felton and Miss Lowell, these letters appear in this volume.

2. From line 40 of Hillard's poem on Longfellow's departure (683.3).

3. See Letter No. 705.

4. Gutzkow (1811–1878), novelist, dramatist, founder of the *Deutsche Revue,* and a leader in the Young Germany movement.

5. The Cambridge edition of *The Spanish Student,* published by Owen, did not appear until the spring of 1843. Longfellow may have been referring to the installments printed in *Graham's Magazine* (705.6).

6. Letter No. 711.

## 713. *To Ferdinand Freiligrath*

[Marienberg] Monday morning. [August 15, 1842]

My dear Freiligrath,

This will be handed you by Mr. Lee of Boston,[1] who is on his way to Constantinople and Egypt. As he proposes to stop for the remainder of the day in St. Goar, I think I cannot do you both a greater pleasure than to make you acquainted with each other. If you have leisure this afternoon, pray climb the *Katze* with him, or the *festung*; and walk up to the Lorelei in the evening.

I am very sorry I have not been able to see you this week, nor to write to you, but really I have been too ill. Since monday last I have had the *grippe* or a *crisis* I do not know which; and have suffered night and day, violent head-ache and tooth-ache, with all the other pleasing ingredients which go to make up that infernal *ragout.* To-day I feel somewhat better; and hope in a few days to be quite well again.

Yours truly, with kind regards to the ladies

Henry W. Longfellow

P.S. Thanks to Helena[2] for the music, which was duly received. Remember me to the Landrath [Heuberger]; and tell him I am heartily, *heartily* tired of staying here; and that I shall never be caught again in a *Hospital* until that *final one* prepared for all poets.

MANUSCRIPT: Longfellow Trust Collection.

1. Henry Lee (1817–1898), a member of the Harvard class of 1836. The date of this letter is established by his movements, for according to Longfellow's MS Journal, he arrived at Marienberg on Sunday, August 14, and spent Tuesday, August 16, at St. Goar.

2. Fräulein von Gall.

## 714. *To Ferdinand Freiligrath*

Marienberg. Aug. 26. [1842]

My dear Freiligrath,

Your precious package and note reached me safely yesterday morning; and I have done nothing since, in my moments of leisure, but read your book upon Immermann.[1] It is exceedingly interesting; and a very appropriate and beautiful monument to his memory. I have read too little of Immerma[n]n's writings to form any judgment of my own in regard to his genius. I must take his fame on credit, for the present, though before long I hope to be better acquainted with him. Many thanks to you for this introduction to his merits.

Why do you think so slightly of that very striking, original, and beautiful poem of yours; "Dread Naught."[2] I assure you I think very highly of it. You should re-touch it here and there; and omit one or two stanzas, and print it in your next collection. Believe me, it is a fine thought, and for the most part well carried out. You must not throw it away.

Thanks also for Hackländer's book. It looks interesting; and I feel quite sure I shall read it with great pleasure; as I certainly shall the two Tales of our fair friend in St. Goar, which I shall begin tomorrow.[3]

When shall we make our Journey to Johannisberg? Before you go to Köln or after you return? The latter would be more convenient for me; — say the 7th or 8th — or in fine, as soon as you get back. But we will discuss that subject more at large, when I see you, which will be in the course of a day or two.

When you write to Hackländer thank him from me for his kindness in sending the book; and say to him I shall send him a return, as soon as possible.

Yesterday in the Kölnische Zeitung appeared Fräulein v. Ploennies's translation of Pulaski's Banner.[4] On the whole it is very good, so far as my recollection of the original serves me, excepting the lines

"When the clarion's music thrills
To the hearts of these lone hills."

— Would it not be proper for me to write her a note, to thank her?

I have begun the *Traubencur,*[5] not *in the place* of my usual diet, but *in addition to it.* As the hour of my departure draws nigh I begin to feel regret at leaving the Rhine, and the new friends I have found here. I shall hate to bid you farewell.

Most sincerely yours, with kind regard to the ladies,

Henry W. Longfellow

MANUSCRIPT: Longfellow Trust Collection.

1. Freiligrath's letter was dated August 24, 1842 ("Longfellow-Freiligrath Correspondence, p. 1237). His book on Immermann was *Karl Immermann. Blätter der Erinnerung an ihn* (Stuttgart, 1842).

2. This poem of thirty-three four-line stanzas, prefaced by Freiligrath's apology, appears in the Immermann volume, pp. 120–126.

3. These books were Friedrich Wilhelm Hackländer's *Vier Könige. — Bilder aus dem Soldatenleben* (Stuttgart, 1841) and Louise von Gall's short novels *Der Neuling* and *Maske,* first published in the *Cottaschen Morgenblatt* (March 21 and 23, and June, 1842).

4. Luise von Plönnies (1803–1872), lyricist and dramatist, entitled her translation "Hymne der pennsylvanischen Nonnen bei der Einweihung von Pulaski's Banner."

5. In his MS Journal entry for August 8, 1842, Longfellow wrote: "Everybody is now talking about the Trauben-cur, which consists in living for a month almost exclusively upon grapes. Some propose to purchase portions of gardens; and eat their eight or ten pounds under their own vineyard."

## 715. *To Catherine Eliot Norton*

Marienberg August 26. [1842]

My dear Mrs. Norton

This is my last letter to you from Marienberg; for the hour of my departure draws near. Alas! I have *no letter* from you to answer; and this all owing to my own want of forethought. I cannot forgive myself for sending those first letters by the way of Havre. I fear they have not reached you yet. No one seems to have heard from me; yet this is my fifth note to you and to all my other correspondents (there are *only eight* of them). I have written at least twice.

Since I last wrote the Convent has been unusually gay. Ten days ago arrived Mr. Harry Lee, Ned Perkins and Sam Eliot. Lee and Perkins have gone to Wiesbaden and left Sam here. The convent walls are again silent and echo no more to the unwonted laugh, which they caught from such gay spirits. Ned is not in the least changed; — he neither lisps nor wears strange suits; but is the same kind-hearted, happy, free, and cordial fellow, as before his travels began. I hardly need tell you, that this is mostly true likewise of Sam; and I am grieved to see that even in health he is not changed. He is in truth very feeble, — very unwell; and I have persuaded him to stay here a few days for quiet and repose during the hot weather. The doctor here has examined his case, and gives it as his opinion, that he has a slight enlargement of the heart; which he thinks can be cured by cold water; though it will take a long, long while to do it. Dr. Mayo, chief surgeon of one of the London hospitals, (who is here for the gout), thinks this treatment the only one, that can cure him. At all events they say that his life for two or three years to come should be one of great quiet.

Unfortunately Sam is very excited and restless. He wants to return home. He wants to start for Paris immediately; and means to leave here in a day or two; — as soon as Ned returns from Wiesbaden. Of course I cannot tell you in a letter all that he says about himself; but I will tell you what most troubles him. He is afraid that his friends at home misjudge him; — that they imagine he is well, and travelling for pleasure to the neglect of duty. You know how conscientious he is; and I assure you this thought seems never to desert his mind, but renders him constantly restless and unhappy. I have tried to persuade him, that this was only his excited fancy; — and have vouched for you, that no severe judgment had been passed upon his conduct under your roof, having so often spoken with you about him. The truth is, he is very nervous; and if you would write him a few lines chiefly on this point, it would soothe him a great deal.

Pardon me for being the messenger of bad news; for bad as they are, I thought it right to send them to you, knowing the lively interest you take in Sam's welfare. You must not be allarmed; but if Sam should return now to Boston he would be no more able to go into business than he was when he left home last Autumn.[1]

I shall remain here a fortnight longer, and then go to London where I hope to find a letter from you, absolving me from the supposed sin of negligence. I shall feel some regret at leaving Marienberg. I shall miss the cold baths in the morning early; I shall miss the strange but now familiar figures that haunt the place; — the old Dutch admiral (the Flying Dutchman) thundering thro' the cloisters at night with his great cane;[2] — the pale, young Jewess, who is carried out in her chair every morning to sit on the terrace, and breathe the fresh air;[3] — the gouty English surgeon,[4] who rides into his chamber on a donkey, and tumbles out of the saddle into bed; — the meek, suffering faces of so many youthful martyrs to disease, teaching constant lessons of patience; — the pretty Miss Gyde, who walks with a stride, like Ellen Tree in the Bandit's Bride;[5] — the Prima Donna of the Düsseldorf theatre, to whom I make love every morning at half-past five o'clock at the fountain in the garden, gallantly filling the tin dipper for her to drink from; (while her husband is lying in his bed bound hand and foot in a blanket);[6] — the Russian Colonel who roars, like a maniac, in the *douche*;[7] the merry music-master, who sings in bed, and in his baths;[8] — and finally, thou, sweet *Jacobina Schmitz,* fair daughter of the Water-doctor at *Marienberg bei Boppard am Rhein*; — born on the margin of this river of romance; — and now just *under the eaves of twenty,* looking forth upon the world with thy tender eyes, dark hair, and green album. All these and many more, I shall recall with interest and a certain kind of painful pleasure, when I look upon their faces no more; for it is one of my weaknesses, to become attached to people and places.

Will you say to Charles, that I have thus far been very successful in collecting coins for him. I have already more than a hundred; among them a *Drei Königs-Thaler,* or Dollar of the Three Kings of Cologne,[9] with the Three Kings Caspar, Melchior and Balthasar adoring the Saviour on one side and St. Peter with a huge key on the other; — sundry other old German coins; and 86 ancient Romans, found under the walls of the Imperial city of Boppard.

Sam, who has the next room to mine has just opened the door to say; "Give my best, best love to Aunt Catherine, and all my uncles, aunts and cousins, — and inform *her* (that is *you*) that as soon as I reach Paris, I shall despatch her a long letter." I beg you to do the same for me; adding Miss Lowell. Inclosed is another poem in German. *Do* look at the signature. The young lady says she is *after* me![10] I hate to close my letter; but there is no remedy. Therefore

Ever sincerely yours
H. W. L.

MANUSCRIPT: Harvard College Library.

1. Samuel Eliot was Mrs. Norton's nephew, which explains why Longfellow discusses his health at such length.

2. See 701.7.

3. The *Dritte Kur-Liste. Juli und August 1842* of the Wasser-Heil-Anstalt Marienberg lists "Frau Cohen mit 2 Fräulein Töchter und Bedienung aus Hannover." Longfellow presumably refers here to one of the daughters.

4. Dr. Mayo.

5. See 705.5. She reminded Longfellow of Ellen Tree (1805–1880), English comedienne and wife of the actor Charles John Kean.

6. The *Dritte Kur-Liste. Juli und August 1842* and the journal entries for August 27 and September 6 identify them as Heinrich Hammermeister (1799–1860) and his wife. Hammermeister, a leading German baritone of the day, eventually emigrated to New York.

7. Herr Dimitri v. Miloradowitsch, K.K. Russ. Oberst a.D. mit Frau Gemahlin und Bedienung aus Kieff (*Dritte Kur-Liste. Juli und August 1842*).

8. Identified in Longfellow's MS Journal as a man named Kroff (August 27, 1842). He is listed as "Herr Kroff. Artist aus London" in the *Zweite Kur-Liste. Mai und Juni 1842.*

9. Longfellow's marginal note at this point: "(date 1688.)."

10. The poem was Luise von Plönnies' translation, "nach H. W. Longfellow," of "Pulaski's Banner," clipped from the *Kölnische Zeitung.* See 714.4.

## 716. *To Jørgen Bølling*

Marienberg bei Boppard am Rhein. Aug. 31. '42

My dear Sir,

Dr. Folderlund,[1] who starts for Copenhagen tomorrow, offers me the opportunity of writing you a line, to inform you of my welfare and to inquire after yours. It is now a long, long time that I have not heard from you; though I have sent you one or two letters. I hope, however, that you have prospered; — that you are well and happy. I hope also to hear from you, as soon as I reach America. To this place you must not write because I leave it in a few days.

Please inform me of all that is new and striking in Danish Literature, since I left you; what new Poets have sprung up, and what new works have appeared.

Do you know our American Minister at Copenhagen, Mr. Jackson?[2] He is a very clever and agreeable person, and if you do not know him I hope you will take occasion to make his acquaintance. Since I saw you I have published two volumes of poems; The "Voices of the Night" and "Ballads and Other Poems." In the latter is a Ballad of an old *Berserk,* which I think would interest you in Denmark. As soon as I return I will send you copies for the Library. I have also in press a drama "The Spanish Student," which I will send when it appears.

I beg you to present my best regards to Professor Rafn and to Fin[n] Magnussen. I recall always with great pleasure my short stay in your beautiful city; and wish it were in my power to pay you another visit at this time. But alas! it is impossible.

Hoping to hear good news from you, I remain

Very truly yours
Henry W. Longfellow.

P. S. I have been here three months, trying the *Wassercur.* Dr. Folderlund will tell you all about it.

MANUSCRIPT: Royal Library, Copenhagen. ADDRESS: Mr. Bölling/Copenhagen/Fav[ore]d by/Dr. Folderlund. PUBLISHED: "Eight Unpublished Letters," pp. 176–177.

1. Carl Emil Tolderlund (1813–1898), a young Danish doctor, had recently completed his training in Copenhagen. Longfellow wrote "Folderlund" here and below, apparently adopting the error of the *Zweite Kur-Liste. Mai und Juni 1842* of the Wasser-Heil-Anstalt Marienberg, which lists "Herr Folderlund, Dr. der Med. u. Chir. aus Copenhagen."

2. Isaac Rand Jackson of Pennsylvania was U. S. chargé d'affaires to Denmark from October 8, 1841, to his death on July 27, 1842 (State Department Records, National Archives). Longfellow had met him in Philadelphia in January 1841 (Letter No. 575).

## 717. *To Josiah Quincy*

Marienberg. September 3 1842

My dear Sir,

When I left you in the Spring, I thought by this time I should have recovered my health and be setting my face homeward. In this I have been disappointed. My recovery has been slower than I expected; and though considerably better than when I arrived here, I am yet far from being well. The Doctor urges me very strongly to remain longer. He thinks it of the utmost importance to my future health, for years to come, that I should do so. He says, that if I look forward to a life of intellectual labor, in his opinion "it is *absolutely necessary* I should give up all thoughts of returning home before next Summer, devoting the time to rëestablishing my health, and avoiding all severe study." I quote these words from a written opinion which he gave me this morning; and in consequence of which I have determined to ask leave of absence until that time, unless the state of my department in College should absolutely demand my return.

I assure you, that I do this with the greatest reluctance. I have no desire to remain here; on the contrary a very strong desire to be at home and at work. Still I wish to return in good health and spirits, and not to lead a maimed life. I fear, and the physician positively asserts, that if I go back now I shall thwart the whole object of my journey; and that if I hope to be well, I *must* go on with the baths.

I have therefore concluded to remain here until I receive an answer from you; promising myself that when I once escape from this hospital I will never enter another until that final one appointed for all the poets.[1]

Will you have the goodness to say to your daughter, Miss [Eliza Susan] Quincy, that I left her package for Mr. Grahame at its address in Havre; and presume it reached him safely. In coming through France it was not in my power to go into Brittany, and avail myself of your letter of introduction to him; the place of his residence lying too far out of my route.[2] From Paris I came through Belgium to this ancient city of Boppard, where I have remained stationary since the first of June.

Perkins and Eliot have been here for a week past. They are on their way to Paris. Eliot is very feeble and nervous. Mrs. Eliot is in Paris, or that neighborhood.

Not far from Boppard is the scene of St. Genoveva's banishment; which is associated in my mind with the beautiful little statue of her, mounted on the deer, by Rauch, which you have in your drawing-room.[3]

With kind remembrances to Mrs. Quincy, and your family,

Very truly yours
Henry W. Longfellow.

MANUSCRIPT: Harvard College Papers, XI, 153–154. PUBLISHED: Higginson, *Longfellow*, pp. 157–158.

1. Longfellow did not receive an answer to his request until he reached London in October, where letters from President Quincy, Sumner, and Felton informed him that the Harvard Corporation, although not demanding his return, would have to stop his salary on November 30. For President Quincy's letter, dated September 30, 1842, see *Professor Longfellow of Harvard*, pp. 47–48. Felton, writing on October 1, added: "I *do* think it important that you should come home. Your department *does* need your influence, superintendence, and instruction."

2. James Grahame (1790–1842), Glasgow-born author of *The History of the United States of North America, from the Plantation of the British Colonies till their Revolt and Declaration of Independence* (London, 1836), 4 vols. had resided in Nantes, but he died suddenly in London on July 3. His *History* earned him a Harvard LL.D. in 1839 and a defense by President Quincy entitled *The Memory of the Late James Grahame, the Historian of the United States, Vindicated from the Charges of Mr. Bancroft* (Boston, 1846). Bancroft had accused Grahame of historical invention.

3. According to the medieval legend, Genoveva von Brabant was falsely accused of infidelity and spent six years in the forest with her son. A tame roe provided nourishment until Genoveva's husband, Siegfried von Treves, reinstated them. Christian Daniel Rauch (1777–1857), the German sculptor, was among many who made artistic use of the legend.

## 718. *To Ferdinand Freiligrath*

[Marienberg] Wednesday. Sept. 7. [1842]

My dear Freiligrath,

As usual, I have only a couple of minutes to write in, as I am just starting for Bornhofen, and the Brothers.[1] But I must not let the afternoon go by, without writing to urge you once more to go with me to the Manœuver.[2] Let not your hard heart resist my appeal!

And thou, of gentler nature and soul more sensitive, — Countess Ida[3] — intercede for me! Tell him, that this is the only opportunity I shall ever have of seeing an army and a Camp (excepting Camp near Bornhofen)![4] Tell him it is hard for me to subdue my Cologne-inclining wishes; and that a *bivouac*, and a night under a tent, and the *reveille* are things to make an impression upon me forevermore.

Have you seen the "Magazin für Auslandische Litteratur"? It has a paragraph on English Hexameters; in which an extract is given from my translation of Tegnér's "Children of the Lord's Supper."[5]

I sent you on Sunday the paragraph from the American paper, in which some Yankee Nodnagel spoke of me, somewhat as the original German Nodnagel spoke of you, though not so much in detail.[6]

The clock strikes three; — signal for our departure towards the ruins. *Denn Adé! adé! adé!*[7]

Ever yours
Henry W. Longfellow

P.S. Doctor Sc[h]mitz has returned from Cologne, full of fire-works, *dejeuné dinatoire* [lunch-dinner] and the King's Speech. He says it was a brilliant affair; and that your name was called out among the other Deputies, and echo answered "*where*?"[8]

MANUSCRIPT: Longfellow Trust Collection. PUBLISHED (*postscript omitted*): "Longfellow-Freiligrath Correspondence," pp. 1239–1240.

1. Sterrenberg and Liebenstein, the "Brothers," are castles above the convent of Bornhofen, between Boppard and St. Goar.

2. Longfellow left Marienberg on September 10 to observe a Prussian army maneuver at an encampment near Bonn, which ended on September 12 with a parade before King Frederick Wilhelm IV. He returned on the 14th. For political reasons Freiligrath could not be persuaded to accompany him.

3. Frau Freiligrath.

4. Longfellow's pun involves the village of Camp, a few miles above Boppard.

5. *Magazin für die Literatur des Auslandes,* No. 104 (August 31, 1842), 416.

6. See 699.4. The "Yankee Nodnagel" is unidentified.

7. "Then adieu! adieu! adieu!" Last line of a "very pathetic ditty in German, where a lover swears eternal fidelity to his mistress," quoted in the MS Journal entry for August 2, 1842.

8. In February 1842, Freiligrath had accepted a small annual allowance (*Deputat*) from King Frederick William IV. He resigned it early in 1844.

## 719. *To Margaret Boies Bradford Eliot*

Marienberg. Sept. 8. 1842

My dear Mrs. Eliot,

It is very late at night for a Marienberger; namely almost ten o'clock; but as Sam [Eliot] starts in the morning, I cannot go to bed without first writing you two or three lines to remind you of my existence and my remembrance of you. I imagine you walking at evening on the stately terrace of St. Germain, beholding the last gleams of sunshine steal from the meadows of the Seine, and dreaming of many things, tho' chiefly of Marienberg, which holds your treasure — that is to say your son. I hope you will find him all the better for his short residence here; and that you will enjoy a happy, quiet Winter together in the noisy *retirement* of Paris.

What my fate is to be I do not yet know. I may possibly go home this Autumn, and that, too, without meeting you, which I shall regret very much. But if I remain in Europe until the Spring, I shall of course see you; as I propose in that case to revisit Paris.

I am following the Water-cure, and the grape-cure and every other cure under the sun, except the *sinecure,* which I am afraid I shall never come to, in this world. And pray tell me, what are you doing? Do you enjoy France? Do you find Paris pleasant? Or are your anticipations disappointed?

Good night, and perhaps, Good bye. But no; I will not say that;

but rather look forward with pleasing forethoughts to meeting you before I return home.

Give my love to William and Margaret. Tell them to learn as much french as they can; and they will never be sorry for it! (Hem! hints for the education of the young.)

Good night. And believe me

Very truly yours
H. W. Longfellow

MANUSCRIPT: Boston Athenaeum.

720. *To Stephen Longfellow*

Marienberg. Sept. 17. 1842

My dear Father,

I write you but a short note to say that I leave Marienberg tomorrow. I am going up the Rhine as far as Frankfort, perhaps as far as Heidelberg; and then return to Cologne; and across Belgium to Ostend, where I shall take steamer for London. I am not so entirely well as I could wish to be. The summer months are not so favorable to the operation of cold water on the system as the Spring and Autumn; so that the results have rather disappointed me. The Doctor urges me to go on with the baths; and I wish I could do so. But my leave of absence expires in October; and unless I can get it prolonged as I hope to do, I shall of course return home next month.

I promise myself great pleasure from my visit to England. You know I am to stay with Dickens while in London; and beside his own very agreeable society, I shall enjoy that of the most noted literary men of the day, which will be a great gratification to me. I hope to have time to run up to Edinborough this time; never having penetrated into Scotland. That however must depend upon circumstances.

It is a very long time since I heard from you. I hope you have been well during the Summer. I wish I could give you such a rest from all care, anxiety and intellectual labor as I have had for some months past. I do not believe any man can be perfectly well in body, who has much labor of the mind to perform. Upon the whole the Summer here has been pleasant to me, tho' the want of intellectual excitement has at times been hard to bear. By way of change, I have made occasional excursions up and down the Rhine. A few days ago I was at the great Prussian camp near Bonn, in which and the neighboring *cantonnements* there was an army of fifty thousand men. But the weather was bad; and upon the whole I was much more fatigued than amused. In a day or two I shall visit a camp of *learned men,* a society that comes together once a year, and this year meets at Mayence.[1] I am curious to see the wild scholars from all quarters of Germany.

I write this note merely to let you know my movements. You may expect a longer letter by the next steamer.[2] Meanwhile much love to you all; and believe me

Very affectionately yours
Henry W. Longfellow

MANUSCRIPT: Longfellow Trust Collection. ADDRESS: Hon. Stephen Longfellow/ Portland/Me/United States of/America. POSTMARKS: FORWARDED BY COATES & CO LONDON/ BOSTON MS SHIP OCT 18

1. Longfellow's "Eintritts-Karte" (ticket of admission) in the Longfellow Trust Collection reveals this to have been the twentieth convention of "der deutschen Naturforscher und Aerzte" (the German Natural Scientists and Physicians).

2. If Longfellow wrote this letter, it is unrecovered.

## 721. *To Charles Sumner*

Marienberg. Sept. 17. 1842

My dearest Charles,

The sun is setting; and it is the last I shall see set over the gardens of Marienberg. I start tomorrow morning early for Bingen, from which point I make a little tour in the Niederwald as far as Johannesberg; and then onward to Mayence to attend the meeting, the great annual meeting of the German *Natur-Forscher* [natural scientists]. I of course am a *Natur-Forscher ex-officio,* having investigated the Marienberg waters to a great depth, and being now on my way to Johannesberg to investigate its wine. I promise myself great pleasure in this assembly of simple-hearted, strange, wild-looking delvers into the mysteries of Nature. You shall hear about it hereafter, if it turns out worth the while.

There rises the moon, broad and tranquil, through the branches of a walnut tree on a hill opposite. I apostrophize it in the words of Faust; "O gentle moon, that lookest for the last time upon my agonies!" — or something to that effect.[1]

*Ten o'clock at night.* My trunk is packed — my bill is paid, my farewells said, and I give you one last thought before going to bed, and one last word. I dispatched to-day to Rotterdam a large box of books to go by first ship to Boston. I know not how it is, but during a voyage I collect books as a ship does barnacles. These books are German, Flemish and French. Among them are a dozen or fifteen on the *Wassercur* for Dr. Wesselhoeft. The box is directed to me; and I wish

Cleveland to find out from his father when it arrives, and pay the expenses. An Invoice of the books lies on top of them. I wish the box to be sent to my room and the books for Dr. W. delivered to him. All this upon the supposition that I do not return this Autumn.

George [Hillard]'s letter of Aug. 1. and Corny[Felton]'s of Aug. 14. are the latest I have received. It is astonishing what has become of all my earliest epistles. I should be sorry to have them lost, they being the *Ausbruch,* (as they say of wine) the first droppings from the grape, before it is pressed.

Tell Corny I have bought him a copy of the Nibelungen Lied, but have not time to get it bound. Tell him I have had a *crisis.* It was like an attack of *grippe* or Influenza; — very much such an attack as I had last October. It lasted about a fortnight. Since then, I am better. I am sorry, however, to say, that I am not yet perfectly well. Begging your pardon for the insult, I do not believe anyone *can* be perfectly well, who has a brain and a heart. You will not be well long, and I consider Corny an invalid, though he is not aware of it.

Good night. Be contented for the moment with this brief missive and take it, without a murmur from yours ever affectionately

H.W.L.

P.S. I have entirely, *entirely* recovered from that attack of *anti-English* spleen; and promise myself great pleasure from my visit to Dickens.

MANUSCRIPT: Longfellow Trust Collection.

1. *Faust,* Part I, "Night," ll. 33–34.

722. *To an Unidentified Correspondent*

[Marienberg, c. September 17, 1842]

With many thanks for your many kindnesses, and this last in particular, I send you, my dear Sir, this amount of your bill and of M. Falckenberg's.[1]

Farewell and God bless you.

Very truly yours,
Henry W. Longfellow.

P.S. Please send the music and Michel Angelo's Sonnets to Freiligrath at St. Goar; and I shall receive them on returning down the Rhein at the end of next week. Freiligrath will pay for the Sonnets, which are not in yr bill.

| | |
|---|---|
| Your account—— | 36.24 |
| Falckenberg's do—— | 6.12 |
| | 43.06 |

On receiving this please, write a note informing me of the same, address Freiligrath, St. Goar.

MANUSCRIPT: Formerly in the Deutsche Staatsbibliothek, Berlin, and now missing; text from "Some Unpublished Longfellow Letters," pp. 184–185.

1. Carl Friedrich Falckenberg, owner of a music store at Gerichtstrasse 8, Koblenz.

## 723. *To Ferdinand Freiligrath*

Nürnberg Sept 24 1842

My dear Freiligrath,

Without any doubt I am in the ancient city of Nürnberg. I arrived last night at ten o'clock, and took my first view by moonlight, strolling *alone* through the broad silent streets, and listening to the musical bells, that ever and anon gave a hint that it was bed time.

To-day has been a busy exciting day. I have seen the best works of Albrecht Dürer, Peter Vischer and other worthies of Nürnberg.[1] I have seen Dürer's House and his grave. Also those of Hans Sachs. The old shoemaker's house is now an ale-house. His portrait is on the sign over the door, with this inscription; "Gasthaus [tavern] zum Hans Sachs." I went in, with my companion (an old doctor from Grätz returning from the Naturforscher meeting at Mayence) and we drank a tankard of ale to the memory of the poet, reading at the same time from a volume of his works, — a venerable folio, the story of "*Der Geist mit den Klapperten Ketten.*" We then made a pilgrimage to his grave. He is literally buried *on top* of his father; it being the fashion here to bury people one upon another, in the same grave, the second driving the first deeper down; — like the infamous Popes in Dante's Inferno.[2]

Specimen of the Nürnberg dialect. *Valet de Place.* Wollen Sie jetz die Kirche ansehen, oder belieben Sie erst *frühzustücken*?

*Ich.* Erst beliebe ich die Kirche *zu ansehen.*[3]

I am taking a solitary cup of tea, in a double bedded room highly suggestive of domestic felicity, up two pair of stairs front in the *Straus,* a poor hotel near the Post. I hope to be drinking tea much more pleasantly with you on the 30th of this month.[4] Till then farewell. With kind regards to the ladies and the Landrath [Heuberger]

Ever truly thine

Henry W. Longfellow.

P.S. What is the meaning of the word *Scheide* in *Scheide Munze* which I find on the coin here? [5]

P.S. Two nights ago, on the way to Würzburg, as we stopped to change horses, the hostler made his appearance with a lantern; whereupon my travelling companion in the *coupé*, a young *Geschäfts-Reisender* [commercial traveler], exclaimed *"Gebt Feuer! Exoriare aliquis!"* [6] He then said you were a "hehrlicher Dichter" [glorious poet]; — and yr. poem on General Leon [7] glorious. He said he did not know you personally, but you had been pointed out to him in Frankfurt once! *Fame!*

MANUSCRIPT: University of Washington Library. ADDRESS: Herrn F. Freiligrath./ St. Goar/am Rhein. POSTMARKS: NÜRNBERG 25 SEP 1842/N $\frac{27}{9}$ I/MAINZ PUBLISHED: "Longfellow-Freiligrath Correspondence," pp. 1241–1242.

1. In his MS Journal for Steptember 24, Longfellow mentions more specifically the bronze canopy by Vischer in St. Sebald's Church and Dürer's paintings in the Germanic Museum. He also reveals that among the "other worthies" were Michael Wohlgemuth, Dürer's master, and Adam Kraft, the stone sculptor.

2. *Inferno,* Canto XIX. St. John's Cemetery contains the grave of Albrecht Dürer, but there is some question that the body of Hans Sachs, the poet, rests in the Sachs plot.

3. "Valet de Place. Would you now like to see the church, or do you wish to *breakfast* first? *I.* First I would like to *see* the church."

4. Longfellow arrived in St. Goar on September 29. After saying goodbye to Freiligrath and his other friends there, he left on October 1 on the first leg of his journey home.

5. Longfellow's query went unanswered. *Scheide* means *"dividing"* or *"parting"; Scheidemünze* is a bit coin or small coin.

6. *"Fire! Arise someone!"* The Latin is from the *Aeneid,* IV, 625; the entire quotation is from Freiligrath's poem "Aus Spanien."

7. Diego Leon (1810–1841), a Carlist cavalry leader whose execution made him a political martyr, was the hero of "Aus Spanien."

## 724. *To an Unidentified Correspondent*

[London] [1] Friday. Oct. 14. [1842]

My dear Sir,

From something which dropped from Mr. Forster [2] yesterday, I have inferred that you expect me on Monday evening. It would give me the greatest pleasure to pass that evening with you; but I shall be prevented by another engagement, which I cannot defer, as many other persons are connected therein. Had I understood you to fix Monday evening, when I left you, I should have set the matter right at once.

At all events, I shall have the pleasure of seeing you again before I leave London. Hoping that you have entirely recovered from your indisposition,

Yours very truly
Henry W. Longfellow

MANUSCRIPT: Clifton Waller Barrett Collection, University of Virginia.

1. Longfellow had arrived in London on October 5, where he was the guest of Charles Dickens for about two weeks. H. W. L. Dana describes this visit in "Longfellow and Dickens: The Story of a Trans-Atlantic Friendship," *Cambridge Historical Society Proceedings*, XXVIII (1942), 69–85.

2. John Forster (1812–1876), biographer, critic, and friend of Dickens, became one of Longfellow's most faithful English correspondents. He is now remembered primarily for his *Life of Charles Dickens* (London, 1872–1874), 3 vols., one of the great biographies of the period.

## 725. *To Charles Sumner*

[London] Sunday. Oct. 16. 1842

My dear Charles,

I write this from Dicken[s'] study, the focus from which so many luminous things have radiated. The raven croaks from the garden; and the ceaseless roar of London fills my ears. Of course, I have no time for a letter; as I must run up in a few minutes to dress for dinner. I can only tell you, that I got your letter last night, and that I shall return in the Great Western. As soon as you get this, therefore, start for New York to meet me. If you cannot, send Hillard, or Felton, or Cleveland or Howe, (for I think he must have more business with the Bible Society about this time). Somebody *must* come. The Great Western sails from Bristol on the 22nd. Dickens goes with me to Bath to dine with [Walter Savage] Landor.

Mr. Rogers[1] has just been here, sitting a half hour with me. He arrived in town last night. We breakfast with him on Tuesday and dine with him on Wednesday.

I am so excited about starting for home that I can hardly hold this pen. I have had a most delightful visit here in London. But alas! the town is quite empty! — and I shall miss seeing many persons whom I desire to look upon.

I have so many, *many* things to say to you, that I am dumb. And let it go at that. I will only add that delighted as I am with London, my desire to be at home again overwhelms every other. I come back with tremendous momentum!

I have read Dicken[s]'s book.[2] It is jovial and good-natured, and at times very severe. You will read it with delight, and for the most part approbation. He has a grand chapter on Slavery. *Spitting* and *politics* at Washington are the other topics of censure. Both you and I would censure them with equal severity to say the least. He gives due laud to the New York oysters ("for thy dear sake, heartiest of Greek Professors!")[3] and says of Howe; "There are not many persons, I hope and believe, who after reading these pages can ever hear that name with indifference."

Love to all. Dont fail one, or two of you to come to New York. Tell my brother I return in the Great Western, that he may write to my father.

Ever most affect[ionatel]y.
H. W. L.

Dickens's kind regards to you all.

MANUSCRIPT: Longfellow Trust Collection. ADDRESS: Chs. Sumner Esq/Boston. PUBLISHED: *Life*, I, 440–441.

1. Samuel Rogers (1763–1855), the poet.
2. Dickens' controversial *American Notes* had just been published in London. Longfellow's presentation copy from Dickens (Longfellow Trust Collection, Houghton Library) is dated October 19, 1842.
3. An allusion to Cornelius Felton.

## 726. *To Ferdinand Freiligrath*

London. Oct. 18. 1842.

My dear Freiligrath,

*Jacta est alea*,[1] and I sail from Bristol for New York in the Great Western on the 22nd; that is to say, on Saturday next. My request to remain in Europe another year was not refused; but granted upon certain conditions. They urge, however my return; and under the circumstances, it is much better for me to go than to stay. Therefore I go; and once more, farewell to you all! — and "Farewell, O Luck of Edenhall!"

After leaving you at Coblenz I journeyed solemnly down the Rhine, and through Belgium to Ostend. Seen in a bright sunshiny day antique Bruges had lost some of its glories; and did not look so old as I remembered it. Nevertheless I finished there the poem on its *Belfry*, which I will send you as soon as it is printed.[2]

I have been in London about ten days; and have enjoyed my visit to Dickens very much. He thanks you most kindly for your poems, which alas! he cannot read; and will send you in a few days a copy of his "American Notes." In the same package I send you "Outre Mer" and the "Spanish Student." Gross's Slang Dictionary,[3] I have not been able to get.

I am sorry to send you so short a note as this. It is only to wave you once again farewell; to thank you again and again for all your kind attentions during the Summer, and to promise a longer letter on reaching home.

My kindest remembrances to your dear wife and to Helena; as likewise to the Landrath [Heuberger] and his family. My bankers in London are *Coates & Co.* 13 Bread Street. Packages to be sent through *Baedeker,* Rotterdam, *not* by way of London. Let me hear from you at your earliest leisure, and believe me

Ever yours
Henry W. Longfellow

MANUSCRIPT: Pierpont Morgan Library. ADDRESS: Mr. Ferd. Freiligrath/St. Goar/ on the Rhine./*Germany* POSTMARKS: PAID/21 10 21/26 N 10 [*remainder illegible*] PUBLISHED: "Longfellow-Freiligrath Correspondence," pp. 1242–1243.

1. "The die is cast." Suetonius, *Caesar,* xxxii.

2. "The Belfry of Bruges" was first published in *Graham's Magazine,* XXII (January 1834), 35.

3. Francis Grose, *A Classical Dictionary of the Vulgar Tongue.* There were five editions between 1785 and 1832. *The Spanish Student* was not available to Longfellow at this time (see 712.5).

## 727. *To John Forster*

[London] Wednesday mor[nin]g. [October 19, 1842]

My dear Forster,

Many, many thanks for your book.[1] I am delighted to take back with me this memorial of you; and shall not only look *at* it, as you suggest, but *into* it as my heart prompts me to do.

Dickens absolutely forbids sending "the jovial offering" of wine. "No — no! the Port will be shaken to the devil before it gets there."[2]

Pray accept the accompanying volumes; — an old affair and not worth much, save as a keepsake.

Looking for you at 4 o'clock, most sincerely and cordially yours
Henry W. Longfellow[3]

MANUSCRIPT: Victoria and Albert Museum, London.

1. John Forster, *The Statesmen of the Commonwealth of England; with a Treatise on the Popular Progress in English History* (London, 1840), 5 vols. See Forster to Longfellow, October 19, 1842 (MS, Clifton Waller Barrett Collection, University of Virginia). The first volume of the work (in the Longfellow House) is inscribed: "Henry W. Longfellow Esqr from his attached friend J. F."

2. Dickens sent instead an offering of punch and Johannisberger to the "Five of Clubs." See Sumner to Ward, November 9, 1842 (*Uncle Sam Ward and His Circle,* p. 360), and Dana, "Longfellow and Dickens," p. 78.

3. Two days after writing this note, Longfellow left London for Bristol with Dickens and Forster, stopping overnight in Bath to visit Landor. His fifteen-day

passage to New York aboard the *Great Western* was a stormy one (described in Letter No. 743). He arrived in New York on the evening of November 6 and proceeded immediately to Cambridge to resume his college duties.

## 728. *To Richard Henry Dana*

Cambridge. Nov. 10. 1842.

My dear Sir

Inclosed is a translation of your Dying Raven in German. Thinking you might like to see it, I send it to you. It is by Freiligrath, the first and foremost of the young poets of Germany.[1]

Yours very truly
Henry W Longfellow

MANUSCRIPT: Longfellow Trust Collection. ENDORSEMENT: Prof. Longfellow/ Novr. 10 — 42 Ans Decr. 1

1. For Dana's answer, see *Life,* I, 442. The translation does not appear in Freiligrath's collected works.

## 729. *To Stephen Longfellow*

Cambridge Nov. 20. 1842

My dear Father,

I have been so very much occupied since my return in seeing my many friends here and in Boston, that I have not had leisure to write you, as I intended. Indeed I hoped and expected to be in Portland before this; but Anne's arrival here has prevented. I have been waiting to take her back with me; and after all it is probable she will not be ready to come. James [Greenleaf] leaves town on Tuesday, and we all think that Anne ought to remain a week or two longer with Mary. I intend to come on Tuesday [November 22]; or at the latest Wednesday; and shall stay till Saturday [November 26].

I find things looking very pleasant here; and on many accounts I am very glad to get back. On other accounts I ought to have staid longer in Germany. The cold water was doing me so much good, that it was a pity to break off before getting thoroughly well. But Fate has so decreed, and here I am, determined to make the best of it.

On the passage home I wrote some poems on Slavery, which I shall publish shortly in a pamphlet.[1] I will bring you a proof-sheet on Tuesday. There are only eight in all; and I hope you will like them.

Hoping to find you all well,

Very affectionately yours
Henry W. Longfellow

MANUSCRIPT: Longfellow Trust Collection. ADDRESS: Hon S. Longfellow/Portland POSTMARK: CAMBRIDGE MS NOV [*date obscured*]

1. *Poems on Slavery* (Cambridge, 1842) was published by John Owen, apparently by December 15.

## 730. *To Henry Russell Cleveland*

Cambridge Nov. 27. 1842.

My dearest Hal,

You cannot imagine how grieved I was on reaching Cambridge to find that you had gone! We crossed each other's track at sea; at least, so near as this, that you sailed from Boston on Sunday morning and I reached New York on Sunday evening. I missed your cordial welcome, your hearty shake of the hand; but found your cordial letter, which was the next thing to seeing you. Many, many thanks for giving me thus a few of your last moments! Would I could repay you in some way, which should go to your heart as your letter did to mine. I waft these good wishes after you. May you return to us hale, hearty and happy — very *robustuous* and very *periwig-pated,* if that be any sign of health.[1]

For my own part, I am somewhat better, though not entirely well. I am afraid, that as soon as I begin to study I shall begin to *pine.* But we shall see.

I returned last evening from Portland where I have been passing Thanksgiving week. Hillard and Felton have been dining with me to-day (Sunday) and are now fast asleep, one on each side the stove, in the large arm chairs. (What is it that puts people to sleep so inevitably in my rooms?) We are going down presently to take tea with your wife, who has Mary Dwight for a visitor. Thence we propose to go up to Mr. Norton's. You see how it is; — I follow in the customary track. Both your wife and Lily are well; — though some days ago the former was suffering from an *extinction de voix,* which came upon her suddenly after a most merry and agreeable dinner she gave us. The Club was present, all save yourself; and Dr. Howe into the bargain. We drank your health — your rapid recovery and swift return.

I am very glad to find, that your father's book succeeded so well. I felt confident it would; and am rejoiced to prove a true prophet.[2] I have already a book in press — a small affair — a collection of Poems on Slavery, which I wrote on my passage home in the Great Western. I shall not dare to send them to you in Cuba, for fear of having you seized as an Abolitionist.

Music flourishes greatly this Winter. The Odeon Concerts are so crowded, that last week the Ticknors, Nortons, Guilds &c were forced to take seats in the upper gallery. A younger Rakemann[3] is here; — so is Miss Sloman. Moreover, we have concerts in Cambridge and, finally, I have brought from Germany *a great Psalm Book,* by the Organist Ring![4] So we go on *crescendo.*

When you get back you will find a portrait of Dickens, by Count D'Orsay,[5] lithographed, awaiting your arrival. Also a full-length of myself by Franquinet, from Graham's Magazine![6] We are getting up a subscription to have Dexter[7] cut his bust of Dickens in marble, to be sent to Mrs. D. The subscription is five dollars; and we of course leave room for you.

The sleepers have waked up, and the tea hour draws near. We shall soon sit by your fireside and talk of you. In what green fields, o'er what flowery meads, through what orange groves are you straying?

Farewell. Write to us, and come home to us as soon as you can. God bless you

Ever yours
Henry W. Longfellow.

MANUSCRIPT: Berg Collection, New York Public Library. ADDRESS: Henry R. Cleveland Esq/Care of De Coninck y Spaulding/Habana

1. Cleveland left New York on November 6, having been ordered to Cuba because of his failing health. "Sumner will tell you all about my case," he wrote on November 4. "You will mourn with us over our fallen hopes, our sudden breaking up, my long pilgrimage, and the final result of all our Cambridge plans." He left Cuba early in 1843 to return home via New Orleans and the Mississippi and died of tuberculosis in St. Louis on June 12, 1843. The italicized words are from Hamlet's soliloquy to the players (III, ii, 9–10).

2. See 642.4 and Letter No. 736.

3. Frederick Rakemann, German pianist and younger brother of Ludwig Rakemann, gave his first concert at the Melodeon on November 29, 1842 (*Daily Evening Transcript*). He was not yet twenty.

4. See 701.14.

5. The portrait of Dickens by Alfred Guillaume Gabriel, Count d'Orsay (1801–1852), artist and leader of fashion in London, is dated December 16, 1841. See Thomas Wright, *Life of Charles Dickens* (New York, 1936), facing p. 121.

6. George Graham had commissioned George Parker (d. 1868), an English engraver then living in New York, to make an engraving of Franquinet's portrait of Longfellow (see Letter No. 499). The engraving appeared subsequently as an illustration for an essay on Longfellow by George Hillard in *Graham's Magazine,* XXII (May 1843), pp. 288–293.

7. Henry Dexter (1806–1876), self-taught American sculptor and painter. Dexter's bust of Dickens, modeled at the Tremont House, "pleased the author and his wife and made a tidy sum for the artist, whose agent sold casts in the different cities in which Dickens lectured" (Albert Ten Eyck Gardner, *Yankee Stonecutters: The First American School of Sculpture 1800–1850* [New York, 1945], p. 63).

## 731. *To Rufus Wilmot Griswold*

Cambridge Nov. 27. 1842.

My dear Sir,

I returned last evening from a visit of a few days in Portland, and found your note and the proof sheet. I cannot express to you in words how truly and deeply I sympathize with you in your affliction. I know from experience how unavailing are consolations from without, in such moments of anguish. I can only say to you, that I feel for you very sincerely, though silently. I have tasted the same cup, and remember its bitterness.[1]

I return to you the proof sheet. I think the stanzas had better be divided, putting only two lines together instead of four. It fills out the page better.

If the M.S. of the Spanish Student was not destroyed, have the goodness to send it to me, by some good opportunity. I mean now to publish it in a volume and think that perhaps some New York or Philadelphia publisher might offer me better terms than Owen can. Could you assist me in this matter? The only point I should insist upon would be to have it printed *here*, uniform with my other volumes.

If Mr. Graham will give me $50 for every article I send him; I will agree to write for no other Magazine than his; this agreement to cease whenever either party gives notice to that effect.

Very truly yours
Henry W. Longfellow.

P.S. Many thanks for the copies of the Portrait. I do not think Franquinet's a very favorable likeness; and am sorry I had not known your design in season to have a sketch made by Cheney here in Boston. He has an admirable style for such things.[2]

I have in press some poems on Slavery; a pamphlet only; and will send you a copy in a few days.

MANUSCRIPT: Historical Society of Pennsylvania. ADDRESS: Rufus W. Griswold Esq/Philadelphia ANNOTATION (*by Longfellow*): Paid. [*deleted*] POSTMARK: BOSTON ||MS|| NOV 28

1. In his note of November 20, 1842, Griswold (then editor of *Graham's Magazine*) had informed Longfellow of the recent death of his wife and enclosed a proof sheet of "The Belfry of Bruges." See 726.2.

2. Griswold had sent him some large paper proofs of the engraving by George Parker (730.6). Longfellow expressed his dislike of the portrait more strongly in Letters No. 735, 739, 741, and 770. See also 744.1.

## 732. *To Henry Russell Cleveland*

[Cambridge] Tuesday morning Decr. 6. '42

My dear Hal,

I write you two words, merely to say that we miss you *demnibly*, and more and more. And in a few days your dear little wife is going away, and the whole establishment, the whole household, once so gay with light hearts and so warm with friendship, is to fade away like the "baseless fabric of a vision."[1] "*Ay de mi, Alhama*!"[2]

Nothing new here. The beautiful cousins — the Pleiades — revolve through their heaven, graceful and bright and with a kind of sphere-like music, harmonious and ruling like other stars the destiny of man; — as the old Spanish says; each a "Doblon ardiente del celestial banco [Fiery doubloon of the celestial bank]."

I have got out of that sentence rather better than I expected when half through. Excuse haste and *Gongorism*. I meant to say that the Nortons, Guilds, Dwights &c were well. So are we all; more or less. We dine with Felton to-day — the Club — and will prove how false is the proverb: "The absent have no friends."

Meanwhile, enjoy yourself and get well; for if you do not, you will be obliged to go to Grafenberg, and drink cold water.

It is a mild Spring-like, bright day; like what you are beholding in Cuba. The mud is knee-deep.

Good bye; and believe me, ever affectionately yours

Henry W. Longfellow

MANUSCRIPT: Berg Collection, New York Public Library. ADDRESS: Henry R. Cleveland, Esq. ANNOTATION (*in another hand*): All well Decbr 6th/Steamer in but no letter from Ned [Perkins]/No news fwd address

1. *The Tempest,* IV, i, 151. Cleveland's wife was about to move from Cambridge to Burlington, N.J., to be with her mother, Eliza Perkins Doane.
2. See 632.2.

## 733. *To William Plumer, Jr.*[1]

Cambridge Decr. 9. 1842.

My dear Sir,

I beg you to receive my best thanks for the copy of your Poems, which you were so kind as to send me. I was already acquainted with the volume; and had always been struck with the air of refinement and classic elegance which pervades it. I am very happy to receive this friendly token from you; and in return will take the liberty of sending you a small volume of "Poems on Slavery," in which I hope you will not find much to condemn, as the spirit in which they are written is that of kindness — not denunciation; — at all events not violence.

Very truly yours
Henry W. Longfellow.

MANUSCRIPT: The Carl H. Pforzheimer Library, New York. ADDRESS: William Plumer Jr. Esq/Epping/N.H.

1. Plumer (1789–1854), a graduate of Harvard in 1809, a member of Congress, 1819–1825, and an ardent Abolitionist, had sent Longfellow a copy of his *Youth, or Scenes from the Past; and other Poems* (Boston, 1841).

## 734. *To John Forster*

Cambridge. Dec 15. 1842.

My dear Forster,

I send you at last a kind greeting from the "*pent-up Utica*"[1] of Cambridge; a greeting I should have sent sooner had I not been absent visiting my father in the East — some hundred miles nearer the Boundary than I am. Immediately on my arrival here I delivered your note and the books to your old friend, and likewise the copy for Bancroft was duly sent. Felton has written to you, and I presume that Bancroft has. At all events I met him in the street not long afterwards and he expressed to me his gratification at your remembrance and his intention of writing.

So here I am once more under my own roof; not so merry and mad as in London, but sufficiently gay for every-day use. I need not tell you how often I think of you, — of Lincoln Inn Fields — Devonshire Terrace &c; nor how often the street lamps of London, and the dinner lamps of my friends gleam through my imagination. When shall I behold them again? Not for many a long year. Let me, however sometimes be present to your thoughts; and let me be present as *meat* since I cannot as *guest* in the persons of a pair of Canvass-back Ducks, which I send you, care of Dickens to whom Felton sends also a pair. I hope you will like them; as I think you will if they arrive in good condition.

I send you herewith a copy of "Poems on Slavery" — a very small book; but which may possibly be made larger hereafter. I must first see the effect of these. They are written in a kindly — not a vindictive spirit. Humanity is the chord to be touched. Denunciation of Slaveholders would do more harm than good; besides, that is not my vein. I leave that to more ferocious natures.

Remember me very affectionately to Dickens, and Mrs. D. Tell them again, for me, how much I enjoyed my visit at their house.

Immense numbers of the "*Notes*" have been sold; so many in a newspaper form, that the booksellers begin to come out in favor of copyright. We are looking eagerly for the new book.[2]

Kind remembrances to Cruikshank, Macready, and Maclise,[3] and to yourself "contenting enjoyments of your auspicious desires"[4] and the sincere and friendly regards of

Yours ever truly
Henry W. Longfellow

MANUSCRIPT: Victoria and Albert Museum, London.

1. It is doubtful that Forster recognized this quotation from an "Epilogue to Cato," by Jonathan Mitchell Sewall (1748–1808), a Massachusetts lawyer and grandnephew of Samuel Sewall. A modification of Sewall's lines served as a masthead motto for Park Benjamin's *The New World*: "No pent-up Utica contracts our powers; for the whole boundless continent is ours."

2. *Martin Chuzzlewit.* See Dickens to Longfellow, December 29, 1842 (*Life,* I, 452).

3. George Cruikshank (1792–1878), caricaturist and book illustrator; William Charles Macready (1793–1873), tragedian; and Daniel Maclise (1806–1870), portrait painter, were all intimately associated with Forster and Dickens and had helped entertain Longfellow during his recent London visit. See Letter No. 743.

4. See 758.1.

## 735. *To Samuel Ward*

Cambridge Dec 18. 1842

Samuel dearest (by way of change in
ringing the *carrillon* of affection),

Did you ever in a circus see a man leap through a paper balloon, tearing his way before him, and falling into the arms of an associate? If you have, then have you some image faint and feeble of the manner in which my heart comes tearing through this letter (as you break the seal) to fall upon yours. Receive it gently; do not let it fall to the ground. As yet I have not *seen* you since my return, — I mean *inwardly,* — and I am looking forward to your visit next Sunday with a desire you will better comprehend when you get here than I can express to you now. To-day Sumner is sitting in the great armchair, that you will then occupy; and at length after this long, long, long separation I shall lay my heart open to you and tell you all my hopes, fears, and plans for the Present and the immediate Future.

And now for a few trifles. Why did you let Griswold have that head of me by Franquinet to engrave for the Magazine? Do you know what the engraver has made of it? Why the most atrocious libel imaginable; a very vulgar individual, looking very *drunk* and very *cunning*! And, moreover, an unredeemed blackguard air hovers over the whole. Now, when I think that forty thousand copies of this thing — this tasteless caricature — are to be printed and distributed through the country as my "counterfeit (*very* counterfeit) *presentment*,"[1] I am in an indescribable agony. I solemnly protest against this whole proceeding, and shall write to Graham this very day to prevent the publication;[2] and will even offer any price within my means to put a stop to this nefarious transaction. I sent you on Saturday a copy of the "Poems on Slavery." I trust that you will like at least the spirit in which they are written. Some of the Bostonians object to the word *stallion* as indelicate! I shall have to get a pair of pantalettes made for that animal.

Write to me straightway; and as often as you can. It is delightful to find your *hand* at the Post-office on my way to lecture.

Jules Janin has written "The American in Paris."[3] Are you his hero?

With kindest regards to the Three Graces,[4] ever yours affectionately

Henry W. Longfellow

Rakemann dines with me to-day. O how I wish you were with us!

MANUSCRIPT: Longfellow Trust Collection. ADDRESS: Samuel Ward Esq/Prime Ward & King/New York. POSTMARK: BOSTON ||MS.|| DEC [?] PUBLISHED: *Life*, I, 442–443.

1. *Hamlet*, III, iv, 54.
2. This letter is unrecovered, but that Longfellow wrote it is verified in Letter No. 739.
3. The edition of this work in the Longfellow House is *The American in Paris: or Heath's Picturesque Annual for 1843* (London, 1843).
4. Ward's sisters.

## 736. *To Richard Jeffry Cleveland*

[Cambridge, 1842][1]

My dear Sir,

Please accept my best thanks for the copy of your Narrative, which you have been kind enough to send me. I have so often expressed to you and to Henry my high opinion of its merits, that I need not repeat it here. Allow me to say, however, that I rejoice with you in the success of the book; and the golden opinions it has won from the reading public, both here and in England. From the beginning I felt confident of this; and remember to have said so more than once while the work was passing through the press. Its republication and very flattering reception in England, as well as at home, prove me to have been a true prophet. Seldom has it fallen to the lot of any man to pass a life of such stirring incidents and to be the historian as well as the hero; to act and then to write.

God bless you, my dear Sir, and may you long live to enjoy your well earned fame.

Yours very truly
Henry W. Longfellow.

MANUSCRIPT: Cornell University Library. ANNOTATION: The above letter was written to my father after receiving his "Narrative of Voyages & Commercial Enterprises" – published in 1842. Mr. Longfellow had assisted my brother in its publication, correcting proofs &c." [2]

1. See 642.4. The date is conjectural but supported by the annotation on the manuscript (below) and by Longfellow's reference to the republication of Cleveland's book in England (1842).

2. The note is by Horace William Shaler Cleveland (1814–1900), a landscape architect and the brother of Henry Cleveland.

## 737. *To John Gorham Palfrey*

[Cambridge, 1842]

My dear Dr.

I accept with great pleasure your invitation to help you devour the *"créature moutonnière"* on Friday.

Yours truly
Henry W. Longfellow.

MANUSCRIPT: Harvard College Library. ENDORSEMENT: 1842/H. W. Longfellow

PART EIGHT

# COURTSHIP'S END

1843

# COURTSHIP'S END

## 1843

LONGFELLOW began the year 1843 with few prospects for release from the worries, pains, and doubts that had harried him since the death of Mary Potter Longfellow in 1835. For almost seven years he had associated that release in his mind with the surrender of Frances Appleton to his recurrent courtship. As a matter of fact, however, he had himself surrendered hope. "*My* Etna *is* burnt out," he wrote to Sam Ward in March, "my Boundary Line is settled. Impassable Highlands divide the waters running North and South. 'Let the dead Past bury its dead!' and excuse me for quoting myself." His congratulatory letter to Samuel Gridley Howe on the occasion of Howe's engagement to Julia Ward emphasized his faith in marriage as an institution that would solve the "great riddle of life." As he put it, "Of course, you seem to us transfigured and glorified. You walk above in the pure air, while Sumner and I, like the poor spirits in Faust, who were struggling far down in the cracks and fissures of the rocks, cry out to you, 'O take us with you! Take us with you!' "

In April he was rescued from this lugubrious state of mind by Frances Appleton's sudden decision to reverse the course of her affection for him. What happened is explained in Longfellow's journal entry for April 13, 1844: "Written be the date in red letters! One year ago I met my beloved Fanny after so long and tedious a separation; and we began once more to draw near unto each other. It was at the Norton's — in the corner window. The day and the Evening shall be kept as a holiday and be blessed for evermore."

During the following month Frances Appleton moved from her former attitude of cool indifference to one of open encouragement; and finally, in a note dated May 10, she surrendered unconditionally. The date is a most important one, for with his engagement Longfellow began the long career of material comfort and spiritual placidity that the public has generally associated with his name. It was a date, certainly, that he would not forget. A year later he commemorated it in his journal with a rhetorical flight: "The Tenth of May! Day to be recorded with sunbeams! Day of light and love! The day of our engagement; when in the bright morning — one year ago — I received Fanny's note, and walked to town, amid the blossoms and sunshine and song of birds, with my heart full of gladness and my eyes full of tears! I walked with the speed of an arrow — too restless to sit in a carriage — too impatient and fearful of encountering anyone! O Day forever blessed; that ushered in this *Vita Nova* of happiness! How full the year has been!"

The marriage took place in the Appleton home at 39 Beacon Street on July 13. Longfellow was too occupied during the following months of 1843 to pay much attention to his correspondence, writing only some 18 or 20 letters after his marriage, of which 11 survive (by contrast, he had written at least 62 letters between January 1 and July 13, of which 56 have been recovered). Since he kept no journal in 1843, his movements after his marriage must be established primarily through the letters and journal of his wife.

After a fortnight in Cambridge — in Longfellow's quarters in Craigie House — the couple spent a week in Portland and a few days in Nahant, visiting the Longfellow and Appleton families. Then they departed on a wedding journey through the Catskills and Berkshires (August 8–19), accompanied on a part of the tour by Charles Sumner, who carried with him a copy of Bossuet's *Oraisons Funèbres*, a symbol perhaps of his own dim prospects for marital happiness. Upon their return to Cambridge, Nathan Appleton arranged for the purchase of Craigie House as a wedding present, and George Washington Greene became the first of a series of guests who were to enjoy the hospitality available in the elegant rooms of the old mansion.

Despite this radical change of fortune, Longfellow did not have complete freedom from worry. His eyes had begun to bother him about the time of his marriage — a condition that forced him to use amanuenses when writing letters — and on or about September 19 he and his wife departed for New York to try the remedies of Dr. Samuel Mackenzie Elliott, a celebrated oculist. A month later he returned to Cambridge, encouraged that he would not lose his eyesight but yet uncured, and finished out the year that marked the beginning of the second half of his life.

738. *To Henry Russell Cleveland*

Cambridge. Jan 1. 1843.

Dearest Hal,

A Happy New Year to you in the tropics — or near the tropics, as the case may be! But wherever you are a very Happy New Year to you. Your friends are in mourning here. Your dear little wife has gone, and left us in darkness. She has borne away the silver candle-sticks, and I have only the fire-light left; — only the red light of that Meleager's fire-brand which smoulders within me. No; I must correct the expression. The Nortons remain, shining peacefully like household lamps, and filling all hearts with their holy light.

Now the flames of all — of the silver candle-sticks — Meleager's fire-brand, and the household lamps — point this night, this new Year's night towards you, like so many tongues of fire, and syllable your name. Accept the friendly greeting, — the *"God-bless-you,"* that they wave and flicker southward for you.

Hillard's Damascus blade — Mary Dwight's flashing scimitar — Sumner's panoply of steel — and Felton's gold spectacles, all reverberate the flames, till like the fiery tongues at Pentecost they all speak to you, and each in its own dialect wishes you a Happy New Year!

I moreover send you some Poems on Slavery; thinking they may furnish you with agreeable topics of conversation with the planters of Matanzas, Habana, and the neighborhood.

Good night. Sumner sits by me curled up like the *Lind-wurm* or dragon of the Northern Romances, and fast asleep in his chair.

Ever yours

H. W. L.

MANUSCRIPT: Berg Collection, New York Public Library.

739. *To Stephen Longfellow*

Cambridge Jan 1 1843

My dear Father,

I send you my most cordial and affectionate greetings — my most sincere wishes for a Happy New Year to all of you at home! I have been so very busy of late, that I have neglected to write; and I find, with a feeling akin to remorse that a whole month has elapsed since Anne's letter was written, and yet it remains unanswered. Pardon me; and I will try to do better hereafter.

How do you like the Slavery Poems? I think they make an impression; — and I have received many letters about them, which I will send to you by the first good opportunity. Some persons regret that I should have written them; but for my own part, I am glad of what I have done. My feelings prompted me and my judgment approved, and still approves.

I have finished my Lectures for the Term; and have my Examination tomorrow. The Term, however, does not close before the middle of next week. I know not when I shall come to Portland, as I have a great many things on hand requiring immediate attention; and for which I must take the leisure of Vacation.

In Graham's Magazine for January I have a poem called The Belfry of Bruges, which I should like to have you see. You will find it copied in the Daily Advertiser.[1] In the next No. is an *un*-likeness of me; reclining in an arm-chair, in a morning gown; — a ridiculous caricature. As soon as it was sent to me I wrote to Graham to have it suppressed; but too late, it was printed, and had cost him some five hundred dollars; and he was not willing to lose so much money. So he promises in some future No. to have a good portrait engraved by a good artist; and thus the matter is left. You will be amused, and perhaps a little vexed afterward, when you see what a picture is distributed over the country to the number of forty thousand as my portrait.

And now good bye for a short season. My love and good wishes to all. I hope Mother's health is now quite restored, and that yours is good.

In haste, affectionately
Henry W. Longfellow.

The portrait was published in the May number.[2]

MANUSCRIPT: Longfellow Trust Collection. ADDRESS: Hon. S. Longfellow/Portland/Me POSTMARK: BOSTON MS JAN 3 PUBLISHED: *Life,* II, 4–5.

1. *Boston Daily Advertiser,* XLVII, No. 15 (December 19, 1842), 814.
2. This postscript was added in pencil at a later date.

## 740. *To Catherine Jane Norton*

[Cambridge] Jan 1. 1843.

My dear Jane,

Will you accept from me these Songs of Schubert, with my best wishes for your happiness. That your whole life may be so harmonious as this music, is the sincere prayer of your friend

Henry W. Longfellow

MANUSCRIPT: Harvard College Library.

## 741. *To Henry Russell Cleveland*

Cambridge. Jan 4 1843

My dearest Hal,

Last evening between the hours of seven and eight I had the extreme pleasure of receiving your most friendly and warm-hearted letter from Matanzas. Decr. 17. which I answer without delay, for fear that as heretofore I may hear of vessels sailing for the West Indies only in season to indite you a short note. This has happened already three times. This time you shall have a letter.

In the first place, then, I wish I were with you. I have a restless, throbbing heart, to which I in vain say "Peace! Peace!" ("Gentlemen may say" &c &c)[1] It is a kind of *King's Evil,* to be cured only by the touch of *one* royal hand, and that royal hand cometh not. Therefore I wish I were away; enjoying with you the gay South; strolling under palm-trees and towering *ceibas,* or journeying on the banks of the Canimar in a *Volante,* whose huge wheels, like the wheel of Fortune, should take us over the rough roads safely. You delight and amuse me so much with your little touches of description, that I look forth from this cage of mine, as a panther from his, into the green field, with indescribable longing in my eyes, and in my heart a kind of faith, that I shall one day be free. Indeed, you make me quite mad with these descriptions; for in my darkest hours — afar off in a southern sea lies a Hesperian isle, flashing in the sun — and waving with broad green leaves, which I shall ere long behold with the bodily eye!

And now let us go back a few days. My arrival in New York was not precisely as you pictured it to yourself. Instead of standing like Park Street church and Steeple on the wharf Sumner and Felton were cosily dining with Howe and Willis at the Globe. It was after dark when the Great Western reached the slip. I went up alone to the Astor House; — thence to Sam Wards, meeting on the way Jack Downing Davis,[2] who insisted on my stopping to *see his wife*! At Ward's I found them — Felton and Sumner. They had been on board the vessel — then to the Astor — and then to Ward. Joyful was the meeting! and the *lovely Louisa* [Ward] made an *impression* in my heart like that made by Fénix in Calderon's Principe Constante, when she lay down in the bed of flowers; (Sobre un catre de carmin, — Hice un foso de *esmeralda*)[3] and *emerald* is the hue of hope. Alas! we ended the night in an *oyster cellar*! precisely as you imagined.

And now I am again in *Castle Craigie!* I have finished a course of lectures in College, and vacation is beginning. I have also published a very small collection of Poems on Slavery a copy of which I sent you by Henry Sumner,[4] who sailed for Havana on Sunday. People here look rather wild at them and "with stiff upper lip snarl dubious." In Grahams Mag. for next month you will find the most ridiculous figure, full length; sitting in an elbow chair in a morning gown, — a vulgar-looking individual with an inebriate eye, and the expression of a cockeral just done crowing; — and underneath you will read

*Henry W. Longfellow* which will lead you to think, that perhaps this was intended for me. And I am constrained to confess, that such is the fact.[5]

So much for what I have done since my return; and what has been done to me. But this is not quite all. We have dined together many times — meaning the club; — first at your house — then at Howe's, (whom we have chosen as a member relying upon your consent) — then here — then at Felton's; — always remembering you in green goblets and brown. But now your noble little wife has gone. It would do your heart good to know and feel truly how much you are both missed here. Charles Perkins will probably take the rooms under me at Craigie House for the next term; — a pleasant arrangement if practicable. We have already projected a grand ball in the summer, as a finale to his college life, and a kind of *last kick* in Head Quarters, which will soon pass into other hands — and I into other lodgings.

Now for your other friends. The Nortons are perfectly well — perfectly serene — perfectly happy. The girls (or as Sam Ward calls them "*Norton's Evidences of Christianity*") are pure and sweet as magnolia blossoms, dewy, fragrant, soiled by no rain, broken by no wind. Felton is more wise, more witty, more joyous, more overflowing with good-fellowship, — more ripe in heart, head, and body than ever. He and Sumner dined with me on Sunday. We had nothing but *Canvass back* ducks and Burgundy — not even a pudding, — and it was one of the most delicious dinners I ever tasted. We drank everybody's health — and then drank it over again; and were very happy. Hillard is as usual — still heart-broken — bowing under the burden —the *infinite* burden of life — a young Hamlet in our own times — with a dark destiny hanging over him.[6] Sumner is in better spirits, and with more heart and hope, than I have seen for a long while in him.

I am right glad to see in the tone of your letter that you have also a stout heart; — and to hear from your own lips, that you are better. But do not let *better* alone. Get well — quite well. Revel in the southern sunshine; and return impregnated with that delicious climate (not the yellow fever.) so that it may exude from every pore of your skin and overflow us, and warm us all.[7]

Now for a chapter of gossip. William Story is engaged to Miss Eldridge — a beautiful girl, like a picture by Sir Peter Lely.[8] Anna Shaw to young Green son of ex-postmaster Green. *Her sister* to a Washington-St shop boy; — romantic attachment contracted in walking around the Common — a look — a bow — a word — a passion —

father obstinate — daughter more so — the consequences are a secret engagement (*Secreto a Voces*) [open secret] and the World says — "how extraordinary."[9] Mrs. Harry Otis is giving Thursday Evenings in imitation of Mrs. Ticknor's Friday Evenings — the Wards[10] in Park Street give a Twelfth Night Party — Bowen has taken the North American — Dr Palfrey is *probably* coming out as Anti-Slavery candidate for Congress[11] — Mme. Calderon has pubd. a very amusing work on Mexico[12] — Dickens's Notes are scattered to the four winds by a blast in Blackwood — and brought together again by Felton in the North American.[13] The Younger Rakemann, a beautiful musician, has been here; — the Academy Concerts are crowded from pit to gallery — and we are all looking forward to your return with great impatience. Bring some of the best Spanish cigars with you — to lie ripening at Pine Bank so that hereafter we may sit by the borders of the Lake, and soothe ourselves with smoke.

Ever yours affectionately
H. W. L.

MANUSCRIPT: Berg Collection, New York Public Library. ADDRESS: Mess. De Coninck & Spaulding/for [*foregoing in another hand*] Henry R. Cleveland Esq/Havana

1. Patrick Henry, "Speech in the Virginia Convention of Delegates, March 23, 1775": "Gentlemen may cry, peace, peace — but there is no peace."

2. Charles Augustus Davis (1795–1867), New York merchant, member of the Knickerbocker literary set, and the author of *Letters of J. Downing, Major, Downingville Militia . . . to Mr. Dwight of the New York Daily Advertiser* (New York, 1834) in imitation of Seba Smith.

3. "On a bed of crimson, — I made an impression of *emerald*." Don Pedro Calderón de la Barca, *El Principe Constante*, II, i.

4. Brother of Charles Sumner. Born in 1814, he "received a mercantile education, travelled in the Southern States, and visited the West Indies and South America" (*Sumner Memoir and Letters*, I, 32). He died in 1852.

5. See 730.6.

6. Hillard's wretchedness seems to have been chronic. Since he "lacked sufficient health, vigor, and money, his divided aims overtaxed him and he never achieved the eminence to which he seemed destined" (*Dictionary of American Biography*, IX, 49).

7. Longfellow's marginal note "Puella loquitur" [a girl now speaks] occurs between paragraphs.

8. William Wetmore Story married Emeline Eldredge (d. 1894) of Boston on October 31, 1843. Lely (1618–1680) was the Dutch-born English portrait painter.

9. Anna Blake Shaw (1817–1878), a daughter of the prominent Boston family, married William Batchelder Greene (1819–1878), soldier, Brook Farmer, abolitionist, and author. Of her three sisters, the one most likely referred to here is Elizabeth Willard Shaw (1823–1850), who married a man named Daniel Augustus Oliver (d. 1850).

10. The family of Thomas Wren Ward.

11. Palfrey was succeeded by Francis Bowen as editor of the *North American*

*Review* in 1843, but he did not become a member of Congress until 1847, when he served one term as a Whig.

12. Frances Erskine Calderón de la Barca, *Life in Mexico during a Residence of Two Years in that Country* (Boston, 1843). William H. Prescott wrote the preface.

13. The attack on *American Notes for General Circulation* appeared in *Blackwood's Edinburgh Magazine,* LII (December 1842), 783–801. Felton devoted his review of the book to a general tribute to Dickens (*North American Review,* LVI [January 1843], 212–237).

## 742. *To George Lunt*[1]

Cambridge Jan. 4 1843

My dear Sir,

I have been so busy for the last week, that I have not been able to answer your favor of Dec 20. until now. I have, however, found time to read your Age of Gold; and am delighted with the elevated spirit it breathes, and the fine poetic passages, which stud its pages, and particularly the solemn and beautiful melodies of its close. I sympathize with you throughout. The theme is one which should be repeated and reëchoed from every good heart and true, through the whole country, for the country seems bent upon disgracing itself in every possible way. I say it with deep humiliation and grief, the American character seems wanting in many of the more generous and lofty traits which ennoble humanity.

I am sorry you find so much to gainsay in my Poems on Slavery. I shall not argue the point with you, however, but will simply state to you my belief, which by the way, you will find more clearly stated in an Article by W. Ware[2] Christian Examiner. Jan. 1843. p.353.

1. I believe Slavery to be an unrighteous institution, based on the false maxim that Might makes Right.

2. I have great faith in doing what is righteous, and fear no evil consequences.

3. I believe that everyone has a perfect right to express his opinion on the subject of Slavery as on every other; nay, that every one ought so to do; until the Public Opinion of all Christendom shall penetrate into and change the hearts of the Southerners on this subject.

4. I would have no other *interference* than what is sanctioned by law.

5. I believe that when there is a *Will* there is a *Way*. When the whole country sincerely wishes to get rid of Slavery it will readily find the means.

6. Let us therefore do all we can to bring about this *Will,* in all gentleness and Christian charity. And God Speed the time.

Feeling almost certain that you will agree with me in this *Credo,* I remain, with sincere regard

Very truly yours
Henry W. Longfellow

P.S. I will send a copy of the Ballads to Fields[3] for you.

MANUSCRIPT: Berg Collection, New York Public Library. ADDRESS: ||George Lunt|| Esq./Newburyport POSTMARK: CAMBRIDGE MS. JAN 4 PUBLISHED: *Life,* II, 7–8.

1. Lunt (1803–1885), Newburyport lawyer, author, and journalist, had just published his *The Age of Gold* (Boston, 1843), a long, didactic, and satirical poem in heroic couplets.

2. William Ware (1797–1852), clergyman and author, was editor and proprietor of the *Christian Examiner.*

3. James T. Fields (1817–1881), at this time senior clerk in the firm of William D. Ticknor & Company (publishers of Lunt's poem, n. 1), became a junior partner in June 1843. When Longfellow began publishing with his firm in 1846, he and Fields established an intimacy that resulted in a lifelong correspondence.

## 743. *To Ferdinand Freiligrath*

Cambridge. January 6. 1843.

My dear Freiligrath, —

Finally from this side of the great ocean I send you my friendliest greetings, with my best and sincerest wishes for a Happy New Year to yourself and your dear wife! I am now in my old rooms again; sitting opposite that same *coquettish* window spoken of by F[r]äulein Von Gall. Close by me on the shelf of my book-case stands the portrait of Freiligrath, in a dark walnut frame, and beside it "Charles Dickens Esquire."[1] On my left hand, the view of St. Goar, given me by our worthy friend the Landrath [Heuberger]. And now surrounded by these reminiscences, let me take up the golden thread of my adventures where I last dropped it, that is to say in London, from which place I wrote you a last farewell, and sent you a copy of Outre-Mer, to which Dickens promised to add his "American Notes." I trust the package was duly sent and received. Otherwise one link in our intercourse, though a small one, is broken.

In London I passed a very agreeable fortnight with Dickens. His wife is a most kind, amiable person, and his four children beautiful in the extreme. In a word, his whole household is a delightful one. At his table he brings together artists and authors; such as Cruikshank, a very original genius; Maclise the painter; — Macready the actor &c &c. We had very pleasant dinners, drank Schloss-Johannisberger, and *cold punch,* (the same article that got Mr. Pickwick into the Pound) and led a life like the monks of old. I saw likewise Mr. Rogers; —

breakfasted and dined with him, and met at his table Tom Campbell, and Mr. Moxon the publisher and Sonneteer.[2] Campbell's outward man disappointed me. He is small and *shrunken,* frost-nipped by unkindly age; — wears a *foxy* wig, and drinks brandy. But I liked his inward man exceedingly. He is simple, frank, cordial; and withal very sociable. Kenyon,[3] Talford,[4] Tennison, Milnes, and many more whom I wanted to see were out of town. Lady Blessington, however, cheered my eyes by her fair presence; — a lady *well preserved,* but rather *deep zoned,* as the Greeks would say; — in St. Goar we should say *stoutish.* Count D'Orsay was [not] in attendance being confined to the house by a severe attack of the *bum-bailiffs;* he only ventures out on Sundays.[5] The Count is a gay youth of thirty-five; — handsome, according to the French notion of beauty; and dressed rather extravagantly. But enough of this. Taking reluctant leave of London, I went by rail-way to Bath, where I dined with Walter Savage Landor, rather a ferocious critic, and author of five volumes of "Imaginary Conversations." The next day brought me to Bristol, where I embarked in the Great Western steamer for New York. We sailed (or rather paddled) out in the very teeth of a violent West-wind, which blew for a week: — "*Frau die alte sass gekehrt rückwärts nach Osten*" [6] — with a vengeance. We had a very boisterous passage. I was not out of my berth more than twelve hours for the first twelve days. I was in the forward part of the vessel, where all the great waves struck and broke with voices of thunder. In the next room to mine, a man died. I was afraid that they might throw me overboard instead of him in the night; but they did not. Well, thus "cribbed, cabined and confined," [7] I passed fifteen days. During this time I wrote seven poems on Slavery. I meditated upon them in the stormy, sleepless nights, and wrote them down with a pencil in the morning. A small window in the side of the vessel admitted light into my berth; and there I lay on my back, and soothed my soul with songs. I send you some copies. In the "*Slave's Dream*" I have borrowed one or two wild animals from your menagerie! [8] Our passage was fifteen days My intimate friends Felton and Sumner were waiting for me in New York; and the day after landing we came back together to Cambridge, where I entered immediately on my College duties, and have been very busy ever since.

And here I am again, as if the summer had been but a dream. I think of you very often; and look at your portrait and then at the picture of St. Goar; — and see you pacing the wintry shore, and "singing out into the dark night." Are you now in your new dwelling? Are you alone? Has Helena departed? Make my peace with her, when you write and say to her, that on again beholding Bruges I saw my error, and now acknowledge that Nürenberg bears away the palm. I did the old town injustice. Let me be duly remembered to her. Likewise to the Heubergers, to whom I shall write soon.

By the first vessel to Rotterdam, I shall send you a small box of books, magazines &c. &c. merely specimens. In Graham's Mag. for February you will find a poem of mine *"The Belfry of Bruges"* — the first of the travelling sketches we spoke about in the steamer on the Rhine. I mean to continue with Günderode, Nürenberg, &c. as soon as I have time.[9] I have been trying to translate some of your poems into English but find them too difficult. Do not fail to send me some copies of the new edition, that I may give them to the lovers of German Poetry here, and make you more known in the wild new World. Mrs. Howitt's translation from the Swedish (or did she translate from a German version? I suspect she did, because she uses such expressions as *"Fetch me the Devil,"* which is very different from *"Devil take me!"*) — this translation, *"The Neighbors"* has been republished here, and is very much liked. It is printed as an extra No. of the *New World*, a newspaper, and sold for *4 groschen*! In this form it will be scattered far and wide over the whole country. A handsomer and dearer edition is also in press.[10]

Again, and again, and again have I read to myself and others your *"Nacht im Hafen,"* that wondrous, untranslateable poem! It meets universal applause. So does the *"Blumen Rache."* When shall I be able to translate them? [11] By the way, if you should translate the Wreck of the Hesperus remember on p. 47. line 3. to read *stove,* not *strove* as there printed.[12]

Jan. 10.

A delicious Spring-like day. I am writing with open window; and wondering whether it is as warm with you. And now, dear old Hector fare thee well. Write to me soon — as soon as possible; and know that I cherish your memory and that of your beloved and lovely wife most tenderly. Keep for me a warm corner by the fireside of your hearts; and think of me as ever your very sincere friend.

Henry W. Longfellow

I have just been gazing at yr. portrait with *considerable tenderness.* God bless you! Be true to yourself; and burn like a watch-fire, afar off there in *your Germany.*

P.S. You will see by my seal, that *another ring* has been created.[13]

MANUSCRIPT: unrecovered; text from photostat, Longfellow Trust Collection. AD-

DRESS: Herrn Ferdinand Freiligrath/St. Goar/am Rhein./Allemagne./via Havre. ANNOTATION (*by Longfellow*): Paid to New York./single. POSTMARKS: OUTRE MER 4 FEVR LE HAVRE/N $\frac{9}{2}$ 4/PAID PUBLISHED: "Longfellow-Freiligrath Correspondence," pp. 1243–1245.

1. The Freiligrath portrait was painted by Johann Heinrich Schramm (1810–1865) and engraved by Carl August Schwerdgeburth (1785–1878). The lithograph of the Dickens portrait by Count d'Orsay was mentioned in Letter No. 730.

2. Longfellow's engagements with Samuel Rogers occurred on Tuesday, October 18, and Wednesday, October 19 (Letter No. 725). Thomas Campbell (1777–1844) had been one of his boyhood favorites (*Young Longfellow*, pp. 17, 18). Edward Moxon (1801–1858), publisher of Wordsworth, Southey, Tennyson, and Landor, among others, was the author of *Sonnets* (London, 1835), dedicated to Wordsworth.

3. John Kenyon (1784–1856), minor English poet and major literary philanthropist. At his death he left a substantial legacy to Robert and Elizabeth Browning.

4. Sir Thomas Noon Talfourd (1795–1854), jurist, dramatist, and friend of Dickens.

5. Lady Marguerite, countess of Blessington (1789–1849), the celebrated Irish-born beauty and novelist, lived at this time in Gore House with the Count d'Orsay. The Count, whose tastes outran his pocketbook, had fallen into debt and was in continual danger of arrest. He went bankrupt in 1849.

6. "The old lady was sitting backwards toward the east." H. R. von Schröter, "Die Geburt der Kolik," in *Finnische Runen*, ed. G. H. von Schröter (Stuttgart and Tübingen, 1834), p. 59. For the possible influence of this work on Hiawatha, see Ernest J. Moyne, *Hiawatha and Kalevala: A Study of the Relationship Between Longfellow's "Indian Edda" and the Finnish Epic.* Folklore Fellows Communication, $LXXX_2$, No. 192 (Helsinki, 1963).

7. Cf. *Macbeth,* III, iv, 24.

8. Hatfield remarks that this refers to "Freiligrath's exotic poems, especially 'Der Mohrenfürst' and 'Scipio' " ("Longfellow-Freiligrath Correspondence," p. 1244, n. 3).

9. Longfellow composed "Nuremburg" in 1844. The reference to "Günderode" is not clear. He may have planned a poem on Karoline von Günderode (1780–1806), a poet and suicide, whose fantastic correspondence with Bettina von Arnim was published by the latter in 1840 as *Die Günderode.*

10. Frederika Bremer, *The Neighbours; a Story of Every-day Life,* trans. from the Swedish by Mary Howitt (Boston, 1843), 2 vols. The suggestion that Mary Howitt may have translated from a German text was also made by Hillard in his review of the book in the *North American Review,* LVI (April 1843), 503.

11. Despite his enthusiasm for these poems, Longfellow continued to find them untranslatable.

12. Stanza 19, line 3. The page reference is to *Ballads and Other Poems.*

13. That is, a seal ring to replace the one lost at Marienberg (Letter No. 707).

## 744. *To Rufus Wilmot Griswold*

Cambridge, Jan. 10, 1843.

My dear Sir:

I am sorry I have not a portrait by Cheney in readiness. Must the engraving be ready for the April No.? Would the delay of a month or two make any difference to Mr. Graham?

As soon as I received your letter I went into town to see Cheney. He is confined by indisposition; and I do not know when he can get the likeness ready. Let us not do the matter in haste. I certainly do not wish to have Thompson's head engraved again. My friends all dislike it; and I am anxious now to have something that will please them. I will therefore have a portrait painted at my own expense, and as soon as possible. Will you wait? and not hurry the matter? If you can, we shall get something worth having. Do you prefer Parker to Cheney as an Engraver? [1]

I fear I can send you nothing for the March No. but will send a poem as soon as I can. I have several in my mind; but have not yet felt in the right mood to put them upon paper.

Thanks for your word about the "Poems on Slavery." I hope, however, you have said nothing to injure your Magazine; for I should be sorry to do that; and I did not think you would like to speak of the book in any way.[2]

Very truly yours,
Henry W. Longfellow.

MANUSCRIPT: unrecovered; text from *Passages from the Correspondence and Other Papers of Rufus W. Griswold* (Cambridge, Mass., 1898), p. 135.

1. Longfellow's unhappiness with the plan to use the engraving of the Franquinet portrait in *Graham's Magazine* had caused Graham and his editor to reconsider. In a letter to Longfellow of January 7, 1843, Griswold had offered to use an engraving of a Cheney portrait if one could be made available. On March 3, with the matter still unsettled, Griswold wrote that Graham had finally been forced to decide in favor of the Franquinet "caricature." It appeared in the May number (730.6). The final paragraph of Hillard's accompanying essay apologizes for its inadequacy: "The likeness which accompanies this, we are sorry to say, is not a very good one. Though correct, perhaps, in the general outline, Mr. Franquinet has failed to give that refined and poetical expression of his original which attracts the regard of every one who sees him in person" (p. 293).

2. Griswold had written: "I thank you for the 'Poems on Slavery.' That last word never is seen in a Philadelphia magazine. You will understand therefore the reason of the brief notice I have made of it. Mr. Graham objected even to publishing the title of the work!" (Letter of January 7, 1843). No notice of the new volume appeared in *Graham's Magazine.*

## 745. *To Julia Ward*

Cambridge Jan. 16. 1843.

My dear Julia,

I solemnly protest against the unworthy name you give me in your note to the "Gentle Doctor." [1] How could your graceful imagination invent it? How could your sweet voice pronounce it? How could your golden pen record it? If the Chinese Proverb be true, that "a coach and six cannot bring back a word once spoken," I beg you to send a coach and seven; or if necessary two coaches. At all events bring it back. And then let your voice like that of the sacred doves in the Dodonean Forest, pronounce a more welcome name, and a better omen.[2]

And then again I hear that you do not like my Poems on Slavery. I wish they were better, that they might better deserve your approbation. Yet be not too severe. Be not inexorable. Be not like the "Sweet Juniper, whose shadow hurteth sore." If you had written them, I would not have criticized them. The next shall be on a more engaging, and less painful theme; and I shall hope for your applause.

We are all eager to hear [about] the ball — the 32 *pounder*.[3] I hope you will let us know all about it, and particularly how you and Louisa are dressed, that we may have you more distinctly before our mind's eye. The forms we know, but we would fain behold the colors you were arrayed in — how

"Gardenia dropped her lucid belles
And rich magnolias closed their purple robes."

Until a gentler name is given me,

Yours
Longobardus.

MANUSCRIPT: unrecovered; text from typewritten transcript, Longfellow Trust Collection (Longfellow House).

1. The nickname coined by Julia Ward was Longobardus. The "Gentle Doctor" was Samuel Gridley Howe.

2. The famous shrine of Zeus at Dodona in Epirus is mentioned in both the *Iliad* and the *Odyssey*. Longfellow's objection to the nickname stems from the fact that Longobardus (Lombard) is a name associated with the Teutonic barbarians.

3. The allusion is explained in Sam Ward's letter to Longfellow of January 6, 1843: "We have a party next Friday [January 20] at No 32 Bond. We trust you will all come on. I can promise you the cream of our New York Belles. Pray say this to Howe, Felton, Sumner and Hillard."

## 746. *To J. G. Jarvis, Jr.*[1]

Cambridge Jan 22 1843

My dear Sir,

I have had the pleasure of receiving your note in regard to the poem of *Excelsior*; and very willingly give you my intention in writing it. This was no more than to display in a series of pictures the Life of a man of genius, resisting all temptations, laying aside all fears, heedless of all warnings and pressing right on to accomplish his purpose. His motto is *Excelsior* — "higher!" He passes through the Alpine village — through the rough cold paths of the world, where the peasants cannot understand him, and where his watch-word is in an "unknown tongue." He disregards the happiness of domestic peace, and sees the glaciers — his fate — before him. He disregards the warning of the old man's wisdom, and the fascination of woman's love. He answers to all "Higher yet!" The Monks of Saint Bernard are the representatives of religious forms and ceremonies; and with their oft-repeated prayer mingles the sound of his voice, telling them there is something higher than forms and ceremonies. Filled with these aspirations he perishes; — without having reached the perfection he longed for; and the voice heard in the air is the promise of immortality and progress ever upward.

You will perceive that *Excelsior*, an adjective of the comparative degree, is used adverbially; a use justified by the best latin writers.[2]

Hoping that this explanation will render the little poem perfectly clear to your mind, I remain

Very truly yours
Henry W. Longfellow.

MANUSCRIPT: Clifton Waller Barrett Collection, University of Virginia. ADDRESS: Mr J. G. Jarvis Jr./Boston POSTMARK: BOSTON MS JAN 23 PUBLISHED: W. Sloane Kennedy, *Henry W. Longfellow* (Boston, 1882), pp. 202–203 [*where the addressee is given as Henry Theodore Tuckerman*].

1. Possibly James Jarvis of 19 Gibbs Lane, Boston (*Boston Directory* for 1843). Jarvis' letter to Longfellow, which occasioned this reply, is dated January 18, 1842 (properly, 1843).
2. See 632.3.

## 747. *To Charles Eliot Norton*

[Cambridge, Jan. 29, 1843][1]

My dear Charles

Inclosed is a note of introduction to my friends in Bond Street, No. 32. whom I wish you to see. You will find their house a very delightful place; and I trust you will pass many very happy hours there.[2]

I most sincerely sympathise with you in your untoward fate; but I know you will bear it like a hero, like a young Frithiof — and deserve to have a *Saga* written about you, (though you probably may not.) Be of good cheer; and by your own courage confirm that of your friend and companion in sorrow Miss Howard,[3] to whom give my best regards and best wishes.

It is Sunday night; or rather Monday morning; for it is after midnight. Of course, I have been at your house this evening (I mean last evening). Sumner and Felton were there; and as neither of them knows the difference between "*B flat*," and "*da capo*," we amused them with German Psalm-tunes, and one or two of Beethoven's Sonatas.

Good night, my dear friend; and believe me

Ever truly yours
Henry W. Longfellow.

MANUSCRIPT: Harvard College Library. ADDRESS: Mr. Chs. E. Norton/New York./ By Mr. Cogswell ENDORSEMENT: Jan. 29. 1843. H. W. Longfellow Esq.

1. Date of Norton's endorsement (see below). Longfellow's remark in the third paragraph puts the date more precisely as the 30th.

2. Longfellow's letter of introduction is unrecovered. Norton had been sent to New York in the middle of his first year at Harvard for treatment of an eye disease.

3. Unidentified. Possibly a member of the family of Dr. John Clark Howard (212.1.).

## 748. *To Catherine Jane Norton*

[Cambridge, January 1843][1]

My dear Jane

I here send you Tennison, and some outlandish music, Dutch, Swedish and Spanish, which I should like to hear you play.

What else can I send you to make you happy?

With kindest regard

very truly
H. W. L.

MANUSCRIPT: Harvard College Library.

1. The date is approximate. Cf. Letter No. 740.

## 749. *To Stephen Longfellow*

Cambridge Feb. 5 1843

My dear Father,

Instead of writing I have sent you one or two newspapers, to inform you of my return and my existence. The last week I have been in Cambridge; the week before, that is, the week after I left you, I passed in Boston with the Ticknors. I had a pleasant visit. Mr. Cogswell was there also; but has gone back again to New York. I told him he ought first to go to Portland, to see his friends there; but he was too busy in Boston. I saw also my old friends the Everetts; who have returned again to Boston. Mr. Everett, you perhaps remember, has been for a year or two past President of a southern College; the College has been burned down; and he has left. Adversity seems to pursue him, wherever he goes.[1]

I shall come again to Portland before long; as soon as I accomplish some work, which I have on hand. But I find vacation a very bad time for working; and cannot bring my mind to bear upon anything with much power.

Tell mother, that I saw Mrs. [Jesse] Sumner a few days after my return; and delivered her message. She says she may perhaps be in Portland again next Summer; and thanks mother very much for her invitation to stay with her, without making any very definite promise to accept.

The long notice of my Poems in the New York Anti-Slavery paper, which I sent you, was written by Mr. Jay, son of Judge Jay. The Judge is now the great anti-slavery Apostle since Dr. Channing's death.[2]

A violent snow-storm began here this morning at about XI o'clock, and is now raging fiercely. We shall be blocked up for some days; and the rail-road impassible.

I have had very pleasant letters from Dickens and Lord Morpeth by the last Steamer; which letters I will bring you, when I come. Have you read Dickens's new book?[3]

President Woods is here. He thinks of putting in claims for the Temple estate for Bowdoin College, as legal heirs. The property is very large; and the question turns upon the point, whether the son of the late Temple Bowdoin, who is a British Officer, can be considered as a citizen of the United States. This Temple Bowdoin was naturalized in 1805. The son was born in England. It is a question of some importance to the College.[4]

Love to all.

Very affectionately yours
Henry W. Longfellow.

Tell little Stephen[5] I have a beautiful officer on horseback for him.

MANUSCRIPT: Longfellow Trust Collection. ADDRESS: Hon. S. Longfellow/Portland.

1. Alexander Everett became president of Jefferson College, Louisiana, in 1842. The *Dictionary of American Biography* gives ill health as the reason for his departure (VI, 221).

2. William Jay (1789–1858), abolitionist and judge of the county court of Westchester County, New York, was the father of John Jay (1817–1894), a young lawyer also engaged in antislavery activities. Longfellow had sent the judge a copy of his *Poems on Slavery,* which elicited the son's favorable review. It appeared in the *National Anti-Slavery Standard,* ed. Lydia Maria Child, III, No. 34 (Thursday, January 26, 1843), 133.

3. *Martin Chuzzlewit.*

4. Rev. Leonard Woods (1807–1878), president of Bowdoin College since

1839, vigorously prosecuted the college's case in this matter and finally won a favorable settlement. The litigation is discussed at some length in Nehemiah Cleaveland and Alpheus Spring Packard, *History of Bowdoin College. With Biographical Sketches of its Graduates from 1806 to 1879, Inclusive* (Boston, 1882), pp. 108–110. See also Letter No. 765.

5. Son of Longfellow's brother Stephen.

## 750. *To Anne Longfellow Pierce*

Cambridge Feb. 15. 1843

My beloved Annie,

Your letter did not reach me till last evening; and the invitation to the Ball was consequently too late. Your wishes shall be attended to as far as possible; and the books prepared for my journey. When am I coming? Why as soon as I dare venture out. The last two days I have been shut up with a cold. We have had strange weather; — freezing, thawing, snowing, raining, in quick succession; and almost everyone has suffered in consequence.

Cheney's portrait is very successful. It is not yet engraved; not even in the hands of the engraver. I wish you could see it; for if it is not good, I would have another made. I should like to have your opinion on the subject. When the engraving is made, I will have some proof copies reserved as you suggest.[1]

I had a letter from Margaret Thacher two days ago; and have answered it to day. She seems well and happy in her solitudes of Acadia; and rejoices in her baby, as a young mother should.[2]

I never saw the American Ballad you speak of, though the old Ballad "Edward! Edward!" I know very well.[3] Nathan Winslow was in the Cars, when I came up, and pleaded guilty, in the name of his daughter Harriet, to the "soft impeachment"[4] of being the grandfather of that poem I like so much

"Why thus longing, thus forever sighing,
For the far-off, unattained and dim;
While the Beautiful, all round thee lying,
Offers up its low perpetual hymn!"[5]

A smile and a new brightness came into the paternal eye of Nathan, when I repeated these lines and asked him if his daughter wrote them; and I really believe that I stand three feet higher in his esteem, than I did before, — Slavery Poems, and all.

The "Ballads and Other Poems" have gone to a fifth edition, which will be published in a few days. "The Neighbors" vol 1. is published; vol 2. will not be out till Saturday.[6]

It is now afternoon; and another snow storm is beginning. I fear the roads will be blocked up again. Still I hope to be with you on Friday or Saturday. Until then farewell. I am sorry to say that I have not been to see Mrs. Mason since you were here; but for your sake will try to do so before coming to Portland.

Yours very truly and affectionately
Henry.

I have not heard from the Commodore [A. S. Wadsworth]; and fear the Music never reached him.

MANUSCRIPT: Longfellow Trust Collection. ADDRESS: Mrs. Anne L. Pierce/care of S. Longfellow Esq/Portland/Me POSTMARK: CAMBRIDGE MS. FEB 16

1. Cheney's portrait now hangs in the Longfellow House. See Plate XI.

2. Francis Storer Thacher, born in Machias, Maine, in October 1842, was the Thacher's first child. He graduated from Bowdoin in 1866, from the Harvard Divinity School in 1873, and died in 1923.

3. Since Anne Pierce's letter is unrecovered, the "American Ballad" cannot be identified. "Edward, Edward," a Scottish ballad, appears in Percy's *Reliques of Ancient English Poetry.*

4. Sheridan, *The Rivals,* V, iii.

5. Stanza 1 of Harriet Winslow's "Why Thus Longing," collected by Longfellow (with the omission of the last four stanzas) in *The Waif* (Boston, 1845), pp. 9–10. Miss Winslow was the daughter of Nathan Winslow, a Portland hardware merchant.

6. See 743.10.

## 751. *To Margaret Potter Thacher*

Cambridge, Feb. 15, 1843.

My dear Margaret, —

I was very much gratified by your brief epistle, which reached me night before last, and brought me the assurances of your kind remembrance. Believe me, I have often thought of you and your husband; and have felt that your new home, though remote from many of your earlier friends, was nevertheless to you the centre of a world of happiness. With your affection, and your "young Astyanax," the "yellow house" becomes a golden palace.[1] For my part, Life seems to be to me "a battle and a march."[2] I am sometimes well, — sometimes ill, and always restless. My late expedition to Germany did me a vast deal of good; and my health is better than it has been for years. So long as I keep out of doors and take exercise enough, I feel perfectly well. So soon as I shut myself up and begin to study, I feel perfectly ill. Thus the Sphinx's riddle — the secret of health — is discovered. In Germany I led an out-of-door life; bathing and walking from morning till night. I was at Boppard on the Rhine, in the old convent of

Marienberg, now a Bathing establishment. I travelled a little in Germany; then passed through Belgium to England. In London I staid with Dickens; and had a very pleasant visit. His wife is a gentle, lovely character; and he has four children, all beautiful and good. I saw likewise *the* raven, who is stuffed in the entry — and his successor, who stalks gravely in the garden.

I am very sorry, my dear Margaret, that I cannot grant your request in regard to Mary's Journal. Just before I sailed for Europe, being in low spirits, and reflecting on the uncertainties of such an expedition as I was then beginning, I burned a great many letters and private papers, and among them this. I now regret it; but alas! too late.

Ah! my dear Margaret! though somewhat wayward and restless, I most affectionately cherish the memory of my wife. You know how happily we lived together; and *I* know that never again shall I be loved with such devotion, sincerity, and utter forgetfulness of self. Make her your model, and you will make your husband ever happy; and be to him as a household lamp irradiating his darkest hours.

Give my best regards to him. I should like very much to visit you; but know not how I can bring it about. Kiss "young Astyanax" for me, and believe me ever affectionately your brother

Henry W. Longfellow.

MANUSCRIPT: unrecovered; text from Higginson, *Longfellow,* pp. 169–171.

1. Margaret Thacher's letter is unrecovered, but it was presumably written from Machias, Maine, where her husband practiced law.
2. Schiller, *Wallensteins Tod,* III, xv, 98–99 (Coleridge's translation).

## 752. *To Samuel Gridley Howe*

Cambridge. Feb. 20 1843.[1]

My dearest Chevalier, —

From the deepest dungeons of my heart, all the imprisoned sympathies and affections of my nature, cry aloud to you, saying "All hail!" On my return from Portland this afternoon, I found your note, and before reading it I read in Sumner's eyes your happiness. The great riddle of life is no longer a riddle to you; the great mystery is solved.[2]

I need not say to you how deeply and devoutly I rejoice with you; — none more so, I assure you. Among all your friends, I am the oldest friend of your fair young bride; she is a beautiful spirit, — a truth which friendship has learned by heart in a few years, and Love has taught you in as many hours!

Of course, you seem to us transfigured and glorified. You walk above in the pure air, while Sumner and I, like the poor spirits in Faust, who were struggling far down in the cracks and fissures of the rocks, cry out to you, "O take us with you! Take us with you!"[3]

In fine, my dear Doctor, God bless you and yours. You know already how much I approve of your choice. I went to your office this afternoon to tell you with my own lips; but you were not there. Take, therefore, this brief expression of my happiness at knowing you are so happy; and believe me

Ever sincerely Your friend
Longfellow

MANUSCRIPT: unrecovered; text from typewritten transcript, Longfellow Trust Collection. PUBLISHED: Laura E. Richards and Maud Howe Elliott, *Julia Ward Howe 1819–1910* (Boston and New York, 1916), I, 76–77.

1. Date from published version of this letter (see above). The typewritten copy in the Longfellow Trust Collection gives the date as February 26, but this is certainly incorrect because Longfellow states in the first paragraph that he had just returned from Portland, and he is known to have been back in Cambridge on the 24th (Letter No. 753).

2. Howe's engagement to Julia Ward had just been announced. They were married on April 26, 1843.

3. Goethe, *Faust*, Part I, xxi, 164.

## 753. *To Julia Ward*

Cambridge. Feb. 24. 1843.

My dear Julia,

When I saw you this afternoon I could not say to you one tenth part of all that was struggling in me for expression; — joy, congratulation, — good wishes — hopes — prayers. There stood the bright Future, opening wide before you its golden gates, like a triumphal arch, and the gentle chevalier leading you by the hand through its illuminated vistas; and I could only salute you, as it were, from afar, and leave unsaid what I most wished to say, you being, as it seemed to my imagination, already beyond the sound of my voice.

Fancy, therefore, this sheet of paper, rolled into a speaking trumpet, and that through it you hear the following words;

"O thou bright Arethusa! so lately Diana's nymph, and now a fountain! A human soul — a new Alpheus, has mingled its waters with thine, — its pure currents having flowed to thee under the deep, salt sea of Life, without being impregnated with its bitterness. Henceforth flow on together, the fountain lost in the river, the river filled by the fountain; and on the surface of this stream be Serenity; — in its depths Tranquillity!"

And now, my dear Julia, after this preliminary flourish, and figure of speech, let me send through the speaking trumpet one sweet, simple, and solemn word; — you have won the heart of a Man — a true, sincere, and noble heart. Rest upon it evermore; it has been tried by love and sorrow; and you know that you can lean upon it for support throughout the remainder of your life. Receive once more my sincere, my earnest wishes for your happiness; and count me ever your friend

Henry W. Longfellow

MANUSCRIPT: Rosalind Richards, Gardiner, Maine. ADDRESS: Miss Julia Ward/ No 3. Park Street

## 754. *To Catherine Jane Norton*

[Cambridge] Sunday noon. [February 26, 1843]

My dear Jane,

Here is the *Spanish Waltz,* which you will find fanciful and pretty. Also a small package for Mr. Giraud,[1] which be kind enough to give him.

Hoping to see you this evening at the "*Stabat Mater,*"[2]

Yours truly
*H. W. L.*

MANUSCRIPT: Harvard College Library. ADDRESS: Miss C. Jane Norton.

1. P. A. Giraud is listed as "teacher French 68 Belknap" in the *Boston Directory* for 1843. He presumably tutored the Norton daughters.

2. The first performance of Rossini's *Stabat Mater* by the Boston Handel and Haydn Society took place at the Melodeon on February 26, 1843, which establishes the earliest date for this letter. It might have been written, however, on any one of the three later Sundays when the performance was repeated — March 5, March 12, and April 2 (Boston *Daily Evening Transcript*).

## 755. *To John Forster*

Cambridge February 28 1843.

My dear Forster,

We were all sadly disappointed when the Acadia arrived and brought us nothing either from you or Dickens. Not a single soul among us had a word from England; and of all the pens mended for reply, only one or two will have a chance of showing their skill. But among them, one shall be mine; and I fall back upon your letter of Jan 3. for which receive my warmest thanks. But alas! *Duc ad me!* what *has* become of the *duc ad me*![1] If the Cunard steamers fail, whom shall we trust?

Meanwhile how wags the brave world in No 58 Lincoln's Inn

Fields? I think very often of your household gods; — your delightful, snug state of *single-cursedness*; the fire-light, wine-light, and friend light in-doors; and the brown cope of heaven out of doors arching above like a huge, smoke-colored Hock-glass turned bottom upwards by jolly Bacchus after drinking a *supernaculum*. The pleasant hours I passed there, and elsewhere with you are still green in my memory and will ever flourish in immortal youth. When shall we again sit together, "drinking the blood-red wine"? [2]

Felton writes to Dickens by this Steamer; I shall by the next. I am sorry to say that dark clouds are descending "upon the house of Agamemnon." Felton's wife is very ill, — dangerously ill. Before her confinement she fell down stairs, (why will women *always* fall down stairs, when in that State?) and has never been well since. As Felton was sitting in his study a few evenings ago, he heard a slight noise at the door, opened it, and his wife tottered in, and fainted in his arms. He called the servants, and carried her up to bed, where she lay quite delirious all night. She is slightly better, but not much. Her constitution seems exhausted; and I much fear, that our next letters, will bring you still worse news. I shudder to think what he has before him! [3]

I was wrong in saying that the Acadia brought us nothing; it brought us Chuzzlewit No 3.[4] The story opens with great freshness and vigor. The Autumn Evening — the strong-minded lady (a kind of Oboë-accompaniment in the family concert) — Tom Pinch's journey to Salisbury — and the arrival of the new pupil — together with the great, moral Pecksniff, are all as the *Reviewers would say*, in Boz's *happiest vein*. The figure of speech about the shadow of the church spire moving round the church-yard, as on a vast dial-plate, I claim as my own; See Preface to Ballads. p. xi. — a very good figure notwithstanding.[5] Of course, the work is pirated here. Two editions appear — one by the Harpers at 3 cents pr. No. And by the way — à propos de bottes, a Boston Publisher is now going round with a subscription paper to induce his fellow publishers to sign in favor of a Copy-right-Law. What will Peter Parley [6] say? I wish Dickens's Publishers would send out a certain number of copies by steamer for the Boston market. I think they would be eagerly bought up. We are getting rather tired of the *shabby style* of publication. The name of "the moral Pecksniff" has been given to our new radical governor *Morton*, not Davis ("Codlin's the friend, not Short.") [7]

And now to descend a note or two. I hope the Slavery Poems did not disappoint you. I have attempted only to invest the subject with a poetic coloring. People here have so long looked upon the ridiculous side of the negro's character (and you have no idea what a *broad* side that is) that their sympathics for the race are deadened. These I have tried to awaken, "by gentle force soliciting" their hearts. This is the point of view from which I want you to look at the poems. Thank you for your promise to notice them in the Examiner. Pray send me the No. Your paper is taken at the Athenaeum in Boston; but two Nos. are missing for January.[8]

I am very sincerely sorry I did not see Milnes. I am sure I should have liked him, for I like the spirit of his poetry, and he carries me along with him, and touches secret c[h]ords within me. I have been speaking with a publisher about an American Edition of his works — of course, supposing he does not object. Nothing definite has, however, been done. And Tennison, too, a more mystic master of the lyre, why did I not see him? And Marston? and Taylor? [9] I sympathize with these men. I should have been delighted to see them. And Talford, likewise; and — but enough! I saw you and Dickens and to see the others can wait another visit. And so, my dear Forster, give me both hands; and believe me ever most cordially yours

Henry W. Longfellow.

P. S. Much love to the Dickenses, — and kiss me all the children, with a double mind for fine little Charlie, whom I can now see as distinctly as if he were standing before me.

Felton will write about Howe's engagement to a fine, young, buxom damsel of four and twenty, who is full of talent, — indeed carrying almost too many guns for any man, who does not want to be *firing salutes* all the time. Felton will laud her to the skies. He thinks there never was such a woman.

MANUSCRIPT: Victoria and Albert Museum, London. ADDRESS: John Forster Esq/ No 58 Lincoln's Inn Fields/London POSTMARKS: B 15 MR 15 1843/ FORWARDED BY HARNDENS PACKAGE EXPRESS|| & FOREIGN LETTER|| OFFICE NO ||8|| COURT ST BOSTON/4E84 MR 15 1843

1. The pun (literally, "Bring to me!") refers to the canvasback ducks sent by Longfellow to Forster in December (Letter No. 734). Forster had not received them when he wrote his letter of January 3 (*Life,* II, 7).

2. "Sir Patrick Spens," l. 2.

3. Longfellow's pessimism was somewhat premature, but Mary Felton did not recover her health and died on April 12, 1845.

4. *Martin Chuzzlewit* was originally produced in twenty monthly installments.

5. The figure apears in Chap. V of *Martin Chuzzlewit.* Longfellow used it in his essay review of *Frithiofs Saga* (*Works,* VII, 320), which in revised form became the preface to *Ballads and Other Poems.*

6. Pseudonym of Samuel Griswold Goodrich (1793–1860), prolific producer of moralistic books for the instruction of the young. In his *Recollections of a Lifetime or Men and Things I have Seen* (New York and Auburn, 1856), II, 355–378, he developed his arguments in favor of an international copyright law.

7. "Honest John" Davis (see 660.3) had recently been succeeded by Marcus Morton (1784–1864), a Democrat, as governor of Massachusetts. The parenthetical quotation is from *The Old Curiosity Shop,* Chap. XIX, and refers to the characters Thomas Codlin and Short Trotters (Mr. Harris).

8. Forster's review — more a discourse on slavery than a notice of Longfellow's poems — appeared in the *Examiner,* No. 1837 (April 8, 1843), 211–212.

9. John Westland Marston (1819–1890) had recently begun his career as a dramatist with *The Patrician's Daughter,* for which Dickens had furnished a prologue. Philip Meadows Taylor (1808–1876), Anglo-Indian officer and correspondent of the London *Times,* was the author of the highly successful *Confessions of a Thug* (London, 1839).

## 756. *To Charles Sumner*

[Cambridge, February 1843]

My dear Charles

When did you write this?[1] I never saw it before. Why have you never shown it to me? It is a true portrait.

Yours truly
H. W. L.

MANUSCRIPT: Longfellow Trust Collection. ANNOTATION (*in another hand*): Feb 1843

1. The following undated newspaper clipping entitled "Misery of a Bachelor's Life" accompanies the letter: "Poor fellow! he returns to his lodging — I will not say to his 'home.' There may be every thing he can possibly desire, in the shape of mere external comforts, provided for him by the officious zeal of Mrs.———, his housekeeper; but still the room has an air of chilling vacancy, the very atmosphere of the apartment has a dim, uninhabited appearance — the chairs, set round with provoking neatness look reproachfully useless and unoccupied — the tables and other furniture shine with impertinent and futile brightness. All is dreary and repelling. No gentle face welcomes his arrival — no gentle hands meet his — no kind looks answer the listless gaze he throws round the apartment. He sits down to a book — alone; there is no one sitting by his own side, to enjoy with him the favorite passage — the apt remark — the just criticism; no eyes in which to read his own feelings; his own tastes are unappreciated and unreflected; he has no resource but himself; all his happiness must emanate from himself. He flings down the volume in despair; hides his face in his hands, and sighs aloud, O! me miserum." The signature "C. *Sumner,*" written in pencil, follows the text of the clipping.

## 757. *To Samuel Ward*

CAMBRIDGE, March 2, 1843.

[O Absalom! my son! How could you send me such a profane song? I had spent the morning in translating a holy Legend from the German of Julius Mosen; and when I paused, instead of an echo from without, I heard that sound of ribaldry, like a loud vulgar ballad from an alehouse!][1]

Thanks for your letter, my dear Sam; though none, absolutely, *utterly* none for the Song. What you say of the Spanish Student is true, in part, at least. The task of adding to it is not agreeable to me; and I am sorely tempted to let it alone. When you come you shall know my plan about it. It is hardly worth while to write about the matter. I will then give you my reasons for using *utterly* and *warm*. They are not changes — these words, — but the original expressions — the first, best words. Be sure they are not used without good and sufficient reason.[2]

*My* Etna *is* burnt out; my Boundary Line is settled. Impassable Highlands divide the waters running North and South. "Let the dead Past bury its dead!" and excuse me for quoting myself.[3]

I was very glad to see Julia. As soon as I heard of her arrival I went in with "Dear Feltonius" to see her. I stayed to dinner, and after dinner took a long walk with her, during which we had a very pleasant conversation, which took a more serious turn, than any I ever before held with Julia. The dinner, however, was *mad* enough; for under the eyes of the *Banker* [Thomas Wren Ward] and his wife, Julia, Mary[4] and I drank "eternal friendship" three times; in imitation of the damsels in Canning's Anti-Jacobin Play: — "A sudden thought strikes me! Let us swear an eternal friendship."[5]

Yes; — it was a pleasant week at the "X Professor's";[6] and I go in tomorrow to pass three or four days more in the same chamber, having accidentally left my slippers there. When will you be here? Let me know precisely: for I am going to Portland again, and wish to time my visit so as not to lose yours. Therefore fix your time; for I must have a long talk with you; and if you come when I am away, it will be a miserable piece of business.

You are slightly mistaken about the "Compagnon du Tour de France." I did begin it; and will finish it ere long, and will then take a glimpse into the Inferno of Mathilde, if you will bring it with you.[7]

"Crows to pick!" did you say? Yes; a whole rookery.

I trust you mean to stay with me when you come. If this is not your plan, I will stay with you — at Park Street Corner, or Tremont House, or wheresoever you choose. Write soon; send the ball bounding back.

Ever thine

HIERONIMUS.

Did the package for Highbee [Higbee] reach him? Julia says it is probably still lying in yr. portmanteau. How is this?

P.S. "In future, Gentlemen, let us have *prose* and *decency*" — Danton in the Assembly.[8] *Therefore* I inclose you another parody, which came by the same mail as the one you sent.

MANUSCRIPT: unrecovered; text from "Letters to Samuel Ward, Part III," pp. 307–308.

1. Ward had sent Longfellow a parody of "Excelsior" (unrecovered) in a letter of February 6, 1843. The translation referred to was either "The Statue over the Cathedral Door" or "The Legend of the Crossbill," both of which were first published in *Graham's Magazine,* XXII (April 1843), 240. See *Works,* VI, 279–281.

2. Ward had objected to Longfellow's substituting "utterly" for "wholly" in line 30 of "Endymion" and "warm" for "clear" in line 12 of "Excelsior."

3. Longfellow quotes from "A Psalm of Life" in this allusion to his romance with Fanny Appleton. Ward had written: "There has been a recent eruption of Mount Etna after a stillness of many years in its crater which it was supposed was *ausgebrandt.* Would that this might prove emblematic of a revival of the Ashburton Treaty zeal in the heart of the student Hieronymus — the only danger would be of crows to pick — each would have some fault to find with the other and it would require oceans of love to drown all discord if its elements were once invoked" (February 6, 1843). The tale of the lovesick student Hieronymus is told by Paul Flemming (Longfellow) to Mary Ashburton (Fanny Appleton) in *Hyperion,* Chap. VIII (*Works,* VIII, 196–205).

4. Mary Ward, daughter of Thomas Wren Ward, had been engaged to Sam's brother, Henry Ward (1818–1840). She later married Charles Dorr of Boston and became a socially prominent hostess.

5. George Canning, *The Rovers,* I, i.

6. That is, ex-Professor George Ticknor. See Letter No. 749.

7. In his letter Ward had written: "I have finished Mathilde. 'Tis a damnable novel and if you will read it I will send it to you. But although there is a remarkable parallelism in our sentiments our tastes are often in antagonism. Thus you never read the Compagnon du Tour de France of George Sand despite my recommendation — while I have devoured half a dozen books at yours." The reference is to Eugène Sue, *Mathilde; Mémoires d'une jeune femme* (Paris, 1841).

8. On March 16, 1794, Danton opposed the recitation of some patriotic verses before the revolutionary convention. "Je . . . demande que dorénavant on n'entende plus à la barre que la raison en prose" (I . . . ask that henceforth only reason in prose be heard in this assembly). See *Discours de Danton,* ed. André Fribourg (Paris, 1910), p. 690. The parody mentioned in the next sequence is missing.

## 758. *To Samuel Ward*

CAMBRIDGE, March 6, 1843.

MY DEAR SAM,

I ought to have written to you long ago on the great event of our Chevalier's conquering the Celestial City; but I have been away from home, and have, moreover, been hoping to see you here, and expecting to hear from you. The event did not surprise me: for the Chevalier is a mighty man of Love, and I noted that on the walls of the citadel (Julia's cheeks) first the white flag would be displayed, and anon the red, and then again the white. The citadel could not have submitted to a braver, better or more humane knight.

Seriously, my dear Sam, and most sincerely do I rejoice in this event. Julia could not have chosen *more* wisely — nor the Doctor so wisely; and I think you may safely look forward to a serene and happy life for your sister. And so God speed them upon Life's journey: "To the one be contenting enjoyments of his auspicious desires; to the other, a happy attendance of her chosen muses." [1]

I write you a very short note this morning, because I am going to hear Sumnerius lecture in the Law School, on Ambassadors, Consuls, Peace and War, and other matters of International Law.

How is it, about the mysterious Highbee [Higbee] package? If you do not send it forthwith, I commission Louisa and Annie to lay their lily hands upon it, remove it from your sac de nuit, where it has been lying long enough, and deliver it to Mr. Highbee in the pulpit!

Write me soon — as soon as you can; and say that you are coming to Cambridge ere long. Life is short. We meet not often; and I am most sincerely,

HENRY W. LONGFELLOW.

MANUSCRIPT: unrecovered; text from "Letters to Samuel Ward, Part III," p. 308.

1. In letters of September 20 and October 5, 1848, to Robert Bigsby (770.5) and Evert Duyckinck, Longfellow attributed this quotation to John Seldon (1584–1654), the English jurist, antiquary, and author.

## 759. *To Catherine Eliot Norton*

[Cambridge, March 9, 1843] [1]

equally so *now*. Do not judge me too severely.

But peace! peace! perturbed Spirit! [2]

I hope Charles's eyes are really better; and Miss Howard's also; and that you will not stay a great while longer in New York. I have been translating some Cantos of Dante for you, since you went away.[3] If there is any merit in the work it is yours. I am also reading Miss Burney's Diary [4] and Evelina; and preparing the Spanish Student for the press and lecturing on Faust and Molière. On Saturday we were at the last Academy Concert.[5] I asked Mr. Norton how he was pleased. He replied with a faint smile (such as heroes of romance always have upon their lips when dying) "Pretty much as usual!" You know how much that is. But he has seen the Comet, which he protests is nothing but a luminous cloud, and no comet at all.[6] Mrs. Felton is much better. Sam Guild has not yet shown himself in Camb; but Elizabeth is at Shady Hill.[7] Spring has begun to-day, for the first time in earnest. Till now a cold, sharp disagreeable West wind has been blowing and chilling us through. I hope it has been more genial, kindly weather with you.

If Mrs. Cleveland is with you, give her my kindest regards. We have heard nothing of late from Henry. Much love to Charles.

Ever affectionately yours
Henry W. Longfellow

MANUSCRIPT: Harvard College Library. ADDRESS: Mrs. C. E. Norton/at Mr. Henry Cowing's/663 Broad Way/New York. ANNOTATION (*by Longfellow*): Single. POSTMARK: CAMBRIDGE MS. MAR 9

1. This letter is fragmentary. Date is from the postmark.

2. Cf. *Hamlet,* I, v, 183.

3. This is the earliest mention in the letters of Longfellow's translation of the *Divine Comedy*, which was published in three volumes, 1865–1867.

4. Five volumes of Fanny Burney's *Letters and Diaries* (London, 1842–1846) had been published in 1842. Her *Evelina* was first published in London in 1778.

5. The last concert of the season sponsored by the Boston Academy of Music, on March 4, 1843, at the Odeon. The program is printed in the *Daily Evening Transcript,* XIV, No. 3868 (Friday, March 3, 1843).

6. The "Great Comet of 1843" is described by Benjamin Peirce in *The American Almanac and Repository of Useful Knowledge, for the Year 1844* (Boston, 1843), pp. 94–100.

7. Samuel Eliot Guild (1819–1862) and his sister Elizabeth Quincy Guild (1821–1894) were the children of Mrs. Norton's sister, Eliza Eliot (Mrs. Benjamin) Guild.

## 760. *To Ferdinand Freiligrath*

Cambridge. March. 15. 1843

Dearest Freiligrath,

On leaving London I wrote you a few lines to say once more farewell; — and since my return have written you once, by the way of Havre, to tell you of my safe arrival among my household gods.[1]

With this I send you a small package, containing Indian *moccasons,* and other Indian matters from Canada. I know that the *mocassons* are too small; for I have still that mysterious strip of paper on which is written in your own hand writing "*Length of my wife's foot!*" But alas! I could get no others; and even these I got by chance. Some of the articles are worked in *wampum,* or porcupine's quills; — the rest in beads; but all are done by the brown fingers of Indian girls, on the banks of the St. Lawrence, and within sound of the roaring Niagara. These little presents I propose to divide as follows;

The black moccasons. }
The bead bag. } To the beloved Ida
The brown moccasons to the eldest Miss Heuberger.
The bracelets to the second Miss Heuberger

The card-case to the youngest Miss Heuberger.

Your wife can easily make the *mocassons* long enough by putting a piece in at the heel.

And Helena! the absent Helena [Fräulein von Gall]! have I forgotten her? Have I broken my vow? Oh no! For her I have an Indian basket — worked with wampum, which I trust will shine on her table in Vienna before many months. But the form is so inconvenient for packing, and the material so frail — birch-bark, that I shall send it in a little box with your books, *via* Rotterdam. If Ida prefers the white moccasons — or the bracelets instead of the bag, let her take them. They are mere trifles; but they will remind you of me; and the Western World, and perchance give rise to a *savage poem* in your teeming brain. Speaking of savage poems you may like to see one. Here it is; written by a Choctaw and translated by a gentleman of Mississippi.[2]

Song of the Ancient Choctaws.

I slew the chief of the Muskokee,
And burned his squaw at a blasted tree,
By the hind-legs I tied up his cur,
He had no time to fondle her.
  Hoo! hoo! hoo! the Muskokee!
  Wah! wah! wah! the blasted tree!

I stripped his skull all naked and bare,
And here's his scalp with a tuft of hair.
His flesh is in the panther's maw,
His bloody bones the wolf doth knaw!
  Hoo! hoo! hoo! the Muskokee!
  Wah! wah! wah! the blasted tree!

A faggot from the blasted tree
Fired the lodge of the Muskokee;
His sinews serve to string my bow
When bent to lay my brethren low.
  Hoo! hoo! hoo! the Muskokee!
  Wah! wah! wah! the Blasted Tree!

*Squaw,* you know, is the Indian for wife. And so here you have a wild ballad, with the war-whoop in it.

For my own part I have written very little since my return. One piece I send you; the *Belfry of Bruges*, published in Graham's magazine, and for which he paid me 75 Prussian Thalers.[3] I have been at work upon the *Spanish Student,* which will shortly appear, much improved.

Your poems excite a great interest here in those to whom I have lent them. I am glad to see that Howit[t] speaks so handsomely of them in his *Rural Life in Germany.*[4]

I shall write you again soon; — with a sketch of our Popular Literature — the republication of English books in cheap form — *alias* piracy, alias "*Yankee scoundrelism*" as the English papers call it.[5]

Much love to Ida the fair, and regards to the Heubergers.

Ever yours
Henry W. Longfellow

This will be handed you by Mr. Muzzy,[6] a very pleasant person, who will answer all your questions about me, and give you a vigorous shake of the hand from me.

MANUSCRIPT: Longfellow Trust Collection.

1. Letters No. 726 and 743.
2. The "gentleman of Mississippi" is not identified. Freiligrath translated the poem under the title "Lied der Alten Tschaktas." See Letter No. 798.
3. See 726.2.
4. William Howitt, *The Rural and Domestic Life of Germany* (London, 1842), pp. 476–478.
5. This letter, if written, has been lost.
6. Artemus Bowers Muzzey (1802–1892), a Unitarian minister and author of numerous moral essays and guides, spent several months in Europe in 1843.

## 761. *To Samuel Ward*

Cambridge March 15 1843.

Dearest Sam,

I write you a very brief note this morning; merely to thank you for your last with the Poem of "monumental brass." It is very forcible — very striking — with some fine thoughts in it. But it breathes an ungenerous spirit — and if the author speaks from his heart he is self-conceited and not magnanimous. Has he a right to say "*Exegi*"?[1]

Of course, you will not take my opinion; but since we have known each other, I have always spoken frankly to you. Take this new token of my candor. Thus you have, as you requested, my "opinion critical and candid."

And now, "Old Gentleman" I rejoice in your severity of soul — but when you speak of your life as being very tranquil and free from emotion — I fancy you do not mean exactly what you say. You, as well as I, can take a motto from the life and lips of Faust:

"Ich bin zu alt um nur zu spielen
Zu jung, um ohne Wünsch zu sein."

But I have to go a line or two farther and add;

Entbehren sollst du! sollst entbehren!" [2]

For the last week I have been plagued with an Influenza, which does not seem disposed to leave me. I am working away however on sundry matters; and have not been into town for a fortnight.

Everybody seems delighted with Julia's engagement. She is wise as well as witty. Howe is a grand fellow; and deserves his good fortune. This everybody feels; and acknowledges.

When you come you of course stay with me; for I cannot now go into town to stay with you. But we are up to our knees in water now. *Á Dios, amigo.*

Thine ever
Victorian.[3]

P. S. Pray dont misconstrue my opinion of the poem. I do not mean to speak harshly — only very plainly. So dont be vexed.

MANUSCRIPT: unrecovered; text from photostat, Longfellow Trust Collection. ADDRESS: Samuel Ward Esq/Prime Ward & King/New York ANNOTATION (*by Longfellow*): ☞ Higbee! PUBLISHED: "Letters to Samuel Ward, Part III," p. 308.

1. According to Ward, the poem — entitled "Exegi monumentum aere perennius" ("I have built a monument more lasting than brass"; Horace, *Odes,* III, xxx, 1) — "flashed a few days since from the soul of a man of letters whom a dark and wealthy lassie had rejected." The poem and its accompanying note are undated. The unnamed poet may have been Ward himself.

2. "I am too old for play/Too young to be without desire"; "Renounce you must! you must renounce!" Goethe, *Faust,* Part I, iv, 20–21 and 23.

3. Longfellow and Ward frequently addressed one another as Victorian and Hypolito, the two students of Alcalá in *The Spanish Student.*

## 762. *To Ferdinand Freiligrath*

Cambridge March 19 1843

My dear Freiligrath,

The bearer of this is the Rev. Mr. Muzzy, clergyman of Cambridgeport, the village that unites Cambridge to Boston. He goes direct to the Rhine; and I cannot let him go, without taking a line to you, for I want him to stop at St. Goar on his own sake, as well as on mine.

You will find Mr. Muzzy a very agreeable companion; and I flatter myself that his being able to tell you all about me will increase his welcome.

If you have time, pray make him acquainted with the Landrath [Heuberger]; and believe me

Ever truly yours
Henry W. Longfellow.[1]

Mr. Muzzy will bring you a letter and sundry small Indian matters for Ida.[2]

Your wife's translation of the "Rainy Day" [is] in a German Newspaper in New York; also in the *Bürger-Freund* at Bremen. Your *Excelsior* has also been reprinted in the New York paper — "Die Deutsche Schnell-Post"; and likewise the "Death of the Flowers."[3] Others of yours are to follow. One of your translations from Tennison I have seen; namely the *Grablied.*[4] It is very good. Have you read "Locksley Hall"? the longest and best poem in Tennison's second volume?

MANUSCRIPT: Henry E. Huntington Library.

1. The direction "over" follows the signature.

2. See Letter No. 760 and n. 6.

3. Freiligrath's translation of Bryant's "The Death of the Flowers" and of "Excelsior" appeared in *Deutsche Schnellpost*, January 25 and 28, 1843. His wife's translation, "Der Regentag," was subsequently published in Freiligrath's *Englische Gedichte aus neuerer Zeit* (Stuttgart and Tübingen, 1846), p. 400.

4. "Ein Grablied" ("A Dirge") was collected in *Englische Gedichte aus neurerer Zeit*, pp. 331–333.

## 763. *To Nathaniel Hawthorne*

Cambridge March 19 1843.

Dearest Hawthornius,

Dont forget that you are to dine with me on Tuesday next — that is to say, the day after tomorrow — at 3 o'clock.

I want very much to see you, and to tell how truly delighted I was with your last story, The Birth Mark. Not the comet himself can unfold a more glorious *tail.*[1]

But you should have made a Romance of it, and not a short story only.

More of that on Tuesday; till when

Yours very truly
H. W. L.

MANUSCRIPT: Connecticut State Library. ADDRESS: Nathaniel Hawthorne/at Dr. Peabody's/West Street.[2]

1. Longfellow read "The Birth Mark" in *The Pioneer, A Literary and Critical Magazine*, ed. J. R. Lowell and R. Carter, I, No. 3 (March 1843), 113–119.

2. Dr. Nathaniel Peabody (1774–1855), dentist of Salem and Boston, was Hawthorne's father-in-law. The Peabody family maintained a home, bookshop, and homeopathic drugstore at 13 West Street, Boston.

## 764. *To Catherine Eliot Norton*

Cambridge March 21 1843[1]

My dear Mrs Norton,

Last evening I had the extreme satisfaction of receiving your kind letter; — four days after its date; and I beg you not for one moment to wrap yourself in the illusion that any letters you receive can give you half the pleasure, that those you write give us. I should not have waited for yours in order to write you again; but for a day or two past I have been busy in writing to Europe, and making up some small packages for my German friends, having an opportunity direct from Cambridge to the Rhine. And now guess who is going! I give you three trials. No, it is *not* Peele Dabney;[2] it is *not* President Quincy; it is *not* Miss Lowell! It is the Reverend Mr. Muzzy of the Port, with his smiling moving face. And this is the most striking thing that has happened since I wrote you; and this has not happened yet.

For the last fortnight I have been in Boston but once. That was to dine with Mrs. Ticknor on Saturday. The guests were young Richard Dana and his wife; and Mr. and Mrs. Crafts.[3] Mrs. Ticknor was unusually well and cheerful. She recommended one of the dishes as a successful attempt of the cook — "quite a *coup*." Mr. Crafts, who was eating thereof, assented, and said "yes, it is what the French call *copper monkey*." All looked very wise, and no one comprehended. Mrs. T. contented herself with saying, she had never heard it called so. Now, what do you imagine he meant? By dint of hard study, I have made it out to be a "*coup pas manqué* [successful attempt]"! This is as good as Louisa Ward's "*donkey shot*" (Don Quichotte) or wicked Julia's insinuation that Hillard called Felton a "very good *raccoon'-ter*" (*raconteur*).

Our friend Miss Lowell has had very sad times since you left us. During that short space of time she has discarded two servants in succession — each departing, like an evil spirit, with maledictions. They mocked her, bade her good bye with grotesque courtesies, — shook their fists in her face, called her "mad Sal — old, drunken, crazy Sal!" and have since gone about town spreading the report of her intemperance. Finally, to eject them from the house it was necessary to send for Mrs. Fay,[4] who "*walked into the kitchen very dignified*" and exorcised the fiends. Nothing for many a day has so strongly excited my indignation, and pity. To think of an old lady exposed to such indignities! What a lonely, what a desolate old age!

How different from this gossip is the Divine Dante with which I begin the morning! I write a few lines every day before breakfast. It is the first thing I do — the morning prayer — the key-note of the day. I am delighted to have you take an interest in it. But do not expect too much; — for I really have but a few moments to devote to it daily; yet daily a stone — small or great is laid on the pile.

The Liverpool steamer is in; and Felton has just come up with a letter from Forster and another from Dickens. The as-yet-unseen friend Forster has had a violent *rheumatic fever*, such as Felton had just a year ago. Sympathy. Dickens's letter is very characteristic, but contains no particular news. I had nothing. Rather a disappointment; as I had made up my mind to several letters. But a letter I did receive two or three days ago from Cleveland, dated at Havana, Feb. 15. He says nothing about his health. He returns by the way of New Orleans. From a Cuban Review he quotes a paragraph about Nat. Willis, who is innocently, and yet comically enough, spoken of as "*Don Juan Willis*."[5]

Hawthorne dined with me to-day. He has just published in the *Pioneer* a remarkable story called the *Birth Mark*. If it falls in your way, pray read it. It very beautifully portrays the madness of a man's looking evermore at a slight defect in the wife of his bosom, till that one defect grows in his imagination so great as to eclipse all her beauty. It is a painful story, but striking.

I heartily wish that the next person you meet in Broad Way might be — myself. It may be Dr. Howe; as he is supposed to have gone in that direction drawn by the "religion of the place." At all events, let me often meet you in thought. Late evening, after the Faculty Meeting I went up to Shady Hill with Felton. The Apthorps[6] were there. A. sang Spanish songs to his guitar. Jane was fascinated. She wants to learn the guitar. Mr. Norton, Felton, Louisa and I, joined in the consert, by playing a "Sonata, arranged for four hands, by Hoyle."[7] A fine piece of music, with *trump-it obbligato*. Do you know it?

I left Jane writing to you, to go by to-day's mail. I told her I should tell you everything, that she did not. Mrs. Cleveland is now with you. Much love to her and to Charles. We shall all be rejoiced to see you on Saturday — and no one more than

Yours very truly and affectionately
Henry W. Longfellow.

Pray observe this letter; thin at the top, and thick at the bottom, as if it had *settled*.

MANUSCRIPT: Harvard College Library. ADDRESS: Mrs. C. E. Norton/New York ANNOTATION (*by Longfellow*): Single. POSTMARK: CAMBRIDGE MS. MAR [*day illegible*]

1. Longfellow first wrote "March 23."

2. Jonathan Peele Dabney (1793–1868), a member of the Harvard class of 1811, was an editor and compiler of hymnbooks and sermons.

3. Richard Henry Dana had married Sarah Watson (1814–1907) after his return from the Pacific and was now practicing law in Boston. Royal Altamont Crafts (1800–1864), merchant and manufacturer, was married to Marianne Mason (b. 1815), whose brother, Alfred Mason, was Longfellow's Bowdoin classmate.

4. Harriet Howard Fay (1782–1847), wife of Judge Fay (518.4).

5. Longfellow altered Willis' title for effect. Cleveland's copy of the Spanish paragraph actually referred to "del joven Americano M. Juan Willis."

6. Robert East Apthorp (1811–1882) and his wife, Eliza Hunt Apthorp (b. 1817). Apthorp was a close friend of Fanny Appleton.

7. Possibly John Hoyle (died c. 1797), English writer on music.

## 765. *To Stephen Longfellow*

Cambridge. March 26. 1843.

My dear Father,

Nothing new since my last. The English Steamer has arrived and brought me no letters, nor has anything transpired here likely to interest you. Graham's Magazine for April is out, and I am happy to say *without* the sketch of me. I hope he will suppress it, and take the new one which is pronounced one of the best portraits ever taken of anybody.[1] I wonder if you will think so. The fifth edition of the *Ballads* goes to press in a few days and the "Spanish Student" in a few weeks. From the latter I expect a good deal, among a certain class of readers. Two hundred and fifty copies of each are to be printed for a London publisher, Edward Moxon, and to be published there.[2]

Have you had any letters from Mary? She has lost in a good degree her zeal for writing. Last winter hardly a day without a note — *nulla dies sine linea*;[3] — but now absence sits more easily upon her; and Mother Greenleaf begins to feel dolefully about getting no letters.[4]

Shall I send you the Nos. of Dickens's new book "*Chuzzlewit*"? I do not think it very amusing yet; but it will no doubt grow better, when he gets fully under way.

The Lovering affair has subsided.[5] The Comet has taken its place. Prof. Peirce has been lecturing upon it;[6] and everybody is watching its great tail.

On Monday night there is a grand Ball in Boston — a subscription ball. I shall go for the purpose of dancing with the *elderly* ladies, who I think are much more grateful for slight attentions than *younger* ones.

Why does not somebody write? Where are Annie's pen-and-ink? Not one letter have I had since the Term began — a month ago. Tell her (Annie) I met Mrs. Crafts formerly Marianne Mason at Mr. Ticknor's at dinner a few days ago. He has lost all his property, and has taken an office in a Factory at Dover. So go the hundreds of thousands.

Dr. Woods has had a shanty erected on the Bowdoin Estate, and taken formal possession. The general impression here is, I think, in favor of the College claim; on the ground that the heirs meant to cut off the College, and keep the property *without complying with the terms of the will.*[7]

Hoping to hear from you soon, and with much love

Very affectionately yours
Henry W. Longfellow

MANUSCRIPT: Longfellow Trust Collection. ADDRESS: Hon S. Longfellow/Portland/Me. POSTMARK: BOSTON ||MS.|| MAR 28

1. The portrait by Cheney (750.1).

2. The *English Catalogue of Books from 1835 to 1863* lists both books as having been published by Moxon in 1843.

3. Proverbial adaptation of Pliny, *Historia Naturalis,* XXXV, xxxvi, 84.

4. Mary Longfellow Greenleaf and her husband lived intermittently in New Orleans at this time (see 639.1).

5. On March 4, 1843, "A personal altercation took place in Washington st. between Dr. Hawes and Prof. Lovering, of Cambridge, in which the latter was rather severely treated, with a cow-skin" (S. N. Dickinson, *The Boston Almanac for the Year 1844,* I, No. 9, 34). Dr. William Hawes (1817–1854), a Boston physician, had graduated from Bowdoin in 1837 and had been known to Longfellow as a student.

6. Benjamin Peirce's lecture took place at the Odeon on March 22, 1843 (Boston *Daily Evening Transcript*).

7. See 749.4.

## 766. *To Anne Sophia Longfellow*

Cambridge April 1 1843

My dear Anne Sophia

I had the pleasure of receiving your amiable letter yesterday afternoon; and send you an answer by the earliest post.

I most heartily and entirely approve of your plan of going to Europe, provided you can have Mary Story,[1] "or some other Mary," equally agreeable to go with you. This is one of those golden opportunities, which seldom come twice in a life time. Follow this beckoning hand before it becomes invisible. You can never hope for another chance so good as this; Dr. Sewall[2] will not be going again next year; and you will never again be so young as you are now.

I should not give you this advice, my dear Sophia, so unhesitatingly and unreservedly, unless I had great confidence in your strong heart and strong head. By such a tour you would be benefitted in many ways and injured in none. But then you must not for a moment think of going without another lady whose company is agreeable to you.

Miss Story would be just the person; for she has great feeling, great intelligence, and all that enthusiasm for things beautiful, which is an essential ingredient in a traveller. She is moreover very amiable; and with her by your side and Europe before you, it would be a wonder indeed if you were not perfectly happy for six months.

I have been imagining Father, when he hears of this plan — walking the room looking at the thermometer and saying every now and then; "Going to Europe?" "Is she crazy?" "She must not think of it!" — and many other dark sayings.

Therefore if you *do* go, you must not go to Maine to take leave of your friends. Avoid painful excitements, when unnecessary.

I venture to present my respects to Dr. Sewall, who has been so much your friend, and so kindly opens for you the golden portals of the Old World. You will excuse my short letter, but I am much in haste and wish to run down to Judge Story's to urge Miss Mary to go with you.[3]

Very affectionately your friend
Henry W. Longfellow

MANUSCRIPT: Berg Collection, New York Public Library. ADDRESS: Miss Anne Sophia Longfellow/Care of Dr. Sewall/Washington POSTMARK: BOSTON ||MS|| APR [*day illegible*]

1. Mary Oliver Story (1817–1849), daughter of Justice Joseph Story.
2. Dr. Thomas Sewall (1786–1845), born in Maine and educated at Harvard, was professor of anatomy at Columbian College (now George Washington University).
3. Influenced possibly by the "dark sayings" of his father, Longfellow later presented his cousin with arguments against making the trip. See Letter No. 777.

767. *To Stephen Longfellow*

Cambridge April 2 1843

My dear Father,

The events of the past week are pretty nearly as follows. On Monday evening a grand ball — very brilliant and very agreeable with fine music and two hundred bouquets on the supper-table, after supper distributed to the ladies. I wished more than once for Marianne to enjoy the scene. On Tuesday a tremendous rain storm, lasting all day.

Wednesday a Lecture on the Comet from Prof. Peirce — very good. Thursday nothing in particular; — Friday a snow-storm. Saturday, April-fool's day. I gave a dinner to Dr. Howe, on occasion of his engagement, — to which dinner the Dr. did not come, — being *snowed up* in New York, thus making April-fools of us, and himself.

In a day or two — that is to say by first opportunity — I will send you the London Monthly Review containing the notice of my poems, which I spoke of in my last.[1] I should like to have you send it back as soon as convenient, as it is from the College Library.

I met your friend Mr. [Leverett] Saltinstall of Salem in the street two days ago. He inquired particularly after you, and says he shall have the pleasure of seeing you this Summer; as he is going to Portland to "try our rail-road."

Judge Story I saw to-day. He looks rather yellow. He says he has reached his "*grand climacteric*" — sixty three — and has pretty nearly made up his mind, that he will not go to Europe.

Day before yesterday I received a note from Anne Sophia, asking my opinion about her going with Dr. Sewall, if Mary Story went — "or any other Mary equally agreeable." I advised her in reply not to let so good an opportunity slip, with the understanding, that she had as above mentioned, some other lady with her. But the plan will probably be given up, as rather impracticable — as the Judge will hardly go.

I hear that Charles Daveis is in town — that is to say in Boston; — but I have not seen him. Nothing new in College. Sam is well — tho' he looks rather pale. We hope to have a visit from Alex. when the weather is a little better. Good news from Mary last week, all well in New Orleans.

Affectionately yours
Henry W. Longfellow.

MANUSCRIPT: Longfellow Trust Collection. ADDRESS: Hon. S. Longfellow/Portland. POSTMARK: BOS||TON MS|| AP||R|| 3

1. A review of *Ballads and Other Poems* appeared in the *Monthly Review,* I, N.S. (February 1843), 249–254; but Longfellow did not mention the notice in his letter of March 26, 1843 (No. 765), which was presumably his last.

## 768. *To Rufus Wilmot Griswold*

Cambridge April. 13 1843.

My dear Griswold

Permit me to present to you my young friend, Mr. Charles Norton, who is a member of our College, but now under Dr. Eliot's[1] care for his eyes.

He takes a most lively interest in literature, and would be pleased to have a glimpse or two into the Literary World of New York. If any good opportunity offers, I trust you will not let it slip. I want him to look a little in the Literary *machinery* at work around him — the Editors' chambers, and publishers' dens, and the *whereabouts* of penny-a-liners. Can you not contrive a kind of Literary Tour about town, to give him a peep at these things?

Do it as you would for myself; for I have a most affectionate interest in my friend, who brings you this.

You may hand him, if you please, the copy of the last edition of your American Poets, which you were kind enough to offer me.[2]

Yours ever very truly
Henry W. Longfellow

P.S. The Spanish Student will be out in a few weeks. It is much improved in many particulars. As soon as it is ready, I will send it to you together with the M.S. as you desired.

MANUSCRIPT: Harvard College Library. ADDRESS: Rufus W. Griswold Esq/New York

1. Samuel Mackenzie Elliott (1811–1873), a graduate of the College of Surgeons in Glasgow, had emigrated to the U. S. in 1833 and built a large practice in New York City as an oculist.

2. The third edition of *The Poets and Poetry of America* (Philadelphia, 1843).

## 769. *To Samuel Ward*

Cambridge April 13 1843.

Dearest Sam,

As I was going down to College yesterday morning I met Sumnerius coming out of his Lecture-room; and the following dialogue took place between us.

*Sumnerius.* (with a knowing smile) There is a new engagement out to-day.

*Longobardus.* Ah! who is it?

*Sumnerius.* Miss Medora Grimes.

*Longobardus.* Ah! to whom?

*Sumnerius.* To that Frenchman.

*Longobardus.* What Frenchman?

*Sumnerius.* An old Frenchman in New York. But you need not make such a mystery about it. You know better than I do. I got at Sam's secret in a moment. When the Chevalier [S. G. Howe] was in New York, Sam asked him to ask me to see Madam Calderon about this Miss Grimes. I saw through the matter at once. And then the other night Sam propounded a romantic case, which I knew at the time could be none other than his own, &c. &c. &c.

*Longobardus holds his peace.*

In the afternoon came your four gloomy lines, saying that all was lost.[1] From my heart of hearts I sympathise with you, my dear Sam; yet when I think out of what a labyrinth you have escaped, I am not sure that this is not one of those disappointments which "are better than success." You now see and feel what a sorrow it was that preyed upon me for so many years. Dont do as I did. Profit by my experience, and make short work with it. Do not hug my fancies of her perfection and your loss.

Her own action in the matter seems to be enough. Cutting down into this white marble in order to make a goddess, you have struck the *blue vein* — you have discovered the blemish.

As Sumnerius has dim glimpses of the truth, or rather knows the truth, would it not be better for you to tell him all — either by letter, or through me? I am afraid he may speak of it to others; and if I tell him not to, I confirm him in his belief.

I write you this in great haste. I wish you were here, that I might bind up your wounds. Be of good cheer. Nothing really *is* so bad as it *seems*. Addio!

Yours evermore and most affectionately
Henry W. Longfellow

MANUSCRIPT: unrecovered; text from photostat, Longfellow Trust Collection. ADDRESS: Samuel Ward Esq/Prime Ward & King/New York. PUBLISHED: *Uncle Sam Ward and His Circle*, pp. 379–380.

1. The note is unrecovered, but in it Ward apparently informed Longfellow of his loss of Medora Grymes, a noted belle and daughter of John Randolph and Suzette Bosque Claiborne Grymes of New Orleans. She had just become engaged to a Frenchman named Delauney. However, Sam Ward finally married Miss Grymes at Staten Island on September 20, 1843. See *Uncle Sam Ward and His Circle,* pp. 387–388.

## 770. *To Stephen Longfellow*

Cambridge April. 16 1843

My dear Father,

Last evening I had the pleasure of receiving your letter and the Review, by hand of Mr. Richardson.[1] I thought you would be pleased with the notice of the poems; tho' I do not think the whole of it in perfectly good taste.

The Spanish Student is in the Printer's hands. But the work of printing goes on so slowly, that I do not believe the book will see the light before July.

Mrs. Seba Smith has published in New York a poem called the "Sinless Child," of which the papers speak very highly.[2] It seems really to be a beautiful poem; and I hope she will gain both fame and emolument by it.

In College no novelty. I have finished one course of Lectures, and am about to commence another. Sam is well. I have seen Aunt Nancy Storrow,[3] but not the Higginsons.

April 23rd.

Graham's Magazine for May has come; with that *caricature,* which I told you about. I feel rather vexed that his forty thousand subscribers and hundred thousand readers should form so disagreeable an impression of me as they necessarily must from that picture. But there is now no remedy save patience. The accompanying sketch was written by Geo: S. Hillard, my intimate friend; who is sincere, yet — as you will see, *very* friendly.[4]

The last steamer brought me a letter from Dr. Bosworth, who tells me the Notice in the Monthly Review was written by Dr. Bigsby, *"L.L.D and Fw. R.S."*[5]

The Play is creeping slowly through the Press; — *very* slowly. Owen is the most negligent and procrastinating of men. The Ballads have been out of print for *three months*; and orders are constantly coming, which he cannot, of course, supply. And yet he lets things drag on, saying that he cannot get the right kind of paper; — as if it were not his business and duty, to look out for this before hand. He is so afraid of losing a cent, that he is losing hundreds. He is penny wise and pound foolish.

Yours with all love
Henry W. Longfellow.

P. S. I think of going to New York on Tuesday to Dr. Howe's wedding.

When is Alex coming this way? I want him to make me a visit soon. Miss Bella[6] gives a party Thursday evening next. I wish he would come on. He can take possession of my rooms. I shall be back Friday.

Bring your Spanish music, when you come, Alex.

MANUSCRIPT: Longfellow Trust Collection. ADDRESS: Hon. S. Longfellow/Portland ANNOTATION (*by Longfellow*): single. POSTMARK: CAMBRIDGE MS APR [*day illegible*]

1. The *Portland Directory* for 1844 lists Israel, Joshua, and Thomas Richardson

as merchants. It was possibly one of them who had returned the number of the London *Monthly Review* mentioned in Letter No. 767.

2. *The Sinless Child and Other Poems* (New York, 1843). Elizabeth Oakes Smith (1806–1893), wife of the author of the "Major Jack Downing" letters, was a native of Portland.

3. Ann Gillam Storrow (1784–1862), older sister of Louisa Storrow Higginson and aunt of Thomas Wentworth Higginson. Known as "Aunt Nancy," she made her home with the Higginson family and was the friend and confidante of Jared Sparks (see *Letters of Ann Gillam Storrow to Jared Sparks*, ed. Frances Bradshaw Blanshard, *Smith College Studies in History*, VI, No. 3 [1921], 185–252).

4. See 744.1.

5. See 767.1. Robert Bigsby (1806–1873), antiquary, subsequently became one of Longfellow's most faithful English correspondents. "Bigsby distinguished himself," says the *Dictionary of National Biography,* "as a virtuoso or collector of curiosities, 'relics and memorials,' as he calls them, of 'illustrious characters' " (II, 489).

6. Unidentified. Possibly a tenant in Craigie House.

## 771. *To Sarah Perkins Cleveland*

[New York]
Wednesday afternoon [April 26, 1843]

My dear Mrs. Cleveland

It is a great shame, that I should be so near you and not be able to take you by the hand! But so it is. I am here to see Dr. Howe properly married to Julia Ward, and the length of my tether permits me to wander into no fair meadows lying beyond, though I may be allowed to look over the fence, as now. How are you? Have you entirely recovered from that fall? I fear not: for I hear that your last letter to the Nortons was not in your own hand. *Do* get well soon; for the idea of seeing *you* ill, is exceedingly disagreeable.

We — (Felton and I) left Boston yesterday afternoon. We were to have taken the *Mohegan* but she blew up a day too soon, as you doubtless saw by the papers. Lucky escape. *Bobby Trueman* was on board of her; but in the alarm threw himself into the sea, followed by his two dogs.[1] No lives lost; so the Steward of the Narraganset informed me. "It was not *a bad burst,*" said I to him. "No," replied he, with great gravity: — "it was a very good one; and seemed to give universal satisfaction."

At supper, the gentleman next to me ate for his meal, *shad and stewed damsons* together.

Thursday morning.

I wrote the above in Sumner's chamber, while waiting for the dinner gong to ring. Now the wedding is over. It passed of[f] well — beautifully. Julia looked and behaved admirably well. But at supper her natural roguery broke out, and seeing Sumner bent over, and intently engaged in talking to a lady, she could not help slipping two or three silver spoons into his coat pocket. (The enchanted princess who heard the mouse in the wall, you remember). Dont say this aloud however; it was an innocent jest, in which we all joined. The wedding was a pleasant one — a very pleasant one.

Good bye, with regards to yr mother and the Rt. Revd. [Bishop G. W. Doane]

Yours very truly
H. W. L.

Felton and Sumner join in kind regards.

MANUSCRIPT: Berg Collection, New York Public Library.

1. The mail steamer *Mohegan* blew a boiler near Hurl Gate, en route from New York to Stonington, on April 24, 1843. According to the *Daily Evening Transcript*, XIV, No. 3913 (April 26, 1843), "One passenger — a full grown man — jumped overboard at the time of the explosion, but was saved." Robert Trueman (1778–1859) was a Boston merchant.

## 772. *To John Forster*

[Cambridge] April 29. 1843.

My dear Forster,

The bearer of this is my friend [Thomas Gold] Appleton, whom I want you to know; as you have many points of character that will make each-other's society agreeable. He will not remain long in London, but he must see the rooms in Lincoln's In[n] fields; where I enjoyed so many pleasant hours.

Appleton is a lover of Art, and Literature — is himself a poet, and admires Tennison as much as you do.

Ever yours truly
Henry W. Longfellow

P. S. If possible make Appleton acquainted with Tennison. This he would like above all things; saving to know Cruikshank, which he would like still more.

MANUSCRIPT: Victoria and Albert Museum, London.

## 733. *To Louise von Gall*

Cambridge. April 29. 1843.

My dear Fräulein,

I could not send you a more agreeable token of my remembrance and regard, than the bearer of this, T. G. Appleton Esq. of Boston.

He will pass a few days in Vienna, and I do not want him to leave it without seeing you. Be kind enough to introduce him to your friend the poet Zedlitz, and any other artists and men of letters, in your city; and in return for your kindness I will acknowledge that the Rhine is greener than the eyes of a jealous lover, that Nüremberg is a finer old place than Bruges, and that I am under great obligations to you, and am

Very truly your friend
Henry W. Longfellow.

P.S. The Indian mocassons I promised you, I have not been able to procure. I shall send you instead an Indian basket of birch bark worked with *wampum*. This will go in a box to Freiligrath, who will forward it to you.[1]

MANUSCRIPT: Longfellow Trust Collection. ADDRESS: Fräulein von Gall/Vienna.

1. See Letter No. 760.

## 774. *To José Cortés*

Cambridge y 30 de Avril de 1843.

Querido Pepe,

Aqúi te mando un amigo mio T. G. Appleton, hombre de mucho talento y de las prendas mas apreciables. Pasará algun tiempo allá en tu Madrid, y se ofreceran muchisimas cosas en las cuales le puedes ser útil. Por el amor que me tienes, y que á él tendrás luego, harás todo le posible para que su visita en la Heroica Villa salga agradable y provechosa.

Tu verdadero amigo
Longfellow.

MANUSCRIPT: Longfellow Trust Collection. ADDRESS: Al Señor Don José Cortés y/Sesti./Calle ancha de San Bernardo/No 48/Madrid

TRANSLATION:

Cambridge April 30, 1843

Dear Pepe,

I am sending you a friend of mine, T. G. Appleton, a man of much talent and the most estimable qualities. He will spend some time there in your Madrid, and there will be many opportunities in which you can be of use to him. Because of the love which you have for me, and which you will soon have for him, you will do everything possible so that his visit in the Heroic Town will turn out to be pleasant and profitable.

Your true friend
Longfellow.

775. *To Ferdinand Freiligrath*

Cambridge April 30. 1843.

My dear Freiligrath,

This will be handed you by T. G. Appleton Esq of Boston, whom you will be happy to see on his own account, and because he is my friend. I have charged him very particularly to stop at St. Goar in order to see you, and your beloved Ida. You will find my friend all on fire with Poetry; and when he departs from you, you must give him a letter of introduction to Uhland and to Zedlitz. "Thus doing" as Sir Philip Sidney says, "your name shall flourish in the printers' shops,"[1] and you shall count me ever your friend

Henry W. Longfellow.

MANUSCRIPT: Longfellow Trust Collection.

1. The peroration to *The Defense of Poesie.*

776. *To Ferdinand Freiligrath*

[Cambridge] April 30. 1843.

My dear Freiligrath

The bearer of this is my particular friend Dr. Howe, who with his lovely young wife and sister,[1] is journeying up the Rhine and stops at St. Goar to see you and Mrs. Freiligrath. I will not launch forth in encomiums upon my friends. I merely ask that they should become acquainted with you and the rest will do itself.

Dr. Howe fought through the Greek revolution, I need not say on which side; and a few years ago was imprisoned by the King of Prussia in Berlin, for assisting the Poles.[2] From this, judge what a chivalrous youth he is.

His wife is a sister of a very dear friend of mine; is full of poetry, and noble impulses, and a thousand other fine qualities, which you will discover.

But *basta*; and believe me ever yours

Longfellow

MANUSCRIPT: Berg Collection, New York Public Library.

1. Anne Eliza (Annie) Ward accompanied the Howes on their European honeymoon.

2. Howe had served as surgeon and soldier in the Greek War of Independence against the Turks; and in 1832 he had spent several weeks in a Prussian prison for attempting to aid a group of Polish insurgents against Russian rule. See Harold Schwartz, *Samuel Gridley Howe: Social Reformer, 1801–1876* (Cambridge, Mass., 1956).

777. *To Stephen Longfellow*

Cambridge May 7 1843.

My dear Father,

I have just been into town to see Sam safe on board the Harbinger.[1] She has just sailed — Sunday noon; — a nice little craft, with blue and white flags flying from her masts. Sam went off, likewise, with flying colors, and made no great display of sentiment. But I am afraid he will before he reaches the Azores, for there goes with him a Miss Rosalie Russel of Milton Hill, — a very pretty damsel, and daughter of the late Hon. Mr. Russel, one of the Commissioners of the Treaty of Ghent.[2] There are two other ladies on board and two gentlemen, of Sam's age, or thereabout. They will have a nice run out to-day; for the wind has just come round West, and is blowing a light breeze.

You probably saw by the papers that Anne Sophia sailed a week ago in the Steamer for Liverpool. I stated to her very clearly all the objections that could be urged against the step; — but seeing she had her mother's approval and Mr. Redington's,[3] and moreover was determined to go, I withdrew these objections; though I could not wholly approve the thing. Indeed I felt about it much as Annie wrote in her last letter. But the affair being now decided, I shall for one put the best face upon it.

Nothing very new. I send by this mail a London Newspaper with a notice of my "Slavery Poems," which please preserve and return at your leisure.[4]

The new editions of the poems are not yet out. The back-water at the Paper-Mill has prevented our getting the paper which we ordered. But in a few weeks all will be right.

Many thanks to Aunt Lucia for the antique chair, I hear she has begged for me; and much love to all.

Very affectionately yours
Henry W. Longfellow.

MANUSCRIPT: Longfellow Trust Collection. ADDRESS: Hon S. Longfellow/Portland/Me. POSTMARK: CAMBRIDGE MS. MAY 8

1. After a year in the Harvard Divinity School, Samuel Longfellow accepted a position as tutor in the family of Charles W. Dabney, U. S. consul at Fayal in the Azores (*Samuel Longfellow, Memoir and Letters*, ed. Joseph May [Boston and New York, 1894], pp. 31–46). He returned to Cambridge in 1844 and completed his Divinity School training in 1846.

2. Jonathan Russell (1771–1832) was U. S. minister to Norway and Sweden in 1814, when he helped negotiate the Treaty of Ghent. He served as a member of Congress, 1821–1823.

3. Asa Redington (1789–1874) of Augusta, judge of the Middle District of Maine, was Anne Sophia Longfellow's stepfather.

4. Possibly a reference to Forster's review in *The Examiner* (755.8).

778. *To Samuel Ward*

Cambridge May. 7. 1843.

My dear Sam,

I fulfilled my promise, and went to Madam Inglis's.[1] I sat on an ottoman by Preciosa's side. She was dressed in white, with a little Greek cap on the side of her beautiful head. We first spoke Spanish, which she said she had almost forgotten; but soon, as the first outworks of conversation were carried, she unsheathed her flashing and trenchant French, that like Antolinez's sword, "illumined all the field."[2] She is a wonderful girl!

But I will not continue in this strain, for I should craze your brain; and I have another object in view. You must be calm. From your own lips, I read you a homily; "*Les choses sérieuses de la vie, pour la vie, ne devraient pas se décider dans un moment* [The serious things of life, for life, should not be decided in a moment]."

Your duty to Medora,
Your duty to yourself,
Your duty to Delaunay,[3]

require you to pause — to remain perfectly quiet. Let this *imbroglio* unravel itself. I urge you the more strenuously to this, because I hear to-day, that she has received a letter — a beautiful and touching one, from her father, — who with[h]olds his consent to the marriage — at least for the present; and says nothing must be done until he comes on in June. Your course is very clear. Do not interfere in any way; — neither by word nor letter, nor the language of looks, nor the language of flowers. SO ACT THAT HEREAFTER YOU MAY LOOK BACK UPON THIS WHOLE MATTER WITH A CONSCIENCE VOID OF OFFENCE.

If you do this, nothing shall harm you; and disappointment will prove no enemy. Indeed you cannot think of acting otherwise; and you need no friend to remind you, that you are to do everywhere, what the soft voice of your little Maddie[4] says you do in Wall-Street. But let me remind you, that

*"Patience et longueur de temps*
*Font plus que force, ni que rage."*[5]

Meanwhile be assured of my warmest sympathies.

Ever yours
Henry W. Longfellow.

P. S. By the way dont forget the "Higbee package"; and excuse me for saying that since your visit I find myself *minus* an umbrella. Do you remember where you left it?

What you told me about G. W. Greene afflicts me seriously. For heaven's sake do something for him. Let not so good an opportunity of lending to the Lord (*"if you like the security"*) escape you.

MANUSCRIPT: unrecovered; text from photostat, Longfellow Trust Collection. ADDRESS: Samuel Ward Esq/(Prime Ward & King)/New York. PUBLISHED: *Uncle Sam Ward and His Circle,* pp. 384–385.

1. To Frances Inglis Calderón de la Barca's where he met Medora Grymes, here referred to as Preciosa (heroine of *The Spanish Student*).

2. Possibly an allusion to José Antolinez (1639–1676), a Spanish painter who died of wounds received in a duel.

3. See 769.1.

4. Margaret Astor Ward (1838–1875), Sam Ward's daughter.

5. "Patience and passage of time/Do more than strength and fury." La Fontaine, "Le Lion et le Rat," *Fables,* II, 11.

## 779. *To John Osborne Sargent*

Cambridge May 10 1843

My dear Sargent,

Inclosed is the autograph you were kind enough to ask for.[1] I am sorry I cannot add a few more; but the few I once had have already been given away.

I have not yet seen Allston. When I do, I will see what can be done in that quarter.

I was very sorry not to see you and Epes, when I was in New York. I called at his office; but my time was so occupied — being a "Wedding Guest" and staying so very short a time in town, that I could do no more.

Hoping nevertheless soon to see you in Cambridge,

Very truly yours
Henry W. Longfellow

MANUSCRIPT: Clifton Waller Barrett Collection, University of Virginia.

1. A copy of "Excelsior" accompanies the letter.

## 780. *To Zilpah Longfellow*

[Cambridge] May 11. 1843

My dearest Mother,

I write you one line, and only one — to tell of the good fortune which has just come to me — namely that I am engaged. Yes, engaged to a very lovely woman — Fanny Appleton — for whom I have many years cherished a feeling of affection.[1]

I cannot say another word — save that she is very beautiful — very intellectual — and very pious — three most excellent *verys.*

Alex will tell you the rest. I hate to *write* of such things.

Ever with great affection yours
Henry.

MANUSCRIPT: Longfellow Trust Collection. PUBLISHED: Edward Wagenknecht, *Longfellow: A Full-Length Portrait* (New York, London, Toronto, 1955), p. 229.

1. Longfellow became engaged on May 10, a date commemorated in his journal the following year (*Young Longfellow*, pp. 421–422).

## 781. *To Anne Longfellow Pierce*

Cambridge May 21 1843

My dearest Annie,

All the week have I been looking for a line from you, and none has come. I hoped your heart would have moved you to write to my beloved Fanny, as I know it would be irresistably drawn towards her did you know her. Now dear Annie, do write to her. Dont let another day go by without it; for fear she should imagine, that you gave her a cold reception into the family.

Monday morning [May 22].

Yesterday, dearest Annie, I began almost a scolding letter to you, being a little disappointed at not receiving a note from you. But upon reflection I find it is my own fault. I should have written to you. But in truth I have had no time. And now what can I say to you of Fanny? I cannot coin my feelings into words. You must see her, and know her, and you will as surely and irresistably love her as you do me; and as warmly too. She is in all things very lovely. I can say no more. Alex, whom I sent as a special Ambassador, must tell you the rest. Everybody is delighted with this engagement, and I more than everybody. Life was too lonely — and sad; — with little to soothe and calm me. Now the Future opens its long closed gates into pleasant fields and lands of quiet. The strife and struggle are over, for a season, at least; and the troubled spirit findeth its perfect rest.

How will you see Fanny? Will you come here; or shall she come there? She longs to know you all; and when you look upon her if all your hearts are not moved with love, it will [be] a marvel indeed.

You must go to Eliza [Potter], and talk to her about this. I have been wishing to write to her; but cannot yet. I have a great deal to tell you; but must wait until I see you.

Farewell. Write to Fanny without delay, all that your warm heart prompts you to say.

Ever thine
Henry.

MANUSCRIPT: Longfellow Trust Collection. ADDRESS: Hon. S. Longfellow./for Mrs. Pierce/Portland/Me. ANNOTATION (*by Longfellow*): Single: POSTMARK: CAMBRIDGE MS. MAY 22

## 782. *To Henry Russell Cleveland*

Cambridge May 22 1843.

Dearest Heinrich

On striped paper, as on a triumphal banner, I send you this greeting, and joyful tidings, which will make my feet beautiful over the Alleganies.[1] Lo! I am engaged to Fanny Appleton! The great vision of my life takes a real shape. I have won not her hand only, but truly and entirely her heart. How this has come to pass, — how the magic circle has narrowed, and narrowed and narrowed, till at last the cloud of vapor fell, and we found ourselves standing hand in hand, — all this I cannot tell you in a letter; but some hints and suggestions, I may perchance breathe into your ear hereafter.

My whole soul is filled with peace and serenity. It returns to her as to its centre. All struggles, all unrest, all indefinite longings — all desires of other things, — all that so agitated me, and sent me swinging and ill-poised through the void and empty space, all this is ended; and the heart hath its perfect rest. Rejoice with me; and come back as soon as you can. Sarah [Cleveland] is quite beside herself with delight; and so is

Your ever affectionate friend
Henry W. Longfellow.

MANUSCRIPT: Berg Collection, New York Public Library. ADDRESS: Henry R. Cleveland Esq/Cincinnati./Ohio. POSTMARK: CAMBRIDGE MS. MAY 23

1. Cf. Isa. 52: 7: "How beautiful upon the mountains are the feet of him that bringeth good tidings."

## 783. *To Isaac Appleton Jewett*

Boston May 23 1843

My dear Jewett,

I have been long, very long your debtor for a most friendly and interesting letter; but the news I now send you is so precious, that it will amply repay you for any delay or seeming neglect.

I am engaged to your beloved and beautiful cousin — Fanny, —

*the* Fanny! What powers have brought this to pass — by what hitherto invisible, golden threads of sympathy the Fates have woven this glorious *"Yes!"* into the dark warp of my life, — by what magic the mist has fallen, and we find ourselves standing hand in hand in the mystic circle — I cannot venture to tell you. Suffice, that it is so; and think with what a jubilant spirit I sit me down to write you this letter!

Were you here you would be touched and amused likewise with the interest everybody takes in the matter. There has been, from the beginning, a spice of romance in it, which has taken hold of several exciteable imaginations, and thanks to my heedless imprudence, the public has been a kind of confident in the whole affair.[1] But now, thank God, this imprudence is forgiven and forgotten by the only one of whom I had to ask forgiveness and oblivion of the past; — and reconciliation falls like peaceful sunshine upon the present.

How will that answer, my dear Jewett, for you, who *"with a very little effort can live the whole domestic career through in your imagination!"* In what terms can one speak of such things to a third person? To your lively imagination, then, I leave this subject; let that be my interpreter, and declare to you all that I feel and hope of joy and tranquillity.

Many thanks for your favorable reception of the "Poems on Slavery."[2] Some people here have been pleased to call them *incendiary,* which certainly they are not; but on the contrary so mild that even a Slaveholder might read them without losing his appetite for breakfast.

Fanny — (who is looking over my shoulder,) begs leave to congratulate you on escaping the fascinations of the *Carneal.*[3] She fears that your ideal theories will be a *mirage* leading you into deserts vast of *single cursedness*; but whether you remain a bachelor or take unto yourself a wife, she sends ever her love to you and[4] wishes you as much happiness as she has been blessed with and hopes to secure until the "feather and the mirror"[5] and far beyond.

I (for I trust your eyes discern the footprints of another pen) take the liberty of anticipating your congratulations, dear Jewett, and thank you for them heartily. 'Go and do likewise'[6] is the best benison I can offer you in subscribing myself your ever attached — tho' by you — terribly neglected coz

Fanny E Appleton.

Very truly your friend
Henry W. Longfellow[7]

MANUSCRIPT: Longfellow Trust Collection. ADDRESS: J. A. Jewett Esq/New Orleans. ANNOTATION: Free/N. Appleton POSTMARK: BOSTON ||MS|| MAY 24

1. A reference to *Hyperion.*

2. Jewett's letter from New Orleans of January 9, 1843, contains an extended comment on this volume.

3. In a letter to Fanny Appleton of April or May, 1843 (the manuscript in the Longfellow House is lost), Jewett had remarked at length on the attributes of a New Orleans lady named Carneal.

4. What follows, through her signature, is in the hand of Fanny Appleton.

5. Until death. Apparently an allusion to King Lear's attempt with looking glass and feather to establish breathing by the dead Cordelia (V, iii, 257–267).

6. Luke 10:37.

7. Longfellow's complimentary closing is written diagonally across the last page of the letter.

## 784. *To John Forster*

Boston. May 24 1843

My dear Forster,

I write you with a heart brim full of gladness; and consequently shall probably make a very silly letter of it. I am engaged to a lady, with whom I have been long in love; and of course the matter so fills my brain, that I can hardly think, speak or write of anything else. I will try, however, to behave with *strict propriety,* and say only that the lady is very fair, and that I am very much enamoured. She is a sister of young Appleton, who has probably handed you a letter of introduction before this. If so, pray treat him, for my sake and in honor of my marriage, with a double degree of kindness. Ask Dickens to do the same. Indeed you would do this for his own sake, as he is a most agreeable fellow, and full of talent and wit. Still I throw in this new inducement and persuasion to kindness. All farther particulars of this affair I leave to Felton's pen; who is in a very tender mood, from shear sympathy.

And now, my dear Forster, many thanks for your kind and excellent notice of the Slavery Poems.[1] I wish I deserved your praises more; but I have a *naïve* way of taking all my friends' commendations *au pied de la lettre,* and thinking, or trying to think, that I do deserve them. Whilst writing these very lines, Mr. Ticknor, at whose home I am staying for a day or two, has opened a letter from Kenyon. It contains the mortifying intelligence that each friend in England to whom I sent these Poems had to pay four shillings postage for them! Now I do assure you, (with the exception of Lord Morpeth's copy,) I inclosed all in one package, directed to my agent in London, with orders, of course, to charge all expenses to me. A certain *gentleman* will put his *hoof* into things. However you and Dickens will exculpate me from all blame in this matter.

The *Spanish Student* will be out in a week or two. It is to be published in London by Moxon.[2] You must find time to read it; for it is much better than the first sketch in Graham's Magazine.

Give the greatest love to the Dickenses; and kiss me all the children; with particular warmth for noble little Charlie.

Felton is hale and hearty. His wife pale and feeble. I have great — nay the greatest fears for her. But let no echo of this come back in your letters to them.

I wrote you by the Hibernia; but as ill luck would have it, was too late for the mail. I rushed down to the wharf; and lo! she was just swinging off. I could not throw my letter on board.[3]

Truly and most cordially
H. W. Longfellow

MANUSCRIPT: Victoria and Albert Museum, London. ADDRESS: John Forster Esq/Lincoln's Inn Fields/London POSTMARK: 8 JU||N|| 43/LIVERPOOL/SHIP

1. See 755.8.
2. See 765.2.
3. This letter seems not to have been sent and is unrecovered.

785. *To Eliza Ann Potter*

Cambridge, May 25, 1843.

My dear Eliza, —

I have been meaning for a week or more to write you in order to tell you of my engagement, and to ask your sympathies and good wishes. But I have been so much occupied, and have had so many letters to write, to go by the last steamers, that I have been rather neglectful of some of my nearer and dearer friends; trusting to their kindness for my excuse.

Yes, my dear Eliza, I am to be married again. My life was too lonely and restless; — I needed the soothing influences of a home; — and I have chosen a person for my wife who possesses in a high degree those virtues and excellent traits of character, which so distinguished my dear Mary. Think not, that in this new engagement, I do any wrong to her memory. I still retain, and ever shall preserve with sacred care all my cherished recollections of her truth, affection and beautiful nature. And I feel, that could she speak to me, she would approve of what I am doing. I hope also for your approval and for your father's. . . . Think of me ever as

Very truly your friend
Henry W. Longfellow.

MANUSCRIPT: unrecovered; text from Higginson, *Longfellow*, p. 172.

786. *To Anne Longfellow Pierce*

[Cambridge] Thursday morning. [June 1, 1843][1]

Dearest Annie,

I know not when I can come down for you; but you must get ready to make Fanny a visit as soon as possible. The Ticknors are going to Gardiner next week; and on their return will take you under their wings, if that arrangement pleases you. That, to be sure, will be rather long to wait; as we are in great haste to see you. Still I do not see how I can get down before next week, if at all. It interferes with my College duties, which I am particularly anxious not to neglect at this time. When can you be spared? If I should appear some night, can you get ready to start the next morning?

Love to all.

Ever yours
Henry.

P. S. The more I think of it, the more you must come. Dont think of saying nay.

MANUSCRIPT: Longfellow Trust Collection.

1. Anne Pierce establishes the date of this letter in her postscript to Zilpah Longfellow's letter to Mary Longfellow Greenleaf of June 2, 1843 (MS, Longfellow Trust Collection, Longfellow House).

787. *To Anne Longfellow Pierce*

[Cambridge, c. June 5, 1843][1]

Dearest Annie,

We are very sorry you cannot come immediately and more sorry for the cause thereof; and I have been from day to day meditating a run to Portland. I shall not, however, be able to accomplish this before next week, on account of engagements of various kinds here.

We are to be married about the middle of July; and shall live for the present in the Craigie house. We shall expect as many of you as possible at the wedding. But above all a visit must you make to my dear Fanny before this month of June is over. Contrive to do this, dearest Annie, I beg of you.

I cannot come to stay more than a few hours. I shall come down at night, and return the next afternoon.

Love to all. In very great haste.

Ever affectionately
Henry

Thanks to Father for his letter.
Fanny's love &c.

MANUSCRIPT: Longfellow Trust Collection.

1. The date is conjectural, but the letter is in response to an unrecovered letter by Anne Pierce in which she declined the suggestion offered in Letter No. 786. In her postscript to Mary Longfellow Greenleaf (786.1.), she remarked that a swollen face, "home habits and *un-loco* motion propensities" kept her from going to Cambridge.

## 788. *To Charles Dickens*

Cambridge June 15 1843

My dear Dickens,

I am afraid you will think I have *repudiated.* It is not so. But of late my heart has turned my brains out of doors. I am to be married in a few weeks; and take the liberty, in consequence, of neglecting my friends. This I trust you will forgive. By the [1]

MANUSCRIPT: Longfellow Trust Collection.

1. The letter is incomplete and was presumably never sent. It is written on what appears to have been a full quarto sheet that was torn in half midway down the leaf. Longfellow used the verso for a rough draft in pencil of his translation of *Purgatorio,* XV, 64–75.

## 789. *To Samuel Gridley Howe*

Boston June 15 1843.

My dear Howe

I ought to have written you by the last Steamer, and to have been the first to tell you of a delightful event in my history which has reached you through the pens of others. Of course, I mean my engagement to Fanny Appleton; the long-loved and never-forgotten Fanny. How it came about, I cannot tell you in detail; suffice it to say, that we have been drawn more and more together of late; — and the *antiquæ vestigia flammæ* [remains of my old passion] burned and burned evermore; — and one morning I awoke and found myself engaged.

Now to you who have so lately entered into the Celestial City, this is enough to give you a vivid picture of what I feel. Were it not so, I should break forth into raptures about my beloved Fanny. Indeed, I feel rather tempted to do so as it is, and to sketch you her portrait as she sits here in front of me writing to her brother; — for you do not know her — you nor Julia nor Annie. Upon second thoughts, however, I will be silent; for I am a little bewildered.

So there you are roving over vast continents and *prairies* of civilization, with your heart and brain both filled full. We have heard of your safe arrival — of your lameness still annoying you, and of your onward march toward London notwithstanding, or rather your intention to march onward. I hope that Julia and Annie find England all they hoped to find it; and that you find yourself among friends wherever you go, as of course you do. Remember me to Forster and the Dickenses — and to Freiligrath on the Rhine. Enjoy yourselves to your hearts' content, and come back to us as soon as you conveniently can.

I have no great news to send you. Our friend Cleveland, as others have already informed you, has been very ill at St. Louis, but by last accounts is better.[1] Sumner is a great recluse; and at the present moment living at the Albion [House] the Paint King having entered his house. He is busy upon an Article for the North American on the Mackenzie case, which article is a mile long — namely some fifty pages! — but it will be very able.[2] President Tyler is to be here tomorrow; and Webster delivers an oration on Bunker Hill, Saturday. I met him at dinner yesterday at the Paiges[3] — black as Erebus. His political friends are rather deserting him.

Good night; it is waxing late; Mr. and Mrs. Appleton have just come in from the Theatre where the Ravels we[re] performing wonders on the tight rope;[4] and I close with best wishes and much love to Julia and Annie; — and likewise to my dear Cousin Annie [Sophia Longfellow] should you meet her again in your travels. I trust you found her a pleasant companion on board ship.

We are to be married on Thursday July 13. so fill your glasses that day, wheresoever you may be, and drink to the health of my beautiful bride. Remember.

Fanny joins me in kindest regards to Julia and Annie, and warmest wishes for your happiness at home and abroad. Farewell. Forgive stupid letters, remembering how hard it is to write, when you are just engaged.

Yours, nevertheless, very truly
Henry W. Longfellow

MANUSCRIPT: Longfellow Trust Collection. ADDRESS: Samuel G. Howe Esq/ care of Baring Brothers/London. POSTMARK: A 29 JU 29 1843

1. Cleveland had died in St. Louis on June 12.

2. Sumner's defense of Alexander Slidell Mackenzie in the *Somers* mutiny affair appeared in the *North American Review,* LVIII (July 1843), 195–242. See 794.2.

3. Rev. Lucius Robinson Paige (1802–1896), author of religious polemics and a former Universalist minister, was the town clerk of Cambridge. The occasion for President Tyler's presence in Boston was the celebration on June 17 of the completion of the Bunker Hill Monument. See Boston *Daily Evening Transcript,* XIV, No. 3958 (Monday, June 19, 1843).

4. The Ravels, a family of French actors, had made their American debut as early as 1832. They were noted for rope walking, pantomimes, and harlequinades.

## 790. *To Lewis Gaylord Clark*

[Cambridge] June 17 1843.

My dear Clark,

Much obliged to you for your note, and your reminiscence of the past.[1] But you are very much mistaken in thinking I am offended. I assure you I am not, at least, not with you. With Graham I am a little so, for that *extraordinary performance on my person.* It is quite inexcusable to have so bad a taste as to think that such an engraving is an embellishment to his Magazine. But he has injured himself more than he has me.

"The Spanish Student" will be published on Monday next. It is enlarged so as to make a volume larger than either of the others. I fancy you will like it. At all events, it now comes forth in a presentable shape, which was hardly the case on its first appearance in Grahams. It was but a child then; and has now more bone and muscle in it.

I was sorry not to meet you in New York when last there; but I had not time to look for you. Indeed, the last two times I have been in your city, I have merely touched foot to the ground and away again. The next time, however, I will make a point of seeing you, and reviving the Past. What have you done with Willis's papers and letters? Is there not to be a volume of them published?[2]

These [lines] in great haste. And yet ere I close a word more. Congratulate me. I am to be married this summer to Miss Fanny Appleton; a lady with whom I have long been enamoured. Of course, I am very happy, and very busy; and have no time for writing letters even. This will account for my not having answered your note sooner.

Very truly yours
Henry W. Longfellow

MANUSCRIPT: Clifton Waller Barrett Collection, University of Virginia.

1. Clark's undated letter appears in *Clark Letters*, p. 144.

2. Clark was editing *The Literary Remains of the Late Willis Gaylord Clark* (New York, 1844). Longfellow wrote a brief notice of it in the *North American Review*, LIX (July 1844), 239–240.

## 791. *To Anne Longfellow Pierce*

[Cambridge] June. 22. 1843.

Dearest Annie

Your letter to Fanny has just arrived. It is rather too bad, that you will not be persuaded to come. I desire so much that you should know this lady of my love! and we are to be married on the 13th of July. So you see there is no time to spare.

Now if you will but consent to come, you shall be as quiet as at home. No parties — no going about to see people — no people coming to see you — in a word, you shall look upon no one's face but Fanny's and mine.

Pray dont be looking for me every night; for I shall come, when I do come, in the early morning train, reaching Portland at 10 or 11 o'clock A.M. But I cannot possibly leave here before next week, if I do at all. I have [been] getting rooms ready in the Craigie House; and there are fifty things to be done every day, principally because I never do them. But the main difficulty is to find two successive days. In short it is impossible. I shall therefore be obliged to come one morning and return the next.

You are all expected at the wedding, of course, without farther invitation. I hope Father and Mother and Aunt Lucia will all be able to come, and Stephen and Marianne.

With much love to you all

Ever most affectionately Your brother

Henry.

MANUSCRIPT: Longfellow Trust Collection.

792. *To Anne Longfellow Pierce*

Boston June 29 1843

Dearest Annie

Your last letter reached me yesterday, just after Fanny and myself had despatched letters to you.[1] Had it reached me sooner, we should have written differently. In future *inclose* everything to Hon. N. Appleton — (*not* direct to his care) but *inclose* to his address, — and there will be less delay. I am now living in Boston; and shall remain here for the present; as I am painting and repairing the rooms in the Craigie House.

Upon second thoughts (you know that I generally act upon *first* ones) I think you may be right in your decision. All things considered, a visit to us in Cambridge would probably be more entirely satisfactory. So it shall be as you say. But do come to the wedding — in suit of sables, if you desire it. The wedding is to be quite unpretending; and I think you will like to be there; — at all events you will like to *have been* there. We shall regret very much not to see Father and Mother — and will not make up our minds to it yet. I think there can be no difficulty about you, Aunt Lucia, Stephen and Marianne.[2]

Write a word or two soon; and dont expect me in Portland before the wedding.

Ever most affectionately,
Henry.

MANUSCRIPT: Longfellow Trust Collection.

1. If Longfellow wrote to his sister on June 27 or 28, the letter has been lost.

2. Zilpah Longfellow's letter of August 7, 1843, to Mrs. A. M. Bartlett of Plymouth (MS, Longfellow Trust Collection, Longfellow House) lists the members of the Longfellow family who attended the wedding and those who did not: "Anne Pierce went up to the wedding, Mary Greenleaf had just returned from New Orleans, they were the only two of the family who attended the ceremony, Lucia [Wadsworth] would not be prevailed upon to go. Mr L and myself were not quite well enough to leave home. Stephen and his wife could not leave their little flock."

## 793. *To Charles Sumner*

[Cambridge, June 1843]

Dear Charley,

I am sorry not to see you. But as to Don Rehadencio[1] — quien sabe? Have I time? How long does he stay in town?

Ever thine
H. W. L.

MANUSCRIPT: Longfellow Trust Collection. ADDRESS: Don Carlos

1. The reading is conjectural, Longfellow having written over and obscured the name. Sumner had asked him to help entertain a visiting Spaniard who was "very voluble in bad and sometimes (to us) unintelligable French" (Letter in the Longfellow Trust Collection, dated "June 43" by Longfellow).

## 794. *To Alexander Slidell Mackenzie*

[Boston, July 1843][1]

My dear Mackenzie,

Pardon my extreme negligence in writing and sending the books I promised you. Since my engagement I have been idle beyond all precedent, a rival of that antedeluvian monster the "*Malidon Robustus, or extinct gigantic Sloth.*" Knowing the cause, you will excuse me.

I am glad to hear from my friend [Samuel Eliot] Guild, that you and your wife are so well; — and that the slight tribute sent you from Boston was acceptable to you. The voice of all upright men — the common consent of all the good, — is with you. Of course, you have seen Sumner's Article in the North American. I have not yet read it, but hear it spoken of by all as very able, and as putting your defence upon stronger and more unassailable grounds than even your own legal advisers did. You will see more, and more my dear Mackenzie, how strongly you are supported in this quarter for maintaining the right at any sacrifice.[2]

I hope you will like the Spanish Student. It is in a different vein from any of my previous writings; "a beaker full of the warm South"[3] — no German fogs or Scandinavian sea-weed about it; — but music, sunshine and odours manifold.

Give my kindest regards to your wife; and remember me on the 13th, which is my wedding day.[4]

MANUSCRIPT: Longfellow Trust Collection. ADDRESS: A. Slidell Mackenzie/New York. POSTAL ANNOTATION: Free/N. Appleton

1. Answered by Mackenzie on July 13, 1843.
2. As captain of the U.S.S. *Somers*, a training vessel, Mackenzie had ordered the execution of three of his crew as mutineers on December 1, 1842. The event became an immediate *cause célèbre*, primarily because one of the mutineers, Philip Spencer, was the son of the secretary of war. On March 28, 1843, a naval court-martial found Mackenzie not guilty of charges and specifications preferred against him by the secretary of the navy, but his acquittal did not satisfy a large segment of the public, and the affair continued to be argued in streets, drawing rooms, journals, and newspapers. For primary source materials, see *The Somers Mutiny Affair*, ed. Harrison Hayford (Englewood Cliffs, N. J., 1959). See also 789.2.
3. Keats, "Ode to a Nightingale," l. 15.
4. The complimentary close and signature have been cut away.

## 795. *To Thomas Gold Appleton*

Portland July 29th. 1843.

My dear Tom,

As Fanny has given me her hand one of the first uses I shall put it to is to answer your most friendly and welcome note.[1] At this present moment I am imitating Homer and Milton, being blind — (pro tem I hope) having strained my eyes by using them in the twilight. The disadvantage of this is that I cannot say to you what I want to about my beloved amanuensis — the first and foremost subject which presents itself in writing to you, — but be of good cheer and fear not. I think — I *know* I comprehend her — (what unwarrantable confidence, printers dev) and shall ever be to her a most loyal, true, and affectionate husband. I regretted as much as any one that you could not be with us on our wedding day. Fanny thinks that I was partly to blame for this because I told you it would be impossible for you to arrive in season, which it seems was not strictly true, as Ned Perkins *did* arrive in season, with his mustache, and "nice friend the Duke," and "nice Italian opera," and "nice Jockey Clubs," — but it all amounts to the same thing for we could not expect that you should make two voyages to see us begin one; and so farewell to this theme until I get the pen into my own hands again.

I hope Charles Dickens Esq and the robust Fo[r]ster made themselves agreeable to you during your stay in London. They are both good fellows in the main; they are both living in a strange hallucination about this country, as you must have seen, but you saw Cruikshank, and perhaps some poets, under their roofs, therefore the object of my letters was answered tho' the letters themselves have not been.

Thanks for the books which arrived safely. I am sorry you did not send the Dante, altho unfinished, as no more of that Commentary will ever see the light, the publisher being dead and the book damned.[2] How shall I reimburse and how much?

Don't pass St Goar on the Rhine without stopping to see Freiligrath. Give him my kindest remembrances and tell him I have written him via Havre de Grace, and the box of books and things is on the way to him. Tell him, likewise, there is a Review of his Poems with many translations in the 121 No of the Dublin University Magazine;[3] but Fanny thinks this is all waste of powder as you will probably never hit St Goar while the Nightingales sing in England.

Fanny and I both rejoice to see that you are enjoying yourself so much. Your description of Mary [Appleton Mackintosh]'s residence — a lovely picture — made us both wish we were with you. We have got pretty well over that now, and wish you were with us. Come back as soon as you can conveniently — you shall have your choice of the rooms at the Craigie, with a season (box) ticket to the cigars, and free admission to the cellar at all hours of the night. We miss you more than you imagine. I will write you again as soon as I get my eyes re-set and all about Fanny and the rest of it.

Affectionately yrs —
Henry W. Longfellow

Read Freiligrath in No 121 of the Dublin Univ. Mag.[4]

MANUSCRIPT: Longfellow Trust Collection. ADDRESS: Thomas G. Appleton Esq./ Care of Baring Brothers & C./London. POSTAL ANNOTATION: pd to Boston POSTMARKS: FORWARDED FROM HARNDEN'S PACKAGE EXPRESS & FOREIGN LETTER OFFICE NO 8 COURT ST BOSTON/A 14 AU 14 1843

1. With the exception of the signature and the postscript, this letter is in Fanny Appleton's hand. Her own letter to her brother follows Longfellow's.

2. Possibly *La Comedia di Dante Alighieri studiata da Ercole Malagoli* (Modena, 1842), of which only Vol. I was published.

3. "Anthologica Germanica. No. XVIII. — Freiligrath's Poems," *Dublin University Magazine,* XXI (January 1843), 29–42.

4. On outside cover in Longfellow's hand.

796. *To George Washington Greene*

[Cambridge] August 21, 1843.

This is really too bad, — that you should have been at home [from Europe] for more than a fortnight without my having the slightest suspicion of it.[1] I did not receive your letter till last night, on my return from an absence of more than a month. The only way to make all right is for you to come immediately to Cambridge, where a room is waiting for you with open arms, — that is, doors.

I write you but a short letter, because, as you perceive, I am obliged to write with the eyes and hand of another. It is the first time in my life that I have been troubled in this way, and I am afraid I do not submit to the dispensation with very exemplary patience.

This is Commencement week. To-morrow are the college performances, and on Thursday an oration by Hillard before the Phi Beta Kappa Society.[2] I want you to hear this; but will my letter reach you in season?

I want to write you about my wife; but she refuses to record any of the fine things that I suggest.

MANUSCRIPT: unrecovered; text from *Life,* II, 13–14.

1. Greene left Rome in the late spring of 1843 to attend to personal affairs in the U. S. He returned to his post in November.

2. George S. Hillard, *The Relation of the Poet to his Age. A Discourse Delivered Before the Phi Beta Kappa Society of Harvard University, on Thursday, August 24, 1843* (Boston, 1843).

797. *To Sarah Perkins Cleveland*[1]

Cambridge Sep 6th. [1843]

Dear Sarah,

I thank you most sincerely for the cane and the volume of poems.

I shall ever preserve and value them in remembrance of you and Henry. The cane will be especially precious to me as so clearly associated with him, and in all my walks will be a companion ever reminding me of my friend.

I find it difficult to say to you how much I sympathize with you in your bereavement. During your short residence in Cambridge Henry and I, as perhaps you remember, were drawn, daily, closer and closer together. When I returned from Europe he was gone but a letter which he left behind him was one of my most cordial welcomes home. We have all lost a most affectionate friend, but let us remember that

"The splendors of the firmament of time
May be eclipsed but are extinguish'd not,
Like stars to their appointed heights they climb,
And death is a low mist which cannot blot
The brightness it may veil." [2]

Fanny joins with me in kindest regards to yourself and Mary Dwight. We hope you will derive much benefit from the sea air.

Very truly yrs
Henry W. Longfellow

MANUSCRIPT: Berg Collection, New York Public Library.

1. Except for the signature, the letter is in Fanny Longfellow's hand.
2. Shelley, "Adonais," stanza 44.

798. *To Ferdinand Freiligrath*

Craigie House. Cambridge Nov. 24. 1843.

My dear Freiligrath

At length I have received news from you. Your two most warm and friendly letters have arrived.[1] The last came three weeks ago, by mail; the first three days ago by Mr. Muzzy, who being a clergyman fulfilled the scripture, making the last first and the first last. Right glad indeed was I to hear from you. The Landrath's long letter, had previously given me some intimations of your doings at St. Goar, of the visitors you have had during the summer; your merry evenings; and of Helen's betrothment, and in my answer which went by the last Steamer, I sent her my felicitations, which please repeat.[2] I am very sorry Mr Muzzy should have been the first to announce to you my engagement, as I hoped and wished to do it with my own hand, but all summer long I have been deprived entirely of the use of my eyes, by an affection of the nerves, and have naturally postponed all letter writing to a more convenient season, which alas! is slow in arriving, as I have not yet recovered any farther than to be able to sign my name. But nevertheless, eyes or no eyes, engaged I was and married I am — I could see clearly enough for that — married to the very Mary Ashburton, whose name *was* Fanny Appleton and *is* Fanny Longfellow. We were married the 16th. [13th.] of last July, and have been married ever since, and if I were writing with my own hand, I should indulge in a little sentiment. But how could I make it flow through another's quill? We are living at my old lodgings in Cambridge. All literary occupation is however suspended. I am as idle as a lord, and have some idea of what a man's life must be who can neither read nor write. I have taken to planting trees and other rural occupations, and am alltogethe[r] rather a useless individ[u]al. To be more particular. We have purchased an old mansion here, built before the revolution, and occupied by Washington as his head quarters when the American army was in Cambridge. It is a fine old house, and I have a strong attachment from having lived in it since I first came to Cambridge. With it there are five acres of land.[3]

[The] Charles River winds through the meadows [in front] and in the rear I yesterday planted an avenue of Linden trees, which already begin to be ten or twelve feet high. I have also planted some acorns, and as the oak grows for a thousand years, you may imagine a whole line of little Longfellow[s], like the shadowy monarchs in Macbeth walking under their branches, through countless generations, "till the crack of doom"[4] all blessing the man who planted them (meaning, the oaks. As to intellectual matters, I have not done much since I left you. A dozen poems on slavery, written at sea, and a translation of sixteen Cantos of Dante is all I have accomplished in that way. I agree with you entirely in what you say about translations. It is like running a plough share through the soil of one's mind; a thousand germs of thought start up (excuse this agricultural figure) which otherwise might have lain and rotted in the ground. Still it sometime[s] seems to me like an excuse for being lazy, like leaning on an other man's shoulder[s]. I am just beginning the publication of a volume of Specimens of foreign poetry, being a selection from the best english translations now existing from the Anglo-Saxon, Icelandic, Danish, Swedish, German, Dutch, French, Italian, Spanish and Portuguese. The object of the book is to bring together in one volume what is now scattered through a hundred and not easily got at. The volume will be of the same size and appearance as Griswold's Poets and Poetry of America. I shall write the introduction and Biographical notices; most of the translations of course, will be by other hands.[5] Some time last summer I sent you a small case of books, containing among other things the "Spanish Student" enlarged and in a more readable shape. Let me thank a thousand times for your package by Mr. Muzzy. Wesselhoft who was a student on the Wartburg and suffered for the ||...||[6] of the German Fleet read to me your fine sonnets[7] with great delight and with loud peals of laughter, the Huhn and Nachtigall.[8] The whole thing is capital. What merry wags you are at St. Goar. I wish I could appear among you, in my Huron dress, with my tomahawk and my "huh, huh, huh, der Muskokee."[9] I would set fire to Ilium, carry off Helena, smoke [the] Apothecary to death, but I forget. *Ilium fuit,* you are now living in your own hired house like St. Paul. From my heart of hearts I hope I may live to see you in it. Don't leave St. Goar, either for Berlin or any other *inn*. It is a delightful place and you illustrate it and render it famous. When I see how much work you do, I am quite ashamed of my own idleness. In a city you could not or would not do half so much. Have you seen the translations from your poems, in the Dublin University Magazine? [10] They are not very literal, but exceedingly spirited, and excite a good deal of commendation from all readers. How remiss I have been in not translating from you for our reviews and magazines, but love and blindness, my dear friend, coming both together were too much for me. We Hurons are proverbially idle, except in battle and the chase. By the way your Muskokee translation, as well as those from Tennyson, are capital, but the Belfry of Bruges did not come in the package. The "Winds" I despatched to Bryant.[11] This will be indeed an ill wind if it does not blow him some good. I am very glad you translated also the preface to the ballads, but the "Troy Whig," ah! the "Troy Whig" was not worth translating.[12] Thank the Landrath for his Poems on the Kaltwasserkur [cold-water treatment] which are very amusing.[13] Thanks to Simrock also for his Macbeth.[14] If there is a spare copy among the books I sent you, pray forward it to him.

And so my dear friend, farewell for the present. My kindest remembrances to your wife and assure her from Mary Ashburton herself that I am wholly mistaken in my impression of her dislike to Germany. She only disliked the Hotel de Hollande in Mainz where she was 7 weeks under the hands of a pompous German doctor and thereby defrauded of the sight of St. Goar and the rest of the Rhine.[15] At all events she is a great admirer of your Poetry and is already disposed to be as true [a] friend of you and Ida as her husband is. Kind remembrances also to Gallina and the Heubergers. Adé, adé! I must now go and bathe in "Gods great waterfall" Niagara! Write to me soon and tell me about your contest with Herwegh of which I have seen some dim intimation in an old German newspaper.[16]

Yrs very affectionately
Henry W. Longfellow

Received yours of Sept[em]b[e]r. 5th Sept. — 24th.

MANUSCRIPT: unrecovered; text from handwritten transcript, Longfellow Trust Collection. PUBLISHED: "Longfellow-Freiligrath Correspondence," pp. 1251–1254.

1. Dated September 5 and 24, 1843 ("Longfellow-Freiligrath Correspondence," pp. 1246–1251).

2. Heuberger's letter, dated June 7-August 20, 1843, is printed in Maria Applemann, *H. W. Longfellow's Beziehungen zu Ferdinand Freiligrath* (Münster, 1915), pp. 28–39. Longfellow's answer is unrecovered.

3. Nathan Appleton purchased the house on October 14, 1843, and transferred the title to his daughter on November 8, 1844 (*Professor Longfellow of Harvard*, p. 50).

4. *Macbeth*, IV, i, 117.

5. *The Poets and Poetry of Europe* was published by Carey & Hart in Philadelphia in 1845.

6. One word is indecipherable. In her *Annals of Brattleboro 1681–1895* (632.6) Mary R. Cabot gives an account of Robert Wesselhoeft's difficulties in Germany before his emigration to the U. S. He had been a member of the Jena Burschenschaft at the time of the Wartburg Festival, October 18, 1817, in commemoration of Luther and the War of Liberation. In 1824, as a member of the Jünglingsbund, a revolutionary society, he had been sentenced to fifteen years in the Fortress of Magdeburg. He was released in 1831.

7. The six sonnets "Flotten-Träume," written in July 1843 and intended as part of a large "Cyklus" of patriotic poems (Freiligrath to Longfellow, September 24, 1843 ["Longfellow-Freiligrath Correspondence," p. 1250]).

8. *Huhn und Nachtigall. Sonettische Eierschnur auf und für Gallina. Dargebracht zum neuen Jahre 1843 von zweien ihrer Verehrer. St. Goar, mit Lurlei-'schen Typen.* These twelve sonnets, composed by Freiligrath and Heuberger and privately printed in Coblenz, included "Bruder Jonathan" (*New Light on Longfellow*, p. 96), in which Longfellow is castigated for his indifference to the attractions of Fräulein von Gall.

9. See Letter No. 760 and n. 2.

10. See 795.3.

11. One of the Tennyson poems was presumably "Die Grablied" (762.4), and the Muskokee translation was "Lied der alten Tschaktas" (Letter No. 760). The other translations were "Der Belfried zu Brügge" and "Die Winde. Nach dem Amerikaner William Cullen Bryant."

12. In his letter of September 5, Freiligrath had written: "Daβ ich das Artikelchen aus dem *Troy Whig* bei uns bekannt gemacht habe, ist Dir doch recht? [Is it all right with you that I have published here the little article from the *Troy Whig*?]" ("Longfellow-Freiligrath Correspondence," pp. 1246–1247). This article, unidentified, was presumably about Longfellow.

13. A pamphlet in the Longfellow Trust Collection entitled *Die Poesie der Kaltwasserkur. Sonettenkranz von Rheinfels. (Als Manuscript gedruckt für befreundete Kurgenossen.)* (St. Goar, 1843). The first poem, "Zueignung," is dedicated to Longfellow.

14. K. Simrock, *Shakspere als Vermittler zweier Nationen. Probeband: Macbeth.* (Stuttgart and Tübingen, 1842).

15. See 367.4.

16. In his satirical poem "Ein Brief" (published in the *Kölnische Zeitung* on January 20, 1843) Freiligrath, a pensioner of King Frederick William IV, castigated the political liberalism of Georg Herwegh. He subsequently reversed his position and in *Ein Glaubensbekenntnis* (Mainz, 1844) declared his sympathy with the liberal movement, which led to his giving up his pension and leaving Germany. See 718.8.

799. *To Stephen Longfellow*

Cra[i]gie House. Cambridge
November 27. 1843 —

My dear Father: —

I hoped ere this to be able to write to you with my own hand but my eyes are still so bad that I cannot venture beyond signing my name.[1] I therefore make pretty poor work of all my correspondance and write as little as possible. I find it very awkward to dictate a letter and therefore trust to Alex to tell you all about us. He will bring you a plan of the house and the adjoining ground and explain to you the projected improvements which will not be very great for the present: — I have been setting out a few trees and trying to transplant some large Elms to take the place of those destroyed by the canker-worms in front of the house. It is getting so late and cold in the season that I don't want to see a tree again till spring.

Fanny is very well and sends much love to you all: I shall try to write you again before long

Affectionately yours.
H. W. L.

MANUSCRIPT: Longfellow Trust Collection. ADDRESS: Hon. Stephen Longfellow/ Portland/Maine/"Politeness of" — /Mr A. W. Longfellow ANNOTATION ON COVER (*by Alexander Longfellow, together with random verses, names, and other jottings*): Brought by the Amanuensis himself from Cambridge Mass. to Portland, Maine. PUBLISHED: *Life*, II, 17.

1. The letter is in Alexander Longfellow's hand.

800. *To Charles Sumner*

[Cambridge] Thursday mor[nin]g. [Nov. 1843][1]

My dear Charles,

I am very sorry to hear, that you are really ill, and confined to the house. Pray keep up your spirits; and all will go well enough. I shall be in to see you soon.

Felton has of course told you of the operation and its result. Think of carrying about one the immense weight of three pails of water! I trust all will go on prosperously there; and that no tumor will be discovered.[2]

Did Hillard tell you of my mad dream?

In great haste

Ever thine
H. W. L.

MANUSCRIPT: Longfellow Trust Collection. ADDRESS: Cha[r]les Sumner Esq/ Hancock Street

1. A tentative date assigned by H. W. L. Dana.
2. Presumably a reference to Felton's wife, who died in April 1845, after being in poor health for several years.

## 801. *To Carey & Hart*[1]

Cambridge Dec 9. 1843.

Gentlemen

Since receiving your last I have sent to New York for the Blackwood and the list of books you mention: but without success. They do not seem to have been left at the Astor House. Will you have the goodness to enquire into this, and have them forwarded to me here?

Do you know who bought Cottle's Edda, in Mr. Jacksons Library?[2] I have sent to England for a copy, but fear it may arrive too late. Could you borrow a copy for me? Send by Harnden, to be forwarded to Cambridge by D. W. Buck's Express, 17 Court St Boston.

Yours truly
Henry W. Longfellow.[3]

say the printers will begin their work. They have had a new type cast for the book. I forgot to say to you that I don't think it will be worth while to import the Dublin University Magazine. I looked the volumes over in New York, and the only ones I shall need are Vols 4th., 9th. and 21st.[4] I think you could borrow these for me.

MANUSCRIPT: New York Public Library (Miscellaneous Papers, Longfellow Folder). ADDRESS: Messrs Cary & Hart/Philadelphia ANNOTATION ON COVER: Will you ascertain when the Box was sent. POSTMARK: CAMBRIDGE MS. DEC 13

1. The letter is in Cornelius Felton's hand, except for the fragmentary postscript.
2. Presumably Isaac Rand Jackson (see 716.2). A copy of A. S. Cottle's *Icelandic Poetry, or The Edda of Saemund* (Bristol, 1797), is in the Longfellow Trust Collection.
3. The manuscript is mutilated. The postscript, continued on the back of the sheet, is in Fanny Longfellow's hand.
4. These volumes contained translations that Longfellow wanted for his *Poets and Poetry of Europe.*

## 802. *To Stephen Longfellow*

Cambridge Dec 17th. 1843.

My dear Father,

It is a long time since we have had the pleasure of hearing from any of you in Portland. We have been reading your praises in the Tribune, today, where we learn that Gen Fessenden is "not flashy but solid."[1] Pray tell Annie she must write oftener, she being the scribe of the family. I have an inkstand for her but as Aleck took his letter with him I have forgotten what the books were which she desired to have. She must let me know in her next.

I sent you by Alex a plan of our house and grounds. We have been setting out a few trees, but frost and snow prevent further operations for the present. We are driven in doors and shall not undertake anything in the way of alterations or repairs until the Spring. We are now making a book for Carey & Hart, Philadelphia, — I say, we — tho' Fanny does all the reading and writing. This book is selections, translated into English, of the European poets, including those of 10 nations, Anglo-Saxon, Icelandic, Danish, Swedish, Dutch, German, French, Italian, Spanish, Portuguese. I write the Introductions and Biographical Notices but shall not make any new translations. The object of the book is to bring within the compass of one volume what is now scattered about in many. The printers begin upon it tomorrow, but it will be a long time before we finish it, as it is to be a volume of 500 pages, 8 vo., in double columns, and will contain an immense deal of matter.

My eyes continue about the same, with very little, if any, progress, but I have confidence in Elliott, and doubt not that in time his remedies will produce the desired effect.[2] Patience, I suspect, will be the greater Oculist of the two after all. We have not heard yet from Mary [Longfellow Greenleaf] but probably shall before long as it is almost time. Nor from Sam; have you had any letters from him? Dont you think he had better go to Europe before he comes back to fit himself for a Professorship, as that seems to be his ambition?[3]

We hope to hear soon that you are all well. Tell Alick or Annie, or both, to write and let us know what is going on in your part of the world. The only novelty with us is the publication of Mr. Prescott's Mexico. It is in three volumes like his former work.[4] We have just commenced it, and it promises to be exceedingly well-written and interesting. It is published by the Harpers of New York who have paid him $7,500 (these cyphers, 'I beg leave to observe' are of Henry's manufacture)[5] for the right of issuing as many copies as they please during one year, at the expiration of which time the copy-right reverts to the Author, a very good bargain for him, and much better than he could have made with any Boston bookseller. Old Judge Prescott had a paralytic stroke a few weeks ago, but is so far recovered as to be out again.[6] You will see by the papers the sudden death of Mr Oxnard.[7] He has been for some time an invalid, tho' no apprehension of so sudden a catastrophe has been felt.

With much love to all in which Fanny joins me.

Very affectionately yrs
Henry W. Longfellow

Annie's receiv[e]d, but not yet read.[8]

MANUSCRIPT: Longfellow Trust Collection. ADDRESS: Hon. S. Longfellow./Portland./Me. POSTMARK: CAMBRIDGE MS. DEC 19

1. The adulatory notices of Stephen Longfellow and Gen. Samuel Fessenden (1784–1869) appeared in an article on Portland men in the *Portland Tribune*, III, No. 36 (December 16, 1843), 290.

2. According to a note in the *Daily Evening Transcript*, XIV, No. 4042 (Wednesday, September 27, 1843), Longfellow had passed some time in New York in September as Dr. Elliot's patient.

3. Samuel Longfellow's ambition remained with the ministry, and he returned to Cambridge without visiting Europe (see 777.1).

4. *History of the Conquest of Mexico* (New York, 1843).

5. Fanny Longfellow inserted the footnote "amanuensis" here. The entire letter, with the exception of the signature and the postscript, is in her hand.

6. Judge Prescott died a year later on December 8, 1844.

7. Henry Oxnard (1789–1843), a Boston merchant.

8. This postscript appears on the address cover in Longfellow's hand.

## 803. *To Carey & Hart*[1]

Cambridge. Dec 24th. 1843.

Gentlemen,

I write to inform you of the arrival of the books from England and of your favor of the 13th. with the prices of the same. I do not wish to complain but it strikes me that they are very high; for instance Cory's Fragments is charged $8.50. A friend of mine bought this work in Boston, the same edition, for $4.00. Cothy's works was published at 16 shillings; you have charged it 6.00. I wish you would have the goodness to run over the list and see if there is not some mistake. Considering the object for which these books have been imported I think you ought to put them to me at cost. I doubt not you will when you see what a serious inroad those already purchased have made into the sum which I am to receive.[2]

Yrs truly,
Henry W. Longfellow

P. S. Would you have the goodness to get from Mr Griswold or Mr Graham the No of their Magazine containing an article of mine on Heine. It was published early in the year 1842 in February or March I think — perhaps January.[3]

MANUSCRIPT: Yale University Library.

1. In Fanny Longfellow's hand, except for the signature.

2. The books referred to are Isaac Preston Cory, *The Ancient Fragments, Containing What Remains of the Writings of Sanchoniatho, Berossus, Abydenus, Megasthenes and Manetho. Also the Hermetic Creed, the Old Chronicle, the Laterculus of Eratosthenes, the Tyrian Annals, the Oracles of Zoroaster and the Periplus of Hanno* (London, 1828); and Walter Davies and John Jones, eds., *The Poetical Works of Lewis Glyn Cothi* (Oxford, 1837). Longfellow's complaint elicited a quick reply from Carey & Hart on December 27, in which they agreed to "make such deduction as we doubt not will be satisfactory to you."

3. March. See 400.2.

## 804. *To Josiah Quincy*[1]

Cambridge Dec 29th [1843]

My dear Sir,

Will you have the goodness to lay before the Corporation, at their next meeting, my request concerning the trees, which I mentioned to you the last time I had the pleasure of seeing you; viz that they would permit me to take from the College grounds 3 elm trees to be placed in front of the Craigie House.

I am endeavoring to replace, as well as possible, the old elms, and find it difficult to obtain many of the size I desire. Some parts of the College ground are so thickly planted that a tree may be removed, here and there, without at all impairing the beauty of the grounds. I therefore request permission to remove any 3 trees that the College Steward shall say may be taken without detriment to the College property.[2]

Yrs very truly,
Henry W. Longfellow

MANUSCRIPT: Harvard College Papers, XII, 26. PUBLISHED: *Professor Longfellow of Harvard*, pp. 50–51.

1. In Fanny Longfellow's hand, except for the signature.

2. The Corporation approved Longfellow's request at a meeting on December 30 (*Professor Longfellow of Harvard*, p. 51).

# SHORT TITLES OF WORKS CITED

# INDEX OF RECIPIENTS

# SHORT TITLES OF WORKS CITED

| | |
|---|---|
| *Boston Directory* | *Stimpson's Boston Directory and City Register* (Boston, Charles Stimpson, Jr., 1837–1843), 7 vols. |
| *Clark Letters* | Leslie W. Dunlap, ed., *The Letters of Willis Gaylord Clark and Lewis Gaylord Clark* (New York, New York Public Library, 1940). |
| *Diary of Clara Crowninshield* | Andrew Hilen, ed., *The Diary of Clara Crowninshield: A European Tour with Longfellow, 1835–1836* (Seattle, University of Washington Press, 1956). |
| *Dickens Days in Boston* | Edward F. Payne, *Dickens Days in Boston: A Record of Daily Events* (Boston and New York, Houghton Mifflin Co., 1927). |
| "Eight Unpublished Letters" | Allen Wilson Porterfield, "Eight Unpublished Letters of Longfellow," *Scandinavian Studies and Notes*, V (1918–1919), 169–180. |
| Higginson, *Longfellow* | Thomas Wentworth Higginson, *Henry Wadsworth Longfellow* (Boston and New York, Houghton Mifflin Co., 1902). |
| "Letters to Samuel Ward" | Henry Marion Hall, "Longfellow's Letters to Samuel Ward," *Putnam's Magazine,* III (October, November, December, 1907), 38–43 (Part I), 165–171 (Part II), 301–308 (Part III). |
| *Life* | Samuel Longfellow, ed., *Life of Henry Wadsworth Longfellow with Extracts from His Journals and Correspondence* (Boston and New York, Houghton, Mifflin Co., 1891), Standard Library Edition, 3 vols. |
| *Longfellow and Scandinavia* | Andrew Hilen, *Longfellow and Scandinavia: A Study of the Poet's Relationship* |

| | |
|---|---|
| | *with the Northern Languages and Literature* (New Haven, Yale University Press, 1947). |
| "Longfellow-Freiligrath Correspondence" | James Taft Hatfield, "The Longfellow-Freiligrath Correspondence," *Publications of the Modern Language Association of America,* XLVIII (December 1933), 1223–1292. |
| *New Light on Longfellow* | James Taft Hatfield, *New Light on Longfellow with Special Reference to His Relations to Germany* (Boston and New York, Houghton Mifflin Co., 1933). |
| "New Longfellow Letters" | Mary Thacher Higginson, "New Longfellow Letters," *Harpers Monthly Magazine,* CVI (April 1903), 779-786. |
| *Poets and Poetry of Europe* | Henry Wadsworth Longfellow, ed., *The Poets and Poetry of Europe. With Introductions and Biographical Notices* (Philadelphia, Porter and Coates, 1871). |
| *Professor Longfellow of Harvard* | Carl L. Johnson, *Professor Longfellow of Harvard* (Eugene, University of Oregon Press, 1944). |
| "Some Unpublished Longfellow Letters" | Amandus Johnson, "Some Unpublished Longfellow Letters," *German-American Annals,* V, N.S. (May and June 1907), 172–192. |
| *Sumner Memoir and Letters* | Edward L. Pierce, ed., *Memoir and Letters of Charles Sumner* (Boston, Roberts Brothers, 1877–1894), 4 vols. |
| *Uncle Sam Ward and His Circle* | Maud Howe Elliott, *Uncle Sam Ward and His Circle* (New York, Macmillan Co., 1938). |
| *Works* | Samuel Longfellow, ed., *The Works of Henry Wadsworth Longfellow with Biographical and Critical Notes* (Boston and New York, Houghton, Mifflin Co., 1886), Standard Library Edition, 11 vols. |
| *Young Longfellow* | Lawrance Thompson, *Young Longfellow* (New York, Macmillan Co., 1938). |

# INDEX OF RECIPIENTS

(References are to letter numbers)